Historical Dictionaries of Ancient Civilizations
and Historical Eras
Series editor: Jon Woronoff

1. *Ancient Egypt*, Morris L. Bierbrier, 1999.
2. *Ancient Mesoamerica*, Joel W. Palka, 2000.
3. *Pre-Colonial Africa*, Robert O. Collins, 2001.
4. *Byzantium*, John H. Rosser, 2001.
5. *Medieval Russia*, Lawrence N. Langer, 2001.
6. *Napoleonic Era*, George F. Nafziger, 2001.
7. *Ottoman Empire*, Selcuk Aksin Somel, 2003.
8. *Mongol World Empire*, Paul D. Buell, 2003.
9. *Mesopotamia*, Gwendolyn Leick, 2003.
10. *Ancient and Medieval Nubia*, by Richard A. Lobban, Jr. 2003.
11. *The Vikings*, by Katherine Holman, 2003.
12. *The Renaissance*, by Charles G. Nauert, 2004.

Historical Dictionary of the Renaissance

Charles G. Nauert

Historical Dictionaries of Ancient Civilizations and Historical Eras, No. 12

The Scarecrow Press, Inc.
Lanham, Maryland, and Oxford
2004

SCARECROW PRESS, INC.

Published in the United States of America
by Scarecrow Press, Inc.
A wholly owned subsidiary of the Rowman & Littlefield Publishing Group, Inc.
4501 Forbes Boulevard, Suite 200, Lanham, Maryland 20706
www.scarecrowpress.com

PO Box 317
Oxford
OX2 9RU, UK

British Library Cataloguing in Publication Information Available

Library of Congress Cataloging-in-Publication Data

Nauert, Charles Garfield, 1928–
  Historical dictionary of the Renaissance / Charles G. Nauert.
    p. cm. — (Historical dictionaries of ancient civilizations and historical
eras ; no. 12)
  Includes bibliographical references.
  ISBN 0-8108-4867-8 (alk. paper)
  1. Renaissance—Dictionaries. I. Title. II. Series.
  CB361 .N35 2003
  940.2'103—dc21

                                                    2003011653

∞™ The paper used in this publication meets the minimum requirements of
American National Standard for Information Sciences—Permanence of Paper
for Printed Library Materials, ANSI/NISO Z39.48-1992.
Manufactured in the United States of America.

Contents

Editor's Foreword

Part of the Renaissance was, as its name denotes, a "rebirth," reaching back to recover and revive the great accomplishments of Ancient Rome and Greece. There was even a glance further back, to the time of the Bible, both the New and the Old Testaments, with the urge for more exact translation from Greek and Hebrew. Had it been nothing more than this harking back and rediscovering, the Renaissance would have been a memorable period. But its impulse was so great and its momentum so strong that it carried on with new, pathbreaking discoveries, concepts, and inventions, producing some of the world's most extraordinary art and architecture, literature and music, and marking major turning points in religion, philosophy, and science. Its impact on the economy, politics, and social relations was equally impressive. Indeed, so much happened, in such a short span, and in a fairly small area, that it is hard to believe and hard to encompass in one volume.

Nonetheless, the *Historical Dictionary of the Renaissance* does give us plenty of information on, and also an excellent feel for, this liveliest of eras. The chronology already shows just how much was being done in multiple fields of activity and different parts of Europe. This is drawn together in the introduction, which helps compose an overall view. But the most important section remains the dictionary, covering all the crucial aspects, yet even then only highlighting the most notable persons, places, and events. These include outstanding artists and architects, writers and philosophers, teachers and scientists (whether in Florence or Rome or other centers), the new art of printing which spread the word, and banking which financed major ventures. There are also the key players, whether popes or religious reformers or secular rulers, from dukes on up to kings and emperors, whose encouragement of war often outdid their contributions to peace. Beyond this, there are fundamental concepts, programs, and movements which affected the times. Since it is hard to stop once you have started reading about the Renaissance, the select bibliography is precious as a source of related and more detailed literature.

This volume, larger than others in the series, and justifiably so, was written by Charles G. Nauert. Presently Professor Emeritus of History at the University of Missouri—Columbia, he spent nearly five decades teaching about the Renaissance and related periods. He has also written extensively, including numerous articles and several books, among them *Agrippa and the Crisis of Renaissance Thought*, *The Age of Renaissance and Reformation*, and *Humanism and the Culture of Renaissance Europe*. He is also the author of the historical notes and introductions for volumes 11 and 12 of *The Correspondence of Erasmus*. Professor Nauert has been active in the historical profession as a member of a number of learned societies, including the American Historical Association, the Renaissance Society of America, the regional New England and Central Renaissance Conferences, the Society for Reformation Research, and the Sixteenth Century Studies Conference. He was the founding general editor of the publication series "Sixteenth Century Essays and Studies," and at its annual meeting in 2002 the Sixteenth Century Studies Conference named him the first recipient of its new award "for Scholarship, Civility, and Service." In 1998 his professional colleagues and former students honored him with a Festschrift, *In Laudem Caroli: Renaissance and Reformation Studies*. Now he honors us with a historical dictionary which contains the essence of a long and fruitful career.

Jon Woronoff
Series Editor

Preface

This dictionary concentrates primarily on the elite or high culture of both Italy and transalpine Europe from the early 14th century to the early 17th century, the period commonly associated with the concept of a renaissance. At its beginning, the Renaissance was often shaped by its medieval precursors even while it disdained them as "barbarous"; hence some entries here deal with topics that are conventionally designated "medieval"—for example, the Florentine poet Dante and the Hundred Years' War. At its peak in northern Europe, the Renaissance was intimately intertwined with the Reformations (plural—both Protestant and Catholic); and some entries given here deal with figures also discussed, from a different perspective, in the *Historical Dictionary of the Protestant and Counter-Reformation* by Professor Hans Hillerbrand in another Scarecrow Press series. Martin Luther and John Calvin, major figures of the Reformation, appear here, but with primary attention to their relation to the Renaissance rather than to their role in the Reformation. Because the Renaissance is primarily a concept in cultural history, this volume treats political, social, and economic topics selectively. For example, Queen Mary I (Mary Tudor) of England has no separate entry here because her reign was too brief to have much influence on the development of English Renaissance culture. She is important for the history of the English Reformation and appropriately appears in Professor Hillerbrand's dictionary. Her half-sister Elizabeth I, however, had a brilliant reign of 45 years, the period when English Renaissance culture (alternatively labelled "Elizabethan") reached full maturity. Hence even though Queen Elizabeth was not personally a very generous patron of the new trends in literature, art, and scholarship, she is included here.

Except for elegant royal ladies like these English queens, most women were shut out from the higher reaches of Renaissance culture. Since fluency in Latin was indispensable for serious intellectual work and only exceptionally privileged women had an opportunity to study Latin, the condition of women in Renaissance Europe has to be approached mainly through the special field of social history, which tends to deal in aggregates rather than individuals and hence produces few topics suitable for a historical dictionary. The spiritual movement of the 15th century known as *Devotio Moderna* produced communities of Sisters of the Common Life alongside the more famous Brethren of the Common Life. But since anonymity and silence were expected of pious women, no prominent female individuals emerge who are comparable to Geert Groote, the founder of the movement, or Thomas à Kempis, the probable author of its most famous book of religious meditations. The literary debate about the proper role of women in society, the *querelle des femmes*, extended through the Renaissance centuries; but it was conducted mainly on terms set by male critics who accused women in general, and certain women in particular, of not being properly silent and submissive. Even most of those who wrote tracts defending women were male, though there were some able female participants. Sadly, one topic of social history that involves the fate of many women is witchcraft, since women were far more likely than men to be accused, convicted, and executed as witches.

For the most part, the individual women who are discussed in this dictionary were members of the educated elite. Even among that privileged group, they were exceptional: writers, a tiny handful of artists (all but one of them, daughters of artists), and a handful of daughters of ruling families who did not stay discreetly in the background as wives, mothers, or nuns but took an active role in politics. Female rulers held office only by default: the hereditary principle of succession put them on the throne, but only because there was no viable male alternative. Queens regnant (as distinct from queens consort, the wives of kings) were rare; and of the handful of female rulers in this period, only two held power that was real, personal, and durable: Queens Isabella of Spain and Elizabeth I of England. Even though their accession to power was tolerated because the alternative was civil war and anarchy, its impropriety as a violation of the laws of God and Nature was a subject of frequent complaint. I have made a special effort to include women, for our society is very interested in the experience of women in past times. Yet it has to be said that even after an effort to find suitable individuals, the women here listed are regrettably few, and nearly all of them were members of the privileged ranks of society.

The bibliography will indicate sources and will supply suggestions for further reading on the general subject and special topics. Any person who wants to locate more detailed information on topics in this field should be aware of three multi-volume reference works that in different ways deal with Renaissance subjects. These are *Encyclopedia of the Renaissance*, edited by Paul F. Grendler, 6 vols. (New York: Charles Scribner's Sons, 1999); *The Oxford Encyclopedia of the Reformation*, edited by Hans J. Hillerbrand, 4 vols. (Oxford: Oxford University Press, 1996); and *Contemporaries of Erasmus: A Biographical Register of the Renaissance and Reformation*, edited by Peter G. Bietenholz and Thomas B. Deutscher, 3 vols. (Toronto: University of Toronto Press, 1985–1987). On specific points that extend beyond my own areas of specialization, I have been fortunate to consult my medievalist colleagues, A. Mark Smith and Lois Huneycutt, and my colleagues in ancient history, Lawrence Okamura and Ian Worthington. The collections of Ellis Library at the University of Missouri–Columbia have been fundamental to my ability to collect information needed for this volume. I am particularly grateful to the library administration for its willingness to assign me a library study in which I can assemble a revolving reference collection specific to the topics of my investigation.

My wife, Jean, has endured my disappearance into my home office almost every evening and many weekends to work on this book; I am happy to dedicate it to her, with my thanks and love.

Charles G. Nauert
University of Missouri–Columbia

Chronology

The question of when to begin and when to end a chronological list of major events of the Renaissance is as open to debate as the scope and significance of the Renaissance itself. In addition, the development of the Protestant Reformation from 1517 creates a whole new set of problems in defining the age. The following list includes only a few major events of the Reformation, since those events are treated fully in another Scarecrow Press historical dictionary. Landmarks in the history of art are included from the late 13th century to the early 17th century. The rather arbitrary starting date is 1250, the death of the last Holy Roman Emperor to have significant political authority in Italy. The terminal events (which, like the condemnation of Copernican astronomy and the imprisonment of Galileo, might well be regarded as part of a post-Renaissance age) are the English civil wars of the 1640s and the end of the Thirty Years' War in 1648. Some dates in the list are approximate.

1250 Death of Emperor Frederick II; most of northern and central Italy is left de facto independent

1267 Guelf party gains permanent control of Florence

1293 Ordinances of Justice (Florentine constitution)

1296–1300 Giotto's frescoes at Assisi, life of St. Francis

1297 Closure of Great Council at Venice

1303 Dante, *De vulgari eloquentia*

1304 Birth of Petrarch

1305–1306 Giotto's frescoes in Arena Chapel at Padua

1305–1377 "Babylonian Captivity" of papacy; popes reside at Avignon, 1309–1377

1321 Death of Dante

1337 Petrarch begins writing *De viris illustribus*; beginning of Hundred Years' War

1341 Petrarch crowned poet laureate at Rome

1343 Approximate onset of 14th-century depression; Florentines defeat attempt by wealthy families to set up a dictatorship

1343–1382 Democratizing reforms at Florence

1347 Cola di Rienzo leads "Roman Revolution" against papal rule of Rome

1348–1350 Black Death strikes most parts of Europe

1360 Treaty of Brétigny suspends large-scale conflict during Hundred Years' War; skirmishes continue

1374 Death of Petrarch

1375 Coluccio Salutati appointed chancellor of Florence

1378 *Ciompi* rebellion at Florence

1378–1402 Giangaleazzo Visconti, duke of Milan

1378–1417 Western Schism divides European Christian churches

1381–1391 Coluccio Salutati, *De laboribus Herculis*

1382 Greater guilds stage coup d'état at Florence; end of democratizing reforms; restoration of control by greater guilds

1397–1400 Manuel Chrysoloras teaches Greek at Florence

1403 Leonardo Bruni, *Laudatio Florentinae urbis*

1409 Council of Pisa fails in effort to end Schism

1414–1418 Council of Constance

1415 Leonardo Bruni writes first part of *History of the Florentine People*; Henry V of England resumes Hundred Years' War

1417 Council of Constance elects Martin V as pope, ending Western Schism

1423 Vittorino da Feltre establishes humanistic court school at Mantua

1425–1427 Masaccio's frescoes, Brancacci Chapel at Florence

1425–1430 Donatello, bronze statue of *David*

1427 Leonardo Bruni appointed chancellor of Florence

1429 Guarino Guarini establishes humanistic court school at Ferrara

1432 Jan van Eyck completes *Ghent Altarpiece*

1434 Cosimo de' Medici returns from exile and establishes Medici political control of Florence

1435 Leon Battista Alberti, *The Elements of Painting*

1440 Lorenzo Valla, *The Elegances of the Latin Language; Declamation on the Forged and Deceitful Donation of Constantine*

1447 Death of Filippo Maria, last Visconti duke of Milan

1450 Francesco Sforza becomes duke of Milan

1453 Fall of Constantinople to Turks; end of Hundred Years' War

1454 Peace of Lodi ends Milanese succession crisis

1454–1455 "Gutenberg Bible" printed at Mainz

1456 Peter Luder returns from Italy; lectures on humanism at University of Heidelberg

1469 Marriage of Isabella of Castile and Ferdinand of Aragon opens way for unification of Spain

1477 Charles the Rash, last duke of Burgundy, killed in battle with Swiss

1478 Pope Sixtus IV founds Spanish Inquisition at request of King Ferdinand and Queen Isabella

1479 Rudolf Agricola returns from Italy to Germany, writes *De inventione dialectica*

1484 Marsilio Ficino, Latin translation of Plato's works

1485 Henry Tudor defeats Richard III in battle of Bosworth

1485–1509 Henry VII, first Tudor king of England

1489 Angelo Poliziano, *Miscellaneorum centuria prima*

1490 Aldus Manutius establishes Aldine press at Venice

1492 Spanish conquest of kingdom of Granada; expulsion of Jews from Spain; Columbus lands at San Salvador in West Indies; Elio Antonio Nebrija, *Gramática . . . sobre la lengua castellana*

1494 French invasion of Italy, conquest of Naples; expulsion of Medici from Florence

1494–1495 Albrecht Dürer's first trip to Italy

1495 Spain and Italian allies drive French out of Italy

1495–1497 Leonardo da Vinci, *The Last Supper*

1498 Savonarola burned as a heretic at Florence; Vasco da Gama lands at Calicut in India; Louis XII renews French invasion of Italy

1499–1512 Machiavelli heads second chancery of Florence

1501–1504 Michelangelo, *David*

1503 Leonardo da Vinci, *Mona Lisa*; Erasmus, *Enchridion of the Christian Soldier*

1506 Donato Bramante designs new St. Peter's basilica

1508–1512 Michelangelo, Sistine Chapel frescoes

1509 Lefèvre d'Etaples, *Quincuplex Psalterium*; instruction commences at University of Alcalá; Erasmus, *The Praise of Folly* (first edition, 1511)

1509–1546 Henry VIII, king of England

1510–1511 Raphael, *The School of Athens*

1512 Spanish troops restore Medici control of Florence

1512–1517 Fifth Lateran Council

1513 Machiavelli, *The Prince* (first edition in 1532); Albrecht Dürer's engravings *Knight, Death, and Devil* and *St. Jerome in His Study*

1515 Publication of Rudolf Agricola, *De inventione dialectica; Letters of Obscure Men* published

1515–1547 Francis I, king of France

1516 Erasmus edits Greek New Testament; Thomas More, *Utopia*

1516–1556 Charles of Habsburg becomes king of Spain

1517 Foundation of *Collegium Trilingue* at Louvain; Martin Luther, *Ninety-five Theses*

1518–1533 Andrea Alciati develops humanistic approach to teaching law (*mos gallicus*) at Avignon and Bourges

1519 Charles of Habsburg elected Emperor Charles V

1521 Diet of Worms; Martin Luther refuses to recant

1524 Erasmus, *On Freedom of the Will*, attacks Luther

1524–1534 Michelangelo, tomb of Giuliano de'Medici

1527 "Sack of Rome" by imperial/Spanish army; Florentine people rebel against Medici control

1528 Baldassare Castiglione, *The Book of the Courtier*

1530 Francis I appoints first Royal Lecturers on humanistic subjects; Spanish army forces Florence to surrender; Medici rule restored

1531 Andrea Alciati, *Book of Emblems*

1532 Florentine republic abolished; Alessandro de'Medici becomes duke of Florence; Rabelais, *Pantagruel*

1534 Rabelais, *Gargantua*; Act of Supremacy recognizes Henry VIII as head of church in England

1534–1541 Michelangelo, *Last Judgment*

1542 Pope Paul III issues bull *Licet ab initio*, founding Roman Inquisition

1543 Nicolaus Copernicus, *De revolutionibus orbium coelestium;* Andreas Vesalius, *De humani corporis fabrica*

1546 Titian, *Pope Paul III and His Grandsons*

1546–1564 Michelangelo designs dome and central plan of St. Peter's basilica at Rome

1549 Joachim du Bellay, *Défense et illustration de la langue française*

1550 Giorgio Vasari, *Lives of the Most Eminent Italian Architects, Painters, and Sculptors*

1555 Religious Peace of Augsburg recognizes legal status of Evangelical (Lutheran) religion in Germany

1556–1598 Philip II, king of Spain

1559 Treaty of Cateau-Cambrésis: France acknowledges Spanish hegemony in Italy

1559–1603 Elizabeth I, queen of England

1562 Pieter Brueghel the Elder, *Peasant Wedding*

1562–1598 French Wars of Religion

1580 Montaigne, *Essays* (books 1 and 2; book 3, 1588)

1585 Philip Sidney, *The Defence of Poetry*

1586 El Greco, *The Burial of Count Orgaz*

1588 Defeat of the Spanish Armada

1589 Henry III, last Valois king of France, murdered

1589–1610 Henry IV, first Bourbon king of France

1590 Posthumous publication of Philip Sidney, *Arcadia*

1599–1602 Caravaggio, *The Calling of St. Matthew*

1599–1607 William Shakespeare produces his major tragedies (*Hamlet, Othello, King Lear, Macbeth*)

1603 Francis Bacon, *The Advancement of Learning*

1603–1625 James I, first Stuart king of England

1607–1615 Carlo Maderno, nave and façade of St. Peter's

1608 Miguel de Cervantes, *Don Quixote*, part 1; part 2, 1615

1616 Roman Inquisition declares Copernican astronomy heretical

1618–1648 Thirty Years' War in Germany

1632 Galileo Galilei, *Dialogue on the Two Chief Systems of the World*; Roman Inquisition compels Galileo to recant, imposes house arrest for life

1642–1649 English civil wars; abolition of monarchy

1648 Peace of Westphalia ends Thirty Years' War

Introduction

"The Renaissance" used to be refreshingly easy to understand. It could be plausibly described as a simple and obvious cultural "rebirth" (the literal meaning of *renaissance*) of advanced civilization after nearly a thousand years when cultural barbarism and political and social chaos had blighted the lives of European peoples. The Renaissance seemed to mark the rediscovery by Western Europeans of the lost cultures of ancient Greece and Rome. Both to scholars and to educated readers who viewed human history from the perspective of the 19th and early 20th centuries, the Renaissance marked the decisive moment when "progress" toward a better state of the world—toward modernity—began, starting in Italy and eventually spreading across the Alps. This was the understanding found in Jacob Burckhardt's *Civilization of the Renaissance in Italy* (1860). He stated flatly that the Renaissance Italian was "the first-born among the sons of modern Europe." The same basic idea had already been expressed in the works of the first great literary and intellectual figure of the Renaissance, the Italian **humanist Petrarch**. As anyone could see, the period described as "the Renaissance" produced some of the masterpieces of modern Western Civilization: the art of the High Renaissance masters (**Leonardo da Vinci, Michelangelo**, and **Raphael**), the books and poems of Renaissance literary giants (Petrarch, **Machiavelli, Rabelais, Cervantes, Shakespeare**), the classical scholarship of those who recovered many forgotten treasures of Latin literature and virtually everything we now possess of the literary treasures of ancient Greece (except Aristotle, who had been discovered 200 years earlier). These centuries (roughly 1330 to 1640) produced masterworks that the educated classes of modern Europe and the Americas regarded as a living part of their own culture.

This was the conventional view of the Renaissance, and for many readers, even well educated ones, it still prevails. But there is a difficulty with it: although it includes many valid judgments on specific points (for example, there really was a spectacular rediscovery of the literary heritage of classical antiquity), it is basically untrue—untrue on many grounds, but especially because of its total misunderstanding of the culture and society that immediately preceded the Renaissance, the **Middle Ages.** The fatal flaw of Burckhardt's picture of the Renaissance is that it took as its point of departure a medieval age that never existed. It is true that in the centuries immediately following the collapse of the Roman Empire, a long period of violent disorders and cultural decline occurred. But some of the classical heritage was preserved, and by the late 11th century, the worst days were past. In the 12th and 13th centuries, western Europe created new and effective political institutions, a powerful if worldly institutional church, a prospering and expanding economy, a rapidly growing population, and a fresh, creative cultural life. The centuries that built the Romanesque and Gothic cathedrals of western Europe, that recovered the writings of **Aristotle** and assimilated their main ideas, and invented the university as a center for high-level education most assuredly were not barbarous. If there ever had been a "Dark Age," it was already past during the great centuries of medieval civilization.

The weaknesses in this traditional but distorted picture of the Middle Ages were already being revealed by a remarkable flowering of medieval studies that was under way even when Burckhardt wrote. As the achievements of the Middle Ages became increasingly well understood, it became hard to regard the Renaissance as simply a rediscovery of "civilization" after centuries when it had somehow got lost. By the 1930s many medieval specialists questioned whether there was ever any Renaissance at all. If there was, maybe it took place during the 12th century, not the 14th, an idea suggested in the title of the influential book by the American medievalist Charles Homer Haskins, *The Renaissance of the Twelfth Century* (1927). In 1940, the Canadian scholar Wallace K. Ferguson called the Renaissance "the most intractable problem child of history"; and his landmark historiographical study *The Renaissance in Historical Thought* (1948) traced the rise, maturation, and fall of the traditional concept of the Renaissance—Burckhardt's Renaissance. A generation of graduate students (including the present writer) pondered what had come to be known as "the Renaissance problem." The very term "Renaissance" became debatable, and many scholars avoided using it at all. The "Renaissance" seemed dead, a term without utility.

And yet, not quite. Whatever the ins and outs of scholarly fad and fashion might dictate, those three centuries that the 19th century confidently called "the Renaissance" really had existed. The artists, poets, **classical** scholars, philosophers, theologians, and politicians whose acts and writings made the period memorable really did do—write—think things that affected all subsequent history, not only European history but the history of the whole world. Ferguson himself did not give up on either the Renaissance or the traditional label. He simply wanted to clarify it and set it onto a sound historical basis. His historiographical masterpiece began by demonstrating that the concept of a Renaissance was a product of the Renaissance itself, not the creation of an Enlightenment anticlerical like Voltaire or a French romantic like Jules Michelet or a Swiss internationalist like Burckhardt. The humanists—that is, the cutting-edge intellectuals of the period, such as Petrarch—were the inventors of the claim that a rebirth of high civilization, inspired and partially caused by recovery of the literary and artistic heritage of classical **antiquity**, was taking place and that they themselves were the creators of this new civilization. Led by Petrarch, they declared that the Middle Ages in their entirety were nothing but a "Dark Age."

Their claim was false or exaggerated as an account of the past, but it was extremely powerful as a value judgment. What was valid in this claim was an unprecedented insight into the nature of historical change, an idea totally lacking in either ancient or medieval times. Petrarch was the first man of any age to realize that the admirable civilization of ancient Greece and Rome had perished during the turmoil that followed the collapse of the western Roman Empire. The culture that grew up during the following centuries may not have been unrelievedly "dark," as he contended, but it certainly was different. The Middle Ages—what Petrarch defined as the "modern age," since he felt still trapped in it—were a distinct (and in his opinion, inferior) civilization, and while he believed that his own society could be vastly improved by learning about antiquity and capturing the mysterious spirit that had made ancient Rome great, he was never so naive as to believe that the dead civilization of ancient times could literally be brought back to life. What could be done, he believed, was to create another high civilization, distinct from the medieval one, that would draw on the riches of antiquity but would be something different from both antiquity and the Middle Ages. A new modern age—our modern age—could be founded and was being founded by himself (no false modesty here!). From the perspective of this new era, the "dark" in-between period would be a "middle" age, and this idea of Petrarch's is the actual source of the term "Middle Ages," which was first used during the 15th century.

Petrarch certainly undervalued the achievements of those "middle" or "medieval" centuries. But he was right to think that that period had overlooked and misunderstood many valuable achievements of the ancients, and he was convinced that the "modern"—that is, medieval—society into which he was born was unspeakably barbarous, corrupt, and disorderly. Petrarch and the generations of humanistic disciples who pursued his dream of a cultural and social revival deliberately set out to do two things: first, to denounce their own time (that is, the age they were trying to leave behind); second, to investigate the riches of ancient literature and so to discover not just additional facts about the Greeks and Romans but the "secret," conceived as an internal spirit, a moral factor, that had made the small cities of Athens and **Rome** (especially Rome) able to dominate the whole Mediterranean world and to create and preserve for centuries the greatest civilization the world had ever known.

The obvious first move was to rediscover the forgotten texts of antiquity that provided evidence about the "secret," the internal dynamic, that had enabled ancient societies to achieve so much. Beginning with Petrarch himself, humanists rummaged through monastic and cathedral libraries, scoured the surviving book collections of the Byzantine Empire, and came up with what they thought was pure cultural gold: forgotten works of some major Latin authors who had been fairly widely known throughout the Middle Ages (such as **Cicero** and St. Augustine); works by other major Latin authors who had been known only at second hand or from fragmentary quotations in other authors (such as the rhetorician Quintilian and the historian Tacitus); and total rediscovery of the whole body of ancient **Greek** literature that is now known to classical scholars but (with one exception, Aristotle) had been virtually unknown throughout the Middle Ages. Only a handful of western Europeans between the seventh century and the end of the 14th could read Greek. Thanks to a great Byzantine scholar, **Manuel Chrysoloras**, who came to Italy and trained a cadre of talented Italian humanists to read Greek, 15th-century Italian readers were suddenly immersed in the treasures of one of the greatest literatures in human history, the literature of classical Greece. From the 15th century through the 16th, because of the hard work of Italian scholars who had learned Greek, classical and Hellenistic Greek literature became available in Latin translations that all educated men (and a handful of privileged women) could read: all of the great tragic and comic dramatists; Greek epic and lyric poetry (including Homer); major historians like Herodotus, Thucydides, and Polybius; works of prose fiction and pastoral romance.

As an extra bonus for a Christian society, command of Greek language also made available the original Greek text of the New Testament and the writings of the early Greek Fathers of the Christian Church, whose works had been little known in the medieval West. In philosophy, previously little but Aristotle's works had been known. Since the 13th century these had become the methodological foundation of **scholasticism**, one of the aspects of medieval "barbarism" that the humanists wanted to destroy or at least modify radically. Now translators made available all the works of other classical philosophers, especially **Plato**, who previously had been known mainly from references in the works of Latin authors. **Marsilio Ficino**, the Florentine philosopher who completed the first translation of the whole body of Plato's works, also translated the works of Plato's later disciples, the **Neoplatonists**, and he drew on these sources to create his own Christianized version of Neoplatonic philosophy, which had great influence in the 16th and 17th centuries, not only on professional philosophers but also—and more importantly—on the poets of all later centuries. If the classical literary tradition as a whole had any value at all for the later development of European civilization, its availability depended on the ancient Latin and Greek texts discovered, edited, and (after the 1450s) printed by humanist scholars.

It is difficult for our unclassical age to realize how profoundly the culture of Europe and America was shaped by this classical heritage. The gain from the humanists' work was not merely quantitative but also qualitative: more was known about ancient thought and society, but in addition, that knowledge was understood in a new way. Typically, medieval thinkers had combed through the ancient texts they knew in order to pick out isolated passages that seemed to bear on some topic they wanted to understand. They regarded such discrete passages as valid statements of the opinion of a particular author on a particular question; they assembled these selections into great, topically organized anthologies. Each selection was taken to be the totality of what such and such an ancient authority (Aristotle, for example) had to say on a particular question under discussion (the immortality of the soul, for example). This was the way in which scholasticism, the intellectual method of the medieval university, functioned. But from the time of Petrarch, some humanists realized that there was a major flaw in this approach to ancient texts. The method was reductive, treating the isolated passage cited as "the opinion" of a particular writer, containing the fullness of his opinion. There was no attention to what the words quoted might mean when viewed in the context of the original source, nor any interest in what the original author's purpose had been and what the extracted words might have meant to the author and his intended audience. The method was ahistorical, totally unaware of the context of a quotation. Inevitably, therefore, since scholastic writers tended to take their "authorities" not out of the original literary source but out of anthologies, medieval use of the ancients often distorted their meaning. Medieval thinkers' unawareness that ancient civilization was different from their own blinded them to the original meaning and often led them into crude, anachronistic misunderstandings.

As they struggled to understand their rediscovered sources, Renaissance humanists developed a sensitivity to the historical situation in which those sources had been produced. They developed a new, historically based critical sense and abandoned the naivete and gullibility typical of medieval authors. They perfected critical methods—both linguistic and historical—for detecting misinterpretations, interpolated or omitted passages, even outright forgeries that medieval thinkers had accepted uncritically. This development reached a peak in the middle and later 15th century in the humanistic scholarship of **Lorenzo Valla** and **Angelo Poliziano** and continued to develop in the 16th century in the scholarly writings of humanists like **Erasmus** and, at the end of the Renaissance, the French scholar **Josephus Justus Scaliger**. The skeptical, critical mentality typical of modern Western thought (a trait very little evident in even the most brilliant medieval authors) stems as much from the critical method of Renaissance humanists as from the slightly later demolition of ancient and medieval scientific beliefs by the great pioneers of modern science such as **Galileo Galilei**, René Descartes, and Isaac Newton.

Renaissance thinkers also gained from their new approach to classical authors many specific ideas that continued to play a role in subsequent Western culture—for example, an appreciation of the active life, as distinguished from the contemplative ideal of the Middle Ages. The humanists' reconsideration of the Roman statesman Cicero led them to understand two ideas that had escaped his medieval readers: first, that a mature and educated person has a moral obligation to participate actively in the social and political life of the community—thus the authority of Cicero called in question the value of a withdrawn, contemplative life such as the life of a monk; second, this moral obligation of a citizen is best fulfilled in a republican political system and not in a monarchy.

The historian Hans Baron contended that early humanism as developed by Petrarch in the 14th century did not become historically significant until the citizens of the republic of **Florence** (one of the few surviving republics in Renaissance Italy) drew inspiration from this "civic" and republican element in Roman culture during the city's fight to preserve its independence in the early 15th century and therefore adopted the humanistic cultural and educational program because it supported and propagated Roman civic values. Even in a predominantly monarchical Europe, a current of republican political principles lurked under the surface of humanism, occasionally becoming visible in the historical writings of **Leonardo Bruni**, in the political philosophy of Niccolò Machiavelli, and again, much later, in the republican ideology that emerged during the English civil wars of the 1640s. Baron's concept of **civic humanism** has been criticized by other scholars. Yet even one of his most persistent critics, Paul Oskar Kristeller, insisted that the central focus of humanist education was not abstract philosophical speculation but moral philosophy and the related study of the arts of effective communication, grammar, and rhetoric—precisely what Baron viewed as the educational preparation needed for leaders of a self-governing republic. Humanist teachers from the 15th through the 17th century attacked traditional medieval education for its concentration on abstract and impractical subjects like metaphysics and natural science, insisting that humanistic schools prepared citizens more adequately for real life by teaching them to understand their moral obligations as citizens and imparting the skills of effective speaking and writing (that is, the skills cultivated in humanistic schools) in order to prepare them to participate in public life, whether as citizens of a self-governing republic or even as advisers of a monarch.

As Baron's critics have correctly pointed out, the humanists' ideal of an obligation to engage in public service and their conviction that a moral and rhetorical (that is, humanistic) education was the best preparation for life was not applicable only to citizens of republics like Florence. Florence may have led the way in the adoption of humanist expression and humanist education by its dominant class, but monarchical courts like the duchy of **Milan** soon saw the utility of the new learning for their needs and began employing humanists as secretaries and counsellors to their rulers and as educators of their children. Humanism quickly became the cultural ideal of courtly societies like those at **Mantua** and **Ferrara**, where humanist schoolmasters founded influential schools to educate the sons (and even an occasional daughter) of the ruler and his closest advisers. This courtly adaptation of Renaissance culture was what made it attractive to the royal courts of northern Europe in the 16th century. Any latent republican implications of humanistic education remained discreetly out of sight unless unusual circumstances arose, such as the chaotic Italian political scene faced by Machiavelli's fellow Florentines or the collapse of the Stuart monarchy in 17th-century England.

Readers of Renaissance literature must understand that the humanists' quest for "renaissance" and "rediscovery" of the ancient past was conceived not as airy theory but as something needed in practical life. Our science-oriented society easily forgets that before the 18th and 19th centuries, scientific studies as pursued by university students of Aristotle seemed abstract, totally inapplicable to real life. Eloquence seemed useful; physics did not. The humanists' rejection of the medieval heritage was not a game; it was a demand for a better world, one more like the great world of **antiquity**.

This hostility to the Middle Ages can be understood only in terms of a reaction to the political and social chaos left behind in Italy after the final collapse of the medieval Holy Roman Empire in the 13th century. Violent internal struggles tore apart the self-governing urban societies of northern and central Italy. By the 14th century, most of them had resolved this political instability by accepting the rule of a *signore*—an authoritarian ruler who solved the problem of political disorder by suppressing political life. Only Florence, among the larger Italian cities, retained a considerable degree of free political life, and historians have speculated whether there is any relationship between this somewhat disorderly but relatively free political condition and the remarkable emergence of Florence from the late 14th century as the major center for the development of humanistic culture and the new Renaissance style of art. Frequent wars among the Italian states placed them all in jeopardy. The two greatest members of the **Medici** family that dominated 15th-century Florence struggled to limit these political rivalries and to preserve peace in order to prevent intervention by non-Italian powers. The whole Italian political system collapsed in 1494 when the king of France invaded Italy in order to assert his hereditary claim to the kingdom of **Naples**, and then was promptly driven out by a counter-invasion dispatched by King **Ferdinand** of Spain. More than 60 years of intermittent warfare between France and Spain for mastery of the Italian peninsula followed, ending in 1559 with the victory of Spain and the beginning of a Spanish domination of Italy that lasted until the 18th century. Whoever won the contest, the Italians lost. The deep vein of pessimism that marks the writings of the two greatest political philosophers of the Renaissance, Niccolò Machiavelli and **Francesco Guicciardini**, is a result of the dawning awareness that Italy no longer controlled its own political destiny.

The undercurrent of pessimism that inspired the humanists' dream of cultural and political renaissance also reflects discontent with the condition of the church. The idea that the Renaissance was anti-Christian or pagan is another of the myths perpetrated by 19th-century writers pursuing 19th-century goals. There is much evidence of deep religious devotion throughout Europe in this period, but the ecclesiastical institution—the church as represented by its leaders—was the subject of constant complaint and repeated waves of agitation for reform. The papacy had emerged more or less victorious from its struggles with the medieval German emperors, but it had also emerged deeply enmeshed in political and other material interests that led to neglect of spiritual matters. The **popes** of the Renaissance centuries functioned more often as shrewd political manipulators and ambitious territorial princes than as inspiring spiritual leaders. Through most of the 14th century, the popes did not even reside in Italy. A line of French popes established residence at **Avignon** (1309–1377) in what is now southeastern France. Scholars like Petrarch and saints like St. **Catherine of Siena** deplored the popes' abandonment of their proper capital and their immersion in worldly politics, and their call for reform of the church from top to bottom began with a demand that the papacy must return to Rome.

Yet when this return did occur in 1377, it was promptly followed by an even worse crisis. A disputed papal election left the church divided between two rival popes. This **Western Schism** (1378–1417) persisted for more than a generation and caused great turmoil in the life of the church. This spiritually devastating situation was resolved only by the extraordinary expedient of a general council convened at **Constance** by the Holy Roman Emperor Sigismund. The council was successful in dethroning the rival popes (by then, there were three contenders) and finally reunited the church by electing **Martin V**, a pope acceptable to all major parties. The schism undermined the prestige of the papacy; it set loose in Europe the doctrines of **Conciliarism**, which challenged the medieval idea of unlimited papal power. Although those who summoned the council sought not only to secure the election of a single pope but also to ensure sweeping reform of the whole church, once the new pope felt secure in his office, he began evading or ignoring the many promises of reform and power-sharing that he had made in order to secure election. Indeed, the popes in the later 15th century became even more enmeshed in the pursuit of wealth and political power than their predecessors. Reform of the church remained an unresolved issue that helped to prepare the way for the collapse of Christian unity during the Protestant **Reformation** of the 16th century.

Concern about political turmoil in Italy and about the corruption of the church was not the only reason why humanists longed to draw on the wisdom of antiquity in order to improve their own world. The 14th century experienced a severe economic downturn that some historians regard as the onset of a severe and persistent **economic depression**. The beginnings of a great drop in population can be documented even before the **Black Death**, the terrible plague that struck much of Europe between 1348 and 1350 and killed about a third of the population. A great financial crisis also predated the plague: in the early 1340s, both of the biggest international trading and banking companies in Florence, the **Bardi** and the **Peruzzi** firms, became bankrupt, and business and industry in the most highly developed parts of Europe (Italy and Flanders) suffered great losses. Historians still debate what impact (if any) the depressed economic conditions had on the development of the new Renaissance culture.

Other important developments that help to explain the desire for cultural and social renewal include the political collapse of the three major European monarchies of medieval Europe. The strong German monarchy of the earlier Middle Ages never recovered its power after the death of Frederick II in 1250. The royal and imperial title had been transformed into a weak elective monarchy in which the emperor had little direct authority over the country as a whole and most real power was in the hands of regional princes, prince-bishops, and self-governng cities. This weakness was permanent. Even when the Emperor **Charles V** became Europe's most powerful ruler during the 16th century, his power rested on the fact that he was also king of Spain, prince of the Netherlands, and hereditary ruler of Austria and other **Habsburg** lands in Germany. In France, the strong monarchy of the 13th century became unstable and faction-ridden, especially after King Edward III of England initiated the **Hundred Years' War** (1337–1453), which was really a whole series of wars involving not only the English king's attempt to secure the French royal title but also a series of internal civil wars among the higher ranks of the French aristocracy that for a time in the 1420s and 1430s seemed likely to end in the permanent division of France between the English king and the duke of Burgundy. France ultimately avoided this disaster and managed to drive out the English, but the country needed at least a generation of internal rebuilding before it could regain its leading role in European politics and cultural life. England eventually also paid a heavy price for its invasion of France. The financial burdens of the war and quarrels about the blame for the final defeat in 1453 led to a series of civil wars among the great English nobles, commonly known as the **Wars of the Roses**. They ended in 1485 with the military victory of the first **Tudor** king, **Henry VII**, who began the process of restoring royal power and stabilizing English government, a process that continued fairly successfully, but unevenly, through the whole 16th century, the period when English Renaissance culture reached its full development.

An important development of the late 15th century was the spread of interest in humanistic learning and Italian Renaissance art into northern Europe. This process began slowly and haltingly, but by the early 16th century, the new Renaissance culture was established in France, England, the Netherlands, and Germany, and had even extended its influence to the eastern borderlands of Latin Christendom, the kingdoms of Poland, Bohemia, and Hungary. The mechanisms for this migration of Renaissance culture across the Alps (and across the Mediterranean to Spain and Portugal) were well established. One of them was the international character of Italian commerce from the 13th century. The trading and banking operations of Italian businessmen spread far beyond Italy. By the 14th century, large colonies of Italian merchants were settled in London, Paris, Lyons, Barcelona, but above all in the cities of Flanders and Brabant, the most economically developed region of northern Europe. Italian firms established branches and subsidiaries in many of these centers. They not only imported and exported merchandise but lent money, especially to rulers who could do them favors. The bankers were inevitably involved in the exchange of money, which became a highly profitable part of their business. The profitability of their business, especially their exchange activity, depended on having the latest information on political and economic events, both at home in Italy and in the transalpine markets; hence information of many sorts constantly flowed back and forth, keeping the insiders of the business world informed of the latest news. The Italian staff of the foreign branches often spent years living abroad and forming personal and cultural relations as well as economic relations with people in the host countries. Italians abroad naturally promoted interest in the art and literature of their homeland, and they also developed interest in the culture of the host countries.

The Catholic Church was another avenue of cultural transfer. By its very nature it was an international organization, with a highly centralized administrative curia at Rome that required the constant shuttling of prelates, diplomats, and financial agents back and forth between Rome and the royal courts and ecclesiastical centers of Catholic Europe. Italian prelates and their staff travelled to the north, sometimes as transient visitors but also as long-term residents, often holding valuable church offices in non-Italian regions. Many of these clerical travellers were men of education and talent. They naturally brought with them their native Renaissance interests, which they continued to pursue in the presence of their hosts. Northern clerics travelled to Rome to petition for papal appointments or to pursue litigation in the church's elaborate judicial system. Some of them had their eyes opened by the wealth, splendor, luxury, and size of Italian cities. Even when tinged with envy and resentment, northern reactions showed awareness that Italy had developed a distinctive new model of civilization.

At least as important as this network of international ecclesiastical connections was the allure of Italian **universities** for northern students. Italian universities were essentially schools of law and medicine, reputedly the best and certainly the most prestigious in Europe. Ambitious and privileged students from north of the Alps came there in increasing numbers, determined to get at **Bologna** or **Padua** or one of several other schools doctorates in law or medicne that would enhance their careers back home. Foreign students rarely came intending to study humanistic subjects; **Ferrara** was a rare exception to this rule, thanks to the great reputation of its leading teacher of humanities, **Guarino Guarini**. But even though they came to study law or medicine, these foreigners spent several years living in cities dominated intellectually by **humanism**. They lived in the midst of the artistic culture of the Renaissance. Many of them were permanently won over to the new learning and the new art they saw in Italy.

German students were the most numerous group, though students came from as far away as Scandinavia and Scotland. Every one of the early humanists who pioneered the integration of humanistic studies into German schools and universities had lived in Italy. **Peter Luder** studied under Guarino at Ferrara and spent at least 20 years in Italy. **Rudolf Agricola** spent a decade there, studying law at Padua and humanities at Ferrara and then becoming organist at the cultivated Renaissance court of the duke of Ferrara. **Conrad Celtis** spent less time— two years—in Italy, but he met the philosopher Marsilio Ficino at Florence and the humanist **Pomponio Leto** at Rome. While he resented the arrogant pose of superiority that many Italians affected, his avowed goal when he began teaching in Germany was to arouse his fellow Germans to capture the leadership in humanistic learning from the Italians. The same story could be told of the pioneers of Renaissance learning in Spain (where their own king ruled Sicily and Naples), England, the Netherlands, Hungary, and Poland. In all of these countries, well-connected graduates of Italian universities rose to wealth and power in royal and ecclesiastical administrations. Once they became rich and influential, such Italian-educated men used their wealth and leisure to encourage interest in humanism and to patronize Renaissance art in their homeland. Thus study in Italy became an important mechanism fostering the growth of interest in Renaissance culture by ambitious youths in each country. France is somewhat exceptional. The incipient humanistic movement led by the royal chancellor, **Jean de Montreuil**, was devastated by his assassination during a palace revolution in 1418 and by the disasters of renewed English invasion. Not until the English had been expelled in 1453 and a new monarch had spent a generation rebuilding the nation was France in a position to pursue interest in Renaissance culture. When it did, the prestige of its own universities made study in Italy less appealing. The first two effective leaders of early French humanism, **Guillaume Fichet** and **Robert Gaguin**, had not studied in Italy, though both of them felt the attraction of the new Renaissance learning.

International relations and dynastic marriages also stimulated northern interest in the new Renaissance culture. The ruling classes of Italy and northern Europe operated in the same political universe and the same marriage pool. The French invasion of Italy in 1494—often mistakenly taken to mark the beginning of the Renaissance in France—had its roots in dynastic marriages between members of the French royal family and Italian princesses. The peak of Renaissance influence in Hungary occurred in part because the Hungarian king, **Matthias Corvinus**, was married to Princess Beatrix of Naples, whose presence and Italian entourage helped to make the royal court at Buda a brilliant center for the diffusion of italianate culture. In Poland also, the marriage of King Sigismund I to Bona Sforza, a daughter of the duke of Milan, made Italian influences powerful at the royal court in Cracow. While Bona was only moderately interested in literature and humanistic scholarship, she actively influenced royal patronage of the visual arts and music and of course favored artists who worked in the Renaissance style. In Hungary, Poland, and also Bohemia, most of the earliest humanists were men who had studied in Italy. Even at times when the royal courts were preoccupied with other matters, native bishops who had studied at Italian universities actively promoted the Renaissance learning.

In all parts of Europe, the new art of **printing** worked to diffuse texts (both classical and contemporary) and speed the diffusion of ideas. Especially important was the ability of printing to reproduce drawings accurately, for illustrated books and engraved prints acted to spread awareness of Italian Renaissance art, both through woodcut imitations of Italian masterpieces and through the production of original prints engraved by the Italian artists themselves, who found a new market in printmaking. The greatest artist of the German Renaissance, **Albrecht Dürer**, made his first trip to Italy in 1494 because both printed copies of Italian art and word-of-mouth reports from travellers convinced him that it would be worth his while to spend a year studying the art of Italy before he settled down in Nuremberg. He met important painters like **Andrea Mantegna** and **Giovanni Bellini**, and his two Italian trips played a major role in transforming him from a promising young painter in the traditional northern style into the great genius of German Renaissance art.

The northern humanists seem to have focused their attention much more strongly than their Italian counterparts on the problem of religious reform. The French humanist **Jacques Lefèvre d'Etaples** and the Dutch humanist Erasmus were the outstanding leaders of this movement. Erasmus in particular became a truly international figure during the second decade of the 16th century. His "philosophy of Christ," a program of a moderate, gradual reform of the church through humanistic education of future curial officials and bishops, may or may not have had a chance to produce meaningful reform, but it had a great appeal to idealistic young humanists of the early 16th century. This development was interrupted by the outbreak of the Protestant Reformation at the end of 1517. The Reformation did not destroy humanism and Renaissance culture, but it significantly changed their direction, not only in the regions that became predominantly Protestant but also in those that remained Roman Catholic. **Martin Luther** himself was educated in the scholastic theology of the late Middle Ages, but he was interested in humanism and made humanistic educational reform (both at the university level and in the Latin grammar schools) a significant part of his reform program. The Renaissance and the Reformation came to be intertwined in complex ways. Nearly all of the major leaders of the Reformation except Luther himself began their careers as young, enthusiastic followers of Erasmus' dream of a moderate humanistic reform within the structures of the old church. But at some early point, each of these leaders became converted to "Evangelical" (i.e., Lutheran) as distinct from "evangelical" (i.e., reformist Catholic) belief. Without the humanists, Luther would never have found the talented collaborators who transformed the Reformation into a mass movement that in parts of Germany and Switzerland, and later in other regions, swept away the authority of the medieval church.

The Reformation goal of regenerating the corrupt contemporary world by recapturing the spirit of early Christianity as found in the Bible was a true product of the Renaissance, but it was simultaneously something else, a religious ideology and a popular social movement that produced lasting changes never envisioned by the pre-Reformation humanists. Yet Renaissance humanism also had an impact on the revived Catholicism of the 16th century. While moderate reformist humanism was almost exterminated by the triumphant conservatives who dominated the papal curia and the Council of Trent from the 1540s, major elements of the humanist educational program, including study of classical languages and literature and even some critical study of the Bible and patristic literature, were cautiously adopted. By the end of the 16th century, the schools of the new **Jesuit** order were active in much of Catholic Europe and offered some of the best humanistic education available.

The Renaissance is also one of the greatest periods in the history of art. Although Renaissance critics like **Giorgio Vasari** regarded the striking changes in style between late-medieval artists like **Duccio** and **Cimabue** and the works of **Giotto** and such great masters of High Renaissance art as Michelangelo as a simple case of rediscovering how to make good art after centuries of artistic incompetence, the true story is far more complex. The artistic Renaissance involved a rethinking of the nature and purpose of art, not just a "rediscovery" of something that had been forgotten. If the story told about **Filippo Brunelleschi** by Vasari is true, and Brunelleschi after losing a major competition to a rival sculptor really did go off to Rome and spend time measuring the proportions of ancient buildings and statues, then perhaps his new mastery of vanishing-point **perspective** is an example of literal rediscovery of an ancient skill that had been lost. Yet no known work of ancient art matches the sophisticated treatment of perspective that emerged suddenly, within about a decade, in the work of Brunelleschi and his Florentine contemporaries **Donatello** and **Masaccio**. There can be no doubt that Brunelleschi and his peers carefully studied the art of classical antiquity. Yet there is plenty of evidence of medieval artists who also studied ancient works. The true spirit of Renaissance art (like the Renaissance in general) sprang from other sources as well as from the example of ancient Rome, and it involved a change in outlook more than simple rediscovery.

The real driving force behind early Renaissance art was the hunger of a wealthy Italian society for artistic beauty. The works of Giotto, and later on, the works of Donatello or Masaccio are not mere repetitions of ancient art, and their creators responded not to some abstract ideology of classical style but to the artists' desire to please themselves and the patrons who paid them. Early Renaissance art conformed to the tastes of a society that was deeply engaged in making a living, rearing its families, and defending its cities from rival powers. So art had to appeal to the tastes of substantial, hard-working, and well-to-do people. These people, like most of the artists, were also pious Christians who wanted their art to reflect their own values, both worldly and other-worldly. Saints outnumber pagan heroes and gods in the paintings of the early Renaissance. Art of the **Quattrocento**, though influenced by Antiquity, was made for the citizens of the day, and many of the greatest commissions came from religious confraternities and guilds and even city governments, not from effete intellectuals driven only by some abstract commitment to a mythical Antiquity. The painters and sculptors themselves were not men of great erudition, and when in the later Renaissance aristocratic intellectuals did call for art that depicted classical myths and heroes, the artist needed guidance from the prince's humanistically educated subject in order to treat classical themes in a properly classical way. Renaissance art was shaped by the ancient past, but it grew out of the life of its own times; and the men (and the few women) who made it were experts in refined manual skills and the artful composition of images, not in humanistic learning. Behind the shift from the art of the early Renaissance, with its reflection of a world similar to the life of its own time (in the works of Masaccio, for example), to the coterie art of the Medicean intellectuals of Florence in the 1480s (illustrated by **Sandro Botticelli**, with his classicized imagery that could be decoded only by the educated elite), there was a change in political and social conditions, not just acquisition of more knowledge about ancient myths. In the end, the greatness of Renaissance art was a product of the turbulent energy and creative power of the society that produced it.

If Renaissance art is difficult to reconcile with the notion that the Renaissance was simply a recovery of ancient civilization, Renaissance music confounds facile explanations even more sharply. First of all, no one then or later really knew what ancient music sounded like, though humanists' study of ancient texts and works of art did produce a few hints about performance practice and instrumentation. Second, even ancient musical theory, the one aspect of music that was written down in texts that people could read, was imperfectly known. In the Middle Ages, the work *De institutione musica / Introduction to Music* by the sixth-century author Boethius was the only ancient text on music that was widely known. His account presented music in terms of abstract numerical relations and cosmic harmony. It made music a branch of philosophy but gave no guide to music that people could listen to. Humanistic translation of Greek texts during the 15th and 16th centuries produced additional knowledge about ancient musical theory, but the main effect of this added information was not a revolution in composition and performance but a series of poisonous squabbles between contemporary theorists. Some (such as **Vincenzo Galileo**, father of the famous scientist) demanded strict observance of classical standards, while others (such as **Gioseffo Zarlino**) defended medieval musical developments such as counterpoint even though no ancient authority mentioned them.

A third reason why the story of "Renaissance music" cannot be told in terms of simple rediscovery is the location of the center of musical innovation. All other Renaissance cultural innovations began in the cities of Italy and eventually spread to Europe north of the Alps. But in music, the decisive innovations began in northern France and the Burgundian Netherlands and spread south to revolutionize the music performed in the churches and secular courts of Italy. The names of the pioneers of Renaissance music are French and Flemish: **Guillaume de Machaut, Guillaume Dufay, Johannes Ockeghem, Josquin des Prés, Heinrich Isaak, Jacob Obrecht, Adrian Willaert**, and **Rolandus Lassus**. All of them were trained in their northern homelands; all of them at some point served the dukes of Burgundy or the kings of France. But nearly all of them spent a major portion of their careers in Italy, attracted by the lavish support available at the courts of rulers like the dukes of Milan and Urbino or at great ecclesiastical establishments like the basilica of St. Mark at **Venice** or the court of the popes at Rome. They not only composed and performed but also taught, exerting a revolutionary impact on native Italian musical traditions and training a generation of Italian disciples like **Andrea Gabrieli, Giovanni Palestrina**, and **Claudio Monteverdi**. Thus the flow of influence in music ran contrary to that in art, humanistic scholarship, and vernacular literature—from north to south. The Italian musicians of the late Renaissance do reflect one direct influence from humanist culture. Efforts to stage ancient Greek dramas in an "ancient" manner led to the combination of music and drama, a process that led directly in the work of Gabrieli and Monteverdi to the invention of opera, one of the great art forms passed by the late Renaissance to the post-Renaissance world of the 17th century.

The proper date for the end of a dictionary focused on the Renaissance is even more debatable than the date for its beginning. Scholarly convention has long identified the lifetime of Petrarch (1304–1374) as the beginning of the Renaissance. If the true hallmark of the Renaissance is devotion to the humanists' dream of recovering the works of ancient civilization and then using this recovered knowledge to inspire and guide a revitalization of the contemporary world, it seems that this rather naive faith in the regenerative power of the classical heritage was waning during the closing decades of the 16th century, even though the remarkable mastery of classical languages and literature, and also the sophisticated techniques of linguistic and historical criticism developed by humanistic scholars, lived on into the 17th and subsequent centuries. **Michel de Montaigne**, for example, had remarkable classical learning and used countless examples from ancient authors to illustrate his meaning, yet he pointedly refused to accept ancient examples as definitive, and he privileged his own personal experience above the alleged wisdom of antiquity. When, a generation later, one comes to **Francis Bacon**, who also had a fine humanistic education but who explicitly declared that in his opinion the "ancients" did not represent the mature, accumulated wisdom of the human race but instead reflected the callow, immature youth of humanity, one might well declare that (for him at least) the Renaissance was over. Even so, certain figures of later date have been conventionally regarded as expressions of Renaissance civilization. **John Milton**, for example, despite his late date, was so constantly guided by the inspiration of classical literature based on his Renaissance education that he usually ranks as a major figure (the last one) of the English Renaissance.

Readers should not be dismayed by the evidence of disagreement and debate among modern scholars reflected in this introduction and in some of the articles in this book. A close and honest look into any other historical period—classical Greece, the Middle Ages, the French Revolution—would reveal the same degree of disagreement. History is messy, inconsistent, conflicted; after all, history is the work of human beings. The challenge to thoughtful readers is to join the debate and learn to appreciate the efforts of people in other places and other ages to face and solve their problems.

The Dictionary

– A –

ACADEMIES. Associations, originally loosely organized and unofficial, formed from about the middle of the 15th century by local groups of Italian **humanists** to promote the growth of humanistic studies and in general the revival of ancient civilization. The use of the term "academy" was a reminiscence of the **Platonic** Academy of ancient Athens. From about 1540, local princes and city governments sometimes sponsored and encouraged such associations, which tended to become more formal than previously. The academies consisted of self-proclaimed leaders of intellectual life, and both before and after the age of public sponsorship, membership in them was a sign of belonging to the intellectual elite. The Roman Academy of the 15th century sprang up as an informal association among the humanists employed in papal administrative agencies. **Pomponio Leto**, one of the most erudite humanists of the day, was its central figure. Pope Paul II suppressed the group in 1468–1469, supposedly because its enthusiasm for ancient culture raised suspicions of pagan religious practices, but more likely because he suspected some of its members of political conspiracy. The organization revived under Popes **Julius II** and **Leo X**, both of whom had been associated with the earlier group, but **Clement VII** suppressed it in the aftermath of the imperial army's sack of the city of Rome in 1527. The most influential of the early informal academies was the so-called Platonic Academy of **Florence**, a loose association of intellectuals dominated by the philosopher **Marsilio Ficino** and devoted to the propagation of Plato's philosophy. This group included humanists like **Angelo Poliziano** and **Cristoforo Landino** but also wealthy patricians and politicians such as **Bernardo Rucellai** and **Lorenzo de'Medici**. By no means all assemblies of local notables and intellectuals called themselves academies: the informal gatherings in the gardens of Bernardo Rucellai in the late 15th century to discuss political questions, meetings that had an impact on the political thought of **Niccolò Machiavelli**, were never called an academy.

By the 16th century, most large Italian cities had several academies, while even small towns had one or two. Most of this activity remained informal, and many academies were short-lived. Some academies specialized in one or a few defined fields of learning, such as Platonist philosophy or natural science; others took the whole of human learning as their subject. In a number of places, local rulers became the patrons of such groups. By 1600 several hundred academies had been founded in Italy, and some major cities had large numbers. For example, **Rome** in the 17th century had 132, a mark of its leading position in Italian cultural life in that period. By no means all academies were serious associations of scholars. Humor and recreation were often more important than scholarly activity. One that was scholarly was the Florentine Academy (about 1540), devoted to preservation of the Tuscan dialect as the literary language for all educated Italians. Its successor, the Accademia della Crusca, founded in 1582, pursued the same goal. There were academies for discussion and perfection of the fine arts, such as the **Carracci** academy founded at **Bologna** in the late 16th century to promote certain stylistic trends in painting, or the Accademia del Disegno in Florence. In the late 16th and 17th centuries, scientific academies like the Accademia dei Lincei at Rome (1603–1630) and the Accademia del Cimento at Florence (1657–1667) were important as centers for critical assessment of Aristotelian science that would not have been tolerated in the tradition-bound universities.

From late in the reign of **Francis I** (1515–1547), French intellectuals encouraged their government to foster academies similar to the Italian ones. While most Italian academies remained essentially local, the growth of centralized royal authority in northern Europe led to the emergence of large, nationally organized academies founded and sometimes even financed by the royal government, such as the Académie Française (1634), devoted to literary and linguistic studies, the Académie Royale des Sciences (1666), devoted to natural science, and the Royal Society of London (1660), which fostered learning in general but increasingly focused its attention on natural science.

The academies of Renaissance Europe were never conceived or organized as schools. Although formal lectures might be delivered, such as those of Ficino on Platonic philosophy, there was never a program of formal instruction. The academies were essentially gatherings of like-minded scholars to discuss ideas and problems in which the members had a shared interest. The most serious ones were historically important because they provided relatively informal settings in which controversial issues and new ideas could be discussed in a way that would have been impossible in **universities** and institutions dedicated to the instruction of youth.

ACHILLINI, ALESSANDRO (1463–1512). Italian physician, anatomist, and philosopher, a moderate follower of the "Averroistic" interpretation of **Aristotle** that dominated philosophical teaching in 15th-century Italy. His philosophy reflects the influence of the English **scholastic** philosopher William of Ockham. Educated at the **University of Bologna**, Achillini taught logic, natural philosophy, and medicine there and at **Padua**. He was an early practitioner of dissection of the human body. His chief medical works were *Humani corporis anatomia / Anatomy of the Human Body* and the posthumous *Annotationes anatomicae / Notes on Anatomy* (1520).

ADRIAN VI (1454–1523, pope 1522–1523). Born Adriaan Floriszoon at Utrecht, he became the outstanding member of the theological faculty at **Louvain** and served as tutor to the future Emperor **Charles V**. This connection drew him into political service to the **Habsburg** dynasty. When Charles inherited the Spanish throne in 1516, Adriaan accompanied him to Spain, where he served as regent during Charles' many absences. He became bishop of Tortosa and a cardinal. In 1522 a deadlocked college of cardinals unanimously elected him **pope**, the last non-Italian chosen until John Paul II in 1978. Although a conservative scholastic theologian, he showed some sympathy for scholarly editions of biblical and patristic texts by **humanists** like **Erasmus**, whom he invited to enter papal service. Adrian was admired for his personal piety and moral integrity and showed awareness of the need for significant reform of the church. Entrenched members of the papal bureaucracy resented him as a foreign intruder and a threat to their lifestyle. His early death prevented him from carrying out his plan for a genuine but conservative reform. He firmly opposed what he regarded as the theological errors and insubordination of **Martin Luther** and other leaders of the **Reformation**.

AGRICOLA, GEORG (vernacular name Georg Bauer, 1490–1555). German writer on metallurgy and mining. Educated in Latin grammar at Leipzig and in medicine at **Bologna**, he wrote on subjects ranging from grammar to weights and measures to the plague, but his work as a physician in a mining town in Bohemia gave rise to an interest in minerals and metallurgy that led to several publications on mines and fossils, culminating in his *De re metallica / On Metals* (1556), a summary of the most advanced knowledge in metal-working and mining, accompanied by hundreds of woodcut illustrations.

AGRICOLA, RUDOLF (Latinized name Roelof Huisman, 1444–1485). Frisian **humanist**. The illegitimate son of a clergyman, he received an excellent grammatical education at Groningen and then studied at the universities of Erfurt, Cologne, and **Louvain**, taking the M.A. degree in 1465 at Louvain, where he began the study of law and became interested in Italian humanism. He was also a talented musical performer and composer. In 1469 he continued his study of law at Pavia in Italy but soon shifted his interest to humanism (*studia humanitatis*). In 1475–1479 he was employed as an organist by the duke of **Ferrara**. Ferrara was a major center of humanistic education, and Agricola studied **Greek** there. He moved back to Germany in 1479, living first at Dillingen, where he completed his major work, *De inventione dialectica / On Dialectical Invention* (not published until 1515). In 1480 he became secretary to the city council of Groningen, but he found both his official duties and the intellectual climate unsatisfying.

In 1482 Agricola accepted the patronage of Johann von Dalberg, bishop of Worms, adviser to the Elector of the Palatinate, and chancellor of the University of Heidelberg. Although linked more closely to the electoral court than to the university, he participated actively in local intellectual life and began the study of **Hebrew**. In 1485, returning from a diplomatic mission to Rome, he fell ill and died. Though his major work remained unpublished until 1515, he left behind a great reputation among German humanists. His *De inventione* *dialectica* became the central text in humanistic reform of the study of dialectic from the time of its publication, and most of the textbooks used for the study of dialectic after the humanists became able to push through reforms of the university curriculum were derived from it. Agricola also published an influential life of the Italian humanist **Petrarch** and a work upholding the value of education in the humanities. He was admired by the humanists of the generation of **Erasmus**, who recalled briefly meeting him while still a schoolboy in Deventer.

AGRIPPA VON NETTESHEIM, HEINRICH CORNELIUS (1486–1535). German **humanist** and polymath, known in his own time principally for his learning in **magic** and other occult sciences. Born near Cologne and educated in liberal arts there, he seems to have studied also at Dôle, Paris, and Pavia and claimed degrees in both law and medicine. He studied **Greek** and **Hebrew** and investigated occult learning that he believed to be very ancient, such as the Jewish mystical thought known as **Cabala** and the **Hermetic** books. In 1510 Agrippa produced the first version of his famous book on magic, *De occulta philosophia / On Occult Philosophy*, which was first printed in 1531–1533. Although he was influenced by the German humanist and Cabalist **Johann Reuchlin** and the occultist abbot **Johannes Trithemius** of Sponheim, his mastery of both humanistic studies and the occult arts increased greatly during six years (1512–1518) spent in Italy. He may have taken a law degree during this period, but he spent most of it studying and lecturing on occult arts and **Neoplatonic** philosophy. His subsequent writings, including the revised version of *De occulta philosophia*, show influence by the Italian Neoplatonists **Marsilio Ficino** and **Giovanni Pico della Mirandola**. Like them Agrippa affirmed the existence of a body of secret learning, originally revealed by God and embodied in the books of the Jewish Cabalists, Hermes Trismegistus, Pythagoras, Zoroaster, and **Plato**. These interests reflect a Christianized religious universalism that acknowledged a divine revelation at the roots of every human culture.

Between 1518 and 1524, Agrippa lived in Metz, Geneva, and Swiss Fribourg as city legal counsellor, medical director of the civic hospital, and city physician, respectively. In this period he displayed sympathy with the Lutheran **Reformation**, though he was a critic of church corruption and clerical arrogance rather than an adherent of Lutheran theology. At Metz Agrippa defended the French humanist **Lefèvre d'Etaples** from attacks by local mendicant friars. In 1524 he moved to Lyon as personal physician to Louise of Savoy, mother of King **Francis I**. Resentment of his outspoken criticism of the queen mother, suspicions of sympathy for **Martin Luther**, and objections to his study and practice of magic caused him to lose favor at court.

During this time of disappointment and financial hardship, Agrippa wrote his second major book, *De incertitudine et vanitate scientium et artium / On the Uncertainty and Vanity of All Sciences and Arts*, first published in 1530. In it he discusses every field of human endeavor and every type of academic learning and concludes that all of them are unreliable and useless; only a simple Christian piety based on the words of Scripture has enduring value.

In 1528 he moved to the Netherlands, where he became historiographer to the governor, Margaret of Austria. Once again, Agrippa's interest in magic, suspicions that he favored the Lutheran cause, and resentment of his caustic attacks on traditional learning and established religious and political authorities cost him the favor of his patron. He left the Netherlands in 1532 to live with a new patron, the archbishop-elector of Cologne, Hermann von Wied. He moved to Lyon in 1535 and was briefly arrested because of his public criticisms of the mother of King Francis. He died at Grenoble later that year.

In his own time and for centuries afterward, Agrippa was famous (or infamous) chiefly for his knowledge and active practice of occult arts such as **astrology** and **alchemy**, but also for his skeptical book on the uncertainty of human knowledge, *De incertitudine et vanitate*. Popular stories about his magical learning and practices made him the subject of legends and bred rumors of diabolical connections. These stories merged with contemporary legends about the German charlatan Georg Faust (ca. 1480–1540), so that the literary figure of Faust in German popular books and in the famous play by the English dramatist **Christopher Marlowe** contains elements derived from the life and legend of Agrippa. He revelled in paradoxical assertions contrary to contemporary opinion, a tendency expressed not only in *De incertitudine et vanitate* but also in his *De nobilitate et praecellentia foeminei sexus / On the Nobility and Superiority of the Female Sex*, which defended the proposition that the female sex is not only equal but actually superior to the male sex, an opinion wildly contrary to prevailing opinion. This little book was frequently reprinted and translated into several European vernaculars during the 16th and 17th centuries.

ALBERTI, LEON BATTISTA (1404–1472). Italian **humanist** and architect, unusual in that he bridged the social gap between the educated humanist and the practicing artist. Born at Genoa as the illegitimate son of an exiled Florentine banker, he studied law at **Bologna** but was more interested in classical studies. His humanistic writings included a Latin comedy and a collection of original dialogues and essays on moral issues, the *Intercenales / Dinner Pieces*. He also produced two vernacular works on love that became very popular in his own lifetime, and a treatise on domestic life, *Della famiglia / On the Family*, that discussed housekeeping, estate management, marriage, and child-rearing. Alberti's literary reputation and his excellent Latin style won him employment at the papal curia. In 1432 he accompanied the curia to **Florence**. There he met the leading Florentine humanists and painters. Although his upbringing in northern Italy made the Tuscan literary language alien to him, he produced the first grammar of literary Italian, *Grammatica della lingua toscana / Grammar of the Tuscan Language*.

Alberti was best known in later times for his *De re aedificatoria / On the Art of Building* (1452), a Latin treatise on the theory and practice of architecture based on the Roman architect Vitruvius. He also wrote a treatise on sculpture and the influential *Elementa picturae / The Elements of Painting* (1435), which contains a clear description of the principles of single-point (linear) **perspective** introduced into Italian art by the sculptor **Donatello** and the painter **Masaccio**. He wrote many other books, including philosophical treatises and a pioneering Latin treatise on cryptography. Alberti also became a successful architect, admired for his design of the Palazzo **Rucellai** in Florence and the church of S. Andrea at **Mantua** and for remodelling the exterior of the church of S. Francesco at Rimini in the classical style.

ALBIZZI FAMILY. Wealthy mercantile family of **Florence** whose head, Maso degli Albizzi, led a junta of wealthy families who seized control of the city by force in 1382. This event reversed a period of democratizing political reform (1343–1382) and left a faction of rich families headed by Maso in charge. While their successes in defending the city from the aggressive **Giangaleazzo Visconti** of **Milan** and conquering the seaport city of **Pisa** made their domination tolerable, there was resentment at the way in which the Albizzi corrupted the republican constitution and put effective control into the hands of a junta.

When Maso died in 1417, his son Rinaldo degli Albizzi (1370–1442) became the faction leader. Unlike his father, Rinaldo had an aloof manner and exerted his political power openly, stirring up resentment even among Albizzi partisans. Faced with political unrest generated by his failed attempt (1429–1433) to conquer the city of Lucca, Rinaldo decided to strike down the most popular potential leader of political opposition, **Cosimo de'Medici**, who had tried to avoid direct confrontation but had opposed the rash attempt to conquer Lucca. Rinaldo had Cosimo put on trial for treason before a special judicial commission (*balìa*). Although the Albizzi dominated the *balìa*, there were enough moderate members that the body decided to sentence Cosimo to exile rather than executing him.

This arbitrary treatment of a popular and respected citizen merely increased resentment. Just a year later, in 1434, a newly selected *signoria* reversed the sentence against Cosimo. Rinaldo attempted an armed coup, but the *signoria* had taken effective measures to prevent his seizure of power. Sympathizers with Cosimo now created a special court (*balìa*) to reform the government. The recall of Cosimo was confirmed, and Rinaldo himself, together with his closest political supporters, was banished. Rinaldo's fall from power marks the beginning of 60 years (1434–1494) of almost unbroken Medici political dominance of the republic.

ALCALÁ DE HENARES, UNIVERSITY OF. New Spanish university formally founded in 1499 by Cardinal **Francisco Ximénes de Cisneros**, archbishop of Toledo. After careful preparation, instruction began in 1508. Although Cardinal Ximénes was a conservative friar, he was determined to reform the Spanish church by fostering deeper spirituality and by creating a new leadership based on merit rather than family influence. This goal implied preparation of an educated elite of future leaders of the clergy. Even though Ximénes was in no way a **humanist**, he realized that this goal meant an emphasis on study of the Bible and therefore provided professorships in **Hebrew** and **Greek**, the two biblical languages. Thus even though founded by a conservative Franciscan theologian, Alcalá became the first university that fulfilled the humanists' goal of **trilingual** (Latin, Greek, and Hebrew) learning.

Ximénes also sponsored scholarly study of the text of the Bible, assembling a team of experts who produced a multilingual edition known as the **Complutensian Polyglot Bible**. Although formal theological instruction was still based on medieval scholastic authors, the emphasis on linguistic study of the biblical sources aligned the university with Renaissance humanism and made Alcalá one of the centers for the growth of humanism in 16th-century Spain.

ALCHEMY. Science (or pseudoscience) that studied the transformation of physical substances from one nature to another and attempted to discover, regularize, and apply the relationships and procedures discovered through observation and experimentation to perform useful works, not only the transmutation of base metals into gold but also the production of chemical medicines. In a general way, it was a precursor of modern chemistry, and until at least the 18th century the distinction between genuine chemical reactions and alchemical transmutations was vague.

Alchemy was known in ancient times, often linked with jewellers and metallurgists; it passed from the ancients to medieval Arabic natural philosophers and from them, along with other Arabic science, to Christian scholars. Its theoretical foundation was belief in a hierarchical organization of the universe, a theory that seemed to support the idea that the material nature of one substance could be transformed into a different substance through some sort of manipulation. The whole field was given credibility by the vaguely **Platonic** idea that the entire universe, inorganic as well as organic, is alive.

Sometimes alchemists sought to apply spiritual forces (angelic or demonic) to facilitate their work, and in that case they were practicing something very close to **witchcraft**. Alchemists observed **astrological** signs and sought to carry out their work when the influences of the stars would favor their goal. The desire for gold and other precious substances (such as gemstones) explains why individuals, even rulers, sometimes granted subsidies to alchemists who promised to increase their wealth.

Although making gold from base metals was the most common goal of alchemists, others sought to produce the "philosopher's stone," which supposedly had the power to heal disease, to prolong life, and to "perfect" metals. Similar medical and material advantage was believed to result from operations that produced the "quintessence" or fifth element. This fifth element was thought to possess great powers, including the power to cure disease and prolong life. Almost always, chemical learning was occult—that is, kept secret—and the alchemist normally claimed to have secret information that would ensure the success of his experiments even though others had failed. A particularly influential practitioner of alchemy was the unconventional physician **Paracelsus**.

ALCIATI, ANDREA (1492–1550). Italian **humanist** and lawyer, educated in classical languages in his native **Milan** and then in law at Pavia, **Bologna**, and **Ferrara**. His *Emblematum liber / Book of Emblems* (1531) was one of the most influential examples of a type of Renaissance publication, the **emblem-book**, that became popular and was imitated throughout late Renaissance Europe. His other claim to fame was as a reformer of legal study. While teaching at the papal university at **Avignon** in 1518, he developed a new approach to jurisprudence inspired by humanism. What set Alciati apart from traditional teachers of Roman law was his application of the critical linguistic and textual methods of the humanists to the standard text of Roman law, the *Corpus Juris Civilis*, while belittling the commentaries and glosses by medieval jurists, which had come to be the main focus of traditional legal education. Just as the humanists did with literary texts, he taught directly from the ancient text, giving a philological and historical exposition. This humanistic approach caused great enthusiasm among his students at Avignon and **Bourges** and came to be known as "the French manner" (*mos gallicus*), in contrast to the traditional "Italian manner" (*mos italicus*) which focused attention on the opinions of famous medieval professors.

Mos gallicus found more followers in French and German jurisprudence than in Italy, though most followers adopted a hybrid approach that combined the new with the traditional. Alciati's development of this new approach to Roman law was strongly influenced by the Florentine humanist **Angelo Poliziano**, by the Dutch humanist

Erasmus, and by his French friend **Guillaume Budé**. He eventually returned to Italy, where he ended his career as one of the most famous law professors of his generation.

ALDINE PRESS. *See* MANUTIUS, ALDUS.

ALDROVANDI, ULISSE (1522–1605). Italian physician and naturalist, known for his travels throughout Europe in pursuit of scientific knowledge and for his publications in that field. He established a botanical garden in 1568 in **Bologna**, where he received his medical degree and later became professor of botany and natural history. His publications in natural history are primarily collections of information, some of it traditional and even mythical but a large part of it based on his personal observations. Subjects covered by his publications included birds, insects, fish, and quadrupeds.

ALEANDRO, GIROLAMO (1480–1542). Italian **humanist** who later became one of the most influential agents of papal opposition to the **Reformation**. A native of Treviso, educated at **Padua**, he began his career in the service of a wealthy cardinal at **Venice**, where he also worked for the famous humanist and printer **Aldus Manutius** and became a friend of **Erasmus**. In 1508 he moved to Paris, where he lectured on **Greek** language and literature. After briefly working for the prince-bishop of Liège, in 1519 Aleandro entered papal service at **Rome**, first as librarian but soon as papal legate to Germany. From his period, his activities increasingly were related to the Protestant Reformation rather than to the Renaissance. During his legatine travels in Germany, he became convinced that the reformist ideas of his former friend Erasmus were the ultimate source of **Martin Luther's** heresies. He remained a powerful figure at Rome down to his death, being named archbishop of Brindisi in 1524 and a cardinal in 1538.

ALEXANDER VI (1431–1503; pope, 1492–1503). Commonly regarded as the worst example of the corruption and worldliness of the Renaissance church, Rodrigo Borja (in Italian, **Borgia**) was born in Spain. He studied canon law in Italy under the patronage of his uncle Alonso, who was a cardinal. The election of Alonso as Pope Calixtus III in 1455 made Rodrigo's fortune. Despite his youth, in 1456 he received the powerful position of papal vice-chancellor and was appointed a cardinal; and he began accumulating church offices that soon made him the wealthiest of the cardinals. Despite his vow of celibacy, he fathered seven or more children (at least one of them after he became pope) by various women. His reputation for political skill, reinforced by the vast wealth which enabled him to offer huge bribes, led to his election as **pope** in 1492. Although several of the preceding popes had been guilty of nepotism, Alexander's use of the papacy to promote the careers of his relatives, especially his own children, surpassed any of his predecessors. Exploiting the struggle between France and Spain for control of Italy, he looked out more for the interests of his family than for the papacy as an institution, attempting to create a hereditary principality in Italy for his favorite son Cesare Borgia and using the marriages of his daughter Lucrezia to advance his political schemes. In legend (and perhaps in fact) Alexander and his children used poison to eliminate hostile cardinals. Although not so great a patron of Renaissance art and learning as his two successors, Alexander was well educated and did commission important paintings and engage in building programs, though (significantly, perhaps) several of the latter involved construction of fortifications. One of his most famous acts as pope was drawing the line of demarcation that separated Spanish from Portuguese claims in the rapidly emerging world of overseas colonization.

ALEXANDER OF VILLEDIEU (ca. 1170–ca. 1250). French grammarian whose *Doctrinale* (1199) became the standard textbook of Latin grammar in medieval **universities**. This collection of doggerel Latin verses became an object of contempt among **humanist** educational reformers who sought to introduce a more **classical** style of Latin. In most places, its replacement by a recent humanistic grammar based on the practices of the best classical authors was a major step toward the new educational program of the Renaissance.

ALIGHIERI, DANTE. *See* DANTE.

ALTDORFER, ALBRECHT (ca. 1480–1538). German painter, active at Regensburg in Bavaria, where he became town architect in 1526. He was a close student of nature and one of the earliest artists to paint landscapes containing no human figures and recounting no story. Influenced by **Lucas Cranach** and **Albrecht Dürer**, he attracted the patronage of the Emperor **Maximilian I** and the duke of Bavaria. His best-known work, *The Battle of Issus*, a colorful, swirling battle scene set into a spectacular landscape of sky, lakes, and mountains, was labelled an illustration of a famous classical event but actually depicted an imaginary encounter of contemporary armies.

AMBROSIAN REPUBLIC. After Filippo Maria, the last **Visconti** duke of **Milan**, died in 1447 without a legitimate heir, the citizens of Milan attempted to restore their medieval republican government, named in honor of St. Ambrose, the city's patron saint. The attempt failed, partly because of rivalries among the ruling group of wealthy families and social tension between rich and poor, but most directly because the new regime hired the prominent *condottiere* general **Francesco Sforza** to defend it. Although Sforza was an able general, he had married the illegitimate daughter of the last Visconti duke. After brushing aside the city's foreign attackers, Sforza seized control and in 1450 forced the city to surrender and accept him as duke.

AMERBACH, JOHANN (ca. 1443–1513). Founder of the most influential publishing firm of Renaissance **Basel**. He was born in Franconia and studied in Paris with Johann Heynlin von Stein, one of the men who introduced the first **printing** press to the French capital; but he probably learned the printing trade at **Venice**. He attracted many educated men to his enterprise, including Heynlin and the humanists **Beatus Rhenanus**, **Johann Reuchlin**, Conrad Pellikan, and **Sebastian Brant**, all of whom worked as editors for him. In association with **Johann Froben** and Johann Petri, he began by publishing traditional **scholastic** textbooks; but the distinctive feature of his activity was his publication of **humanistic** and patristic texts. His younger partner Froben continued and expanded this publishing program. His youngest son, Bonifacius (1495–1562), studied law at Freiburg-im-Breisgau under **Ulrich Zasius** and at **Avignon** under **Andrea Alciati**. Bonifacius became professor of civil law at Basel and was highly influential in the field of jurisprudence because he achieved a synthesis of Alciati's *mos gallicus* with the traditional *mos italicus*, which emphasized study of medieval Italian jurisprudence. An intimate friend of **Erasmus**, Bonifacius corresponded with many of the leaders of European intellectual life.

AMYOT, JACQUES (1515–1593). French **humanist** scholar and poet, known for his translations of **Greek** literature into Latin and French, especially his French versions of the *Parallel Lives* (1559) and *Moralia* (1572) of Plutarch. In 1557 he became tutor of the sons of King Henri II. Rewarded for his services with the abbacy of a monastery, in 1560 Amyot became grand almoner of France and in 1570 bishop of Auxerre. Although Amyot worked to preserve the Catholic faith against Protestant attacks, his loyal support of the monarchy during the French Wars of Religion brought upon him the hostility of the extremist Catholic League.

ANDREINI, ISABELLA (1562–1604). Famous actress in the Italian *commedia dell'arte* tradition, also celebrated as a poet and author of prose literature. Born at **Padua** to a family of **Venetian** origin, Isabella Canale became the leading actress of the highly regarded Gelosi theatrical company. She became a star performer because of her beauty, her acting ability, and her mastery of singing and instrumental music. She was also praised for her irreproachable personal life. In 1578 she married Francesco Andreini, another leading member of the Gelosi company, and she died at Lyon in 1604 while returning to Italy from a triumphant series of performances in Paris. In 1588 she published a successful pastoral tale, *Mirtilla*. Her collected *Rime / Poems* were first published in 1601, and after her death, her husband published a collection of her letters (1607) and an edition of her collected works (1625).

ANGELICO, FRA. *See* FRA ANGELICO.

ANGUISSOLA, SOFONISBA (1527–1625). Italian painter noted for religious scenes and especially for portraits. She was the first **woman** painter to establish an international reputation and to leave behind a significant body of work, and also one of the few not to be trained by a father who was an artist. The daughter of a Piedmontese nobleman, she studied under a respected artist of Cremona. By 1559 King **Philip II** of Spain invited her to his court, where she became lady-in-waiting and drawing instructor to the queen. Most of her Spanish portraits were later destroyed by fire. Her best-known surviving painting portrays her three sisters playing chess.

ANTIQUITY. *See* CLASSICISM.

ANTONINO, SAINT (Antonio Pierozzi, 1389–1459). Son of a Florentine notary, he was attracted to join the Dominican order in 1405 by the preaching of the anti-humanist friar **Giovanni Dominici**; and he remained suspicious of **humanistic** culture even though he became close to one of the humanists' great patrons, **Cosimo de'Medici**. He gained a reputation for piety, learning, and administrative ability and became prior of San Marco in 1436. In 1446 Pope **Eugenius IV** appointed him archbishop of **Florence**. Unlike many bishops of his time, he was no absentee but became an energetic pastor to the citizens, struggling to reform the morals and deepen the piety of a rich and worldly society.

As archbishop of one of the world's most active centers of capitalism, Antonino had to deal with the discord between the ordinary practices of the business world (such as charging interest on loans) and the laws of the medieval church, which regarded business activities, like all aspects of life, as subject to its moral and legal control. His numerous writings, such as his *Summa moralia / A Compendium of Morality*, are **scholastic** and traditional in manner and content. Antonino approved certain types of credit transactions but denounced many of the subterfuges by which businessmen tried to conceal their morally and legally questionable practice of charging interest. He was widely revered in his own lifetime as a holy and principled pastor and was canonized in 1523.

ARETINO, PIETRO (1492–1556). Italian writer, born to a poor family in Arezzo but by 1517 settled at **Rome**, where he found wealthy patrons. A skilled vernacular poet, he first became notorious for his satirical verses or *pasquinades*, which were sufficiently offensive that in 1525 one of the victims of his ridicule attempted to assassinate him. After a brief period in **Mantua**, he settled permanently at **Venice**, which on account of its tolerance of individual expression and its flourishing printing industry proved to be an ideal place for his satirical skills. Switching from poetry to prose, Aretino ridiculed many aspects of current Italian society, such as literary **Petrarchism**, **Neoplatonism**, and the sexual hypocrisy of a society that lauded Christian asceticism but freely indulged in promiscuous hetero- and homosexual practices. He became so famous for his sharp pen that many of his patrons supported him as much out of fear of being attacked as out of respect for his literary talent. To a considerable degree, Aretino functioned more as a literary blackmailer and extortionist than as a respectable author.

ARGYROPOULOS, JOHANNES (1415–1487). Byzantine scholar who became a respected teacher of **Greek** language, literature, and philosophy in Italy. He settled at **Florence**, where he taught at the **university** and helped a number of prominent Italian **humanists**, including **Cristoforo Landino** and **Angelo Poliziano**, perfect their Greek and study the Greek text of ancient philosophers. Although sometimes regarded as a precursor of the fashion for **Plato** that culminated in the **Neoplatonism** of **Marsilio Ficino**, his own teaching was based on **Aristotle**, whom he wanted to make available in improved Latin texts based on the original Greek.

ARIOSTO, LUDOVICO (1474–1533). Italian Renaissance poet, productive in lyric poetry and in comedies inspired by **classical** drama, but known chiefly for his epic *Orlando furioso / Roland Gone Mad* (first published in 1516). It was a best seller in the author's lifetime and by 1600 had gone through more than a hundred editions. Although inspired by the work of an earlier poet, **Matteo Boiardo**, the poem reflects the author's reaction to the tension between two genres, the traditional medieval romance (still popular in Renaissance Italy) and the classical epic. The poem is structured as an epic and begins and ends with echoes of Vergil's *Aeneid*, but the insanity that overwhelms the hero Roland in the middle of the poem prevents the standard classical progression to an epic conclusion and expresses the poet's awareness of disharmony between the medieval and the classical literary heritage.

Ariosto grew up at the court of the **Este** dukes of **Ferrara**, where his father was a military officer. The death of his father in 1500 forced him to support the family by entering the service of the ruling family, first in the household of the Cardinal d'Este and later in the service of the duke, who made him a provincial governor. His writings, including the *Orlando*, show that while he mastered Latin language and literature thoroughly, he was also somewhat critical of **humanism** as a fashionable court culture, regarding it as pretentious and sometimes morally dangerous.

ARISTOTLE / ARISTOTELIANISM. The importance of the newly rediscovered philosophical works of **Plato** in the literature and learning of the 15th and 16th centuries often causes students of the Renaissance to forget that the philosophy of Aristotle (384–322 B.C.), which had been rediscovered by the Latin West in the early 13th century and had become the philosophical basis for all study of philosophy and theology, remained dominant throughout the Renaissance. Plato may have been translated and frequently read; he (or his disciples, the **Neoplatonists**) may have had a powerful influence on poetry and other literary genres. But Plato was not taught—at least not formally and systematically. All philosophical instruction in the universities continued to be based on the logical method of **Aristotle** and also was influenced by other aspects of his philosophy. In particular, Aristotle, who was a great systematizer of ancient scientific knowledge, provided the only systematic body of well-organized knowledge and theory for the study of natural science. Not until the middle of the 17th century, when the work of **Galileo Galilei**, **Johannes Kepler**, and Isaac Newton made Aristotle's scientific works hopelessly obsolete and provided the basis for a whole new approach to the study of the natural world, was the stranglehold of Aristotle on systematic philosophy and science broken.

The Latin Aristotelian texts taught in the universities were products of the **Middle Ages**, most of them translated in the 12th and early 13th centuries by Christian scholars who went to Spain and Sicily in order to find the manuscripts and to acquire the linguistic skills they needed. Nearly all of these medieval translations were based not on the Greek originals but on Arabic translations produced in the earlier Middle Ages. Although by the 13th century nearly all of the Aristotelian works now known had been made available in Latin, those translations were often defective. Renaissance scholars by the 15th century had become keenly aware of these defects. Once the

Italian **humanists** had learned to read Greek, there was an effort to retranslate Aristotle directly from the Greek and to eliminate the ambiguities and errors of the traditional Latin texts.

This push for better translations was led by some of the most influential humanists of the **Quattrocento** such as **Leonardo Bruni**, **Ermolao Barbaro**, and **Angelo Poliziano**; and many new translations were made by émigré Greek scholars such as **George of Trebizond** and **Johannes Argyropoulos**. At the turn of the 16th century, the French humanist **Lefèvre d'Etaples** and several of his followers published new Latin editions of Aristotle for **academic** use, though many of the translations were the work of Italian and refugee Greek scholars during the preceding hundred years. This text-based reform of Aristotelianism in the long run proved hard for even the most conservative **scholastic** philosophers to resist, and during the early 16th century many of the new translations came into use.

Renaissance Aristotelianism also produced new directions in the interpretation of Aristotle, in part because of the influence of ancient Greek commentaries that were now becoming available. There was a revival of interest in the interpretation of Aristotle given by the greatest Arabic philosopher of the Middle Ages, Averroës (in Arabic, ibn Rushd), who had already been known in the 13th century but had aroused much opposition because his interpretation of Aristotle clashed with Christian doctrine. The leaders in this revival were three professors at the **University of Padua**, Nicoletto Vernia (ca. 1420–1499), Agostino Nifo (ca. 1470–1538), and Marcantonio Zimara (ca. 1475–1532). The most controversial philosopher of the early 16th century, **Pietro Pomponazzi**, was striving to reinterpret Aristotle when he wrote his famous treatise *On the Immortality of the Soul*. Even such important pioneers of the new science of the 17th century as **William Harvey** in medicine and Galileo Galilei in physics and astronomy began their scientific work as Aristotelians, though they (especially Galileo) took the steps that would destroy the authority of Aristotle as the guide to all scientific and philosophical questions.

Just as the influence of Aristotle in most fields of study was waning, theorists of literature were rediscovering Aristotle's *Poetics*, a text that had been known but little regarded before 1500, and were making it the basis of a new literary aesthetic that was applied both to the composition of new literary works and to the critical evaluation of old ones. In English literature, both **Sir Philip Sidney's** *Defense of Poesie* and the preface to **John Milton's** *Samson Agonistes* represent an essentially Aristotelian philosophy of poetic composition.

ASCHAM, ROGER (ca. 1515–1568). English **humanist** and teacher. A poor boy from Yorkshire, educated at Cambridge University at a time when enthusiasm for **Greek** language and **Ciceronian** eloquence was colored by growing commitment to religious reform based on the Bible, he first attracted the patronage of the royal court in 1545 by presenting to King **Henry VIII** his patriotic and erudite dialogue *Toxophilus / Lover of the Bow* in praise of the traditional English military art, archery. In 1548 the court appointed him tutor to Princess Elizabeth. He retained favor at court under Edward VI and even the Catholic Mary I (despite his Protestant sympathies) as Latin secretary, and the accession of his former pupil as Queen **Elizabeth I** confirmed his tenure in office. His treatise on education, *The Scholemaster*, published in 1570 by his widow, became an influential statement of Renaissance educational ideals as developed in England.

ASTROLOGY. Pseudoscience that sought to understand the effects of forces thought to emanate from celestial bodies (planets, moon, sun, and stars) on earthly bodies and souls. Its origins go back to the ancient Babylonians, who closely observed the movements of the celestial bodies, thus founding the science of astronomy as well as astrology, two fields that were often closely intermingled. The data observed by astronomers were recorded in tables showing the position of the planets as they appear to revolve around the earth. The whole circle of the visible heavens (the zodiac) is divided into 12 pie-shaped wedges, called "houses," and the basis for all efforts to create a real science out of astrology is that the planets appear to move in a regular and predictable pattern around the circle, spending a specific and equally predictable amount of time in each of the "houses" as they make their annual rotation around the earth. Each of the 12 segments or "signs" (for example, Capricorn, Aquarius, Pisces) of the zodiac is assumed to have certain qualities that produce effects on earthly objects. Likewise, each of the planets has specific characteristics (Mars, for example, is obviously warlike).

The combination of these forces as a planet moves into, through, and out of one of the signs is what the astrologer attempts to study.

The particular planet in ascendancy at the time of a person's birth, joined to the house or sign in which it is located at that moment, places an indelible stamp on the character of the person that affects his or her life. The effects exerted on earthly things by the various houses and the various planets are in fact purely conventional. For example, no astrologer could really offer any explanation why the planet known as Mars should have a warlike effect. Indeed, the use of ancient pagan gods for the names of the planets shows that astrology was closely linked to relics of ancient religious beliefs that no one in the **Middle Ages** or the Renaissance really understood.

The most obvious application of this body of learning was in "judicial astrology," that is, the making of general or even very specific predictions about the fate of the individual seeking astrological advice. For an individual whose date and place of birth were known, specific locations of certain planets in the zodiac at the time of birth would indicate that certain dates would be favorable, and other dates unfavorable, for certain types of activity—for starting a new business, setting out on a journey, or getting married, for example.

Since the medieval church insisted that people's moral responsibility for their own acts was based on their exercise of free will, astrological predictions of future events were inherently contrary to the church's teaching. Although in practice the clergy were just as likely to seek astrological advice as anyone else, any predictions that claimed to determine absolutely events occurring in the future were sinful and unlawful. On the other hand, merely trying to determine favorable and unfavorable days for undertaking a proposed action was theoretically no more objectionable than using meteorological conditions to pick favorable and unfavorable days. Some critics of astrology conceded that the position of celestial bodies did affect events on earth, while arguing that there was no valid way of determining what those effects were and hence no validity in judicial astrology. One of the most famous objectors to astrology, **Giovanni Pico della Mirandola**, raised an objection that was very difficult for astrology's defenders to refute. The notion that the celestial bodies are "superior" to terrestrial beings and hence are able to "govern" them is based on a verbal equivocation: a planet is "higher" than a human soul only in the spatial sense; in the **Platonic** hierarchy of being, the human soul, being spiritual, is "higher" and hence more powerful than the planet.

Although predicting the future was its most obvious application, astrology was also applied in the practice of medicine. Medieval and Renaissance physicians regularly took the date of the patient's birth—and its supposed astrological consequences—into account when they made diagnoses and prescriptions. In a sense, astrology was conceived as nothing more than applied astronomy. The practice of **magic** employed astrological influences as one of its principal foundations.

AVIGNON. City on the Rhone River, seat of the papal curia from 1309 to 1378. Although now a part of France, in the **Middle Ages** and Renaissance the city was part of the county of Venaissin, which was a fief dependent on the papacy. After his election in 1305, Pope Clement V, a Frenchman by birth, decided that political conditions in central Italy were too disturbed for him to go at once to **Rome**. He spent several years in France but in 1309 he settled in Avignon to get out of territory controlled by the King Philip IV. Although Clement intended to move to Rome as soon as conditions permitted, he never found conditions favorable. Between 1309 and 1378, a total of seven **popes** administered the "Roman" bishopric from Avignon, which they gradually developed into a luxurious and heavily fortified papal capital. All seven of these popes were French. They filled administrative offices and especially the college of cardinals (which elected future popes) full of Frenchmen: 113 of the 134 cardinals appointed in this period were French. Inevitably, each time a pope died, the French electoral majority produced another French pope.

The Avignonese popes were often perceived as subject to French influence. This situation caused loud complaints about the "captivity" of the papacy. In addition, since these popes were unable to establish effective control over their estates in and around Rome, the traditional revenues of the papacy were greatly reduced, precisely at a time when the need to develop Avignon as a new capital imposed new financial burdens. These needs were one reason why the papacy in this period ruthlessly sought to increase old sources of revenue and to discover new ones. People all over Europe complained that the papacy had become a greedy institution interested only in squeezing money out of the faithful. Critics likened the French "capture" of the papacy to the Babylonian captivity of the ancient Hebrews, and many earnest reformers (including figures as diverse as the humanist **Petrarch** and the mystic **St. Catherine of Siena**) demanded that the popes must return to Rome as the first step in a sweeping reform of the church "in head and members." Each of these popes promised to return to Rome as soon as possible; some of them even meant it. Pope Gregory XI had pledged at his election to make the return. Finally, late in 1377, he left for Italy, entering Rome in January 1378. But he was old and infirm, and he died in March. The subsequent papal election produced not one but two rival popes, one of whom stayed in Rome while the other (a Frenchman elected by the French majority) returned to Avignon, ushering in an even more troubled period in the history of the church, the **Western Schism**.

– B –

"BABYLONIAN CAPTIVITY." *See* AVIGNON.

BACON, FRANCIS (1561–1626). English philosopher, essayist, and royal official, knighted by King James VI and eventually raised to the peerage. The son of a high-ranking official of Queen **Elizabeth I**, under James VI he rose to be lord chancellor, the highest position in the state. Although Bacon was avid for high office and its social and financial rewards, he was also deeply committed to the improvement of education, especially the study of the natural sciences. During his studies at Cambridge **University** (1573–1575), he became convinced that the traditional scientific method of **Aristotle** was worthless and that a new science founded on a new scientific method must replace it. His book *The Advancement of Learning* (1603) set forth this program of drastic educational and scientific reform.

Despite his many political duties, Bacon continued to publish on this theme, attempting without great success to clarify his concept of a new intellectual method. He projected a total reconstruction of science, a work called *Instauratio magna / The Great [New] Beginning* (1620); but he completed only a few fragments, notably the introductory section, also called *Instauratio magna*, and a sketch of his new logic, the *Novum Organum*. He also realized that one of the goals of a new natural science should be the application of scientific knowledge to improving the quality of human life, an idea developed in his scientific utopia, *The New Atlantis*.

Bacon's interests were not limited to natural science. His best known literary work is his *Essays*, published between 1597 and 1625, which dealt with social and ethical questions and introduced into English literature the informal essay pioneered in French literature by **Michel de Montaigne**. Bacon also wrote an influential biography of the first Tudor king, **Henry VII**. Although he was educated in the **humanistic** learning of the Renaissance, in many respects Bacon represents a passage from Renaissance to post-Renaissance thought. He no longer shared the Renaissance conviction that the improvement of learning depended on rediscovery of lost classical learning but instead declared the contribution of ancient philosophical and scientific knowledge to be exhausted. He linked the further advancement of humanity to his program of a new learning based on natural science.

BADE, JOSSE (Jodocus Badius Ascensius, ca. 1461–1535). Influential editor and publisher, born in Flanders but settled in Paris from 1499 and active as a printer from 1503. He published several of the earlier writings of the **humanist Erasmus** as well as the works of other humanists and major **classical** authors and is usually regarded as a humanistic publisher. In reality, however, he was official printer to the conservative **University** of Paris from 1507; and while he did produce many humanistic texts, he just as gladly issued works of traditional **scholastic** learning and attacks by conservative theologians on Erasmus, **Lefèvre d'Etaples**, and other humanists.

BAÏF, JEAN-ANTOINE DE (1532–1589). French poet known especially for his experiments in adapting classical rules of prosody to the writing of French verse. He was a member of the influential group of poets known even in their own time as *La Pléiade*.

BALDUNG GRIEN, HANS (ca. 1484–1545). German painter and printmaker, trained in the workshop of **Albrecht Dürer** in Nuremberg. He spent most of his active career in Strasbourg, but he lived in Freiburg for several years while working on the altarpiece for its cathedral. His paintings and engravings often were intended to disturb and shock the viewer, and recurrent themes in his work include **witchcraft** (a notable example is his woodcut of 1510, *The Witches' Sabbath*) and death.

BANDELLO, MATTEO (1485–1561). Italian courtier and author, born in Lombardy. He entered the Dominican order at Genoa about 1504 but eventually abandoned his monastic vows and pursued a career as court poet at the princely courts of **Ferrara** and **Mantua** and in the household of a **Venetian** general, Cesare Fregoso. In 1537, while in France, he dedicated an Italian translation of Euripides' *Hecuba* to the great patron of the French Renaissance, **Margaret of Navarre**. He became a particular favorite of the **women** of the courts he served, dedicating his many love poems (supposedly platonic) to them. He is best known, however, for a highly popular collection of racy vernacular stories, the *Novelle / Tales*, which were published between 1554 and 1573. These tales were modelled on **Giovanni Boccaccio's** *Decameron*. **Shakespeare** drew on several of them for plots and characters in plays such as *Romeo and Juliet*, *Much Ado About Nothing*, and *Twelfth Night*. In 1542, following the death of Fregoso, Bandello returned to France and in 1550 became bishop of Agen.

BAPTISTA MANTUANUS (1448–1516). Spanish-born monk and poet active in Italy, originally named Baptista Spagnolo. He studied at **Mantua** and **Padua** and became tutor to the children of the **Gonzaga** dynasty of Mantua. His early poetry was secular, largely devoted to praising the Mantuan court, but he abandoned his courtly life and entered the Carmelite order with such success that in 1513 he was elected general of the order. His later poetry was profoundly Christian, and many conservative **humanists** (such as **John Colet** in England) who had reservations about letting young students read pagan poetry recommended using Mantuanus' works instead since they were **classical** in language and form but thoroughly Christian and morally pure. His *Eclogues* became a widely used school text, and he came to be known as "the Christian Vergil."

BARBARO, ERMOLAO (the Younger, 1453–1493). The most distinguished Venetian **humanist** of the 15th century, member of an influential noble family of **Venice**, educated in part by his uncle Ermolao the Elder (1410–1471), who had entered papal diplomatic service and was made a bishop. An outstanding Latin stylist and **Greek** scholar, young Ermolao lectured at Venice on **Aristotle**; and his commentary (*Castigationes*) on the *Natural History* of Pliny the Elder was a foundation for later scholarship on that author. Also influential was his handbook for diplomats, *De officio legati / The Duties of an Ambassador*. Barbaro served Venice as a diplomat and became ambassador to the papal curia in 1490, but his acceptance of a papal appointment as patriarch of Aquileia in 1491 led to his permanent exile since the republic strictly forbade its citizens to accept foreign honors and appointments, especially ecclesiastical positions in Venetian territory, without approval of the home government. He died of plague in 1493.

BARBARO, FRANCESCO (1390–1454). Venetian **humanist** and political figure, grandfather of Ermolao the Younger. His public career included governorship of several subject territories, ambassadorships, and military commands. He was also a learned humanist, educated by Gasparino Barzizza and the famous schoolmaster Guarino da Verona and familiar with the leaders of contemporary **Florentine** humanism. His principal work, *De re uxoria / On Marriage*, discusses how to choose a wife and outlines the duties of the wife of a **Venetian** aristocrat.

BARDI. Florentine banking family. By 1310 they were the wealthiest family in **Florence**. They and the other two leading family banks, the **Peruzzi** and the Acciaiuoli, maintained branches at locations stretching from England and the Netherlands to North Africa and the Middle East. The company's basic operating capital belonged to the family and a few close partners, but money was also received on deposit from outsiders. The foreign branches were operated by salaried employees or by individual partners sent abroad. The firm traded in agricultural commodities and industrial products, especially woollen textiles, for which Florence was a major center of production, but they drew much of their profit from fees levied on exchange of currency. These fees also served as a legal screen behind which they concealed the practice of usury (charging interest on loans), a practice outlawed by canon law. Conducting large-scale commercial and credit business over great distances was risky. The Florentine banks flourished because they had better and more current economic information than those they did business with.

Extension of credit was the most risky activity of all, and in the 1340s the Bardi and other leading banks discovered this to their sorrow. Both firms made the mistake of lending vast sums to King Edward III of England during the 1330s as he prepared for the conflict with France that became the **Hundred Years' War**. The bankers soon realized that they had extended too much credit, but since they had already lent so much, they felt compelled to lend more, lest they lose what they had already lent. They also continued lending because they needed royal licenses for the export of medieval England's great international product, wool, and lending to the king was the price they had to pay for permission to export. By 1343, when it became obvious that Edward was not going to score a speedy victory, the king repudiated his debts to the unpopular foreign bankers.

The amounts lost were enormous: 900,000 gold florins owed to the Bardi and 600,000 to the Peruzzi, none of it ever repaid. Both firms, and also several other Italian banks, were ruined; and since they also held money on deposit from wealthy individuals throughout Italy, their collapse spread financial loss far beyond their membership. The Peruzzi bank went into bankruptcy in 1343; the Bardi struggled on for three more years but were also liquidated. Smaller firms survived the crash and by the end of the century rose to great wealth and power. The new masters of Florentine banking were the **Pazzi**, **Rucellai**, Strozzi, and **Medici**, though these firms never had the vast capital assets of the banks that perished in the 1340s. Some economic historians have concluded that this collapse of the early Florentine banks was a major cause of a great **depression** that lasted beyond the 1340s.

BAROQUE. Modern term, used most frequently in art history, to describe a post-Renaissance style that continued many of the elements of High Renaissance style while developing and exaggerating other characteristics. Some art historians also insert a transitional phase, which they call **mannerism**. Both of these terms were originally applied in a pejorative sense: "mannerism" or "mannered style" implies "artificial," while the word "baroque" originally meant "contorted" or "grotesque." In a rough sense, *mannerism* is used to categorize the work of some Italian artists of the middle and late 16th century, while *baroque* is conventionally applied to the art of the 17th century. But these delimitations are vague, and the terms themselves are debated.

Even more debatable is the effort of historians of other subjects to extend the terms *mannerism* and *baroque* to fields other than art, though in the history of music the term baroque has become well established. Particularly in the case of baroque art, there are sharp regional differences. Some art historians identify three different lines of development, a "**Counter-Reformation**" style found in Spanish, Italian, south German, and Flemish painting from the late 16th through the 17th century; a "Protestant Baroque" style, exemplified chiefly in the 17th-century art of the Dutch Republic; and a "Courtly Baroque" style in the art of France and England. The term baroque is standard in discussions of art and music of the 17th century.

BASEL, COUNCIL OF (1431–1449). Pope **Eugenius IV** reluctantly convened this general council of the church because of pressure from European rulers and many of the lower clergy to obey the decree *Frequens* of the **Council of Constance** which mandated the calling of frequent general councils. The council opened in 1431 and was dominated by supporters of **Conciliarism**, the belief that a general council, not the **pope**, is the supreme authority in the church. The most extreme conciliarists intended to develop councils into a regular representative assembly that would compel the popes to share the absolute power they had claimed since the 13th century. Councils, they believed, would also enact tough reform legislation that would overcome the foot-dragging of the popes, curial officials, and bishops who stood to lose by reform of the church.

An immediate and pressing problem for the council was relations with the **Hussite** movement of Bohemia. Some at the council wanted to follow a conciliatory policy of negotiation and compromise on the issues that separated the Hussites from other Christians; others wanted to use the council to condemn the Bohemian heresies and to impose that decision by armed force. Another urgent problem arose from the negotiations of Pope Eugenius IV with the leaders of the Greek Orthodox church. He wanted to move the council to Italy and to bring the Orthodox leaders, including the Byzantine emperor and the patriarch of Constantinople, there in order to reunify the whole Christian church. The pope's efforts to move the council to Italy set off bitter conflict. Eventually the pope called a rival council (the **Council of Ferrara-Florence**).

At Basel, the struggle between those who wanted to preserve papal absolutism and those who wanted to transform the church into something like a parliamentary monarchy was bitter. The pope's short-lived success in negotiating reunion with the Greeks, as well as the fear of many bishops that the university theologians and canon lawyers in the council were trying to make the church a democracy, divided the council. Eventually, moderate conciliarists such as **Nicholas of Cusa**, Aeneas Sylvius Piccolomini (the future Pope **Pius II**), and the pope's own legate, Cardinal Giuliano Cesarini, withdrew. As the moderates departed, the radicals gained the upper hand. Because Pope Eugenius defied them, they declared him deposed from office and proceeded to elect a new pope, who took the name Felix V. Thus the council itself seemed guilty of reviving the schism. All of the major European rulers rejected this action. After the death of Eugenius in 1447 and the election of **Nicholas V** as the next pope, Felix abdicated; and in 1449 the remaining members of the Council of Basel voted to endorse the election of Nicholas and then dissolved their assembly. This disastrous end of the council greatly weakened the whole Conciliar movement.

BEATUS RHENANUS (Beat Bild von Rheinau, 1485–1547). German **humanist**, closely linked to the greatest of the northern humanists, **Erasmus**, and to the press of **Johann Froben** at **Basel**. Although Erasmus was the star of the Froben press, known internationally for his textual editions, Beatus handled much of the laborious detail involved in making the editions excellent. He was born in the Alsatian city of Sélestat and received an excellent humanistic education in the city's distinguished school. He studied at Paris (1503–1507), where his talent was recognized by leading humanists such as **Lefèvre d'Etaples**. In 1511 he moved to Basel and began working as an editor and proofreader for Froben. Although he became closely identified with the scholarship of Erasmus, Beatus was also a productive editor in his own right, preparing important editions of the Roman historian Velleius Paterculus (1520), the patristic theologian Tertullian (1521), and an influential collection of historical texts on the early church, *Auctores historiae ecclesiasticae* (1523), as well as an influential commentary (1526) on the *Natural History* of Pliny the Elder.

Beatus remained in touch with his home town of Sélestat, which was easily accessible from Basel, and in 1527 he moved back there, though he still did work for the Froben press and made occasional visits to Basel. In his later years, he produced a scholarly book on early German history, *Rerum Germanicarum libri tres / Three Books of German Affairs* (1531) and also published editions of two major Roman historians, Tacitus and Livy. Since Beatus was a strong supporter of Erasmus' hopes for a peaceful reform of the church, his initial reaction to **Martin Luther** was favorable. Concern about the division of the church, the uprising of the peasants in 1525, and the growing strength of the Evangelical reformers in Basel itself gradually alienated him from the Protestant movement, even though his own private opinion inclined toward **Reformation** doctrines.

BEAUFORT, LADY MARGARET (1443–1509). The mother of the first **Tudor** king of England, **Henry VII**. She was descended from King Edward III and in 1455 married Edmund Tudor, earl of Richmond. John Fisher, bishop of Rochester, became her spiritual adviser and encouraged her to use her wealth to support education. She endowed professorships in theology at both Oxford and Cambridge **Universities** and in 1503 endowed a university preachership at Cambridge. Bishop Fisher persuaded her to give much of her estate to Cambridge, where she founded Christ's College (1505) and endowed St. John's College (1511).

BECCADELLI, ANTONIO (1394–1471). Sicilian **humanist** and poet, often known as Panormita from the Latin name for his birthplace, Palermo. He studied law and classical literature in several northern Italian cities. His book of sexually suggestive poems, *Hermaphroditus / The Hermaphrodite* (1425) attracted much notoriety, especially because of its explicit homosexual references. It was condemned and burned by the church as immoral, but the leading political figure of **Florence**, **Cosimo de'Medici**, was happy to accept the dedication. The work has often been cited as evidence that the culture of Renaissance Italy was irreligious and morally corrupt. Beccadelli was admired for his **classical** learning and his skill as a poet. In midlife he accepted the patronage of King Alfonso V of **Naples** and Sicily, and he spent the rest of his life at Alfonso's court, composing a laudatory biography of his patron.

BELLINI. Family of **Venetian** artists whose works influenced the emergence of a distinctive Venetian Renaissance style of painting. Jacopo (ca. 1400–1470) studied with **Gentile da Fabriano** (ca. 1370–ca. 1427), a talented painter who worked in a late Gothic style. While much of Jacopo's work has perished, the surviving paintings show that he had retained the skills of his teacher in depicting color and light but had also mastered the theory and technique of linear **perspective** described in the treatise on painting by **Leon Battista Alberti**. Jacopo is best known for training his two sons, Gentile (ca. 1429–1507) and Giovanni (ca. 1431–1516). Gentile was knighted by the Holy Roman Emperor Frederick III (ruled 1440–1492) and was selected to restore the depiction of early Venetian history in the doge's palace and to paint an official portrait of each new doge (works which have perished). He also was sent to Istanbul in 1479 to paint for Sultan Muhammad II. His portrait of the sultan survives. Gentile produced many paintings of public processions in Venice. But the family's greatest painter was the younger brother, Giovanni, who adopted the Netherlandish practice of painting in oils and opened the way for the Venetian High Renaissance style of painting brought to completion by the greatest Venetian master, **Titian**, who was his pupil.

BELON, PIERRE (1517–1564). French naturalist. Though born to a poor family, he found aristocratic and royal patronage that not only enabled him to study at the **University** of Paris but also financed his extensive travels through Europe and the Near East to observe natural phenomena. His two famous works were *La Nature et diversité des poissons / The Nature and Variety of Fish* (1551) and *L'Histoire de la nature des oyseaux / Description of the Nature of Birds* (1555).

BEMBO, PIETRO (1470–1547). Venetian humanist and cardinal, noted for his lyric poetry, his editions of earlier Italian authors, his **classical** scholarship, and his excellent style in both Latin and the Tuscan vernacular. Born to patrician parents and sent as a youth to study in **Florence, Rome**, and Bergamo under a number of distinguished **humanists**, including the Venetian **Ermolao Barbaro**, he also went to Sicily to study **Greek** under Constantine Lascaris, whose Greek grammar he edited for publication. He became a leading representative of the purist movement in Latin composition known as **Ciceronianism**, a viewpoint developed in his *De imitatione / On Imitation* (1513) but opposed by some contemporary humanists, most notably **Erasmus** of Rotterdam. Bembo was close to the humanists and **Neoplatonic** philosophers who dominated the intellectual life of Florence in the late 15th century. In his own writings he espoused Neoplatonism. He emphasized the concept of **Platonic** love in his vernacular dialogues *Gli Asolani / The Asolans* (1505).

For several years beginning in 1506, he lived at the elegant and highly intellectual court of **Urbino**. His interest in Platonism is reflected in the *Book of the Courtier* by his friend **Baldassare Castiglione**, a dialogue that is set in the court at Urbino and presents Bembo as a defender of Platonic love against the misogynistic contempt of **women** expressed by several of the characters.

Bembo's pure Latin style (and his aristocratic connections) in 1514 secured for him a position as Latin secretary to the Medici Pope **Leo X**. His efforts to attain higher church offices were disappointed, and in 1519 he moved to **Padua**. He spent most of the 1520s and 1530s living at Padua and **Venice**. Despite his reputation for writing elegant Ciceronian Latin, he was also interested in vernacular literature. In 1501 and 1502 he published with the Venetian printer **Aldus Manutius** critical editions of the poems of **Petrarch** and **Dante's** *Divine Comedy*, and both his edition of Petrarch and his own poems promoted the growth of **Petrarchism**. An important product of his interest in vernacular literature was his *Prose della volgar lingua / Prose Works on the Vernacular Language* (1525). In it he discussed the relative merits of writing literary works in Latin and in Italian and also defended the excellence of the Tuscan dialect as Italy's literary language. His views on language had great influence on contemporary authors. The poet **Ariosto**, for example, revised his epic poem *Orlando furioso* in accord with the standards set forth by Bembo. Bembo's *Rime / Collected Poems* (1530) exemplified this ideal. In 1529 Bembo became historian and librarian to the Venetian Republic. He produced *Historia Veneta, 1487–1513*, a continuation of a work by an earlier author. It was published posthumously in both Latin and his own Italian translation.

Although his philosophical works, especially *Gli Asolani*, upheld the asexual and purely spiritual ideal of Platonic love, which was also attributed to him in Castiglione's *Courtier*, in real life Bembo had a number of lovers, including the woman to whom he dedicated *Gli Asolani*, **Lucrezia Borgia**, daughter of Pope **Alexander VI**. He was consistent in regarding women as fully human persons deserving respect, a view also attributed by Castiglione to his character "Bembo." Bembo took a vow of chastity in 1522 in order to preserve his eligibility for benefices, but from 1513 until her death in 1535, he maintained an enduring connection with a woman with whom he had three children. Under Pope Paul III, Bembo was promoted to the rank of cardinal, ordained to the priesthood, and made a bishop. The influence of one of his female admirers, the aristocratic and highly intellectual poet **Vittoria Colonna**, probably had much to do with his sudden advancement. This relationship, unlike some of the others, seems to have been purely spiritual and was based on mutual interest in Petrarchan style and Neoplatonic philosophy. Bembo spent much of these last years at Rome, where he played an active role in curial affairs.

BERNARDINO OF SIENA, SAINT (1380–1444). Franciscan preacher, noted for his denunciation of the moral corruption and violence of Italian society. A dramatic preacher, skilled at using symbolism and public rituals to heighten the effect of his words, he was especially appealing to **women**. First attracted to religious life after nursing the sick during a plague at Siena in 1400, he became a friar in 1402 and vigorously promoted the strict Observant movement within his order. In 1438 he was elected vicar general of the Observant Franciscans in Italy. After his death, his relics produced reports of miracles, and he was canonized in 1450.

BEROALDO, FILIPPO (the Elder, 1453–1505). Humanist lecturer and author, professor of rhetoric at the **university** of his native city, **Bologna**, from 1472 to his death. He travelled extensively and during a year in Paris (1476–1477), he made a great impression on his French audiences, an early example of success by a humanist lecturer in the most famous northern university. He edited and commented on many **classical** authors, and his sample collection of letters was often used by humanist lecturers as a textbook for courses on rhetoric.

BESSARION, JOHANNES (ca. 1403–1472). Greek clergyman and **humanist**, born at Trebizond in Anatolia. He became a monk at **Constantinople** in 1423 and a priest in 1430, winning a reputation for erudition. In the following decade he moved to a monastery at Mistra in the Peloponnesus and was educated in **Platonic** philosophy by **Georgios Gemistos Pletho**. He also became fluent in Latin and in 1438, after becoming bishop of Nicaea, was a member of the Greek delegation that attended the **Council of Ferrara-Florence**. He strongly favored the union of the churches proclaimed there and in 1439 returned to Constantinople in a vain effort to persuade other leaders of the Greek church to accept the union. Pope **Eugenius IV**

named him a cardinal in order to strengthen his claim to be a mediator between the eastern and western churches.

After the Byzantines repudiated the union in 1440, Bessarion returned to Italy and spent the rest of his life in the West. His theological writings upheld the validity and orthodoxy of the agreements reached at Florence. After the conquest of Constantinople by the Turks in 1453, he campaigned for a crusade to recapture the city. Proud of his Greek heritage, the pagan part as well as the Christian, he bequeathed his library to the republic of **Venice**, the Italian city most closely linked to the Byzantine past.

Bessarion's household at **Rome** became a major center of humanistic scholarship by both refugee Greeks and Italians. The cardinal himself made a fresh translation of **Aristotle's** *Metaphysics* and other Aristotelian works. In the conflict that broke out between philosophical followers of Plato and followers of Aristotle, he upheld a mediating position, arguing that the two philosophers agreed on most important issues. He criticized his own mentor, Pletho, for exaggerating their disagreements and promoting Plato's authority above Aristotle's, but in response to a work by another exiled Greek scholar, **George of Trebizond**, which denounced Plato, he published a rebuttal, *In calumniatorem Platonis / Against a Slanderer of Plato* (1469), in which he expounded Plato's philosophy in a way that showed its compatibility with Christianity. This book was an important influence on the rise of **Neoplatonism** and had particularly strong influence on the Neoplatonist **Marsilio Ficino** and his disciples at **Florence**.

BINCHOIS, GILLES (1400–1460). One of the major composers associated with the flowering of music at the court of the dukes of **Burgundy** in the 15th-century Netherlands. Although he produced much liturgical music, he is best known for his secular *chansons* (songs) accompanying poems of courtly love. Probably born near Mons, he became organist in a church there and later for a long period served as chaplain to Philip the Good, duke of Burgundy (reigned 1419–1467).

BIONDO, FLAVIO (Flavius Blondus, 1392–1463). A native of Forlì, Biondo was a notary, civil servant, and professional scribe at **Venice** but was important because of his **humanistic** and historical writings. Although his Latin style was mediocre, his eagerness to explore and describe the **antiquities** of Italy led to important literary works. He gained the favor of Pope **Eugenius IV** and was active in the **Council of Ferrara-Florence**, but he lost favor under the next **pope** and found support at several princely courts. His major work, *Historiarum ab inclinatione Romanorum libri / History since the Fall of Rome* (1453), also known as the *Decades*, covered the history of Italy from 410 to the 1440s. It is important because it articulates the emergent Renaissance concepts of the fall of **Rome** and a fundamental break between ancient history and the "modern" (that is, medieval) period. As an account of medieval Italy, it is important for its critical use of sources and for its presentation of history as a series of secular events rather than as a fulfillment of the decrees of divine providence. Also important was his *Italia illustrata*, which linked the greatness of ancient Rome to the emergent greatness of modern Italy. He engaged in a controversy on the history of Latin language, contending that the complex Latin found in classical literature really was spoken by all classes, not just an educated elite, a view contrary to the opinion of **Leonardo Bruni** that **classical** Latin was too complex to have been used by ordinary Romans. His *Roma instaurata / Rome Restored* (1481) is a topography of ancient Rome.

BISTICCI, VESPASIANO DA (1422–1498). Florentine bookseller who supplied the intellectuals and wealthy patrons of his time with manuscript books produced by a large team of professional scribes. Little is known about his early life except that he was born at **Florence** and began business as a member of the stationer's **guild**. His shop became a favorite meeting-place for local **humanists** and bibliophiles. He heartily disapproved of the newfangled **printed** books and sold his bookshop in 1480 when he saw that the market for handwritten books was shrinking. In retirement he produced several works, including moral treatises and a book about famous ladies, but his major work was *Vite d'uomini illustri / Lives of Illustrious Men*, a collection of short biographies of the leading men of his time that presented the lives of the upper-class men who were his own best customers. Appropriately for an author who hated printed books, the *Lives* remained unprinted until 1839.

BLACK DEATH. Pandemic disease that swept through most of Europe and the Middle East between 1347 and 1350. First recorded in the Crimea in 1347, the epidemic was carried westward to Italy and then swept northwest into France, the Netherlands, England, Germany, Poland, and Russia, with 1348 being the peak year in Italy and the mainland of western Europe. The plague also devastated Egypt and the rest of Muslim North Africa. Contemporary descriptions and modern medical history agree that the principal disease involved was bubonic plague, so called from the buboes, or swollen lymph glands, that appeared in the groin or under the armpits of victims and then turned black. The course of the disease was rapid. Some patients recovered, but for the great majority, infection ended in death after only a few days.

Bubonic plague is caused by an organism, *Yersinia pestis*, that does not spread directly from person to person but involves a trilateral passage from infected rat to flea to human victim. Being spread by rats and fleas, the epidemic was primarily a phenomenon of the summer and waned or disappeared in cold weather. Well-documented instances in which plague spread actively during the winter suggest that a second illness, pneumonic plague, was concurrent with the bubonic plague, so that the total epidemic may have involved both diseases. Cities seem to have been harder hit than rural districts, though this impression may be a function of better record-keeping in cities. There is considerable evidence that communities of people living together in crowded quarters, such as in cathedral chapters and monasteries, suffered especially heavy losses. Some monasteries lost virtually every member.

The plague came suddenly and unexpectedly, and as news of it spread, panic ran through society, especially since medical treatment proved useless and no one understood the mechanisms of transmission. There are contemporary accounts of children abandoning infected parents and parents abandoning infected children. The mortality described by contemporary writers like **Petrarch** and **Giovanni Boccaccio** (his *Decameron* is set in the plague year of 1348) is so great that historians long regarded it as grossly exaggerated. But recent demographic studies not only confirm the horror but even suggest that it may have been worse than the most lurid contemporary descriptions claim. Not all parts of Europe were affected. The city of **Milan**, most of the Netherlands, and the kingdom of Bohemia suffered lightly, while neighboring regions were devastated. Where sources permit careful demographic study, the conclusions are that between 20 and 60 percent of the adult inhabitants of affected communities died during the few days or weeks when the infection raged locally. Figures for Europe as a whole are little more than guesses, but it is probable that between 25 and 30 percent of the total population of Western Europe perished.

Something so horrible clearly seemed to be a judgment of God, and people sought through prayers and processions the safety they could not find through medicine. City governments and other political authorities tried to guard against the plague by shutting their gates to travellers from outside, not realizing that their city walls offered no protection from the movements of the infected rats and fleas that were the agents of contagion. In some places, panic-stricken populations accused local **Jews** ("the usual suspects" in any medieval disaster) of poisoning the local wells and massacred them. In many regions, European population had already begun a sharp decline from the high populations of the 13th century, the result of the great famines of the early 14th century and also of the economic **depression** that was evident by the early 1340s. But the Black Death greatly accelerated the decline, and many cities suffered remarkable and long-term declines in population. **Florence**, for example, had grown from a small town to a metropolis of perhaps 120,000 by the end of the 13th century; after the Black Death, its population may have shrunk to 40,000. Its population rebounded, but the city remained much smaller than its medieval peak throughout the Renaissance.

Although the great epidemic of 1347–1350, "the Black Death" of history and legend, was the greatest demographic disaster in European history, unmatched even by the wars and massacres of the 20th century, bubonic plague became endemic in European populations and seems to have recurred about once in every generation, striking particularly hard at that part of the population born since the last outbreak. There was a second wave of plague in Italy in the 1360s, another about 1400. In England, there were serious recurrences in 1360–1361, 1368–1369, and 1374. Mortality in these later plagues was still high: at Florence in 1400 as much as 28 percent of the population may have perished. Periodic epidemics of bubonic plague became a regular feature of European life throughout the 15th, 16th, and 17th centuries, and while the authorities eventually perfected techniques of isolation and quarantine that may have helped to limit the spread of plague, neither those techniques nor the efforts of physicians achieved true control.

Gradually, plague disappeared from western Europe after 1660. The great London plague of 1665 was the final outbreak there. The disease persisted in eastern Europe until the 18th century, and there have been localized outbreaks in Asia and Africa in recent years. The causes of the disappearance of the disease in Europe are debated just as hotly as the causes of the initial epidemic. What remains beyond dispute, however, is that the initial onset of bubonic plague in 1347–1350 was a shattering blow to both the population and the psychological self-confidence of Europe at the very outset of the Renaissance.

BOCCACCIO, GIOVANNI (1313–1375). One of the three great Italian authors of the 14th century (along with **Dante** and **Petrarch**) who established the Tuscan dialect as Italy's literary language. Born near **Florence** to a merchant employed by the **Bardi** bank and a woman whose name is unrecorded, Giovanni was legitimized and educated by his father, who sought to educate him as a banker and later as a canon lawyer. From an early age, however, the youth discovered his own interests in literature and **classical** studies. His father's transfer to the **Naples** branch of the Bardi bank brought Giovanni into the literary circles of the royal court there. He also was able to study classical literature at the local university.

His own early writings reflect a combination of interests: in the medieval love poetry of the Neapolitan court, in the classical literature of ancient Rome, in the Bible, and in the encyclopedic compilations of the Middle Ages. Boccaccio wrote both verse romances (such as *Filostrato*, a source for **Chaucer's** *Troilus and Criseyde*) and lengthy prose fiction (such as the *Filocolo*, a popular tale of love and adventure).

In 1341 his father's employer recalled him to Florence. The son found the shift from an elegant royal court to an austere republic devoted to money-making difficult, but in time he became a Florentine patriot and strove to glorify its greatest literary figures, Dante and Petrarch. One of the most enduring and influential of Boccaccio's early works was *Fiametta* (1343–1344), a prose tale sometmes called the first psychological novel. Contrary to custom, it had a female narrator. His masterpiece was the *Decameron* (1348–1351), a collection of prose tales supposedly told by ten wealthy young men and women who had fled Florence to escape the **Black Death**. Although many of the individual stories have become famous and influenced later writers, the work is not just a haphazard collection of tales but a unified book in which the character of the narrators and the interplay among members of the group are developed skillfully.

Boccaccio was also strongly drawn to the classical interests of his fellow **humanists** and produced additional works in Latin. In 1350 he finally met Petrarch, whose works he had long admired. Petrarch encouraged him to write more scholarly books. Boccaccio responded by continuing his series of Latin eclogues (*Bucolicum carmen*). But he did not share Petrarch's disdain for popular literature. Where the two men agreed most fully was in defining the pursuit of literature as a goal worthy of a wise man's life. Boccaccio composed three works reflecting his own classical studies: *Genealogia deorum gentilium / Genealogy of the Pagan Gods* (1350–1373), which became a standard work of reference on Roman and **Greek** mythology, and two biographical collections, *De casibus virorum illustrium / Fates of Illustrious Men* (1355–1373) and a counterpart for the biographies of famous **women**, *De mulieribus claris* (1361). In addition, he wrote biographical sketches of both Dante and Petrarch and late in life delivered a series of public lectures on Dante's *Divine Comedy*.

BOIARDO, MATTEO MARIA (1441–1494). Italian **humanist** and poet, best known for his romance epic *Orlando innamorato / Roland in Love*. Boiardo was brought up at **Ferrara** and at a castle belonging to his grandfather. He lived at the court of Ferrara, where he was a close associate of Duke Ercole I and served the prince as a military commander and regional governor. His early poetry was in Latin, but he also wrote vernacular pastoral eclogues and a book of love poetry modelled on **Petrarch**. His famous epic merges two traditional romance themes, the Carolingian and the Arthurian, in an account of the love of the hero Orlando for a Saracen princess. It draws on Greek, Latin, French, and Italian material from several genres. It had great influence on epic poetry in the following generations and inspired many sequels; the *Orlando furioso* by **Ariosto** is the most famous of the latter.

BOLOGNA, CONCORDAT OF (1516). Treaty between Pope **Leo X** and King **Francis I** of France, settling several disputes between the

French church and the **papacy**. The kings and higher clergy of France had long upheld the principle of **Gallicanism**, which recognized the general authority of the **pope** but in most respects regarded the French church as an autonomous, self-governing religious community, particularly in matters of appointments to office and taxation. In 1438 this theory had been made part of French law by the **Pragmatic Sanction of Bourges**. The papacy had always condemned these "Gallican" ideas and the closely associated doctrines of 15th-century **Conciliarism**, which taught that a general council, not the pope, was the ultimate authority in the church. The predecessor of King **Francis I**, Louis XII, had convened an antipapal **Council of Pisa** in 1511 as part of his war with Pope **Julius II**, using the threat of deposition by the council as a means of bringing pressure on the pope. This effort had failed, for the "false council" of Pisa received little support outside of France. At first Francis continued this political conflict with the new pope, Leo X, and in 1515 scored a major military victory over an anti-French alliance that included the pope. After his victory, Francis found it advantageous to negotiate a deal with the pope in order to detach him from his allies. The **Concordat of Bologna** was the result.

The king abandoned the moribund council. He abandoned the principles of "Gallican liberties" and acknowledged papal supremacy over the Gallican Church. In return, he gained control over the appointment of nearly all high-ranking clergymen, subject only to a nominal right of the pope to reject a nominee he found unqualified. This provision enabled Francis to strengthen his political position in France by using ecclesiastical patronage to buy the loyalty of powerful families in the French aristocracy. For the French clergy, the Concordat betrayed the traditional French support for Conciliarism and undermined Gallican liberties. Both the supreme judicial court, the Parlement of Paris, which had to register treaties, and the University of Paris resisted, but the king ruthlessly employed his constitutional supremacy to override their opposition and silence protests.

BOLOGNA, UNIVERSITY OF. The older of the two greatest **universities** of medieval and Renaissance Italy, known especially for the study of law but also possessing a highly regarded faculty of medicine. The university came into being by natural growth, beginning in the late 11th century, and like its northern counterpart, Paris, it worked out its institutional structures gradually in the middle decades of the 12th century. The city government granted financial support based on a tax on goods imported for sale; it appointed a commission that chose professors, set salaries, made regulations, and defined the privileges and exemptions of students and faculty. In practice, however, the students constituted the heart of the institution. The *universitas* or association of students was the university, and though the professors provided professional expertise and certified students for degrees, in many respects they were employees of the student **guild**. This type of organization, a university of students, was typical of universities in Italy and Mediterranean Europe, unlike the structure of northern universities like Paris, which originated as an association of teachers.

Because Bologna was essentially a school of law and medicine, its students entered at a more advanced educational level and at a more mature age than in the north. Italian students matriculated in their late teens, while most students at Paris and other northern universities entered at about age 13. This difference in age of students probably was a major reason why Italian students played a more powerful role in university governance than was true of northern institutions. In the 15th century, students of law outnumbered students of the combined faculty of arts and medicine, but during the 16th century, medicine became the largest branch of the university. Bologna had no theological faculty at all until the late 15th century, another respect in which it was typical of Italian universities and unlike the northern ones. The fame of Bologna spread across the Alps, and nearly a third of the students were non-Italians. Germans were the most numerous foreign group, but the reputation of Bologna spread everywhere: a doctorate in law from Bologna was the most desirable degree in the profession, just as a medical doctorate from **Padua** had the highest prestige in that field.

Since the city of Bologna was legally a part of the **Papal States** and experienced repeated attempts by the Bentivoglio dynasty and the **popes** to establish control, local political life was unstable and often violent. The university was so highly regarded, however, that it prospered in spite of the unstable political situation.

BORGIA. Spanish noble family, originally named Borja. The election of Alfonso de Borja as Pope Calixtus III (1455–1458), the first Spanish **pope**, made the family's fortune and attracted its leading members to Italy since Pope Calixtus relied on his kinsmen and his Spanish advisers to help him administer the papacy. His nephew Rodrigo became a cardinal and papal vice-chancellor and was enriched by many ecclesiastical benefices, eventually winning election as Pope **Alexander VI** in 1492. Alexander earned the reputation of being the most corrupt pope of the Italian Renaissance. Two of Alexander's several children became important historical figures in their own right. The first of these was **Cesare Borgia** (1475–1507), who became a cardinal and commander of the papal army under his father. Cesare received many valuable ecclesiastical appointments but was never ordained as a priest and was later permitted to marry a French princess. He also received the French duchy of Valentinois and is often referred to by contemporaries (**Niccolò Machiavelli**, for example) as Duke Valentino. In the opening years of the 16th century, backed by his father's authority and assisted by a French army, Cesare set out to create a hereditary Borgia principality in the province of Romagna, which was nominally a part of the **Papal States**. Ruthless in his use of violence and deceit, Cesare eliminated potential rivals by military conquest and murder. The unexpected death of his father in 1503 caught him at a vulnerable moment, and the election of the anti-Borgia Pope **Julius II** caused his enterprise to collapse. Cesare was arrested and sent to Spain by order of King **Ferdinand** of Spain. Although he managed to escape in 1506, he was killed in a minor skirmish the following year.

The younger sister of Cesare and daughter of Pope Alexander, Lucrezia Borgia (1480–1519) became infamous for her own political ambitions and, like her brother, was reputed to have poisoned those who stood in her way. Rumors of incest with her father and brother seem to be a fabrication of the family's enemies. In reality, she was more the pawn of her ambitious kinsmen than an independent political force. At age 12 she was married to the ruler of a minor principality, the lord of Pesaro. When a more advantageous opportunity arose in 1497, the pope annulled her first marriage and married her to an illegitimate son of the king of **Naples**. When this second husband became a political liability, Cesare had him murdered. A third marriage followed in 1501, by far the most splendid, to Alfonso d'**Este**, who became duke of **Ferrara** in 1505. At Ferrara, Lucrezia became the head of a brilliant court that included figures such as the poet **Ariosto**, the scholar-**printer Aldus Manutius**, the painter **Titian**, and the humanist **Pietro Bembo**, who became her lover and dedicated his first major work to her. Her charitable activities as duchess gained her the love of the people. She gave birth to seven children and died in 1519 at the birth of the last one.

BOSCÁN, JUAN (ca. 1490–1542). Catalan poet and **humanist**. He received a humanistic education at the court of King **Ferdinand of Aragon** and tutored the future Spanish general and governor of the Netherlands, the Duke of Alva. In 1526 his encounter with the **Venetian** ambassador Andrea Navagero, a noted humanist and poet, awakened his interest in imitating Italian poetry in his own language, and he and his close associate **Garcilaso de Vega** pioneered the introduction of **Petrarchan** themes and Italian verse forms into Spanish literature. He is also known as the translator of the famous *Book of the Courtier* by **Baldassare Castiglione**, a book that shaped the ideas and manners of the Spanish court for the rest of the century.

BOSCH, HIERONYMUS (ca. 1450–1516). Dutch painter, born at 's Hertogenbosch. The son of a painter, he seems to have spent his whole life in 's Hertogenbosch, though some art historians find evidence of a trip to Italy. Details of his life are scarce. Even his date of birth is little more than a guess; he was reputed to be an old man when he died in 1516. Much of his work continues the "Flemish style" of late Gothic painting that flourished in the southern Netherlands and northern France throughout the 15th century. His talent was recognized in his own lifetime, and he attracted the patronage of aristocrats and higher clergy and became a wealthy man. Many of his works treat the life of Christ and the saints or present moral allegories, for example *Christ Carrying the Cross* and *St. John on Patmos*.

But Bosch's subsequent fame rested on other paintings that presented moral allegories in an irrational and hallucinatory form, deeply laden with sensual and sexual images that seem to depict human beings as enslaved to their bodily appetites and offer no hint of redemption. The images are so strange that some art historians interpret them as evidence of his membership in a secret heretical sect. In any case, there is a jarring discord between the beauty of the works and the strange monsters and repulsive actions depicted. Two famous examples of this genre of painting are *The Last Judgment* and *The Garden of Earthly Delights*. Their meaning remains uncertain, but his work attracted attention and found a market. In the late 16th century, both **Philip II** of Spain and his cousin the Emperor **Rudolf II** admired and collected Bosch's works.

BOTTICELLI, SANDRO (1444/5–1510). **Florentine** painter most closely associated with the intellectual circle of **Lorenzo de' Medici** in the later 15th century. A pupil of **Fra Filippo Lippi**, in his own time he was renowned for his draftsmanship and for the beauty of his paintings. His works were influenced by contemporaries like **Andrea Verocchio** and **Antonio del Pollaiuolo**, but he developed a style distinctly his own, marked by shallow modelling of figures and lack of concern with deep space that seem to represent a deliberate rejection of the solidly three-dimensional pictures of earlier Renaissance painters. Botticelli painted many traditional religious scenes, such as the early *The Adoration of the Magi*, which reflects the influence of Lippi, and *The Coronation of the Virgin*, as well as a series of paintings executed at **Rome** in 1480–1482 as part of the original decoration of the Sistine Chapel. But he is best known for allegorical paintings depicting themes from classical mythology for the Medici circle, such as *Primavera* (ca. 1478) and *The Birth of Venus* (ca. 1485). The latter was perhaps the first depiction of a nude goddess since ancient times. These works were by no means intended to glorify ancient paganism but are allegories in which the figures embody the abstractions of the **Neoplatonic** philosophy fashionable in the Medicean circle. Especially as he became a "court painter" to Lorenzo, Botticelli's works took on some of the ethereal, otherworldly look of late-medieval court painting, yet they also bear clear traces of the influence of other Renaissance art. These allegorical works were created for an elite audience of insiders and if they had been put on public display would not have been meaningful to most Florentines.

Botticelli's later paintings, however, done after the fall of the Medici from power in 1494 and after the artist had become attracted to the anti-Renaissance preaching of the friar **Girolamo Savonarola**, moved away from the ethereal mood of the allegories and also away from non-Christian themes. Eventually, Botticelli destroyed some of his worldly paintings and from about 1501 stopped painting altogether. By the early 16th century, Botticelli's work had lost its earlier popularity, and he was virtually forgotten until art historians in the 19th century rediscovered his work.

BOURGES, PRAGMATIC SANCTION OF. *See* PRAGMATIC SANCTION OF BOURGES.

BOUTS, DIERCK (ca. 1415–1475). Netherlandish painter, born and probably trained in Haarlem but located for most of his career in Louvain, where he married into a wealthy family and became a prosperous citizen. Outstanding among his works is the triptych *The Holy Family*, in the church of St. Peter in Louvain. In this and other works, theologians from the **university** advised him on the iconography. Several of his paintings were sold abroad and played a role in popularizing the Netherlandish style in Italy and elsewhere.

BRACCIOLINI, POGGIO (1380–1459). Florentine **humanist**. A provincial by birth, he settled in **Florence** shortly before 1400 and became a professional notary. He is commonly regarded as the principal creator of the elegant **humanistic script** that became the common hand for **classical** manuscripts in the Renaissance and later was the model for all typographical fonts known as roman. Between 1404 and 1453, Poggio was employed at the papal curia in **Rome**, eventually rising to the influential position of apostolic secretary. He always regarded himself as a Florentine, however, and he was known to contemporaries as Poggius Florentinus. In 1453 he became chancellor of the Florentine republic, a position previously held by such prominent humanists as **Coluccio Salutati** and **Leonardo Bruni**.

During his attendance at the **Council of Constance**, Poggio visited many northern monastic libraries in search of unknown classical works and made a number of important discoveries, including the *Familiar Letters* and several orations by **Cicero**, nine comedies of Plautus, the *De rerum natura* of Lucretius, and the *Institutio oratoria* of Quintilian. Quintilian's *Institutio* had a great influence on subsequent humanistic conceptions of Latin style, rhetoric, and education. Poggio was probably the most successful of all the Italian humanists of his time in finding lost works of Latin literature.

He also produced original works, including many letters to humanist friends (notably a sympathetic account of the execution of the **Hussite** leader Jerome of Prague at the Council of Constance), and a collection of humorous tales, the *Facetiae*, often cynical and anticlerical in tone. Though it scandalized many people, this collection circulated widely. He also wrote an influential description of the city of Rome and a history of Florence, continuing the work of Leonardo Bruni. Although Poggio wrote a literate, supple, and correct Latin style, it did not measure up to the more rigorously classical standards of the mid-15th century. In later life he found his literary reputation and his scholarly standards challenged by ambitious younger rivals. This generational rivalry led to a number of bitter literary conflicts, notably with **Lorenzo Valla**.

BRAHE, TYCHO (1546–1601). Danish astronomer, known primarily for his fresh and highly accurate observations of the orbits of the planets. After study at Copenhagen and several German **universities**, he settled in an isolated castle belonging to his family and devoted himself to scientific work. His earliest major achievement was his careful tracking of a "new star" (a supernova) never previously observed. This object caused great excitement among astronomers; it was bright enough to be seen even by day and remained clearly visible for more than a year. His observations clearly established that it was beyond the moon, thus challenging the prevailing belief that the superlunary universe was perfect and unchanging. His book (1573) reporting these observations caught the attention of astronomers throughout Europe. Other observations by Brahe also challenged traditional astronomy, including his demonstration that the comet of 1577 did not follow the circular orbit required by current theory and cut across several planetary orbits. Brahe's observations also noted many discrepancies between the actual location of planets and their locations as predicted in current planetary tables.

Although these discoveries confirmed the widespread uneasiness of 16th-century astronomers about traditional astronomy, Brahe found the heliocentric theory of **Nicolaus Copernicus** too radical and devised an alternative theory (the "Tychonic system") that tried to account for his discoveries without removing the earth from the center of the universe. According to this theory, the other planets revolve about the sun rather than the earth, but the sun and planets still revolve about the earth. Brahe was the last major astronomer to reject the

Copernican system, and also the last to function without the assistance of the telescope. Brahe also had elaborate apparatus for **alchemical** experiments, but little is known about this work. He was a painstaking mathematician, carrying out intricate calculations by lengthy arithmetical procedures since his generation still lacked the mathematical discoveries (logarithms, for example) made in the following century. Because he was compiling fresh experimental data unmatched by any contemporary, the brilliant German mathematician **Johannes Kepler** accepted his invitation to join him in Denmark and entered his service again when Brahe moved to the court of the Emperor **Rudolf II** in Prague. Although Kepler disagreed with Brahe's rejection of Copernican astronomy, Brahe bequeathed all of his papers to him when he died in 1601, thus putting into the younger man's hands the vast body of fresh experimental data that became one of the foundations of his books supporting the Copernican hypothesis.

BRAMANTE, DONATO (1443/4–1514). Italian artist, known principally as an architect. He originally worked at **Urbino** and **Milan** as a painter, but his service to the duke of Milan led to involvement in architectural work, beginning perhaps with paintings and drawings of buildings. By the early 1480s he had become an architect for the ruler's building projects. After the collapse of **Sforza** rule at Milan, he entered papal service at **Rome**, where his design of the small structure known as the Tempietto (1502) marked his emergence as the leading architect of the High Renaissance style. Bramante was also influenced by the architectural drawings of his friend **Leonardo da Vinci**.

His success with the Tempietto led to his appointment as chief architect to Pope **Julius II**. His first project was a plan for the extensive remodeling of the papal palace, but the most significant assignment of his career was to design the new St. Peter's basilica. In 1506 Bramante proposed a gigantic centrally planned building topped by a great dome on pendentives, with four identical façades. It was inspired not only by ancient Roman architectural theory but also by the ancient Roman Pantheon and by the sixth-century basilica of Haghia Sophia at Constantinople. Later papal architects, especially **Michelangelo** and **Carlo Maderno**, greatly modified his plan. Yet the mature Renaissance architectural style was created by Bramante, and later Renaissance architectural theorists, such as **Giorgio Vasari**, referred to him when they wanted to demonstrate architectural perfection.

BRANT, SEBASTIAN (1457–1521). German **humanist** and poet, a native of Strasbourg, educated in liberal arts and law at **Basel**. After graduation he taught there in both of these faculties and in 1496 received a professorship of civil and canon law. He also worked as an editor for several Basel publishers. In 1498 he published a collection of Latin poems. His lasting fame, however, depends on his vernacular *Narrenschiff / Ship of Fools* (1494), which humorously criticized various social classes and professions and was soon translated into Latin, French, Dutch, and English. In 1501 Brant moved back to Strasbourg, first as a legal adviser to the city government and then as the city's secretary. The Emperor **Maximilian I** appointed him an imperial councillor, and he served on several diplomatic missions.

BRETHREN OF THE COMMON LIFE. *See DEVOTIO MODERNA.*

BRONZINO, AGNOLO (1503–1572). **Florentine** painter of the late sixteenth century, court painter to Duke Cosimo I de'**Medici**. He also had a reputation as a poet. Classed among the Italian **mannerist** artists by modern art historians, he is best known for his portraits, such as the portrait of Duchess Eleanora of Toledo and her son Giovanni, wife and son of his patron Duke Cosimo.

BRUEGHEL, PIETER (the Elder, ca. 1525–1569). The principal Dutch painter of the 16th century. Though highly educated, closely linked to leading **humanists**, and patronized by the **Habsburg** rulers, he concentrated many of his paintings on the life and customs of the lower classes. A trip to **Rome** and **Naples** in 1552–1553 left him not with the usual northern artist's interest in contemporary Italian art but with an interest in landscape, perhaps derived from Venetian landscape paintings but in his case vividly expressed in the background of depictions of peasant groups (for example, *The Return of the Hunters*, *The Blind Leading the Blind*, and *Peasant Wedding*) which present an unromanticized view of the life of ordinary folk. Though his work continues traditional Flemish realism, there are also many signs of the influence of the fantastic and psychologically disturbing works of **Hieronymus Bosch**. He also painted religious and allegorical scenes, but his own religious beliefs remain elusive, perhaps a reflection of the religious tensions of a society undergoing spiritual upheaval and living on the brink of civil war. Nevertheless, the Habsburg rulers found his work appealing, so that many of his finest works are now in Vienna. The family artistic tradition continued with his sons, Pieter the Younger (1564–1638) and Jan the Elder (1568–1625), for at least two additional generations.

BRUNELLESCHI, FILIPPO (1377–1446). Florentine artist, initially active as a sculptor but known principally as the creator of the early Italian Renaissance architectural style. According to a story told by two later Renaissance authors, after he was defeated by **Lorenzo Ghiberti** in 1401 in a competition for design of new bronze doors for the Florentine baptistery, he and his friend the sculptor **Donatello** travelled to **Rome** and studied the monuments of ancient Rome. This study enabled Brunelleschi to define the mathematical principles and proportions on which the ancient **classical** style was based. Whether this story is literally true or not, he seems to have been the first person to understand the mathematical principles of linear **perspective**.

Back in **Florence** by 1417, Brunelleschi again competed against Ghiberti for the daunting task of designing the huge dome called for by the original architect of the cathedral but left unbuilt because no one could contrive a design for such a gigantic dome. This time Brunelleschi won the competition, largely because in addition to his familiarity with ancient Roman architecture, he had become a skilled mathematician and structural engineer. His dome won because of an ingenious design that not only called for a lighter, less stress-intensive structure but also would be much cheaper and faster to build. This success led the wealthy **Medici** family to choose him to design the sacristy (the family's burial chapel) of the church of San Lorenzo and then to rebuild the entire church. Though the new structure is reminiscent of the traditional Tuscan Romanesque style, it reflected classical architectural practice in its elegant and harmonious proportions. On a much smaller scale, strongly redolent of elements drawn from Roman architecture and yet representing a clearly modern design, was the Pazzi Chapel, commissioned by another wealthy Florentine family. Brunelleschi's subsequent works included the churches of Santo Spirito and Santa Maria degli Angeli. The latter was the earliest domed, central-plan church of the Renaissance. The engineering skills that Brunelleschi applied to designing the cathedral dome were also put to use in improving the design of the organ in the cathedral, designing a new type of river boat, designing an aqueduct, building stage machinery, and designing fortifications.

BRUNI, LEONARDO (1370–1444). Florentine **humanist** and chancellor. Born at Arezzo, in the early 1390s Bruni migrated to **Florence**. He intended to study law, but he had the good fortune to be drawn into the circle of the Florentine chancellor **Coluccio Salutati**, where he became imbued with humanistic literary ideals and took advantage of the opportunity to learn **Greek** under the eminent Byzantine scholar **Manuel Chrysoloras**. This instruction was crucial not only for Bruni's development but also for the further development of Italian humanism, since the ablest of Chrysoloras' pupils became the first generation of Italian scholars to attain an effective mastery of the **Greek** language and hence to gain full access to the masterpieces of Greek literature. Bruni seems to have become deeply attached to Florence, but in 1405 he left the city to become apostolic secretary at **Rome**. He spent nearly all of the following decade in papal service.

In 1415, after the **Council of Constance** forced the **pope** he was serving to resign, Bruni returned to Florence. He began work on his greatest literary production, *Historiarum Florentini populi / History of the Florentine People*, a history of the city from Roman times. During this period (1415–1427) as a private citizen, he produced a number of treatises on moral and scholarly subjects, of which the most important was *De recta interpretatione / On the Correct Way to Translate*, in which he challenged the medieval practice of translating ancient texts word for word. Bruni himself became a skillful translator, producing many Latin versions of Greek authors, including a series of biographies from Plutarch, speeches by Demosthenes and other Greek orators, a few of **Plato's** dialogues, and **Aristotle's** moral and political works. His most influential translation, however, was a letter of one of the major Greek patristic authors, St. Basil of Caesarea, whose *Epistula ad adolescentes / Letter to Young Men* (1401) encouraged young Christians to study the best works of ancient pagan literature. Renaissance humanists used this translation as justification for their study of pagan authors; hundreds of manuscript copies still survive.

From an early date, Bruni had become interested in both history and current politics. His *Laudatio Florentinae urbis / Panegyric on the City of Florence* (1403) praised the city as the heir of the tradition of republican government that had made ancient Rome a powerful and civilized city, and he later produced several other works, of which the most important was the *History of the Florentine People*, that also glorified not only Florence but also its republican constitution. The *Laudatio* was written just after a military crisis that threatened to subordinate Florence to the duke of **Milan, Giangaleazzo Visconti**, and some modern historians have cited it to explain the adoption of republican ideals of active citizenship by the city's leading intellectuals, a group that previously had regarded involvement in civic life as a hindrance to the higher calling of scholarship.

This concept of "civic humanism," and even Bruni's personal commitment either to Florence or to republican political ideals have been challenged by other modern historians who have correctly observed that he did not hesitate to pursue a career in the autocratic papal curia at Rome. Yet it is also true that in 1415, after his appointment at Rome ended, he chose to come back to Florence, secured Florentine citizenship (which was not readily granted to non-natives), and devoted much of the rest of his literary career to his history of Florence. In the history, he restates his "republican" ideology, arguing that Rome had grown powerful and achieved literary greatness under republican government and that the rise of the emperors from the time of Julius Caesar and Augustus had introduced a crushing tyranny that snuffed out the free intellectual life of republican Rome and ultimately led to the dissolution of Roman power. Defenders of the concept of "civic humanism" view the literary and historical works of Bruni as marking the moment when humanism became the dominant cultural ideal of the Florentine ruling class.

Florentines of his own time admired Bruni's political ideas. Impressed by the early sections of his *History of Florence*, they granted him citizenship and made him the official historiographer of the city. In 1427 the *Signoria* (governing council) appointed him to the city's most important administrative office, chancellor of the republic, a powerful position that he held for the rest of his life. Critics have rightly pointed out that the republicanism that Bruni extolled was not a democracy but an oligarchy based on the constitutional rule of the middling and wealthy property-owners (and in practice, on behind-the-scenes domination by a faction of rich merchants); but then neither the Florentine leaders nor Bruni himself ever claimed to endorse democracy, which they rejected as an unworkable political form that put power into the hands of the rabble. Bruni's writings defend the Florentine constitution as a mixed government, with some limited participation by all property-owning residents but with effective control safely in the hands of the well-to-do, the educated, and the competent. His own career was based on his embrace of this kind of social and political milieu. Starting life as a poor immigrant from a provincial town, he transformed himself into one of the most admired members of the ruling elite, a status marked at his death by the elaborate state funeral that the *Signoria* arranged and by the impressive marble tomb that the republic commissioned for him in the Franciscan church of Santa Croce.

BRUNO, GIORDANO (1548–1600). Italian philosopher, famous in his own time for his publications on religion, natural philosophy and magic, but most commonly remembered in later times as a "scientist" burned at the stake in **Rome** for heresy. Born at Nola in southern Italy, he became a Dominican friar in 1565. In the schools of his order, he ran into trouble when his reading of banned books by **Erasmus** led to his arrest on suspicion of heresy. Early in 1576 he escaped from custody and began an itinerant career. He moved first to Rome and then north of the Alps to Geneva (where he had a brief and stormy career as professor of theology in the Calvinist university), then to several places in France, including Paris. His publications at Paris dealt with systems of memory (*De umbris idearum / On the Shadows of Ideas* and *Ars memoriae / The Art of Memory*) and with the mnemonic writings of the medieval Catalan philosopher Ramon Lull. In these works Bruno rejected traditional **Aristotelian** psychology and claimed to have invented a far superior new method of learning.

In 1583 Bruno moved to England, where he lectured on Copernican astronomy at Oxford and then settled in London, publishing additional works on memory and on the cosmological implications of **Copernicus'** heliocentric theory (especially *La Cena de le ceneri / The Ash Wednesday Supper*). Other Italian-language publications at London in 1584, including *De l'infinito, universo, e mondi / On the Infinite Universe and Worlds* and *Spaccio della bestia trionfante / Expulsion of the Triumphant Beast*, presented his speculations about human nature and his view of the world as an emanation from God. His radical **Neoplatonic** and **Cabalistic** thought dismissed traditional Christianity as a muddle of superstitious ideas. His *De gli eroici furori / On Heroic Frenzies* (1585) continued the exposition of his anti-Christian ideas and extolled Platonic love as the true path to contemplation of God. In the autumn of 1585 Bruno returned to France, where he publicly disputed against the prevailing Aristotelian philosophy. In 1586 he moved to Germany, where he lectured at Wittenberg on Aristotle, then spent periods lecturing at Prague, Helmstedt, Frankfurt, and Zürich.

Bruno had associated with Calvinists at Geneva and with both Calvinistic Puritans and Anglican theologians at Oxford, but his unconventional ideas alienated both groups. At Wittenberg, although he converted to the Lutheran faith, his radical religious beliefs soon caused him to be excommunicated. While he was at Frankfurt, a Venetian aristocrat invited him to come to **Venice** and teach his patron his art of memory. He moved there in August 1591. Some biographers have called the invitation itself a trap, designed to lure him back within reach of the **Inquisition**. About a year after he settled in Venice, his patron had him arrested by the Venetian Inquisition. In 1593 the far more strict Roman Inquisition had him extradited to Rome, where, after seven years of incarceration and a lengthy trial, he was condemned as an unrepentant heretic and burned at the stake early in 1600.

Bruno probably always thought of himself as a loyal Catholic who wanted to lead a drastic reform of Catholicism. The problem was that he wanted to preserve the authoritarian structures of Catholicism while transforming it into a philosophical religion based not on the Bible or church tradition but on his own peculiar blend of Neoplatonic mysticism and the philosophy of **Hermes Trismegistus**. Bruno's strong interest in **magic** rested on his confidence that an understanding of the religion of the Egyptians, transmitted by the **Jewish** Cabalists, the Zoroastrian oracles, the Hermetic books, and the philosophy of **Plato** and the Alexandrian Neoplatonists, would lead humanity to a harmonious relationship with God and a control over physical nature that would improve both the eternal destiny and the earthly life of the human race. Although anticlerical historians of the late 19th century attributed his execution to his support of Copernicus and his belief in an infinite universe, thus making him into a martyr of modern science, the real cause of his execution was his speculative philosophical and theological ideas.

BUDÉ, GUILLAUME (1468–1540). The most famous French **humanist** of the first half of the 16th century. Born into a recently ennobled family of royal officials, he studied law at Orléans but left without taking a degree. In 1491 he underwent a sort of secular conversion to humanistic learning, acquiring his outstanding mastery of **Greek** largely through independent study. He also resumed his study of law, but this time on his own, making his mastery of **classical** Latin and Greek the key to a radically new, philologically based approach to the Roman civil law (Corpus Juris Civilis). These ideas constituted a rejection of *mos italicus*, the medieval Italian tradition of legal education, and called for application of humanistic skills to interpretation of the legal texts, a method that came to be known as *mos gallicus* (the French manner), introduced from about 1518 by the teaching of Budé's Italian friend **Andrea Alciati** at **Avignon** and later at Bourges.

Though Budé never either taught or practiced law, his first major publication, *Annotationes in Pandectarum libros*, a linguistic explication of the pandects, became a landmark of Renaissance jurisprudence. In it he applied the philological methods developed by the Italian humanists **Lorenzo Valla** and **Angelo Poliziano** to explain legal terms that medieval law professors had debated endlessly. In 1515 he published another widely admired book, *De asse*, which began as a study of Roman coins, weights, and measures, but grew into a vast compilation of information on the material basis of Roman life.

Budé was an intensely patriotic French citizen, resentful of the arrogant superiority assumed by many Italian scholars, and he dreamed of making France rather than Italy the center of Renaissance culture. He had followed other members of his family into royal service in 1497, when he became secretary to King Charles VIII, but he was not very active at court under Louis XII. The succession of the young king **Francis I** to the throne in 1515 filled him with hope that the new ruler would become a great patron of Renaissance learning. Not until 1522, however, did he become a regular participant in royal administration, being appointed a master of requests. This position involved spending much time in attendance on the royal court. Budé used his connections there to agitate for the founding of a **trilingual college** (teaching classical Latin, **Greek**, and **Hebrew** language and literature) at Paris on the model of the famous trilingual institutions founded at **Alcalá** and **Louvain**. In 1517 and again in 1524 Budé participated in unsuccessful attempts by King Francis to attract the Dutch humanist **Erasmus** to the French court, perhaps with the idea of making him the star attraction of such a new royal college. In 1530 Budé finally attained partial success, when the king provided salaries for royal lecturers on Hebrew and Greek, the small beginings of what later became the **Collège Royal**.

Budé intervened to calm a nasty scholarly quarrel between Erasmus and the most important of the older French humanists, **Jacques Lefèvre d'Etaples** in 1517–1518. From 1516 until the late 1520s, Erasmus and Budé conducted an extensive correspondence. Contemporaries universally regarded them as respectively the greatest Dutch and the greatest French humanistic scholar, but there was always an undercurrent of tension over the implied question of which of the two was the greater. Budé found in Erasmus' dialogue *Ciceronianus* (1528) a reference to himself that he took to be slighting, and Erasmus, in turn, resented the failure of an important new book of Budé on the Greek language, *Commentarii linguae graecae* (1529), to include a courteous acknowledgment of Erasmus' edition of the Greek New Testament.

Though they shared a common love of classical literature and the Greek language, the two humanists were very different. Budé's French patriotism did not square with Erasmus' explicitly cosmopolitan internationalism. While Erasmus employed satire and humor as a means of advancing ideas, Budé was an intense, humorless, and rather narrow man, perhaps superior to Erasmus in mastery of Greek but not his equal in catching the inner spirit, as distinguished from the technical details, of Greek language and literature.

Until the **Reformation** became an issue in France in the 1530s, Budé had relatively little to say about religion, though like Erasmus he could be critical of clerical abuses and corruption. Erasmus, on the other hand, was more interested in the spiritual regeneration of Latin Christendom than in any other issue. Only in 1535, when a native French Protestant movement was beginning to emerge, did Budé write directly and at length on religion. His *De transitu Hellenismi ad Christianismum / The Transition from Hellenism to Christianity* reiterated his earlier criticisms of clerical corruption but denounced the Protestant reformers. He strove to demonstrate that the humanistic scholarship that he cherished was in no way subversive of Catholic orthodoxy and if properly subordinated to Christian goals was a valuable resource for the defense of the Catholic faith. The provisions of his will in 1540 confirm that he was a pious and obedient Catholic. The later decision of his widow and children to go into exile at Calvinist Geneva represents the conditions of a later generation and does not indicate that Budé himself ever favored Protestantism.

BURGUNDY, DUCHY OF. Strictly speaking, the duchy of Burgundy was a large fief held in feudal tenure from the king of France and located in east-central France. But in the 14th and 15th centuries, the term also designated a much larger political unit, including the original duchy but also incorporating most of modern Belgium and the Netherlands. This powerful state developed expansionist ambitions that endangered the territorial integrity of both France and the German Empire. It originated in 1364 when King John II of France granted the duchy of Burgundy to his younger son Philip the Bold as a virtually independent principality. John then secured for Philip the adjacent Free County of Burgundy, a fief of the German Empire, and arranged for him to marry the heiress of the count of Flanders, the richest, most industrialized, and most urbanized part of northern Europe. Duke Philip and his descendants began acting like rulers of a sovereign kingdom, negotiating with foreign powers and scheming to expand their principality. Some of its regions were French-speaking; some spoke Flemish and Dutch. Each province had its own regional courts, assemblies, and other institutions. The rulers created central judicial, representative, and administrative agencies for the Netherlandish provinces, but until the 16th century, these efforts at centralization had little effect.

Since the dukes were still members of the French royal family, they became major players in the turbulent factional politics of the French court during the **Hundred Years' War**. During the second phase (1415–1453) of that conflict, Duke Philip the Good (1419–1467) allied himself with the English king, Henry V, and negotiated a division of all of northern France between himself and Henry, whom he recognized as king of France. Burgundy's defection from this English alliance in 1435 was a major turning point in the struggle to drive the English out of France. The last independent duke of Burgundy, Charles the Rash (1467–1477), tried to seize those parts of northern France and western Germany that separated his Burgundian from his Netherlandish territories. This attempt led to conflict with the Swiss Confederation, and Charles died in battle against the Swiss. His only child, Mary of Burgundy, sought to preserve her principality by marrying **Maximilian** of **Habsburg**, the heir of the German emperor. King Louis XI of France seized the duchy of Burgundy but was unable to conquer the Free County of Burgundy and the Netherlandish provinces. Thus Mary and her husband Maximilian remained rulers of most of the Burgundian lands. Mary died a few years later, leaving her son Philip as her successor, under the regency of his father. In 1496 Maximilian negotiated Philip's marriage to Juana, daughter of **Ferdinand** and **Isabella**, the rulers of Spain.

The son of Philip and Juana, Charles (the future emperor **Charles V**), became the heir to Spain and its many territorial claims in Italy and the Americas, to the hereditary Habsburg lands in Germany, and to the Burgundian territories, including the Netherlands. Charles grew up in the Netherlands, gained his first political experience there, and originally spoke no language except French, the language of the Burgundian court. Although he inherited the Spanish crown in 1516 and was elected Holy Roman emperor in 1519, initially his political goals and closest advisers were Burgundian. Charles continued to press for development of central judicial and administrative agencies, despite growing uneasiness among the local elites over his policy of centralization. He had grown up among the Burgundian aristocracy and retained their loyalty, even though by the late 1520s it was becoming obvious that he was making Spain rather than the Netherlands the foundation of his rule.

Under his son **Philip II**, a thoroughly Spanish king, the latent conflict between royal centralization and Burgundian regionalism became more obvious. Local resistance to the centralizing policies of the crown and to the ruler's efforts to extirpate heresy produced a movement of protest in the mid-1560s, civil disorders in 1566, and a full-scale civil war after 1568. Ultimately, the leaders of the resistance movement declared independence from Spain in 1581. The Spanish army eventually regained control of the southern provinces, leaving the Burgundian lands permanently divided between the independent United Netherlands and the Habsburg-ruled Spanish Netherlands (known as Belgium since 1830, when it became an independent kingdom).

BUSCHE, HERMANN VON DEM (**Hermannus Buschius, ca. 1468–1534**). German **humanist**. Descended from a noble Westphalian family, he studied at Münster and at the famous school at Deventer directed by **Alexander Hegius**, then briefly under **Rudolf Agricola** at Heidelberg before a period of study in Italy under **Pomponius Laetus** at **Rome** and the elder **Filippo Beroaldo** at **Bologna**. Thus his education was directed by some of the most distinguished humanists of the day. Although he entered the University of Cologne in 1495 intending to study law, he became an itinerant teacher of Latin grammar, rhetoric, and poetry for brief periods at a number of German schools and **universities**. He also published poems and other writings. Busche agitated for a sweeping reform of the liberal arts curriculum of the German universities in order to increase attention to humanistic studies.

In 1502 he became one of the original faculty of the new University of Wittenberg, and the following year he lectured at the University of Leipzig, where he received a baccalaureate in law. Busche's open disdain for traditional academic studies led to his expulsion from Leipzig and later from the University of Erfurt. While teaching at Erfurt he established a lasting connection with the influential humanist **Mutianus Rufus** and the latter's Erfurt disciples, **Ulrich von Hutten** and **Crotus Rubianus**. Between 1506 and 1516 Busche again taught at Cologne, where he became one of a circle of outspoken humanist critics of **scholastic** learning and engaged in a bitter feud with a more conservative humanist, **Ortwin Gratius**. During the famous controversy between the humanist **Johann Reuchlin** and the theological faculty and Dominican friars of Cologne, Busche became an outspoken defender of Reuchlin. Although he was only marginally involved in composition of the satirical attack on the Cologne theologians, *Epistolae obscurorum virorum*, he probably contributed a number of authentic local details to Crotus and Hutten, the principal authors. The selection of Ortwin Gratius as the butt of the satire may well be an echo of Busche's earlier conflict with him. In 1518 Busche published an influential defense of humanist learning, *Vallum humanitatis / The Fortress of the Humanities*.

By 1521, when he attended the Diet of Worms, Busche had become an outspoken defender of **Martin Luther**. While at **Basel** in 1522, he joined a group of pro-Lutherans in publicly breaking the Lenten fast. When the new Lutheran University of Marburg opened in 1527, he became professor of poetry and classical literature. In 1533 he debated for the Lutheran cause against the revolutionary Anabaptists in his native region at Münster.

BYRD, WILLIAM (1540–1623). English composer, born in London and probably trained in the Chapel Royal under **Thomas Tallis**. He became organist and choirmaster at Lincoln cathedral (1563–1572), and in 1572 he was named a gentleman of the Chapel Royal and organist conjointly with his teacher, Tallis. In 1575 Queen **Elizabeth I** granted the two of them a privilege (a legal monopoly) for the publication and sale of printed music. Byrd's compositions included much music for the services of the Church of England, though Byrd and his family remained Roman Catholics. In the early 1590s he retired to Essex, but he continued composing and publishing religious and secular music, both vocal and instrumental. His Anglican service music, his few but highly regarded masses, and his motets are leading examples of English contrapuntal music of the late Renaissance.

BYZANTINE EMPIRE. *See* CONSTANTINOPLE, FALL OF.

– C –

CABALA (also written Kabbalah). A body of **Hebrew** mystical speculation, purporting to represent an ancient oral tradition of biblical interpretation and meditation that contained secret insights into the true spiritual meaning of Scripture. Originally, cabalistic writings were esoteric — something to be divulged only to persons who were intellectually and spiritually prepared to seek direct experience of God. The earliest cabalists passed their doctrines on by word of mouth, but eventually the texts were written down. There is considerable evidence of mystical practices and secret (sometimes quite unorthodox) beliefs going all the way back to the first century B.C. One of the earliest cabalistic texts to be preserved, *Sefer Yetzirah / The Book of Creation*, was probably written between the third and sixth centuries. It contains speculation on the elements of which the world is composed, which are identified as the 10 primordial numbers (the *sephiroth*) and the 22 letters of the Hebrew alphabet, which are symbols for the forces through which God made the world. This secret knowledge is believed to confer power over the universe; hence *Sefer Yetzirah*, like many cabalistic works, is linked to **magic**—that is, to efforts to gain practical control over material things—as well as to mystical contemplation.

Cabalistic learning flourished in Italy and Spain in the 13th and 14th centuries. One of the most influential scholars, Abraham Abulafia (1240–after 1291), born in Spain, spent several years travelling in the Middle East and Italy in quest of spiritual enlightenment. After returning to Spain about 1270, he studied *Sefer Yetzirah* and wrote several commentaries on it. From other cabalists he also learned techniques of biblical interpretation based on manipulation of the numerical values of letters and words in the Hebrew Bible, seeking to learn the true name of God and the names of the *sephiroth*. The greatest medieval cabalistic book was the *Sefer ha-Zohar / Book of Splendor*, which claimed to have been written in the second century but in fact was compiled by an anonymous mystic in 13th-century Spain.

In the later 15th century, a number of Italian Christian scholars, mainly **Neoplatonists** interested in mystical speculation, studied Cabala. The most important of these was **Giovanni Pico della Mirandola**, who learned Hebrew and sought religious truths in cabalistic texts. Like most of the early Christian cabalists, Pico interpreted these treatises in a Christian sense. A similar desire to prove Christian truths out of cabalistic literature motivated the first important Christian cabalist from north of the Alps, **Johann Reuchlin**, and the Christian cabalist who most aggressively pursued the idea that magical power could be obtained from the Cabala, **Agrippa von Nettesheim**. Cabalistic learning was suspect among traditional theologians because of its Jewish origins, because it was often associated with doctrines (transmigration of souls, for example) incompatible with Christian belief, and because of its links with magic.

CALVIN, JOHN (1509–1564). French religious reformer. Although identified mainly with the Protestant **Reformation**, Calvin began his intellectual development as a follower of **humanism**. Born at Noyon in northern France, he studied liberal arts at the University of Paris and law at Orléans and Bourges. He was more interested in the new humanistic movement and in the vague ideas of religious reform associated with it than in the traditional academic curriculum. At Paris he studied with a prominent humanist, Mathurin Cordier; at Orléans he received private lessons in **Greek** from the German humanist Melchior Wolmar, who was already a follower of **Martin Luther**; at Bourges he studied with the humanistic reformer of legal studies **Andrea Alciati**. After his father's death freed him to pursue his own goals, Calvin returned to Paris (1531) to study the Greek language, the Bible, and classical literature. In 1532 he published his first book, a humanistic commentary on the treatise *De clementia* by the Roman Stoic philosopher Seneca. Like many young French humanists of his time, he admired the biblical humanism of **Lefèvre d'Etaples** and **Erasmus** and probably had read some works of Luther. As late as 1532 he still seems to have regarded himself a Catholic.

Sometime between 1532 and 1535, however, Calvin changed from reform-minded Catholic humanist into committed Protestant. Twice, in 1533 and 1534–1535, he left Paris during periods when the authorities were actively hunting heretics. During the second of these exiles, Calvin spent several months in the Protestant city of **Basel**, where in 1535 he wrote the first version of his masterpiece of Protestant theology, *Institutes of the Christian Religion*, published the following year. After a few months at the court of the French-born duchess René of **Ferrara**, who sheltered a circle of Protestant sympathizers, he returned briefly to France and then began an exile that lasted for the rest of his life and transformed him into a major Protestant theologian and the leader of the Reformation in Geneva, where he spent most of his remaining years.

Nevertheless, Calvin's humanist background remained evident. Aside from his frequently reprinted *Institutes*, his principal theological works were his commentaries on the Bible. In them he applied the humanistic techniques of historical and linguistic analysis to probe the Scriptures. Also reflecting his humanist background was his emphasis on humanistic education as the essential preparation for leaders of religious reform. This commitment to education in the humanities culminated in the founding of the **Genevan Academy** in 1559.

CAMDEN, WILLIAM (1551–1623). English antiquary and educator. After study at St. Paul's school and Oxford, he became a teacher and headmaster at Westminster School. In 1597 he became a herald. His employments provided leisure for the antiquarian researches into the English past which produced *Britannia* (1586), an influential topographical survey of the country, and *Annales* (1615), a history of the reign of **Elizabeth I** down to 1588.

CAMOENS, LUIS VAS DE (1524/5–1580). Portuguese soldier and poet. Although he produced Portugal's greatest epic poem, *The Lusiads* (1572), and a body of lyric poetry, relatively little is known of his life except that after involvement in a street brawl he was imprisoned and sent as a soldier to India, where he spent nearly 20 years. His epic poem is modelled on the *Aeneid* of Vergil and traces the rise of Portuguese nation to greatness, culminating in the heroic exploits of its explorers and soldiers.

CAMPANELLA, TOMMASO (1568–1639). Italian philosopher, poet, and utopian political theorist. He entered the Dominican order in 1582. He was a brilliant student but soon turned against the dominant position of **Aristotle** in philosophy. His discovery of the anti-Aristotelian "nature-philosophy" of **Bernardino Telesio** led him to write several works defending Telesio from his critics. This got him in trouble not only with his order but also with the **Inquisition**. In 1594 at **Rome**, he was compelled to recant his errors. Sent back to his friary in Calabria, Campanella became involved in a popular uprising against Spanish rule and was arrested in 1599 and condemned to death on charges of both heresy and treason. Since the church's law forbade execution of mentally ill people, he successfully pretended to be insane, but he was held in jail for nearly 30 years. During this period he wrote most of his important books and poems. In 1626, having attracted the sympathy of Pope Urban VIII, Campanella was freed and permitted to go to Rome. In 1634, fearing that the pope had turned against him, he fled to France. He was cordially received by Cardinal Richelieu, the king's chief minister, and given a small pension. He lived in Paris for the remaining years of his life.

The philosophical principles expressed in works like *Philosophia sensibus demonstrata / Philosophy Proved from the Senses* (1591) derived in part from Telesio's efforts to found a new philosophy based on sensory knowledge rather than abstract reason. But Campanella's philosophical system was complex. It attempted to construct a picture of the real world that corresponded with the trinitarian nature of God. Ultimate reunion of the soul with God was the supreme goal of life. Some aspects of his thought suggest animism, the belief that all things in the universe have souls; at other times, he seems inclined to pantheism, the belief that all things are part of the divine essence. An affirmation of occult forces (**magical** and **astrological**) is implicit in his view of reality.

Yet none of the theoretical parts of his philosophy was so radical as his social and political philosophy, expressed in his most famous book, *La Città del sole / The City of the Sun* (written in 1602, published in 1623). Even though the Catholic church and the Spanish monarchy were responsible for persecuting him, Campanella's ideal human society was an absolute and autocratic world-monarchy ruled by a just and philosophical **pope**. This ruler would rigidly discipline every aspect of life, imposing **communism** of property, obligation to labor, and strict regulation of sexual practices. His ideal society would be based solely on merit. Even women would be eligible for every office not requiring physical strength beyond their ability. The stability and prosperity of this society would be based on education, natural science, and technology. Campanella also wrote many poems, and a number of these were published.

CAMPIN, ROBERT (documented, 1406–1444). Leading painter of the city of Tournai in Flanders, usually regarded as identical with the so-called "Master of Flémalle," creator of an outstanding painting, the *Merode Altarpiece* (ca. 1425) that marks a significant breakthrough from the Flemish paintings of the late-medieval International Gothic style to the mature Franco-Flemish style of the 15th century. The work is also notable for its depicition of prosperous burghers rather than great aristocrats, its sympathetic depiction of St. Joseph as a simple craftsman, and its pioneering use of oil paints instead of the tempera medium typical of medieval painting.

CAMPION, THOMAS (1567–1620). English poet and composer. His devotion to ancient Roman prosody appears in his *Observations in the Art of English Poesie* (1602), which attacks the medieval use of rhyme and urges modern poets to follow **classical** practice. On this issue he engaged in a literary duel with a rival poet, Samuel Daniel, author of *A Defence of Ryme* (1603). His own poetry, however, only occasionally abandons the use of rhyme and accentual meter. He also wrote four books of *Ayres*, in which he created both lyrics and music. He was one of the leading composers of the masques that were fashionable in his time, and he published five books of airs for the lute.

CAPITANO DEL POPOLO. An official elected in many Italian communes of the 13th and 14th centuries, normally acting as the chief executive of the combined local **guilds** in opposition to the old patrician families that dominated the government of most cities in the early period of the independent **communes**. The *capitano del popolo* assumed a mediating role in relations between various guilds, acquired informal extra-legal powers in order to restrain the disfranchised noble clans (the grandi), and in many places ended by becoming the *signore*, or dictator, of the city. Examples of the ascension of *capitani del popolo* to hereditary rule include the Carrara dynasty at **Padua**, the della **Scala** at Verona, the **Gonzaga** at **Mantua**, and the Della Torre and **Visconti** families at **Milan**. At **Florence**, however, which was exceptional in its successful resistance to the rise of a dictatorship, the power of the *capitano* was restrained by a requirement to have his decrees ratified by a council of citizens.

CARAVAGGIO. One of the leading figures of early **baroque** painting at **Rome**. His proper name was Michelangelo Merisi (1571–1610), but he was called Caravaggio after his home town near **Milan**. He received his early training under a Milanese master, but he developed a highly personal style notable for its naturalism and its dramatic contrasts of light and darkness. Some of his best early work was done in a chapel of the church of S. Luigi dei Francesi, notably *The Calling of St. Matthew*, which shows traits of both the older **mannerist** and the new baroque style. This presentation of a scene from the New Testament in terms that reflect the life of the lower classes shocked many contemporaries, who found it irreverent. In his own time, Caravaggio's paintings were regarded highly by other artists and sophisticated patrons but not widely appreciated by the general public. He worked in Rome from about 1593 to 1606, when he fled from Rome after committing murder. He spent most of the rest of his life in **Naples** and Malta. Though known to be a fugitive, he retained the favor of the highest ranks of society.

CARDANO, GIROLAMO (1501–1576). Italian physician, mathematician, and natural philosopher. Born in Pavia and educated there and at **Padua**, he supported himself during his student years as a gambler. One of his later writings, *Liber de ludo aleae / Book on Games of Dice*, presented a sophisticated discussion of the mathematics of probability, though it had little influence since it was not published until the following century. After graduation, he practiced medicine near Padua and in 1534 moved to **Milan**, first as a teacher of mathematics and later as a medical practitioner. From 1543 to 1560 he was professor of medicine at the University of Pavia. Cardano's interests extended to many branches of natural philosophy, including mechanics, geology, and hydrodynamics. He realized that the trajectory of a projectile is a parabola; he noted that the presence of marine fossils on dry land proves that mountainous regions had once been ocean floor; he suggested that the earth's water is constantly recirculated from rain to rivers to oceans to clouds and back to rain.

Cardano was especially gifted as a mathematician. His first mathematical publication, *Practica arithmeticae / Arithmetical Practice* (1539), showed great skill in manipulating equations. He was one of a number of contemporaries who studied quadratic equations, and his book *Ars magna / The Great Art* (1545) summarized his own work and that of several others on that topic, though it also involved him in a bitter controversy with **Niccolò Tartaglia** even though he gave Tartaglia full credit for his pioneering contributions. In 1560 Cardano moved from Pavia to **Bologna**. There he was imprisoned in 1570 by the **Roman Inquisition** on suspicion of heresy, but he was released and spent his final years at **Rome**, supported by a papal pension.

CARRACCI. Family of **Bolognese** artists active in the late 16th and early 17th centuries. They led a rebellion against the style known as **mannerism** and developed a more naturalistic style subsequently labelled **baroque**. The family is also important because they founded the Accademia dei Caracci, inspired by the Florentine Accademia del Disegno, the first officially recognized school for educating artists. Ludovico (1555–1619) and his cousins Agostino (1557–1602) and Annibale (1560–1609) were the first of the family to become painters and achieved great fame both through paintings done separately and through collaborative projects including a series of much-admired paintings in the **Farnese** Palace at **Rome**.

CARVAJAL Y MENDOZA, LUISA DE (1566–1614). Spanish religious poet. Born into the powerful Mendoza family and reared by relatives after she was orphaned, she felt a strong calling to religious work but was not willing to become a nun. Instead, she lived an austere single life and ministered to the poor. Distressed by the loss of Christian unity, she decided to travel to England and work for the reconversion of the English to the Catholic faith, a plan that she carried out beginning in 1605, with the encouragement of the **Jesuit** order. She was twice imprisoned for preaching in the streets and attempting to form a convent in her home but managed to remain in England until her death. Her religious poetry, published posthumously, includes sonnets and ballads and often took the form of dialogues.

CASAUBON, ISAAC (1559–1614). French classical scholar, regarded as the most skilled Hellenist of his time. A Protestant in religion, he taught **Greek** in Geneva and at the **University** of Montpellier and in 1600 was invited to the French court, where he became keeper of the royal library but disappointed the hopes of King Henry IV by refusing to convert to Catholicism. He began as primarily a student of **classical antiquity** but gradually shifted his interests to early Christian history. He spent the last period of his life at the court of James I of England, who had him write polemical works in defense of the Anglican religious settlement. Casaubon published several critical editions of Greek authors but was best known for his last publication, *De rebus sacris et ecclesiasticis exercitationes / Exercises on Sacred and Ecclesiastical Matters* (1614). This work attacked the strongly Catholic account of early church history in the *Annales* of Cardinal Cesare Baronio. Its most famous chapter demonstrated that the **Hermetic** texts which Renaissance **Platonists** attributed to a divine revelation made to the Egyptians long before the birth of Christ were a series of forgeries made in the late classical period.

CASTAGNO, ANDREA DEL (ca. 1423–1457). The most talented **Florentine** painter of the generation following **Masaccio**, whose style influenced him greatly. He thoroughly assimilated the techniques of **perspective** defined by **Filippo Brunelleschi** and first successfully applied to painting by Masaccio. The technical mastery demonstrated in his *Last Supper* (ca. 1445–1450) was confirmed by his *David*, completed about five years later.

CASTIGLIONE, BALDASSARE (ca. 1478–1529). Italian writer and diplomat. The son of a professional soldier who served the marquis of **Mantua**, Castiglione received a **humanistic** education but began his career as a military officer and diplomat. In 1504, having met Duke Guidobaldo of **Urbino** while visiting **Rome**, he entered the service of that prince and went on embassies to England, **Milan**, France, and Rome. His later diplomatic service took him back to Rome in 1523 as Mantuan ambassador, and in 1524 Pope **Clement VII** appointed him papal nuncio to the court of **Charles V** in Spain, where he spent the rest of his life and died of plague in 1529.

Castiglione was a skilled practitioner of courtly poetry and was active in organizing performances of plays at court. But his literary masterpiece was *The Book of the Courtier*, published in 1528. The book is a series of imaginary dialogues set at the court of the duke and duchess of Urbino, where he had spent much of his early adult life. It reflects the elegant and highly intellectual court, and many of the interlocutors are real people he had known there. Both men and women participate in the witty discussions held as an amusement for the courtiers during long evenings together. The game is to define the characteristics of the perfect courtier and the perfect court lady. The imaginary pictures of both gentleman and lady represent a high ideal of aristocratic life, with emphasis on development of a broad range of skills, not only physical and artistic but also poetic and intellectual. The final topic of conversation is the proper conduct of the courtier in matters of love, and this discussion culminates in the explanation of the ideal of **Platonic** love by **Pietro Bembo**, who in real life had articulated that ideal. Castiglione's book was a great literary success. It was translated into Latin and nearly all of the major European languages, largely because its portrait of the ideal courtier and court lady served as a book of manners for aspiring aristocrats.

CATHERINE OF SIENA, SAINT (1347–1380). Italian mystic, daughter of an influential Sienese family, canonized in 1461 and declared to be a doctor of the church in 1970. From childhood she was deeply spiritual, and at age 16 she became a Dominican tertiary, living in self-imposed solitude for three years and then becoming active in ministry to the sick and poor. She experienced a spiritual marriage to Christ and in 1375 received the stigmata, signs of Christ's wounds.

Deeply devoted to the church and to the papacy and distressed by the frequent wars among Italian cities, she went to **Avignon** to visit Pope Gregory XI, and in response to her prophecies he returned to **Rome**. Her influence extended far beyond Siena. Many people, both men and women, acknowledged her holiness and looked to her for inspiration. She became a trusted adviser to Pope **Urban VI**. Catherine's great popularity is reflected in the many Renaissance paintings depicting events in her life. She is recognized as the first female author to write in the Tuscan dialect. Her surviving writings include several hundred letters to popes, secular princes, and prisoners; an influential mystical treatise, *Il libro della divina dottrina / A Treatise on Divine Providence* (1377–1378); and a collection of prayers. Despite her lack of formal schooling, she was familiar with the Bible and the works of such doctors of the church as Saints Augustine, Gregory the Great, Bernard of Clairvaux, and Thomas Aquinas. Her letters, which addressed contemporary religious and political problems, including the need for reform of the church, were published in 1500 by the Venetian **humanist** and **printer Aldus Manutius**.

CAXTON, WILLIAM (ca. 1422–1491). The first Englishman to practice the new art of **printing**. A native of Kent and a member of the Mercers' Company of London, he spent many years living abroad, chiefly at Bruges in the Netherlands. In 1470 he moved to Cologne and took charge of a printing firm. After printing several books there, he returned to Bruges and founded a new printing shop. About the end of 1473, he brought out the first book printed in English, a translation of a French historical romance, *Recuyell of the Histories of Troy*. In 1476 Caxton moved back to England and set up shop at Westminster, near the royal court. There he printed about a hundred titles, of which the most famous is the first edition of **Chaucer's** *Canterbury Tales* (1477); but his products also included works of religious edification, English translations of lives of the saints (notably the *Legenda aurea* of Jacobus de Voragine), a book on chess, *Aesop's Fables*, and *Reynard the Fox*. At the very end of his life, he translated into English a book of the lives of the ancient Christian Desert Fathers, published by his successor Wynkyn de Worde.

CELESTINA. See ROJAS, FERNANDO DE.

CELLINI, BENVENUTO (1500–1571). Florentine sculptor and gold-smith, now best known for his *Autobiography*, first published in 1728. Apprenticed as a goldsmith in **Florence**, he had a brilliant but unstable career, largely because of his own moral irregularities, which he admitted, often boastfully, in his autobiography. He is commonly regarded as one of the greatest sculptors who worked in the **manner-ist** style. As early as 1516 Cellini had to leave Florence and move to Siena because of his involvement in a brawl, and his autobiography describes his many acts of violence, including murder. He worked for several years in several Italian cities, including **Rome**. He left Rome after it was looted by the imperial army in 1527 but later returned and worked in the papal mint on the design of commemorative medals. Al-though he was charged with the murder of another goldsmith, Pope Paul III pardoned him. Cellini fled Rome in 1535 to escape arrest, worked in several Italian cities, visited France, was arrested while back in Rome, but escaped and eventually moved to France.

There he won the favor of King **Francis I** and created a grand-scale bronze sculpture of a nymph for the palace at Fontainebleau, his earliest surviving large-scale work. Also from this period is his gold saltcellar, an elegant example of his work as a jeweller. In 1545 Cellini returned to Florence and created for Duke Cosimo I a grand-scale bronze statue of Perseus holding the severed head of Medusa, probably the finest of his large works. He also demonstrated his mas-tery of carving in marble by incorporating an ancient marble torso be-longing to the duke into a statue of Ganymede.

Cellini's difficult personality and disorderly life, as well as the changing tastes of his patron, caused him to lose favor at court, and although his life-size *Crucifix* (1562) again demonstrated his mastery of work in marble, he never regained the generous patronage he en-joyed in his early career. He was an overwhelming personality. That personality is reflected in all of Cellini's literary work, which in-cluded the only two of his works published in his own lifetime, trea-tises on goldsmithing and sculpture, as well as a substantial body of poetry, not published until modern times, and his famous *Autobiog-raphy* (1728), which was widely translated into other languages. This work contributed significantly to the exaggerated idea of undisci-plined individualism, violence, sexual irregularity, and irreligion that dominated much writing about Renaissance Italy during the 18th and 19th centuries.

CELTIS, CONRAD (1459–1508). German **humanist** and Latin poet. Born near Würzburg to a peasant family, he acquired a university education despite his poverty, receiving a B.A. degree at Cologne (1479) and an M.A. at Heidelberg (1485), where he was attracted by the presence of **Rudolf Agricola**. He then taught poetry for brief periods at Erfurt, Rostock, and Leipzig, publishing his first work, *Ars versificandi / The Art of Versification*, at Leipzig in 1486. Celtis spent the years 1487–1497 travelling, the first two years in Italy, where he met important scholars such as **Marsilio Ficino** at **Florence** and **Pomponio Leto** at **Rome**. In 1489 he went to the University of Cracow to study natural philosophy, astronomy, and mathematics.

Beginning in 1492, Celtis taught at the **University** of Ingolstadt, where his inaugural lecture, published in 1492, laid out his program of reforming German education by emphasizing humanistic studies over traditional **scholastic** learning. His avowed goal was to make Germany, rather than Italy, the center of humanism. His criticism of the traditional university curriculum irritated many faculty colleagues, but they were probably more alienated by his habitual drunkenness, his numerous love affairs (reflected in his poems), and his frequent absenteeism. Despite his personal faults, his reputation as a scholar and a talented poet won him a professorship at the University of Vienna in 1497, and he remained there until his death, working to carry out the plan of the Emperor **Maximilian I** to support humanistic studies by founding a new academic unit, the College of Poets and Mathematicians. Maximilian's goal, shared by Celtis, was to create a new elite of young humanists to administer a revitalized German monarchy.

Celtis published a book of love poetry, the *Amores*, in 1502. He also discovered an important text that demonstrated the presence of **classical** learning in medieval Germany, the six Latin dramas written by a 10th-century German nun, Hrosvitha of Gandersheim, and in 1500 he published the *Germania* of the Roman historian Tacitus, which extravagantly praised the ancient Germans. Celtis dreamed of publishing a comprehensive historical and geographical survey of all of Germany, but he completed only one part, a description of the city of Nuremberg (1502). After his death, his students published a collection of his odes (1513).

Celtis' greatest importance is his association of the past and future greatness of Germany with his enthusiasm for the study of classical languages and literature. In pursuit of this goal, he promoted the founding of humanist sodalities at several places in southern and southwestern Germany. These sodalities did much to promote the study of humanistic subjects in German schools and universities, and their positive early response to the teachings of **Martin Luther** was one reason for the rapid diffusion of the German reformer's ideas among educated Germans.

CERETA, LAURA (1469–1499). One of the rare female **humanists** and authors of Renaissance Italy. She was born to a prominent family of Brescia and educated at home and in a convent school. As was customary for women of her class, she married at age 15 but was left a childless widow when her husband died of plague. She devoted her life to study and writing. She met many of the humanists who lived in and near Brescia and addressed to them and others a series of letters discussing literary topics. Many of the men to whom she wrote refused to reply to her letters. She also attempted to meet and encourage other educated **women**. Her letters to humanists were often autobiographical, revealing her desire for a respected place in the all-male world of learning. She sought to establish a social environment in which educated women could participate without risking their reputation for moral uprightness.

CERVANTES SAAVEDRA, MIGUEL DE (1547–1616). With the possible exception of the dramatist **Lope de Vega**, Cervantes was the greatest literary figure of the Golden Age of Spanish literature. He is world famous as the author of the two-part comic novel, *Don Quixote* (1605, 1615). Although born in the **university** town of **Alcalá de Henares**, he was unable to secure a higher education because of his family's poverty. In 1569 Cervantes fled to Italy in order to avoid having a hand amputated as punishment for involvement in a brawl. He became a member of the household of a Spanish cardinal at **Rome** and in 1570 enlisted in the Spanish army. He fought heroically in the famous naval victory over the Turks at Lepanto (1571) but was wounded and lost the use of his left hand. Returning to Spain by sea in 1575, he and his brother were captured by Moorish pirates and sold into slavery at Algiers. He had to remain in captivity until 1580, when he finally was able to purchase his liberty. He started writing toward the end of his captivity, producing a memoir of his resistance and his attempts to escape. Eventually he won appointment to the unglamorous job of tax collector, a difficult task that twice got him arrested on suspicion of embezzlement.

Cervantes began writing plays and in 1585 published a pastoral romance, *La Galatea*. He married in 1584 but had no legitimate children, and his effort to secure a government position in the American colonies failed. Not until 1605, when he published the first part of *Don Quixote* at age 58, did Cervantes win recognition as an author. He followed the royal court to Madrid in 1606 and spent the rest of his life there. He published many works during this period, including a dozen short prose narratives, a long autobiograpical poem, eight plays and eight interludes (none of which were produced on stage), and the second part of *Don Quixote*. His widow published his romance *Los trabajos de Persiles y Sigismunda* in 1617.

Don Quixote was by far Cervantes' most successful work, a favorite among Spanish readers for many centuries, and later translations won an international following. Its satirical attacks on the fashion for preposterous tales of chivalry, its memorable characters (especially Don Quixote himself and his squire Sancho Panza), its varied pictures of the life of Spanish people, and its long series of amusing episodes guaranteed its popularity among the masses, while its subtle discussion of the distinction between reality and illusion has intrigued more sophisticated readers.

CESALPINO, ANDREA (1525–1603). Italian physician and botanist, born at Arezzo and educated at **Pisa**, where he studied both anatomy and botany. In 1565 he became director of the botanical garden at Pisa, and in 1569 he was appointed professor of medicine. He moved to **Rome** in 1592 as professor of medicine and personal physician to Pope Clement VIII. His medical publications show him to be a confirmed supporter of the traditional authority of **Aristotle**, but also to be eager to discover new ways to apply Aristotelian principles to scientific problems. His most original work was in botany. His *De plantis libri XVI / Sixteen Books on Botany* (1583) followed the classification principles of Aristotle and his disciple Theophrastus. Surprisingly for the work of a physician, this botanical book provided no illustrations and rarely discussed medicinal applications. He seems to have coined the phrase "circulation of the blood," and his discussion of that topic vaguely foreshadows the subsequent work of **William Harvey**.

CHAMBERS OF RHETORIC. Literary societies formed in many cities of France and the Netherlands in the 15th and 16th centuries by middle-class citizens who wanted to encourage the growth of poetry and drama. Few of them were innovative, but they organized public celebrations and encouraged development of both drama and poetry. In the Netherlands, they fostered the growth of a national vernacular literature.

CHAPMAN, GEORGE (1560–1634). English poet, dramatist, and translator. His comedies *All Fools* (1605) and *The Widow's Tears* (1612) were successful on the London stage, and his classical education (probably at Oxford) is reflected in his tragedy *Bussy d'Ambois* (1607), which shows the influence of the Roman dramatist Seneca, though it also reflects his interest in the recent history of France. He is most widely known as a translator of classical literature; his translation of Homer was long regarded as the best English text of the Homeric poems.

CHARLES V (1500–1558). King of Spain (1515–1555) and Holy Roman Emperor (1519–1555). Charles was the most powerful ruler in 16th-century Europe. As the descendant of the German **Habsburg** dynasty, of the rulers of the united Spain created by his grandparents **Ferdinand** and **Isabella**, and of the powerful dukes of **Burgundy**, in his youth he collected, by inheritance and election, a vast empire that dominated much of Europe and considerable parts of the Americas. Born and reared in the Netherlands, and originally speaking only the French language of the Burgundian court, he became ruling prince of the Netherlands at the age of six and was declared of legal age in 1515, when he took charge of the government. In 1516, after the death of his grandfather Ferdinand, he became hereditary king of Spain, a position that also made him king of **Naples** and ruler of the Spanish colonies in America. The death of his Habsburg grandfather **Maximilian I** in 1519 brought him title to the hereditary Habsburg principalities in Germany; it also made him the prime candidate to succeed Maximilian as emperor, a position to which he was elected in 1519 in rivalry with King **Francis I** of France. His electoral victory was won not by his descent from the German Habsburgs (he understood no German) but by the enormous bribes with which he bought the votes of a majority of the seven electoral princes.

Charles aspired to develop his imperial title into a strong German monarchy, while also maintaining control over the Netherlands (where he grew up), Spain, and Naples. He took seriously the universalist claims of his imperial title. Personally devout and firmly Catholic though sympathetic to **humanist** reformers like **Erasmus**, he nevertheless clashed frequently with the **popes**, partly over ecclesiastical patronage in his territories but mainly over his determination to transform the imperial title into an effective control over all of Italy, a policy bitterly resisted by the popes. The chief hindrance to his success was the determination of France to resist his attempts to regain French fiefs lost by his Burgundian ancestors in the mid-15th century, and also to keep him from creating a unified German monarchy that would dominate western and central Europe. Charles's task was complicated by the Lutheran **Reformation** and the decision of a number of the German princes and the great majority of self-governing German towns to support **Martin Luther's** reforms. Charles attempted to enforce the decree he proclaimed at the Diet of Worms in 1521 outlawing Luther and all who supported him.

Despite his great military power and revenues, however, he never gained enough military power in Germany to make good his threats to extinguish heresy by force. The constant opposition of the French king Francis I, who felt threatened by Charles' ambitions, helped to frustrate his policy. Only in 1546, at one of the rare moments when he had forced the French to stop meddling in German politics and had won political and financial support from the pope, was Charles finally able to concentrate his military power in Germany, defeat the Lutheran princes in the Schmalkaldic War (1546–1547), and compel those princes to accept an interim religious settlement that was intended to re-establish Catholicism eventually throughout Germany. Even this victory proved ephemeral. The French king resumed his encouragement of the anti-Habsburg German princes, the one major Lutheran prince who had joined the imperial side in the war defected, and by 1552 the Lutherans had forced Charles' brother Ferdinand to agree to a settlement that preserved Lutheranism in Germany. After many decades of struggle against the Lutherans, the French, and the **Ottoman Turks**, Charles decided to abdicate. He turned control of Germany over to his brother Ferdinand, who received the imperial title. He abdicated control in the Netherlands, Spain, and Naples in favor of his son **Philip II**. In 1556 he withdrew to a monastery in Spain.

Although by no means an intellectual, Charles did have some sympathy for the humanistic learning of the Renaissance, especially for the moderate reform ideas of the German and Dutch humanists who did not turn Protestant. He was a great admirer and patron of the artists of the Renaissance.

CHARRON, PIERRE (1541–1603). French philosopher. Educated in both **humanist** and **scholastic** subjects at Paris, and then in law at Orléans, Bourges, and Montpellier, and ordained as a priest, he settled in southwestern France and became chaplain to **Margaret of Navarre** and a close friend of **Michel de Montaigne**. He sought to encourage an end to the French Wars of Religion by drawing a distinction between the realm of faith and the realm of reason. His book *Les trois veritez / The Three Truths* (1593) discussed the basic truths of Christianity, while his *De la sagesse / On Wisdom* (1601) discussed the theme of human reason as something distinct from religion though subordinate to it. *De la sagesse* was an influential work of **Neostoic** moral philosophy. It was usually interpreted as defining a secular moral code distinct from religion, though that was not Charron's intention.

CHAUCER, GEOFFREY (ca. 1340–1400). The greatest poet of medieval English literature, and the first widely influential poet since Anglo-Saxon times to write mainly in English rather than French. He is enduringly famous as the author of the *Canterbury Tales*, a collection of verse narratives supposedly told by a band of pilgrims on their way to visit the shrine of St. Thomas à Becket at Canterbury. The poem is remarkable for the socially diverse collection of characters portrayed, for its subtle portrayal of human character, and for its skillful and original treatment of stories that were often traditional folk tales and sometimes were borrowed from earlier authors. The poem is also notable for the anticlerical satire that reflects popular criticism of the clergy, a theme found in much late-medieval literature.

Although Chaucer is usually defined as a medieval author, his great poem shows familiarity with writers of the early Italian Renaissance such as **Giovanni Boccaccio**. Also important is the role of his writings in establishing the East Midlands dialect of Middle English as the dominant form of the English language. Yet Chaucer knew French language and literature well and was influenced by medieval French literature. One of his early works was an adaptation of the famous French poem *The Romance of the Rose*. He was also influenced by late medieval and early Renaissance Italian literature—his *Troilus and Criseyde*, for example, was adapted from a work of Boccaccio.

Chaucer was born into a prosperous London mercantile family (his father was a vintner) and as a boy became a page at the royal court. He made several journeys abroad, sometimes in military service and sometimes on diplomatic missions. One of these missions took him to Italy, where he may have met Boccaccio and **Petrarch**. He secured a lucrative governmental appointment as a royal customs officer, served as a member of Parliament, and advanced his family in social rank from prosperous middle-class to the outer fringes of the aristocracy.

CHEKE, JOHN (1514–1557). English **humanist** and teacher. One of the most brilliant of the Cambridge scholars who fostered the study of **Greek**, Cheke became the first regius professor of that language at Cambridge in 1540. Strongly sympathetic to Protestantism, he became tutor to the future King Edward VI in 1544 and had an important role in the education of the prince to be a Protestant ruler. He sat as a member of Edward's first Parliament and was ordained to the clergy in 1549. Upon the premature death of the young king in 1553, Cheke was involved in the attempt to block the succession of the Catholic Mary **Tudor** and was arrested after she gained control of the government. He fled to the Continent, lived in both **Basel** and Strasbourg, and taught Greek in the latter place. Arrested by the government of **Charles V** while travelling in the Netherlands, he was sent back to England as a prisoner and was forced to abjure his Protestant beliefs by threat of torture.

CHRISTIAN HUMANISM. *See* HUMANISM.

CHRISTINE DE PIZAN (1364–1430). French author. Although born in **Venice**, Christine moved to France as a child when her father became court **astrologer** and medical adviser to King **Charles V**. Christine may have received some formal instruction from the tutor who taught her brothers, but since she married when she was 15 and gave birth to three children before the death of her husband of plague in 1390, she must have acquired most of her remarkable learning through independent reading. Her husband's death left her with very limited means. She became a writer in order to find patrons and win financial support. Her best-known works were defenses of female character against the misogyny of an influential poet, Jean de **Meung**, who had written a continuation of the *Romance of the Rose*. In her most influential work, *Le livre de la Cité des dames / The Book of the City of Ladies* (1405), she shows the influence of **Giovanni Boccaccio's** book on famous **women**. At the request of the duke of **Burgundy**, Christine undertook a history of the deeds of King Charles V (1404). After the outbreak of civil war among factions of the aristocracy, she wrote several works pleading for the restoration of peace. Christine eventually retired to a Dominican convent at Poissy where her daughter was a nun, but she remained active in literature and wrote the first literary work devoted to the praise of **Joan of Arc**.

CHRISTUS, PETRUS (ca. 1410–ca. 1472). Flemish painter, a disciple of **Jan van Eyck**, some of whose unfinished works he may have completed. His paintings demonstrate some of the earliest examples of the use of linear **perspective** in northern art. His *Portrait of a Young Woman* (ca. 1450) has the meticulous attention to detail typical of Flemish painting but also has a sensuous spirit and an inwardness not common in his time and place.

CHRYSOLORAS, MANUEL (ca. 1350–1415). Greek-born scholar, teacher, and diplomat, important in the history of the Renaissance as the first teacher to make a group of Western pupils sufficiently skilled in **Greek** that they could continue the development of Greek studies on their own. Born into an aristocratic family at Constantinople and renowned as a scholar, he became a friend of the Byzantine emperor Manuel II and in 1394 was sent to Western Europe to seek military and financial support against the **Ottoman Turks**. At **Venice**, Chrysoloras met a friend of the Florentine chancellor **Coluccio Salutati**, who persuaded the Florentine republic to employ Chrysoloras to teach Greek in the city. He reached **Florence** in early 1397 and stayed there until early spring of 1400.

What made Chrysoloras more successful than earlier Greek language teachers in Italy was his broad mastery of ancient literature, Latin as well as Greek. He was fluent in Latin and hence could communicate with his Italian pupils far better than the masters who had tried to teach Greek to early **humanists** like **Petrarch** and **Giovanni Boccaccio**. Chrysoloras' reputation spread rapidly, and not only Florentines but also humanists from other parts of Italy came to study under him. **Leonardo Bruni**, one of the leading humanists of the next generation, abandoned the study of law to study with Chrysoloras because such an opportunity to learn Greek might never come again. Thus Chrysoloras opened the way to the permanent establishment of Greek studies among Western European humanists. Many of the most successful teachers of Greek in the next generation had been his pupils. He also influenced the humanists' ideas about translating texts. He was critical of medieval translators' practice of translating word for word. He argued that a good translation must convey the sense, not the words, of its original.

About 1403 Chrysoloras returned to Constantinople, where he continued teaching and welcomed a number of Italian scholars who came east to learn Greek in its homeland. He made at least two later diplomatic missions to Italy and about 1405 became a convert to the Roman Catholic form of Christianity. In addition to seeking military assistance for his homeland, he also worked for the reunion of the Greek and Latin churches. Between 1407 and 1410 he travelled widely in northern Europe. He lectured on Greek literature at the **University** of Paris, but unlike Italy, where the growth of humanism had made many scholars realize the importance of Greek, neither Paris nor the other northern universities he visited felt the excitement that Chrysoloras' teaching had aroused in Renaissance Italy. In 1414 he accompanied the pope's delegation to the **Council of Constance**; while there, he fell ill and died, being then buried in the Dominican church in Constance.

CICERONIANISM. The tendency of Renaissance **humanists** to define Cicero (106–43 B.C.) as the sole model for good Latin style. Marcus Tullius Cicero was the most influential ancient Roman prose author. Medieval knowledge of his works focused primarily on his philosophical writings. For **Petrarch**, Cicero continued to be conceived primarily as a wise philosopher. Petrarch also admired Cicero's Latin style, but he made no attempt to purge his own Latin of words and usages not found in Cicero's works. Yet his discovery of Cicero's orations and personal letters initiated a major shift in the perception of the Roman author. These orations and letters revealed that the Cicero whom Petrarch had revered as a moral philosopher interested only in wisdom and virtue was also an ambitious politician eager for power and fame. In the early 15th century, humanists also found manuscripts of Cicero's mature works on rhetoric.

Thus the image of Cicero changed from that of scholarly moral philosopher to that of ambitious statesman, eloquent orator, and supreme master of Latin style. By the beginning of the 15th century, his reputation as the unquestioned authority for all questions of Latin style and vocabulary was growing rapidly. This stress on Cicero as the perfect model for writing Latin was the foundation of what later came to be called Ciceronianism. The early "Ciceronians" did not utterly reject Latin words and grammatical constructions found in other ancient authors, but following Cicero whenever possible seemed the safest way to attain an excellent style.

This emergent Ciceronianism did not pass unchallenged. **Lorenzo Valla**, himself one of the most brilliant Latinists of his time, caused a scandal when he openly declared that the recently discovered rhetorician Quintilian was a better guide to good Latin than Cicero. In the later 15th century, the **Florentine** humanist **Angelo Poliziano** criticized those who attacked his writings as insufficiently Ciceronian. Like Valla, he practiced a consciously eclectic style, looking to other ancient authors in addition to Cicero for models and not hesitant to accept words and structures never found in a known work of Cicero.

The Venetian scholar **Pietro Bembo** in 1512 argued that Cicero ought to be the model for all who wanted to write good Latin. The humanists at the papal curia in **Rome**, who made their reputations and their professional careers as experts in **classical** Latin, were notoriously devoted to a narrow and restricted brand of Ciceronianism. As the influence of Italian humanism spread across the Alps, some natives of northern Europe also began judging Latin style according to Ciceronian models. The young Netherlander **Christophe de Longueil** spent years among the Ciceronians at Rome and became a sharp critic of contemporary authors who did not write Ciceronian

Latin. Other northerners, however, resented the Italians' claim to a monopoly on good style. Their most eloquent spokesman was the Dutch humanist **Erasmus**, whose dialogue *Ciceronianus* (1528) made Longueil a particular target of criticism. Erasmus humorously treated Ciceronianism as a disease needing to be cured. In a more serious vein, he defended a model of good Latin that was far less narrow. While he admired Cicero, his own preferences among modern Latinists were those who had adopted an eclectic style, such as Valla and Poliziano. Erasmus' main argument was that because society had changed greatly since ancient times, language must be adapted to express new realities—in particular, the religious change from Roman paganism to Christianity. Accompanying his criticism of the Italian Ciceronians was his conviction that most of them, especially the arrogant curial secretaries at Rome, had very little real religious spirit and in practice lived, thought, and wrote like pagans. A sharp controversy followed the publication of Erasmus' book.

Despite such criticisms, Ciceronianism not only survived but grew in the middle decades of the 16th century. In 1535 Mario Nizzoli published a dictionary of Ciceronian words to guide those who wished to avoid any non-Ciceronian terms. Probably because the practice of defining Cicero as the standard was more easily teachable to students than Erasmus' eclectic style, which depended on a sophisticated taste that few writers possessed, Ciceronianism dominated (and still dominates) the teaching of Latin. Cicero's works were used as schoolbooks. Protestant educational reformers like **Philipp Melanchthon** at Wittenberg and **Johann Sturm** at Strasbourg, as well as Catholic educators in Italy and Spain, upheld Ciceronian standards, and the **Jesuit** order, which became a major force in Catholic education, officially adopted Ciceronian standards in its schools.

CIMABUE (ca. 1250–after 1300). One of the major painters of the late-medieval *maniera greca* (Byzantine manner) that dominated Italian art during the 13th century. His work *Madonna Enthroned* at **Florence** is a significant example of the adaptation of Byzantine artistic style to Italian taste. Renaissance artists believed that he was the master who trained **Giotto**, the late-Gothic painter whose work is commonly thought to mark the first great step toward the Italian Renaissance style of painting.

CIOMPI. Florentine term for unskilled wool-carders employed in the woollen industry, one of the lowest-ranking social and economic groups. Their violent rebellion in 1378 was a memorable incident in the troubled political and economic history of 14th-century **Florence**. After the failure of the attempt by a group of wealthy merchants to put a military dictator into power in 1343, the **guilds** representing the middling elements of the population had compelled the guilds of rich businessmen to grant them an increased share in the city's government. Encouraged by this development, the *Ciompi*, who were totally excluded from a political voice and were suffering from low wages and unemployment, sought a voice of their own in government. When they were turned down in 1378, the *Ciompi* rebelled and forced the regime directed by the 21 established guilds to grant them the right to organize two new guilds and thus to gain some voice, though not a very powerful one, in the political system. The members of the 14 lesser guilds, however, resented the new privileges of this propertyless group and tried to limit their gains. In 1382, since tension between the *Ciompi* and the middling classes was paralyzing local government and threatening further violence, rich conspirators from the seven greater guilds staged a coup d'état, dissolved the two new guilds of the *Ciompi*, and then used their military force to restore order. Within a few years, the wealthy guilds had managed to carry through a "reform" of the political system that reduced the representation of the lesser guilds on the ruling executive council and restored the dominance of the rich over the political system.

CITY-STATE. *See* COMMUNE.

CIVIC HUMANISM. *See* BRUNI, LEONARDO; COMMUNE; HUMANISM.

CLASSICS. Some familiarity with the literary works of ancient **Rome** continued from late **antiquity** throughout the **Middle Ages**, but even well-educated medieval scholars were familiar with only those parts of Latin literature that seemed germane to their own society, and they knew at first hand almost none of the literary masterpieces of ancient Greece. In addition, medieval thinkers often understood the works of ancient authors in ways that impress modern students as strangely anachronistic. The work of **Petrarch** revived interest in rediscovering the whole corpus of ancient Latin literature—that is, the "**classics**"—because he and his followers identified Roman literature with the sophisticated, highly civilized society that had produced it, and longed to restore familiarity not only with that literature but also with the values reflected in it. Thus the classics became "the classics" because they were thought to be markers of high civilization. The Petrarchan dream of restoring the power and culture of ancient Rome was closely linked to enthusiasm for discovering, diffusing, and learning from the writings of the ancient authors—that is, from the classics.

This reverence for ancient literature was one of the principal characteristics of the Italian Renaissance, and while it began to mature only with the lifetime of Petrarch, evidence of its growth in northern Italy can already be found in the writings of a number of influential authors of the late 13th century. Beginning with the work of Petrarch himself, the classicizing **humanist** scholars of the 14th and 15th centuries rediscovered unknown works even of classical Latin authors who had been relatively well known in the Middle Ages, such as Cicero, while works of other ancient Latin authors whose works were virtually unknown, such as Livy and Quintilian, were brought to light by Petrarch's successors. The restoration of a knowledge of **Greek** language by the teaching of **Manuel Chrysoloras** at the turn of the 15th century opened the way to a parallel rediscovery of Greek classical literature. The invention of **printing** in the mid-15th century diffused the rediscovered Latin and Greek classics (along with other books) among the educated classes of all of western and central Europe. *See also* CICERONIANISM; GREEK LANGUAGE AND LITERATURE; HUMANISM.

CLEMENT VII, POPE (Giulio de'Medici, 1478–1534). Elected **pope** in 1523. An illegitimate and posthumous son of the murdered **Giuliano de'Medici**, Giulio was brought up with the sons of his uncle **Lorenzo de'Medici**, educated by the **humanist** Gentile Becchi, and committed to the service of his cousin Giovanni when the latter became a cardinal in 1492. When **Giovanni de'Medici** became pope as **Leo X** in 1513, he made Giulio archbishop of **Florence** and a cardinal. From 1519 Giulio also managed the Medici family's restored control of Florentine political life. Although his humanistic education and early exposure to the artistic patronage of his Medici relatives created great expectations of his becoming a munificent patron of Renaissance art and humanistic studies, his many political and financial setbacks, culminating in the Sack of **Rome** by the army of the Emperor **Charles V** in 1527, meant that Pope Clement had neither the leisure nor the financial resources to accomplish much in the field of culture—or, for that matter, in the field of church administration and reform, since his desperate fiscal situation blocked any possibility of reforming the abuses rampant in the Roman curia because reform inevitably would mean reduced income for the papal treasury. Despite his promising background, Clement was largely a failure as a patron of Renaissance culture.

COLET, JOHN (1467–1519). English **humanist** and reform-minded clergyman. He was an outspoken (but strictly Catholic) critic of the worldliness and neglect of duty typical of many English clergymen. Born the son of a rich London merchant, Colet studied at Cambridge **University** and spent three years in Italy, where he became familiar with the writings of the philosophers **Marsilio Ficino** and **Giovanni Pico della Mirandola**. He then entered Oxford University and received a doctorate in theology. His father's influence won for him the important office of dean of St. Paul's cathedral as soon as he had the theological degree. Colet's inherited wealth made it possible for him to re-found St. Paul's school in a way that emphasized literary study but in many respects was not typical of humanistic education, since Colet's religious traditionalism made him critical of the practice of exposing young students to the pagan religious beliefs and the questionable moral tone found in much classical literature. Although the new St. Paul's School ultimately became an important center of humanist education in England, this was done, mostly after Colet's death, by headmasters who quietly abandoned Colet's insistence that his school should avoid pagan authors and should concentrate its studies on Christian authors.

Colet in 1510 delivered before Convocation (the assembly of the clergy) a powerful and brutally frank sermon attacking the worldliness of many of the clergy and urging reform. Though he meant well and was widely admired as a morally upright and well-educated clergyman, Colet was also resented by many, for he was often rude and unfairly critical of others. But his acknowledged religious orthodoxy, his narrow but genuine learning, and his eloquence as a preacher made him widely admired. He was insistent on the central role of the Bible in religious life, and in a course of lectures at Oxford produced commentaries on biblical books that were much admired. He encouraged his friend **Erasmus** to become a biblical scholar, but unlike his Dutch friend he had very little awareness of the crucial role of **Greek** for any serious student of the New Testament.

COLLÈGE ROYAL. The present-day Collège de France has long regarded itself as the descendant of the pre-revolutionary Collège Royal and traces its foundation back to a group of lecturers appointed by King **Francis I** in 1530 to promote **humanistic** studies in France. In reality, however, the king merely appointed four leading scholars to teach publicly in Paris on the humanistic subjects to which each was assigned. These lectureships had an ill-defined and often troubled relationship with the well-established and predominantly anti-humanist **University** of Paris, which tried to establish its own supervisory power, guaranteed by its 13th-century charter, over all higher-level teaching in Paris. Two of the initial lecturers taught **Greek** and two taught **Hebrew**, the biblical languages. Additional appointments in the next few years added lectures in mathematics and in **classical** (that is, **Ciceronian**) Latin. The so-called Collège had no corporate structure, no degree-granting function, and until the early 17th century not even a building of its own: the lectures were held in various buildings of the university.

The king's act in initiating this series of lectureships was partly the result of agitation by French humanists, especially **Guillaume Budé**, who were inspired by the founding of **trilingual** (Latin-Greek-Hebrew) colleges at **Alcalá** in Spain and **Louvain** in the Netherlands. Francis, who fancied himself a great patron of arts and letters, announced a plan to create a similar French institution as early as 1517, but his political and territorial ambitions, which involved him in costly wars, delayed the first steps toward fulfillment of the plan until 1530.

COLONNA, FRANCESCO (ca. 1433–1527). Italian writer and Dominican friar, educated in Dominican schools and at the **University**

of **Padua**. The work for which he is remembered, *Hypnerotomachia Poliphili* (1499), is a vaguely allegorical romance, written in a language that is neither normal Italian nor Latin but seems to be the author's own invention, based on the Venetian dialect, but blending in words taken from Latin and even from **Greek**. Although contemporaries discovered what they thought were profound mysteries in the book, its literary success rested in large part on the elegant and evocative woodcut ilustrations that the publisher of the first edition, the Venetian printer **Aldus Manutius**, added to the text. It was reprinted in 1545 and thereafter repeatedly, both in Italy and abroad.

COLONNA, VITTORIA (ca. 1492–1547). Italian poet, born into one of the most ancient and powerful noble families of **Rome**. She married the marquis of Pescara, ruler of a small principality, and lived at **Naples** while her husband pursued his career as a military commander. At Naples she presided over a court society that included many of the leading intellectuals of her time, and she became famous for her intellect, personal virtue, and piety. She concentrated on intellectual and spiritual matters even more strongly after her husband died in 1525. Her devoutness drew her close to a number of reform-minded Catholic clerics and laity.

These close associates were known as the *spirituali*, including important figures like Gasparo Contarini, Bernardino Ochino, **Reginald Pole**, and **Juan de Valdés**, two of them cardinals and all of them inclined to think of religion as essentially an inward, personal experience. Colonna also became close to the artist **Michelangelo**, who wrote poems addressed to her and shared with her a mutual love that remained purely spiritual. She and several of her Roman circle were attracted to the Lutheran doctrine of justification by faith, though only one of the inner group (Ochino) ended by becoming a Protestant. Her spiritualizing ideas and sympathy for reform brought her under the suspicion of the **Inquisition** in the 1540s. Her poems have caused her to be ranked among Italy's leading female poets, and their publication (without her approval) in 1538 made her a much-admired author.

COLUMBUS, CHRISTOPHER (in Italian, Cristoforo Colombo; in Spanish, Cristobal Colón; 1451–1506). Italian-born Spanish navigator, explorer, and colonial administrator, conventionally recognized as the discoverer of the Americas. Although recent criticisms by ethnic groups who feel victimized by European imperialism rightly point out the defects of Columbus as a colonial administrator, he remains a great seaman and explorer. The claim that he did not "discover" America because its inhabitants were not lost is verbal sophistry: perhaps in one sense he did not "discover" America, but he certainly was the first to establish a route leading from Europe to the Americas, an event that has had enormous consequences (both for good and for ill) not only for the Americas but for all parts of the world.

Beginning with his first voyage of 1492–1493, Columbus led four expeditions to the Americas, discovering several of the islands of the Caribbean on his first voyage and exploring the region from Cuba in the north to the northern coast of South America on his three subsequent voyages of 1493–1496, 1498–1500, and 1502–1504. On his second voyage, he founded the first permanent European settlement in the New World on Hispaniola, the predecessor of modern Santo Domingo. Columbus' original goal had not been the discovery of new islands or continents but finding a direct route to Japan and China. Despite the obvious differences between the peoples and lands that he found and his best information on East Asia, he never fully realized that he had discovered a portion of the earth completely unknown to Europeans.

Columbus was born at Genoa in Italy, the son of a weaver. From an early age he went to sea. He had little or no formal education. In 1476 he was shipwrecked off the coast of Portugal. He then settled in Lisbon, which was Europe's greatest center of maritime exploration. He sailed on Portuguese ships, and made at least one voyage to a Portuguese trading post in West Africa and another to England, Ireland, and perhaps Iceland. He married a Portuguese woman in 1479 and from about 1482 lived for a time at Funchal in the Madeiras.

It remains uncertain just when Columbus conceived his plan to reach the fabled riches of China by sailing due west rather than pursuing the Portuguese enterprise of seeking a way to Asia by way of South Africa. Although he may still have been illiterate when he reached Lisbon in 1476, he learned to read not only vernacular languages but also Latin, and he seems to have read widely. In Lisbon he must have matured, if not even invented, his plan to sail west to Asia. His connections with his wife's family gave him ready access to the maritime experience of Portuguese explorers of West Africa. Columbus was also well informed about medieval and **classical** geographical theory; he knew the description of China by Marco Polo, and his plan may have been influenced by correspondence with the prominent **Florentine** geographer **Paolo Toscanelli**. From about 1483 he vainly attempted to persuade the king of Portugal to support his plan. About 1485–1486 he went to Spain and again was unsuccessful in selling his plan, though the Spanish rulers were sufficiently attracted to appoint a commission to study the project. Though the commissioners knew perfectly well that the earth was spherical, they concluded (correctly, as things turned out) that the distance was too great and the direct route to East Asia was not feasible. Queen **Isabella**, however, seems to have remained interested, and after Spain had completed its conquest of Granada in 1492, the rulers agreed to provide financial backing, even conceding his ambitious demands for personal and economic gain from any lands that he discovered. Although Columbus' failures as a colonial administrator eventually led the rulers to revoke some of the concessions they had granted, leaving Columbus bitterly aggrieved, he died a wealthy man.

Except through his contacts (probable but disputed) with Toscanelli and his use of printed editions of classical texts on geography, Columbus had little contact with the high culture of the Renaissance. His dream of using his anticipated fortune to finance a crusade to recapture Jerusalem as well as his hope of converting China to Christianity show him to be in most respects a man of the late **Middle Ages** rather than a participant in the Renaissance culture of his Italian homeland.

COMMUNE. Italian term for the self-governing city-states of late-medieval and early Renaissance Italy. The commune originated as a spontaneous organization of the citizens of an urban community. At its origin, such a commune had no legal status but assumed de facto control of the city and sometimes also control of the surrounding countryside. This development was a result of the struggle between **popes** and emperors during the 12th and 13th centuries, which brought about the collapse of effective control of northern and central Italy by the emperors or any other external political authority and left the cities practically independent.

Although the formation of communes was almost always led by wealthy landowners and merchants, the early communes were organized as republics in which most inhabitants who owned property and belonged to one of the guilds had some political voice. During the 13th century, these informal urban communities came to be more systematically organized as city-republics which might acknowledge some nominal subordination to the emperor, the pope, or some other external authority but in practice were independent republics. From the late 13th to the middle of the 15th century, military threats from outside and internal social conflict caused most of these republics to accept the rule of a *signore*, or dictator. In the same period, many of the smaller cities of northern and central Italy were conquered by larger ones, so that the northern and central Italy of the communes gave way to medium-sized territorial states. **Florence** and **Venice** were the most important of the cities that resisted the tendency toward princely rule and retained their republican form of government through all or most of the Renaissance. The consolidation, rivalries, and wars of these independent states form the political background for the cultural developments of the Italian Renaissance.

In many respects, the political condition of Italy was similar to the political condition of ancient Greece, in which the independent *poleis* (city-states) provided the social and political background for the growth of classical Greek civilization. Renaissance Italians did not fail to note this similarity. In particular, living in fully or largely self-governing cities made the Italians regard themselves as citizens rather than subjects. Many of them found in the political and social thought of the ancient Greeks and Romans a set of ideals and values that they attempted to assimilate into their own urban life, a development that some modern historians have labelled "**civic humanism**." This development helps to explain the attractiveness of Roman and **Greek** literature, and especially republican political thought, to the political elites of Renaissance Italy. *See also* HUMANISM.

COMPLUTENSIAN POLYGLOT BIBLE. A six-volume, multilingual edition of both the Old and New Testaments, edited by a group of Spanish scholars working at the new **University** of **Alcalá** (in Latin, *Complutum*) under the patronage of the archbishop of Toledo, Cardinal **Francisco Ximénes de Cisneros**. His financial support and political connections made it possible for the editors to consult the best Hebrew, Aramaic, **Greek**, and Latin manuscripts then known, including materials borrowed from the Vatican Library in **Rome**. Three scholars from the large Spanish community of converted Jews had charge of the **Hebrew** text; a learned Byzantine refugee, Demetrius Ducas, and a conservative Spanish theologian, Diego López Zúñiga, were the leading editors of the Greek New Testament; and a number of **humanists**, including **Juan de Vergara** and **Herman Nuñez de Toledo y Guzmán**, directed the work on the ancient Greek text of the Old Testament. Although Cardinal Ximénes was eager to use the new art of printing to make a vastly improved text of the Bible available to scholars, he did not favor the philological criticism that had grown up among advanced humanist scholars, and he instructed the editors to present the traditional texts, modified only in cases where reliable ancient manuscripts made limited revisions unavoidable. One of Spain's most talented younger humanists, **Elio Antonio de Nebrija**, who worked on the text of the New Testament, argued against this conservative mode of editing but was overruled and eventually resigned from the project. Hence the Greek New Testament prepared for the edition was extremely conservative; the editors regularly preferred readings that backed the traditional Vulgate Latin text and that also preserved wording used by traditional **scholastic** theologians.

Thus despite having access to a body of manuscript sources that far surpassed the manuscripts available to the Dutch humanist **Erasmus**, who was preparing a rival Greek edition of the New Testament, the Complutensian New Testament was based on outmoded philological standards. Even so, it was a remarkable achievement in biblical scholarship. Its printed text of the Greek New Testament was ready for publication and sale at the very beginning of 1514, more than two years earlier than Erasmus' more famous edition, but difficulties in securing papal approval for publication caused the distribution of the Complutensian New Testament to be held up until 1520. Hence Erasmus' more philologically sophisticated and more critical edition became the first published edition of the Greek New Testament and had a far greater long-term impact on New Testament scholarship than the Spanish publication.

CONCILIARISM. The theory that a general council (rather than the **pope**) is the supreme and ultimate authority in the Christian church.

This theory was rooted in the practice of the early church, especially in the role of the ecumenical councils of the fourth and fifth centuries in defining the doctrines of orthodox Christianity. The growing tendency of the bishops of **Rome** to claim absolute supremacy eclipsed the idea of conciliar power but did not entirely destroy it. Several popes of the 12th and 13th centuries held councils, but these were carefully controlled and posed no serious challenge to papal sovereignty. Medieval canon law provided that in some special cases the Holy See could be outranked by a council. In general, such ideas of conciliar power covered only great emergencies.

The terrible crisis of the **Western Schism** (1378–1417), which produced two rival lines of popes, moved even moderate canonists, bishops, and secular rulers toward acceptance of Conciliarism. The abortive **Council of Pisa** (1409) attempted to put these theories into practice but merely added a third pope to the prevailing confusion. The **Council of Constance** (1414–1418), summoned by the Emperor Sigismund, was able to end the Schism. It was dominated by academic canon lawyers who wanted to use the occasion not only to restore unity but also to compel reluctant popes to undertake a thorough reform of the church and to establish a permanent role for representative councils in the constitution of the church. They attempted to achieve this end by enacting the decree *Haec sancta* in 1415, which declared that a general council of the whole church was superior to any part of the church, even the pope. In 1417 the council also enacted the decree *Frequens*, which required all future popes to summon a general council at least every 10 years. Although the pope elected at Constance, **Martin V**, was required to swear obedience to these decrees, neither he nor his successors accepted them as valid. Long before the end of the 15th century, papal absolutism had been restored.

Although many canon lawyers and reformers remained devoted to Conciliarism, the general acceptance of Conciliarism had been a product of the Schism, and the end of the Schism, by resolving the immediate crisis, weakened favor for conciliar ideas. Conciliarism remained influential in some northern universities, especially at Paris, and among some reformers who saw that the popes showed little enthusiasm for sweeping reforms and wanted to use a council to compel reform. The acceptability of Conciliarism was also damaged by the failure of the **Council of Basel**, particularly by the council's rash attempt to dethrone and replace Pope **Eugenius IV**. Individuals and rulers occasionally used the threat of a council to bring pressure on popes, notably the convening of the **Council of Pisa** by Louis XII of France in 1511. Fear of conciliar doctrines was still powerful at Rome and does much to explain the reluctance of the popes of the **Reformation** era to summon a council early enough to make a credible response to the early Protestant Reformers.

CONDOTTIERI. Italian term for the mercenary captains who during the later **Middle Ages** and the Renaissance provided most of the armed forces of the Italian states. The term is derived from the word *condotta*, the contract between an employing ruler and the commander. Nearly all European armies from the later Middle Ages down to the French Revolution were composed of professional soldiers who fought for hire. In Italy, these hired professionals were not citizens of the state that hired them. Their critics, such as the **Florentine** political theorist **Niccolò Machiavelli**, charged that such mercenaries were interested only in their pay and plunder, that they avoided serious combat and merely made a show of anything more dangerous than skirmishing, and that they would betray their employers if that seemed advantageous.

Most of these charges are untrue. As long as their salaries were paid regularly, most mercenaries gave loyal service. The states made their contracts with established commanders (*condottieri*) who already had a private military force. In the late 13th and 14th centuries, many of the *condottieri* and their troops were foreigners from regions such as the Balkan peninsula, Germany, or France. Discharged English and French soldiers seeking work during the frequent truces in the **Hundred Years' War** were especially common in the later 14th century, and the most respected *condottiere* of that period was an Englishman, Sir John Hawkwood. By the 15th century, most of the troops and their commanders were Italians.

Although these mercenary captains came from all ranks of society, most of them were nobles. A number of the most important were rulers of small Italian states who not only earned money but also safeguarded their independence by making themselves useful to larger neighbors: the rulers of **Urbino**, **Ferrara**, and **Mantua** were the most important of these. Small mercenary bands were most dangerous to society when they were unemployed and might turn into brigands. The one major mercenary force of Renaissance Italy not usually called *condottieri* were the Swiss soldiers who constituted the backbone of papal armies and also provided infantry to the kings of France. Although the Swiss fought on foot, most mercenary armies were predominantly cavalry.

CONSTANCE, COUNCIL OF (1414–1418). General council of the Roman Catholic Church, assembled in order to end the **Western Schism** that had divided Latin Christendom since 1378. The disputed papal election of 1378 had produced two rival **popes** whose successors competed for the loyalty of a divided Christendom. Many attempts had been made to settle the division by negotiation or compromise, but all had failed. A growing number of leading clerics and rulers eventually concluded that only a general council representing the whole church would have the authority needed to depose the rival popes and restore unity.

Since there was no generally recognized pope to summon a council, the Holy Roman Emperor Sigismund, the highest-ranking secular ruler in Christendom, brought the council together, with the reluctant co-operation of a third pope, John XXIII, who traced his title to the abortive **Council of Pisa**. Sigismund's council was dominated by university-trained doctors of theology and canon law, who attended in great numbers and established their right to vote. Most of these academic intellectuals supported the theory of **Conciliarism**. This group intended to depose all three rival popes and reunify the church, but they also had additional goals. They intended to enact legislation mandating a sweeping reform of church abuses. The more radical of them were determined to use the council to make the teachings of Conciliarism a permanent part of the church's constitution.

In 1415 the council enacted the decree *Haec sancta* (sometimes called *Sacrosancta*), which declared that a general council received its authority directly from Christ and that "all men, of every rank and condition, including the pope himself, are bound to obey it." In 1417, realizing that future popes would resist calling such a powerful institutional rival into session, the council enacted a second decree, *Frequens*, that required future popes to summon a general council at least every 10 years. The council also was eager to suppress the new **Hussite** heresy in Bohemia, and its first major achievement was to arrest and execute the Bohemian reformer **John Huss**. The council succeeded in deposing Pope John XXIII when he attempted to dissolve it. Legislation to enact significant reform of the church proved far more difficult to enact, for each interest group present wanted reform to begin at the expense of somebody else. The struggle over reform was so sharp that in 1417, fearing that the council might split apart before it had ended the Schism, the members accepted the voluntary abdication of the Roman pope and acted to depose the **Avignonese** pope; then it elected a new pope, **Martin V**, who gained general acceptance. This election meant that the Schism was finally at an end.

The council's successes consisted of its execution of Huss, the removal of all three rival popes and the election of a new one, and the two constitutional decrees *Haec sancta* and *Frequens*. The success of the decrees was illusory since Martin V, despite his pledge to uphold *Haec sancta*, never truly accepted it as valid. Although he and his successor did summon additional councils as required by *Frequens*, they did so with great reluctance. Once the crisis of the Schism was past, most moderate Catholics abandoned any serious commitment to conciliar ideas. The only unqualified success of the council was the end of the Schism. As for the issue of church reform, the council had been unable to agree on a workable program, and the new pope informed the council that he would take charge of reform, a promise that he did little or nothing to fulfill after the council adjourned.

CONSTANTINOPLE, FALL OF. In the year 330, the first Christian emperor of **Rome**, Constantine the Great (306–337), dedicated a new capital of the Roman Empire on the site of the Greek town of Byzantium. After his death, it came to be known as Constantinople, "the city of Constantine." By the sixth century, though the western empire at Rome had ceased to exist, his successors had reorganized the eastern provinces into a powerful and fervently Christian state that became a bulwark of Christendom against the expansion of the Muslim Arabs and Turks into Europe. This empire always referred to itself as "Roman," but modern scholars generally call it "Byzantine."

After a disastrous military defeat by the Seljuk Turks in 1087 cost the empire control over the Anatolian peninsula, the empire became increasingly weak. The Western crusades from the 11th through the 14th centuries never tilted the balance of power back in favor of the Byzantines, and the misdirected Fourth Crusade (1203–1204) ended by attacking and plundering Constantinople itself. From 1204 to

1261, a puppet regime installed by the crusaders ruled at Constantinople. This foreign domination was overthrown in 1261, but the enfeebled empire gradually lost control of its Balkan, Greek, and island territories, some to the Turks and some to Italian cities like **Venice**.

By mid-15th century the emperors controlled only the immediate environs of the capital city and a few scattered outposts in Greece and the islands. In 1453 the Turkish sultan Muhammad II (1451–1481) made a final attack on the city, which fell to the Turks on 29 May 1453 and, renamed Istanbul, became the capital of the **Ottoman Empire**. The Turkish conquest of Constantinople in 1453 has sometimes been misinterpreted as the cause of the Renaissance, which supposedly was begun by Greek scholars who fled with their books and their knowledge to western Europe. It would be more accurate to say that the fall of Constantinople marks the beginning of the end for direct influence of Byzantine scholars on the development of Renaissance civilization. The establishment of **Greek** studies by the teaching of **Manuel Chrysoloras** at **Florence** from 1397, followed by a flow of scholars, diplomats, churchmen, and teachers, had by 1453 made the Westerners largely self-sustaining in terms of access to Greek literature.

CONTRAPPOSTO. Italian term for a technique developed by ancient Greek sculptors to represent the human figure standing at ease in a relaxed and natural stance. It was based on an intentional assymetry of stance, with one leg carrying most of the body's weight and the other leg free. Although based on depiction of the body at rest, the technique was also fundamental to realistic representation of the body in motion. This technique first appeared in early Greek **classical** sculpture (early fifth century B.C.) and was widely used throughout the classical period but fell out of use in medieval sculpture. Its rediscovery in the early 15th century is attributed to the **Florentine** sculptor **Donatello**. At least, it first appears in his work, notably his bronze *David*, executed about 1425, which is reminiscent of classical statuary in its *contrapposto* stance. In painting, the use of *contrapposto* first appears in the work of **Masaccio**, most strikingly in *The Tribute Money* (ca. 1427) but also in the nude figures of Adam and Eve in his *Expulsion from Paradise*.

CONVERSO. In medieval and Renaissance Spain, a **Jew** who had converted to Christianity. Under the relatively tolerant rule of the Muslim conquerors of Spain, a large Jewish community played an important part in Spanish life. This tolerance and prosperity continued for several centuries in regions reconquered by the Christians. During the 13th and 14th centuries, however, pressure from the clergy for conversion and incidents of persecution became more frequent. In 1391 a series of riots and massacres swept through the peninsula. Often, conversion was the price paid to stay alive. Pressure for conversion grew throughout the 15th century and achieved great success. Thousands of Jews became *conversos*, and they began to prosper within the Christian society, rising to high office in government service, education, medicine, business, and even the clergy. The most successful even married into the aristocracy. Yet the "old Christians" realized that many of those converted had changed religion only out of fear. While many *conversos* did become true converts to their new religion, some secretly continued to practice their ancestral faith.

Concern about backsliding *conversos* culminated in the founding of the **Spanish Inquisition** in 1478. Since experience suggested that the continued presence of Jews in the country encouraged *conversos* to relapse secretly, in 1492 the rulers ordered the expulsion of all unconverted Jews. Large numbers went into exile in Portugal and especially in Muslim North Africa, but the majority converted, either sincerely or out of fear. Despite (or probably because of) the success of many *conversos* in gaining wealth, political influence, and high office in church and state, Spanish society watched them closely. The Inquisition was the institution created to detect and punish those who relapsed into Jewish religious practices. During the 16th century, *conversos* suffered both covert and open discrimination, including exclusion from an increasing number of high offices in church and state and from the most prestigious colleges in the Spanish universities, the ones that controlled access to the highest offices in the country.

COPERNICUS, NICOLAUS (1473–1543). Polish astronomer, best known for his theory of the universe that placed the sun, rather than the earth, at the center of the system. Born in the Polish city of Torún and orphaned at an early age, Copernicus was supported by an uncle who became a bishop. The uncle sent him in 1491 to the **University** of Cracow. Through his uncle's influence, he secured a lifetime appointment as one of the canons of the cathedral chapter at Frauenburg

(Frombork). In 1496 the chapter sent him to the **University of Bologna** to study canon law, but he was also able to study astronomy there, and his first recorded astronomical observation was made there in 1497. After returning home to Frauenburg in 1501, he received permission to return to Italy in order to study medicine at **Padua**. He received a doctorate in canon law from the University of **Ferrara** in 1503 and also was qualified to practice medicine before returning to spend the rest of his life at Frauenburg.

Copernicus became widely known as an expert astronomer and made a number of important astronomical discoveries, though his major achievement was not in discovering new data but in rethinking the theoretical foundations of astronomy. His Italian education gave him the competence in **Greek** that allowed him to publish Latin translations of Greek books and to consult the Greek text of Ptolemy's major astronomical work, the *Almagest*, a work not yet available in Latin.

Copernicus' later fame rests on his book *De revolutionibus orbium coelestium / On the Revolutions of the Celestial Spheres* (1543), but he had worked for much of his life seeking to discover a view of the universe that challenged the complicated and self-contradictory system of the Hellenistic astronomer Ptolemy, the universally acknowledged authority in astronomy. As early as 1513 he wrote a short work, *Commentariolus / Little Commentary*, that put forward many of the ideas elaborated in *De revolutionibus*. His new system made a rather simple suggestion—that if one reversed the positions that Ptolemy and nearly all subsequent astronomers assigned to the earth and the sun, putting the sun instead of the earth at the center, many of the troublesome complications of astronomy were resolved.

Yet since his proposal would challenge many philosophical and religious ideas associated with the idea that the earth was the center of the universe, Copernicus hesitated to publish his new system. His pupil Georg Joachim Rheticus, who had published a summary of his ideas under the title *Narratio prima / Preliminary Account*, finally persuaded Copernicus to publish his major treatise. The work was dedicated to Pope Paul III, and publication was arranged by a Lutheran minister, Andreas Osiander, who added a preface presenting Copernicus' new theory not as literally true but as a hypothesis useful in simplifying astronomical calculations.

Although his book attracted considerable attention, most astronomers rejected it not just because it flew in the face of traditional learning but also because its theories raised certain objections that Copernicus himself could not explain. In particular, Copernicus' continued adherence to the Ptolemaic belief that the orbits of the planets must be perfectly circular prevented his system from providing the greater accuracy in the calculation of orbits that he anticipated. Though well known to professional astronomers, his ideas were rejected by most of them. In the long run, the importance of *De revolutionibus* is that it defined the problems that astronomers of the next four or five generations—**Tycho Brahe**, **Johannes Kepler**, **Galileo Galilei**, and Isaac Newton—would resolve as they developed a new science of astronomy based on his heliocentric theory.

CORNARO, CATERINA (1454–1510). Venetian-born queen of Cyprus. Descended from one of the most ancient Venetian noble families and also from the Comnenus dynasty that ruled Trebizond on the Black Sea, in 1472 she married James II, king of Cyprus. Her husband died not long after the wedding, and their infant son died a year later. Since her husband was the last representative of the Lusignan dynasty, Caterina then ruled the island as queen. Several of the powers active in the eastern Mediterranean longed to annex this strategic island. In 1489 **Venice** browbeat her into ceding the island and accepting the Italian town of Asolo in exchange. As ruler of Asolo, she introduced a number of reforms, commissioned palaces and works of art, and gathered a court circle noted for its poets. The humanist **Pietro Bembo** made this court the setting for his dialogues on love, *Gli Asolani / The Asolans*.

CORREGGIO (1489/94–1534). Professional name of the painter Antonio Allegri, born in the small Lombard town of Correggio. Probably trained by an uncle and influenced by the works of **Andrea Mantegna**, **Leonardo da Vinci**, **Raphael**, and **Michelangelo**, he spent most of his career at Parma and developed a style notable for its emotional sensuality and the use of colors offset by the technique of chiaroscuro. His work is often interpreted as a precursor of the **baroque** style, and though his paintings were not especially influential in his own century, about 1600, as **baroque** style matured, they began to be highly regarded. His fresco *The Assumption of the Virgin* on the dome of Parma cathedral is a striking example of his religious painting, but his later work, done for the duke of **Mantua**, was erotic in spirit and was dominated by pagan mythology.

CORVINUS, MATTHIAS (1440–1490). A younger son of János Hunyadi, king of Hungary, he successfully contended for the succession against the **Habsburg** Emperor Frederick III and ruled as king from 1458 to 1490. In 1469 he also became king of Bohemia. Given a **humanist** education and influenced by Italian conceptions of a ruler as well as by his family's military tradition, he made his capital at Buda a center for humanists from many parts of Europe and assembled the famous Corviniana library. His marriage to a Neapolitan princess in 1476 was linked to an expansionist foreign policy that extended his lands westward but led to neglect of the threat from the **Ottoman Turks** on his southern border that contributed to the Turkish conquest of most of Hungary in 1526.

COUNCIL OF TEN. The most notorious of the group of councils that governed the republic of **Venice**. Founded in 1310 as a reaction to an unsuccessful uprising against the power of the city's noble families and the exclusion of non-noble citizens from any voice in government, the Council was a guarantor of political stability, always on the lookout for conspiracies aimed against the domination of the political system by the nobility. It was notorious for its use of spies, secret diplomacy, and the assassination of those who endangered the interests of Venice. For most of its existence, members were selected by the Great Council for one-year terms and were not allowed to serve consecutive terms. Napoleon Bonaparte abolished the council in 1797 after his army gained control of Venice.

CRANACH, LUCAS (the Elder, 1472–1553). German painter, printmaker, and illustrator of books. He was born at Kronach in Bavaria and trained by his father but came under the influence of the greatest German Renaissance artist, **Albrecht Dürer**. He lived for about two years in Vienna, where he absorbed the influence of the **humanist** circle dominated by **Conrad Celtis** and began producing religious paintings and landscapes. His well-known *Flight into Egypt* (1504) combines a religious theme and a landscape in a way that attracted attention from other German artists. About 1504 he settled in Wittenberg, where he became court painter to Frederick the Wise, elector of Saxony. Cranach was strongly attracted to **Martin Luther** and the Protestant **Reformation**. He painted several portraits of Luther and made illustrations for Luther's German Bible and for Lutheran religious tracts. Luther did not approve the iconoclastic policies of many other Protestant leaders. He endorsed Cranach's work and encouraged him to create a style appropriate for Evangelical religious sentiment.

Cranach became a successful artistic entrepreneur, employing his sons Hans and Lucas the Younger as well as a number of apprentices in a large and productive workshop. Later in life he also painted allegories that incorporated mythological and secular elements such as female nudes that show the influence of Italian art, but without capturing the cultural and iconographic sensibility of his Italian predecessors. In the best-known of these allegories, *The Judgment of Paris* (1530), the theme and the gently erotic female nudes express Italian influence, but Paris appears as a German knight in modern armor; and the three nude damsels are naked Northern women, not classical nudes, while the background is a clearly German landscape.

CROMWELL, THOMAS (ca. 1485–1540). English politician who rose from humble origins to become a trusted servant of King **Henry VIII**'s most powerful government minister, Cardinal **Thomas Wolsey**. After Wolsey's fall from power in 1529, Cromwell replaced him and became even more powerful. His efficiency and decisive personality soon made him the dominant person in political life. He arranged the divorce of the king from Queen Catherine of Aragon; the acquiescence of both Parliament and the clergy in declaring Henry head of the English church and abolishing papal authority; the suppression of the monasteries and the confiscation of their properties by the crown; and the publication of the first English-language Bible to appear with the approval of the government and clergy. Modern historians have often regarded the administrative agencies that he created to administer the former monastic lands and establish royal control over the church as a decisive step away from the personal administrative structure of the medieval monarchy to a more impersonal and institutionalized administration that foreshadows modern English government.

Cromwell's own religious views leaned toward Protestantism, but as a servant of a king who continued to favor Catholic doctrine even after his break with **Rome**, he had to move slowly and cautiously. He collaborated with the new archbishop of Canterbury, Thomas Cranmer, to authorize the official English Bible, to modify some of the doctrines of the medieval church, and gradually to introduce the doctrines of Continental Protestantism. In these efforts, Cromwell employed the services of a number of writers with **humanist** backgrounds and arranged for the publication of English translations of works of **Erasmus** and other humanists who had favored reform of the church and had sharply criticized ecclesiastical corruption.

Cromwell was raised to the peerage as earl of Essex, but his foreign policy of close relations with the German Protestant princes, culminating in the marriage of the king to the German princess Anne of Cleves, whom the king found unacceptable, led to his sudden fall from power in 1540. He was arrested, attainted by act of Parliament, and executed. Yet both his administrative reforms and his transformation of the English church into a national institution under the control of the monarch endured.

CROTUS RUBIANUS (Johannes Jäger, 1480–ca. 1545). German **humanist**, one of the circle of Erfurt humanists who were close to **Mutianus Rufus**. Born to a peasant family in Thuringia, Crotus (a **classicized** name he adopted in 1509) studied at the University of Erfurt, where he was acquainted with young **Martin Luther** and became a close friend of **Ulrich von Hutten**. Sometime after he received his B.A. degree in 1502, he and Hutten moved to Cologne, where he matriculated in 1505 but stayed for only a year before returning to Erfurt and completing the M.A. degree in 1507. He became a priest and from 1510 was headmaster of a school attached to the abbey at Fulda.

Crotus was a skillful Latin poet, much admired for his poems in praise of Erfurt (1507) and his *Bucolicon* (1509). He became an outspoken supporter of the humanist **Johann Reuchlin** during the latter's conflict with the Dominican theologians of Cologne and was the principal author of the famous satirical attack on the Cologne theologians, *Epistolae obscurorum virorum / Letters of Obscure Men* (1515). His satire ridiculed the narrowness, pretentiousness, and self-serving conservatism of his antagonists but avoided the savage personal attacks typical of the second part of the satire, published in 1517 and written mainly by Hutten. In 1517 he went to Italy and obtained a doctorate of theology at **Bologna**.

Crotus returned to Germany in 1520 and became professor of theology at Erfurt. As the elected rector of the **university** for the winter term 1520–1521, Crotus enthusiastically welcomed Martin Luther when Luther passed through town on his way to his hearing at the Diet of Worms. Though initially sympathetic to Luther, Crotus was unwilling to support open defiance of church authority.

In 1524 he entered the service of Albert of Brandenburg-Ansbach, grand master of the Teutonic Knights. In this capacity, he played a role in carrying out Albert's decision to turn Lutheran, secularize his ecclesiastical principality, and transform his state into the hereditary duchy of Prussia. But Crotus was personally reluctant to endorse the change of religion and left Albert's service in 1530. A year later he entered the service of Albert's kinsman, Albert of Brandenburg, archbishop-elector of Mainz. His subsequent activity as an anti-Lutheran pamphleteer cost him the friendship of a number of humanists, such as **Eobanus Hessus** and Justus Jonas, but he became close to other humanists who had supported Luther only briefly but then became defenders of the Catholic church.

CUSA, NICHOLAS OF. *See* NICHOLAS OF CUSA.

– D –

DANTE (Dante Alighieri, 1265–1321). Italy's greatest poet, known principally for his epic poem depicting his own spiritual conversion, *La divina commedia / The Divine Comedy* (written 1304–1319). Although he ended by being a great literary figure, his intention was to be a leading citizen of **Florence**, his native city. He fought in the city's armies, married and reared a family there, and held major public offices. In 1302, after a hostile political faction had seized control of the city, Dante was falsely accused of corruption and forced into exile.

Even as a young man, Dante had been interested in intellectual matters. He attended philosophical lectures in the Dominican friary and even before his exile gained a reputation as a vernacular poet. His lyrics perfected the new style of love poetry known as the *dolce stil nuovo* ("sweet new style"), a phrase coined by Dante himself. His early *La vita nuova / New Life* (ca. 1293) is a hallmark of this style. A collection of philosophical tracts, *Il convivio / The Banquet* (ca. 1304–1308), written afer his exile, shows the influence of Cicero and Boethius as well as the **scholastic** philosophy he had acquired from his studies with the Dominicans. Shortly after he left Florence, he wrote a Latin treatise, *De vulgari eloquentia / On Vernacular Eloquence*, that praised his native Tuscan dialect as the ideal language for literary works, and his own poems, more than any other single factor, contributed to the establishment of Tuscan as the Italian literary language.

Dante also wrote on politics. The chaotic political condition of Italy in his time convinced him that Christian society needed to be reorganized under the authority of a single ruler, a new Roman emperor. His Latin treatise *De monarchia / On Monarchy* presented philosophical arguments for the creation of one imperial government for the whole world that would restore peace, compel the corrupt and worldly **popes** to return from **Avignon** to Italy and reform the church, and defend Christian religion from unbelievers. This book bluntly criticized the popes and was condemned by the papal curia; it was not printed until after the Protestant **Reformation**.

Dante's crowning achievement, however, was his epic *The Divine Comedy*. The poem, written in three parts, describes the spiritual journey of Dante himself, caught in a mid-life crisis of despair. In it he is rescued from an aimless and worldly existence and guided through *Inferno* (Hell), *Purgatorio* (Purgatory), and *Paradiso* (Paradise), the three states of soul defined by medieval theology. It is significant that in his pilgrimage he is led from worldly despair and through Hell and Purgatory by the Roman epic poet Vergil, who symbolizes both the strength and the limitations of human reason; also significant that Vergil (Reason) cannot take him to his ultimate goal but can lead him only through Purgatory, where the blessed Beatrice (the girl Dante had loved as a young boy), symbolizing divine grace and sent by the Virgin Mary, takes over the role of guide to Heaven. This epic of the human soul has a cosmic significance, yet it also has many other points to make along the way. For most readers, the journey through Hell has seemed the most interesting, probably because there Dante takes the opportunity to settle scores with the corrupt politicians who had sent him into exile, the corrupt businessmen who put material gain above the salvation of their souls, and the corrupt popes who had prostituted their high office in pursuit of worldly power.

In many respects, Dante's works are typical products of medieval civilization at its peak. His dependence on the thought of **Aristotle** and the greatest medieval Aristotelian, Thomas Aquinas, is one example. Nevertheless, in other respects, Dante's life and work point ahead to the conditions that would produce Renaissance civilization. He was not a member of the clergy but an educated layman, able to acquire an advanced philosophical education and to address major issues of both eternal and worldly life. From the perspective of later Renaissance humanists, his major defects were that he wrote in the vernacular rather than in Latin, that the style of his Latin works was not classical.

Nevertheless, among Florentines, there was never any question of his greatness. His books, and especially his *Commedia*, were widely circulated in manuscript, printed (1472) within a few years of the introduction of printing, and frequently reprinted. Both **Petrarch** and **Giovanni Boccaccio** praised him; Boccaccio lectured on his works at Florence and wrote the earliest biography; and the three of them, together, became the "Three Crowns" of Florentine literature. One of the leading figures among the Florentine **Neoplatonists, Cristoforo Landino**, developed his lectures on Dante into an extensive commentary (published in 1481) that interprets the *Commedia* in terms of Neoplatonism. Most humanists of the 15th and 16th centuries (especially non-Florentines) were less favorable. The first great figure of 16th-century **Ciceronianism**, the Venetian humanist and poet **Pietro Bembo**, was dismissive when comparing Dante to Petrarch, criticizing him for attempting to write a epic poem in the vernacular and for addressing philosophical and theological questions far beyond his competence and also beyond the proper scope of poetry.

DATINI, FRANCESCO (ca. 1335–1410). Italian merchant born at Prato near **Florence** but for many years resident in the papal court at **Avignon**, where he began his career as an office boy for a Florentine merchant. He founded his own trading and banking company and accumulated great wealth. After his return to Prato in 1382, he had branches and commercial correspondents in several European cities and engaged in commerce that extended from England to the eastern Mediterranean. In these activities, he was typical of successful Italian merchants. What makes him historically unique is that he preserved his business and personal correspondence, account ledgers, and other business documents. These survive and provide unequalled insight into the activities, style of life, and mentality of the Italian merchants who dominated the economic life of early Renaissance Europe. The charitable foundation that he willed to his city for the support of poor children still survives.

DECEMBRIO, PIER CANDIDO (1399–1477). Milanese **humanist**, most often remembered as a critic of the **Florentine** humanist and chancellor **Leonardo Bruni**. His *Panegyric* of **Milan** (ca. 1436) was a pro-Milanese and monarchist response to the republican and pro-Florentine outlook represented in Bruni's writings. It was written during Decembrio's many years of service (1419–1447) as secretary to **Filippo Maria Visconti**, the last Visconti duke of Milan, a dangerous enemy of the Florentine republic. Decembrio also wrote a life of his patron and produced a great number of translations from **Greek** into Latin and from Latin into Italian. Decembrio also became known as the author of a large correspondence in Latin, much of it written in his role as chancellor. After his patron's death in 1447, Decembrio spent some time in papal service, then lived at the court of King **Alfonso V** of **Naples**, and finally at the court of the **Este** dukes of **Ferrara**.

DEE, JOHN (1527–1608). English natural philosopher, **alchemist, astrologer**, and mathematician, famous for his learning in scientific and **occult** subjects, but also suspected as a person whose occult interests might involve contact with evil spirits. These suspicions were deepened by his efforts, with the aid of his "scryer" or medium Edward Kelly, to establish communication with angels in order to learn about the world of nature. The son of a London merchant, Dee received an excellent **humanistic** education and took B.A. and M.A. degrees at Cambridge, but natural philosophy and the occult sciences became his principal interest. Although he won some patronage from

English politicians such as William Cecil and Robert Dudley, he never gained much financial support from his own sovereigns, and he died in relative poverty. Dee travelled widely in Europe seeking financial support. He spent several years at the court of the Emperor **Rudolf II** in Prague but eventually returned home when he realized that the emperor was interested only in his ability to transmute base metals into gold. He left behind a reputation for profound learning. His large library eventually was acquired by the Bodleian Library at Oxford.

DELLA CASA, GIOVANNI (1503–1556). Italian author and churchman, most famous for his *Galateo* (1558), a book of manners that promotes a set of values for personal life emphasizing the importance of education, wealth, and social standing for those who have to cope with the unpredictability of human life. A native of **Florence**, Della Casa studied law at **Bologna** and in 1531 settled in **Rome**, where at first he led a dissolute life. He undertook a clerical career merely as a way to guarantee a comfortable life, but about 1537, the year when he published a book on whether a man should marry, he seems to have changed into a hard-working and earnest servant of the papal curia, where he gained high office. In 1544 Della Casa became archbishop of Benevento. Sent as papal nuncio to **Venice** that same year, he struggled to persuade the independent-minded Venetian government to be more active in enforcing Catholic orthodoxy and in censoring the press, and he succeeded in establishing a Venetian **Inquisition** in 1547 and in persuading the state to tighten control of the press. His collected vernacular poems were published posthumously in 1558, and he also wrote a number of treatises on moral and political questions.

DELLA PORTA, GIACOMO (1541?–1604). Italian architect, a native of **Rome** and a pupil of **Michelangelo**. He completed several unfinished projects of Michelangelo, including the dome of St. Peter's basilica. His outstanding original achievement was the design of the façade of the Gesù, the mother church of the **Jesuit** order, an influential example of **baroque** Counter-**Reformation** architecture. The floor plan and general design of the Gesù were the work of his older associate Giacomo Vignola.

DELLA QUERCIA, JACOPO (ca. 1374–1438). The leading sculptor of Renaissance Siena. Although his early work was done in the late medieval style now known as International Gothic, he came under the influence of **Donatello** and produced sculptures in early Renaissance style that are notable examples of the treatment of the nude human figure. His work strongly influenced the sculpture of **Michelangelo**. Della Quercia's most famous and best-preserved work is the series of reliefs on the portal of the church of San Patronio in Siena.

DELLA ROBBIA, LUCA (1400–1482). Florentine sculptor. Though generally associated with the early Renaissance style, he still manifested the influence of the late Gothic sculptor **Nanni di Banco** (ca. 1381–1421), who may have been his teacher. His most famous work is the series of marble reliefs of singing angels produced in the 1430s for the *Cantoria* (singers' pulpit) of the cathedral in **Florence**. Later, he turned to the production of less costly reliefs done in terra cotta, notable for their graceful design and their striking contrast of white and bright blue glazes. This technique and medium led easily to routine reproduction, and the terra cotta reliefs of his late years were virtually factory products, produced in great numbers for sale to private collectors and small-town churches. This business was continued by his nephew Andrea (1435–1525) and Andrea's sons through the first quarter of the 16th century.

DEPRESSION, ECONOMIC. Since the 1940s many economic historians have contended that the older economic history of late medieval Europe, which explained the new culture of the Renaissance as a byproduct of a prospering urban capitalism centered in northern Italy, was fundamentally erroneous because it had missed the onset of a major economic crisis that marked the end of an age of rapid economic growth and caused widespread business failures and chronic unemployment in Italy and the southern Netherlands. Many of these revisionist historians also contended that the depressed economic conditions, clearly evident before the middle of the 14th century, were followed by a long period of economic stagnation rather than by the dynamic growth attributed by older historiography to Renaissance Europe. While the economic depression was uneven and some areas (Catalonia, Bohemia and neighboring parts of Hungary and

Poland, the textile-producing regions of England, and the towns of southern Germany) continued to grow and prosper, these represented catching up by regions that were relatively undeveloped before 1300. Even these growing regions experienced slowing growth by the late 14th and early 15th centuries.

Historians who accept the existence of this depression explain its origins largely in terms of structural limitations on growth imposed by the technological, social, and political realities of the late **Middle Ages**. They regard the major famine that struck northwestern Europe in the second decade of the 14th century as evidence that population had exceeded the capacity of a stagnating economy, and they dismiss the terrible mortality of the **Black Death** at mid-century as just an aggravating incident, not a fundamental cause, of the depression. They insist that unmistakable signs of the downturn were evident long before the plague. The stagnant economy, not the plague, explains the remarkable decrease in populations in Italy and throughout most of western Europe that is usually linked to the plague itself. Defenders of the theory note that the decrease in population was not followed by the population rebound that normally would be expected after the plague, and they point out that many of the leading Renaissance cities (**Florence** is a striking example) did not regain their pre-1300 population levels until the 19th century. The onset of the crisis (but not the underlying cause) was the series of bankruptcies of Italian banking and commercial companies (such as the **Bardi** and **Peruzzi** firms of Florence).

In terms of cultural history, the revisionists suggest that students of the Renaissance should view its social foundations not as a dynamic, growing economy but as a reduced and rather stagnant, though still wealthy, mercantile capitalism that was dominated by a defensive mentality and sought to secure the position of its leaders by control of political authority and by investment of resources in such symbols of high status as patronage of art and literature.

This economic reinterpretation of the Renaissance is by no means universally accepted. Virtually no one now denies that there was a serious economic crisis in the mid-14th century and that it was not caused primarily by the Black Death. What remains debatable is the depth of the economic downturn and its persistence, particularly the timing of renewed growth. There seems to be agreement that by the later 15th century, prosperity had returned to most regions. Europe as a whole seems to have had an expanding economy through most of the 16th century, though the period from about 1520 also suffered from a severe price inflation that fed social, political, and religious unrest. This general prosperity continued until the onset of a more universally recognized economic depression about 1618, which persisted until mid-century and formed the economic background of the wars and political upheavals of the early 17th century.

DES PÉRIERS, BONAVENTURE (ca. 1510–ca. 1544). French author, notorious for his satirical dialogues *Cymbalum Mundi / The Cymbal of the World* (1537), a work influenced by the ancient satirist Lucian and apparently intended to demonstrate that disputes over intricate questions of Christian doctrine are a distraction from the true essence of religion. This book impressed contemporaries as an open attack on Christianity and was banned soon after publication. Des Périers also wrote a collection of short narratives, *Nouvelles récréations et joyeux devis*, published posthumously in 1558, that is somewhat similar to the *Heptaméron* of **Margaret of Navarre**, whom he served as valet de chambre. It presents a lively and sometimes ribald picture of life in the courtly society of the time. In his younger years, Des Périers collaborated with the French Protestant Pierre Olivétan on his French translation of the Bible. Des Périers also was a poet and made translations of **Plato** and Terence. His premature death about 1544 was believed to be a suicide.

DES PREZ, JOSQUIN (ca. 1440–1521). Franco-Flemish musician, generally regarded as the greatest composer of the early 16th century. Probably born along the northern border of France, he worked as a professional singer at **Milan** cathedral (1459–1472), as a musician at the ducal chapel there (1472–1476), and between 1486 and 1494 lived at **Rome** in the service of Cardinal Ascanio **Sforza** and then at the papal chapel. He returned to France, probably at the royal court, from 1501 to 1503, became director of the chapel of the dukes of **Ferrara** in 1503, but in the following year returned permanently to France, where he was provost of Notre Dame at Condé-sur-l'Escaut. Josquin's music blends his original Franco-Flemish style with Italian influences. His surviving works, found both in manuscript and in contemporary printed music, include 18 masses, 100 motets, and 70 secular vocal works. He was by far the most famous composer of his age. **Martin Luther**, who was himself skilled at music, called him "the master of the notes," and a later 16th-century author compared his dominance of music to the mastery that **Michelangelo** exercised in the visual arts.

DES ROCHES, MADELEINE (1520–1587), and CATHERINE (1542–1587). French poets, mother and daughter. Madeleine from her youth showed an interest in literature, and she transmitted it to her daughter. From about 1570 they became active as writers. Their careers developed together, and the closeness is symbolized by their death on the same day during an epidemic. Madeleine Neveu was born near Châtellerault into a family of judicial officials (*gens de robe*) and married twice, first to a legal procurator named André Fradonnet about 1539 at Poitiers and, after his death in 1547, to another French legal official, François Eboissard, seigneur de la Villée et **des Roches**. Catherine was a child of the first marriage but took her stepfather's surname.

From about 1570 mother and daughter held a literary salon at Poitiers and developed reputations as poets. Their friends included a prominent kinsman, Scévole de Sainte-Marthe, the great French **humanist Josephus Justus Scaliger**, and the poet **Pierre de Ronsard**. The residence of the royal court in Poitiers in 1577 and the national assembly of legal officers (*Grands Jours*) there in 1579 spread their literary reputation to other parts of France. Their first collection of poetry, *Les oeuvres de Mesdames des Roche, mère et fille*, was published in 1578, shortly after the death of Madeleine's second husband; a second edition appeared in 1579. Another collection, *Secondes oeuvres*, appeared in 1585, followed the next year by *Missives de Mesdames Desroches*, in which they published not only poems but also literary letters. Madeleine's poems are full of sadness and demonstrate that she sought consolation in religion and **Platonic** philosophy. Catherine's poems are more moralizing and didactic. Catherine never married but devoted her life to her literary work and her close companionship with her mother.

DEVOTIO MODERNA (Modern Devotion). A late medieval movement of personal spiritual regeneration and concern for preaching and social ministry to the poor in northwestern Europe. Its followers also favored reform of the institutional church, but in a way that emphasized the need to avoid heresy and to obey superiors. The movement was founded by Geert Groote (1340–1384), the son of a prominent family of Deventer in the Netherlands. He had an excellent **scholastic** education, primarily at the University of Paris (M.A., 1358). After graduation, he studied canon law, natural philosophy, and theology at Paris, and perhaps also at Cologne and Prague. Though not ordained as a priest, in 1368 he obtained a valuable canonry at Aachen and settled down to the conventional career of a wealthy cleric. In 1372, after a nearly fatal illness, he renounced his study of **magic** and vowed to spend the rest of his life in the service of God. He resigned his lucrative benefices and adopted a self-denying way of life.

In 1374 Groote turned his family home in Deventer into a shelter for poor women and lived for several years as a guest of a Carthusian monastery. Eventually, he concluded that God was calling him to be a preacher to the general populace. He secured ordination as a deacon in order to qualify for permission to preach but never became a priest. Between 1379 and 1383 he worked as an itinerant preacher. His sermons were so critical of the morals and privileges of the clergy, openly denouncing those who lived with women in violation of their vows, that the bishop of Utrecht revoked his license to preach. Though he appealed to the **pope**, he obeyed the bishop's order and withdrew first to a monastery and then to a small community of his disciples at Kampen.

In the meantime, a priest at Deventer who had become his disciple, Florens Radewijns (1350–1400), resigned his own benefices and formed in his own house a community (a commune) of Groote's followers. They led a life in common, working in the secular world (often as professional copyists) and pooling their earnings. They elected a rector but did not organize as a formal monastic community, preferring an informal association, inspired by the example of the early Christian church at Jerusalem. There were no binding vows, and decisions to enter or to leave the community were a matter of personal calling. Because of their commitment to share a common life, they came to be known as **Brethren of the Common Life**.

Other communities were soon organized in imitation of the Deventer group, and the rules established by Radewijns at Deventer were adopted by the others. Occasionally such a local group decided to take formal monastic vows; one such community was the Augustinian monastery at St. Agnietenberg, where **Thomas à Kempis**, the probable author of *The Imitation of Christ*, was master of novices. Groote and Radewijns were also interested in the spiritual and material needs of poor **women** converted by their preaching, and a number of communities of Sisters of the Common Life were the result. The communities, both male and female, sought no endowed income or charity but supported themselves by their own labor. These semi-monastic communities of men and women arose spontaneously, without formal canonical status, and were a matter of great concern to the ecclesiastical authorities, who worried that heretical doctrines and immoral styles of living might prevail within communities (especially the communities of women) that were not subject to a monastic rule. The communities did seek approval from diocesan bishops, but suspicions of them remained strong among the higher clergy and the monks. There was pressure on them to reorganize as monastic communities.

In the face of this pressure, since he was by no means hostile to monasticism, Groote shortly before his death advised some of his followers to organize a monastery under the established rule for Augustinian canons. In 1387 these followers formed an Augustinian monastery at Windesheim, committed to strict observance of the Augustinian rule, and this monastery became the center for a group of Augustinian houses known as the Windesheim Congregation. It received papal approval in 1395. By the end of the 14th century, the *Devotio Moderna* consisted of three distinct but closely linked organizations: 1) the Brethren of the Common Life; 2) the Sisters of the Common Life; and 3) a group of reformed Augustinian monasteries belonging to the Windesheim Congregation. All three movements spread from their original center in the northern Netherlands into the southern Netherlands, northern France, and northwestern Germany. Many of these communities were disbanded during the **Reformation**, and in 1568 Pope Pius V ordered all remaining communities of Brethren and Sisters either to adopt a formal monastic rule or to disband.

Historians of the late medieval church have often associated the rise of the *Devotio Moderna* with a growing hunger for personal spirituality among the people of northwestern Europe, chiefly in the socially troubled urban centers. Desire for an effective response to spiritual needs and to the problems of urban poverty inspired idealistic young men like Groote and caused such communities to spread. It also led many of them to draw a sharp contrast between their life and the worldly lives of many wealthy clergy. Hence their preaching often took on an anticlerical tinge. Yet some historians have overemphasized and misinterpreted this critical side of the movement. The Brethren were determined to be humble and obedient as well as devout. Their close links to the Augustinian order show that they had no revolutionary agenda and in no way were precursors of the Protestant Reformation.

Another common misunderstanding has to do with their attitude toward intellectual life and their activity in education. Although Groote himself repudiated the scholastic learning he had acquired at Paris, he and his movement had no intention of challenging the traditional formulations of orthodox doctrine. They were cool to higher education because they thought that it implied a kind of intellectual arrogance that was incompatible with the simplicity and humility of the early New Testament Christians. Being largely an urban movement, they realized the value of literacy and did not extend their coolness toward university learning into hostility to education in general. The copying of books—mainly books of prayer and meditation—was regarded as a pious act and became a source of income for many of the communities. Later, some communities became publishers of spiritual tracts.

A second misunderstanding is the idea that because they encouraged literacy and the production of books, the Brethren became a major force in education, even a center for the diffusion of Renaissance interests in **classical** learning. The "schools of the Brethren of the Common Life," of which some historians have made much, represent exaggeration and even distortion of the record. Some communities of Brethren did organize schools to meet the needs of boys from their towns, and as time passed, the number of such schools increased. But the Brethren were not precursors of the teaching orders of Counter-Reformation Catholicism. Instead of opening schools, many communities provided hostels in which boys from out of town could live in a pious and moral environment while attending schools operated by town governments or by wealthy cathedral chapters and collegiate churches. The prime example of this misunderstanding concerns the relation of the Brethren at Deventer to the famous school of St. Lebwin's church, the school attended by the young **Erasmus**, **Rudolf Agricola**, and other prominent Renaissance **humanists**. St. Lebwin's was an excellent school for its time. Its largely medieval curriculum was enriched by attention to humanistic studies, especially during the long tenure of **Alexander Hegius** as its headmaster. But the school was never under the control of the Brethren. Since the Brethren discouraged their members from attending universities, the only qualified teachers they had were men (Groote himself would be an example) who had been converted to the common life after their formal education.

DIAS, BARTOLOMEU (ca. 1450–1500). Portuguese explorer, the first European captain to round the Cape of Good Hope (1487–1488) and to realize that he had reached the southernmost point of Africa. His accurate reports facilitated the voyage by **Vasco da Gama** that reached India in 1498. Dias also supervised the construction of the four ships specially built for the later expedition, though he did not receive command of the undertaking. In 1500 he accompanied the second Portuguese expedition destined for India, commanded by Pedro Alvares Cabral, which swept so far to the west that it found the coast of Brazil. Dias drowned in a storm off that coast before the fleet continued to India.

DOLCE STIL NUOVO. A type of pre-Renaissance Italian lyric verse developed in the second half of the 13th century, spiritualizing the earlier tradition of courtly love poetry, which had been more explicitly sexual in tone. The *Vita nuova* of **Dante** was the most famous expression of the new style, which was a powerful influence on the lyric poetry of **Petrarch**, and on all later Renaissance love poetry. *See also* PETRARCHISM.

DOLET, ETIENNE (1509–1546). French **humanist** and **printer**, notorious in his own time for the boldness with which he denounced traditional learning in his own French and Latin writings and for the controversial or forbidden books (many of them written by early French Protestants) that he published after he established his own printing firm at Lyon in 1538. Educated at Paris and **Padua**, he also for a time worked for the French ambassador in **Venice** and studied law at Toulouse. Arrested on suspicion of heresy in 1543 because of his publication of dangerous books, he was released and then re-arrested in 1544. He spent two years in prison and was burned at the stake in 1546, a fate that won for him a reputation as a martyr for intellectual freedom, Renaissance learning, and evangelical religion.

DOMINICI, GIOVANNI (1357–1419). Florentine friar and popular preacher. He was prior of the influential Dominican convent of San Marco at **Florence** and became an outspoken critic of the books and ideas of the circle of **humanists** who surrounded the humanist chancellor of Florence, **Coluccio Salutati**. His *Lucula noctis / The Firefly* (1405) was an attack on the humanists' claim that study of pagan classical literature would strengthen Christian faith. He argued that Christians (and certainly schoolboys) should not study pagan books at all, since such study would only confuse them and weaken their faith. His challenge distressed Salutati, who was a deeply religious man who began having second thoughts about study of the classics, even though he wrote a tract refuting Dominici and defending such study as a support for genuine faith.

DONATELLO (ca. 1386–1466). Popular name of the Florentine sculptor who is generally regarded as the first and greatest figure of early Renaissance sculpture. Born Donato di Niccolò di Betto di Bardi, he is first documented in 1401 as an assistant to the sculptor **Lorenzo Ghiberti** during work on the first of Ghiberti's two famous sets of bronze doors for the baptistery at **Florence**. By 1408 he seems to have been working independently.

From an early point in his career (for example, his marble free-standing *St. Mark*, executed in 1411–1414), Donatello demonstrated a mastery of the classical technique of ***contrapposto*** that gave his figures an air of movement and life unequalled since the **antiquity**. He also executed important work in low relief such as *The Feast of Herod*, produced at Siena about 1425, that demonstrated mastery of the principles of single-point **perspective** discovered by his friend **Filippo Brunelleschi**. Donatello also mastered sculpture in bronze, of which his most striking example was the nude David (1425–1430), a startling expression of his consciousness of the anatomical structure concealed under the clothing of earlier subjects such as the *St. Mark* and the statue for Florence cathedral known as *Il Zuccone* (1423–1425). Later in his career, Donatello spent 12 years working at **Padua**, but he then returned to Florence. His ability to create attention-catching figures infused with personality and a sense of life survived throughout his career. His last works, such as the emaciated *St. Mary Magdalene* (1445–1455) executed for the Florentine baptistery, demonstrate that he retained his ability to portray deep emotion and to create dramatic effect. Donatello was famous in his own lifetime, and his works did much to shape sculpture by later Renaissance artists.

DONATION OF CONSTANTINE. *See* VALLA, LORENZO.

DONNE, JOHN (1572–1631). English poet, one of the most important of the group known as metaphysical poets. Born into a Roman Catholic family, in his youth he managed his education at Oxford and the law schools (the Inns of Court) carefully so that he could avoid taking the oath of supremacy that acknowledged the monarch's position as head of the church, which was required of all recipients of degrees. He travelled on the European continent before settling down to the study of law and seems to have recanted his Catholicism while at the Inns of Court. He served in a naval expedition against Spain and won appointment as private secretary to a high government official. His clandestine marriage to a niece of his patron cost him his official favor and threw him and his family into poverty.

Under James I, however, Donne's fortunes improved, helped by two tracts defending the Anglican church and criticizing Roman Catholicism. In 1615, encouraged by the king, he was ordained as a clergyman; in 1616 he became official preacher and theological lecturer at Lincoln's Inn; and in 1621 he became dean of St. Paul's cathedral. He often preached in the presence of Kings James I and Charles I, and his published sermons are among the finest English sermons of the 17th century.

Donne's poetry, much of it love poetry written in his youth, and some of it written on the theme of death during his later years, is notable for its striking figures of speech and its passionate spirit. After several centuries of being out of fashion among critics, his work was rediscovered by English-language poets of the early 20th century.

Since that rediscovery, Donne has come to be regarded as a major lyric poet. Little of his verse was published in his lifetime, and only a few of his sermons. Shortly after his death, his son published three volumes of his sermons. Though many of his poems had circulated in manuscript, most of them were collected and published in editions of 1632 and 1635. The best of his poems, such as the elegy *The Second Anniversary*, are among the most widely admired lyrics in the English language.

DOWLAND, JOHN (1562–1626). Dowland and **Thomas Campion** rank as the leading English composers of songs for the lute. Dowland is noted for his subtle melody and for the verse that he wrote for the vocal part of the performance. His air *Flow, My Tears* was his best-known song in the reign of **Elizabeth I** and led him to compose a whole series of *Lachrymae / Tears* (1605) that conveys the spirit of melancholy that the composer wished to express.

DRAYTON, MICHAEL (1563–1631). English poet known for his historical verse but also for his pastorals and sonnets. His outstanding work was *Poly-Olbion*, a topographical survey of Britain. Many of his historical poems dealt with figures and events from the medieval period of English history.

DU BARTAS, GUILLAUME SALLUSTE (1544–1590). French Calvinist poet and playwright. Born into a noble Gascon family and given an excellent **humanistic** education, he became a Calvinist and was closely associated with Henry of Navarre, the military and political leader of the Huguenots during the French Wars of Religion (1562–1598). The influence of his works on Protestant poets at home and abroad (including **John Milton**) was facilitated by the translation of his verses into several other languages. His poem *La Sepmaine / The Week* reflects the sufferings caused by the religious wars. Other Calvinist writers admired him as a model for literature written in conformity with Reformed Christian principles. His plays, such as *La Judit / Judith*, dealt with biblical themes, and despite his roots in earlier French court poetry, he rejected the licentiousness of that genre and also the use of pagan themes as unacceptable for Christian authors.

DU BELLAY, JOACHIM (ca. 1522–1560). French poet, second only to **Pierre de Ronsard** among the group of court poets known as *La Pléiade*. Like others of this school, he strove to capture and express the spirit of the great poets of **classical antiquity** in his native language. He is best known for a prose manifesto, *Défense et illustration de la langue française / Defense and Illustration of the French Language* (1549), which advocated a program to enrich both the language and its literature through imitation of ancient **Greek** and Latin literature as well as works of the Italian Renaissance. Among his poems, the collection of sonnets known as *Les Regrets* is most highly regarded.

DUCCIO DI BUONINSEGNA (ca. 1255–before 1319). Sienese painter, a major representative of the *maniera greca*, or Byzantine style, of late medieval painting that prevailed in Italy during the 13th century and forms the background for the innovative style of **Giotto** that traditional art historians regarded as the first great step toward Renaissance art. Duccio's best-known work is an altarpiece for the main altar of Siena cathedral, featuring *The Madonna Enthroned* as its central panel and popularly called the *Maestà* (Majesty).

DUFAY, GUILLAUME (ca. 1397–1474). Flemish composer and singer, associated with the court of the dukes of **Burgundy**, though he seems not to have been a regular member of the ducal chapel. He began as a choirboy at Cambrai cathedral and from 1420 to 1457 served several Italian rulers, including the duke of Savoy and Pope **Eugenius IV**. He received from the **pope** a valuable canonry in the cathedral at Cambrai and spent some of the period after 1439 and probably all his later years in that city. He was an unusually well educated man and had a degree in canon law from the **University of Bologna**. His compositions included both secular songs and liturgical music. While in Italy, he composed a motet for the ceremonies held in 1436 to consecrate the magnificent dome designed and built by **Filippo Brunelleschi** for the cathedral of Santa Maria del Fiore at **Florence**.

DUNSTABLE, JOHN (ca. 1385–1453). The outstanding English composer of the first half of the 15th century, famous not only in England but in Italy and elsewhere. He was a married layman but was closely linked to the great monastery at St. Albans and through it, to Duke Humphrey of Gloucester, younger brother of King Henry V and an important early English patron of **humanists**, both English and Italian. Most of his surviving music (more than 70 pieces) is liturgical and was originally intended solely for vocal performance. The sweetness of the music composed by Dunstable and his English contemporaries was greatly admired by contemporaries.

DÜRER, ALBRECHT (1471–1528). The most famous artist of the German Renaissance, active as a painter and engraver. Born at Nuremberg, the son of a goldsmith, he began to study that craft under his father but was apprenticed (1486–1489) to a prominent local painter, **Michael Wolgemut**. Upon completing this training, he became an itinerant craftsman, working at **Basel** and Strasbourg, especially on woodcut illustrations to illustrate books. In 1494 he returned to Nuremberg and married, but that autumn he made the first of two historically important trips to Italy, where he was strongly influenced by the work of **Andrea Mantegna** and **Giovanni Bellini**. Bellini in particular became his friend and taught him the Venetian style of using color.

Dürer settled down in Nuremberg in 1495, beginning a highly successful career as a painter and engraver. Although he was a skilled painter and exemplified the reshaping of the traditional German style by the influence of Italian Renaissance art, the rapid growth of his fame throughout Europe was the result of his productivity and skill as a maker of printed engravings which served to diffuse both his new Renaissance style and his reputation far and wide. By the time of his second trip to Italy (1505–1507), he was already a well-known artist. He returned to Nuremberg early in 1507 and in 1512 became official painter to the Holy Roman Emperor **Maximilian I**. He and his apprentices produced a set of 192 woodcut illustrations for the *Triumphal Arch*, an illustrated book planned by Maximilian to advertise the achievements of his reign. In 1520–1521 Dürer made a journey to the Netherlands in order to secure confirmation of his imperial pension by the new Emperor **Charles V**. On this journey, which is recorded in his diary, he was greeted as a major artist and was able to meet the expenses of his trip by the sale of prints. He spent his last years back home in Nuremberg, concentrating on portraits of wealthy and famous persons.

Dürer became a close friend of the Nuremberg **humanist Willibald Pirckheimer** and was the only local artist who formed an integral part of the city's circle of humanist intellectuals. From about 1519 he became increasingly committed to the religious ideas of **Martin Luther**. In 1526, when the city became officially Lutheran, he presented to the city council two panels containing his noted portraits of the *Four Apostles*.

Dürer represents not only the influence of Italian art on the Germanic north but also the emergence of the artist as an intellectual as well as a craftsman. He published several theoretical and practical treatises on art, including books on measurement, on fortification, and on the proportions of the human body. He was one of the most prolific artists of the Renaissance. His best-known paintings include his early self-portrait (1500), which is reminiscent of 15th-century Flemish paintings, his *Adam and Eve* (1507), which shows the influence of Venetian art, and his *Four Apostles* (1526), which is clearly the work of a man who has assimilated the technical skills and much of the aesthetic sensibility of the Italian Renaissance. Perhaps even greater, and certainly more widely available, were his many engravings, of which the most admired are *The Four Horsemen* (1497–1498), *Knight, Death, and Devil* (1513), *St. Jerome in His Study* (1513), *Melencolia I* (1514), the *Triumphal Arch of Maximilian* (1515), and several portraits of prominent personages of his time, including Cardinal Albrecht von Brandenburg (1519), Frederick III of Saxony (1524), and three portraits done in 1526: the humanist **Erasmus**, the Protestant leader **Philipp Melanchthon**, and his fellow townsman and friend, Pirckheimer. Dürer worked in other media as well, designing stained glass windows and fountains. Also admired are the watercolor landscapes he painted on his way back to Germany during his first visit to Italy.

DU VAIR, GUILLAUME (1556–1612). French politician and moral philosopher. Trained in both law and theology, he remained Catholic and was concerned about the rapid spread of Protestantism in France before and during the Wars of Religion (1562–1598), but the excesses of the Catholic League made him into a Politique, the group of Frenchmen (mostly Catholic) who regarded the preservation of national unity and domestic tranquillity as more important than the forcible extirpation of heresy. He had served as a member of the highest judicial court, the Parlement of Paris, during the violent coup d'état staged at Paris by extremist members of the Catholic League in 1588. Du Vair became a trusted adviser to the new King Henry IV, serving as intendant of justice in Marseille, and becoming *premier président* of the Parlement of Provence. Under Louis XIII he became keeper of the seals and bishop of Lisieux. His contemporary fame rested partly on his eloquent oratory, notably his *Exhortation à la Paix / An Exhortation to Peace* (1592), supporting the moderate royalist Politiques against the extremist Catholics.

Du Vair was also a highly regarded moral philosopher, defending a **neo-Stoic** philosophy that blended ancient Stoicism with Christian faith and emphasized the duty of public service as second only to Christian faith. These ideas were best expressed in his *La philosophie morale des Stoiques*, his *Exhortation à la vie civile*, and his *Traité de la constance et consolation ès calamités publiques*. In these books he criticized citizens who reacted to the civil wars by retreating into private life and abandoning public service.

– E –

EBREO, LEONE. *See* LEONE EBREO.

EDUCATION, HUMANISTIC. *See* HUMANISM.

EGUÍA PRESS. Spanish publishing firm, named for its owner, Miguel de Eguía (ca. 1495–after 1548). The firm had several locations, but its most famous center was the university town of **Alcalá**. Eguía began as an apprentice of the **printer** Arnaldo Guillén de Brocar, who moved to Alcalá to serve the new university founded there by Cardinal **Ximénes de Cisneros**. Eguía became manager of the press and official printer to the **university** after the death of Brocar in 1523. He also operated presses in Valladolid and Toledo. About 130 publications by him have been identified. He was especially important for publication of Spanish versions of works by **Erasmus**, giving rise to an enthusiasm for the Dutch **humanist** that flourished in Spain during the late 1520s and 1530s but had died away by mid-century as conservative churchmen refused to tolerate Erasmus' frank discussion of church corruption and reform ideas. Eguía also published the works of native Spanish humanists like **Juan de Valdés**. He was strongly committed to the personal spirituality of the mystical movement known as Illuminism. In 1531 his association with Illuminism and with the works of Erasmus led to his arrest on charges of being a secret Lutheran. He spent two years in prison but was eventually acquitted.

EL GRECO. Popular nickname of the late Renaissance painter Domenikos Theotokopoulos (ca. 1541–1614), who was born in Crete but moved to **Venice**. There he assimilated the characteristics of Italian Renaissance painters, especially **Titian** and **Tintoretto**. In 1570 he moved to **Rome**, where he enjoyed the patronage of Cardinal **Alessandro Farnese**. Loss of this support caused him to move to Spain in 1577, where he received a valuable commission at Toledo but got into trouble when he refused to alter the painting to suit the preferences of the cathedral chapter and had to sue for his fee. Nevertheless, he was one of the artists chosen to paint altarpieces for the royal basilica of El Escorial, for which he produced *The Martyrdom of St. Maurice and the Theban Legion*. Once again, the work displeased his patron, King **Philip II**, who disliked the painting on both stylistic and religious grounds. El Greco returned to Toledo and about 1585 established a workshop. An important commission there was *The Burial of the Count of Orgaz* (1586). El Greco also painted a considerable number of portraits, of which the most striking depicts an important scholar and close friend of the artist, *Fray Felix Hortensio Paravicino*. El Greco's highly individual style combined the Byzantine tradition with the use of brilliant colors he had learned at Venice and with a unique illusionism that made his paintings transcend natural appearances in order to express spiritual reality.

ELIZABETH I (1533–1603). Queen of England from 1558. A daughter of King **Henry VIII** and Anne Boleyn, she grew up at court under the cloud of her mother's execution on charges of adultery, lived a life sheltered from politics during the brief reign (1547–1553) of her half-brother Edward VI, and then lived in great danger during the reign of her half-sister Mary I (1553–1558) both because of her known Protestant sympathies during a time of Catholic restoration and also because, as the childless queen's next heir, she became the unwilling focus of plots by religious and political opponents of Mary. Although the England she took charge of in 1558 was militarily, financially, and politically weak, Elizabeth surrounded herself with statesmen of great ability and by the end of her long reign had made England a stable monarchy, a major European power, and the international leader of Protestantism. She reversed Mary's religious policy, restoring the independent status of the Church of England as it had existed at the end of her father's reign and maintaining a moderately Protestant and tightly controlled national church that pleased neither the relatively few zealous defenders of Catholicism nor the increasingly numerous Protestant extremists, commonly called Puritans.

Elizabeth made her court the center of an elegant aristocratic society that became noted for its italianate and **classicizing** poetry and for its musical life. Especially after the defeat of the Spanish Armada in 1588, the queen became the symbol of England's emerging greatness, and throughout subsequent centuries, her reign has been associated with political and military success and with the brilliant achievements of the era that came to be called "Elizabethan." Although the queen herself was not a very generous patron, her astute political leadership and the large number of wealthy patrons and talented artists and authors drawn to London by the presence of her court made the Elizabethan age one of the high points in English history and the supreme moment of Renaissance civilization in England. Elizabeth received an excellent **humanistic** education under the direction of Roger Ascham, had a good command of **Greek**, Latin, French, and Italian, and as a young woman translated literary works of **Margaret of Navarre** and **Erasmus** from French and Latin. She often surprised foreign ambassadors with her mastery of languages and her familiarity with classical literature.

ELYOT, THOMAS (ca. 1490–1546). English author and diplomat, a major figure in English cultural life during the reign of **Henry VIII**. Elyot was educated in law at the Inns of Court and won the patronage of Henry's principal government minister, Cardinal **Thomas Wolsey**. About 1523 he became clerk of the royal council, and in

1530 he was knighted. His most famous work, *The Boke Named the Governor* (1531), articulated the values of a successful ruling class and argued that a good **classical** education was the best way for a youth to prepare for a life of service to the ruler.

ELZEVIER PRESS. One of the greatest publishing firms of the late Renaissance. Founded in 1583 by Louis Elzevier (1546–1617), a Protestant refugee from **Louvain** who settled in Leiden after working for the press of **Christophe Plantin** at Antwerp, the firm benefitted from its location in Leiden, home of a new university founded in 1575. By 1592 Elzevier was fully engaged in publishing, though he always contracted the printing to other firms. Almost all of his publications were in Latin, and his production of editions of classical literature was one of the foundations of his success. The other was his introduction of printed catalogs of books offered for sale by auction. After Louis' death in 1617, his sons Matthias and Bonaventura continued the firm, and his grandson Isaac became official printer to the university in 1620.

The golden age of the Elzevier press occurred under the partnership between Bonaventura and Abraham Elzevier, a son of Matthias, especially after they purchased Isaac's company in 1625. In addition to classical editions and academic dissertations, the new partnership became the publisher of choice for prominent scholars not only from the Dutch Republic (**Gerardus Johannes Vossius**, Hugo Grotius, and Daniel Heinsius, for example) but also for foreign scholars, including **Galileo Galilei**. The press continued until 1713. An offshoot of the Leiden firm was founded by Louis II Elzevier at Amsterdam; it concentrated on the publication of contemporary authors including Thomas Hobbes, **Francis Bacon**, Pierre Gassendi, **John Milton**, and René Descartes. There were also branches at The Hague and Utrecht, founded by other descendants of the original Louis Elzevier. The elegant products of the Amsterdam press in the 17th century, particularly its beautifully printed small-format editions of **classical** authors, had already become collectors' items by the 18th century.

EMBLEMS. Collections of woodcut illustrations, each accompanied by a title and an epigrammatic verse, usually with a more or less obvious allegorical meaning. The fashion for these books goes back to the popularity of the *Emblemata / Emblems* published by **Andrea Alciati** in 1531. The genre first became popular in France but soon spread to the Netherlands, Germany, England, Italy, and Spain. Editions of Alciati's collection, often revised to meet local tastes, appeared in all of those countries, both in the original Latin and in the vernacular. Imitations by other compilers began being published from about 1540. Later in the 16th century, there were specifically Catholic and Protestant books of emblems. Although the accompanying texts were rarely distinguished examples of poetry, the engraved illustrations were often done with great care. The emblem-book probably derived from manuscript collections of pictures, each with its associated motto, known in 15th-century Italy as *Imprese* and in France as *devises*. Emblems also influenced the development of court masques, and there are many references to emblems in other genres of Renaissance literature.

ENCINA, JUAN DEL (ca. 1468–1530). Spanish poet, playwright, and musician. He studied law at the University of Salamanca and became a cathedral chorister, but the foundation of his literary career was his service at the court of the duke of Alba, where he was in charge of providing entertainment. He wrote most of his numerous poems and his 14 verse dramas for the court between 1492 and 1500. He also gained an ecclesiastical appointment in 1500 through papal patronage but was not ordained as a priest until 1519.

ERASMUS, DESIDERIUS (ca. 1467–1536). The most famous Northern European **humanist**, probably the greatest **classical**, biblical, and patristic scholar of the early 16th century, also important for his sharp criticism of religious corruption and for his efforts to bring about a moderate and peaceful reform of the church. His mastery of classical languages and sharp wit enabled this illegitimate son of a priest to become an internationally famous scholar whom **popes**, kings, bishops, and great nobles were eager to attract into their service. He received a sound classical education at St. Lebwin's school at Deventer in the Netherlands. After the death of both parents, he and his elder brother, probably with some reluctance, agreed to enter a monastery. Erasmus was ordained as a priest in 1492. He never adapted comfortably to monastic life, and eventually, having been permitted to live outside the monastery in order to pursue his education and to serve as secretary to an aristocratic bishop, he was able to get a papal dispensation granting permission to live independently and to dress as an ordinary secular priest.

In 1495 his patron, the bishop of Cambrai, sent Erasmus to Paris to study theology. This experience did not lead to a degree but did give him a lifelong aversion to the traditional **scholastic** theology taught there. His patron lost interest in him, and he earned his way by tutoring well-to-do youths. Some of his earliest works on Latin style, as well as his *Familiar Colloquies*, had their beginning in handbooks that he prepared for his own pupils. One of these pupils, a young English nobleman, invited him to visit England in 1499, and this introduction into the lifestyle of wealthy and educated Englishmen strengthened his determination to pursue a literary career.

On this first trip to England, he laid the foundations for lifelong friendships with Englishmen of high rank and great intellectual ability, including the humanists **John Colet** and **Thomas More**, the archbishop of Canterbury, and two future bishops. Colet encouraged Erasmus to stay at Oxford as lecturer on the New Testament, but Erasmus declined, convinced that without a mastery of **Greek** (a need that Colet did not understand), he could make little progress in understanding the New Testament. After his return to Paris, Erasmus worked hard to improve his command of Greek. Through his connections at the English court, he got the opportunity to travel to Italy in 1506 as tutor to the sons of the Italian-born physician to King **Henry VII**. He was able to travel widely in Italy, spending time at **Rome**, where he met many of the humanists associated with the papal curia, and at **Venice**, where he became one of the humanists gathered at the press of the great Renaissance publisher **Aldus Manutius**. This group included a number of exiled Greek scholars and other specialists on the editing of classical and patristic texts. This experience deepened Erasmus' knowledge of Greek language and literature. An outstanding example is the new edition of his collection of ancient maxims, the *Adagia / Adages*, which was greatly increased in size but, more important, enriched by the infusion of Greek maxims and literary references. His visit to Italy gave him a mature appreciation of his own talents and the self-confidence to press ahead with his commitment to the study of the New Testament and the Greek Church Fathers.

In 1509, learning of the accession of the young **Henry VIII** to the throne, he hurried to England in anticipation of a great increase in royal patronage for humanists. These hopes were not fulfilled, since Henry was far too involved in wars and diplomacy to give much help to foreign scholars. Nevertheless, Erasmus stayed in England until 1514. For much of this period he worked as lecturer in theology and Greek language at Cambridge University. In 1514 he returned to the Netherlands, where his growing literary reputation won him an appointment as honorary councillor to the future Emperor **Charles V**.

In 1517, after Charles had departed for Spain to establish his rule as king of Spain, Erasmus settled in **Louvain**, site of the region's only university. His type of textually based biblical scholarship, requiring mastery of Greek and implicitly critical of traditional medieval scholasticism, was not welcome among the Louvain theologians, who regarded his famous edition of the Greek New Testament (1516) as a challenge to the authenticity of the biblical text on which medieval Catholic doctrine and practice were based. His role in encouraging and organizing a new institute devoted to humanistic studies, the **Trilingual College** (which taught classical Latin, Greek, and **Hebrew**), was resented. Worst of all, the emergence of the early **Reformation** in Germany stirred up charges that Erasmus' frank criticisms of corruption in the church were the source of **Martin Luther's** heresies.

Erasmus' editorial work had already brought him into contact with the **Basel** publisher **Johannes Froben**, and he travelled to Basel twice in order to supervise editions being published there, including two of his greatest editorial achievements, the complete works of St. Jerome and the first edition of the Greek text of the New Testament (both published in 1516). In 1521 he moved permanently to Basel. He found Basel a congenial environment, with a flourishing printing industry and a large community of humanistic scholars. As a new member of the Swiss Confederation, the city was somewhat sheltered from the bitter controversies generated by the Reformation in Germany. Erasmus stayed in Basel until the city adhered to the Reformation in 1529. Then he moved to the small and safely Catholic university town of Freiburg-im-Breisgau. His close ties to friends at Basel and to the Froben press eventually drew him back to Basel, where he spent the last few months of his life and died in July 1536.

Erasmus' scholarly achievement included not only his work on ancient Greek and Latin patristic authors (St. Jerome above all, but also Origen and Saints Ambrose, Basil, Cyprian, Chrysostom, Hilary, and Irenaeus) and several editions of his epoch-making Greek New Testament, but also important editions of classical Latin authors. These editions, plus the vastly expanded 1508 edition of the *Adages* (which continued to grow larger and richer with each succeeding edition), formed the basis of his reputation as the greatest scholar of his time. His early works included a number of books that long remained standard textbooks for youths who wanted to master the art of speaking and writing good classical Latin, such as *De copia / On Style* (1512), *De conscribendis epistolis / On Letter-Writing* (1522), and especially the *Colloquia / Colloquies*, a collection of dialogues that originated as a simple manual of Latin conversation but evolved into a lively set of dialogues that functioned like essays to discuss controversial topics of great concern to Erasmus and his contemporaries (first published in a pirated edition of 1518; first authorized edition, 1519). Erasmus also published (1529) an abridgment of the *Elegances* of the Italian humanist **Lorenzo Valla**, a useful guide to classical Latin style; a collection of *Parabolae sive similia / Similes* (1514), and a collection of literary anecdotes or apothegms (1531), all of them intended to help authors to develop a good Latin style and to provide a stock of stories and examples that authors could draw on for their own compositions.

Many of Erasmus' works dealt with current religious questions, expressing a characteristic Erasmian conception of religion. They appealed greatly to many educated people of his time but later became the basis for accusations that he was the source of Luther's heresies. Although all of his published works were written in Latin and hence were addressed to an educated rather than a mass audience, within the limits imposed by language they became popular and influential. His most famous satire was *Encomium Moriae / The Praise of Folly* (first edition 1511; revised editions in 1514 and 1521), a sophisticated and satirical monologue that addresses many contemporary problems but focuses heavily on the faults of the church and the clergy. His *Colloquies* set forth in dialogue form many of the same ideas about the need for reform of spiritual life and the institutional church. Erasmus also produced religious works more serious in tone.

His own ideal of a Christian faith focused on personal spiritual experience and on a morality of love and concern for other people, which he called "the philosophy of Christ," found its most influential expression in *Enchiridion militis Christiani / Handbook of the Christian Soldier*, which first appeared in 1503. It became a best-seller and was frequently reprinted, not only in Latin but in translations into English, Czech, German, Dutch, Spanish, and French. Also treating religion in a serious vein were his *Paraclesis*, a short and simple presentation of his concept of true Christian piety, prefaced to the first edition of his Greek New Testament in 1516, and his *Methodus sive ratio theologiae / Method or Form of Theology*, originally published as the preface to the second edition of the New Testament in 1519 but soon separately printed. Erasmus also wrote tracts discussing practical issues of church life, such as *De esu carnium / On Eating Meat* (1522), which discussed mandatory fasting, and *Exomologesis* (1524), a discussion of confession.

His initial reaction to Martin Luther's theology and defiance of church authority was guarded. Erasmus recognized that some of Luther's teachings would eliminate abuses that he himself had criticized, but from a very early date, he feared that others of Luther's ideas threatened the unity of the church and created a danger of social upheaval. He finally concluded that he must speak out against Luther, and his *De libero arbitrio / On Free Will* (1524) challenged Luther's belief that human dependence on divine grace was incompatible with freedom of the will. This open criticism of Luther disappointed many humanists who had become Lutherans, but it did not silence the criticisms from conservative Catholics, who were offended both by Erasmus' continued assertions that some of Luther's doctrines were correct and by his continuing criticisms of the old church.

Erasmus remained deeply concerned by the split in the church and longed to see it ended, not by a victory of one faction over another but by emphasis on the many beliefs that all Christians held in common and by peaceful negotiation rather than violence. His *De sarcienda ecclesiae concordia / On Mending the Peace of the Church* (1533) pleaded for a peaceful resolution of the religious crisis. Erasmus was a consistent defender of the value of peace, advancing pacifist ideas in *Querela pacis / The Complaint of Peace* (1517), in a famous and lengthy essay called *Dulce bellum inexpertis / War Is Sweet to Those Who Have Not Experienced It* (1515), and in a work on war against the Turks. Erasmus was interested in a pastoral, practical type of Christianity, and for that ideal he wrote works of practical advice like *Institutio Christiani matrimonii / Foundations of Christian Marriage* (1526) and *De vidua Christiana / The Christian Widow* (1529). His *Paraphrases* on nearly all books of the New Testament attempted to restate the central meaning of the sacred texts in terms comprehensible to ordinary people.

This sort of moderate, reformist Catholicism exposed Erasmus to attacks by both sides of the religious conflict, with Catholics accusing him of conceding too many points to the Protestants, while Protestants accused him of being too cowardly to face the consequences of his own best principles. In the end, however, his reputation fared better among Protestants, even though he firmly refused to join them. Luther's humanist colleague **Philipp Melanchthon** acknowledged Erasmus' great learning and his sincerity. In the Catholic world, as the leadership of the church turned increasingly conservative, he came to be viewed with hostility because of his open criticisms, his insistence that many of Luther's early proposals were valid, and his contention that much of the blame for the religious schism fell on the church's worldly, unspiritual leaders. He always retained a following among Catholics, but in many Catholic regions, such as Spain, by 1550 the possession of Erasmus' books or favorable mention of his name and ideas came to be treated as evidence of heresy.

Erasmus travelled widely throughout western and central Europe, lived for extended periods in various places, and hence conducted an active correspondence. Several thousand of his letters survive and constitute a valuable documentary source not only for his own development but also for the political and religious history of his time.

ESTE, HOUSE OF. Princely dynasty which ruled the city of **Ferrara** from 1240 to 1598 and played an important part in Italian diplomacy and warfare. Originally ranked as marquises, they were made dukes of Modena and Reggio by an imperial grant of 1452 and in 1471 were elevated by the **pope** to the rank of dukes of Ferrara. The dynasty formed a brilliant and culturally attractive court. Under Borso (ruled 1450–1471) and Ercole I (1471–1505), the court was the center of a distinctive Ferrarese style of painting. Both Ercole I and his son Alfonso I (1505–1534) were lavish builders of palaces and churches. Borso collected an excellent library of classical and humanistic manuscripts, and the Este court became an active center of theatrical performances and public pageants.

In 1429 Duke Niccolò III persuaded the prominent schoolmaster **Guarino Guarini** to become tutor to his son Leonello, and the excellent court school thus created became famous throughout Italy, rivalled only by the other major court school conducted by **Vittorino da Feltre** for the marquis of **Mantua**. Both schools attracted aristocratic pupils from throughout Italy and even from abroad. The school at Ferrara became the foundation for a revived local university, with Guarino teaching the *studia humanitatis*, that is, the central academic subjects associated with Renaissance **humanism**.

ESTE, ISABELLA D' (1474–1539). Marchioness of the Italian principality of **Mantua** and a noted a patron of arts and literature. Brought up as the daughter of Duke Ercole I of **Ferrara** and given the rare privilege of sharing the **humanistic** education given in the court school founded by **Guarino Guarini**, she became famous for her learning. In 1490 she married **Francesco Gonzaga**, marquis of Mantua. She bore six children and carefully prepared the girls to become prominent princesses or nuns, and her sons to pursue careers as soldiers or clerics. She collected books and paintings by leading authors and artists of her time. During her husband's frequent absences for military service, Isabella administered the state and gained a reputation for justice. She also ruled during the interval between Francesco's death and the majority of their son Federico II. *See also* ESTE, HOUSE OF.

ESTIENNE FAMILY. French publishers and printers who created one of the most famous publishing firms of Renaissance Europe, noted for its publication of **classical**, biblical, and **humanistic** texts. The firm was founded at Paris by Henri I (ca. 1470–1520), whose publications embraced both medieval **scholastic** theology and humanism. His most famous humanistic author was **Jacques Lefèvre d'Etaples**. When Henri died in 1520, his widow turned management over to her second husband, Simon de Colines. In 1526 Robert I (1503–1559), a son of Henri I, took control and developed the press into one of the largest publishers in Europe, producing a total of about 500 titles. His editions included famous editions of the Bible in **Greek**, Latin, and **Hebrew**. In 1539 King **Francis I** appointed Robert as royal printer. The Paris theologians, however, found some of the notes in Estienne's Bibles heretical, and in 1550 Robert moved to Geneva, where he continued to publish Bibles and became a major printer of Protestant theologians, especially **John Calvin**. When Robert moved to Geneva, the Paris operations came under the control of his brother, Charles (ca. 1504–1564), who served as royal printer from 1551 to 1561.

At Geneva, Robert I was succeeded by his eldest son, Henri II (1528–1598), a scholar of immense erudition and a publisher who specialized even more than his predecessors in the printing of Greek texts. His major publication was *Thesaurus linguae Graecae* (5 vols., 1572), which still remains a reference work of value for Greek scholars. He produced important editions of classical Greek authors and also continued his father's program of publishing Calvinist books. The Paris branch continued under the leadership of Robert II (1530–1571), who also succeeded to the title of royal printer. It continued under his widow and his son (Robert III) until 1631. The Geneva branch was headed by Paul (1566–1627) and then by Paul's son Antoine (1592–1674), who converted to Catholicism and moved back to Paris. He became royal printer and continued publishing until 1664.

EUGENIUS IV. Pope from 1431 to 1447, during the final stage of a serious challenge to papal absolutism by supporters of the theory of **Conciliarism**. Born as Gabriele Condulmer at **Venice** about 1383, he pursued a career at the papal curia after his uncle Angelo Correr became a cardinal and then was elected pope as Gregory XII (1406–1415). Gabriele became bishop of Siena in 1407 and a cardinal the following year. He never studied at a **university** and showed little interest in the new **humanist** culture. At his election, he promised to lead the reform of the church "in head and members" and to continue the church council that had already begun its sessions at Basel.

Eugenius attempted to dissolve the **Council of Basel** at the end of 1431, but the repudiation of this action not only by the council itself but also by most of the major European rulers forced him to back down. His relations with the council remained troubled. He refused to accept conciliar decrees declaring the supremacy of a council over all other authorities in the church and empowering a council to enact reforms without papal approval. In the papal bull *Doctoris gentium* (1437) he reasserted the papacy's claim to unlimited monarchical power over the church and ordered the council's sessions transferred to **Ferrara** in Italy. The great majority of the council rejected this order and in June 1439 formally declared Eugenius deposed. The pope's hand was strengthened by the agreement of the Greek Orthodox leaders to attend the council at Ferrara in order to reunify the eastern and western churches. The union proclaimed in 1439 ultimately fell through, but this apparent success helped Eugenius win the support of most of the major European rulers, especially since the decree of deposition and the election of a rival pope by the council made the council seem responsible for a new schism.

Eugenius solidified his power by negotiating a series of concordats (treaties) with individual governments, granting broad control of church appointments to the secular rulers in return for recognition of papal supremacy. Official support for the Council of Basel dwindled, though great numbers of clergy in northern Europe, especially the educated ones, continued to support the principles of Conciliarism. Eugenius also faced great difficulty in maintaining control of the city of Rome, where some of the local nobility in 1434 staged a coup d'etat that forced the pope to flee to **Florence**, disguised as a monk. He did not return to Rome until 1443, an exile of nine years, two-thirds of which were spent in Florence.

EXECRABILIS. Papal bull issued by Pope **Pius II** on 18 January 1460, forbidding anyone to appeal from a decision of a **pope** to a future general council of the church. The end of the **Great Schism** of the Western church in 1417 had removed the crisis of disunity that had strengthened **Conciliarism**, the theory that a general council of the church, rather than the pope, was the supreme authority in the church. With the final disbanding of the Council of **Basel** in 1449, both the driving force behind Conciliarism and the political backing for any extreme action to enforce its theories had been weakened.

Nevertheless, much opinion among educated clergymen north of the Alps still held that the supremacy of councils over popes, formally adopted by the decree *Haec sancta* of the **Council of Constance** in

1415, was a permanent part of the law of the church. The popes had always opposed this doctrine, but they hesitated to revoke the decree openly since actions of the Council of Constance had been the basis for the end of the Schism and the election of **Martin V** as pope in 1417.

After the end of the Council of Basel, popes **Nicholas V**, Calixtus III, and Pius II found that disgruntled secular rulers and clergymen sometimes appealed from papal decisions to the meeting of the next general council (which would have occurred every 10 years if the popes had lived up to Martin V's promise to the Council of Constance). Hence Pius II's immediate goal in issuing *Execrabilis* was to stop the practice of appealing his decisions to a future general council. His long-term goal was even simpler: it was to weaken and ultimately destroy the foundation of the Conciliarist view of authority within the church and to reaffirm the view of the medieval popes that the pope's authority rested entirely on his position as successor to St. Peter and hence was absolute and not answerable to any council or any other human agency. Pius II's decree was resented in many places, and from time to time rulers still threatened to convene a council against the pope's will and make him answerable to it. Other persons (**Martin Luther** in 1520, for example) still issued public appeals from an unwelcome decision of the pope to a future general council.

EYCK, HUBERT AND JAN VAN. *See* VAN EYCK, HUBERT AND JAN.

– F –

FALLOPPIO, GABRIELE (1523–1562). Italian physician and anatomist, best known as discoverer of the Fallopian tubes, but also important for other anatomical discoveries concerning the female reproductive organs. In addition, he studied the anatomy of the brain and eyes, provided the earliest accurate description of the inner ear, and studied the larynx, respiration, and the action of muscles. A native of Modena, educated under **Andreas Vesalius** at **Padua**, he became professor of anatomy at Pisa in 1548 and in 1551 moved to the **University** of Padua.

FARNESE, HOUSE OF. Family of Italian nobility. Originally soldiers and landholders in southern Tuscany and the **Papal States**, the Farnese rose to princely status after Alessandro Farnese was elected Pope Paul III (1534–1549). Pope Paul was the first post-**Reformation pope** who seriously addressed the need for reform of the church, but he was also a scandalous nepotist, putting three of his own grandsons onto the college of cardinals and making another grandson prefect of the city of **Rome.** In 1537 he organized the new duchy of Castro in the papal domains and made his son Pier Luigi (1503–1547) its duke. In 1545 he again used the church's lands to create the duchy of Parma and Piacenza with Pier Luigi as its first duke.

Pope Paul also used his influence to win brilliant marriage alliances with Italian princely families, as well as with illegitimate offspring of the Emperor **Charles V** and the French king Henry II, for his relatives. The most famous of this group of ambitious papal kinfolk was Cardinal Alessandro Farnese (1520–1589), who received many lucrative appointments. Alessandro was a man of great ability, a skilled diplomat, a great collector of art, and a generous patron of writers and artists. The pope had begun construction of a magnificent palace in Rome even before his election, and Alessandro completed it. Alessandro also brought about the building of many churches at Rome.

In the branch of the family that ruled Parma, another Alessandro Farnese (1545–1592) was reared at the court of Spain and became a famous military leader, eventually serving as Spanish governor in the Netherlands during the Dutch war of independence. While he was unable to reconquer the seven northern provinces, which became the United Netherlands, he managed to consolidate the southern part of the region into a state that remained under Spanish rule until the 18th century. This Alessandro eventually became duke of Parma (1586–1592). The Farnese dynasty continued to rule Parma until 1731, when the succession passed to the Spanish Bourbon dynasty through descent from a Farnese princess.

FEDELE, CASSANDRA (1465–1558). Venetian author and one of the relatively few Renaissance **women** who were able to obtain a thorough **humanistic** education. Her father, Angelo, introduced her to Latin grammar and study of the Roman orators. He regarded her as a child prodigy and arranged for her to be tutored in **Greek**, philosophy, natural science, and logic. As a young woman she delivered public speeches to the **University** of **Padua**, the Venetian Senate, and the doge, and when she was only 22, her first book was printed, a collection of four letters with one of her orations (1487). As a woman, Fedele could not participate fully in the intellectual and academic life of her time, but she became a great letter-writer, corresponding on intellectual matters with humanist scholars at Padua and other places in Italy, including the chancellor of **Florence**, **Bartolomeo Scala**, and his daughter **Alessandra**. One of the most distinguished Florentine humanists of the late 15th century, **Angelo Poliziano**, described Fedele as second only to his friend **Giovanni Pico della Mirandola** in learning, and perhaps even his equal. Yet this high praise also underlines her uniqueness and implies that few women could ever be suited for study at such a high level. Fedele also corresponded with Italian and other European rulers. Her correspondence with Queen **Isabella** of Spain raised the possibility that Fedele might receive an academic appointment in Spain, but the Venetian Senate forbade her to emigrate. She married in 1498 and after the premature death of her husband in 1520 was left an impoverished and childless widow. For several decades both her city and the **popes** from whom she sought assistance ignored her. Eventually, when she was 82 years old, Pope Paul III interceded with the Venetian government, which appointed her prioress of an orphanage associated with a local church, and she lived the rest of her life there. In 1556, now remarkable for her great age as well as her erudition, she delivered a public oration welcoming the queen of Poland to **Venice**. This was her last public appearance. In addition to the small book she published in 1487, she left a collection of letters and orations which was posthumously published in 1636. Although she became the most famous learned woman of her time, she accepted the conventional belief that women are naturally inferior to men.

FERDINAND OF ARAGON (1452–1516). King of Aragon as Ferdinand II (1479–1516). His marriage to Princess **Isabella** of Castile in 1469 made him king consort of Castile after she became queen of that country in 1474, and his inheritance of Aragon in 1479 was the decisive step that made Ferdinand and Isabella the first king and queen of a united Spain. For many purposes the two kingdoms remained separate, but the royal marriage ensured that their descendants would rule both kingdoms. The **Spanish Inquisition**, founded in Castile in 1478 and extended to Aragon in 1483, was the only institution (except for the persons of the king and queen) common to both kingdoms. After Isabella's death in 1504, Ferdinand's authority in Castile came to an end, and the crown passed to their daughter, Juana, and her husband Philip the Handsome of **Burgundy**, a member of the **Habsburg** dynasty. But Ferdinand soon regained control of Castile as regent because of the death of Philip in 1506 and the mental illness of Juana, who was set aside in favor of her young son **Charles** of Ghent, born in 1500. Ferdinand acted as regent for the child, who grew up at the court of his Burgundian ancestors in the Netherlands while Ferdinand retained control of both Castile and Aragon.

Like his wife Isabella, Ferdinand was a ruler of great ability, though their interests were very different. While Isabella was deeply religious and gave great attention to issues of church reform and Castilian domestic policy, Ferdinand was a secular politician mainly interested in foreign policy and military affairs. He consolidated his control of Spain and in 1492 successfully completed the conquest of the last Islamic principality left in Spain, the kingdom of Granada. Aragon had long functioned as a Mediterranean power with special interests in Italy because its king had direct rule over Sicily and Sardinia and also because an illegitimate branch of its royal family ruled the kingdom of **Naples**. Ferdinand responded to the French invasion of Italy in 1494 by coming to the aid of his cousin King Alfonso in 1495 and forcing the French out of Naples. From that time until the definitive establishment of Spanish hegemony in Italy in 1559, Spain was the principal rival of France for control of the peninsula.

When the French throne passed in 1498 to King Louis XII, who had a hereditary claim to **Milan** as well as Naples, Ferdinand negotiated a secret treaty with Louis, agreeing to permit French seizure of Milan and to join the French in dethroning his cousin King Federico of Naples and dividing the kingdom between France and Spain. He then picked a quarrel with the French occupying force and in 1503 sent an army that crushed the French. This time Ferdinand kept the whole Neapolitan kingdom for himself. It remained under Spanish rule until the 18th century. In 1512 during another war with France,

Ferdinand conquered most of the small kingdom of Navarre, including all of the region lying south of the Pyrenees mountains. Thus Ferdinand showed himself a ruthless but effective expansionist, adding Granada and Navarre to the Castilian lands and annexing all of Naples in 1503. He became a major figure in European politics and won the grudging admiration of the Florentine political philosopher **Niccolò Machiavelli**. Ferdinand shares some responsibility for the establishment of the **Inquisition** and its systematic use to destroy the large **Jewish** community in Spain, but this action was probably more the work of the queen, who dominated religious policy.

The enterprise of transatlantic exploration and the beginnings of Spanish colonialism in the Americas seem to have resulted from the initiative of Isabella rather than Ferdinand. Geography dictated that Castile would play the leading role in the new American colonies. In the long run, Ferdinand's greatest accomplishment was his dynastic diplomacy, expressed not only in military action but also in the advantageous marriages he negotiated for his children. His marriage of Juana to the **Habsburg** heir to Burgundy and the Netherlands was the act that brought his grandson Charles to the throne of Spain, Naples, Burgundy, and the Netherlands and prepared the way for his election as Holy Roman Emperor (**Charles V**) in 1519. Ferdinand's last great act was his careful preparation for Charles to succeed him in 1516 as the universally acknowledged sole heir to Spain and its dependencies.

Although Ferdinand's connection with Sicily and Naples made him aware of Renaissance art and **humanistic** learning and led him to become a patron of the artists and scholars who introduced the new culture into Spain, he is not a major figure in the emergence of the native Spanish Renaissance. His fame rests on his military, political, and dynastic exploits, not on his cultural policies.

FERRARA. City of north-central Italy, the capital of a duchy ruled from the 13th to the end of the 16th century by the princely house of **Este**. In theory the city was subject to the **popes**, and the papacy took direct control in 1598. The city grew and prospered during the Renaissance, reaching nearly 33,000 inhabitants in 1601. The Este dynasty conducted an ambitious program of building, not only of their own palaces but also of churches and charitable institutions. The rulers purchased or commissioned paintings by Italian masters and also by artists of the Flemish school such as **Rogier van der Weyden**. In the middle of the 15th century, a distinct Ferrarese school of painting developed, of which Cosmè Tura (1430–1495) and Francesco della Cossa (ca. 1435–ca. 1477) were the most prominent.

Probably the outstanding achievement in the city's cultural life was the creation of a famous school of **humanistic** studies at the ducal court by the renowned teacher **Guarino Guarini** under the patronage of Duke Niccolò III in 1429. This school attracted students from princely and wealthy mercantile families throughout Italy and even from north of the Alps. In the middle of the 15th century, the school was further expanded into a university, though its original reputation rested largely on the teaching of Guarino.

FERRARA-FLORENCE, COUNCIL OF. General council of the Latin Church summoned by Pope **Eugenius IV** in 1437. It convened at Ferrara on 8 January 1438. The sessions were soon moved to Florence, where the city's political leader, **Cosimo de' Medici**, offered financial support. The primary (and only avowed) goal of the **pope** was to complete negotiations with the Byzantine emperor John VIII Palaeologus and the leaders of the Orthodox Church for a reunion of the Latin and Greek branches of the church, which had been divided since the 11th century. The second goal, not openly acknowledged, was to undermine the authority of the independent-minded **Council of Basel**, which had refused to let the pope transfer its sessions to Ferrara or any other place in Italy and which was reasserting the doctrines of **Conciliarism**, which taught that the supreme authority within the Catholic Church is not the pope but a general council.

The Byzantine emperor, the Patriarch of **Constantinople**, and a large delegation of other churchmen and scholars came from Constantinople to Florence. There were a number of theological and liturgical issues to be resolved. The most difficult of these was the Greeks' refusal to acknowledge the superiority of the pope as bishop of **Rome** over all other bishops. The Greek Orthodox church held that supreme authority was shared by all bishops and especially by the bishops of the oldest dioceses, of whom the Roman bishop was only one. Eventually, the Byzantine delegation, which was desperate for Western political and military aid against the **Ottoman Turks**, yielded on these issues. On 6 July 1439 the conciliar decree *Laetentur coeli / The Heavens Re-*

joice was proclaimed, theoretically ending the centuries-long separation of the Greek and Latin churches. In the east, the reunification proved abortive, because the majority of the people and clergy rejected the terms of the union. But the apparent success in ending the schism between east and west did much to weaken support for the Council of Basel and to solidify Pope Eugenius' reassertion of the papacy's claim to absolute sovereignty over the whole church. The council moved to Rome in 1442, as negotiations continued with a number of smaller separated eastern churches.

Far more lasting than the abortive reunion of churches were the cultural effects of the presence of the large Byzantine delegation. A revival of interest in ancient **Greek** language and literature had already taken hold in some parts of Italy (notably **Florence** and **Venice**) at the end of the 14th century, and the growing group of Western specialists in Greek found contact with the visiting Byzantines both inspiring and useful. Several of the visitors had been involved in efforts to deepen modern Greeks' awareness of their own classical heritage. The most influential of these was **Georgios Gemistos Pletho**. A considerable number of Greek clerics who were deeply committed to the union with the Latin church remained in Italy. The most famous of these was the archbishop of Nicaea, **Johannes Bessarion**.

FICHET, GUILLAUME (1433–after 1490). Paris theologian. He was born in Savoy and from an early age was attracted to the Latin works of **Petrarch** and to the ancient Roman poets. He studied at **Avignon** and then at Paris, where he received a doctorate in theology in 1468. At Paris he taught the traditional **scholastic** courses in logic and theology, but he also gave well-attended evening lectures on **classical** authors. A diplomatic mission to **Milan** in 1469–1470 gave him firsthand experience of the new **humanistic** culture of Italy. Largely because of his desire to spread interest in ancient literature, he joined with another theologian, the German Johann Heynlin von Stein, to bring German printers to Paris and establish the first press in France within the building of the Sorbonne. Fichet probably met Cardinal **Johannes Bessarion** while he was in Italy and certainly corresponded with him and introduced him to the **university** faculty when Bessarion came to Paris to preach a crusade to recapture **Constantinople**. Neither Fichet nor his collaborator Heynlin stayed in Paris.

Heynlin moved to the University of **Basel**, and in 1472 Fichet followed Bessarion back to Italy, where he was given a position in the papal curia at **Rome**. His introduction of the art of **printing** to France greatly helped him promote the study of classical Latin language and literature at Paris. The year of his death is unknown, but he was still living at Rome in 1490.

FICINO, MARSILIO (1433–1499). **Florentine** translator and **Neoplatonic** philosopher, associated with the **Medici** family, who became his patrons. The son of a personal physician to **Cosimo de'Medici**, he received a medical rather than a **humanistic** education. Thus although the great philosophical influence on his intellectual development was the works of **Plato** and the Hellenistic Neoplatonists, he also had a firm grounding in the philosophy of **Aristotle**. His studies of late classical Platonists and of Christian Platonists aroused his interest in the works of Plato himself, few of which had been translated into Latin. In order to study Plato and his disciples, Ficino took up the study of the **Greek** language and by the end of the 1450s and the early 1460s was able to make Latin translations for his own use. Cosimo de'Medici, who was interested in philosophy and literature, heard of Ficino's reputation and in 1462 asked him to translate all of the works of Plato. Cosimo soon also asked him to translate a collection of short philosophical treatises attributed to a fictitious Greek sage known as **Hermes Trismegistus**, the so-called Hermetic literature. Ficino rapidly completed the translation of these brief texts, now known as the *Corpus hermeticum*. He also continued working on the arduous task of translating all of Plato into Latin. By 1468 he had completed rough drafts of all of the texts. In 1484 a revised text was **printed**, the first edition of Plato's works ever to be printed in any language. This translation remained the standard text of Plato used by readers of Latin until the 18th century.

As he struggled with the translation of Plato, Ficino also struggled to reconcile his growing enthusiasm for the philosophy of this pagan philosopher with his Christian faith. His ultimate resolution of this problem was a conviction that Plato, with his emphasis on spiritual things and his belittling of the material world, was not only compatible with Christian faith but had been sent by divine providence to bring philosophers closer to the essential beliefs of Christian faith.

The symbolic act marking resolution of his own spiritual conflict was his decision to be ordained as a priest in 1473.

Ficino made his conviction of the harmony between Platonism and Christianity the foundation of his own philosophical works. His *Theologia Platonica de immortalitate animae* (1474; published 1482) followed the structure of a medieval scholastic treatise but drew heavily on those whom he called "the ancient theologians." Its principal goal was to set forth convincing proofs of the immortality of the human soul. In 1474 he published concurrent Italian and Latin versions of another work dealing with his faith, *De Christiana religione / On the Christian Religion*. Other important works, all based on Platonic philosophy, were his commentary on the *Symposium* of Plato, called *De amore / On Love* (circulated in manuscript from 1469); *De triplici vita / On Threefold Life* (1489), which contained his attempt to reconstruct the dangerous subject of **magic** in a way that banished evil spirits and relied on spiritual preparation to release the powers of the human soul; and a large collection of Latin letters (1495) in which he applied his Platonic principles to various issues. Ficino continued his work as a translator of late Platonic (Neoplatonic) works, including the *Enneades* of Plotinus (1492), the most influential ancient Neoplatonic philosopher; a volume of translations from other representatives of ancient **Neoplatonism** such as Porphyry, Iamblichus, Synesius, Proclus, and Psellus (1497); and a new translation (1496) of the works of the Christian Neoplatonist known as Dionysius the Areopagite (now called pseudo-Dionysius). Ficino lectured on the works of these authors and on Plato himself to a select group of admirers, the "Platonic **Academy** of Florence" (which was not a formal educational institution), and his commentaries on Plato, cast in a dialogue form borrowed from the philosopher himself, were published in 1496.

Finally, though he is always remembered solely as a philosopher, Ficino was also a physician and published one influential medical treatise in Italian, *Consiglio contro la pestilenza / Advice against the Plague* (1479; published in 1481). His emphasis on the importance of spiritual rather than material reality made him as a physician especially interested in the relations between medicine and religion, and his philosophical works (especially *De vita*, with its potentially dangerous discussion of "spiritual magic") had implications for the treatment of depression and other psychological disorders. He was critical of the conventional and materialistic implications of the influential science of **astrology** and published an attack on judicial astrology, yet his own medical and philosophical doctrines take for granted the influence of the celestial world on earthly affairs.

Ficino believed in the concept of *prisca theologia*, the idea that God had made direct revelations of religious truth to all the ancient peoples, not just the **Jews**, and that the writings attributed to such shadowy ancient sages as the Persian Zoroaster, the Egyptian Hermes, and the Greek Pythagoras represented this "ancient theology" which extended back before the beginnings of recorded time. In his opinion, much of this ancient wisdom had culminated in the philosophy of Plato. Ficino's interpretation of Plato was heavily influenced by his study of the so-called Hermes Trismegistus and by the genuine works of the Alexandrian Neoplatonist Plotinus. His brand of Neoplatonism is very different from the Platonism of Plato himself. Nevertheless, his achievement in translating not only Plato but also the principal ancient Neoplatonist philosophers into Latin, the universal language of scholars, was a major contribution to the assimilation of ancient culture into Renaissance culture.

FILELFO, FRANCESCO (1398–1481). Italian **humanist**, noted for his excellent command of **Greek** language and his valuable collection of rare Greek manuscripts. A native of Tolentino, he studied law and rhetoric at the University of **Padua** and taught there for a time. In 1420 he travelled to **Constantinople** to perfect his knowledge of Greek. He stayed there for seven years, studying Greek with **Manuel Chrysoloras** and eventually marrying his teacher's daughter Theodora. He and his family returned to **Venice** in 1427 with a rich haul of Greek books, including many **classical** texts not yet known in the West.

In 1428 Filelfo became teacher of rhetoric and moral philosophy at the **University of Bologna**. Disruption of the university by civil war caused him to move to the University of **Florence** in 1429. His lectures there on Greek authors drew large crowds and attracted the favor of leading citizens, including **Cosimo de'Medici**, Palla Strozzi, and the chancellor **Leonardo Bruni**, He lost the favor of Cosimo in 1431. In 1433 he survived an attempted assassination, and when the

Medici returned to power in 1434, he left town. He taught at Siena (1435–1438) and survived another attempt at assassination.

In 1439 Filelfo became court poet to the duke of **Milan** and professor of rhetoric at Pavia. For most of the rest of his life he lived under the patronage of the **Visconti** and then the **Sforza** dukes of Milan. He was a prolific author. His works included his Horatian *Satyrae*, two Plutarchan dialogues, a Vergilian-style epic poem called the *Sforziad* in honor of the new Milanese ruling family, several collections of letters and poems, a treatise on moral philosophy, and a collection of his own letters. He translated a number of ancient Greek texts into Latin.

FLETCHER, JOHN (1579–1625). English dramatist. This son of a bishop of London enjoyed his greatest success in the works he wrote in collaboration with Francis Beaumont (ca. 1584–1616). The most highly regarded of the dozen plays they wrote together were *Philaster* (1610) and *The Maid's Tragedy* (ca. 1611). Fletcher also wrote about 16 plays by himself and collaborated with several other dramatists, perhaps including **Shakespeare** (*The Two Kinsmen* and *Henry VIII*).

FLORENCE. Principal city of the Italian region of Tuscany, located on the Arno River. Although other cities of northern and central Italy also played an important role in the development of Renaissance culture, Florence was the most creative center for the **humanistic** learning and artistic styles that constitute the principal features of the Italian Renaissance. During the wars between **popes** and emperors in the 12th and 13th centuries, most citizens favored the **Guelf** (pro-papal) cause against the **Ghibelline** (pro-imperial) cause. By the 12th century, Florence had become a self-governing **commune**, with its own elected magistrates. Lacking access to the sea, Florence remained rather small in the early 13th century, but it grew rapidly in the later 13th and early 14th centuries, attaining a population estimated at about 120,000 on the eve of the **Black Death**, which devastated the city in 1348. By 1427 Florence seems to have declined to a mere 40,000 inhabitants; and it did not regain its pre-plague population until the 19th century.

The city's power and wealth rested primarily on commerce and industry. The production of high-quality woolen and silk textiles and the development of trading and banking firms that bought and sold goods throughout Europe were the foundation of its prosperity. Economic and political life was dominated by **guilds** of wealthy merchants and industrialists. The city had 21 recognized guilds; seven of these ranked as greater guilds (*arti maggiori*) and consisted of professional men or wealthy merchants and bankers. The other 14 guilds, officially classed as the lesser guilds (*arti minori*), were made up of shopkeepers and skilled artisans. The right to an active role in politics was restricted to members of the guilds, and for nearly all of the Renaissance period, the seven greater guilds held a majority of positions on the councils that governed the city. Perhaps 15 percent of the total population, and a considerably higher proportion of adult male guild members, were eligible to hold public office.

The fact that such an unusually large proportion of the population had some chance of exercising political office may explain why Florence, unlike almost every other Italian commune except **Venice**, retained its republican institutions until its republican constitution was replaced by a duchy imposed by foreign troops in 1532. Excluded from guild membership and hence from politics were inhabitants who did not own businesses or property and supported themselves by working as unskilled laborers. In the 13th century, the guilds still had to share power with a nobility (the *grandi*) whose high social and political rank was based on ownership of landed estates. These nobles, many of whom were Ghibellines, maintained fortified houses and bands of armed retainers, and were notorious for using violence against their social inferiors. The guildsmen's struggle to uphold the city's de facto independence against the Ghibellines was linked to their desire to compel the *grandi* to obey the laws like other citizens.

The middle decades of the 13th century were a violent and unstable period, since both Guelfs and Ghibellines, aided by outside military forces, enjoyed periods of political dominance. In 1267 the Guelfs permanently gained control of the city. They made the Guelf party the only legal political party; they made it a crime for anyone whom the Guelf party declared to be a Ghibelline to hold public office; and they passed laws imposing heavier penalties on nobles who committed crimes of violence than on ordinary citizens. By 1293 the guilds had worked out a series of laws, the Ordinances of Justice, which remained the basis of the republican constitution until the republic itself was suppressed by force in 1532. This republican system put effective control of the government into the hands of the seven wealthy guilds behind a façade of participatory republicanism, while preserving a limited voice for the 14 lesser (but much more populous) guilds. The central institution of government was the *Signoria*, a council that was chosen not by election (which the Florentines regarded as an aristocratic practice) but by drawing lots. The membership of the new *Signoria* was determined by drawing names until the eight district members (the *priori*) and one at-large member (the *gonfaloniere della giustizia*) were selected. The term of office was brief, only two months, and at the next drawing, current members and their close kin were ineligible. Since six groups of nine citizens were selected each year, a large number of male citizens would serve at least once in a lifetime on the *Signoria*.

At most periods, some system was used to ensure that more than half of the *Signoria* came from the seven greater guilds—that is, from the wealthy classes. Various advisory committees and boards advised the *Signoria*, and there were other boards that dealt with executive matters like military preparations and internal security. Continuity was promoted by a staff of civil servants headed by the chancellor of the republic, a position that from the late 14th century usually was awarded to a distinguished humanist. Special boards (*balìe*) were set up whenever need arose—for the administration of a war, for example, or development of a new system of taxation. In very extraordinary circumstances, the *Signoria* might authorize the calling of a *parlamento* or assembly of all citizens (that is, all guild members) which could set up new *balìe*, change or suspend laws, decree the arrest of dangerous persons, or take other actions it deemed necessary. Such assemblies were often prearranged by a group who wanted to seize power and give their actions an aura of legality.

On three occasions, most notably in 1343, wealthy conspirators brought in a foreign mercenary captain and attempted to create a military dictatorship, yet the Florentines loved their republican constitution and on each occasion employed mob violence to thwart these conspiracies. Social tension caused by the mutual suspicions between rich and poor citizens was a constant threat to internal stability. After the failure of the attempt to set up a dictator in 1343, the lesser guilds demanded a change in the balance among the guilds so that their groups, which included far more citizens, would hold a majority on the *Signoria*. A severe economic **depression** at the same time weakened the wealthy classes, and for about 40 years Florence was somewhat more democratic than it had been previously or would be in the future.

The unorganized workers in the textile industry (the ***Ciompi***), afflicted by severe underemployment, agitated for a voice in government. In 1378 a rebellion of the *Ciompi* seized control of the city and forced the ruling groups to agree to organize two additional guilds in order to ensure some political representation of the poorer classes. The workers' reforms also required employers in the textile trades to guarantee at least a minimum quota of cloth production so that there would be jobs for the poor. These successful demands frightened the wealthier classes, who viewed them as an attack on private property, but the middle and lesser guilds were even more frightened than the rich by this bid for power by their social inferiors. Because of these fears, the lesser guilds relaxed their restrictions on the rich, and in 1382 a group of wealthy conspirators brought in a mercenary army, seized control of the city by force, suppressed riots by the *Ciompi*, and abolished the two new guilds of unskilled workers. Within a few years, the greater guilds also changed the laws that had guaranteed a majority on the *Signoria* to the lesser guilds. This marked the end of the period of democratizing reforms. From that time until the abolition of the republican constitution in 1532, the greater guilds once again controlled the *Signoria* and thereby also controlled the city government. The middle and lesser guilds were still guaranteed a minority voice, but the propertyless workers were completely excluded.

After the coup of 1382, power increasingly fell into the hands of a faction of rich clans led by the **Albizzi** family. During the closing years of the 14th century and the first quarter of the 15th century, the success of this oligarchical regime in defending the city from the threat of conquest by the duke of **Milan, Giangaleazzo Visconti**, made their dominance tolerable. They also fulfilled a long-standing goal of Florentine foreign policy by conquering the seaport city of **Pisa** in 1406. But the arrogance of the Albizzi clan was resented, most bitterly of all by the other wealthy families (such as the **Medici**) who were effectively excluded from real power. A humiliating defeat in an unprovoked war intended to annex the independent city of

Lucca in 1429–1433 shook the self-confidence of the rulers, and the Albizzi decided to make a pre-emptive political strike by arresting **Cosimo de'Medici**, head of one of the excluded mercantile families, who had come to be the focal point of hostility to them. He was accused of conspiracy, put on trial, and was fortunate to avoid a death sentence and to be sent into exile instead.

The aristocracy since the 1380s had sustained its political control by devising ways of corrupting the selection of the new *Signoria*. In 1433 the *Signoria* holding office was favorable to the action against Cosimo. But despite the regime's ability to distort the drawing of the *Signoria*, it never had total control. Since each *Signoria* held office for only two months, the degree of Albizzi control varied from term to term. Exactly one year after the action against Cosimo, the lottery produced a new *Signoria* dominated by men who resented the Albizzi and disapproved of the attack on the Medici. This *Signoria* cancelled the sentence of exile, invited Cosimo to return home, and soon exiled the Albizzi.

Cosimo now organized a new ruling faction of anti-Albizzi clans and devised new methods of reducing even further the chances that the lottery for the *Signoria* would bring his family's political rivals back into power. Although Cosimo himself held office only occasionally and carefully avoided the kind of public flaunting of political power that had stirred up resentment against the Albizzi, he manipulated the government from behind the scenes and remained the dominant political force until his death in 1464. The period of Medici dominance (1434–1494), which lasted through the lives of his son Piero and his grandson Lorenzo, was just as oligarchical as Albizzi rule. The Medici were more sensitive to public opinion, less greedy for the trappings and material advantages of political power, and far more successful in maintaining the fiction that the republican constitution was functioning as it had been designed to do. Under Piero and especially under Lorenzo, the family's control became more overt, and after an assassination attempt killed his brother and wounded him, Lorenzo introduced some constitutional changes to solidify Medici control. But the regime remained generally popular and survived until the combination of the French invasion of 1494 and the ineptitude of the new Medici leader, Piero di Lorenzo, produced a popular uprising that drove the Medici into exile.

A twofold attempt to reform the govenment followed the expulsion of the Medici. The revolutionaries abolished a special executive council created by Lorenzo to consolidate his control, and there was pressure from the lesser guilds to end or reduce the dominance of the greater guilds. This reform movement received a peculiar twist because of the emergence of the eloquent revivalist preacher, **Girolamo Savonarola**, a Dominican friar, who favored a popular government and sought to bring about not only political but also moral reform. For most of 1494–1498, he dominated politics though he held no public office. Unfortunately for himself, however, his pro-French foreign policy ran counter to the interests of the worldly Pope **Alexander VI**, who supported his internal opponents and eventually excommunicated him. His enemies were then able to accuse him of heresy and execute him.

The wealthy classes now came forward with a more moderate reform policy, which kept power safely in their own hands but attempted to stabilize government by creating an executive authority stronger than the constantly-changing *Signoria*. While preserving the old system, they had their leader, a patrician named **Piero Soderini**, elected *gonfaloniere della giustizia* (head of the *Signoria*) for life. Soderini tried to make the government somewhat more equitable toward the non-aristocratic classes. He also pursued a pro-French foreign policy that sought to preserve the city's independence. But the defeat of a French army in 1512 made it possible for pro-Medici exiles to bring in Spanish and papal troops, overthrow Soderini's regime, and call the Medici back to power. During the years (1513–1521) when the papacy was held by Pope **Leo X**, a son of Lorenzo de'Medici, the ultimate authority in Florence was the pope. Medici control lasted until 1527, when local republicans took advantage of a war between another Medici pope, **Clement VII**, and the Emperor **Charles V**, and again sent the Medici into exile. But in 1529 Pope Clement restored friendly relations with the emperor. A Spanish army besieged Florence and in 1530 forced it to surrender.

The Medici were restored to power by this foreign intervention. This time they decided to exercise their control openly and directly. In 1532 the pope's nephew Alessandro was declared head of state, and shortly afterwards, the republican constitution was abolished. Under Duke Cosimo I (1537–1574), Florence became the capital of the grand duchy of Tuscany, a medium-sized principality closely linked to Spain. It remained the center of an active literary, intellectual, and artistic life, but the center of late Italian Renaissance culture had shifted to papal **Rome** and to the last great republic left in Italy, Venice.

The importance of Florence in the Renaissance is not primarily in its troubled political experience but in its brilliant cultural achievements. From the period when **Coluccio Salutati** became chancellor of the republic down through the career of the later humanistic chancellor **Leonardo Bruni** and on into the period of Medici dominance, Florence became the liveliest center for the development of Renaissance humanism. Likewise, Florence was a major center for the artistic work of the first great painter associated with the coming Renaissance, **Giotto**, and in the generation of **Filippo Brunelleschi**, **Lorenzo Ghiberti**, **Donatello**, and **Masaccio** in the first half of the 15th century, the city was the principal center for the rise, spread, and maturation of early Renaissance art, culminating in the works of the great artists of the High Renaissance. Cultural historians have often speculated whether the exciting, unstable, and (by Italian standards) relatively popular form of government had any causal effect on the city's vibrant cultural life. Florentines themselves, especially from the time of **Niccolò Machiavelli**, believed that their own political "liberty" was the major cause of their city's greatness.

FLORIO, JOHN (ca. 1553–1625). English author and teacher, best known for his Italian-English dictionary, *A World of Words* (1598) and for his translations, notably the essays of **Michel de Montaigne**. He was born in London to a family of refugee Italian Protestants and developed connections with the literary circle of **Sir Philip Sidney**. After teaching at Oxford, he became tutor in Italian to the wife of King **James I**, Anne of Denmark, and also to the elder son of the king and queen, Henry, prince of Wales.

FONTANA, LAVINIA (1552–1614). Italian painter, a native of **Bologna** and daughter of the painter Prospero Fontana. She has the largest extant body of work by any female artist active before 1700, a considerable achievement for a **woman** who also bore her husband (a minor painter named Paolo Zappi) 11 children. By 1577 she had gained a reputation as a painter of portraits at Bologna, and she also produced many paintings on religious themes. Her altarpiece, *The Holy Family with Sleeping Christ Child* (1589), was produced for the Benedictine monastery linked to the Spanish royal palace, El Escorial, under the patronage of **Philip II**. Her last major commission was a *Martyrdom of St. Stephen* painted at **Rome** for the basilica of S. Paolo fuori le Mure. Other paintings on religious themes include *Noli me tangere* (1581) and *The Vision of St. Hyacinthus* (1600) at S. Sabina in Rome.

FONTE, MODERATA. *Pseudonym*; *see* POZZO, MODESTA.

FRA ANGELICO (Guido di Pietry, ca. 1400–1455). Italian Dominican friar and artist, known especially for the frescoes he painted in 1437–1452 for the monastery of San Marco in **Florence**; the best known part of that cycle is *The Annunciation*. He was noted for his personal piety and for the tender religious spirit and delicate figures of his paintings. His personal style was far more traditional than that of many contemporary artists, continuing the use of gilding and brilliant coloring typical of painters who lived a century earlier. Although most of his paintings were produced for Dominican convents in Tuscany, he worked on a more lavish scale when the **pope** commissioned him to produce paintings for (old) St. Peter's and the Vatican palace in **Rome**. Except for paintings done for the cathedral in Orvieto and a series on the lives of Saints Stephen and Lawrence in the private chapel of Pope **Nicholas V** at the Vatican palace, little of the work he did outside of Florence survives.

FRACASTORO, GIROLAMO (ca. 1478–1553). Italian physician and anatomist. Born into a noble family of Verona, he studied at the **University of Padua**, including not only **Aristotelian** philosophy and medicine but also **classical** Latin language and literature. He also had a strong interest in astronomy and mathematics. He became lecturer in logic at Padua in 1501 and in 1534 retired to his family's country villa, spending his time practicing medicine and studying. He later became official physician to the Council of Trent. His reputation as a scientist rests partly on his lengthy Latin poem *Syphilis sive morbus gallicus / Syphilis or the French Disease* (1530), an early contribution to the literature on the new disease of **syphilis**; the title of his book became the name of the illness. His other major contribution is a study of contagious disease, *De contagione et contagiosis morbis* (1546), in which he tried to classify the ways in which diseases spread. His medical works were critical of the common practice of attributing disease to **occult** qualities.

FRANCIS I (1494–1547). King of France from 1515. His reign is associated with the flowering of Renaissance culture in France. Born to the duke of Angoulême and his wife Louise of Savoy, he and his sister Marguerite (usually known in English as **Margaret of Navarre**) were educated in the new Renaissance learning that was being introduced from Italy. Unlike his intellectual sister, Francis did not pursue learning closely and was more attracted to the usual avocations of the high nobility, sports and hunting. After succeeding his cousin Louis XII in 1515, Francis pursued his hereditary claim to the duchy of **Milan** and reopened the struggle against Spain for hegemony in Italy that filled his reign with costly wars. In the long run, these turned out to the advantage of his rival, the Emperor **Charles V**. From the early 1530s, his government faced the rapid spread of Protestantism in many parts of France, and despite his sympathy for some moderate reform humanists such as **Lefèvre d'Etaples**, he attempted to suppress the new heresy, though with only partial success.

Francis has a reputation as a great patron of Renaissance art and scholarship. He was an active builder of palaces, and his new chateaux in the Loire valley at Amboise, Blois, and Chambord show strong traces of Italian Renaissance architectural influence. In 1519 he invited the elderly **Leonardo da Vinci** to France, where he died in 1521. The ruler later acquired several works of Leonardo, notably the *Mona Lisa*. Francis employed the sculptor **Benvenuto Cellini** and continued to patronize traditional Flemish and French painters, especially for portraits.

Francis was a patron of the new **humanist** learning, making the leading French humanist of his time, **Guillaume Budé**, a member of his household and an adviser on cultural matters. The king acquired a large library, including many **classical** works in **Greek** and Latin. He attempted without success to persuade the greatest humanist of the age, **Erasmus**, to settle in France. Urged on by Budé, he repeatedly promised to found a special college devoted to classical studies, but perhaps because of his costly wars, he took no action to fulfill these promises until 1530, when he agreed to subsidize two lecturers in Greek and two in **Hebrew**, soon supplemented by a lecturer in Latin language and literature and one in mathematics. Although the king provided no institutional framework or facilities for their lectures, these lectureships did encourage the spread of humanism among educated Frenchmen and are conventionally regarded as the origin of the later **Collège Royal**.

FRANCO, VERONICA (1546–1591). Venetian courtesan and poet, the daughter of a procuress and a merchant. Because of her father's ancestry, she had a certain degree of social standing and eventually became a semi-respectable, high-class prostitute in the 1560s, exchanging poems with prominent male poets of her time. She compiled anthologies of their poems and in 1575 published a volume of her own poems, which (contrary to the usual conventions of Italian poetry) are sexually explicit and assert her literary as well as her sexual independence. In 1580 she published a collection of letters, *Lettere familiari a diversi / Familiar Letters to Various Persons*, that reflects the influence of ancient authors like **Cicero** and Seneca. In 1580 she was charged with engaging in **magic**, and though she was acquitted, the accusation damaged her reputation and she died in poverty.

FREQUENS. Decree enacted by the **Council of Constance** in 1417, requiring the **pope** to convene another general council within five years, a second one seven years after the first, and then a council every 10 years. This decree was a deliberate attempt to limit the autocratic power of the popes and to introduce the general council as a representative assembly expressing the general interests of the entire Christian community. It was inspired by the principles of **Conciliarism**. Although the pope elected at Constance, **Martin V**, pledged to observe the decree and did actually summon councils in 1423 and 1431, the papacy remained profoundly hostile to this effort to make the council a permanent element in the constitution of the church. After the failure of the **Council of Basel**, later popes denied the validity of this decree and summoned councils only when they wanted to.

FROBEN, JOHANN (1460–1527). **Basel** printer, head of the great-est northern Renaissance publishing and **printing** firm of the early 16th century, which continued under the direction of his heirs and associates until 1587. Froben was a master printer and successful businessman, not a scholar, but he realized the market value of high-quality **humanistic** publications and made his firm the most respected publisher of **classical** and humanistic books north of the Alps. He learned his trade in Nuremberg but in 1491 moved to Basel and began printing. In 1494 he entered a partnership with Johannes Petri and the leading Basel printer of the preceding generation, **Johannes Amerbach**. After the death of his partners, Froben took full control of the press but brought in as a new partner his father-in-law, the bookseller Wolfgang Lachner, who was an astute busi-nessman and looked after the commercial side of the business while Froben handled the authors and editors and the process of production.

By 1510 his press had become the center of a large circle of hu-manist scholars, mostly German and Swiss, who wrote and edited texts for publication. Some of these were **Beatus Rhenanus**, **Heinrich Glareanus**, Johannes Oecolampadius, and Conradus Pellicanus, the two latter destined to become important leaders of the early Swiss **Reformation**, but his greatest acquisition was the leading humanist of the century, **Desiderius Erasmus**, who found in the Froben press the ideal outlet for his scholarly publications. From about 1515, Froben became almost the exclusive publisher used by Erasmus. The landmarks of Froben's work as publisher of Erasmus, both first issued in 1516, were the famous **Greek** edition of the New Testament and the collected works of the greatest scholar among the ancient Latin Church Fathers, St. Jerome. In 1521 Erasmus moved from the Netherlands to Basel, where he en-joyed the lively intellectual activity and impressive linguistic skills of the young humanists employed by Froben and found a stimulat-ing milieu in which to work. In large part because of the value (both personal and financial) of Erasmus to the firm, Froben gen-erally avoided the publication of works by **Martin Luther** and other leaders of the Reformation, leaving that lucrative market to other Basel printers. After Froben's death in 1527, the firm contin-ued to flourish under the direction of his son Hieronymus.

FUGGER FAMILY. Mercantile and banking family of Augsburg, noted for their role in financing European governments but also as patrons of art and scholarship. Their rise began in the 14th century with Hans Fugger, a cloth merchant. The true founder of their greatness was Jacob Fugger (1459–1525), who transformed the family from important local businessmen into a major force in European economic and political life. The secret of Jacob's rise to fame was his lending large sums of money to the **Habsburg** dynasty, especially the Emperor **Maximilian I** and his grandson **Charles V**, in order to finance the wars, dynastic marriages, and other political schemes that made the Habsburgs the most powerful rulers in 16th-century Europe. As security for these loans, Fugger received control of valuable mining properties in central Europe, establishing a stranglehold on the mining and processing of silver and copper ore. He also became financial agent for the **popes**, a responsibility that involved the bank in the financial administration of the infamous St. Peter's indulgence of 1517 which evoked criticism of indulgences by **Martin Luther** and thus precipitated the Protestant **Reformation**. As the Habsburgs' dynastic expansion brought the Netherlands, Spain, and southern Italy, as well as Spain's rapidly growing empire in the Americas, under their political control, the Fugger bank, together with some other Augsburg firms, provided loans that made it all possible.

The bank was still rich and powerful under the direction of Jacob's nephew Anton Fugger (1493–1560), but the insatiable demands of the Habsburgs for money and their inability to pay the costs of their empire led to a series of governmental bankruptcies (the first in 1557) that eventually undermined the power of the bank, though members of the family, which had been granted noble status, remained personally wealthy.

The Fugger family were also important patrons of the arts, employing major painters like Hans Burgkmaier, **Hans Holbein**, **Albrecht Dürer**, and **Giulio Romano**. They built chapels for churches, urban and country palaces for the family, and they created the Fuggerei, a community of more than 50 houses designed to provide decent housing for Augsburg workers. Members of the family also became major collectors of ancient coins, bronzes, and marbles, accumulated a major library, and patronized musicians and composers, of whom the most famous was Orlando di Lasso (**Roland de Lassus**).

– G –

GABRIELI FAMILY. Prominent musicians of **Venice**, closely connected with the basilica of St. Mark and distinguished as performers, composers, and teachers. Andrea Gabrieli (ca. 1520–1586) may have begun as a singer at St. Mark's as early as 1536, but the first solidly documented event of his career there is his becoming second organist in 1564; he was promoted to first organist in 1585. Noted for his effort to make music dramatic, Andrea published his first madrigal in 1554. The first published collection devoted exclusively to his work was the *Sacrae Cantiones / Sacred Songs* (1565). He also composed sacred music, including both masses and motets. He provided music for a dramatic presentation of an Italian translation of Sophocles' *Oedipus Rex*, and the republic itself commissioned him to compose music for celebrations of the great naval victory at Lepanto (1571) and for a state visit by King Henry III of France. His most distinguished pupil was his nephew **Giovanni** (1557–1612), who succeeded him as second organist of St. Mark's in 1585 and wrote both sacred and secular music. Giovanni never became first organist and seems to have been recognized as a greater composer than performer. He spent four years (1576–1580) at the court of the duke of Bavaria.

GAFORI, FRANCHINO (1451–1522). Italian priest and composer, influential for his writings on musical theory. His *Practica musicae* (1496) describes current rules for composing and provides useful clues about the time-value of notes in Renaissance performances. His treatise *De harmonia musicorum instrumentorum* (1518) shows that he had Latin translations of **Greek** musical treatises made, so that he was less dependent than earlier theorists on the late-**classical** author Boethius. Gafori was also a prolific composer. In 1484 he became choirmaster in the cathedral at **Milan**, where he spent the rest of his life.

GAGUIN, ROBERT (ca. 1423–1501). French monk, diplomat, and **humanist**, generally considered the leading figure among the first generation of Paris humanists. Born in the Pas-de-Calais and educated at a school of the Trinitarian order, he entered a monastery of that order and in 1457 went to Paris to study at the university. In 1480 he received a doctorate in canon law. From 1463, frequent travel on business for his order, which was active in ransoming captives of the Turks and other prisoners of war, took him to many parts of Europe. In 1473 Gaguin was chosen general of his order. This new prominence and his French patriotism led to frequent service as an ambassador for French kings. He was a close friend of **Guillaume Fichet** and probably was involved in the creation of the first French **printing** press at the University of Paris as well as in bringing the printer **Josse Bade** to Paris.

Gaguin was devoted to the study of **classical** Latin literature and produced French translations of Caesar (1485) and Livy (1493). His literary fame, however, rested mainly on his *Compendium de origine et gestis Francorum / Compendium on the Origins and Deeds of the Franks* (1497). The work was strongly pro-French and aroused criticism in England by **Thomas More**, **John Colet**, and John Skelton. Gaguin was an important influence on the early career of the Dutch humanist **Erasmus**, who at that period was still just an obscure young monk with a taste for Latin literature. Gaguin encouraged Erasmus' classical studies and provided him his first chance to appear in print.

GALILEI, GALILEO (1564–1642). Italian mathematician, astronomer, and physicist, one of the principal figures in the 17th-century reconstruction of physical science. His writings and his work are also important in the development of ideas about scientific method. He was born at **Pisa**, the son of a prominent Florentine musician, **Vincenzo Galilei**. He studied **classical** languages at the monastery of Vallombrosa. In 1581 he matriculated as a medical student at the **University** of Pisa, but he left without a degree in 1585 and worked as a private teacher of mathematics. He was already interested in mathematical and physical science and in 1589 became professor of mathematics at Pisa. In 1592 he accepted a professorship at the **University of Padua**, the Venetian state university, where he spent 18 productive years and wrote on astronomical, physical, and mathematical subjects.

Learning of the invention of the telescope in the Netherlands, in 1609 Galileo designed and built one of his own. The discoveries resulting from his observations were startling, including the existence of mountains on the moon and the satellites of the planet Jupiter. Both of these discoveries contradicted prevailing astronomical theory. His experiments in physics and astronomy at Padua led to his observation of sunspots and discovery of the phases of Venus and his demonstration that Venus rotates around the sun, not the earth, thus providing strong evidence in favor of the heliocentric astronomy of **Copernicus**. He set forth these findings and his discovery of sunspots (another blow to the credibility of traditional astronomy) in his *Sidereus nuncius / The Starry Messenger* (1610).

Galileo's astronomical discoveries attracted the patronage of the grand duke Cosimo II of Tuscany, and in 1610 he left Padua for **Florence** and became mathematician and philosopher to Cosimo. At this point Galileo openly became a supporter of Copernicus. This position aroused opposition from the Dominican friars, who charged that teaching that the sun stood in the center of the universe and the earth moved around it was contrary to the Bible. Under attack from them, he wrote a famous *Letter to the Grand Duchess* (1615) demonstrating that Copernican astronomy was not contrary to Scripture. This letter set forth what came to be an influential conception of the relation between natural science and religious authority.

By 1616, however, the **Inquisition** at **Rome** had declared the idea that the earth moved to be heretical, and Galileo received a formal warning from one of his critics, Cardinal Robert Bellarmine, while officials of the Inquisition stood by to serve an injunction against him if he refused to submit. He did agree never again to teach or defend the forbidden opinion. At this time also, the Congregation of the Index forbade publication of Copernicus' *De revolutionibus* until it was purged of errors (basically, of its author's opinion).

The accession of a new and much friendlier **pope**, Urban VIII, in 1623 encouraged Galileo to dedicate to the pope a work that upheld Galileo's opinion on the orbit of comets, *Il saggiatore / The Assayer*. The pope's gracious acceptance of this dedication encouraged Galileo to continue refining his Copernican ideas. During the rest of the 1620s, he worked on what became his most famous book, *Dialogo sopra i due massimi sistemi del mondo / Dialogues on the Two Chief Systems of the World*. Because of the ban on defenses of Copernican astronomy, he had difficulty getting permission to publish it and eventually had to add a preface and concluding note declaring that the Copernican system was a purely mathematical hypothesis and not a provable scientific conclusion. The book was then licensed and published in 1632.

Pope Urban regarded this publication as a violation of Galileo's promise to write impartially on the Copernican question. The Inquisition prohibited sale and any further publication of the *Dialogues* and summoned Galileo to Rome to answer charges that he had defended Copernicanism even though it had already been condemned. He eventually was compelled to plead guilty to a lesser charge that he had rashly produced a defense of Copernicus without intending to do so. The pope himself insisted that Galileo must be compelled to take an oath declaring that he did not believe in the motion of the earth; he was forced to abjure his former opinion, and he was then sentenced to house arrest for the rest of his life and forbidden ever to write again on Copernicanism.

In the last decade of his life, being confined to his country villa, Galileo shifted his scientific work from astronomy to dynamics. The result was a book, *Discorsi e dimostrazioni matematiche intorno a due nuove scienze / Two New Sciences*, which he smuggled out of Italy to Holland and published at Leiden in 1638. Not until the 19th century did church officials lift the ban on Copernican astronomy, and when a new edition of the Index of Forbidden Books appeared in 1835, Galileo's *Dialogues on the Two Chief Systems of the World* had at last been removed.

GALILEI, VINCENZO (ca. 1520–1591). Though most famous as the father of the astronomer and physicist **Galileo Galilei**, Vincenzo was also a prominent musician, active mainly in **Florence** and noted as a composer, theorist, and performer on the lute. He became involved in a heated controversy with his own teacher, **Gioseffo Zarlino**, over the relation between contemporary music and ancient musical theory.

GALLICANISM. A set of beliefs and practices in the French Catholic Church that conceived the church in France as an autonomous, self-governing branch of the universal church. It acknowledged the nominal supremacy of the **popes** but rejected papal intervention in filling church offices, in taxation of the clergy, and in some questions of religious practice. The widespread charges of corruption in the late medieval church, which popular opinion blamed mainly on the popes, encouraged this resistance to papal meddling in local affairs. Gallican tradition also supported the ideas of **Conciliarism**, which attributed ultimate authority in the church not to the popes but to a general council. Gallicanism was encouraged by the kings of France, who wanted to preserve their control of appointment to valuable church offices. In 1438 the French bishops supported King Charles VII's enactment of the **Pragmatic Sanction of Bourges**, a document defining the legal rights of the autonomous Gallican church.

Although a king of France had issued the Pragmatic Sanction, the kings upheld Gallicanism only when it suited their political purposes. In 1516 the new king, **Francis I,** and a new pope, **Leo X**, negotiated the **Concordat of Bologna**, in which the pope acknowledged some French claims to administrative autonomy. But the Concordat acknowledged the right of the king, rather than the clergy of the diocesan cathedral chapters, to appoint French bishops, subject to confirmation by the pope. The treaty was a betrayal of the principle of an autonomous church, since the independence of the clergy was now threatened not by a distant pope but by a close-at-hand king who exploited his control of church patronage to reward his favorites.

Gallicanism still survived as an ideal, but in reality it had life only when the kings, for reasons of their own, fostered it, as happened when they resisted papal efforts to extend the decrees of the Council of Trent to France or to block royal efforts to end the religious civil wars by granting toleration to the large Protestant minority. Gallicanism remained a force in French society through the 17th and 18th centuries. In general, however, once the kings had gained control of church appointments and properties under the Concordat of Bologna, they preferred to negotiate specific issues directly with the papacy.

GAMA, VASCO DA (ca. 1469–1524). Portuguese explorer, the commander chosen to lead the expedition of 1497–1499 that reached the port of Calicut in India in May 1498 and thus completed Portugal's search for a route to India by way of South Africa. He was a member of an influential aristocratic family. The fact that he rather than the more obscure **Bartolomeu Dias** received the command of the fleet suggests that he had considerable maritime experience, though it is possible that his preferment arose solely from his social rank. Upon his triumphant return home in 1499, he was given many honors, including membership on the royal council, designation as admiral of India, and the rare and extremely exalted rank of count. He also led the fourth Portuguese expedition to India in 1502–1503 and made a third trip in 1524 as viceroy of India, but he died there on Christmas Eve of the same year.

GANSFORT, WESSEL (ca. 1419–1489). Dutch **humanist** and theologian, closely linked to the spiritual movement known as *Devotio Moderna*. A native of Groningen, about 1432 he went to Zwolle, where he lived in a house of the **Brethren of the Common Life**, first as a pupil and later as a teacher, and became a close friend of **Thomas à Kempis**, the probable author of the famous book of meditations, *The Imitation of Christ*. In 1449 he matriculated in the University of Cologne (B.A. 1450, M.A. 1452). He then spent several years travelling, first in Germany, where he associated with other influential scholars, including **Johann Reuchlin** and the theologian Gabriel Biel, and then in Italy, where he lived and studied at **Rome, Venice, and Florence**. He spent most of the years 1458–1470 at Paris, continuing his study of philosophy and theology. In 1475 Gansfort returned to the Netherlands and spent the last years of his life there, frequently as a guest 'of monasteries at Zwolle and Groningen. The latter, a Cistercian convent, was the center for meetings of an informal association of humanists known as the Academy of Aduard, a group that included pioneering northern humanists such as **Rudolf Agricola** and **Alexander Hegius**.

Gansfort's writings include several works on religious meditation, the most influential being *Scala meditationis / Ladder of Meditation*, and he became known (and in the opinion of some contemporaries, dangerous) because of his rejection of medieval **scholastic** theology. His works emphasized the importance of inward, personal devotion expressed in moral action, and he affirmed the central role of the Bible as the source of Christian life and doctrine. Both **Martin Luther** and **Erasmus** later found some similarity between his beliefs and those of Luther. Modern scholars have had difficulty defining the influence of his works on the origin of Protestantism. Several of them were collected and published at **Basel** and Wittenberg in 1522. His treatise on the Eucharist (*De sacramento eucharistiae*) was one of the sources of the rejection of the Catholic doctrine of transubstantiation by later Protestants and influenced the eucharistic doctrine of the reformer of Zürich, **Huldrych Zwingli**.

GARCILASO DE LA VEGA (ca. 1501–1536). Spanish poet and soldier. His literary output was modest in quantity but decisive in establishing an Italianate poetic style modelled on **Petrarch** as the standard of excellence for Spansh poetry of the Golden Age. His literary mentor, the poet **Juan Boscán**, preceded him in the adoption of Petrarchan style and persuaded him to use it. Most of Garcilaso's poems were dedicated to the Duke of Alba, who sheltered him during times of disfavor at court. Garcilaso was of noble birth and spent most of his career not as a poet but as a courtier and soldier in the service of the Emperor **Charles V**. In 1520 he became a member of the king's guard; in 1523 he was made a knight of the aristocratic Order of Santiago; and in 1525 he was married to a lady-in-waiting to the emperor's sister whom the emperor had provided with a rich dowry.

Unlike his brother Pedro, who supported the anti-**Habsburg** Comunero Rebellion in 1521 and was exiled from Spain, Garcilaso supported King Charles against the Comuneros, attended him on his trip to be crowned emperor by the **pope** in 1530, and served in several military expeditions. But he irritated the ruler by remaining in touch with his exiled brother and in 1531 was exiled for attending a wedding of his nephew which the emperor had opposed. He spent this exile in **Naples**, where he deepened his familiarity with Italian poetry and probably produced most of his poems. He eventually won a pardon from the emperor, who made him governor of a castle in Calabria. In his last years, he served on several military expeditions against the Moors and the French, and he died in 1536 from wounds suffered near Marseilles.

GAZA, THEODORE OF (ca. 1415–ca. 1476). Greek **humanist** and author. Born and educated at **Constantinople**, Gaza favored the union of the Latin and Greek churches negotiated at the **Council of Ferrara-Florence** and in 1440 emigrated to Italy, where he found employment as a Greek copyist at **Milan** and then as an assistant teacher at the school of **Vittorino da Feltre** in **Mantua**. In this period he worked to acquire fluency in Latin, the international language of learning in Western Europe. In 1446 he became teacher of **Greek** at the University of **Ferrara** and also studied medicine there. The emigré Greek scholar and cardinal **Johannes Bessarion** helped him win the patronage of Pope **Nicholas V**, who hoped to sponsor the translation of all of Greek literature into Latin. After the **pope's** death in 1455, Gaza continued working as a translator, at **Rome** under the patronage of Bessarion and then at the court of the King of **Naples, Alfonso I**. His most important work as a translator was his new version of works of **Aristotle**, especially the zoological treatises, and of Aristotle's pupil Theophrastus.

Renaissance humanists dissatisfied with the inelegant and sometimes mistranslated medieval versions of Aristotle hailed his new translations and agitated for their use in place of the traditional ones, since they were prepared directly from the Greek. Also important was Gaza's grammar of the Greek language (first printed at **Venice** in 1495). The Dutch humanist **Erasmus** regarded this as the best Greek grammar available and published his own translation of the first two books into Latin (1516). In the philosophical controversies of the later 15th century, Gaza supported the **platonizing** interpretation of Aristotle put forward by his patron Bessarion against the defense of medieval Aristotelianism by his fellow Greek exile **George of Trebizond**. Gaza also translated several ancient Latin authors, notably Caesar and Cicero, into Greek, and wrote several treatises, letters, and orations in both Greek and Latin.

GEBWILER, HIERONYMUS (ca. 1473–1545). Alsatian **humanist** and schoolmaster. Born at Kaysersberg and educated at **Basel** and Paris (B.A. 1493, M.A. 1495), in 1501 he became headmaster of the famous Latin school at Sélestat, where he attracted several pupils who later became influential humanists, including **Beatus Rhenanus, Bonifacius Amerbach** of Basel, and his own eventual successor as headmaster, Johannes Witz (Sapidus). In 1509 he moved to Strasbourg as headmaster of the cathedral school, being determined to make the school into an ideal **classical** Gymnasium. He abandoned the traditional Latin grammar book of the Middle Ages, the *Doctrinale* of Alexander de Villa Dei, and adopted a new humanist grammar by Johannes Cochlaeus. Gebwiler published editions of the Epistles of Horace and comedies of Plautus for use in teaching Latin, as well as an annotated edition of the commentaries on Aristotle's *Physics* by the French humanist **Lefèvre d'Etaples** and an edition of the historical work *De inventoribus rerum / On the Inventors of Things* by the Italian humanist **Polydore Vergil**. He opposed the Protestant **Reformation**, and when the movement won control of Strasbourg in 1525 he left to become director of a school in Haguenau.

GENEVAN ACADEMY. School founded by the city of Geneva in 1559 at the urging of the city's religious leader, **John Calvin**, who had been a young **humanist** before his conversion to Protestantism and remained convinced that a sound humanistic education was the essential foundation for true theology. Modelled on the earlier Protestant school at Strasbourg directed by **Johannes Sturm**, the **Academy** had two sections. The larger part, the "private school, was a secondary academy devoted to the teaching of Latin and **Greek** language and literature and the elements of logic as preparation for **university** study. This branch primarily aimed to meet the needs of sons of local citizens, though it also attracted students from other places.

The second section was the "public school," initially organized as a seminary for the training of Protestant clergy but eventually enriched with faculties of medicine and law, developments that Calvin anticipated but did not live to see. Although this section conferred no formal academic degrees, it functioned as a high-level university and soon attracted Protestant students from all over Europe, thus extending the school's influence (and Calvinist religion) throughout northern Europe, especially to France, where a certificate of attendance at Geneva became the best qualification for appointment as a pastor in the growing number of clandestine Protestant churches. Calvin was able to recruit a brilliant faculty of young scholars, most of them humanists exiled from France, and headed by Theodore Beza, who became Calvin's successor as leader of the Genevan church.

GENTILE DA FABRIANO (ca. 1370–1427). Italian painter, generally regarded as the greatest Italian painter of the late-medieval style known as International Gothic. He worked mainly in **Venice** but also in Siena, Orvieto, **Rome**, and **Florence**. He seems to have been uninfluenced by the new Early Renaissance style being developed in Florence by **Masaccio** at the very time when Gentile was working there on his most famous painting, *The Adoration of the Magi* (1423). The glowing color, lavish draperies, and exquisitely fine detail of this work are reminiscent of the works of the Flemish school, though Gentile executed his painting, an altarpiece, on a monumental scale rather than in the form of manuscript illuminations typical of northern art at the same period. **Jacopo Bellini**, one of the founders of the distinctive Venetian Renaissance style, was his pupil.

GENTILESCHI, ARTEMISIA (1593–1652/3). One of the first female painters since ancient times to attain recognition as an important artist. She was the daughter of a pupil of the artist **Caravaggio** and was born and trained at **Rome**. Her paintings of biblical **women** such as Bathsheba and Judith depict dramatic and often violent scenes and present women as heroic and independent characters. The first of several paintings depicting the murder of Holofernes by Judith (1612–1613) is particularly violent, celebrating the heroine who saved her people by seducing and killing their oppressor. Though trained at Rome, Gentileschi also worked in **Florence** and **Naples** and spent three years in England, where she and her father worked together on commissions from King Charles I. Unlike most early female artists, she was able to attract noble and royal patrons. Modern commentators have attributed some of the violent spirit of her paintings to her rape at age 16 by a painter her father had hired to teach her the art of perspective, an incident that led to a scandalous trial in which the offender was found guilty but got off with a light punishment.

GEORGE OF TREBIZOND (1396–ca. 1472; Latin name, Trapezuntius). **Humanist** and philosopher, born on the island of Crete. He settled in **Venice** in 1416 and initially worked as a **Greek** scribe. His study under the famous schoolmaster **Vittorino da Feltre** gave him a mastery of Latin rare among Greek emigrés, and by 1420 he was appointed to teach Latin grammar at Vicenza. He is now best known for the hostility to the philosophy of **Plato** and the strong defense of **Aristotle** expressed in several works, especially his *Comparatio Platonis et Aristotelis / Comparison of Plato and Aristotle* (1458). This book accused the humanist circle patronized by the Greek-born Platonist Cardinal **Johannes Bessarion** of undermining the foundations of medieval Aristotelian theology. It also attacked the pagan message concealed in the thought of the contemporary Greek Platonist **Georgios Gemistos Pletho** and warned of the danger to orthodoxy if a Platonist like Bessarion were ever elected **pope**. The book precipitated a sharp controversy between defenders of medieval

Aristotelianism and supporters of **Neoplatonism**, and it provoked a strong rebuttal from Bessarion.

Converted from Orthodoxy to Roman Catholicism about 1427, Trebizond conducted his own school at Venice (1428–1436) and published books on rhetoric and logic that established his reputation as a teacher and scholar. The work on logic, *Isagoge dialectica*, was widely used as a textbook in northern Europe during the 16th century. In 1438 he began teaching at the University of **Florence** but soon became an official of the papal curia, which was located in Florence at that period. He ultimately rose to the rank of papal secretary. **Pope Nicholas V** employed him as a translator of Greek patristic and pagan authors; his retranslations from Aristotle became particularly influential. Trebizond's loss of the pope's favor forced him to leave Rome and work for King **Alfonso** of **Naples** (1452–1455), but he resumed his position as papal secretary after Nicholas V's death in 1455 and remained there for the rest of his career except for a brief and unsuccessful tenure as a teacher in Venice and a trip to Constantinople (1465–1466), where he attempted in vain to convert the sultan Muhammad II to Christianity.

GESNER, CONRAD (1516–1565). Swiss scholar who specialized in natural philosophy. Born in Zurich, a godson of the Reformer **Huldrych Zwingli**, he studied theology there and **Hebrew** at Strasbourg, then studied medicine at **Bourges**, Paris, and **Basel**. He worked as professor of **Greek** at the Protestant academy in Lausanne (1537–1540) and obtained his medical doctorate in 1541. Next he studied botany at Montpellier and then settled in Basel to practice medicine, though he continued to travel widely in pursuit of knowledge about plants and animals. Gesner's massive *Historia animalium* (1551–1558) was an influential encyclopedia of knowledge about natural history. Based on his own observations and on information sent by other scholars in response to his inquiries, it challenged the work of the same name by **Aristotle**, which had been the standard authority since ancient times. His book was alphabetical in arrangement and had numerous illustrations. It reflects the author's love of the outdoors and shows some effort to criticize fabulous accounts drawn from ancient authors: he dismissed descriptions of tritons and sirens as fictions but accepted reports of fabulous creatures like the fishman. Gesner carefully cites his sources, either ancient texts or modern descriptions, and differentiates between what he knew from personal observation and what he accepts on the authority of others. He never completed either this work or a parallel study of plants, though his materials for the latter were published by one of his disciples.

GHIBELLINES / GUELFS. Party names of the two rival factions that arose in many Italian **communes** during the wars of the 12th and 13th centuries between the German emperors and the **popes**. The Ghibellines supported the efforts of the emperors of the Hohenstaufen or Waibling dynasty (the word "Ghibellini" is an attempt to render the latter name in Italian) to establish political control of northern and central Italy; the Guelfs were named for the Welf dynasty of Saxon dukes whom the popes favored in an effort to block the consolidation of imperial power in Italy. Most Italian cities were internally divided by this conflict between popes and emperors. The wealthier classes generally feared that the unstable republican constitutions of the communes would lead to political control by the lower classes and hence to attacks on private property. The Guelf families (by no means limited to the poor) generally favored local independence and looked to the popes for support since the papacy had long struggled to block the incorporation of Italy into a powerful imperial monarchy. Within each city, the struggle was nominally over foreign policy—which side in the larger conflict the local government would support—but in fact the division was also influenced by local family rivalries.

Each side when it gained the upper hand employed exile, confiscation of property, execution, and assassination in an effort to destroy its rivals. The 13th century was especially bloody as many cities experienced alternating periods of Guelf and Ghibelline control. Although the great struggle between popes and emperors was largely over with the death of the last powerful medieval emperor, Frederick II, in 1250, the factions long outlived the larger conflict that had produced them. Membership in either the Guelf or the Ghibelline party became a matter of family tradition. Rivalry between Guelfs and Ghibellines was one of the sources of the violent struggles for power that eventually caused most Italian communes to abandon their republican constitutions and accept the rule of a *signore* (dictator) who would suppress internal violence.

The struggle between Ghibellines and Guelfs was especially significant in the political development of **Florence**, one of only two large Italian states that resisted the tendency to accept despotic government. The chaotic experience of mid-13th century, a period marked by foreign intervention, mass exile of defeated factions, and deliberate use of political power to impoverish political rivals, ended in 1267 when, with the aid of French troops, the local Guelfs permanently seized control of the city. The Guelfs destroyed the power of the local Ghibellines by large-scale confiscation of property and imposition of exile. Eventually they adopted a constitution that made it unlawful for any person of Ghibelline political persuasion (essentially, anyone whose ancestors had been Ghibellines) to hold public office. The Guelf political party acted as a sort of shadow government, basing its influence on the party's legal power of declaring individuals or families to be Ghibellines, thus banishing from political activity any politician who seemed to endanger the interests of the wealthy merchant families who dominated both the party and the government.

GHIBERTI, LORENZO (1378–1455). Florentine goldsmith and sculptor, known in his own time for his skill in casting bronze statues. His workshop trained a number of leading younger artists, notably **Donatello** and **Paolo Uccello**. Though trained as a goldsmith, he established his reputation as a sculptor by winning the competition held in 1401–1402 for the design of a set of bronze doors for the north portal of the Florentine baptistery. Upon completion of this massive project in 1424, in 1425 he received the commission for a second set of doors for the east portal. These two sets of doors are among the supreme achievements of Renaissance sculpture. Ghiberti's early work is less aesthetically and technically typical of Renaissance sculpture than the work of his pupil (and later rival) Donatello, yet the baptistery doors reflect his careful study of ancient sculpture. The first set of doors continued the International Gothic style of the late **Middle Ages**, but Ghiberti was sensitive to fashion. Hence the second set, popularly known as "the Gates of Paradise" and completed by 1452, reflects the spirit and techniques of the Early Renaissance style. Ghiberti produced other important bronze statues in **Florence** and Siena. He was fully aware of the implications of the work of **Filippino Brunelleschi**, his principal rival in the competition of 1401–1402, and while Brunelleschi was the inventor of the system of single-point **perspective** that marks the emergence of a fully Renaissance art, Ghiberti mastered and codified its principles in his *Commentarii / Commentaries* (ca. 1450), a pioneering autobiography that discusses both ancient and contemporary art.

GHIRLANDAIO, DOMENICO (ca. 1449–1494). Florentine painter best known for the cycle of fresco paintings executed late in his career in the church of Santa Maria Novella. These frescoes are notable for their portrayal of his contemporaries and for depicting details from ordinary Florentine life. He headed a large workshop with a number of apprentices, of whom the most famous was **Michelangelo**. Ghirlandaio was one of the most popular painters of the last quarter of the 15th century and executed commissons from many wealthy Florentine families.

GIBBONS, ORLANDO (1583–1625). English composer and keyboard artist. Born at Oxford into a family of musicians and reared in Cambridge, where he took a baccalaureate in music in 1606, he received a position in the choir of King's College, Cambridge, in 1596 and became organist in the Chapel Royal in 1605. In 1623 he became organist at Westminster Abbey, providing the music for the funeral of King James VI and composing music for the wedding of the new King Charles I. Gibbons composed a large number of vocal and instrumental secular pieces, but he is best known for his music composed for services of the Anglican Church.

GILBERT, WILLIAM (1540–1603). English scientist, best known for his study of magnetism. In his principal work, *De magnete / On the Magnet* (1600), he contended that the earth itself is a great magnet and attempted to explain the phenomena of astronomy as the effects of magnetism. Educated at Cambridge (B.A. 1564, M.D. 1569), he became a successful medical practitioner in London and served as physician to both Queen **Elizabeth I** and King James I. Gilbert's work involved much carefully recorded experimentation. In both *De magnete* and his second major work, *De mundo / On the World*, he explicitly rejected the scientific authority of **Aristotle**.

GIOLITO PRESS. Venetian publishing firm of the 16th century, active from 1536 to 1606, founded by Giovanni Giolito (d. 1540). Especially in the time of its second director, Gabriele, the firm outstripped competitors because of sensitivity to the changing tastes of consumers and strenuous efforts to keep prices low, symbolized by the adoption of a compact **italic** type font that reduced **printing** costs. The press sought a mass market by concentrating on vernacular publication. Its products included many editions of favorite Italian authors like **Ludovico Ariosto**, **Petrarch**, and **Giovanni Boccaccio**, and such popular contemporary authors as **Pietro Aretino**, **Paolo Giovio**, Ortensio Lando, and Lodovico Domenici. The press also published vernacular histories, sermons, and devotional works. Under the pressure of Counter-**Reformation** Catholicism, in the later 16th century it avoided "dangerous" titles and increased its production of devotional and liturgical books. It also undertook an economy-size series of translations of **Greek** and Latin **classics** into Italian.

GIORGIONE (Giorgio Barbarelli da Castelfranco, 1475–1510). Venetian painter of the late 15th century, especially influential because of his use of oil paint. Details of his life and career, and even the dating of his works, are debated. He seems to have studied at **Venice** under **Giovanni Bellini**. Three works now universally attributed to him are *Boy with an Arrow*, *Three Philosophers in a Landscape*, and *The Tempest*; not quite so securely attributed is the sensuous *Sleeping Venus*. The art historian **Giorgio Vasari** remarked on Giorgione's skill at painting without making a preliminary drawing.

GIOTTO DI BONDONE (ca. 1266–1337). **Florentine** painter, regarded by most subsequent Renaissance artists and critics as the first great figure of "modern" (i.e., Renaissance) art. Although more recent interpreters have reservations about this view because they are aware of the similarities between his work and the medieval style of his immediate predecessors, they concede that in many respects his work points to the principal characteristics of the Renaissance art that developed in the early 15th century. Giotto was immensely famous in his own lifetime, mentioned by authors such as **Dante**, **Petrarch**, and **Boccaccio**. At the peak of his career the republic of Florence named him overseer of the workshop of the city's cathedral, the city's most distinguished artistic appointment, which had previously been held only by architects and sculptors. Later Renaissance historians and artists like **Filippo Villani**, **Lorenzo Ghiberti**, and **Giorgio Vasari** regarded Giotto as the one who replaced what they regarded as the crude "**Greek** style" of the late 13th century with the "modern" style of their own time. Vasari in particular made canonical the opinion that Giotto's work marks the crucial turning-point in the "recovery" of the spirit of ancient art.

Very little is known about Giotto's early life, and even the attribution of some of his famous paintings has been disputed. Nevertheless, he left behind a substantial body of work that is almost certainly his own, as well as other paintings in which the division between the master and his apprentices is not clear. A story told by Ghiberti and Vasari claims that Giotto was a peasant boy whose skill at drawing attracted the attention of the leading Florentine painter of the preceding generation, **Cimabue**, a master who worked in the medieval style known as *maniera greca*; Cimabue persuaded the youth's father to let him become an apprentice, and in time, the pupil outstripped the master. Whether the story is true or not, the influence of Cimabue's *maniera greca* on Giotto's paintings is evident, even though he developed far beyond that style.

Most of Giotto's work is in the form of frescoes, wall-paintings done on wet plaster, though a small number of panel-paintings also survive, including one of his best-known, the *Madonna Enthroned* (ca. 1310). The main body of his work, however, is in two great cycles of fresco paintings. One is a series of 38 scenes from the life of Christ and the Virgin Mary in the Arena Chapel at **Padua**, done about 1306 (the most famous of these is *Christ Entering Jerusalem*). The second is a cycle of scenes from the life of St. Francis painted in the upper church of San Francesco in Assisi. Different historians date this cycle between the 1290s and the 1320s. Perhaps the most famous individual painting from this series is *St. Francis Preaching to the Birds*.

What distinguishes Giotto from the Florentine painters who preceded him, and thus makes him a progenitor of the later Renaissance style, is a series of characteristics markedly different from medieval painting. The first of these is his simplification of traditional scenes—his paintings exclude the extraneous details that tend to clutter the work of late-medieval painters; his scenes concentrate on the essentials and skillfully focus the viewer's attention on a single theme. A second characteristic is what critics have called the "tactile values" of his pictures: the pictorial space and the figures placed within it create an illusion of three-dimensional depth as if the viewer could reach into the picture-space and touch them. Third, his paintings, while not having the sophisticated single-point **perspective** created by **Filippo Brunelleschi** and **Masaccio** a century later, present an illusion of three-dimensionality that gives the figures a rounded, lifelike appearance rarely found in Western painting since ancient times. This third characteristic probably reflects both the artist's familiarity with surviving works of ancient sculpture and painting and with the sculptural work of late-medieval artists like Nicola and Giovanni Pisano.

GIOVANNI DA BOLOGNA (1529–1608). French-born sculptor (originally Jean de Boulogne), a native of Douai who settled in Italy about 1555 and under his italianized name became the leading sculptor working in the **mannerist** style at **Florence** in the closing decades of the 16th century. His best-known work, *The Rape of the Sabine Women* (1583), shows the twisted forms and exaggerated emotionalism that is typical of the mannerist art.

GIOVIO, PAOLO (1483–1552). Italian historian and biographer. Born into the ruling patriciate of Como and educated under the direction of his **humanist** brother Benedetto, he studied at **Padua**, where he took a doctorate in arts and medicine in 1511, and then migrated to **Rome**. There he began as a lecturer on philosophy but soon became personal physician to Cardinal **Giulio de'Medici**, the future Pope **Clement VII**, who made him bishop of Nocera in 1527. His position at the papal curia facilitated his decision to make himself the historian of his own times. His major historical work, *Historiae suae temporis / History of His Own Times* (1550–1552), covered events from 1494 to 1547. Much of this work depends on his own observations and his discussions with contemporary participants. Giovio also wrote biographies of Popes **Leo X** and **Adrian VI** and a number of military figures. Also influential was his *Elogia* (1546, 1551), a collection of gossipy character-sketches of famous people, each accompanied by an engraved portrait of the subject.

GIULIO ROMANO (Giulio Pippi de' Giannuzzi, 1499–1546). Generally regarded as the most important pupil of the painter **Raphael**, he worked under his master's direction on the murals in the Vatican Palace down to Raphael's death in 1520, but from the first painting that he completed on his own, the *Battle of Constantine* (1521), his work moved away from Raphael's strongly **classical** style and expressed the characteristics of the **mannerist** style that became fashionable during the middle decades of the 16th century. In 1524 he left **Rome** to enter the service of **Federico Gonzaga**, marquis of **Mantua**, serving not only as a court painter but also as an architect and head of a busy artistic workshop. His most famous work at Mantua was the design of the Palazzo del Tè (1527–1530), a recreational palace whose architectural details display the artist's mastery of the details of classical style but whose general design displays the irregularities typical of the new mannerist style.

Giulio also gained both fame and notoriety for a set of 16 pornographic drawings done at Rome, showing couples engaged in sexual intercourse in various positions. The drawings circulated privately but were soon published as a set of engravings, leading to imprisonment of the engraver but not the artist. Although the prints were declared illegal, a second edition appeared, this time accompanied by sexually suggestive poems by the Venetian satirist **Pietro Aretino**. These prints had a strong influence on erotic art in the later Renaissance.

GIUNTI PRESS. Italian **printing** and publishing firm, founded at **Venice** in 1489 by Lucantonio Giunti (1457–1538), but brought to prominence by his business partner and brother Filippo (1456–1517), who transferred his shop to **Florence** in 1497. Lucantonio had published liturgical and medical books, but Filippo produced mainly **humanistic** works and editions of **Greek** and Latin **classics**, as well as Italian vernacular authors. His most notable classical publication was the first Greek edition of Plutarch's *Lives* (1517). His branch of the family continued in business until the early 17th century. In addition, his descendants founded presses in Spain and France. The original Venetian branch continued as a separate firm until the middle of the 17th centry, carrying on its original tradition of publishing liturgical, medical, and other professional books.

GLAREANUS, HENRICUS (Heinrich Loriti, 1488–1563). Swiss **humanist** and writer on musical theory. Born near Glarus and educated in both the **scholastic** and humanist traditions at the **University**

of Cologne, he inclined increasingly to the humanist side, sympa-
thizing with **Johann Reuchlin** during his controversy with the
Cologne theologians, being crowned poet laureate by Emperor **Maximilian I** in 1512, and becoming a close friend of the future Protestant Reformer **Huldrych Zwingli**. In 1514 he settled in **Basel**, where
Erasmus hailed him as a leading Swiss humanist. He worked as a
schoolmaster in Basel, Paris, and finally Freiburg-im-Breisgau,
where he moved in 1529 and remained for the rest of his life, holding a professorship of poetry and training a long line of Swiss humanists. A close friend and admirer of Erasmus, he agreed with the
Dutch humanist in rejecting the Protestant **Reformation**.

Glareanus was admired for his Latin poems, his editions and commentaries on **classical** texts (especially works on music, history, and
mathematics), and his geographical books, of which the best known
is his publication of a map of the world in 1510 derived from the cos-
mographer Martin Waldseemüller that shows rather accurately the
contours and place-names of the Atlantic coast of America. He is
most remembered, however, for his publications on musical theory,
Isagoge in musicen (1516) and *Dodecachordon* (1547), in which he
defined 12 rather than the usual eight modes of music and strove to
bring contemporary musical theory and practice into conformity with
classical and early Christian theory. Although he travelled widely,
Glareanus was a patriotic Swiss citizen and sought to enhance the
cultural life of his homeland. He abandoned his youthful plan to become a priest, but as a firmly Catholic layman, after his settlement in
Freiburg he strove to encourage Catholic reform and to strenghen the
Catholic party in Switzerland.

GOES, HUGO VAN DER. *See* VAN DER GOES, HUGO.

GOÏS, DAMIÃO DE (1502–1574). Portuguese **humanist**. Born into a
family of the lower nobility, after his father's death he became a page
at the court of King **Manuel I**. He entered diplomatic service in 1521
and soon became secretary for the Portuguese trading center in
Antwerp. Later he served on an embassy to England. Even as a youth
at the Portuguese court, he had become interested in the diversity of
customs and beliefs of various peoples, attracted particularly by his
contact with an Ethiopian emissary to King Manuel. His residence in
Antwerp, a center for world trade, fostered these interests, and he

made the acquaintance of the humanist and geographer **Cornelius Grapheus**, who assisted him in his study of Latin. Grapheus' sympathy for the **Reformation** did not offend Goïs. During a diplomatic mission to Denmark and Prussia in 1531, he visited Wittenberg and heard **Martin Luther** preach, and he formed a durable friendship with **Philipp Melanchthon**.

Conversations with the exiled Swedish archbishop of Uppsala, Johannes Magnus, aroused Goïs' concern for the sufferings of the Lapps, who refused to become Christians because of mistreatment by their Swedish landlords. On his return from the Baltic region, Goïs completed his first publication (1532), a collection that included a letter of 1514 from the ruler of Ethiopia to King Manuel of Portugal and also Goïs' own tract pleading for more humane treatment of the Lapps. In 1531 he enrolled in the **University of Louvain**. His travels also brought him to Freiburg-im-Breisgau in 1533 to visit **Erasmus**. King John III had decided to appoint Goïs treasurer of the royal commercial center in Lisbon, but he chose to abandon his diplomatic and commercial career and received royal permisson to return to his studies in Louvain. During a second visit to Erasmus in 1534, his open expression of sympathy for some Protestant doctrines aroused hostility in Catholic Freiburg and forced him to depart. His interest in Ethiopian Christians led to publication of *Fides, religio, moresque Aethiopium / The Religion and Customs of the Ethiopians* (1540), which criticized the papacy's refusal to recognize the Christian faith of the Ethiopians. From Freiburg, he moved to Italy in 1534 to continue his study of languages at **Padua**. In memory of Erasmus' death, he published at **Venice** in 1538 a Portuguese translation of one of the humanist's favorite works of Cicero, *De senectute*.

That same year, Goïs returned to Louvain. He participated in the defense of Louvain against French attack in 1542 and was captured and held as a prisoner for more than a year. King John III of Portugal then made him royal archivist (1545), with a commission to write the chronicles of the reigns of kings John II and Manuel I. These vernacular chronicles, published in 1566 and 1567, established his reputation as a historical writer. But a Portuguese **Jesuit** who had heard him mention his good relations with the Lutherans made several efforts to initiate prosecution of Goïs by the **Inquisition**, and in 1572, after the death of his royal patron John III, Goïs was tried and convicted for his contacts with the Wittenberg reformers and with Erasmus. He was imprisoned and died two years later. Goïs was also a talented musician, and a few of his compositions survive.

GÓNGORA y ARGOTE, LUIS DE (1561–1627). One of the major poets of the Golden Age of Spanish literature. His early education was with the **Jesuits**, and at Salamanca he secured broad **classical** education but failed to earn a degree because of his disorderly lifestyle. His father than secured him a benefice in the cathedral at Córdoba. Although his bishop accused him of drunkenness and neglect of his liturgical duties, he achieved a great reputation as a poet. His florid and complex Spanish style, characterized by Latinate grammatical constructions and the introduction of words taken from Latin and **Greek**, founded a tradition in Spanish literature known as Gongorism. In 1617 he was appointed a royal chaplain and moved to Madrid, but the position yielded an inadequate income, and he moved back to Córdoba. There he died in 1627 while at work on an edition of his poems.

Góngora produced poetry in a variety of genres. Most of it received favorable notice, though his attempts at writing drama were failures. His ambition was to reshape Spanish into a literary medium comparable to the classical languages, a goal reflected in the title of his works published shortly after his death, in which he is called "the Spanish Homer." Perhaps his most famous poem is *La fábula de Polifemo y Galatea*, a pastoral based on Ovid's *Metamorphoses*, parodying not only its classical source and the Italian poet **Petrarch** but even Góngora's own style.

GONZAGA DYNASTY. Ruling house of the Italian city of **Mantua** from 1328, first as *signori* (lords) of the city and from 1433 with the more elegant title of marquis, conferred on Ludovico II (1412–1478) by the Holy Roman Emperor Sigismund. By that time, the principality had become a small but relatively powerful state in Lombardy. The most famous member of the dynasty was Francesco II (1466–1519), who became a mercenary captain, or *condottiere*, in the service of the Republic of **Venice** and the **papacy**. His talented wife, **Isabella d'Este**, administered the principality during his many absences. In 1530 the Emperor **Charles V** promoted Federico II (1500–1540) to the rank of duke, but the dynasty and the state were frequently overshadowed by imperial power. After the death of the last direct descendant of the ruling family, Vincenzo II, in 1627, the principality declined, becoming involved in an internal dispute between two branches of the dynasty. In 1707 the last Gonzaga duke, Ferdinando Carlo, was exiled and the duchy reverted to the **Habsburgs** as an imperial fief. During the later 16th century, several members of the family were active in the Catholic reform movement. Elisabetta Gonzaga, a daughter of Federico I, married the duke of **Urbino**, became a notable patron of literature, and appears as the leading figure in the famous book of Renaissance court manners, *The Book of the Courtier*, by the Mantuan **humanist Baldassare Castiglione**.

GOSSAERT, JAN (ca. 1478–ca. 1533; also called Mabuse). Flemish painter. His visit to Italy in 1508 helped to introduce Italian elements into his typically Northern style of painting. **Classical** detail in his paintings *Adam and Eve* and *Neptune and Amphitrite* (both about 1516) reflects this influence, while earlier works like his *Adoration of the Magi* and *The Upright Judges* are done in a more traditional Flemish style.

GOURNAY, MARIE DE (1565–1645). French author and feminist, best known as the protégée of **Michel de Montaigne**, who first met her in 1588 and was so impressed with her intelligence and learning that he regarded her as almost an adoptive daughter. Born into a noble but poor family, she resisted pressure from her mother to abandon her intellectual ambitions and marry. Largely self-taught, Marie mastered Latin language and literature and later studied **Greek**. Her reading of Montaigne's *Essays* was her great source of intellectual awakening. Yet Montaigne's endorsement left her with mixed feelings. She welcomed his interest but nevertheless also felt overshadowed by his fame. One of her principal works, the tragic romance *Le proumenoir de Monsieur de Montaigne / The Promenade of Monsieur Montaigne* (1594), was dedicated to his memory but dealt with the theme of betrayal and male treachery and was written in a genre that he disapproved. In 1595 she published an influential edition of his *Essays*, including a preface that described her own struggle against misogyny. She created an influential literary salon in Paris and continued writing, including explicitly feminist essays such as her work on the equality of men and **women** (1621).

GOZZOLI, BENOZZO (1420–1497). Florentine painter, trained by **Fra Angelico.** His major work, the *Journey of the Magi*, executed about 1460 for **Piero de'Medici,** demonstrates full mastery of the sophisticated **perspective** of mature **Quattrocento** art, but the bright colors, multiplicity of human figures, and elegant courtly mood suggest the influence of the last great representative of the International Gothic painting in Italy, **Gentile da Fabriano.** *The Journey of the Magi* depicts a splendid aristocratic procession in which the artist portrayed not only his patron Piero but also Piero's father Cosimo and his sons Giuliano and Lorenzo; other figures from the Medici circle include Gozzoli himself, **Fra Angelico, Pico della Mirandola,** and **Angelo Poliziano.**

GRAPHEUS, CORNELIUS (ca. 1482–1558). Flemish **humanist,** born at Aalst. Little is known about his education. He studied in Italy and seems to have had an M.A. degree, perhaps from an Italian **university.** In 1515 he settled in Antwerp, married, and by 1520 had become one of the secretaries to the city council. His open sympathy for **Martin Luther** led to his arrest in 1522, and he was compelled to make written and public recantations. After a period in prison, he returned to Antwerp in 1523, first working as a schoolteacher and then in the printing shop of his brother Johannes. In 1540 Grapheus regained his position as town secretary. He had a great contemporary reputation as a Latin poet and was a friend of **Erasmus** and many other Dutch humanists. A number of his Latin publications are historical in nature, describing events in Antwerp, visits by the emperor, and other matters of local interest.

GRATIUS, ORTWIN (d. 1542). Ortwin van Graes was born no later than 1480 at Holtwick in Westphalia, descended from a noble family that had fallen onto hard times. An uncle who was a priest at Deventer paid for his education at the chapter school of St. Lebwin, directed by the famous schoolmaster **Alexander Hegius.** In 1501 he matriculated at the University of Cologne (B.A. 1502, M.A. 1506). In 1507 he became a member of the faculty of arts, where he continued to teach for the rest of his life. About 1512–1514 he was ordained as a priest.

Gratius seems to have remained poor for his whole life, and probably in order to supplement his meager income from teaching, he began working as an editor and proofreader for local publishers, first for Heinrich of Neuss, who printed Gratius' own *Orationes quodlibeticae* (1508) and *In laudem divi Swiberti epigrammata*. In 1509 he moved to the Quentel press, where he edited a number of **humanist** works and **classical** texts, including Cicero's *De officiis* with the commentaries of **Erasmus**. Gratius is best classified as a rather conservative humanist, with a genuine sympathy for moderate church reform. His late work *Fasciculus rerum expetendarum ac fugiendarum / Collection of Things to Be Sought and to Be Avoided* (1535) endorsed a program of moderate Catholic reform explicitly conceived in the spirit of Erasmus.

His undeserved reputation as a foe of humanistic studies is a result of his support of the attack by the converted **Jew** Johann Pfefferkorn and the Cologne theologians on the famous humanist **Johann Reuchlin**. An earlier quarrel with the humanist **Hermann von dem Busche** over Busche's use of an elementary Latin grammar for teaching at the **University** of Cologne was probably more important than his editorial work in support of Pfefferkorn in Gratius' being selected by the authors of the *Letters of Obscure Men* as the butt of most of the scurrilous humor in their pro-Reuchlin satire. This satire demolished Gratius' standing as a respectable scholar and unfairly gave him a reputation for being an ultra-convervative obscurantist. His two attempts to defend himself, *Lamentationes obscurorum virorum* and *Epistola apologetica* (both published in 1518), failed to restore his good name among humanist scholars.

GREEK LANGUAGE AND LITERATURE. Although occasional individuals in medieval Western Europe knew some Greek, for the most part that language and the extensive literature written in it (Christian as well as pagan) were inaccessible to Western scholars from late Roman times until the end of the 14th century. Very few Greek philosophical works were available in Latin until the wave of translations of philosophy and science, mainly works of **Aristotle**, that occurred in the late 12th and early 13th centuries. Nearly all of those translations originated in regions recently reconquered from Islamic rule, such as Sicily and Spain, and the majority of the new Latin versions rested not on the original Greek but on Arabic translations made several centuries earlier. Not even the Latin crusaders' conquest of **Constantinople** in 1204 and the subsequent rule of the Byzantine capital by puppet governments backed by the crusaders and their Venetian allies was sufficient to stimulate Western scholars to learn Greek and investigate either Greek **classical** literature or the Greek Church Fathers. The earlier stages of the classical revival in northern Italy during the 13th and 14th centuries focused solely on Latin language and Latin literature.

The most learned **humanists**, such as **Petrarch**, realized that the Roman authors had admired and imitated earlier Greek literature. Petrarch had a manuscript of the most famous work of ancient Greek poetry, Homer's *Iliad*, but he could not read it. Despite his efforts, he never learned to read the language. His Florentine contemporary **Boccaccio** arranged for a Calabrian, Leontius Pilatus, to come to **Florence** and teach Greek, but Pilatus was not a very assiduous teacher, and his students gained only a smattering of the language. The possibilities of mastering Greek were very limited. Greek manuscripts were rare, books of Greek grammar written for Latin-speakers even rarer, and the reference aids that modern students of language take for granted (bilingual dictionaries, tables of verb forms, bilingual texts) were virtually nonexistent.

The leading successor to Petrarch's interests, the Florentine chancellor **Coluccio Salutati**, was convinced that adequate understanding of the Latin classics was impossible without access to their Greek sources. He prevailed on the city government to hire a distinguished scholar from **Constantinople, Manuel Chrysoloras**, to introduce regular instruction in Greek. Chrysoloras was a skilled teacher and (perhaps even more important) sufficiently fluent in Latin that he could communicate effectively with his Italian pupils. He arrived in Florence in 1397 and taught there for three years; then he taught at both **Milan** and Pavia before returning to Constantinople in 1403. By the time of his departure, he had laid the foundations needed to make competent instruction in Greek language and literature permanently available in the Latin West—first in Florence, but eventually in a number of Italian cities. His own merits as a teacher were one cause for his remarkable success. Even more important was the growing realization among leading humanists that without Greek, their scholarship on Latin classical literature was crippled.

News of Chrysoloras' arrival caught the attention of younger humanists, many of whom set aside other activities in order to seize the opportunity to learn Greek. **Pier Paolo Vergerio** resigned his professorship of logic at **Padua** to study under Chrysoloras. **Leonardo Bruni** abandoned the study of law. Other humanists, such as **Guarino da Verona** and **Francesco Filelfo**, even followed Chrysoloras back to Constantinople in order to perfect their mastery of the language, acquire manuscripts, and familiarize themselves with the Greek literary works referred to by their favorite Latin authors. These new Hellenists felt honor-bound to put their new skills to work by creating Latin translations of Greek works hitherto known only by title and occasional excerpts in Latin authors. This process of translation continued through the 15th and 16th centuries. In addition, some Greek authors whose works had been available in Latin during the **Middle Ages**, such as Aristotle, were now retranslated directly from Greek. Leonardo Bruni produced a number of influential translations. Both Vergerio and Guarino became famous schoolmasters and established regular instruction in Greek as an integral part of the curriculum for the better sort of Latin grammar-schools.

During the first half of the 15th century—and well before the fall of Constantinople to the Turks in 1453—a substantial number of Byzantine scholars followed Chrysoloras' path to the Latin West, seeking to better their personal fortunes by catering to the growing interest in Greek. Thus the fall of Constantinople was by no means the beginning of access to Greek language and literature by Westerners. By 1500 Italy had become well supplied with competent Hellenists, not only Greekborn ones but also native Italians. Only a few Italian humanists could read Greek with great ease, however, and even fewer could write it well, but the new translations into Latin made the treasures of Greek literature lastingly accessible to Western scholars. This acquisition of ancient Greek literature was one of the permanent contributions of the Renaissance to the civilization of Western Europe. During the 16th century, the spread of interest in humanistic learning north of the Alps produced a similar wave of enthusiasm for Greek studies there.

GROCYN, WILLIAM (ca. 1446–1519). English **humanist**. Educated at New College, Oxford, where he matriculated in 1481, he became reader in divinity at Magdalen College. In 1488 he went to Italy for further education, studying Greek at **Florence** and **Rome** under **Angelo Poliziano** and Demetrios Chalcondylas. Ordained as a priest after his return, he taught **Greek** at Exeter College, Oxford, becoming the first person in England to teach that language publicly (as distinguished from private tutoring). He was a friend of both **Thomas More** and **Erasmus.** At his death, he left a substantial library, but none of his own writings survives.

GROOTE, GEERT. *See DEVOTIO MODERNA.*

GRÜNEWALD, MATTHIAS (d. 1528). German painter, also active as an architect and engineer. Virtually nothing is known about his early life and training. He was probably born in Würzburg, but even this is uncertain. The growing fashion for italianate styles, evident in the work of his contemporary **Albrecht Dürer**, probably explains why this great painter, whose work is clearly Northern rather than Italian in inspiration, was largely overlooked in his own century and virtually forgotten until the 20th century. His earliest identifiable paintings, such as his *Mocking of Christ*, date from about 1504–1506. Between 1508 and 1514 he served as court painter to the archbishop of Mainz. By far his best-known work is the polyptich or altarpiece commissioned for the chapel of a monastery near Isenheim in Alsace, and its most famous segment is a *Crucifixion* scene. Unlike the works of Dürer, Grünewald's paintings do not reflect a direct influence from Italy. They continue many features of Northern art of the 15th century, yet they also show the sophisticated use of perspective, the physical treatment of the human figure, and the simplified, thematically unified composition that are generally taken to be signs of influence from Renaissance Italy.

GUARINI, GUARINO, of Verona (1374–1460). Humanist and educator, best known as the headmaster of a famous humanistic school at the court of the duke of **Ferrara**. Though born into a poor family, he received an excellent Latin education in his native Verona and then at **Padua** and **Venice**. When the Byzantine teacher **Manuel Chrysoloras** passed through Venice in 1403, Guarino followed him to Constantinople and spent five years studying there (1403–1408). After he returned to Italy about 1408, he struggled to establish himself as a teacher in **Florence** or Venice. In 1418 he married a wealthy woman of Verona. With the backing of his wife's family, he opened a successful boarding school in Verona and in 1420 was hired by the city to lecture on rhetoric and newly discovered works of **Cicero**.

In 1429 Guarino accepted an invitation of the ruler of Ferrara to become tutor to the heir to the throne, on condition that the court school also be open to other promising students. His school, which attracted the sons of prominent families from many parts of Italy, was one of the two earliest and most influential humanist schools in Italy; the other was the similar school formed at the court of **Mantua** by **Vittorino da Feltre**. In 1442 Guarino became professor in the revived University of Ferrara, which became a popular place of study for early humanists from Northern Europe. After Guarino's death in 1460, his youngest son, Battista, continued his work in Ferrara. Although Guarino was denounced by some monks for teaching pagan authors, he declared that familiarity with ancient literature was necessary for any person who wanted to understand the works of the ancient Church Fathers.

Because Guarino's mastery of **Greek** was far superior to that of most Italian humanists of his generation, his translations of Greek literary texts, especially Plutarch's *Lives* and Strabo's *Geography*, were of special importance. As a schoolmaster, he regarded fluency in a style of Latin modelled on the language of Cicero as fundamental. His students also read the works of other major Latin authors and received at least some instruction in Greek language and literature. He contended that this kind of literary education would encourage the moral growth of students and hence prepare them to become worthy persons and good citizens. *See also* **CICERONIANISM**.

GUELFS. *See* GHIBELLINES / GUELFS.

GUEVARA, ANTONIO DE (ca. 1480–1545). Spanish author. He was educated at the court of the heir to the Spanish throne and became a Franciscan friar in 1504. He was appointed bishop of Granada in 1529 and in 1537 was moved to the see of Mondoñedo. Despite his monastic vocation, he retained his close ties with the royal court, remaining active in political matters, advising the Spanish military reformer Gonzalo de Córdoba and becoming an outspoken supporter of the new **Habsburg** king, **Charles V**, during the rebellion of the *Comuneros* (1519–1521). Guevara was a famous preacher and in 1521 was appointed court preacher by the emperor. In 1525–1526 he preached to the nominally converted Moriscos of Valencia and Granada. But much of his activity was political; he spent more time at court than in his diocese. In 1535 he accompanied the emperor on his military expedition to Tunis and subsequently on his journey to Italy and France.

Guevara's first major literary work was his *Libro áureo de Marco Aurelio / Golden Book of Marcus Aurelius*, written by 1524 and circulated in manuscript. An unauthorized printed edition appeared in 1528. Closely related was his *Relox de príncipes / Dial of Princes* (1529). Both of these works were didactic and moralizing books written as historical narrative. They blended his own ideas with materials borrowed from **classical antiquity**. His collection of vernacular letters, *Epístolas familiares*, was widely read and was one of the favorite modern books of the French essayist **Montaigne**. His works had a major influence on the development of 16th-century Spanish prose.

GUICCIARDINI, FRANCESCO (1483–1540). Florentine politician, historian, and political theorist. Born into a prominent family, he received a **humanistic** education, studied law at **Ferrara** and **Padua**, and then took up a political career that began with service to the reformed republican regime headed by **Piero Soderini**, which he served as ambassador to King Ferdinand I of Spain. His career survived the overthrow of Soderini and the restoration of the **Medici** to power. He accommodated himself to Medici rule and soon entered the service of the Medici pope, **Leo X**. Under Leo, he served as governor of Modena, where his good sense and firm hand made him an outstanding success. Under the next Medici pope, **Clement VII**, he governed the province of Romagna. He was less successful as an adviser on diplomatic matters, being involved in the pope's ill-starred decision to attempt to expel Spanish power from Italy. During the ensuing war, he was one of the commanders whose actions led to the disastrous Sack of **Rome** by the troops of **Charles V** in 1527. His service to the Medici caused the revolutionary regime that ruled Florence from 1527 to 1530 to banish him and confiscate his property.

When Spanish troops restored the Medici to power, Guicciardini was one of the officials commissioned to punish the leaders of the defeated republican regime. He then served Clement VII as governor of

Bologna. After the pope's death in 1534, he returned to Florence and became an adviser to the first duke of the city, Alessandro de' Medici. When Alessandro was murdered by a conspiracy in favor of his cousin Cosimo, Guicciardini was a leader in arranging the peaceful acceptance of Cosimo as duke but was soon eased out of power. He spent the final three years of his life in retirement, working on his *History of Italy*, which was largely completed by the time of his death, though his heirs delayed publication until 1561 because of the sensitive political issues that it treated.

Both as a historian and as a political theorist, Guicciardini was far less sympathetic to the Florentine republican tradition than his older friend **Niccolò Machiavelli**. His personal preference was for continuation of a republican form of government dominated by the rich rather than for the openly monarchical regime created by the Medici during the 1530s, but he had no sympathy for the radical republicanism of the anti-Medicean party, and both before and after the suppression of the republican constitution, he proved fully willing to serve the Medici. He shared Machiavelli's acceptance of raw power and self-interest as the basis for government, but his thought was less influenced by theoretical considerations and distinctly less open to granting any but the most nominal power to citizens outside the inner circle of wealthy aristocratic families.

Guicciardini's *History of Florence* (written in 1508–1509 but not published until the 19th century) shows that even at the outset of his career he favored a strong ruler who would tie himself closely to the high aristocracy; but the *History of Italy*, as his last work, shows that while his political preferences had remained the same, he had become profoundly pessimistic, lacking even the limited optimism of Machiavelli, though fully sharing his friend's cynicism about human motivation and religion. His other major work, a set of informal *Ricordi* or maxims, confirms the pessimism of his thought. He no longer thought that there was any possibility for Florence to be governed by his own aristocratic class and concluded that it was wiser to accept the city's subordination to despotism than to struggle against the inevitable.

GUILD. An association of merchants or craftsmen in a medieval or Renaissance city, intended to regulate relations among those who practiced the same occupation and to safeguard the common interests of its members and also (in theory) the general interest of the whole community. Guilds developed gradually and spontaneously as industrial production and commerce grew, and they were common by the 11th and 12th centuries. In many towns, the earliest guild was an association of all who traded or produced goods for sale. Since most early medieval towns were ruled by some external authority (a feudal lord, an imperial vicar, or a bishop) who provided few or no services but regarded the townspeople as subject to his laws and taxes, the early guilds acted to provide basic necessities such as fortifications, potable water, and reliable supplies of food. In many places, the guild of merchants gradually became the real local government and struggled—sometimes by paying money and sometimes by force of arms—to reduce or even to eliminate the authority of the overlord. Since the wealthy merchants dominated the guild, the new town governments were also dominated by the rich. In Italy, many local regimes also faced the problem of incorporating the urban nobility, a military caste of owners of landed estates who were not involved in commerce or industry and who often refused to obey the city's laws. The leaders of the guilds (the *popolo*) strove to reduce the privileges of the nobility—above all, to compel them to abandon the practice of enforcing their will by armed force and to demolish their fortified urban houses. These struggles took place in nearly every self-governing Italian **commune** and were especially important in the early history of the republic of **Florence**.

The rise of guilds was important in many parts of Europe, even in regions where cities remained subject to royal authority. Not every large city had guilds. In some places, the rich merchants who dominated local government regarded them as potential sources of political opposition. Nuremberg in Germany, for example, suppressed its guilds in 1349. There, all regulations governing commerce and industrial production came from the city council, and there were no guilds to form and enforce rules of their own. In most cities, however, people engaged in the same trade did develop guilds. In some places, guilds dominated local government. In other places, guilds had little or no political power but were allowed to organize and to regulate their professional activities, always subject to the authority of the city council.

In towns that remained small, all guilds were craft guilds, organizations of self-employed artisans who managed both the production and the retail sale of their own wares — for example, bakers, butchers, and shoemakers. Members of such craft guilds produced exclusively for local consumption. Their rules forbade production by non-members and excluded competing goods imported from outside. They supervised methods of production, hours of labor, maintenance of quality, number of apprentices and journeymen, and prices. The guilds also regulated the training of apprentices and the admission of journeymen, young men who had completed their apprenticeship, to the status of independent masters and members of the guild. By the 15th century, in many guilds the established masters created barriers to attaining master status, both in order to limit competition and in order to maintain a pool of skilled laborers available for hire. In some trades, journeymen who were not sons of established masters might be compelled to remain wage-laborers for their entire lives.

Such craft guilds also developed in the large cities that became centers of international trade, but these cities also developed guilds of merchants who traded outside the city and directed the production of exportable products. Members of such guilds were no longer simple merchants; their guilds were associations of mercantile capitalists. The craft guilds tried to ensure that all members would have relatively equal incomes and standards of living: no one would starve, but no one would be allowed to get more than his fair share of the total business. The merchant-capitalists could never be effectively regulated in this way because their business extended beyond the city's jurisdiction. Particularly in the textile trades of Italy and Flanders, wealthy merchants controlled the market outlets for the products of local craftsmen. Thus the merchant-exporters could control the prices they paid for work by artisans even though in theory the artisans were self-employed craftsmen. City guilds and even city governments often tried to outlaw this tendency of large-scale merchants to evade local regulation and to reduce self-employed artisans to the level of de facto employees, but since the exporters alone had access to the foreign markets, they were immune to local control.

This distinction between the privileged guilds of wealthy businessmen and the humbler craft guilds was highly developed in Florence, where it was built into the political system. The right to participate in politics and to hold public office was limited to members of the 21 officially recognized guilds. But except for about four decades (1343–1382) of democratizing political reforms that ended in a coup d'état by the rich merchants, the seven greater guilds (*arti maggiori*), composed of the international merchants on whose activities the prosperity of the city depended, were guaranteed a majority on the ruling council (*Signoria*) and thus controlled public policy on all issues on which they were agreed. The much more populous 14 middle and lesser guilds (*arti minori*) had some voice on the *Signoria*, but the rich guilds controlled the government. As in nearly all cities that had guilds, the very poorest Florentines, casual wage-laborers who had no skilled trade, owned no property, and had no guild of their own, were totally cut out of political life. The *Ciompi* rebellion of 1378 in Florence was an attempt by these unorganized and unskilled laborers to form guilds and so to gain a voice in local politics, but within four years the rebels had been put down by armed force and had lost all the gains that they made in 1378.

In addition to their economic and political function, guilds were also important in urban religious and social life. Many guilds paid special honors to the patron saint of their craft, maintaining an altar or chapel in one of the parish churches, attending services together on the saint's feast day, and assessing members for the financial support of such communal activities. They required members to attend services on religious feast days and to be present at the funerals of members. They also provided social welfare services for guild members who suffered from disabling illness, for widows and orphans of deceased members, and for other cases of special need among their members.

GUTENBERG, JOHANNES (ca. 1398–1468). Johann Gansfleisch von Gutenberg is usually and probably correctly identified as the inventor of the art of **printing** with movable type. Born at Mainz in western Germany to a socially prominent but impoverished family, in 1534 he moved to Strasbourg after a political upheaval in Mainz exiled his family. At Strasbourg he was enrolled in the **guild** of goldsmiths and no later than 1439 was involved in a lawsuit concerning a secret process of some sort. He seems to have struggled against poverty throughout his life and was repeatedly involved in litigation, usually over business matters but also including a breach-of-promise lawsuit brought by a Strasbourg woman of good family. Sometime between 1444 and 1448, Gutenberg returned to Mainz and resided there until his death.

The exact history of what he did, when he did it, and where he did it is obscured not only by lack of records but also by large numbers of forged documents produced in later centuries. Yet it seems clear that even though other individuals were experimenting along similar lines, Gutenberg was the first to perfect the technology of letterpress printing, and that his membership in the goldsmiths' guild at Strasbourg was related to his early experiments in the casting of metallic type. The early traditions of the printing industry point to him as the true inventor, and works of contemporary historians also attribute the new art to him. He probably invented the alloy of lead, tin, and antimony that was used successfully to cast individual letters that could be used for printing and then be reused repeatedly. He also devised an ink, derived from the oil-based paints used by northern European painters, that would adhere to the metallic letters. At least as important as the type faces and the ink was the organizational method devised for storing the type, setting it by hand and locking the assembled lines into a metallic chase, breaking down and redistributing the metallic letters after use, adapting the existing winepress to the task of printing, and training a whole class of laborers to engage systematically in an industrial process that had never been done before. The development must have involved repeated instances of trial and error, and the experimental nature of the process no doubt explains why Gutenberg repeatedly had difficulty with business partners and investors who expected marketable products far more rapidly than he could produce them.

His principal backer after he returned to Mainz was a wealthy goldsmith, Johann Fust, who provided him large sums of money and in 1455 sued him for failure to produce books by some new technique. Despite his technological competence, Gutenberg remained strapped for cash, and it was his former partner, Fust, associated with his son-in-law Peter Schoeffer, who founded the first financially successful printing firm, using typographical material that must have been provided by Gutenberg. They produced books not only for the local market but also for sale abroad; Fust died in 1466 while on a business trip to Paris, no doubt to market products of the new press. This firm of Fust and Schoeffer remained active into the early 16th century.

The object conventionally identified as "the first printed book" is the so-called Gutenberg Bible, a Latin Vulgate Bible probably printed in 1454–1455 and certainly completed by 1456, when a local illuminator completed decoration of a copy and noted the date on the copy. The first book with a printed date was an elaborate and costly edition of the Psalms produced for liturgical use on order of the archbishop of Mainz, not by Gutenberg but by his former associates, Fust and Schoeffer. It bears the printed date of completion, 14 August 1457. Historians of printing have noted that both of these early volumes were remarkably perfect in form, bearing little evidence of being the product of a new and still experimental technology. The first clearly datable product of the new art was not a book at all but a set of blank forms provided by the clergy to penitents who secured ecclesiastical indulgences in return for contributions for a papal crusade for the reconquest of **Constantinople**, which fell to the **Ottoman Turks** in 1453. These blanks had the name of the purchaser and the date of purchase filled in by pen, and surviving copies bear handwritten dates from 1454 and 1455. There are even earlier fragments of more technologically primitive printing, including a fragment of an astrological calendar for 1448 (hence presumably printed the preceding year) that is technologically much less advanced. The identity of the printer or printers who produced these early fragments is uncertain. *See also* **PRINTING**.

– H –

HABSBURG DYNASTY. Multinational European ruling family, originally regional counts in the duchy of Swabia. Their importance increased greatly when they inherited the frontier mark of Austria in 1246, but their broader importance began with the election of Count Rudolf as Holy Roman Emperor in 1273 at the end of the Interregnum, a period of nearly a quarter-century when no claimant to the imperial throne gained general recognition. By 1273, the actual power of the emperor outside his hereditary principalities was very limited.

As emperor, Rudolf so skillfully exploited the imperial office that the high-ranking nobles who made imperial elections refused to choose another Habsburg.

With one exception, the electors avoided the Habsburgs until 1438, when Albert II became the third Habsburg emperor. When he died after only a year in office, the electors turned to his cousin, Duke Frederick of Styria, whose long reign (1440–1493), though inglorious in many respects, marks the beginning of an incredibly successful series of dynastic marriages that eventually transformed the dynasty into the most powerful ruling family in Europe. Frederick III's son and heir **Maximilian** (emperor, 1493–1519) was wed to the richest heiress of 15th-century Europe, Duchess Mary of **Burgundy**. She had inherited not only the Franche-Comté of Burgundy but also the richest and most economically developed part of northern Europe, the Netherlands. The only child of Mary and Maximilian, Prince Philip (nicknamed "the Handsome"), married Juana, daughter of the first king and queen of a united Spain, **Ferdinand I** and **Isabella**; the eldest son of Philip and Juana in 1516 succeeded his Spanish grandparents as king of Spain, and then in 1519 was elected emperor with the title of **Charles V**. Charles's accession to the imperial throne meant that the Habsburg dynasty now spanned Europe, including Spain (and its dependency the kingdom of **Naples**, plus its emerging colonial empire), the Low Countries (modern Belgium and the Netherlands), the archduchy of Austria, and a large number of other German principalities. This vast Habsburg empire posed an acute threat to other European rulers, especially the kings of France, whose realm was almost entirely surrounded by Habsburg-dominated territories.

The major limitation on Charles V's power was the unwieldiness of the collection of principalities that he had inherited, the difficulty of mobilizing his theoretically vast resources in one place and at one time for decisive action. Charles himself, despite his genuine devotion to duty, found his vast empire burdensome and ultimately frustrating. Long before his abdication in 1555 and retirement in Spain, he arranged that his territories would be divided. The hereditary Habsburg lands in southern Germany and eastern Europe, together with the imperial title, went to his younger brother Ferdinand, while the Spanish throne, along with its attached principalities in Naples and other parts of Italy, and the Burgundian and Netherlandish territories, went to his son, Philip II. This division into a German / Austrian branch and a Spanish branch continued down to the extinction of the direct line of Spanish Habsburgs in 1700.

Long after the Renaissance period, the Habsburgs controlled the imperial title, with one partial exception in the 18th century, until the old empire was abolished by Napoleon in 1806 and the Habsburgs were consoled with the new title of emperors of Austria, a title they held until the monarchy was abolished in 1918 at the end of World War I. In reality, the last Habsburg emperor who conducted a truly imperial policy in Germany was Ferdinand II (1619–1637), whose sponsorship of the Catholic cause during the Thirty Years' War (1618–1648) was in part an attempt to reduce the other German princes to subjection and to revive imperial power in Germany. After the defeat of that effort, the later Habsburgs, first as titular Holy Roman emperors and later as emperors of Austria and kings of Hungary, developed the old archduchy of Austria and the contiguous hereditary provinces into the nucleus of a powerful multi-national state, dominated by ethnic Germans.

Throughout their long history, the Habsburgs were consistent defenders of the Roman Catholic faith, in some cases out of personal devotion but also for political reasons, since their major role in Germany after the **Reformation** was as leader of the portions of the country that had remained Catholic.

HARVEY, WILLIAM (1578–1657). English physician, famous in the history of medicine as the discoverer of the circulation of the blood. His discovery appeared in his principal publication, *De motu cordis / On the Motion of the Heart* (1628). His theory undermined the theoretical foundations of traditional Galenic medicine. He studied medicine at Cambridge and at **Padua** in Italy, the most famous medical school of the Renaissance. He then worked at St. Bartholomew's Hospital in London and also lectured on medicine. Beginning in 1618, he served as royal physician to Kings James I and Charles I.

Observing from animal studies that that the valves in the circulatory system permit the blood to flow in only one direction, he calculated the volume of blood pumped out of the heart at each beat and concluded that the amount of blood passing through the heart was so great that the same blood must circulate repeatedly through the veins and arteries. His work is also important in the field of scientific methodology, for he permitted his quantitative calculations of the volume of blood to overrule the lack of any experimental demonstration of a connecting link between the venous system and the arteries. Not until a generation later, after the invention of the compound microscope, was there experimental confirmation of the blood's circulation when the capillaries linking veins and arteries in the lungs were discovered.

HEBREO, LEONE. *See* LEONE EBREO

HEBREW LANGUAGE. Although the early Christian church accepted the Hebrew scriptures (known to Christians as the Old Testament) as part of its own divine revelation, relatively few early Christian biblical scholars learned Hebrew, and most Christians relied on the ancient **Greek** translation (the Septuagint) used among Greek-speaking **Jews** settled in Egypt. Saint Jerome (ca. 340–420), the reputed author of the standard Latin translation of the whole Bible (the Vulgate), did master Hebrew and consulted both the Hebrew Bible and the Jewish biblical commentators, but after his time, relatively few theologians in the Latin church used either the Hebrew Scriptures or commentaries produced by Jewish scholars. In the 14th century, the Franciscan theologian and biblical commentator Nicholas of Lyra (ca. 1270–1349) learned Hebrew and cited Jewish commentators, but in general, Western theologians worked in isolation from Jewish biblical scholarship and also from the original Hebrew text. This neglect of the language and its literature is especially striking because significant communities of Jews lived in many parts of western Europe. Religious prejudice, not lack of opportunity, was the cause of Christian theologians' ignorance of Hebrew. A rich literature, embracing not only biblical studies and religious tracts but also secular themes and literary genres, flourished within these Jewish communities, especially in Italy, Spain, and Portugal.

By the 15th century, however, as **humanistically** educated Italians were beginning to show interest in the original Greek text of the New Testament, some of them were also attracted to study of the Hebrew Old Testament. Some humanists regarded Hebrew as a third classical language, alongside Greek and Latin. Beginning with **Bologna** in

1460, a few Italian universties founded professorships of Hebrew, positions often filled by former Jews who had been converted to Christianity. **Lorenzo de'Medici**, the political leader of **Florence**, studied Hebrew under a Jewish teacher; and a young Christian scholar, **Giovanni Pico della Mirandola**, took on the task of mastering the Hebrew language and the religious writings of the Jews, both biblical commentary and the mystical texts known as **Cabala**.

As Renaissance learning spread to Northern Europe, interest in Hebrew also grew, though more slowly than interest in Latin and Greek. In the 1490s, the German humanist and lawyer **Johann Reuchlin** visited Italy, became intrigued by the cabalistic books, and learned Hebrew so that he could adapt Jewish mystical writings to his own Christian faith. His interest in Hebrew language and literature became the target for attack by several conservative theologians and members of religious orders. A bitter and disruptive controversy broke out in the second decade of the 16th century between Reuchlin and his critics, the Dominican friars and the theological faculty of the University of Cologne.

Nevertheless, during the second decade of the 16th century, pressure to provide regular **university** instruction in Hebrew and to make mastery of both Greek and Hebrew a standard part of the academic curriculum that prepared students for the study of theology increased. Where the **Reformation** gained the upper hand, study of Hebrew became mandatory for students of theology. Similar progress in regions that remained Catholic was less general, but by the end of the 16th century, at least some Catholic as well as Protestant theologians were well versed in the Hebrew language, the Hebrew Bible, and some parts of Hebrew exegetical and theological literature.

HEGIUS, ALEXANDER (ca. 1433–1498). German **humanist** and schoolmaster, a leader in the introduction of humanistic subjects into the curriculum of the Latin grammar-schools of northwestern Europe. Nothing is known of his early life other than his birth at Heek in Westphalia, but at some point in his career he studied with **Thomas à Kempis**, probable author of the famous devotional book *The Imitation of Christ*. After teaching at Wesel (1469–1474) and at Emmerich, where he studied **Greek** with his friend **Rudolf Agricola**, about 1483 Hegius became headmaster of the highly regarded chapter-school of

St. Lebwin's church at Deventer. His most famous pupil there was the young **Erasmus of Rotterdam**, though it is unlikely that a pupil so young as Erasmus had much direct instruction from the headmaster. Hegius also taught many other well-known German and Dutch humanists, including Johannes Murmellius, Gerard Geldenhouwer, **Ortwin Gratius**, Johann Butzbach, and **Hermann von dem Busche**. Although he was personally close to the spiritual movement known as *Devotio Moderna* and to the local community of the **Brethren of the Common Life**, he remained a layman until near the end of his life.

By later standards Hegius would be regarded as a very conservative educational reformer, but he was critical of the complex medieval handbooks on logic that most humanists disdained. He collaborated with one of his assistants to produce a commentary on the traditional textbook of Latin grammar, the *Doctrinale* of **Alexander de Villa Dei**, attempting to make the old book more effective in the classroom. Hegius also produced a collection of poems and several other short Latin works, most of which were published shortly after his death.

HENRY VII, king of England (Reigned 1485–1509). First king of the **Tudor** dynasty. His military victory over King Richard III brought an end to the 30 years of sporadic civil war known as the **Wars of the Roses**. Henry was a shrewd and calculating politician, skilled at exploiting the traditional powers of the monarch in order to guard against anti-Tudor conspiracies and to keep the higher aristocracy under far closer control than any of his 15th-century predecessors had been able to do. He was also frugal in spending money and notoriously ruthless in exploiting the financial rights of the crown. Hence he placed his new dynasty on a sound financial basis that was one of the principal reasons for its survival.

Henry's reputation for stinginess was reflected in the modest scale on which he acted as patron to the new Renaissance culture. He employed one Italian **humanist** of considerable talent, **Polydore Vergil**, as historiographer and patronized a handful of other humanists, most of them Italian. One or two buildings were built under Italian inspiration, though none of these survives. His most significant surviving architectural monument is the beautiful royal chapel he built at Westminster Abbey, but it was constructed in the traditional English

Gothic style. Henry also extended patronage to a limited number of English scholars, including the vernacular poet John Skelton and the Italian-educated humanist and physician **Thomas Linacre**, who became physician to the king and also tutor to Henry's eldest son Arthur, Prince of Wales.

HENRY VIII, king of England (reigned 1509–1547). Born the second son of **Henry VII**, the younger Henry became heir to the throne when his brother Arthur died. He also was married to Catherine of Aragon, the young widow of his brother, despite church laws forbidding such a marriage. A papal dispensation was secured on the grounds that the marriage of Arthur and Catherine had never been consummated and hence was not a legal impediment. Henry VIII is most famous (or infamous) for his many marriages. Although the first marriage seems to have been reasonably happy, the queen's failure to bear a male heir to the throne gradually made the king discontented. As only the second of the Tudor monarchs, in a nation that had experienced 30 years of dynastic civil war before their accession, Henry was desperate for a male heir. One child of Henry and Catherine survived infancy, the future Queen Mary I, but since no female heir had ever successfully claimed the English throne without a period of civil war, Henry had real cause to seek a divorce (under canon law, essentially an annulment).

The failure of Pope **Clement VII** to approve Henry's petition for a dissolution led first to attempts by Henry to exert pressure on **Rome** and then to a decision to sever all ties between the church in England and the papacy and to make the king himself "under Christ, the head of the church in England." The upshot was the secession of England from obedience to the papacy and the gradual adhesion of the country to the Protestant side in the **Reformation** despite the king's personal preference for the liturgical practices and doctrines of the medieval Catholic church. Despite his own conservatism in religion, Henry VIII became a major figure in the history of the Protestant Reformation.

After the break with Rome, Henry married not just one but a succession of wives. The second of these, Anne Boleyn, disappointed him yet again when she gave birth to another girl, the future Queen **Elizabeth I**. But the king later accused her of adultery, and she was executed. His third wife, Jane Seymour, did give birth to a son, the future King Edward I, but died in childbirth. Two more marriages were also unsuccessful. His sixth wife, a widow named Catherine Parr, outlived him.

Henry was mainly interested in gaining military glory and playing an active role in European politics. The religious changes he introduced were very limited as long as the conservative king himself lived. Although he unwillingly played a major role in the history of the Reformation and willingly tried to play a major role in international diplomacy, his share in the development of Renaissance culture in England was rather limited. **Humanists** like **Erasmus** had expected him to be a patron of the new learning, but Henry soon demonstrated that he was far more interested in politics and war than in humanistic studies or thoroughing reform of the church. During his reign, humanistic studies became increasingly prominent in the universities and the better Latin grammar-schools, but the king did relatively little to foster this development. Several persons close to him, such as the humanists **John Colet** and **Thomas More**, the physician **Thomas Linacre**, **Thomas Cromwell** (his principal adviser during the 1530s), and the royal secretary **Sir Thomas Elyot**, fostered the new learning, but their patronage was their own personal action and did not draw the king into a major role in promoting the Renaissance.

HENRY, PRINCE OF PORTUGAL (1394–1460). Fourth son of King João I of Portugal. In the English-speaking world he is known as "Henry the Navigator," though he ventured to sea only for military expeditions against the Muslim rulers of Morocco. His public career began in 1415 when he accompanied his father on a campaign to conquer the Moroccan port of Ceuta, where the Portuguese established a military outpost. His experience in North Africa convinced him that overland trade routes across the Sahara Desert led to lands of great commercial value. In 1418 Henry became governor of the Algarve, Portugal's southernmost province. He established himself at Sagres on the coast, building a castle, an astronomical observatory, and a chapel. Between 1420 and the 1440s his captains explored and began planting colonies in the offshore Atlantic islands, the Madeiras, the Canaries, and the Azores.

Sometime not long after he settled at Sagres, Henry also began sending ships south along the African coast. In 1434 one of his captains got past Cape Bojador, which seems to have been both a topographical and a psychological barrier to further progress. Once the expeditions reached tropical Africa, there were commercial profits from the trade in gold, ivory, pepper, and slaves to justify the expense and risks of exploration. Henry continued sending his captains farther and farther south until his death in 1460. By that time, exploration of West Africa had become so well established that it continued without his leadership, though more slowly. Only under King João II (1481–1495) was there again an active leadership to promote rapid progress, culminating in the expedition of **Bartolomeu Dias** that in 1488 reached and passed the Cape of Good Hope and the expedition led by **Vasco da Gama** that reached Calicut in India in 1498.

Although historians have speculated about Prince Henry's activities and intentions, relatively little is known for sure. The Portuguese seem to have deliberately kept information about their discoveries secret. Henry gathered mapmakers and geographers at Sagres, and Portuguese shipbuilders developed new types of sailing ships better suited to long voyages far from home. Whether Henry from the very first was seeking a way around Africa into the Indian Ocean remains uncertain. He certainly was interested in colonial trade with West Africa, and even before his death, Portugal had set up fortified trading factories in the region and developed a profitable trade with the Guinea coast. By the end of the 1470s, Spanish interlopers were trying to exploit the same region, and the important fort at Elmina was established in 1482 to keep Spanish traders out of the region. Henry was a deeply religious man, and conversion of the natives to Christianity was among his motives.

HERMETICA / **HERMES TRISMEGISTUS.** A collection of pseudonymous **Greek** treatises, believed during the Renaissance to be a distillation of the learning and religious wisdom of ancient Egypt and attributed to a mythical author named Hermes. Egypt in Hellenistic and Roman times produced a large body of religious and theosophical works and an even greater body of literature dealing with magical and medicinal spells, amulets, and images. Most of these writings were composed in Greek, and they were linked to the Egyptian god Thoth, a deity identified by the syncretistic Greek-speakers with their own deity Hermes. The epithet *trismegistos* ("thrice-greatest") was frequently applied to this deity, and the writings themselves were either attributed to the god himself or believed to be inspired by him. Although actually composed late in the history of ancient Egypt, contemporaneously with the spread of Christianity, they were believed to contain the secret wisdom of the Egyptian priests, whose beliefs and ceremonies were thought to go back to the very beginnings of human civilization. Strictly orthodox Christians opposed this literature as pagan, but some Christians regarded it as true wisdom, providentially designed by God to prepare the world for acceptance of Christianity.

The magical *Hermetica* are usually short texts, often little more than brief incantations. Most of this literature has been lost, but a large body of it still survives in either Arabic or Latin translations. These works were generally feared as having diabolical sources and spiritually dangerous consequences. Far more respectable were the so-called philosophical *Hermetica*, of which 17 treatises (of widely varying philosophical content despite their false attribution to a single author) survive in Greek. One additional Hermetic tract, the *Asclepius*, of which only a few fragments survive in Greek, had already been translated into Latin by the fifth century, and it had been known to some medieval Latin authors. In addition, a collection of excerpts from other treatises that are now lost survived in an anthology compiled in the fifth century by Stobaeus. Most of the philosophical *Hermetica* reflected the influence of **Neoplatonism** on late Egyptian thought, especially in their tendency to denigrate the corporeal aspects of human nature and to glorify the spiritual. Despite their recent origin, they claimed to go back to the very beginnings of human civilization, even to antedate Moses.

The revival of **Greek** studies in 15th-century Italy and the resultant interest in all sorts of Greek literature embraced the *Hermetica*, in large part because the one text already known in Latin, the *Asclepius*, was attractive to spiritually inclined Italian intellectuals who sought ancient religious enlightenment that could be fitted into a Christian world-view. In 1462 **Cosimo de'Medici** provided a Greek manuscript containing 14 of the treatises to his protégé **Marsilio Ficino**, who was already working on his Latin translation of the works of **Plato**. Ficino quickly prepared a Latin translation of these 14 tracts, which he labelled *Pimander* from the title of the first of them. The book was printed in 1471 and frequently reprinted, not only in Italy but also in France, where the influential **humanists** Symphorien

Champier and **Jacques Lefèvre d'Etaples** promoted interest in "Hermes" and published several of the treatises. Their Hermetic themes seemed, at least superficially, to be compatible with Christianity, and the allure of ancient Egyptian wisdom was irresistible. Not until the late Renaissance, in 1614, did the French Protestant humanist **Isaac Casaubon** apply philological criticism to demonstrate irrefutably the late date and questionable authorship of the *Hermetica*. Even after Casaubon, a considerable but diminishing number of European authors still sought spiritual inspiration from the Hermetic treatises.

HESSUS, HELIUS EOBANUS (Eoban Koch, 1488–1540). German Latin poet. Born in Hesse, the son of peasants, he managed to secure an education with the aid of the Cistercian abbot whom his father served. He entered the University of Erfurt in 1504 (B.A. 1506, M.A.1509) and became a leading figure among the young Erfurt disciples of **Mutianus Rufus**. This group agitated for sweeping reform of the university curriculum to replace traditional **scholastic** subjects with **humanistic** ones. Hessus' first significant poetic work, *Bucolicon*, an eclogue, appeared in 1509. His *Heroidum Christianarum epistolae* (1514) published 22 letters by female saints. Between 1509 and 1514 he served as secretary to the bishop of Pomerania and then made brief stays at two universities in eastern Germany, Frankfurt-an-der-Oder and Leipzig, before returning to Erfurt, where he was hailed as Germany's leading Latin poet.

Hessus and his friends became outspoken supporters of the Hebraist **Johann Reuchlin** during the latter's conflict with the Cologne Dominicans. In 1518 Hessus was appointed professor of poetry, and a few months later he led a group of Erfurt **humanists** who travelled to **Louvain** to honor the leading Northern humanist, **Erasmus**. Hessus commemorated this visit in his poem *Hodoeporicon* (1519). His university lectures on the Roman rhetorician Quintilian attracted large numbers of students. When **Martin Luther** passed through Erfurt on his way to the Diet of Worms in April 1521, Hessus greeted him in the name of the university and published a collection of elegies expressing support for him. Hessus remained a supporter of Luther, though this allegiance did not interrupt his friendship with Erasmus even after the later openly opposed Luther.

Since Hessus found that neither his poetry nor his lectures at Erfurt produced much income, in 1523 he began the study of medicine. Although he never completed a degree, his studies did produce a poem on medicine, *Bonae valetudinis conservandae praecepta / Advice for Preserving Good Health* (1524), which was widely read. In 1526 he became a teacher in Nuremberg, where he stayed until 1533. In 1533 he resumed his teaching at Erfurt. Finding the universty in decline, he moved to the new Protestant university at Marburg in 1536 and spent the rest of his life there. His verse paraphrase of the Psalms (1537) was frequently reprinted, and his Latin version of Homer's *Iliad* was published in the year of his death.

HILLIARD, NICHOLAS (1547–1619). English goldsmith and painter of miniatures. As a client of the wealthy Protestant merchant John Bodley, he fled to **Geneva** during the Catholic restoration under Queen Mary I (1553–1558). Under her Protestant successor, **Elizabeth I**, he was active as a court painter, though he spent the late 1570s in Paris in hopes of gaining more income there. He returned to England about 1578. He continued to be active as a painter of portraits and acknowledged the influence of **Albrecht Dürer** and **Hans Holbein the Younger** on his art. Hilliard produced jewelry as well as paintings. Under Elizabeth, he was involved in making the second great seal for the queen, and under James I he received a grant of monopoly to produce, engrave, and print royal portraits.

HOBY, THOMAS (1530–1566). English diplomat. Educated at Cambridge and widely travelled on the Continent, he became known as a master of languages and a translator. In 1566 he became **Elizabeth I's** ambassador to France but died later that same year. His most famous translation was **Baldassare Castiglione's** *Book of the Courtier*, completed in 1552–1553 but not published until 1561.

HOLBEIN, HANS (the Elder, ca. 1460–1534; the Younger, 1497–1543). German painters, both natives of Augsburg. Little is known about the early life of Hans the Elder. His early work was in the late-medieval style prevalent in southern Germany and influenced by **Rogier van der Weyden** and other Netherlandish painters. By about 1500, his sequence of paintings of Christ's Passion for the church of Saints Ulrich and Afra at Augsburg showed signs of Italian Renaissance influence. His best known work, *The Martyrdom of St. Sebastian* (1516), shows a simplification of design that also suggests Italian influence. He trained his sons Ambrosius and Hans as painters. Hans became the most successful member of the family.

Hans the Younger studied with his father until 1516, when he moved to **Basel** as a journeyman employed by the local artist Hans Herbst. In 1519 he was received into the Basel **guild** of painters. He illustrated several books for the printer **Johann Froben**, who recommended him to his leading author, **Erasmus**. Erasmus commissioned portraits of himself to be sent as gifts to friends and patrons, including William Warham, archbishop of Canterbury. In 1524 Holbein visited the French court, where he was exposed to the works of **Leonardo da Vinci**. He spent the years 1526–1528 in England, warmly recommended by Erasmus and employed by **Thomas More** and other English courtiers for portraits. His return to Basel in 1529 coincided with the political victory of Protestantism, and he felt torn between producing conventional Catholic religious paintings and producing woodcut illustrations for anti-Catholic tracts. His earlier trip to England may have been intended to test the market for his services there, and in 1532 he returned to London. A notable work of this period was *The Ambassadors* (1533), depicting two French ambassadors to England. From 1532 to 1538 Holbein was official painter to King **Henry VIII**, and his portrait of Henry himself (1536) is the most widely known image of the English monarch. He also designed title pages of books and jewelry for the court and was active as a portrait painter.

HOWARD, HENRY, EARL OF SURREY (ca. 1517–1547). English poet, associated with his friend **Sir Thomas Wyatt** (1503–1542) in the introduction of the sonnet, a form developed in Italy during the 13th century and perfected in the works of **Petrarch**, into English poetry. Wyatt became familiar with the sonnet during travels in France and Italy in 1526–1527 and used the genre in his own writing, beginning with a free translation of many of Petrarch's *Rime* into English sonnets. He introduced a characteristic English modification into the rhyming scheme of the sestet (the last six lines) of the fourteen-line sonnet. He also produced poetry in such forms as the satire and

the rondeau. Surrey adopted the sonnet and is usually credited with perfecting it. The work of both Wyatt and Surrey, together with that of several contemporaries, was included in an influential collection published in 1557 by Richard Tottel under the title *Songes and Sonettes* but usually known as *Tottel's Miscellany*. The first 32 pages of the collection presented Surrey's poems. This publication established both the reputation of the author and the popularity of the sonnet form in England. Surrey is also famous for his translation of portions of Vergil's *Aeneid* into English blank verse (first edition ca. 1554), both because his translation itself was greatly admired and because he seems to have originated the use of blank verse (that is, omitting the use of rhyme, as in **classical** poetry) in English. Surrey had the ill fortune to be the son of the Duke of Norfolk, the leading conservative nobleman under **Henry VIII** and a determined opponent of the king's religious policy. In 1547 Surrey was arrested on patently specious charges of high treason, condemned, and beheaded at the age of 30.

HUMANISM/HUMANIST. Humanism was the principal intellectual movement of the European Renaissance; a humanist was a teacher or follower of humanism. In the simplest sense, the term "humanism" implies that a certain group of school subjects known since ancient times as the *studia humanitatis* (humanistic studies) provides the best preparation for life and should become the central focus for the education of the ruling classes. The American scholar Paul Oskar Kristeller, who developed this definition of humanism, defined these "humanistic studies" as five: grammar (that is, the grammar of Latin, the language of education), rhetoric (the study of the art of effective communication and persuasion, both written and oral), moral philosophy (the art of making responsible choices in everyday life), poetry (which implied the reading of ancient literature), and history (regarded as a source of examples showing the consequences of moral choices).

The "humanists" regarded these subjects (especially the first three) as the studies most practical for real life, contrasting them with the more theoretical subjects that had received greatest emphasis in medieval grammar schools and **universities**, such as logic, metaphysics, and natural science, subjects that dealt with abstract and theoretical issues rather than the issues faced daily by the ruling classes of the Italian cities. Humanists took as their immediate goal the revival of the **classical** Latin and **Greek** languages and literatures, but this goal was intimately linked with the broader purpose of transforming all aspects of European civilization along lines inspired by study of ancient literature, in other words, the goal of bringing about a cultural renaissance or rebirth.

Some recent scholars have associated the origins of this classicizing intellectual movement with the emergence of self-governing urban republics in northern and central Italy in the late **Middle Ages**. Leading citizens of these republics found that the older medieval culture, attuned to a society dominated by clergy and aristocratic warriors, did not meet the needs of a rapidly developing urban milieu. Initially, the higher culture of the Italian cities was dominated by men trained in law and the art of *dictamen*, the composition of formal Latin letters, orations, and documents needed for political, diplomatic, legal, and commercial life. But by the end of the 13th century, there was a new interest in ancient Latin literature and a desire to create a modern Latin literature modelled on the heritage of ancient **Rome**. This interest in the classics spread from poetry to various prose genres, and by the end of the 14th century, humanism had come to imply a reorientation of pre-university education in order to emphasize the *studia humanitatis*. Student slang called teachers of these subjects *humanistae* (humanists), but the term also covers people of many professions who shared the enthusiasm for ancient languages and literatures. The abstract noun, "humanism," was a coinage of a much later period, originating in early 19th-century Germany, but the terms "humanist" and "humanistic studies" have their roots in the language and life of the Renaissance itself.

Sometimes, notably among humanists living in the republic of **Florence** and inspired by the humanist chancellors **Coluccio Salutati** and **Leonardo Bruni**, humanism was linked to the aristocratic republican ideology of **Cicero** and other leaders of the ancient Roman Republic. The example of Roman ideals of citizenship was used to inspire Florentine resistance to threats to the city's independence by the **Visconti** dukes of **Milan**. Some modern scholars have defined a subtype, "civic humanism," and contend that there was an undercurrent of hostility to monarchy and at least a latent preference for republican forms of government inherent in the admiration for Cicero and republican Rome shared by all humanists. The thought of Salutati, Bruni, and **Niccolò Machiavelli** does display some evidence of republican political ideology. In general, however, humanism seems to have been neutral on the relative merits of republicanism and monarchy. The ideal of humanist education as the best preparation of young men for political duty was easily adapted to the politics and court life of the monarchical regimes that prevailed in most Italian cities and in virtually all of transalpine Europe. The well-educated humanist could become the adviser to a prince just as well as he could be the active citizen of a republic. In either case, however, the excellence of humanistic education as useful preparation for public service could be upheld.

In any case, the educational goals of humanistic education were clearly secular, intended to prepare boys from the urban elites to take their proper role in society. This secular orientation caused later scholars of Renaissance civilization to define humanism as a non-religious or even anti-religious philosophy of life that viewed a fulfilling earthly life as the goal of human activity and either rejected religion entirely or marginalized it as a set of rituals and superstitions that fostered the maintenance of social order. This definition of humanism as a secular philosophy of life is implied in the work of the most influential historian of the Italian Renaissance, Jacob Burckhardt, but it is essentially a product of Enlightenment and 19th-century thought and has little following among recent historians of humanism.

From the end of the 14th century, humanistic culture was enriched by a growing interest in Greek language and literature. Renaissance humanists enthusiastically hunted for surviving works of ancient literature that had been unknown to educated people of the Middle Ages. After the 1450s, the new art of **printing** contributed greatly to the diffusion and development of humanistic culture. During the 15th and 16th centuries, humanists developed sophisticated techniques of textual, linguistic, and historical criticism that often challenged medieval beliefs and practices. Thus humanism came to imply certain assumptions about intellectual method that, while not constituting a formal system of philosophy capable of replacing medieval **scholasticism**, tended to erode confidence in traditional learning and exercised a generally solvent effect on established systems of belief.

As humanism spread into northern Europe during the late 15th and early 16th centuries, humanists like **Lefèvre d'Etaples** and **Erasmus** extended their scholarly interests to embrace study of the documents of ancient Christian religion, giving rise to a movement sometimes called "Christian humanism" or "biblical humanism." This humanism aspired to apply knowledge about both pagan and Christian **antiquity** to produce a general reform and renewal of the church and Christian spirituality. "Christian humanism" was closely linked to the origins of the Protestant **Reformation**, which split the humanists into Protestant and Catholic camps but did not destroy the dominance of humanistic subjects and classical learning over the education of European elites. *See also* SCRIPT, HUMANISTIC.

HUNDRED YEARS' WAR. Series of wars between France and England that began with the decision of King Edward III of England to invade France in 1337 and lasted sporadically until 1453, when the French finally drove the English armies from French soil. The war fell into three main periods: a period of active fighting from 1337 down to a truce signed in 1360, a period of relatively little military action, interrupted only by occasional raids, from 1360 to 1415, and a final determined effort of the English under King Henry V to either conquer all of France or divide it with their ally the duke of **Burgundy**, a phase in which France was pushed to the very brink of defeat. This war is conventionally defined as part of medieval rather than Renaissance history, but its course coincided with the rise of Renaissance civilization in Italy.

The causes that produced war were essentially medieval: the awkward feudal relationship between the kings of England (who held many feudal principalities, including all of the great duchy of Guienne, as fiefs under the suzerainty of the king of France) and the kings of France, who longed to end the anomalous situation in which the English king controlled more French territory than did the French king himself. Because of frequent intermarriages between royal families, Edward III regarded himself rather than Philip VI as the rightful heir to the French throne. Although Edward's claim to the French throne was useful mainly as a device to attract allies among dissident French nobles, this dynastic issue was another product of medieval conditions, and in the final phase of the war, Henry V (unlike Edward

III) seems to have intended to enforce his right to the French throne and to have had a systematic military plan to conquer northern and central France city by city and establish himself as king.

The war was fought with the military organization and methods typical of the later Middle Ages, and while the use of artillery during the siege of cities in the final phase of the war does represent the beginning of a shift toward modern military technology, the many English victories resulted mainly from their effective use of archery and their adoption of tactics suited to exploit the use of archers in the face of the traditional French reliance on heavy cavalry.

The war affected Renaissance Italy most decisively near its beginning, when the inability of Edward III to repay the enormous loans he had received from Italian banking firms to finance his war precipitated a severe financial crisis in the commercial cities of northern and central Italy (*see* DEPRESSION, ECONOMIC).

France suffered terrible losses of life and property during all periods of active fighting and even during times of truce, since discharged mercenary soldiers continued to ravage the countryside as brigands. England, which held the military upper hand in the opening phases of the conflict, eventually also suffered financial and political exhaustion. In terms of Renaissance culture, the damage inflicted on France seems to have retarded a growing interest in ancient **classical** civilization that was evident during the early 14th century. Only after the invaders had been ejected in 1453 was France able to resume these interests. Thus the timing of the spread of Renaissance culture into France was affected by the war.

HUSS, JOHN (Jan Hus, ca. 1370–1415). Bohemian priest and religious reformer, educated at the University of Prague and in 1402 appointed preacher in the Bethlehem Chapel in Prague. He became an extremely popular preacher, highly critical of the worldliness and corrupt lives of the clergy. Huss also became interested in the theology of the English heretic **John Wyclif**, whose ideas had spread among some Czech theologians. His surviving sermons, however, are dominated by concern for moral reform and do not uphold the doctrines for which Wyclif had been condemned. His influence rested in part on resentment by ethnic Czechs against the traditional dominance of the national church by the large German minority.

Huss' agitation for reform of the church eventually led the Archbishop of Prague to try to silence his sermons. His defiance of this attempt was backed by mobs of supporters. In 1409 the king transferred control of the local university from the German scholars, who had traditionally been dominant, to the Czechs. Most of the Germans soon left for Leipzig, where they founded a new university, and Huss himself was elected rector of the Czech university. The claim of his opponents that he was a follower of the doctrines of Wyclif (whose works had been condemned in 1403) was at best an exaggeration, though books written by Wyclif were circulating among Czech theologians. But Huss did protest against the burning of Wyclif's books and as a result was excommunicated. He appealed first to the **Roman** curia and then to the authority of Christ, but he was never in personal danger, since not only the king but also the overwhelming majority of the Czech-speaking population supported him.

In 1412, when Pope John XXIII proclaimed an indulgence to raise money for his war against the king of **Naples**, Huss denounced the indulgence as a perversion of the crusade. The **pope** responded by laying Prague under an interdict as long as Huss was allowed to live there. Huss relieved the city of this burden by leaving for a self-imposed exile in the countryside, where he wrote several treatises dealing with simony, clerical immorality, and the authority of the church hierarchy but also spread his ideas among the rural population. In 1414 the **Council of Constance**, assembled to end the **Western Schism**, invited him to appear and explain his position. Although the Holy Roman Emperor promised him safe conduct, once he arrived in Constance, the council declared that promises made to heretics were not binding. Huss was imprisoned, faced with demands to recant his teachings, and upon his refusal to accept the accuracy of the supposedly Wycliffite passages extracted from his books, was burned at the stake.

News of the execution of Huss led to a national uprising of the Czech people. Efforts of the local hierarchy to use force against his followers were resoundingly defeated, and when later popes attempted to mount crusades against the **Hussites**, the crusading armies were crushed.

HUSSITES. Followers of the Bohemian (Czech) religious reformer **John Huss**. After his betrayal and execution as a heretic by the

Council of Constance in 1415, his followers rose up against the church. Angry crowds attacked churches and convents; priests and monks were massacred; and officials of King Wenceslaus who tried to arrest Hussite leaders for heresy were killed by mobs. When the new king, the Emperor Sigismund, tried to take possession of Prague with the aid of a German army in 1420, an army of radical peasants defeated his army and forced him to flee.

Under the pressure of external attack, the Hussite movement split into two factions. The more moderate group, the Utraquists, constituted chiefly by the middle and upper classes, set limited goals, reflecting their understanding of the actual teachings of Huss. They demanded little more than the repression of blatant corruption in the church and the administration of communion to the laity in both kinds (*sub utraque specie*). The latter demand came to be the symbolic marker of their movement. The more radical faction was known as the **Taborites**, recruited mainly from the poorer classes and named from the town of Tabor in southern Bohemia. They demanded a drastic restructuring of the Bohemian church that would subject the clergy to secular law and authorize the confiscation of church property. They rejected any belief or practice not literally commanded in the New Testament; they recognized only two sacraments, baptism and communion; they elected their own bishops and priests and permitted laymen as well as clergy to preach. They rejected belief in purgatory, opposed indulgences and prayers for the dead, repudiated veneration of saints, and destroyed pictures and statues in churches. They also provided the most fervent soldiers for the national army commanded by an experienced Czech soldier, Jan Zizka.

Thus Bohemia became bitterly divided into three groups, those who wanted to restore medieval Catholicism, those who wanted some limited reforms and the granting of communion in both kinds to the laity (the Utraquists), and the Taborites. In effect, the Taborites demanded a social revolution as well as sweeping ecclesiastical reforms. Civil war among these factions became endemic for almost 20 years, complicated by repeated efforts by imperial officials and papal legates to invade the country and restore Catholic orthodoxy by force. The Taborite-dominated armies repeatedly defeated these mainly German invaders. The last crusade, led in 1431 by Cardinal Giuliano Cesarini, ended in humiliating defeat. Eventually, in 1433 and 1434, the Utraquists, who were more numerous, overwhelmed the Taborite army and entered into negotiations with King Sigismund which in 1436 produced the *Compactata* (Compacts of Prague) that guaranteed religious tolerance to both Utraquists and Catholics. The **papacy** never regarded the emperor's concessions as lawful, but in effect the treaty made Bohemia the first European nation in which the religious unity of medieval Christendom came to an end. The Utraquists remained a large and legally recognized religious group into the age of the **Reformation**, and the defeated Taborites survived as small sectarian groups that re-emerged as radical Protestants in the 16th century.

HUTTEN, ULRICH VON (1488–1523). German **humanist** and Latin poet. Born into a family of imperial knights, Hutten was educated at the Benedictine abbey of Fulda and intended for a monastic career. In 1505 he fled from the monastery and spent several years engaged in humanistic studies at several German universities, eventually receiving a bachelor of arts degree from the University of Frankfurt an der Oder. His *De arte versificandi / On the Art of Writing Poetry* (1511) demonstrated his mastery of ancient Latin prosody and was frequently reprinted. Moving to Vienna in 1511, Hutten came under the influence of the patriotic humanists patronized by the Emperor **Maximilian I**. This contact aroused his interest in politics and transformed him into a literary partisan of Maximilian against his foreign enemies. Hutten visited Italy in 1512–1514 and again in 1515–1517, but the experience served merely to confirm his resentment of Italians' disdain for Germans as a nation of barbarians.

Hutten also became an outspoken defender of the German Hebraist **Johann Reuchlin** against attacks by the theologians and Dominican friars of Cologne. A number of young humanists interpreted the attacks on Reuchlin as evidence of a plot to destroy humanistic studies in Germany, and in 1515 and 1517 some of this group published a savage satire defending Reuchlin and depicting his foes as a pack of ignoramuses and hypocrites. This book was the *Letters of Obscure Men*, a collection of fictitious letters addressed by imaginary members of the Cologne faculty to their friend **Ortwin Gratius**. The first part of the collection was probably the work of the Erfurt humanist **Crotus Rubeanus**, while the second part, far more personal and vituperative in its attacks, was probably Hutten's work. Inspired in part by his ardent German patriotism and in part by his experiences in Italy and his conviction that the Italian-dominated papal curia was deliberately exploiting and humiliating the German nation, Hutten began what he called his war against the Romanists, a series of satirical Latin poems denouncing the tyranny exercised by **Rome** over Germans and calling for reform of the church.

Hutten's initial denunciation of conditions in the church was exclusively political and nationalist in tone. When he first heard reports of **Martin Luther's** Ninety-five Theses, he contemptuously dismissed the controversy as just another squabble among rival monks. But when Luther showed remarkable courage in upholding his convictions, Hutten changed into an outspoken defender of the Saxon reformer. After being excommunicated in 1521, Hutten took shelter with the imperial knight Franz von Sickingen and encouraged Sickingen's unsuccessful attack on the estates of the archbishop of Trier. After Sickingen's death from injuries suffered in battle, Hutten fled to Switzerland, first to **Basel** and then to Zürich, and eventually died of a long-standing **syphilitic** infection in 1523. Hutten's espousal of Luther's cause produced a bitter break with the leading figure of reformist humanism, **Erasmus of Rotterdam**. Among German patriots of the 19th century, when the country was struggling to attain political unity, Hutten was interpreted as a tragic hero who had defended his nation's freedom but had been overcome by Roman deceit and conspiracy.

– I –

INNOCENT VIII (Giovanni Battista Cibò). Pope from 1484 to 1492, generally classed as one of the worldly popes who tolerated corruption in the church and neglected spiritual matters and church reform in their pursuit of wealth and power. As a patron of the arts, he is remembered for the construction of the Villa Belvedere at Rome, a building inspired by Roman architecture and decorated by paintings by **Bernardo Pinturicchio** and **Andrea Mantegna**. He is also notorious as the first pope who openly acknowledged his own illegitimate sons and daughters (begotten before his ordination to the priesthood) and used his authority to advance their careers.

INQUISITION. Judicial agency created under papal authority for the discovery, prosecution, and punishment of heresy and certain other acts defined as criminal under canon law, such as bigamy and sodomy. Christianity had always exercised the power to expel members who rejected its doctrines or moral requirements. After it became the official religion of the **Roman Empire** during the fourth century, imperial legislation made the local bishops judges over their community. In the first half of the **Middle Ages**, the bishop or his judicial deputy dealt with cases of heresy but never claimed the right to take a defendant's life. In the early 13th century, after the suppression of the Albigensian heresy in southern France by a crusade authorized by Pope Innocent III, the Roman curia concluded that the local bishops had been too lax. Since the Albigensian heretics of southern France remained stubborn and elusive, in 1233 Pope Gregory IX began appointing special inquisitors in some regions, charged with the duty of suppressing heresy.

Although the procedures followed by these inquisitors seem harsh when evauated by modern standards, they were modelled on the practices of Roman law. An inquisitor began by publicizing a grace period of 30 days during which heretics could identify themselves, abjure their errors, and be reconciled to the church. After this interval, all good Christians were supposed to denounce known heretics. Because of fear that powerful individuals would intimidate potential accusers, the names of accusers and their testimony were kept secret. Accused persons were, however, invited to present a list of personal enemies who might have made false accusations. In cases where there was substantial suspicion of heresy, the judges had the authority to interrogate the accused under torture, another procedure borrowed from Roman law. Inquisitors were fully aware that using torture could be a means of getting the testimony one wanted rather than getting the truth. Torture was regarded as a last resort, but it was used.

Being charged before an inquisitorial tribunal was a serious matter. Yet a substantial proportion of defendants was acquitted. Of those found guilty, most were assigned modest penalties and then released under supervision. For a person who had been condemned previously and had relapsed into heresy, however, a sentence of death was virtually certain. Although theoretically, being a church court, the inquisitorial court did not execute condemned heretics, in such cases guilty persons were "relaxed to the secular arm"—that is, to the secular government—which was then expected to carry out the execution.

Although historians have often used the term "inquisition" loosely, the medieval inquisition was not a formal institution but merely a number of individuals (usually Dominican or Franciscan friars) commissioned to investigate and punish heresy in a region. They were not active in all parts of Europe, and where they were active their efficacy was often questionable, though they did succeed in exterminating the Albigensian heresy. There was no institutional network, no systematic communication between inquisitors, and no system of supervision to ensure that their work was effective or free from abuses. In addition, since diocesan bishops still retained their own judicial authority, there were often conflicts of jurisdiction in the investigation and prosecution of heretics. *See also* PORTUGUESE INQUISITION, ROMAN INQUISITION; SPANISH INQUISITION.

ISAAK, HEINRICH (ca. 1450–1517). Netherlandish composer. Although born in the duchy of Brabant, he followed the pattern common in the lives of many Netherlandish composers by making his career abroad. His most important employment was in **Florence** during the high point of the Florentine Renaissance under **Lorenzo de'Medici**. He served the Medici family but was also a singer in the chapel of San Giovanni and in the cathedral choir. After Lorenzo's death in 1492, he was employed by the Emperor **Maximilian I**. In the emperor's service, Isaak enjoyed relative freedom of movement and lived at Vienna, Innsbruck, and Constance. He also spent time at the court of Ercole d'**Este**, duke of **Ferrara**, and he spent the last years of his life back in Florence, where he had married the daughter of a prosperous butcher.

Isaak produced many musical compositions, both religious and secular. His *Choralis Constantinus*, a set of liturgical offices covering the whole ecclesiastical year, is a remarkable synthesis of the tradition of Flemish music out of which his own career developed. One of his most admired works was his musical setting of the lament for the death of Lorenzo de'Medici composed by the Florentine **humanist** and poet **Angelo Poliziano**. Isaak's secular compositions are even more highly regarded than his ecclesiastical music. They include settings for vernacular poems by Poliziano and a number of three-part and four-part German songs.

ISABELLA, QUEEN OF SPAIN (1451–1504). Queen of Castile from 1474. Her marriage to **Ferdinand**, heir to the crown of Aragon, in 1469 and the subsequent ascension of Ferdinand to the Aragonese throne in 1479 meant that for the first time, both of the major states of Spain were under the rule of a single royal couple. While each of them functioned as the primary ruler in his or her own kingdom, they ruled as a team, making their marriage more than just a personal union of two kingdoms but rather the foundation of a developing national community. Hence the reign of Isabella and Ferdinand laid the foundations for a powerful European state, which by the beginning of the 16th century had become the most powerful kingdom in Christian Europe. The children of their marriage became heirs to both parts of Spain. The marriage of their daughter Juana to Philip of **Habsburg**, son of the Emperor **Maximilian I**, hereditary prince of the Netherlands and heir to the numerous Habsburg territories in the German Empire, made their grandson Charles (Charles I of Spain, **Charles V** as emperor) the most powerful ruler in 16th-century Europe.

While Ferdinand generally took the lead in matters of foreign policy, becoming a leading figure in the wars and diplomacy of the early 16th century, Isabella concentrated her efforts on Castilian domestic policy. In 1492 she and Ferdinand completed the conquest of the last Islamic principality left in Spain, the kingdom of Granada. They founded the **Spanish Inquisition**, and it became the first public institution that exercised power over both halves of Spain. Their policies also included the expulsion of the remaining unconverted **Jews** from Spain in 1492 and forcible (though for a long time mainly nominal) efforts to convert the Muslim population to Christianity; the sponsorship of **Christopher Columbus'** discovery of the route to the Americas in 1492; and the organization of the first set of institutions for the new American colonies. Isabella and Ferdinand also asserted royal supremacy over the higher nobility, acted to suppress brigandage and civil disorder in Castile, organized a powerful national army, and assured the crown of adequate tax revenues to meet the costs of domestic and foreign policy.

Isabella was deeply religious, and while her religious zeal led to policies like the persecution of Jewish and Muslim minorities and the creation of the Inquisition, it also embraced efforts to reform the church, to ensure the availability of educated men for service in ecclesiastical and royal administration, and to promote devout, well-educated, and competent men to high positions in the church. In recognition of their liberation of southern Spain from Moorish rule and their many actions to favor the church, Ferdinand and Isabella received papal designation as "their Catholic Majesties" and have been known as "the Catholic Monarchs" ever since their own time.

ITALIC SCRIPT. *See* SCRIPT, HUMANISTIC.

– J –

JANUS PANNONIUS (1434–1472). Hungarian **humanist**. His vernacular name was Janus of Czezmicze. He was a nephew of János Vitéz, bishop of Oradea, an early Hungarian humanist who directed the education of his nephew and in 1447 sent him to Italy for further study. He remained in Italy for 11 years, starting in the school of **Guarino Guarini**. While in Italy, he began writing poetry and eventually gained recognition as a talented poet. In 1454 he began studying canon law at the University of **Padua**, but it is uncertain whether he completed a doctorate. When **Matthias Corvinus** became king of Hungary in 1458, Janus returned home and soon became an influential figure among the court humanists. He became canon of the cathedral chapter of Oradea and in 1460, bishop of Pécs (German name, Fünfkirchen). He was a member of the royal council, chancellor to the queen, and influential in the king's cultural policy. As ambassador to the curia in 1465 he sought financial aid against the Turks from Pope Paul II. In 1469–1470 he was governor of a province, but because of disagreement with the king over foreign policy he became involved in a conspiracy against the ruler and when it was discovered fled to Italy. He died of plague near Zagreb while on his way to exile. Despite their quarrel, King Matthias admired Janus' poetry and arranged for his works to be collected. These works were printed several times during the 16th century.

JESUIT ORDER (officially, the Society of Jesus). Roman Catholic religious order organized by Ignatius Loyola (1491–1556) and authorized by the bull *Regimini militantis ecclesiae* issued by Pope Paul

III in 1540. The goal of the new order was to restore the power and unity of the Catholic church, and it became one of the primary forces opposing Protestantism in Germany and elsewhere. Its first members had strong missionary ambitions, and the society later became active in efforts to introduce Christianity into India, China, and Japan. At the Council of Trent, Jesuit theologians backed the conservatives who promoted an uncompromising reaffirmation of traditional doctrines and of practices challenged by the Protestants. The order laid particular emphasis on the authority of the **pope** as successor to St. Peter and guarantor of unity and orthodoxy.

Loyola himself was not much attracted to **humanism**, and he was sharply critical of the most famous non-Italian humanist of the century, **Erasmus**. Yet the Jesuits became deeply involved in educational work, and their schools developed a strong tradition of humanistic studies. Their commitment to education began in 1548 with their first school at Messina in Sicily. Within little more than a decade, they recognized education as their principal activity. By the end of the century, they were in charge of a large number of schools and also had created at **Rome** a distinguished institute for study of theology, the *Collegium Romanum*. In several regions, particularly in Germany, they took control of colleges, or even the whole faculties of liberal arts, in established **universities**. But their most successful institutions were secondary schools designed to produce well-educated laymen, well-prepared candidates for the clergy, and candidates for university study who would have the best possible preparation for success in the higher faculties (law, medicine, and theology).

In their schools, the Jesuits developed a program of studies that fulfilled most of the aspirations of earlier humanist educational reformers. While they avoided study of authors like Erasmus who had been openly critical of the church, they developed in their graduates a fluent mastery of **classical** Latin, introduced a reasonably thorough study of **Greek**, and had their students read a considerable body of ancient Latin and Greek literature. They adopted from the best contemporary French grammar schools a sequential plan of study in which each level prepared students for the next. But they followed the lead of some earlier humanist reformers in regarding the humanistic subjects, such as grammar and rhetoric, as suitable for the lower levels of study, while the curriculum of their own schools culminated in study of **Aristotelian** philosophy (including natural science) that traditionally had been introduced only in the universities. The plan of study and the methods followed were closely defined in regulations that culminated in the *Ratio studiorum / Plan of Studies* (1599). By the 17th century, Jesuit schools were widely recognized as among the best in Europe.

JEWS. Western and central Europe had had Jewish residents since Roman times, and even though anti-Jewish prejudice had led to repeated instances of mob violence, legal discrimination, and pressure for conversion, those communities never entirely disappeared over any broad area and for any extended time, with the exception of Spain and Portugal after the expulsion of all unconverted Jews in 1492 and 1496 respectively. Wherever they lived, Jews constituted separate communities that in the eyes of the law were resident aliens theoretically under the protection of the ruler.

Jews were excluded from occupations that required membership in **guilds** (most of which had a religious element) and also in most regions from ownership of agricultural land. Hence the only occupations open to them were marginal ones, including mercantile activity and moneylending, since trade was regarded as ethically questionable and canon law forbade Christians to lend money at interest. Wealthy Jewish merchants with good business connections and liquid assets were useful to rulers, who relied on them for loans and financial services and hence granted them some protection while in many cases also exploiting the threat of popular violence to extort gifts and favorable terms on loans. Local Jewish communities generally regulated their own religious and family matters.

The larger communities often contained learned scholars, usually specialists in biblical interpretation, philosophy, medicine, and such occult arts as **astrology** and **magic**. From the second half of the 15th century, beginning in Italy, some Christian **humanists** became interested in **Hebrew** language and in several fields of Jewish learning. Prominent examples were **Giovanni Pico della Mirandola** in Italy and **Johann Reuchlin** in Germany. In return, Jewish scholars like Yohanan Alemanno of **Florence**, who had assisted Pico's study of Jewish learning, became interested in the revived **Platonism** found in the translations and original treatises of **Marsilio Ficino**. Another prominent Jewish scholar, exiled from Portugal, was **Leone Ebreo**, whose *Dialoghi d'amore / Dialogues on Love* explored the Platonic idea of love and tried to relate Renaissance **Neoplatonic** thought to the Jewish mystical writings known as **Cabala**.

As the large Jewish populations of Spain and Portugal were dismantled by persecution, conversion, and exile, Italy became the principal center of Jewish life in western and central Europe. **Rome** in particular had a large and highly cultivated Jewish population since the **popes**, although imposing many limitations, rejected a policy of forced conversion. At **Venice**, Rome, and other places Jews were permitted to live only in an officially defined ghetto. The pressures of living separate from the rest of society and of constantly facing the threat of having their privileges further restricted may explain the intense mystical developments and the many Messianic prophecies that arose within Jewish communities, especially from the late 16th century.

JIMÉNEZ DE CISNEROS, FRANCISCO. *See* XIMÉNES DE CISNEROS, FRANCISCO.

JOAN OF ARC (d. 1431). Peasant girl who, in 1429, arrived at the court of the French king Charles VII (1422–1461), claiming to have been divinely commissioned by the voices of saints to maintain the king's cause against his rival, King Henry V of England. Although both Joan and the **Hundred Years' War** that she played a major role in bringing to an end are conventionally regarded as belonging to medieval history, her role in stimulating the French ruler to action did much to rally French support behind King Charles. Although Joan herself was captured in battle by the **Burgundian** allies of England, sold to the English, and condemned and executed as a **witch** by a church court, the renewed French consciousness that she both expressed and stimulated created the foundation for emergence of French Renaissance culture. Up to the French Revolution, the monarchy avoided acknowledging her share in French recovery, but in the 19th century, French nationalists transformed her into a national hero, the church reversed her condemnation, and in 1920 she was canonized as Saint Joan.

JONES, INIGO (1573–1652). English architect. He began his artistic career as a painter for aristocratic patrons and as a maker of ecclesiastical furnishings. He toured Italy in 1598, visited Denmark in 1603, and collaborated with the playwright **Ben Jonson** in designing court masques for Anne, queen of King James I. In 1613 he accompanied an English embassy to celebrate the marriage of the king's daughter to the Elector Palatine in Heidelberg and then made a second trip to Italy. Guided by the writings of the Italian architect **Andrea Palladio**, he studied ancient monuments. Back in England in 1615, he became surveyor of the king's works and produced a number of designs for buildings (most of them never built) intended to transform London into a magnificent royal capital. His most famous surviving building is the Banqueting House (1619–1622) at Whitehall, designed in a **classicizing** style inspired by Palladio.

JONSON, BEN (1572–1637). English dramatist. Born in Westminster and educated at Westminster School, after a period of soldiering in Flanders he became an actor and playwright in 1597. Imprisoned for killng another actor in a duel, he was converted to Roman Catholicism in prison but 12 years later returned to the Church of England. His most highly regarded plays, all comedies, were *Volpone, or The Fox* (1606), *The Alchemist* (1610) and *Bartholomew Fayre* (1614). Also influential were two tragedies inspired by **classical** models, *Sejanus* (1603) and *Catiline* (1611). Jonson was a learned and prolific author, not only of plays but also of of poetry and literary criticism. Although his published works were sometimes critical of his contemporary **William Shakespeare**, he also wrote a number of passages acknowledging the greatness of his older friend. Many of his plays and several masques were published in a folio edition dated 1616. In later life his works fell out of fashion, and he died in poverty, but he was buried in Westminster Abbey.

JULIUS II, POPE (Giuliano della Rovere, ca. 1445–1513; pope from 1503). Giuliano's uncle Francesco provided for his education and upon being elected **pope (Sixtus IV)** in 1471 made Giuliano a cardinal and soon conferred on him many valuable benefices. He acted as papal ambassador on several occasions, but his most obvious talent was as an administrator and military commander, beginning with his service as legate in the province of Umbria in the **Papal States**. Giuliano had considerable influence over his uncle's successor, Pope

Innocent VIII. With the next pope, **Alexander VI** (1492–1503), he had a poor relationship and eventually withdrew to France. He was one of those who encouraged King Charles VIII to undertake the invasion of **Naples** in 1494 that precipitated a series of political crises and wars in Italy that lasted for more than half a century. His strong personality and reputation for aggressive defense of the papacy's political claims was the basis for his own election as pope in 1503, and he even exceeded the expectations of the cardinals who supported him.

Julius is known as "the warrior pope," engaging in a complex set of diplomatic and military adventures that threw most of Italy into turmoil but generally advanced the temporal power of the papacy. His assertive personality and militarism were sharply criticized in the famous satire *Julius exclusus*, published anonymously but usually attributed to the Dutch **humanist Erasmus**. Julius called the last general council of the Latin church to meet before the **Reformation**, the **Fifth Lateran Council**, which met in **Rome** and continued under Julius's successor, **Leo X**. Although his private life was far more respectable than that of his predecessor Alexander VI, and his warlike actions were aimed at extending the political authority of the papacy in Italy rather than at exploiting papal power in the interests of his own kin, Julius did continue the tendency of Renaissance popes to function as secular leaders at the expense of their pastoral responsibilities.

Julius' historical significance probably rests more on his actions as a patron of the arts at the peak of the Renaissance than on his work as a spiritual or even a political leader. His major commissions were the construction of the Belvedere courtyard in the Vatican, designed by **Donato Bramante**; the paintings by **Raphael** in the papal apartments, notably *The School of Athens*; and the work that may well be the high point of Renaissance painting, the frescoes on the ceiling of the Sistine Chapel, painted at the pope's insistence by a reluctant **Michelangelo**. The Sistine ceiling was completed in 1512. Michelangelo's sculptural project for the pope's tomb was never finished on account of the great cost, and only one of the parts completed, the statue *Moses*, was finished by Michelangelo's own hand. Julius also made the decision to tear down the ancient basilica of St. Peter and to replace it with a gigantic church built in the Renaissance central-dome style, designed by Bramante and begun in 1506, though not completed until the following century and considerably modified by several later architects. The famous portrait of the pope by Raphael (1511–1512) captures the personality of the elderly but still energetic and strong-willed pontiff.

– K –

KEPLER, JOHANNES (1571–1630). German mathematician and astronomer. His family relocated to the Protestant state of Württemberg while he was still a small child. This principality had developed a strong educational system, and young Kepler benefitted from a scholarship to an excellent Latin grammar school. He then entered the **University** of Tübingen intending to become a minister, but he studied there with a mathematician who accepted the new heliocentric astronomical system of **Copernicus**. Kepler had not intended to focus on mathematics, but the university recommended him as a teacher of mathematics in a Protestant seminary in Graz, a predominantly Catholic city. His added duties as district mathematician required him to draw up **astrological** calendars.

Kepler's first mathematical publication, *Mysterium cosmographicum / Secret of the Universe* (1596), suggested that the truth of Copernicus' system of astronomy was confirmed by his conclusion that the orbits of each of the planets in the Copernican system could be inscribed as tangents to one of the five geometrical solids of Euclidean geometry. The book attracted attention, and Kepler was invited to become an assistant to the Danish astronomer **Tycho Brahe**. Although Brahe opposed Copernicus' heliocentric theory and supported a compromise between it and the old Ptolemaic system, Kepler knew that Brahe had amassed a vast treasure of precise astronomical observations in his observatory and was eager to gain access to these important new data.

When Brahe left Denmark to become court astronomer to the Emperor **Rudolf II**, Kepler returned to Graz but found that the **Habsburg** archduke was increasing pressure on local Protestants to turn Catholic. Hence he rejoined Brahe at Prague, where in 1601, following Brahe's death, he succeeded to the position of imperial mathematician. He continued to fulfill Brahe's official duty of compiling tables of the planetary orbits. By 1605 he had completed work on another major book,

Astronomia nova / The New Astronomy, though publication was delayed until 1609. In this book Kepler demonstrated many complex relations among the planetary orbits. Many of these had no particular usefulness but two of them stated what are now known as Kepler's first two laws of planetary motion. In this book for the first time he abandoned his youthful belief that the force that moved the heavens was spiritual and attempted to derive all motions from purely material, physical forces.

KRZYCKI, ANDRZEJ (d. 1537). Polish poet, statesman, and bishop, known in Latin as Andreas Cricius. Born into a noble family but orphaned at an early age, he was educated under the direction of his maternal uncle, Bishop Piotr Tomicki, an influential royal official. He studied in Italy, probably from 1498 to 1503, and heard the lectures of two famous **humanist** professors at **Bologna**, Codro Urceo and **Filippo Beroaldo the Elder**. The bishop of Poznán became his patron, and he entered holy orders and received several valuable benefices. In 1512 Krzycki became secretary to Queen Barbara Zápolyai and after her death became a protégé of King Sigismund's second wife, the Italian princess Bona **Sforza**. In 1523 he became bishop of Przemysl but spent nearly all of his time at the royal court in Cracow. He represented the king in negotiations that led to the secularization of the state of the Teutonic Knights in Prussia, a dependency of the Polish crown. Despite this political mission, which made Prussia a Protestant duchy, he was personally opposed to the **Reformation**. Later he was promoted to the bishopric of Plock (1527) and still later to the archbishopric of Gniezno.

Throughout his career, Krzycki supported humanism. He was also a highly regarded Latin poet and published a number of works, some of them occasional poems for his royal patrons, others being epigrams and satiric verses directed against his political antagonists. His verses included parodies of church hymns and popular religious verse. Much of his work, especially his erotic poems, remained unpublished but circulated in manuscript. He also published two prose works against **Martin Luther**. He was a great admirer of the Dutch humanist **Erasmus** and sought to persuade him to visit Poland. He respected the Lutheran leader **Philipp Melanchthon** and tried to bring him to Poland in order to woo him away from Luther.

– L –

LABÉ, LOUISE (ca. 1524–1566). The pen name of the poet Louise Charly, born into a well-to-do family of rope-makers at Lyon and given a classical education unusual for any **woman** of her time. Her collected poems, published in 1555, include three elegies and 24 love sonnets written in the **Petrarchan** style, as well as a prefatory manifesto on the rights of women and a mythological prose dialogue, *Débat de Folie et d'Amour / Disputation of Folly and Love*, written in the manner of the Renaissance *facetia*. Her work shows familiarity with Catullus and Ovid. She places herself firmly in the tradition of Renaissance lyric and satire but provides ironic commentary on the conventional language of love devised by and for men.

LABODERIE, GUY LEFÈVRE DE (1541–1598). French poet and biblical translator. His mastery of **Greek, Hebrew**, Arabic, Chaldean, and Syriac brought him into touch with the older scholar and **Cabalist Guillaume Postel**, whose influence led to the selection of Laboderie and his brother Nicolas to participate in editorial work on the great **polyglot Bible** published by the Antwerp printer **Christophe Plantin**. While living in Antwerp he became associated wth the underground antinomian religious sect known as the Family of Love, but at the same period, he was also close to the **Jesuit** community at **Louvain** and dedicated several poems to them. He published French translations of the spiritual poems of the **Florentine Neoplatonist Marsilio Ficino** (1578) and a poem on poetic and musical theory and the orgins of civilization, *La galliade*, as well as a French translation of the widely admired work of **Pico della Mirandola** commonly known by the title *Oration on the Dignity of Man*. Laboderie's erudition made him an able translator, but his erudite etymological references made some of his work inaccessible to most readers.

LA BOÉTIE, ETIENNE DE (1530–1563). French **humanist**, author, and translator. He was educated in law and had a public career in the Parlement of Bordeaux. He translated classical texts by Plutarch and Xenophon into French. His *Mémoire sur la pacification des troubles / On the Pacification of the Civil Wars*, though not published until the 20th century, took a conservative stance on the problems of the

French Wars of Religion, insisting that since two rival religious could not coexist peacefully in the same society, only Catholicism should be legally permitted despite his repugnance to the use of force to suppress intellectual disagreements. His best-known work, *Discours de la servitude volontaire / On Voluntary Servitude* (1574), denounces tyranny and was used by the Huguenot party in the civil wars to justify their cause, even though it also maintained that individuals are obligated to submit to the traditional laws of their country. La Boétie is best known in French literary history as an intimate friend of **Michel de Montaigne**, who devoted one of his most famous essays, "On Friendship," to the memory of their friendship.

LANDINO, CRISTOFORO (1424–1498). Humanist, professor of poetry at the University of **Florence**, and prominent member of the **Platonic Academy** of Florence, an informal association of scholars led by the **Neoplatonic** philosopher **Marsilio Ficino**. Landino's dialogue *Disputationes Camaldulenses / Disputations at Camaldoli* (ca. 1472), dealing with the relative merits of the active and the contemplative life, is perhaps the earliest Platonic dialogue written in the Italian Renaissance. He also published works in Italian, including a translation of the *Natural History* of Pliny the Elder and an edition of Dante's *Divine Comedy* with commentary. His commentaries on several classical Latin poets circulated among his associates but were not published.

LANYER, AEMILIA (1569–1645). English poet, the daughter of an Italian musician employed at the court of Queen **Elizabeth I** and his English wife. She was left alone at age 18 when her mother died. She became pregnant by a cousin of the queen, Lord Hunsdon, and in 1592 was married off to a court musician, Alfonso Lanyer, who acted as father to her son. Early in the new century, she lived for a time in the household of Margaret Clifford, dowager countess of Cumberland, and produced a much-admired book of poems, *Salve deus rex Judaeorum/Hail God, King of the Jews* (1611). It contains several dedications, all addressed to **women**. The title-poem deals with the passion of Christ from the viewpoint of the women who followed him, and it contrasts their loyalty and piety with the wickeness of men in the Gospel accounts of Jesus' life. For a time Lanyer supported herself by teaching school.

LASKI, JAN I and JAN II. Uncle and nephew, members of an influential family of Polish nobility who were leaders in the church and also in encouraging Renaissance learning in their country. Jan I (1455–1531) entered the service of the Polish king in 1496 and rose to high position in the church. In 1510 he became archbishop of Gniezno and as such, primate (senior prelate) of the Polish church. He attended the **Fifth Lateran Council**, made a pilgrimage to Jerusalem, and played a prominent role in domestic politics and European diplomacy. After the **Reformation** began in eastern Germany, Bishop Laski opposed the spread of Lutheran ideas in Poland. He also educated his nephews and supported their careers in royal service and in the church.

Of the nephews, Jan II (1499–1560) was the most important in the cultural and religious history of his time. He accompanied his uncle to **Rome** for the Lateran Council, studied in Vienna, **Bologna**, and **Padua**, and became an enthusiastic supporter of humanistic studies, particularly the Christian **humanism** of **Erasmus**. On his second visit to Erasmus at **Basel** in 1525, he lived in Erasmus' house for six months, paying his own expenses and arranging to purchase most of Erasmus'personal library. The books were to remain in Erasmus' possession during his lifetime. Aided by his uncle's influence, young Jan obtained a number of valuable benefices in the Polish church. Although critical (like Erasmus) of **Martin Luther's** rashness, he found Luther's more moderate and more humanistic colleague **Philipp Melanchthon** very appealing. In 1539 he moved to **Louvain**, attracted by the *philosophia Christi* of reform-minded Dutch Catholics. While at Louvain, he married the daughter of a merchant, a step that forced him to forfeit his ecclesiastical offices in Poland. He then moved to Emden in northwestern Germany, working to improve local education. Laski returned to Poland in 1541, affirming on oath that he was an orthodox Catholic. But when he returned to Emden, he openly broke with Catholicism and became superintendent (Protestant bishop) of the churches of East Friesland. He opposed the pro-Catholic religious settlement (the Augsburg Interim) imposed on Germany in 1548 by the **Emperor Charles V** and accepted the invitation of the Anglican Archbishop Thomas Cranmer of Canterbury to settle in England. There he became superintendent of the congregations of foreign Protestants (mostly German and Dutch) settled in

London. After Queen Mary I restored Catholicism in England (1553), he returned to Emden. In 1556 he went back Poland, where he attempted to unify the growing but disunited Protestant groups with a religious system based largely on the theology of **John Calvin**. Laski's influence had much to do with the Calvinist theology of most Polish Protestants, who remained an influential minority, especially among the aristocracy, until the 17th century.

LASSUS, ROLAND DE, also Orlando di Lasso (ca. 1530–1594). Composer and musical performer. Born at Mons in the southern Netherlands, he studied music there. His beautiful voice was so admired that he was kidnapped three times by patrons who wanted his services as a singer. In 1544 he travelled to Italy in the service of the Spanish viceroy of Sicily. In 1552 he became choirmaster in the church of St. John Lateran at **Rome**. Called home by the illness of his parents, he remained in the North after their death and settled in Antwerp. Eventually Lassus became a chapel singer in the service of Duke Albert V of Bavaria at Munich and remained there for the rest of his life. More than a thousand of his compositions survive, covering every contemporary genre except instrumental music. This number includes more than 500 motets and 60 masses and other liturgical music. He also composed musical settings for Italian-language madrigals and for poems by several contemporary French poets. The diffusion of his compositions in printed form enhanced his reputation as the greatest composer of his time.

LATERAN COUNCIL, FIFTH (1512–1517). The last general council of the Western church before the outbreak of the Protestant **Reformation**. It was summoned to **Rome** by **Pope Julius II** in order to eclipse a schismatic council convened at **Pisa** (also in 1512) by King Louis XII of France, the Emperor **Maximilian I**, and a number of dissident cardinals. The goals of the Lateran Council were to restore the unity of the church, to end warfare among Christian powers, to organize a crusade against the Turks, to extirpate heresy (the **Hussite** heresy in Bohemia), and to reform church and society. After the death of Pope Julius in 1513, the new pope, **Leo X**, continued the council.

It was a splendid gathering, marked by sermons delivered by famous **humanist** preachers and advocates for moderate reform of the church, and it was well attended, though the overwhelming majority of the bishops attending were Italians, who in general backed papal authority. Under the even-tempered Pope Leo, the dispute with the French king that had caused the convocation of the rival body at Pisa was settled by the **Concordat of Bologna** (1516). Although the Lateran Council endorsed the Concordat, no French delegates came to take part in its final sessions. The ordinary diocesan bishops hoped to secure greater authority within their dioceses, to restrict the special exemptions granted by the papacy to the mendicant orders, and to create a college of bishops sitting permanently at Rome to look after their interests, but they made very few gains.

As for reform of worship, the council advocated preaching of the Gospel guided by the interpretations of the ancient Church Fathers and the medieval doctors of theology—that is, pretty much the status quo. It noted that the new art of **printing** created a potential danger to orthodox faith and morals and commanded local bishops to supervise the press in their dioceses. **University** professors of philosophy were required to uphold the church's traditions on topics such as the immortality and unity of the soul, the unity of truth (that is, that truths taught by reason must conform to the truths taught by religion), and the creation of the world.

These latter requirements in effect made the doctrine of the soul's immortality and the creation of the world by God dogmas of the Catholic faith rather than just the doctrine traditionally held by the faithful. They were directed against the secular, non-religious interpretation of **Aristotle** and his ancient and medieval commentators by professors in Italian universities, such as **Pietro Pomponazzi** at Bologna. Although later defenders of the record of the pre-Reformation church have rightly pointed out a number of conciliar measures encouraging reforms of doctrine and practice, the council failed to prepare the church to face the Protestant Reformation, which broke out little more than six months after the council's adjournment.

LATINI, BRUNETTO (ca. 1220–1294). Florentine notary, poet, and political leader. He is best known from his appearance in Canto 15 of **Dante's** *Inferno* as one of those punished for sodomy. Despite his condemnation to eternal punishment, Dante treats him with great respect as an admired master. His principal literary work, written in

French rather than Italian, was his *Trésor* (full title, *Li livres dou tresor*), written ca. 1262–1266. In 1260 he had been sent as Florentine ambassador to Castile. Before his return, he learned that the **Ghibelline** party had seized control of Florence. Hence he stayed in France until the restoration of his own **Guelf** party to control made return safe. His *Trésor* was written during that exile. Latini later wrote a handbook of good social conduct called *Tesoretto / The Little Treasure*, in which he parodied an influential French vernacular poem, the *Roman de la rose / **Romance of the Rose***. Although Latini is conventionally classsified as a medieval rather than a Renaissance author, recent scholarship on the origins of Italian **humanism** has caused him to be regarded as one of the earliest Florentine authors who might be regarded as a humanist, in the Renaissance sense of the term.

Latini made a number of translations of **classical** texts from Latin into the Tuscan dialect that was soon to emerge as the literary vernacular understood throughout Italy. About 1260–1262, during his political exile in Paris, he translated part of one of Cicero's rhetorical works, *De inventione*, into Tuscan as part of his own work on rhetoric. After returning to Italy in 1267, he translated three **Ciceronian** orations as models of eloquence for modern orators. In his translations of Cicero, Latini regards rhetoric as more than just style in oral discourse; rather, it is a source of civilization because it is essential to the governance of a republic and hence an important influence on the moral and political virtues necessary for the kind of **communal** government that had developed in Florence. He made his Ciceronian translations in the hope that familiarity with these texts would help his fellow citizens manage their own republic. He also conceived rhetoric as dealing primarily with oration rather than written discourse. Unlike the expatriate **Petrarch** but much like Cicero himself, Latini regarded political involvement as the proper duty of a citizen and saw oratory as a tool that enables the statesman to give moral guidance to society. Thus he laid the foundation for the growth of interest in the classics (often in vernacular translations) among members of the Florentine ruling class. His French-language *Trésor* stated flatly that the communal (that is, republican) form of government is "by far the best."

LAZARILLO DE TORMES. Spanish prose novel, published in 1554 and commonly regarded as the first picaresque novel, a genre that became popular in later 16th-century Spain. The name of the author is unknown, though the character of the work suggests a person of considerable education. It is written as an autobiography and follows the eponymous hero through a series of employments by disreputable masters from whom he learns that one can advance in society only through deception. The book exercised influence well beyond its country of origin, for it was soon translated into Latin and into several European vernaculars.

LEFÈVRE d'ETAPLES, JACQUES (ca. 1453–1536). French **humanist**, known in Latin as Faber Stapulensis. He was a major influence on the "evangelical" religious reformers of the early 16th century and on the earliest French Protestants, though he never broke his own connection with the Roman Catholic church. Born at Etaples in Picardy, he studied at Paris (B.A. 1479, M.A. 1480) and became a teacher in the faculty of liberal arts. He also studied **Greek** under an exiled scholar, Georgius Hermonymus. His first published work was an introduction to **Aristotle's** *Metaphysics* that is notable for its rejection of the vast body of commentaries produced by medieval **scholastic** philosophers and for its emphasis on the original Aristotelian text and its skill at explaining the ideas of Aristotle clearly. Though about 1491 he considered entering a monastery, Lefèvre remained a secular priest.

In 1491–1492 he made the first of three trips to Italy, where he met the Venetian humanist **Ermolao Barbaro** and the **Florentine** philosophers **Marsilio Ficino** and **Giovanni Pico della Mirandola**. Barbaro's influence inspired him to reform the teaching of Aristotle at Paris by publishing his original texts in Greek and adding a series of commentaries on them. Though also attracted by the Florentines to **Platonist** and **Neoplatonic** philosophy, he soon returned to his Aristotelian orientation. He retained a lively interest in the **Hermetic** literature, which he accepted as a genuine expression of the religious wisdom of the ancient Egyptians, and in the works ascribed to Dionysius the Areopagite, another late-**classical** forgery that he accepted as a product of the apostolic age and whose author he mistakenly identified with St. Denis, the patron saint of France.

Upon his return to teaching in Paris, Lefèvre began publishing revised Aristotelian texts and commentaries. He regarded Aristotle, though a pagan, as inspired by the spirit of God and profoundly compatible with Christian belief. He also developed an increasing interest in the Bible and the works of the early Christian Church Fathers. He became the center of a group of younger disciples who shared his interest in Aristotle and collaborated with him in publishing not only Aristotle but also ancient texts on logic and mathematics. Shortly after 1500 he retired from active teaching and became a protégé of a former student, Guillaume Briçonnet, abbot of the famous monastery of Saint-Germain-des-Prés.

There Lefèvre resided as a guest of the abbey and devoted himself to full-time scholarly work. He concentrated on study of the Bible and in 1509 published *Quincuplex Psalterium / Fivefold Psalter*, a critical study of the Psalms, and in 1512, his commentaries on the Epistles of St. Paul. His work on the Bible conceived religion (much like his contemporary **Erasmus**) as spiritual and based on grace rather than external and based on ritual. In 1511, if not previously, he met Erasmus at Paris. They established friendly relations but were never particularly close, and after a quarrel provoked by Lefèvre's sharp criticism of Erasmus' interpretation of a passage in Hebrews and aggravated by Erasmus' humiliating demonstration of the superficiality of Lefèvre's textual scholarship, the relationship (despite a formal reconciliation arranged by their mutual friend **Guillaume Budé**) remained civil but distant. Nevertheless, Lefèvre's scholarly work on the Bible was warmly greeted by most humanists and by those theologians who were open to the value of applying humanist textual criticism to Scripture (the young **Martin Luther** among them) but was eclipsed by the publication of Erasmus' annotated edition of the Greek text of the New Testament in 1516.

Lefèvre's textual approach to study of the Bible earned him the hostility of conservative Paris theologians, and his short tracts criticizing certain beliefs about two female saints, Mary Magdalene and Anne, that were based solely on legend and had no foundation in Scripture called forth bitter accusations of impiety and even of heresy. Lefèvre (unlike Martin Luther and Erasmus) was no fighter, and his reaction was to withdraw from Paris and move to the diocese of Meaux, where his patron Guillaume Briçonnet had become bishop. Briçonnet, inspired by Lefèvre's idea of a moderate reform of religion led by diocesan bishops, had undertaken a reform of his own diocese. Lefèvre became one of his advisers. But the movement, which emphasized preaching of Gospel-based doctrine to the common people, attracted several radical reformers who were influenced by the thought of Luther. It eventually led to popular riots against the traditional practices. Conservative critics charged that the bishop and his advisers were unleashing a dangerous religious radicalism that would produce heresy and social unrest. At this period, Lefèvre and others of his associates were in touch with radical agitators like Guillaume Farel and were reading the works of German Reformers.

Eventually, the Parlement of Paris, the mendicant orders, and the Paris faculty of theology collaborated to break up the Meaux reform movement. The bishop himself was called before a court to answer charges of reckless actions that promoted heresy, and several of his advisers, including Lefèvre himself, fled to the Protestant city of Strasbourg (a German imperial city not yet annexed by France). Lefèvre did not return to France until the king, who together with his sister **Margaret of Navarre** had protected the evangelical humanists from attacks by conservatives but who had been a prisoner of war in Spain, was back in France to restrain the theologians and the Parlement of Paris.

In addition to his support of the abortive diocesan reform at Meaux, Lefèvre had infuriated religious conservatives by publishing further biblical commentaries and by publishing in 1523 his own French translation of the New Testament, followed in 1530 by a translation of the whole Bible (printed, however, across the border in Antwerp because of the censorship in France). When he returned from Strasbourg in the spring of 1526, Lefèvre avoided the storm-center of controversy at Paris. The king appointed him director of the royal library at Blois and tutor to the royal children. In 1530 he moved into even deeper shelter at Nérac, the residence of the king's sister Marguerite, queen of the semi-independent principality of Navarre. There he lived quietly, avoiding controversy.

Lefèvre's personal doctrines, though somewhat vague on questions like the relation between faith and good works, probably never quite conformed to the doctrinal standard characteristic of Reformers like Luther, but his emphasis on the importance of inner religion rather than external actions, his questions about the validity of the sacraments unless backed by faith, and his criticism of the use of religious images and prayers to the saints suggested tacit support for the German heresies. He had been a house guest of the German Protestant theologian Martin Bucer during his exile in Strasbourg. In the end, unlike many of his young disciples, he found much to admire in the German Protestants but was unwilling to break away from the traditional church.

LELAND, JOHN (ca. 1506–1552). English poet, antiquary, and topographer. He studied at St. Paul's school under the **humanist** grammarian **William Lily** and then at the **universities** of Cambridge, Oxford, and Paris. His Latin poetry attracted patrons at the court of King **Henry VIII**, and the king appointed him royal antiquary and sent him out to study ancient sites and records. Though sympathetic to the **Reformation**, he was dismayed by the threat to books and documents caused by the king's dissolution of English monasteries. He urged Henry to take personal charge of the libraries and ensure their preservation. This effort preserved some, but far from all, of the rare library materials. In 1546 Leland published a volume of *Englandes Antiquities*, but most of his work, including copious notes describing in detail the localities that he visited, remained unprinted, mainly because of his mental breakdown. In the 18th century, his topographical notes were published under the title of *Itinerary*, a vast but disordered body of details about the landscape and **antiquities** of many parts of England in the time of **Henry VIII**.

LEMAIRE DES BELGES, JEAN (1470–1525). French poet and **humanist**, a transitional figure between the vernacular *rhétoriqueurs* of the 15th century and later French humanists. His works reflect growing French interest in Italian Renaissance culture and the Tuscan language, embracing both **classical** authors and the writings of contemporary Italian humanists. His principal work was a romantic and fictionalized historical narrative, *Les illustrations de Gaule et singularitez de Troyes* (the first book was published in 1511; the complete work in 1524). This was a blend of mythical and actual historical accounts of the origins of France since pre-Roman times, in which Lemaire tried to link the origins of France with ancient Troy, a historical myth promoted by a number of early French humanists.

LEO X, POPE (Giovanni de'Medici, 1475–1521; pope 1513–1521). The second son of **Lorenzo de'Medici**, Giovanni was intended from boyhood for a career in the church. He received a humanistic education under the direction of **Angelo Poliziano** and other **humanists** and was made a cardinal at age 14 by **Pope Innocent VIII**. He studied canon law at **Pisa**, receiving his doctorate at age 17. He then settled in **Rome**, serving as papal legate on several occasions and making an extended trip to Germany, the Low Countries, and France in 1499–1500. He continued to serve as a diplomat under Pope **Julius II**. Giovanni was elected pope on 9 March 1513, being promptly ordained to the rank of priest on 15 March and to the rank of bishop on 17 March in preparation for his coronation as pope on 19 March. Although widely praised as a man of peace, he took a hard line in establishing stronger control over the outlying parts of the Papal States, removing the duke of **Urbino** from office in 1516 and replacing him with his own nephew, the younger Lorenzo de'Medici. He longed to reduce the influence of non-Italian powers in Italy, first allying himself with the Spanish against the French, then with the French against the Spansh, and again with the Spanish in the last year of his reign. Thanks to the action of Pope **Julius II** and the Spanish in overthrowing the reformed republican regime that dominated **Florence** after the Medici were driven out in 1494, he was the real ruler of Florence throughout his pontificate, exercising control through various relatives. As pope he continued the **Fifth Lateran Council** called by his predecessor and brought the council to its conclusion in 1517.

Leo had been prepared from childhood to be an ecclesiastical prince and also to be an active patron of the arts and of humanistic scholarship. His career as ruler of the **Papal States** was moderately successful while his patronage of the visual arts was outstanding since he had at his disposal both **Michelangelo** and **Raphael**, two of the greatest artists of the Renaissance. Raphael painted a famous portrait of the pope with two of his cousins.

But nothing had prepared Leo to cope with the profound theological issues raised by **Martin Luther** in Germany, and the pope's clumsy efforts to silence Luther and either secure his recantation or bring him to trial for heresy did much to ensure that the religious upheaval in Germany would rapidly grow out of control. At the crucial period when popular opinion in Germany was rallying around Luther, Pope Leo was far more concerned with his own efforts to block the election of **Charles** of **Habsburg**, king of Spain, as Holy Roman Emperor than with the spiritual issues involved in the Saxon heresy.

Indeed, he assiduously cultivated the Elector of Saxony, Frederick the Wise, who was protecting Luther, because he needed the highly respected elector's support in his vain effort to get virtually anyone other than the Habsburg candidate elected to the imperial throne. This policy was dictated partly by the pope's failure to grasp the seriousness of the religious issues in Germany but mainly by the way in which Italian political questions, not theological ones, were of concern to him.

Leo did make an effort to enforce some of the modest program of monastic reform enacted by the Lateran Council, but he did not enforce the council's reforms of the central administrative system of the church, the Roman Curia, because these reforms involved giving up abuses that were important sources of revenue for the papacy. The financial requirements of his military operations, his luxurious court, and his patronage of the arts caused him to extend the sale of administrative offices, dispensations, and indulgences that the conciliar reformers had sought to abolish or reduce.

LEÓN, LUIS DE (ca. 1527–1591). Spanish poet, biblical scholar, and monk. Born into a prosperous *converso* family, he became an Augustinian friar in 1544. He was educated at Salamanca, where he studied philosophy, theology, and biblical languages, and became professor of theology in 1561. Despite his fame as a scholar, Fray Luis came under attack from the Spanish **Inquisition** on charges of "Judaizing," by which his accusers and judges did not mean that he practiced **Jewish** religion but that he taught that at several points the Hebrew text of the Old Testament revealed mistranslations in the traditional Latin Vulgate Bible. Such a critical attitude smacked of the ideas of the **Erasmian humanists** and the Lutheran heretics. He compounded the offense by supporting the use of rabbinical commentaries on the Hebrew Scriptures. The fact that his family were *conversos* undoubtedly encouraged the attacks. Fray Luis vigorously defended himself and was eventually let off with a mild caution against certain dangerous tendencies in his teaching. He promptly resumed his career as professor of theology at Salamanca. But in the interim, he had had to spend nearly five years in solitary confinement.

Fray Luis was also a distinguished poet, writing poems in both Latin and Spanish that were not published until 1631 but circulated in manuscript during and after his lifetime. They are now regarded as a landmark in the use of Spanish for lyric poetry and as one of the works that make the late 16th century the Golden Age of Spanish literature. He also produced a prose dialogue, *De los nombres de Cristo / The Names of Christ* (1583) that presented biblical themes for the use of pious Spanish readers who were forbidden to have the Bible itself in their own language. He published Latin commentaries on several parts of the Bible. The most famous and most extensive of these was his commentary on the Song of Songs (1580–1582). Fray Luis's commentaries on Obadiah and Job contended that those books of the Old Testament contained prophecies of the Spanish discovery and settlement of America.

LEONARDO DA VINCI (1452–1519). Tuscan painter, sculptor, scientist, and engineer, the oldest of the three most famous artists of the Italian Renaissance. He was also a polymath whose insatiable curiosity led him to investigate many aspects of his world. Born near the Tuscan town of Vinci, the son of a notary and a peasant girl, he was reared by his paternal grandfather and sometime before 1472 was apprenticed to the Florentine painter and sculptor **Andrea Verocchio**. His earliest surviving painting, an *Annunciation*, dates from 1473. Perhaps the best known of his early paintings is his portrait *Ginevra de'Benci* (ca. 1475). Leonardo left **Florence** around 1482 and by 1483 was in **Milan**, where he began the earlier version of his *Virgin of the Rocks*. He sought the patronage of the duke of Milan, **Ludovico Sforza**; his letter applying for employment emphasized his skills as a civil and military engineer as well as his qualities as an artist. By 1489 he was at work on a huge equestrian statue of Ludovico's father, **Francesco Sforza**; many sketches survive in his notebooks, but the statue was never completed. His most famous painting of this period was the fresco *The Last Supper*, painted (ca. 1495–1497) for a monastery patronized by the Sforza dynasty.

The fall of the Sforza from power ended Leonardo's stay in Milan. He travelled to several cities, including **Mantua**, where he made a portrait of the duchess **Isabella d'Este**. He then spent about two years in Florence, undertaking several projects but finishing little. Next he went to **Rome**, serving **Cesare Borgia**, the ambitious son of **Pope Alexander VI**, as an architect, engineer, and city planner. Returning to Florence in 1503 after the death of the Borgia pope, he was commissioned to produce a battle scene, *The Battle of Anghiari*, commemorating a great Florentine military victory of the preceding century. The painting has been completely destroyed, though copies by other painters survive. Leonardo also began his most famous portrait, the *Mona Lisa*, whose subject was the wife of a prominent Florentine citizen. In 1508 he completed the second version (the London version) of the *Virgin of the Rocks*. By 1508 he was frequently employed by the French governor of Milan. Another political upheaval at Milan forced him to renew his migrations, going first to Florence and then to Milan, but he completed few of the projects he undertook. In 1517 he accepted the invitation of the new king of France, **Francis I**, to move to the French court. He designed settings for court ceremonies and worked on plans for a new royal palace, but he died in 1519 without completing his French projects.

Leonardo was constantly at work, not only on works of art but on scientific investigations of many kinds. Many of these are preserved in his voluminous notebooks, not published until centuries afterward but in themselves constituting a masterpiece in the art of drawing. The most numerous drawings were anatomical, often based on dissections. Leonardo was also interested in mechanical contraptions of all kinds. He made many drawings of flying machines and other machines including a horse-driven armored vehicle, a multi-barreled gun, and other military devices. His notebooks include studies in the science of optics, in mathematics, and in geology. His investigations of fossils, especially of marine shells found on mountain tops, caused him to speculate on geology and on the power of water to shape the earth.

The price paid for Leonardo's many-sided interests was that he completed only a relatively small number of the paintings and statues he undertook, and of these, many have perished. Nevertheless, his rather few completed and surviving paintings are monuments of High Renaissance art at its peak. The scientific findings documented in his notebooks constitute a problem for historians of Renaissance science: the drawings are accurate and clearly prove that he knew scientific facts not "discovered" until later times, yet the notebooks were not published until centuries later, so that it remains questionable whether his discoveries had any significant impact on later scientific investigators.

LEONE EBREO (also Hebreo; ca. 1460–1521). Jewish physician and author, born at Lisbon, the son of a prominent physician and scholar, Isaac Abravanel. In 1483 the father was forced into exile, and Leone joined him in Spain, followed by a second exile when Spain in 1492 expelled all Jews who refused to convert to Christianity. He may have met the philosopher **Giovanni Pico della Mirandola** on a visit to **Florence** and probably spent time in **Venice**, but it is certain that he lived for at least two periods in **Naples**, where in 1501 he became physician to the Spanish viceroy Gónzalo de Córdoba. Strongly influenced by Renaissance **Neoplatonic** thought, in his *Dialoghi d'amore / Dialogues on Love* (probably written about 1502 but not published until 1535) Leone maintained that love was the force that gave rise to all life. He presents a conception of the universe that is influenced by Jewish **Cabalistic** mysticism. His *Dialogues* had considerable influence on later Renaissance authors, including the Spanish writer **Miguel de Cervantes** and the Portuguese poet **Luis Vas de Camoens**. Leone also wrote poems, first published along with his *Dialoghi*, honoring his father and in one case lamenting that his son had been compelled by the king of Portugal to convert to Christianity.

LESCOT, PIERRE (ca. 1515–1578). French Renaissance architect, best known as the designer of the Cour Carrée / Square Court of the Louvre palace in Paris, begun in 1546 for King **Francis I**. This palace is the finest surviving example of the "**classic**" phase of French Renaissance architecture and represents a successful synthesis of Italian influences with the older French style of chateau. The building had sculptures by Jean Goujon, with whom Lescot collaborated closely. Other surviving works are the Fontaine des Innocents in Paris and the Hôtel de Ligneris (Musée Carnavalet).

LETO, POMPONIO (1428–1498). Calabrian-born **humanist**, known in Latin as Julius Pomponius Laetus. Born the illegitimate son of a count, he became so profoundly devoted to Roman **antiquity** that he abandoned his vernacular name and came to be known only under his **classicized** name. He moved to **Rome** in the 1450s, studied Latin under the great stylist **Lorenzo Valla**, and became professor of rhetoric at the **University** of Rome. His home became the gathering place for a group of like-minded enthusiasts for ancient Rome known as the **Roman**

Academy, all of whom took classical-sounding Latin names and referred to Leto as *pontifex maximus*. In part they were a study group, discussing ancient history and ancient archaeological remains, staging plays by Plautus and Terence, and critiquing each other's Latin writings. But they also revived celebration of the Palilia, the ancient festival commemorating the founding of the city of Rome.

In 1467, while in **Venice**, Leto was arrested and charged with sodomy. The following year, he was turned over to authorities at Rome and, together with other members of the Roman Academy such as the humanist **Bartolomeo Platina**, he was brought to trial on charges of sodomy, conspiracy against papal rule of the city, and trying to revive ancient pagan religion. **Pope** Paul II himself presided over one of the two trials. While some of the accused may have been involved in sexual irregularities and re-enactments of ancient religious rituals, the real cause of the prosecution was the pope's fear of political conspiracy against his rule over Rome. Eventually, the defendants were discharged without punishment and Leto was restored to his professorship.

Under the next pope, **Sixtus IV**, Leto revived the Roman Academy, but this time it was organized as a specifically Christian religious sodality, and while it still observed the Palilia, it also honored several Christian saints whose feasts fell at about the same time as the Roman festival. The group's practice of founding sodalities to promote classical studies was a model for later associations of the same kind in both Italy and Northern Europe. Pomponio edited several classical authors and lectured on most of the ancient Latin authors most admired for their style of writing. Leto attracted able students, of whom **Ermolao Barbaro the Younger** became the most famous.

LETTERS OF OBSCURE MEN. Satirical collection of imaginary letters supposedly addressed by several **scholastic** theologians and monks to **Ortwin Gratius**, a Cologne **humanist** who had supported the theologians and Dominican friars of Cologne in their efforts to prosecute the humanist and **Hebrew** scholar **Johann Reuchlin** on charges of impiety. The Latin title is *Epistolae obscurorum virorum.* The first part was published anonymously in 1515. The imaginary letter writers, some of whom bore the names of real persons associated with the attack on Reuchlin while others had ridiculous names that suggest lower-class ancestry and depraved morals ("Piggy," "Honeylicker," "Bottleclinker"), comment on the Reuchlin case and in doing so display themselves and those who agree with them as ignorant, hypocritical, and morally base. The Latin of the letters is a parody of the everyday Latin of the medieval university. The intention is to make the targets of the satire appear ignorant and ridiculous. The letters also pretend to reveal the existence of a vast conspiracy among monks and theologians to destroy **classical** learning and persecute all humanists.

Although the work was published anonymously, virtually everyone knew that some humanists sympathetic to Reuchlin must have produced it. Modern studies have established that the satire was the work of a group of young humanists, all of them having some association with the University of Erfurt and also with the older humanist **Mutianus Rufus**, a canon of Gotha who exerted a radicalizing influence on his young disciples. The poet **Crotus Rubianus** is thought to have originated the form of the attack and to have written most or all of the letters printed in 1515, which are light and humorous in tone and refrain from direct attacks on real individuals. The humanistic knight **Ulrich von Hutten** probably was the author of seven new letters added to a reprint of 1516 and of all of the second part of the work, published in 1517. These added letters are more blunt, naming real individuals both as depraved and ignorant foes of Reuchlin and as good humanists who support Reuchlin. The intention of the second part was to interpret the conflict as a life-and-death struggle between humanism and **scholasticism**. Another young humanist, **Hermann von dem Busche**, may have written some of the letters and probably arranged for the book's clandestine publication. In their choice of **Ortwin Gratius** as the butt of the satire, the authors were also settling personal scores. The book was an overnight sensation among German intellectuals and by presenting the Cologne theologians as contemptible, base, and ignorant, probably weakened the prestige of scholastic theologians on the eve of their confrontation with **Martin Luther**.

LILY, WILLIAM (ca. 1468–1522). English **humanist** and teacher, first grand master of the reorganized St. Paul's school founded by **John Colet**, dean of St. Paul's cathedral. After graduation from Magdalen College, Oxford, in 1486, Lily went on pilgrimage to

Jerusalem, stopped on Rhodes to study **Greek**, and then spent several years perfecting his skills as a **classical** scholar at **Rome** and **Venice** before returning to England. In 1512 Colet chose Lily as head of the new school. While he was fully in sympathy with Colet's intention to create a pious and explicitly Christian spirit for the school, he did not fully share Colet's reservations about using pagan classical authors as readings for grammar-school students. Lily gradually subverted Colet's preference for studying ancient Christian authors and began the transformation of the school into a first-class center for classical studies. He was a friend of **Thomas More**, with whom he published *Progymnasmata* (1521), Latin translations of Greek epigrams. For Colet's school, Lily produced *Grammatices rudimenta / Rudiments of Grammar* (first published in 1527 but used in the school from about 1513) and several other grammatical works which in 1540 were brought together into a comprehensive Latin grammar book, *Institutio compendiaria totius grammaticae*. King **Henry VIII** made Lily's *Institutio* the textbook required for use in all English schools, and it retained this official status well into the 17th century.

LIMBOURG BROTHERS. Three brothers, Paul, Herman, and Jan, active as painters in Paris and at the court of the dukes of **Burgundy** in the late 14th and early 15th centuries. Not much is known about their lives or even their dates; all three were dead by 1416. They are remembered for two sets of manuscript illuminations for aristocratic devotional books (books of hours), *Les Belles heures* (ca. 1408) and *Les très riches heures du Duc de Berry* (1413–1416). The latter work is especially famous for the remarkable scenes of contemporary life illustrating the change of seasons throughout the year. Their genre, miniatures executed in manuscript books, is distinctly medieval, and they exemplify the last phase of medieval Gothic painting, the International Style. The Limbourgs' books of hours were created for private use by members of the French royal family and hence were not likely to be known to the public. But work of this type, especially in its rich colors and its use of the new technique of oil painting, had great influence on the development of painting in 15th-century Italy; and the scenes of both peasant life and aristocratic life, though idealized, provide vivid images of society in northwestern Europe.

LINACRE, THOMAS (ca. 1460–1524). English **humanist** and physician. He grew up in Canterbury and studied at Oxford before going to **Florence** (1487–1493), where he studied **classical** languages under Demetrius Chalcondyles and **Angelo Poliziano.** He then took a medical doctorate at **Padua** in 1496. He became an assistant to the **Venetian printer Aldus Manutius,** working on Aldus' **Greek** edition of **Aristotle** and a Latin translation of Proclus' *De sphaera / On Spheres.* Though offered a position teaching medicine at Padua, he returned to England and after 1509 became physician to King **Henry VIII** and tutor to the king's daughter, Princess Mary. He lectured at Oxford and in 1518 founded the Royal College of Physicians. Linacre's goal as a humanist-educated reformer of medicine was to make ancient Greek medical authors available to contemporary physicians, especially in England. He translated several works of the major Greek medical authority, Galen, into Latin between 1517 and 1523. His influence helped to establish the theory of humors and complexions as the basis of medical practice in England. He corresponded with many of the leading humanists of his time, not only Englishmen like **Thomas More, John Colet,** and **William Lily** but also leading Continental figures such as **Erasmus** and **Guillaume Budé.** He also produced a Latin grammar, originally devised for Princess Mary. Recognizing the backwardness of English medical education in comparison to Italy's, he founded lectureships in medicine at both Oxford and Cambridge.

LIPPI, FRA FILIPPO (ca. 1406–1469). Florentine painter and Carmelite monk. His early work (for example, *Madonna Enthroned,* 1437) shows the influence of **Masaccio** but also suggests the influence of the sculptors **Donatello** and **Lorenzo Ghiberti.** His use of color, well exemplified by his *Adoration* (ca. 1459), suggests exposure to contemporary Flemish art. The evolution of his style is important because he exercised considerable influence on the next generation of artists, especially on his own pupil **Sandro Botticelli.** His many Madonnas are typical of the girlish image and wistful beauty of Florentine Madonnas of the **Quattrocento. Cosimo de' Medici** was an important patron. The paintings of events in the lives of St. John the Baptist and St. Stephen done for the cathedral at Prato, especially the *Death of St. Stephen,* are other well-known examples of his work.

Unlike the pious Dominican painter **Fra Angelico**, Fra Filippo led a disorderly personal life, marked by an early conviction for forgery and his elopement with a nun by whom he had two children, one of whom also became a successful painter, Filippino Lippi (ca. 1457–1504), who was his father's pupil.

LIPSIUS, JUSTUS (1547–1606). Dutch-born **humanist**, one of the great **classical** scholars of the late Renaissance, also historically important for his philosophical works advocating a Christianized form of Stoicism, often labelled **Neostoicism**. His life (as well as his religious affiliation) was repeatedly upset by the violence associated with the Dutch War for Independence, which disrupted both the southern Netherlands (in which he was born) and the northern provinces which eventually gained their independence from Spain. Lipsius received his preparatory education at a **Jesuit** college that was part of the **University** of Cologne. He then studied at **Louvain**, where he entered the service of Antoine Perrenot, Cardinal Granvelle, whom he accompanied as secretary on a mission to **Rome** for King **Philip II** of Spain. This Roman experience contributed to his first book, *Variae lectiones / Various Readings*, a collection of critical commentaries on ancient Latin authors. In 1570 he returned to Louvain but soon left because of the civil war.

In 1572 Lipsius became professor of history and rhetoric at the University of Jena, a position that required profession of Lutheran religion. In 1573, however, he married a Catholic woman whom he had met at Louvain. He returned to the Catholic faith and soon moved back to Louvain, where he received the licentiate in law. The editions of Tacitus' historical works completed there helped to make him famous throughout the world of humanist scholarship. In 1578 he accepted a professorship at the Protestant University of Leiden in the rebellious northern provinces. While in Leiden he continued his prolific work as a classical scholar and again became a Protestant. Twice he was elected rector of the university. In 1591, however, Lipsius converted back to the Catholic Church. After his reconversion, he returned for a time to Leiden, which was religiously tolerant, but in 1592 he became professor of history and Latin language and literature at Louvain. In 1595 he also became official historiographer to Philip II of Spain. During this period at Louvain he published

Catholic devotional tracts and books on political philosophy and Roman history. He also brought out expurgated editions of some of his earlier books that contained passages no longer acceptable for a professor at a Catholic institution.

Lipsius' greatest skills were in the field of philology, and his editions of Tacitus and Seneca influenced the text of those authors for several centuries. He produced important commentaries on classical (mainly Latin) authors. His work as a philosopher (shaped by his close study of the greatest author of ancient Roman Stoicism, Seneca) emphasized the value of Stoicism as a political doctrine that could help contemporaries cope with the international and civil wars that were tearing Christian Europe apart. Lipsius' most popular book of Stoic philosophy was *De constantia / On Constancy* (1584). A second book promoting Stoicism was his *Politica* (1589). Some contemporaries noted cynically that it was strange for a man who had so obviously changed his own religious identity in accord with the demands of his career to be the author of a book in praise of constancy. Yet his promotion of a Christianized Stoicism as a philosophy suitable for a man of culture and moderation contributed to the Stoic ethical code that dominated the mentality of the European ruling classes during the following centuries.

LOLLARDS. Followers of the 14th-century English theologian and heretic **John Wyclif**. After Wyclif's death in 1384, the English ecclesiastical courts forced most of his university followers to recant their heretical doctrines, and during the reign of Henry IV, a Parliamentary statute made heresy a capital offense. Ownership of an unauthorized copy of the Bible in English came to be regarded as *prima facie* evidence of heresy. The Lollards' educated leadership had been destroyed or silenced by the 1420s, but the movement survived as a clandestine sect of simple, pious people, many of them artisans and small merchants. What held the underground groups together was mainly rejection of the authority of the official clergy and insistence on laymen's free access to the Bible in English translations made by Wyclif's early followers.

Lollardy was a phenomenon of the later **Middle Ages** and had no connection with Renaissance culture. But clusters of Lollards survived, sometimes in significant numbers, in various parts of England,

and there were still Lollards in England in the early 16th century. An issue debated among historians of the early English **Reformation** is whether Lollard beliefs contributed to the spread of Lutheranism and prepared the way for the official Reformation begun by **Henry VIII** in the 1530s.

LONGUEIL, CHRISTOPHE DE (ca. 1488–1522). French-Netherlandish **humanist**, born at Mechelen in Brabant to a local woman and an aristocratic French bishop who was French ambassador to the Netherlands. In 1497 his father sent him to study at the University of Paris. After his father's death in 1500 Longueil left school and began a military career, first in the service of King Louis XII of France, then in the service of Philip the Handsome, duke of **Burgundy**. After Duke Philip died in 1506, Longueil studied law at **Bologna** (1507) and then at Poitiers (1508–1510). His interest in natural science led to his being appointed to lecture on Pliny the Elder, a classical authority on scientific matters; he also lectured on the Pandects, a branch of Roman law. Pope **Leo X** granted Longueil a brief of legitimation, making him eligible for an honorary papal appointment and pension. In 1514 he received a doctorate in law from the **University** of Valence and delivered an oration in praise of law that was published there. He moved to Paris and was appointed to the Parlement of Paris. There he assisted the humanist and publisher Nicolas Bérault with a collection of various scholars' notes and commentaries on Pliny.

In order to perfect his **Greek**, Longueil went to **Rome**, where he studied with Janus Lascaris and Marcus Musurus. He met other influential figures at the Curia, including **Pietro Bembo**, and associated with the Roman **Academy**, a sodality of enthusiasts for study of Roman **antiquities**. His acceptance among this group was a tribute to the pure **Ciceronian** style of his Latin. The discrepancy between his earlier expressions of French patriotism and his aspirations to be recognized at the curia as truly "Roman" involved him in an unpleasant personal conflict with rivals at Rome, and for a time he went back to France. He returned to Italy in 1519, first to **Venice** and the following year to **Padua**, where for a time he lived as a guest of Bembo. After the death of Pope **Leo X**, Longueil became the protégé of **Reginald Pole**, a cousin of **Henry VIII** of England. While a house guest of Pole at Padua, he fell ill and died. Pole wrote a biographical sketch that was prefixed to an edition of several of Longueil's works and letters.

During his brief life, Longueil acquired a great reputation on account of his ability to write Ciceronian Latin. He was highly regarded by the influential French humanist **Guillaume Budé**, but his relations with the even more famous Dutch humanist **Erasmus** were cool, for Erasmus endorsed a more open, moderately eclectic style of Latin and was critical of those humanists (mostly Italians at the Roman curia) who regarded Cicero as the only proper model both for style and vocabulary. Since Longueil was the leading non-Italian supporter of this Ciceronianism, and since he was circumspectly but obviously critical of Erasmus' own Latin, an undercurrent of hostility grew up between them. Though Erasmus expressed regret at Longueil's premature death, when his *Ciceronianus* (1528) was published, repudiating the sterile purism and artificiality of the "Ciceronian" style of Latin, Longueil was a target of his criticism.

LOPE DE VEGA (Lope Félix de Vega Carpio, 1562–1635). Spanish poet and playwright, commonly regarded as Spain's greatest dramatist, and together with his older contemporary **Miguel de Cervantes Saavedra**, one of the authors whose work defines the Golden Age of Spanish literature. One of his disciples claimed that he had written 1,800 plays. About 314 plays are securely attributed to him, and 187 others are attributed with some plausibility. Born at Madrid, the son of a master embroiderer, Lope was a child prodigy, composing verses orally before he could write, reading Latin as well as Castilian when he was five, and writing his first play at age 12, possibly as part of his studies in a **Jesuit** college. At age 14 he entered the service of the bishop of Ávila and later served the Marquis of Las Navas. He studied at the **University of Alcalá** and during his service to Las Navas may also have studied at Salamanca.

Lope participated in a military expedition to the Azores but in 1588 was banished from Madrid for eight years because of his libellous poems attacking one of his mistresses who had thrown him over for a rich lover. He secretly returned to Madrid and married a woman there in 1588, the same year in which he enlisted in the Spanish Armada against England. He served as secretary to several high nobles, including the duke of Alba and (from 1605) the duke of Sessa. He received a royal pardon in 1595, forgiving his unauthorized return to Madrid during his "exile."

Lope's residence in Valencia during part of that exile introduced him to a lively theatrical world, and when he returned to Madrid he brought innovations that changed theater in that city. He rebelled against the effort of learned critics to impose the **classical** set of three unities on drama, writing a tract, *Arte nuevo de hacer comedias en este reino / New Art of Playwriting in this Kingdom* (1609), which defended several practices forbidden by classical theory, such as use of comic relief and subplots in serious dramas. He reduced the number of acts from five to three, took plot material from Spanish history and legend as well as from more traditional religious and mythological sources, presented cross-dressing female characters on stage, and in general paid heed to what pleased theatergoers rather than to theorists.

His plays are far too numerous to be enumerated here, but some of the most highly regarded may be listed: *El caballero de Olmedo / The Knight from Olmedo* (1620–1625) is based on a popular ballad and models one of its characters on a character in the popular prose romance *La Celestina* by **Ferdinando de Rojas**; *Fuenteovejuna* is based on 15th-century Castilian history; the comedy *Perro de hortelano / The Dog in the Manger* (1613–1615) is an ingenious work influenced by the style of classical comedy; *El castigo sin venganza / Punishment Without Vengeance* (1631) is based on a popular Italian novella.

Although most famous as a dramatist, Lope was also a productive poet and prose author. He wrote several hundred sonnets, some of which appeared in anthologies with the works of other poets, some of which were published in his own collections. One of his epic poems, *La Dragontea*, was directed against the English privateer Francis Drake and reflects his own experience as a member of the ill-fated Armada expedition. Lope also wrote prose fiction, including a pastoral novel, *La Arcadia* (1598); *La Filomena* (1621) and *La Circe* (1624), two examples of mythological themes; and *La Dorotea* (1632), his own account of one of his many adulterous love affairs. Although in many respects he was a pious man and in 1614 was ordained a priest, he had many mistresses and begot many children out of wedlock. He did acknowledge and support his children. Despite his humble social origins, he was by far the most successful literary figure of Spain in his time.

LORENZETTI, PIETRO (ca. 1280–ca. 1348) and AMBROGIO (after 1290–1348). Sienese brothers, prominent artists succeeding to the position of **Duccio** and **Simone Martini** as Siena's leading painters. Pietro is known for his frescoes in the council chamber of his city, while Ambrogio's works include frescoes in the lower church at Assisi. Both brothers worked in the last great medieval artistic style, International Gothic, though their work also shows the influence of the greatest **Florentine** painter of the preceding generation, **Giotto**, who is often viewed as a precursor of the artistic Renaissance.

LORRIS, GUILLAUME DE. *See ROMANCE OF THE ROSE.*

LOSCHI, ANTONIO (ca. 1368–1441). Italian **humanist**, a native of Vicenza, educated in law at **Padua** but best known for his career as chancellor to the duke of **Milan, Giangaleazzo Visconti**, during a period of war between Milan and **Florence**. He wrote a political tract attacking the Florentines' claim that the war involved a struggle between republican liberty and monarchical tyranny. This *Invectiva in Florentinos*, probably written about 1397–1398 and directed against the Florentine propaganda diffused in the official letters of the Florentine chancellor **Coluccio Salutati**, praised monarchy as a better guarantor of peace and social order than republican government. It argued that unification of northern Italy under the rule of the Visconti dukes would shelter the peninsula from military intervention by foreign powers.

Loschi also argued that the Florentines' eagerness to gain political control over neighboring cities gave the lie to the city's pretense of being the defender of Italian liberty. In response, a number of Florentine humanists, including Salutati himself in his *Invectiva contra Antonium Luschum* (1403), defended the record of their city in upholding political freedom. Yet Loschi was by no means a personal enemy of Salutati. He had been one of the young humanists who clustered around Salutati during the years when Salutati made Florence the center of the new humanist culture. In 1406, after the death of Giangaleazzo, Loschi moved to **Rome** and became a curial official.

LOUVAIN, UNIVERSITY OF. The first and (until the late 16th century) only university in the Netherlands. Founded in 1425 with faculties of liberal arts, law, and medicine, it was authorized in 1432 to add a faculty of theology, thus acquiring all four of the faculties traditionally found in a medieval **university**. As the only university in a large and wealthy region, Louvain became a flourishing institution. Its statutes and customs were modelled on the practices of Paris, Cologne, and Vienna, and many of the earliest faculty were graduates of those institutions. The university was committed to the realist tradition (*via antiqua*) of philosophical and theological teaching. Although Louvain was a bulwark of medieval **scholasticism**, by the late 15th century it did have **humanist** teachers. In 1517 the Collegium Trilingue (**Trilingual College**), a special institute for the study of the languages essential to humanistic scholarship (classical Latin, **Greek**, and **Hebrew**), was founded by a legacy from a wealthy royal official. The Dutch humanist **Erasmus**, who resided in Louvain from 1517 to 1521, played an advisory role in founding the new institute and recruiting its earliest faculty. The faculties of arts and theology resisted the incorporation of the new college into the university, but within a few years it had become an important part of the school, confirming and strengthening the reputation of Louvain as an excellent center for humanistic education.

After 1517, professors from the faculty of theology played an important role in the struggle against the spread of Protestant doctrines in the **Habsburg** Netherlands. While the university suffered during the religious strife and civil wars of the later 16th century, it recovered its importance as a leading Catholic institution during the 17th century.

LOVATI, LOVATO DEI (1241–1309). Paduan notary and judge, one of the first Italian poets in several centuries to write in Latin rather than in the literary languages previously current in northern Italy— French, Provençal, and several regional Italian dialects. Although conventionally classified as a "pre-humanist," he did most of the things usually regarded as typical of later **humanists**, not only by writing original Latin poetry but also by his admiration for **classical** Latin literature and his interest in the **Roman antiquities** of his own community. About 1283 he discovered an ancient tomb that he mistakenly claimed to be that of Antenor, the mythical founder of **Padua**. Lovati was especially devoted to the Roman dramatist Seneca, and his study of that Seneca led him to write a treatise in which he explained the nature of classical Latin poetical meter, an subject that had been completely misunderstood during the **Middle Ages**.

In his Latin verse, Lovato sought to recapture the diction of classical Latin, though his prose writings, mostly related to his work as a judge and notary, used the prevailing medieval Latin of his profession. He was one of the few earlier classical scholars to be mentioned favorably by **Petrarch**. His prominent role in Latin literary culture is especially important because he was a layman, writing at a time when north of the Alps most higher culture was still dominated by the clergy. Because he was a layman and was active in the political life of what was then a republic, his poems dealt with questions of family life and civic politics in a way that later became typical of the "civic" and secular humanism of the 15th century.

LUCAS VAN LEYDEN (1494–1533). Dutch painter, active at Leiden and Antwerp. He was especially important for the quality of his woodcuts and engravings, which were strongly influenced by **Albrecht Dürer**. His paintings suggest Italian influence. Among his best-known paintings are a genre painting, *The Chess Players*, and a biblical scene, *Lot and His Daughters*.

LUDER, PETER (1415–1472). One of the "wandering poets," educated Germans who moved about the country in the decades after 1450 teaching poetry or other literary subjects relevant to Renaissance **humanism**, and trying to create a Renaissance culture in Germany. He sought to inspire young Germans to emulate their Italian contemporaries by abandoning traditional medieval **university** subjects and mastering **classical** Latin style and literature. Educated at Heidelberg, about 1434 Luder went to Italy and studied humanistic subjects at the University of **Ferrara** under **Guarino da Verona**. He lived in Italy for nearly 20 years before returning to Germany in 1456.

Luder began his migratory teaching at Heidelberg that year by announcing that the subject of his course would be the *studia humanitatis*, "that is, the books of the [ancient] poets, orators, and historians." He announced that he intended to restore the purity of the Latin language, which had fallen into medieval "barbarism." Subsequently he lectured at Ulm and the universities of Erfurt and Leipzig. After returning to Italy and completing a doctorate in medicine, he settled in **Basel**, where he lectured on both poetry and medicine and served as town physician. He acted as a diplomatic representative for the duke of the Tyrol and in 1470 lectured at Vienna.

The peripatetic nature of Luder's career may well have been due to his excessive drinking, his love affairs (thoroughly advertised in his Latin poems), and the hostility of conservative faculty to a teacher who challenged the **scholastic** tradition, but the main cause was probably that since the new subjects did not form part of the curriculum of studies required for degrees, students could not afford to spend much of their time attending lectures on such topics. Hence the potential public for such lectures at any one place was limited, and after teaching for a term or two, he had exhausted the paying audience and had to move on to another place.

LUIS DE LEÓN. *See* LEÓN, LUIS DE.

LURIA, ISAAC (1534–1572). Jewish **cabalist**. Born in Jerusalem and educated not only in cabalistic mysticism but also in the **Jewish** law, he considered the *Sefer Zohar / Book of Splendor*, a work written in Spain in the 13th century but then thought to date from the second century, to be the most authoritative cabalistic text. By 1554 he was living in Egypt, where he became a judge of the religious court of Ashkenazic Jews. In 1569 he moved back to the Holy Land, settling at Safed.

Luria became famous both for his mastery of the Cabala and for his knowledge of the religious law. Most of his small body of writings consisted of commentaries on the *Zohar*, though he also wrote some poems. His teachings emphasized the inner experience of the soul, and he also had strong messianic expectations. He did not earn his living as a teacher or legal scholar but as a merchant, a profession he followed throughout his life.

LUTHER, MARTIN (1483–1546). German religious reformer. His challenge to prevailing practices and doctrine precipitated the spiritual and social upheaval now known as the Protestant **Reformation**. Although in many respects he was a product of the **scholastic** university education he received in his youth, Luther was still a man of his generation, affected by the rising interest in ancient language and literature and expressing regret even in his later years that he had never learned to write Latin in the **humanist** style. After he had become a monk and had received his doctorate in theology, Luther still experimented with the humanist fashion for adopting a **classical** substitute for a German surname: for a time he signed letters to friends as "Eleutherius," a name with a **Greek** ring to it.

Luther's practice as professor of biblical theology at Wittenberg suggests acceptance of humanist ideas of educational reform. He focused his lectures on the text of Scripture rather than on the many layers of commentary created by medieval scholarship. This textual emphasis was not due to humanist influence alone. There was already a strong biblical strain in the popular piety of Germanic Europe, and Luther's monastic superior and mentor, Johann von Staupitz, had already concentrated on the sacred text itself while he was teaching at Wittenberg. But openness to humanist ways of approaching the Bible is evident in Luther's eagerness to apply the new scholarship of biblical humanists like **Lefèvre d'Etaples** and **Erasmus** in his lectures. When Erasmus' edition of the **Greek** New Testament was published in 1516, Luther promptly bought a copy and made it, rather than the traditional Latin Bible, the decisive authority in his classroom teaching. Finally, Luther conceived his central theological doctrine, that man is justified before God by faith alone and not by any kind of action ("good works") done by human effort, as a restoration of the original and ancient doctrine taught by Christ and most clearly expressed in St. Paul's Epistle to the Romans. This desire to go back to the ancient text, and particularly to privilege the original Greek over the Latin translation, conformed to the general desire of Renaissance humanists to return to the ancient sources.

Luther was also linked to the Renaissance by the warm and early support he received from most German humanists, even many who eventually broke with him when they realized that his movement would shatter the unity of the church. The rapid spread of Luther's ideas throughout Germany was made possible by humanist advisers to publishers who printed his early writings and created a popular image of him as a man of God. It is essentially correct to say that without the support of the German humanists in its early stages, there would have been no Reformation.

Luther attracted the humanists in part because he was the leader in a substantial reorientation of the curricula in liberal arts and theology at Wittenberg that conformed closely to humanist ideas of educational reform. In close collaboration with the young humanist hired as Wittenberg's first regular professor of Greek, **Philipp Melanchthon**, he carried through a significant number of changes in the course of study. Subsequently he backed Melanchthon's work as educational adviser to German princes and city councils who wanted to introduce humanistic reform into German **universities** and grammar schools. Even though it is fair to say that Luther was not a humanist, his openness to humanistic ideas about theological study and general education and the positive reception he had from most humanists (especially the younger ones) make his relation to Renaissance humanism an integral part of his role as leader of the movement for religious reform.

LYLY, JOHN (ca. 1553–1606). English dramatist and author of a prose romance, *Euphues: The Anatomy of Wit* (1578), which was his first and most influential published work. This moralizing and allegorical tale was important for its elaborate and highly artificial prose style, which dominated the English prose literature of his time. The book was immensely popular, though now regarded as almost unreadable because of the obscurity of his style. Lyly's plays, produced under the patronage of the Earl of Oxford, dealt with the same themes as *Euphues*, moral tensions produced by conflicts between love and duty and by tension between the demands of society and the will of the individual. His plays were produced at court and were successful in their time, but they never won the royal patronage that he expected, and he died largely neglected by the new Stuart court.

– M –

MACHAUT, GUILLAUME DE (1300–1377). French composer, poet, and priest. He was the most prominent composer in the style known as *ars nova* / "the new art" that dominated French music in the first half of the 14th century. He began his career as secretary to King John of Bohemia, who was killed in 1346 in the battle of Crécy. He then joined the French royal court and eventually became canon of the cathedral at Rheims. In his own time, Machaut was famous both as a poet and as a musician. Like *ars nova* music in general, his compositions, even those composed for liturgical use, sounded more secular than the music of the preceding century and were criticized as lascivious and as so complex that the liturgical text was obscured by the music. He wrote both monophonic and polyphonic music, for both secular and religious purposes, using many genres including motets, *lais*, *chansons balladées* or *virelais*, and *rondeaux*. Machaut was particularly important in the development of the form known as the *ballade*. Of special significance is his composition of one of the earliest polyphonic musical settings for the Ordinary of the mass, his *Messe de Notre Dame*, which may have been written for the coronation of King **Charles V** in 1364.

MACHIAVELLI, NICCOLÒ (1469–1527). Florentine political theorist, statesman, and historian, commonly regarded as the greatest political thinker of the Renaissance. His keen analysis of the realities of power and the foundations of political success was so often denounced as immoral that the term "Machiavellian" still implies ruthlessness in the pursuit of power and unscrupulousness in the means adopted. The real Machiavelli was a far more subtle and nuanced thinker than the modern term implies, though his system of political thought, based on his insider's view of the workings of Italian statecraft, began with the assumption that unless a political leader can gain office and keep it, no gentler political virtues are of any account. Although often depicted as an apologist for tyranny and violence, Machiavelli preferred a republican form of government in which an elite of well-born and prosperous leaders shared authority with representatives of the lower (but not the very lowest) orders of society — essentially the system of government that he believed to have ruled the ancient **Roman** republic.

Machiavelli received an excellent **humanistic** education under the supervision of his father, who himself was an admirer of ancient literature. The son came of political age just as Medicean dominance of **Florence** collapsed and new leaders tried to devise political reforms that would provide a strong executive authority while preventing any one faction or family from becoming as powerful as the **Medici** had been. He witnessed the radical and unstable phase of this reform effort when the Dominican friar **Savonarola** dominated the city. After the fall of Savonarola in 1498, Machiavelli was appointed to an important civic office as head of the second chancery. He also became secretary to the government commission that managed foreign policy and accompanied several embassies abroad. After 1502 he became close to **Piero Soderini**, a moderate aristocrat who was elected *gonfaloniere* (head of the central governing council, the *Signoria*) for life.

Even before Soderini's rise to power, Machiavelli had agitated for the creation of a local militia made up of citizens, arguing that reliance on mercenary troops had been the source of the inability of the Italian states to cope with the invasions by French and Spanish rulers. Soderini authorized him to organize such a militia, which was successful in restoring Florentine rule over **Pisa** in 1509 but proved no match for the powerful army, mostly Spanish troops, sent by Pope **Julius II** and King **Ferdinand I** of Spain in 1512 to conquer Florence, oust Soderini and restore the Medici to power. Unlike most civil servants under Soderini, Machiavelli was summarily dismissed from office, fined heavily, and forbidden to leave Florentine territory for a year. In 1513, when a plot against the Medici was discovered, he was arrested and tortured, but apparently there was no evidence that he had been involved.

The fall of Soderini's regime was essentially the end of Machiavelli's political career. He was perfectly willing to accept the restored Medicean leadership, but his known republican sympathies made the new rulers mistrust him. He was commissioned indirectly by the Medici to write a *History of Florence*, a work that he completed in 1525 and dedicated to the Medici pope, **Clement VII**. His work on this project brought about a partial reconciliation with the Medici but never led to a significant political appointment. In 1527, when the army of the Emperor **Charles V** plundered Rome and held the pope himself captive, the Florentine people, still loyal to their republican constitution, again overthrew the Medici. Machiavelli offered his services to the revolutionary regime, but his recent association with the Medici made him mistrusted, and his offer was declined. He died a few weeks later.

Politics was life to Machiavelli. Despite his fine humanistic education, he was interested in action, not in literature. After his release from imprisonment in 1513, he had nothing better to do than think and write, mostly about his own personal experience and the thing that interested him most, political power. In the last 14 years of his life, he turned out a brilliant collection of literary works, mostly about politics but also including comedies, poems, a novella, and his *Florentine Histories*. His two comedies, *Mandragola* (1518) and *Clizia* (1525) are among the principal achievements of the early Renaissance Italian theater. His *Florentine Histories* provide a well-informed and thoughtful analysis of the background of the political instability that afflicted contemporary Italy. His *The Art of War* (1519–1520) presented his case for a citizen army and also sought to adapt to modern conditions the military wisdom of the ancient Romans.

But his most important works are *The Prince* (ca. 1513; first published in 1532) and *Discourses on the First Ten Books of Titus Livius* (usually dated 1514–1517), a pair of tracts in which he put forward his ideas on politics, based primarily on his own experience of Italian political reality, and secondarily on his reading and ruminations on the history of ancient Rome. *The Prince* is often taken to be a cynical and self-serving endorsement of tyrannical government. In reality, especially when read in the light of the *Discourses*, it is nothing of the kind. Rather, it seeks to define those policies that will enable a ruler to gain and hold onto political power, even in the most adverse circumstances. While its underlying view of human nature and human political behavior is bleak and cynical, Machiavelli is aware that the real basis of any successful political system is the support of the common people. Since the people expect very little from government, Machiavelli argues that it is very easy for an intelligent ruler to win the loyalty of the people. Machiavelli urges his ideal ruler to develop and rely on the military resources of his own populace, who in a crisis will fight for him (and themselves) with a determination unknown to even the most skilled mercenary troops. He evaluates religion exclusively as a political force and warns that the ruler must manipulate that force by seeming to be pious even if he personally is not. At the end of a coldly rational dissection of the secrets of political success, Machiavelli concludes with a passionate appeal to the Medici princes to take advantage of Italy's desperate condition by placing themselves at the head of the whole Italian nation and leading the nation to throw off the yoke of foreign conquest.

While a cursory reading of *The Prince* may make it seem incompatible with Machiavelli's lifelong devotion to a moderate republican government, the *Discourses* suggest an underlying unity of thought.

Of special importance is the concept of historical cycles enunciated in the *Discourses*. All human societies, he argues, eventually pass through three stages of political organization, and no human institution endures forever. Like ancient Rome, they begin as monarchies, eventually overthrow their kings under aristocratic leadership when royal government becomes oppressive, and finally drive out the aristocrats when they become corrupt, ending with a popular government (a democracy, in modern terminology but not in Machiavelli's). Each of the three fundamental types of constitution (as defined by **Aristotle**) eventually declines into a degenerate form: monarchy becomes tyranny, aristocracy (rule of the best and most public-spirited citizens) becomes oligarchy (rule by the rich, who exploit the community for personal gain), and popular government degenerates into what Machiavelli calls "democracy," or mob rule. Since the final state, rule by an undisciplined mob, leads to unbearable social disorder, ultimately a strong man will take power and restore order, thus founding a new monarchy and initiating the next cycle of political change. This cycle will be repeated, over and over again, as long as the community remains independent. The underlying cause of this endless cycle of political forms is the inherent wickedness of human nature and the resulting propensity of rulers to exploit those whom they rule.

Yet it is possible for a wise "lawgiver" (the monarch who brings to an end each phase of mob rule and restores strong government) to erect safeguards that may delay (but never permanently prevent) the inevitable ruin. The secret of political longevity is the creation of a "balanced" government in which an authoritarian ruler, a powerful aristocracy of the rich and well-born, and the common people share authority so that each of the three social elements acts to restrain misuse of power by the other two. This concept of a mixed government, combining monarchical, aristocratic, and popular elements, implies a system of checks and balances similar to the idealized (and largely mythical) Roman republic described by the Hellenistic historian Polybius (whose works were one of the rediscoveries of 15th-century humanistic scholarship). Polybius' history of Rome, written to explain how the single city of Rome could have come to rule the whole Mediterranean world, is a major source of the idea of cyclical rise and fall of political systems that is at the heart of Machiavelli's *Discourses*.

Machiavelli also believed that the third stage of his cycle, a republic ruled by its own citizens, could avoid mob rule and endure only if the people themselves had "virtue," a term implying public-spiritedness and willingness to put the general interest of society ahead of the interest of any one class, clan, or faction. This idea of the need for "virtue" in the people explains why Machiavelli in *The Prince* was willing to encourage the emergence of an authoritarian leader despite his personal preference for a republican constitution. Not all societies have the virtue required for stable, workable republican government. Looking at the chaotic Italian society of his time and the recent conquest of the Florentine republic by foreign troops, Machiavelli concluded that Florentine society was too morally corrupt to rule itself and that for the present crisis, acceptance of rule by a powerful leader might be necessary as a short-term expedient in order to get rid of foreign conquerors and provide internal stability. Viewed in the light of his cyclical theory of political change and his view of human nature, *The Prince* seems to represent not a betrayal of Machiavelli's republican principles but an expedient required by the realities of a harsh age. Neither *The Prince* nor the *Discourses* endorses the unrestrained power of a tyrant as a permanent solution to the problems of human society.

These two political works constitute the most powerful defense of a limited republican constitution written in the Renaissance. Machiavelli was not, however, addressing the masses of Italy. All of his works were written in the Tuscan vernacular, but they were intended to circulate privately among people with enough experience and judgment to find the correct lessons in his writings. None of his political or historical writings was published in his lifetime. Only *The Art of War*, a practical manual on how to organize for war under the guidance of Roman examples, was published while he lived.

MADERNO, CARLO (1556–1629). Italian architect who in 1603 was given the task of bringing the construction of the basilica of St. Peter in **Rome** to completion and changing the pure central-dome plan conceived by **Bramante** and perfected by **Michelangelo**, his greatest predecessors in designing the church, into a basilican form. This task involved designing the present nave and the façade at the west end of the church.

MAGIC. The Renaissance was the golden age of belief in magic, defined as an organized science focused on the understanding and practical application of observed phenomena that cannot be explained by conventional, rationalistic philosophy and science but nevertheless are confirmed by actual experience. Thus magic was conceived as a sort of supreme science, embracing not only the rationally explicable aspects of experience but also all sorts of phenomena which were believed to have real existence but seemed to violate the rules of reason. The word *magic* served as a blanket term for a whole bundle of what modern thought would label pseudosciences. **Astrology**, one of those pseudosciences, sought to discover, understand, and make use of the physical and spiritual influences exerted by the stars and planets on the earth. It was closely linked to magic because the influence of the stars was one of the basic forces that must be taken into account by anyone who wanted to control the occult powers that were the basis of magic.

What is most significant about the place of magic and related subjects like astrology and **alchemy** in the civilization of the Renaissance is that the attraction of these subjects was not limited to culturally and intellectually marginal groups and individuals but was taken with great seriousness by some of the leading minds of the age. There was a popular, unintellectual magic that consisted of nothing but collections of spells, enchantments, and substances, often used to cure disease or to gain control over individuals—for example, to provoke love. But both magic and astrology also were serious subjects, studied by learned and intelligent scholars.

Many of those who studied magic attempted to establish a clear distinction between "natural magic," the study of phenomena that could be observed by the senses but could not be rationally explained by traditional **Aristotelian** science (the action of a magnet on iron was often used as an example) and "spiritual magic," magical operations that involved words and incantations and hence seemed to involve bringing intelligent spiritual beings into action to assist the magician. Use of spiritual forces seemed dangerous since those forces might well be evil demons seeking to lure the soul of the *magus* (practitioner of magic) to its damnation. Although some magicians tried to distinguish between use of good demons and use of evil demons, any demonic or spiritual magic was risky since evil demons were deceitful and might disguise themselves as good ones. Attempts to practice "astral magic," that is, the application of occult forces shed upon the earth by the celestial bodies, were also debatable, since some of these presumed forces seemed material and natural (the use of sunlight to bleach linen, for example) while others were thought to be spiritual and hence involved all the objections to practicing demonic magic.

The credibility of magic was enhanced by the fact that belief in magic and astrology had also been an important aspect of the **classical** civilization that the Renaissance intellectuals admired. Hence study of ancient texts—or of postclassical texts that claimed to be ancient—reinforced interest in the occult sciences. The greatest support for the intellectual credibility of magic was the rediscovery of ancient **Neoplatonic** texts that provided a philosophical basis for magic. The crucial step toward an effort to transform magic from crude charms and rituals employed by unlearned sorcerers into an intellectually defensible science was the work of the **Florentine** philosopher **Marsilio Ficino** in translating the works not only of **Plato** himself but also of the Hellenistic and **Roman** Neoplatonists. The exaggerated emphasis on the spirit-world found in some of these texts stimulated interest in spiritual magic, while Ficino himself, a physician as well as a philosopher, sought to incorporate traditional material substances into a system of thought that embraced both natural magic and spiritual magic. His treatise *De vita coelitus comparanda / On Drawing Life-forces down from the Heavens*, the last part of a larger work called *De vita / On Life* (1489), provided a philosophical basis for study of magic as a real science. Despite his effort to be cautious and orthodox, Ficino practiced a kind of demonic magic that probably violated the laws of both the church and the Roman state. He regarded magic as the supreme form of philosophy and traced its origins through an unbroken chain of enlightened souls from the Persian sage Zoroaster and the Egyptian sage **Hermes Trismegistus** through the **Greek** philosopher Pythagoras to Plato, and from Plato through the Neoplatonic tradition down to his own rediscovery of the Neoplatonic and Hermetic writings.

A second major Renaissance influence on this effort to make magic respectable by giving it ancient sources and a philosophical foundation was Ficino's friend **Giovanni Pico della Mirandola**. He also emphasized the dangers of using occult powers for corrupt and worldly goals and taught that only the properly prepared and spiritually oriented soul could avoid diabolical traps. His interest in **Jewish Cabala** involved an effort both to justify magical learning and to provide a set of symbols, the letters of the **Hebrew** alphabet and the words of Hebrew Scripture, that could be safely used for magical works because of its scriptural foundation. Pico differed from Ficino and from nearly all other scholars of philosophical magic by his rejection of astrology. In fact, he produced a tract, *Disputationes adversus astrologos / Disputations against the Astrologers* (posthumously published in 1513) that challenged the theoretical basis for both scholarly and popular belief in astrology.

The interest in magic (and usually also in astrology) aroused by these Florentine Neoplatonists continued into the 16th and 17th centuries. The German scholar **Agrippa von Nettesheim**, who studied Ficino's works closely and was influenced by Pico's writings to study Jewish cabalistic books, produced the most comprehensive attempt to systematize all the magical learning of **antiquity** and the **Middle Ages** and enrich it with doctrines of Ficino and Pico. His *De occulta philosophia libri tres / Three Books of Occult Philosophy* (1533) was republished several times later in the century. Another influential book on magic was *De naturalium effectuum causis sive de incantationibus / On the Causes of Natural Phenomena, or On Incantations* by the Aristotelian philosopher **Pietro Pomponazzi**. He solved the problem of demonic magic by dismissing all possibility of action by spiritual agents on material substances. He described a magical science that involved only the action of natural agents on material objects. He attributed a major role to astrological influences, which he likewise redefined to eliminate the possibility of spiritual forces, reducing celestial influences to the purely material level. Later authors who wrote on magical themes included three late Renaissance philosophers, **Giordano Bruno**, **Giambattista della Porta**, and **Tommaso Campanella**. These and other occultist philosophers drew most of their underlying magical ideas from Ficino and Pico. Sharply different from all the others was the German physician **Paracelsus**, who borrowed some ideas from the Florentine Platonists but also drew on materials provided by the uneducated classes, including alchemy, metallurgy, and popular theology.

The shaky foundations of magic's claim to be a genuine science were evident to the English philosopher-scientist **Francis Bacon**, who tried without much success to reform and preserve whatever was good and useful in magic while purging the science of its ancient philosophical sources and attempting to base it on empirical knowledge. Even more destructive was the work of a number of mathematicians and scientists brought together in Paris by the monk Marin Mersenne, a translator of **Galileo** and an associate of both René Descartes and Blaise Pascal; by the 1630s he and his friends had essentially abandoned the basic magical premise that nature is full of spirits and can be understood and controlled by spiritual forces. Henceforth, throughout the 17th century, magic gradually lost its Renaissance aura of intellectual respectability and came to be dismissed by the educated classes as mere superstition or fraud.

MALDONADO, JUAN (ca. 1485–1554). Spanish **humanist** and clergyman. At the University of Salamanca, he studied wth one of the leading Spanish humanists of the early 16th century, **Elio Antonio de Nebrija**, and with the Netherlandish scholar **Christophe de Longueil**. After ordination to the priesthood, he settled in Burgos, where he won the favor of Bishop Juan de Fonseca and became diocesan examiner of candidates for ordination. His first literary work was a history of the recent Comuneros rebellion (1520–1521) against the **Emperor Charles V**, *De motu Hispaniae / On the Spanish Rebellion*, which was presented in manuscript to the future King **Philip II** but never published in the author's lifetime. The first printed edition appeared at **Rome** in 1572.

In the 1520s Maldonado was one of the many Spanish humanists inspired by **Erasmus** and corresponded with the Dutch humanist. Maldonado favored moderate religious reform under the leadership of well educated diocesan bishops. But by the early 1530s he had concluded that Erasmus' satirical attacks on corrupt members of the clergy and the religious orders were reckless and ill-considered. At this point he declared that Erasmus' *Colloquies* were unsuitable for students and that of all of Erasmus' original works, only his Paraphrases of the New Testament were free from the danger of encouraging heresy. Maldonado also wrote a Latin comedy, *Hispaniola*, two tracts critical of Erasmus, and a collection of short works, including his *Pastor bonus*, a work sharply critical of the Spanish clergy. His turning against Erasmus is especially significant because he did not reject humanistic studies in general; indeed, he taught the humanities at a Latin school in Burgos from 1532.

MANETTI, GIANNOZZO (1396–1459). Florentine **humanist**, orator, and diplomat, best known in his own century for his treatise *De* *dignitate et excellentia hominis / On the Dignity and Excellence of Man*, written at the request of King Alfonso V of **Naples** while Manetti was **Florentine** ambassador there. The book is the ablest of a number of treatises written as responses to an earlier work, *On the Misery of the Human Condition*, written in the late 12th century by Lotario di Segni, who later became Pope Innocent III. Pope Innocent's book emphasized the fleeting nature of human happiness and was intended to show that all worldly goods are unreliable and that only God can give lasting happiness. Pope Innocent also announced a never-fulfilled plan to write a second treatise on human happiness. The pope's tract had come up in Manetti's conversations with the king, and when he completed his book, he dedicated it to Alfonso. Although his treatise does indeed glorify human nature, it is by no means devoid of religious sentiments. His emphasis on the suitability of an active life for humans is compatible with his own career as an active participant in Florentine politics. He believed strongly that political involvement was morally obligatory for the citizen of a republic, and his own role in the political life of his city brought him fame but also much criticism.

In 1453 Manetti, unwilling to be silenced by the growing political power of **Cosimo de'Medici**, openly opposed Cosimo on a question of foreign policy and was forced into exile. He spent two years at **Rome** as secretary to **Pope Nicholas V** and in 1455 was appointed as a councillor to King Alfonso, who provided him with a palace and a large secretarial staff to assist him in translating **Greek** works into Latin. He also undertook a fresh translation of the Old Testament from **Hebrew**, though he completed only the text of Psalms. Manetti was both a humanist admirer of ancient languages and literature and a pious Christian, who near the end of his life wrote a book *Contra Iudeos et gentes / Against the Jews and Gentiles*, which asserted that Christianity was the fulfillment of the best elements in both **Jewish** religion and the wisdom of the ancient pagan sages.

Although most Florentine humanists of the earlier 15th century viewed their humanistic culture and the values that governed their lives in a predominantly secular frame of reference, Manetti was notably devout. He had studied Greek with **Ambrogio Traversari**, a humanist who was also a member of the strict Camaldolesian religious order and whose scholarship focused on ancient Greek patristic authors. He became expert not only in classical Latin and Greek but also in Hebrew, a rare attainment for a Christian scholar of his generation. He also wrote historical and biographical works, including literary assessments of the work of the three great Florentine intellectuals of the preceding century, **Dante**, **Petrarch**, and **Boccaccio**; also a life of the humanist **Niccolò Niccoli**; and a life of his patron Pope Nicholas V. Manetti made new translations of the ethical writings of **Aristotle**. Perhaps the most intriguing of his translations, however, is his translation of the New Testament from Greek, apparently made independently of the famous textual notes on the Greek New Testament made by **Lorenzo Valla** a few years earlier. Manetti may have known of Valla's annotations, since both men were living at the papal curia in 1453–1457, yet his work appears to be independent. His translation survived only in a few manuscripts and has never been printed.

MANNERISM. Term used by art historians to label a style of painting, sculpture, and architecture that arose in the 1520s as a variant of the style of High Renaissance masters such as **Leonardo da Vinci**, **Michelangelo**, and **Raphael**. The death of Leonardo in 1519 and of Raphael in 1520 is a rough benchmark for the stylistic change perceived by later historians, and while Michelangelo lived much longer, his style underwent significant changes in the 1520s so that his own development has often been expressed in terms of a shift from Renaissance to mannerist art. The end of mannerism is far more vague than its beginning. About the end of the 16th century, historians of art identify the emergence of the style known as **baroque**, though the change from mannerist to baroque style seems to have been gradual and is often hard to describe objectively.

"Mannerism" as a label for a style and a period is rooted in the Italian noun *maniera*, used by the pioneer art historian **Giorgio Vasari** to mean "style." The principal characteristics of art designated as mannerist are deliberate striving after bizarre effects, violent emotion, emphasis on movement, vivid colors, and exaggerated subjectivity. The mannerist artists chose certain elements in the style of the Renaissance masters and sought to be innovative by developing these further or even exaggerating them. The new style began with extreme, shocking distortion in the work of two young **Florentine** painters, **Rosso Fiorentino** and **Jacopo da Pontormo**, in the 1520s. Early examples are Rosso's *Descent from the Cross* and Pontormo's *Joseph with Jacob in Egypt* (1518). Both of these paintings use exaggeration and violence to flout the stable and composed images typical of the Renaissance masters. Less violent and less extreme are the works of **Parmigianino**, who in his self-portrait of 1524 toys with the distortion caused by his own image in a convex mirror. A clear example of mannerist distortion is Parmigianino's *Madonna with the Long Neck* (ca. 1535). The painting is full of strange details that deliberately challenge the viewer's expectations.

Other painters whose works exemplify the mannerist style are **Bronzino** and **Tintoretto**, the first Venetian painter to be associated with mannerism, while the greatest of the mannerist painters was **El Greco**, a native of Crete who reached the peak of his career in the Spain of **Philip II**. In sculpture, **Benvenuto Cellini** and **Giovanni da Bologna** provide early and later examples of mannerist style. In architecture, examples of mannerism include the Uffizi Palace at Florence, designed by Giorgio Vasari, and the Palazzo del Tè at **Mantua**, designed by **Giulio Romano**.

MANTEGNA, ANDREA (1431–1506). North Italian painter, trained at **Padua** but also influenced by **Florentine** artists, especially the sculptor **Donatello**, who worked in Padua while Mantegna was an apprentice, and by the treatise *Della pittura* by **Leon Battista Alberti**, who provided the earliest clear description of the principles of vanishing-point **perspective**. Mantegna must also have closely studied **Roman** monuments available in northern Italy, an influence evident in his frescoes in the Church of the Eremitani at Padua, such as *St. James Led to His Execution*, the most important product of his early period. His *St. Sebastian*, painted shortly after he left Padua to become court painter to **Ludovico Gonzaga**, marquis of **Mantua**, also uses **classical** architecture as background but demonstrates a new attention to color which is usually attributed (though without decisive evidence) to popular interest in the colorful paintings of the Flemish style that had developed in Florence and **Venice** between 1430 and 1450. Mantegna's most important work for the marquis of Mantua was the set of frescoes depicting the ruling family painted between 1465 and 1474 in the Camera degli Sposi of the palace.

Mantegna continued to work for Ludovico's successor Federigo and especially for Federigo's wife, **Isabella d'Este**. He undertook a series of allegorical paintings for Isabella's new palace. Except for the short-lived **Masaccio**, Mantegna was the most talented painter of the early Renaissance (or **Quattrocento**) style, and the length of his life meant that he had considerable influence on later artists. His marriage to a sister of the Venetian painters **Gentile** and **Giovanni Bellini** extended his influence to Venice, and his work as a printmaker spread his influence not only throughout Italy but also into northern Europe, where **Albrecht Dürer** was affected by his prints.

MANTUA. City of Lombardy in northern Italy, located on the Mincio River, with a population estimated at about 30,000 in the Renaissance. It was the capital of a duchy created in 1328 when Luigi **Gonzaga** established a hereditary principality that continued to be ruled by his dynasty until 1707. In 1433 the Emperor Sigismund raised Mantua to the status of a marquisate and a fief of the Holy Roman Empire. Located in territory coveted by powerful neighbors such as **Venice** and **Milan**, Mantua was frequently in danger of conquest but was saved by the careful diplomacy of the rulers, who created a powerful army and made themselves useful to other powers as mercenary captains (**condottieri**). From the late 15th century, the struggle between the French **Valois** and the Spanish **Habsburg** dynasties for control of northern Italy further complicated the effort to remain independent, but the Gonzaga allied themselves with the Emperor **Charles V**, who ultimately established Spanish hegemony over Italy.

The marquises of Mantua also conducted an active cultural policy that made their state an important center of Renaissance art and learning. Gianfrancesco Gonzaga (1395–1444) brought the noted teacher **Vittorino da Feltre** to his court to establish a **humanistic** school for the education of the ruler's children and other local boys, and it soon attracted sons of prominent families from many parts of northern Italy. The Gonzaga also patronized the arts, attracting **Antonio Pisanello, Andrea Mantegna, Leon Battista Alberti**, and **Giulio Romano** to embellish their court at various periods of the 15th and 16th centuries. Especially in the time of Francesco Gonzaga (1466–1519) and his wife **Isabella d'Este** (1474–1539), the court of Mantua was recognized as one of the most splendid centers of literary and artistic life in Italy.

MANTUANUS, BAPTISTA. *See* BAPTISTA MANTUANUS.

MANUTIUS, ALDUS (vernacular name, Aldo Manuzio, ca. 1452–1515). Italian **humanist** and teacher who became the greatest **printer** and publisher of the Italian Renaissance. Born at **Rome**, he taught at **Ferrara** and Carpi, and about 1490 moved to **Venice**. There he gave up teaching and promoted a plan to publish editions of **Greek classical** authors. In 1495 he entered a partnership with an established publisher, Andrea Torresani, and later married his partner's daughter. The **Aldine Press** published editions of both Latin and Greek authors in a small format and at a cost low enough that the editions were affordable by great numbers of humanists. The small **italic** type faces used for Latin books, modelled on the cursive script used in chancery schools, and the cursive Greek letters of the Greek editions exerted strong influence on the appearance of classical and humanistic texts throughout the 16th century.

The press published first editions of many ancient Greek authors. It also published Italian vernacular works and texts by postclassical authors, including the Latin stylist and vernacular poet **Pietro Bembo**, the collected works of the humanist **Angelo Poliziano**, and the letters of the popular religious writer St. **Catherine of Siena**. The editorial work on Aldus' publications was done by a talented group of local and visiting humanists, including a number of exiled Greek scholars and such non-Italian luminaries as **Erasmus**, who matured as a Greek scholar while working in the Aldine printshop. Aldus' dream of organizing a formal **academy** of humanists devoted to writing and even speaking Greek was never realized, but the press did attract a significant community of scholars and became a major center for the editing and interpretation of ancient texts. The publication of classical editions was not particularly lucrative, and there were periods when the press was not very profitable.

After Aldus' death in 1515, his father-in-law Torresani continued to publish under the Aldine imprint. While humanists often charged that Torresani cared only about money and not scholarship, he had provided much of the capital that made the firm possible, and even though he kept an eye on the balance sheet, he continued the general program of producing editions of classical authors and modern writers. Although the publishing activity was in abeyance after the death of Torresani in 1528, from 1533 one of Aldus' sons, Paulus, revived the firm and continued as a publisher at both Venice and Rome until his death in 1574. Under Aldus' grandson (also named Aldus) the Aldine imprint continued down to the end of the 16th century. *See also* PRINTING.

MARGARET OF NAVARRE (1492–1549). French writer of poetry and prose, sister of King **Francis I**, and (after her second marriage in 1527) queen of Navarre. She is sometimes called Margaret (or Marguerite) of Angoulême since her brother was duke of Angoulême before he succeeded to the French throne in 1515; sometimes also Margaret of Alençon, from the title of her first husband. Margaret was very close to her brother and had even more political influence than was usual for a king's sister. She was deeply religious, but unlike her mother Louise of Savoy, whose piety was conservative, Margaret was sympathetic to the movement to reform the French church along lines suggested by **humanist** reformers. She sheltered protégés like **Lefèvre d'Etaples**, Gerard Roussel, and Bishop Guillaume Briçonnet when they came under attack by conservative theologians who accused them of Lutheran sympathies.

Margaret was active as a writer in French, though only a little of her work was published until after her death. Her long, meditative poem *Le miroir de l'âme pécheresse / Mirror of the Sinful Soul* was published in 1531 and republished in 1533 along with a second religious poem, *Dialogue en forme de vision nocturne / Dialogue in the Form of a Nocturnal Vision*; this combined publication was condemned by the faculty of theology of the University of Paris for its similarities to the doctrines of **Martin Luther** on grace, faith, and free will. This censure caused her brother to exile the leader of the theologians' attack, Noël Béda, to a remote province. Two years before her death, Margaret published a collection of poems whose title embodied a pun on her name, *Les marguerites de la marguerite des princesses / Pearls from the Pearl of Princesses* (*margarita* is the Latin word for pearl). Like most of her work, these poems are deeply religious and provide allegories about the Christian life.

Her most famous work, however, is a collection of prose tales published some years after her death, the *Heptaméron*, which was modelled on **Giovanni Boccaccio's** *Decameron*. It provides both inspiring stories of heroic devotion to Christian faith and scandalous tales of fraud, adultery, and sexual seduction, and the characters who are the storytellers are often identifiable with members of the court society of which she was an intellectual and literary ornament. Her grandson Henry IV in 1589 became the first king of the Bourbon dynasty which occupied the French throne down to the French Revolution.

MARINELLA, LUCREZIA (1571–1653). Venetian poet. She spent her entire life in **Venice**, first as the daughter of a learned physician who gave her access to his library and thus made possible her literary development, and then as the wife of a physician. She wrote both secular and sacred poems. Several of them recount the lives of saints, yet two of the most successful were pastoral dramas, *Amore innamorato e impazzato / Cupid in Love and Driven Mad [by love]* (1598) and *Felice Arcadia / Happy Arcadia* (1605). Her principal poetic work was an epic inspired by **Torquato Tasso**, *L'Enrico overo Bisantio Acquistato / Henry, or Byzantium Won* (1635). She also wrote commentaries on poetry, including her own *Felice Arcadia*, and a rebuttal of a harshly antifeminist poem by Giuseppe Passi.

MARLOWE, CHRISTOPHER (1564–1593). English playwright and poet, also known as a translator of Latin poetry (Ovid and Lucan) into English. Educated at the King's School in Canterbury and at Corpus Christi College, Cambridge, he began his career as a dramatist with *Dido, Queen of Carthage* (ca. 1587), with Thomas Nashe as co-author. His *Tamburlaine the Great* was performed in 1588 on a public stage at London by the Lord Admiral's Men and attracted much favorable attention. His other plays include *The Jew of Malta*, *Edward II*, *The Massacre at Paris*, and *Doctor Faustus*; the latter is probably his most important play. The dates and chronological order of his plays are uncertain. He led a disorderly life, being arrested and tried for manslaughter and forgery, and was accused both of planning to go over to the underground Catholic movement and of being an atheist. He was stabbed to death in a tavern brawl.

MAROT, CLÉMENT (1496–1544). French poet, son of a poet who wrote in the medieval *rhétoriqueur* style. Clément was early attracted to **humanism** and the evangelical religious style of his patron, **Mar-**

garet of Navarre. About 1527 he abandoned traditional medieval verse forms and rhetorical practices and developed a simple but elegant poetic style that influenced subsequent French poetry. He was suspected of sympathy for Lutheran religious ideas and was arrested in 1526 on charges of breaking the Lenten fast and again in 1527 but was released on orders of Margaret's brother, King **Francis I**. With the encouragement of Margaret he made metrical translations of the Psalms. After the scandalous Affair of the Placards (1534), in which posters denouncing the Catholic mass as idolatrous were posted in and around the royal court, he sought safety from the ensuing repression by withdrawing first to the kingdom of Navarre and then to **Ferrara**, where the king's cousin Renée de France was duchess and a sympathizer with **Martin Luther**. At Ferrara he came under the influence of Italian poets, including **Petrarch** and **Pietro Bembo**.

In 1536 Marot abjured his doctrinal errors and returned to France. In 1538 he published his *Oeuvres / Works*, including several of his metrical Psalms, and in 1541 added several new translations and dedicated the expanded edition to the king. In 1543 the Paris faculty of theology condemned his *Cinquante Psaumes de David / Fifty Psalms of David*, but the condemnation did not prevent their frequent republication. Eventually they were adopted for use by many congregations of the emerging Protestant movement. Late in 1542 he fled the country again, perhaps because the humanist printer **Etienne Dolet** had published his early allegorical satire *L'Enfer / Hell*. He lived for two years in Geneva and then moved to Savoy. He died suddenly at Turin in 1544. In addition to producing what are probably the first sonnets written in French, influencing the metrical structure of later French poetry, and publishing collections of poems organized by genre (an innovation in his time), in 1526 he edited the famous 13th-century French poem *Romance of the Rose*.

MARTIN V (Oddone Colonna, 1368–1431; pope from 1417). A member of a powerful family of the Roman aristocracy, Colonna was elected **pope** by the **Council of Constance** (1414–1418) in order to end the **Western Schism** which since 1378 had divided Latin Christendom between allegiance to two, and for a time three, popes. His election represented a triumph for the principle of **Conciliarism**, the theory that a general council, not the pope, was the ultimate authority in the church, and before his election Martin had to pledge to undertake reform of the church and to commit himself to summon periodic church councils which would have limited the autocratic powers claimed by the popes of the High **Middle Ages**. Once he was elected, however, Martin distanced himself from Conciliarism; he summoned the promised council at **Pisa** in 1423 but did not attend it in person, and when it proved to be poorly attended, he dissolved it. In 1431, under intense pressure from bishops and secular rulers, he called another council to meet in **Basel**, but he died before it convened.

Martin was a shrewd political manipulator, able to persuade secular princes to give him military support that enabled him to regain control of the disorderly city of **Rome** but unwilling to undertake any reforms that would significantly restrict his own claim to absolute power over the church. He reorganized the central bureaucracy of the papacy into an overwhelmingly Italian institution, not only in membership but also in outlook. Both the pope and his servants sought to rebuild the centralized power of the papacy, leaving many of the spiritual and organizational issues that had arisen in the later Middle Ages still unresolved.

MARTINI, SIMONE (ca. 1284–1344). Italian artist, trained at Siena by **Duccio** but active also in **Naples**, Assisi, and the papal court at **Avignon**. Unlike his Florentine contemporaries, who were dominated by the influence of **Giotto**, he continued to paint in the elegant courtly style known as International Gothic. His best-known works are his small panel painting *The Road to Calvary* and his delicate and aristocratic tempera painting of the Virgin Mary, *The Annunciation*, a work probably done at Avignon and clearly influenced by French Gothic painting. He was aware of the new Renaissance literary culture represented by **Petrarch**, for another of his works is the frontispiece done for Petrarch's own manuscript of Vergil's *Aeneid*, and he is mentioned in two of Petrarch's poems.

MASACCIO (1401–ca. 1428). Florentine painter. Despite the small number of paintings he completed before his premature death at age 27, Tommaso di Giovanni di Simone Guidi, nicknamed Masaccio, was one of the most influential painters in the history of art. He was born and trained in **Florence** and seems to have understood before any other painter the significance of the principle of vanishing-point **perspective** first applied to sculpture by his fellow Florentines **Filippo Brunelleschi** and **Donatello**. The attribution of a number of very early paintings sometimes ascribed to him is an open question, but between 1525 and 1527 he produced a series of frescoes for the Brancacci chapel in the Carmelite church of Santa Maria Novella that exemplify full mastery of the decisive turn in painting associated with his name. The most striking of these frescoes are *Holy Trinity with the Virgin and St. John*, *The Expulsion from the Garden*, which depicts the nude and despairing Adam and Eve being driven out of Eden by the angel, and *The Tribute Money*, a pictorial representation of an incident from the life of Christ. Each of these three paintings shows mature and sensitive control of the characteristics that art historians define as typical of the early Renaissance (or **Quattrocento**) style.

MASSYS, QUENTIN (1466–1530). Flemish painter. Born and trained at **Louvain**, he travelled to Italy to study the works of art about which he had heard and came back with increased skill in the technique of **perspective** but otherwise did not fundamentally change the style of painting he had learned from his Flemish predecessors. He was highly regarded as a painter of portraits, and his twin portraits of the Dutch humanist **Erasmus** and his friend Pieter Gillis (1517) are well known.

MAXIMILIAN I, Holy Roman Emperor (1459–1519; emperor from 1493). The first member of the **Habsburg** dynasty to gain a pan-European reputation, he brought his family to unprecedented power through a series of brilliant dynastic marriages. Maximilian was the son of Frederick III, one of the most futile of the weak emperors of the later Middle Ages. He received a careful education that raised his sights above the goal of merely preserving Habsburg rule over their hereditary principalities in Germany. Although he was frequently short of cash and never able to mobilize power comparable to that of the kings of France, England, and Spain, Maximilian became a major figure in European political life. The key to his success was a series of advantageous dynastic marriages, beginning with his own marriage to Mary of Burgundy, heiress of the powerful state of **Burgundy**, which included the Netherlands, the wealthiest region in northern Europe. After Mary's death in 1482, Maximilian retained control of the Burgundian lands as regent for their son Philip the Handsome. He then arranged a marriage between Philip and Juana, a daughter of **Ferdinand** and **Isabella** of Spain. The child of that marriage, Charles of Habsburg, succeeded his Spanish grandfather as King Charles I of Spain in 1516, became ruler of the scattered hereditary states of his family in Germany after Maximilian's death, and was elected Holy Roman Emperor (**Charles V**) in 1519.

Maximilian also began a financial relationship with the **Fugger** banking firm of Augsburg, based on using the royalties from mines (mostly of copper and silver) located on Habsburg lands in central Europe as collateral for loans that financed his wars and other political actions. In his time, this relationship was on a small scale, but after his grandson Charles became ruler of Spain, the Habsburg / Fugger relationship was secured by the revenues from the new Spanish colonies, especially from silver mines in Mexico and Peru.

Maximilian appreciated the political usefulness of a well-conceived cultural policy that presented him as a restorer of Germany's lost greatness. His patronage of **humanists** and especially of artists such as **Albrecht Dürer** associated him and his dynasty with a growing national self-awareness among the educated classes of Germany. In this case, too, the great beneficiary of what he began was his grandson Charles, who was elected emperor in 1519 over the rival contender, **Francis I** of France, in part because the Habsburg prince was regarded as "German" even though he spoke no German and had spent most of his life at the French-speaking court of the Netherlands and in Spain.

During his own reign, Maximilian faced many problems. In the east, he pursued ambitions to win the throne of Bohemia and made treaty arrangements that in the next generation brought the throne of that kingdom to the Habsburgs. He also tried unsuccessfully to become king of Hungary but arranged a dynastic marriage that once again paid off in the next generation, when his grandson, Archduke **Ferdinand of Habsburg**, managed to salvage the western section and the title of king of Hungary after the death of his brother-in-law Louis of Hungary in battle against the Turks in 1526. In the west and northwest, Maximilian faced border disputes and dynastic claims against the kings of France, as well as political unrest and one serious uprising in the Netherlands, a collection of provinces which had long traditions of local self-government and resisted any efforts either to assert close control over them or to subject them to taxes. Finally, Maximilian was one of the rulers involved in the series of international wars in Italy precipitated by the French attempt to claim their king's inheritance of **Naples** in 1494. In Germany itself, he faced war against the Swiss, who had become independent in all but name.

As emperor, Maximilian had very limited power over any territory except the scattered hereditary lands of his own dynasty. He tried with only limited success to persuade the Imperial Diet (*Reichstag*) to accept some direct taxation, but they insisted that each state would collect the "common penny" itself. He did establish a central judicial court that gained some recognition throughout the country, and he proclaimed an internal peace intended to end warfare among the states and brigandage in the countryside. The electoral princes and other great nobles, however, though they talked about the need to establish internal peace and to strengthen the kingdom, had no intention of letting Maximilian centralize power in his own hands, and since he was chronically short on cash and already overcommitted by the expense of his military efforts in Italy, he was unable to remedy the inherent weakness of the imperial office. His greatest success in Germany did not come to fruition until after his death, when his grandson Charles V became emperor and with the ability to draw on his Netherlandish and Spanish resources was able to play a more powerful role in German politics.

MEDICI FAMILY. Florentine mercantile and banking family that played a significant part in local politics and from 1434 dominated the political system of **Florence** through a combination of careful political alliances and outright corruption of the electoral system. Although officially they were just one of the wealthy merchant families who shared political leadership, between 1434 and 1494 the Medici exercised an increasingly overt hegemony over the city. In 1494 after proving weak in the face of the French invasion of **Naples**, the current Medici leader was exiled; in 1512 the Medici were restored to power by a papal and Spanish army, and after they had been again ejected by a popular uprising in 1527, they were again brought to power by foreign troops in 1530. This time they suppressed the old republican constitution and openly became despotic princes as dukes of Florence (1532) and later as grand dukes of Tuscany.

The family's political rise began very hesitantly under the first head of the family to make the Medici a major European banking and mercantile power, Giovanni di Bicci de'Medici (1360–1429), who preferred to avoid politics and to concentrate on his international banking business. As a prominent citizen, however, he came to be perceived by the ruling **Albizzi** faction as a potential threat to their control of the republic. This hostility emerged openly in the career of his son Cosimo de'Medici (1389–1464). Arrested on trumped-up charges of political conspiracy in 1433, Cosimo was fortunate to escape execution and merely to be exiled. In 1434 a swing of the electoral lottery brought into power a group of citizens who resented the arbitrary treatment he had suffered and the arrogance of the Albizzi leaders. Hence in 1434 he was called back from exile, the Albizzi were exiled, and Cosimo and his political allies established a long-lasting control over the political machinery. He crafted a political system in which he occasionally held leading public offices for the normal two-month term but usually remained in the background, allowing others in the group of families that suported him to hold the public offices and exercise nominal control. Only in foreign policy, where in the 1450s he pushed through a revolutionary realignment of alliances among the Italian states, did he play a consistently dominant role. With Cosimo begins the family's history as great patrons of **humanistic** learning and the fine arts.

His son and successor, **Piero di Cosimo** de'Medici (1416–1469), nicknamed "the gouty," was far less effective, in part because of chronic ill health, but he was able to put down two conspiracies by disgruntled opponents. At his death in 1469, his son Lorenzo di Piero de'Medici (1449–1492) took charge of the family's political and financial interests despite his youth. Lorenzo, who received the popular nickname "the Magnificent," was challenged by families kept out of power by his grandfather and father, including the exiled Pazzi and Salviati families. Lorenzo's foreign policy ran counter to the interests of Pope **Sixtus IV**. The **pope** supported the dissidents and may have been a leading participant (as some of his close associates certainly were) in a plot (the **Pazzi conspiracy**) to remove the Medici from power by assassinating Lorenzo and his younger brother **Giuliano**. The attempt occurred in April 1478 as the brothers attended mass in the cathedral. Giuliano was stabbed to death; Lorenzo was wounded but survived. In reaction, a mob of citizens hanged several of the conspirators, including the Archbishop of **Pisa**. The killing of this high-ranking clergyman served as an excuse for the pope to excommunicate Lorenzo and lay the whole city under an interdict. War inevitably followed, in which the pope was supported by the king of Naples. Although the Pazzi conspiracy rallied popular support behind Lorenzo, the military situation of the city was dangerous. Lorenzo skillfully negotiated a political settlement and then organized a new league between Florence, **Milan**, and Naples that forced the pope to agree to peace. This alliance served to stabilize Italian politics for a whole generation by restraining the aggressive ambitions of Italy's two rogue states, the **Papal States** and **Venice**, which sought to expand at the expense of the other Italian powers.

Lorenzo became an active patron of learning and the arts, supporting the humanist scholars **Angelo Poliziano** and **Cristoforo Landino**, the **Neoplatonic** philosopher **Marsilio Ficino**, the painter **Sandro Botticelli**, and a number of other writers, philosophers, and artists who made the unofficial "court" in Lorenzo's household a major center of Renaissance culture. Lorenzo was genuinely interested in the work of the scholars and artists whom he patronized and was himself a talented poet writing in the Italian vernacular. This court society produced writings and art directed not to the tastes and interests of the general public but to the concerns of a restricted elite.

Lorenzo's one area of failure was in the banking business that had been the basis of his family's rise to power. The semi-independent branch banks that Cosimo had formed in Lyon, Bruges, London, Venice, and several other Italian cities, as well as the papal court, proved hard to control, especially when the senior executive in Florence was neither personally experienced in their complex banking operations nor interested enough to supervise the branch managers closely. In Lorenzo's time, several branches got into serious financial difficulties, and even Lorenzo's ability to use his control of the Florentine government to help his business (whether this went so far as embezzling public funds is debated) was not enough to return the branches and the home office to a sound footing. When the Medici were driven from power and exiled in 1494, the business collapsed. Lorenzo seems to have inherited the ill health that had plagued his father, and he died at the age of 43.

His son Piero di Lorenzo de'Medici (1471–1503) succeeded to his political leadership. Piero had been reared almost as a prince and had not developed the kind of close personal links that his ancestors had formed with the heads of other wealthy Florentine families. He managed to take charge of the government when his father died in 1492, but when he faced his first major crisis, the French invasion of Italy in 1494, he acted so ineptly and indecisively that Florence not only was humiliated by the passage of the French army through its territories but also was threatened with becoming a French satellite. The citizens reacted by rioting and overthrowing the Medici regime and expelling its leaders from the city.

In exile, the leader of the Medici was Piero's younger brother, **Giovanni**, who had been made a cardinal at age 13. Giovanni enjoyed the favor of Pope **Julius II**, and in 1512 an army raised by the pope and King **Ferdinand** of Spain besieged Florence and forced it to surrender, ending the reform efforts of the anti-Medicean leader **Piero Soderini** and restoring the Medici to power. The election of Cardinal Giovanni as the first Medici pope, **Leo X**, in 1513 strengthened the family's control of the city. Policy was directed from **Rome**, and local administration was handled first by the pope's nephew Lorenzo and then by his cousin Giuliano, who despite his illegitimate birth was made a cardinal and sent as papal legate to Florence. The Medici retained control of the city after Giuliano's election as Pope **Clement VII** in 1523 and during the intervening pontificate of **Adrian VI**, but the unsuccessful foreign policy of Pope Clement and the ensuing sack of Rome by an imperial army in 1527 encouraged the Florentines to make another effort to end Medici control and restore their old republican constitution.

A Spanish army in 1530 forced the city to surrender after a long siege; several of the anti-Medicean leaders were executed, and Alessandro de'Medici (1510–1537) was given control of Florence in 1531 and allowed to assume the title of duke of Florence in 1532. The republican constitution was abolished. Alessandro was assassinated in 1537 by a conspiracy led by his kinsman Lorenzino, and since there was no direct Medici heir, the leaders of the pro-Medici aristocracy turned to a more distant relative, **Cosimo**, a youth of 18. Despite his youth, he proved to be a skilled politician. He ruled as duke of Florence (1537–1569) and near the end of his reign secured papal approval to change his title to Grand Duke of Tuscany. Under this title, the Medici ruled their principality until the last Medici grand duke died without heirs in 1737. The European powers then transferred the duchy to the family of the dukes of Lorraine.

MELANCHTHON, PHILIPP (1497–1560). German **humanist, Reformation** leader, and educational reformer. He was born at Bretten in the Rhenish Palatinate. His original German name was Schwarzerd, hellenized to create his **classical** surname. He was the great-nephew of the famous humanist **Johann Reuchlin,** who closely supervised his education and prepared him for a scholarly career. A precocious youth, he attended the **University** of Heidelberg and received his B.A. degree at age 14. He qualified for the M.A. degree but was deemed too young to be graduated and so moved too Tübingen, where he did receive the M.A. and taught for several years in the faculty of arts.

In 1518 Melanchthon was appointed to the new professorship of **Greek** at the University of Wittenberg, largely because his uncle Reuchlin promoted his candidacy. His youthful appearance dismayed some of the faculty, including the rising theological star of the university, **Martin Luther,** but his inaugural lecture (*De corrigendis adolescentiae studiis / On Reforming the Education of Youth*) was such an eloquent plea for the value of a humanistic education that these doubts were resolved. Melanchthon, already widely regarded as the crown prince of German humanism on account of his relation to Reuchlin and his precocious academic success, soon became an academic star in his own right. Although his uncle Reuchlin was hostile to the Reformation, Melanchthon became an enthusiastic supporter of Luther, commenced study in the faculty of theology, and in 1519 received the baccalaureate in that field. His main interest, however, was in humanistic studies. He offered occasional courses in theology but never attempted to gain the doctorate. He was at heart a grammarian and rhetorician—a humanist—not a theologian. Yet his *Loci communes* (1521) was the first systematic statement of Lutheran theology and remained an influential book.

As Luther became increasingly preoccupied with his own legal defense against charges of heresy, Melanchthon took over the ambitious program of reforming the university curriculum along humanist lines, in which the first step had been his own employment to teach Greek and the creation of a parallel professorship of **Hebrew**. Melanchthon spent his whole academic career in Wittenberg. In the face of many humanists' concerns about anti-intellectual tendencies in popular Protestantism, his presence and his tracts defending humanistic education as the basis for any sound reform of religion did much to relieve the worries of moderately conservative humanists that the Reformation movement would destroy the recent gains of humanistic education. Melanchthon himself became the author of many textbooks in both humanistic and scientific subjects, and he prepared editions of classical authors for use in universities and grammar schools. From the mid-1520s, he made frequent trips to other parts of Germany to advise rulers on the reform of existing schools and the founding of new schools aimed at providing pupils with a humanistic education. His work in promoting educational reform won for him the nickname *Praeceptor Germaniae* ("Preceptor of Germany").

In Wittenberg itself, he led a second wave of academic reforms in the 1530s intended to make Wittenberg more clearly both a Lutheran and a humanistic university. After the disruption of the university by the defeat of Electoral Saxony in the Schmalkaldic War of 1546–1547, he led a further revision of the academic program that helped to preserve Wittenberg's role as a leading Protestant university.

Melanchthon was also an important figure in questions of religious reform. Although more cautious and less outspoken than Luther, he firmly backed Luther against both Catholics and radical Protestants. He was a leader in the formal visitations of Saxon churches by commissioners appointed by the Saxon ruler to survey the spiritual and financial condition of local parishes. He insisted that the churches must have well-educated and well-paid preachers to teach the ill-informed common folk the central doctrines of Christian religion. He supported Luther's recommendation that each city government had an obligation to provide sound elementary education to every boy—and every girl.

In 1530, during the negotiations attempting to restore religious unity at the Diet of Augsburg, Luther, being under a legal sentence of outlawry, could not attend; Melanchthon took his place and drafted the fundamental summary of the Lutheran faith (the Augsburg Confession) laid before the emperor and the members of the Diet. Melanchthon was a temperamentally conciliatory person and retained friendly relations with many moderate and reform-minded Catholics, including the greatest figure of Northern humanism, **Erasmus**. He opposed the more radical reform ideas of **Huldrych Zwingli** and Johannes Oecolampadius, especially their eucharistic theology. Yet he admitted that on many other doctrines they agreed with him and Luther, and during his later years, when Luther was dead and he was the principal successor to Luther's leadership, he remained so friendly with the Swiss Sacramentarians (followers of Zwingli) that other, more conservative Lutherans accused him of being a Zwinglian heretic. After the victory of the Emperor **Charles V** in the Schmalkaldic War, Melanchthon favored a cautious and moderate policy. He regarded many of the ideas and practices that the emperor was trying to enforce in Lutheran parts of the country as *adiaphora* (non-essential matters) on which the Lutherans could make some concessions without betraying their basic doctrines. Thus he was frequently attacked both as too radical because of his lack of enthusiasm for attacking Protestant "Sacramentarians" and as too close to the Catholics because he was recommending limited obedience to some of the imperial policies intended to bring Protestants back into the Roman Catholic church.

In 1541–1542 Melanchthon was the principal Lutheran participant in a series of colloquies at which Lutheran, Catholic, and Reformed (Zwinglian) theologians attempted to define areas of agreement and reach compromises on areas of disagreement so that the Christian church could be reunited. Melanchthon and the papal representative signed an agreement on justification by faith that they hoped would provide a basis for reunion. This agreement (which left several other major issues unresolved) was rejected both by Luther and by the **pope**. Despite open attacks by self-proclaimed "real Lutherans," who regarded him as weak in dealing with both Catholics and Sacramentarians, Melanchthon remained the leading figure of Lutheranism following Luther's death in 1546.

MEMLING, HANS (ca. 1430–1494). Flemish painter, born in Germany and initially trained in the Rhineland, probably at Cologne. He moved to Flanders, where he seems to have studied under **Rogier van der Weyden**. Eventually he settled in Bruges, where he became highly regarded as a painter of religious scenes and portraits. His

Saint John Altarpiece at Bruges, especially its central panel, *The Mystical Marriage of St. Catherine of Alexandria*, suggests the influence of **Jan van Eyck**, who worked in Bruges, as well as the continuing influence of van der Weyden. Memling's work was known and admired in Italy, an example of the openness of Italian connoisseurs to Northern painting even at a time when their own native art was entering its period of greatest creativity.

MENA, JUAN DE (1411–1456). Castilian royal secretary and poet. Although sometimes associated with the beginnings of **humanist** culture in Spain, he is more properly regarded as an influence on the rise of a national literature. He studied at Córdoba, Salamanca, and **Rome** and developed an interest in **classical** literature reflected in his translation of the *Iliad* into Castilian verse. King Juan II and the royal favorite Alvaro de Luna were his patrons. His poetry used traditional Castilian meter rather than new forms borrowed from Italy. He developed an inflated poetic diction, much admired in his day, that was remote from everyday speech, using complex syntax and a vocabulary in which Castilian words were arbitrarily assigned meanings identical to that of their Latin source. His poetry is full of allegory and subjects derived from classical mythology. His most famous poem was *Laberinto de la fortuna / The Labyrinth of Fortune*, a didactic allegory in which the past and present of Castile are presented as if in a prophecy.

MERCATOR, GERARD (1512–1594). Flemish mathematician and mapmaker, based in **Louvain**. His large engraved map of Europe in 1554 was his outstanding work, but he is most important because he devised the method of projecting maps of a spherical Earth onto a flat surface by making the parallels and meridians intersect at 90 degrees. This Mercator's Projection was simple and reasonably accurate for the parts of the globe usually mapped by Europeans of his time, but it causes increasing distortion of regions the nearer they lie to the south and north poles.

MEUNG, JEAN DE. *See ROMANCE OF THE ROSE.*

MICHELANGELO (1475–1564). Probably the greatest and certainly the most versatile of the three artists commonly held to represent the peak of High Renaissance art. Born in a small Tuscan town, the son of a local magistrate, Michelangelo di Lodovico Buonarroti was apprenticed in 1488 to one of the leading Florentine painters, **Domenico Ghirlandaio**, who taught him not only the technique of fresco painting but also the skills in drawing that Ghirlandaio regarded as fundamental to good artistic work. He did not complete his apprenticeship and never organized a conventional artist's workshop. Instead, probably through his father's influence, he became a member of the household of **Lorenzo de'Medici**, the dominant political figure in **Florence** and the principal patron of arts and learning. He spent two years (1490–1492) there and studied at close hand Lorenzo's rich collection of ancient and contemporary works of art. He also met the leading intellectuals of the day, including **Marsilio Ficino, Giovanni Pico della Mirandola, Cristoforo Landino**, and **Angelo Poliziano**. He shared this circle's enthusiasm for **Neoplatonism**, especially the Neoplatonic dualism which regarded spirit as the true reality and body as the mere outward appearance through which the spiritual found expression. Although he never mastered Latin, he was exposed to the world of literature and philosophy and had a more highly developed awareness of **humanistic** culture and Neoplatonic philosophy than any other artist of his generation.

After Lorenzo's death in 1492 and the expulsion of the Medici from Florence in 1494, Michelangelo needed to find new patrons. Being convinced that he was of noble ancestry, he had no intention of adopting the career of an artisan by organizing a workshop and earning his living by manual labor. He viewed his art as the expression of his mental conceptions, not as a handicraft. He followed the Medici into exile at **Bologna**, then in 1495 moved back to Florence. In 1496 he made his first trip to **Rome**, where he studied ancient works of art and began working for cardinals and other members of the papal curia. His maturation as a sculptor was incredibly rapid. He quickly gained a commission for a large sculpture that became the earliest of his masterpieces, the *Pietà* (1497–1500), which marked his emergence as a great sculptor. His next major commission was his *David* (1501–1504), which made such an impression that the civic officials at Florence relocated it in front of the seat of local government as a symbol of the city's liberty. The *Pietà* and the *David*, one of them a moving religious image of the Virgin Mary's grief and the other a powerful figure that not only represented but perhaps surpassed the best male nude statues of **antiquity**, established his reputation for life.

Michelangelo's problem now was not how to get commissions but how to hold off the many powerful and wealthy individuals who wanted his services. The most insistent of these patrons was Pope **Julius II**, who called him to Rome to design and execute a gigantic tomb for the **pope**. The project was never completed, in part because of the enormous cost. Michelangelo struggled with it long after the pope's death in 1513. The eventual product was a relatively modest tomb in one of the Roman churches. The only parts of the original plan to be completed were the seated *Moses* (ca. 1513–1515), which did become part of the tomb, and two remarkable male nudes, *Bound Slave* (sometimes called *Dying Slave*) and *Rebellious Slave*, both brought close to completion in 1513–1516 but never finished and never actually incorporated into Julius II's monument. Michelangelo was frustrated by the pope's distraction from the tomb project by the costly scheme to tear down the old Basilica of St. Peter and replace it with a modern church and by his even more costly wars.

Michelangelo left Rome but soon was summoned back. His next task was a huge bronze statue of Julius in the conquered city of Bologna (a work destroyed by the citizens when they rebelled against papal rule). He found that the pope now wanted him to put off the tomb project and to paint a cycle of frescoes on the ceiling of the pope's private chapel. Michelangelo had already produced some well-regarded paintings, but he thought of himself as a sculptor. He was reluctant to undertake this demanding project, but Julius insisted. Hence between 1508 and 1512, Michelangelo spent most of his working days reluctantly producing what many art historians regard as the greatest single work that he or any other artist ever made, the frescoes of the Sistine Chapel ceiling. He conceived a harmonious sequence of images depicting the relation between humanity and God from the beginning of time down through the fall of Adam and Eve and the ultimate salvation of the human race, and drawing on **Jewish**, **classical**, and Christian themes and forms.

The Medici popes **Leo X** and **Clement VII**, whom Michelangelo had known when he was living in Lorenzo's house, commissioned him to design a new burial chapel in the family church at Florence, and from 1524 to 1534 he spent much of his time on that project, completing the sculpture for two of the planned four tombs. Especially striking is the statue (not intended to be a portrait) representing Giuliano de'Medici and the accompanying mythological figures of Day and Night. At the same period he carried out one of his earliest major architectural commissions, the Laurentian Library at Florence.

In the last three decades of his long life, Michelangelo dedicated more time and effort to architecture than to any other branch of the arts. For Pope Paul III he redesigned the Campidoglio, the central piazza of ancient Rome, commonly regarded as one of the greatest examples of Renaissance urban planning. Paul III also brought him back to the Sistine Chapel to paint the last of his great frescoes, *The Last Judgment* (1534–1541). This crowded, dark, and ominous picture represents a remarkable shift in Michelangelo's style of painting, not in the techniques of execution but in the conception, which reflects his own inner spiritual turmoil. The contrast between the brooding *Last Judgment* and the dynamic, optimistic Sistine ceiling that he painted for Julius II is often used to illustrate the shift (in this case, within the same artist) from the Renaissance to the **mannerist** style of art.

His last great commission, on which he spent his closing years and for which he would accept no pay, was his redesign and continuation of the great basilica of St. Peter, originally planned by **Donato Bramante** in 1506 under Julius II. Michelangelo significantly changed the design and was solely responsible for the great dome which still dominates the structure; the church that now exists is essentially his work, despite the decision made after the Council of Trent to transform its shape from the Renaissance central-plan structure to the medieval basilica form, a change made in the early 17th century by **Carlo Maderno.**

In addition to being the greatest and most versatile artist of the Renaissance, Michelangelo was a vernacular poet of considerable talent. His poems, like his designs, reflect the many cultural forces at work in his mind, including his Neoplatonic philosophy, his reverence for the civilization of the classical world, his deeply spiritual Christian piety, and his conflicted homosexual longings. Fifty of the poems are addressed to a young Roman aristocrat, the first large body of homoerotic poetry in any Western language. Many also celebrate his intense but asexual relationship with a remarkable aristocratic woman, **Vittoria Colonna**, member of an ancient Roman noble family and an active figure in the spiritual life of groups of devout and intellectual Catholics in Rome and **Naples**. The poems were not published until 1623, and then in a carefully expurgated edition, but they also circulated in manuscript. Michelangelo was the most famous artist of his time, enthusiastically hailed by the art historian **Giorgio Vasari** as the greatest figure of the Renaissance.

MIDDLE AGES. Historical term used in all Western languages to designate the thousand-year period from the disintegration of the ancient Roman political and social system in the fourth and fifth centuries to the beginning of the Renaissance. The term was totally unknown to medieval people themselves, who conceived themselves as still living at the latter end of the ancient Roman world. It was coined in the 14th and 15th centuries by the **humanists** of the Renaissance, beginning with the most famous early humanist, **Petrarch**, to characterize an age of decay, barbarism, and inferior civilization lying between two happy ages of high civilization, the ancient **classical** world and the new world of cultural rebirth (the "Renaissance") which they thought they were bringing into being in their own time. Although the pejorative implication of the term (implying an inferior age lying between two good ones) is totally unjust to the creative and dynamic society of the actual Middle Ages, the term itself has endured, now used mainly as a neutral label for the whole period of history but still occasionally used with pejorative implications in popular discourse.

MIDDLETON, THOMAS (1580–1627). English dramatist, a younger contemporary of **William Shakespeare**. He often wrote in collaboration with other playwrights such as William Rowley and Thomas Dekker. He also produced many masques and pageants for public occasions. Educated at Queen's College, Oxford, he began his literary career as a poet in 1597 and soon became an active writer for the flourishing London theater. He wrote comedies, both romantic and realistic, and tragedies. His works include *The Changeling* (1622), which was his most famous tragedy; *The Roaring Girl* (ca. 1610); and *Women Beware Women* (1621). In his own time, the most noticed of his plays was his savage attack on Spain and the Spanish ambassador in London, *A Game at Chess* (1624), written at a time when the king was considering a Spanish princess as a bride for the future King Charles I. The drama played to packed and enthusiastic houses nine consecutive days until the government closed it down. Modern quantitative analysis of Jacobean plays has also identified Middleton's probable authorship of some passages in two Shakespearean plays, *Macbeth* and *Timon of Athens*, and has identified him as the probable author of a very influential play, *The Revenger's Tragedy* (1607).

MILAN. Principal city of the Lombard plain from late **Roman** times through the **Middle Ages** and Renaissance. In the 12th century, when the cities of northern Italy resisted the efforts of the German Holy Roman Emperors to establish control over the region, **Milan** led the resistance. In 1162, after a two-year siege, the Emperor Frederick I (Barbarossa) ordered the city levelled to the ground. But it soon recovered and resumed its role as head of the anti-imperial Lombard League. In the 13th century, Milan was the scene of an internal power struggle between two aristocratic clans, the Della Torre and **Visconti** families. In 1277 the Visconti faction, in the person of their candidate for the archbishopric of the city, Ottone Visconti, gained control, and Archbishop Ottone succeeded in getting his great-nephew, Matteo Visconti, elected as commander of the local armed forces. In effect Matteo became lord of the city and was able to keep his office even after the archbishop's death.

With one brief interruption, the Visconti family managed to maintain its power over the city, while also purchasing from the German emperors a series of local and regional titles that gave them a claim to political authority beyond the city's borders. In 1317 Matteo assumed the title of *dominus* (lord or **signore**) of Milan. The citizens' own council in 1330 confirmed this title for his descendant Azzo. Under the greatest figure of the dynasty, Giangaleazzo Visconti (ruled 1378–1402), the ruler engaged in an aggressive policy of conquest and diplomacy that made Milan the greatest power in northern Italy. Giangaleazzo married his children into both the French and the English ruling families and in 1395, again for a cash payment, received from the emperor the title of duke of Milan. Giangaleazzo's ambitions made Milanese territorial expansion a threat to Italy's two most important surviving republics, **Venice** and **Florence**. Although his sudden death in 1402 caused a temporary period of weakness, Milan remained a powerful state, and under his second son, Filippo Maria, fear of Milanese expansion again drove the two republics into an alliance that claimed to uphold Italian liberty against Milanese "tyranny."

Filippo Maria died in 1447, leaving no legitimate heirs and only an illegitimate daughter to claim his throne. The citizens of Milan declared the ducal title abrogated and their old republican constitution restored. Unfortunately for them, other powers, especially Venice, rushed in to seize whatever territories they could, and the king of France claimed the ducal throne on the basis of his descent from one of Giangaleazzo's daughters. The republican government hired Francesco **Sforza**, the ablest of the Italian mercenary generals (*condottieri*), to defend the city. But Sforza was married to the illegitimate daughter of the last Visconti duke and soon seized power, declared himself and his wife hereditary duke and duchess, and continued the monarchical system established by the Visconti.

The seizure of power by Sforza precipitated a military and diplomatic crisis that was resolved by the decision of the leading political figure at Florence, **Cosimo de'Medici**, to oppose the efforts of Venice and the **papacy** to overthrow Sforza and seize Milanese territory. Fearing French or imperial intervention in Milan, Cosimo abandoned traditional Florentine alliances with Venice and the papacy and accepted Sforza's control over Milan. Together, he and Sforza, supported by the king of **Naples**, compelled the other two major states to sign the Peace of Lodi (1454) and enter an Italian League (1455) that sought to prevent conflict among the Italian states and thus to discourage foreign intervention.

Sforza retained his duchy down to his death in 1465 and passed the title on to his incompetent son Galeazzo Maria, who was assassinated in 1476. Even then, the throne was preserved for Galeazzo Maria's young son, under the regency of his mother. But the young duke's uncle, Ludovico Sforza, nicknamed *il Moro* ("the Moor"), forced himself into the position of regent and refused to surrender control to his nephew. Ludovico sought to block the emergence of an alliance against his usurpation by encouraging the ambitious young king of France, Charles VIII, to enforce his dynastic claim to the throne of Naples. The resulting French invasion of Italy and temporary conquest of Naples in 1494 marked a new and disastrous stage in the political life of Italy, which ended by becoming a battleground for a long struggle between France and Spain for control of the peninsula.

At first, Ludovico Sforza seemed to have been the greatest winner, since the French invasion prevented the other Italian powers from forming a coalition against him. But in 1498 the French throne came into the hands of Charles VIII's cousin Louis XII (1498–1515), who was directly descended from a Visconti princess. The new king decided to enforce not only his claim to Naples but also his hereditary claim to Milan, and his invasion in 1499 led to French occupation of Milan and the brief establishment of a French-controlled regime there. Ludovico Sforza ended his life as a prisoner in France. The French were unable to retain control of Milan for very long. The Italian powers, aided by King **Ferdinand** of Spain, restored the Sforza dynasty to power. King **Francis I** of France (1515–1547) reconquered Milan in 1515 and held the duchy until his disastrous defeat by the imperial army at Pavia in 1525. Then the Sforza dukes returned, but only as pawns of Spanish power, and when Francesco II Sforza died in 1535, the Emperor **Charles V** claimed the duchy as an imperial fief and made it part of the **Habsburg** empire. It remained subject to the Spanish crown until the 18th century.

In cultural terms, Milan could not match the innovative record of the rival city of Florence, but from the time of Giangaleazzo Visconti in the late 14th century, the Milanese court employed **humanists** as secretaries and propagandists and encouraged humanistic scholarship and education. The Sforza court in the later 15th century was a generous patron of the arts. The original designer of the new basilica of St. Peter at **Rome, Donato Bramante**, began his career in Milan, and **Leonardo da Vinci** painted his *Last Supper* for a monastery near Milan and was employed by the Sforza rulers as a military engineer and architect. The Sforza dukes also were generous patrons of music and created a ducal choir that was involved in many musical innovations and employed a number of the greatest Renaissance composers, of whom **Josquin des Prez** was the most famous.

MILTON, JOHN (1608–1674). English poet, political figure, and author of tracts on political and religious issues. Though his life is totally contained in the 17th century and so falls chronologically into a post-Renaissance age, his prodigious mastery of Renaissance **humanistic** learning and the Protestant theology of the **Reformation** has caused him to be conventionally treated as a very late representative of the Renaissance in England. The son of a distinguished musical composer of the same name, he received a superb classical education and studied at Christ's College, Cambridge. He published his first poem in 1632. He had intended to enter the clergy, but his strong Puritan sympathies made him unwilling to conform to the Church of England. He published poetry in English, Latin, and Italian and in 1638–1639 travelled on the Continent, meeting many prominent scholars and literary figures and even visiting the aged **Galileo Galilei** during the astronomer's years of house arrest following his condemnation by the **Roman Inquisition**.

Milton's hostility to the authoritarian tendencies of Archbishop Laud's church and King Charles I's secular administration made him support the Puritan side in the English civil wars that broke out in 1642. In 1649, after the victory of the revolutionaries, he became secretary of foreign tongues for the Council of State, the man responsible for correspondence (normally in Latin) with foreign powers. He also emerged as a political pamphleteer, defending the republican government and insisting that the king was not above the law and could be held responsible for unlawful acts. In 1652, however, Milton became totally blind, though he continued his government work with the aid of a secretary.

Milton always regarded poetry as his true calling and from an early age aspired to succeed in what literary theory regarded as the highest and noblest form of literature, epic poetry. His collected poems published in 1645 contained his early lyric and religious poems, including several sonnets in Italian. His prose works were not limited to political controversy; he also wrote on religion, including a notorious treatise on divorce that gave limited endorsement to legal divorce with the right of remarriage in cases where a marriage had broken down irretrievably. His most admired prose work, however, is *Areopagitica* (1644), a defense of intellectual freedom particularly directed against the censorship traditionally exercised by the English state over the press.

Milton's close association with Oliver Cromwell and the other republican leaders who abolished the monarchy and executed King

Charles I made it inevitable that he would be one of the few individuals not included in the general amnesty promised by the new king, Charles II, when the monarchy was restored in 1660. What saved him from execution was partly the recognition of his greatness as a poet and partly his blindness. Only after the Restoration in 1660, now out of office and out of official favor, did he concentrate on his lifelong ambition of producing the great poetic epic that English literature had lacked. The result was *Paradise Lost*, not an epic of warlike heroism or a returning hero's wanderings but an epic of the relationship between humanity and God, focused on the sin of Adam and Eve, their eviction by God from the Garden of Eden, and God's promise to send a savior who would redeem humanity. Milton's other major poems were a shorter epic, *Paradise Regained*, and a poem in dramatic form, *Samson Agonistes* (both published in 1671). Even while subject to close censorship and operating in a society that now shunned his political and social ideas, Milton in these final epic poems firmly restated his commitment to human dignity and human freedom.

MONTAIGNE, MICHEL DE (1533–1592). French moral philosopher and author, commonly regarded as the inventor of the personal essay as a literary genre. His father was a wealthy lawyer who had risen to the minor nobility. The father was himself attracted to **classical** and **humanistic** learning but was not very skilled in Latin. He devised a unique system of education for his infant son, surrounding him with a German tutor and a household of servants who spoke only Latin to the child, so that until he was six, Montaigne himself spoke only Latin. He was sent to study at the Collège de Guyenne, one of the best of France's Latin grammar schools. Subsequently he studied law, probably at Toulouse, and at age 21 began work as a lawyer, holding a magistracy in the Parlement de Guyenne (the supreme judicial court of southwestern France) at Bordeaux.

Montaigne found this judicial career dull and unfulfilling. Since he was sufficiently wealthy to live off his private fortune, he retired in 1571 and moved to his estate at Montaigne, intending to spend the rest of his life reading, thinking, and writing. In 1580–1581 he undertook a long foreign tour for self-education, visiting Germany, Switzerland, and especially Italy, where he met many of that country's leading literary and philosophical figures. His scholarly retreat was interrupted by service as mayor of Bordeaux (1581–1585), a difficult task in a period when the country was torn by civil war between Protestants and Catholics. Though personally loyal to his country's traditional Catholic faith, he despised the violence and fanaticism of extremists on both sides of the conflict. Because of his candor and honesty he came to be respected and trusted by moderates on both sides, including the Protestant leader Henry of Navarre, the future King Henry IV, who used Montaigne to conduct confidential negotiations between rival factions.

In 1569 Montaigne published his first work, a French translation of the *Natural Theology* of Raymond Sebond, a Catalan theologian of the 15th century who undertook to prove by rational demonstration all the doctrines of the Catholic faith, an effort that Montaigne regarded as futile and that had led to censure by the church because he left no room for faith. Montaigne also wrote a journal of his travels abroad. Yet his great literary work is his three books of essays, the first two published in 1580, revised and republished several times, and reissued with a third book in 1588. He continued revising and adding to the text until his death, and a posthumous edition incorporating all of the later additions was published in 1595 under the editorship of the intellectual noblewoman **Marie de Gournay**.

Although the essays deal in an idiosyncratic and deliberately unsystematic way with a broad range of topics, the real subject of all of them is the author himself as he thinks about his own varied experience. The work reflects Montaigne's profound mastery of classical literature, the result of years of thoughtful reading, yet he had no intention of presenting or systematically endorsing the ideas of any author. One of his most famous essays, "Of Education," insists that the proper goal in reading the classics is not to memorize facts about them but to use them for the formation of one's own beliefs. Though the search for truth is characteristic of human nature, the finding of truth (in the sense of absolute and indisputable truth) is highly questionable. Montaigne was strongly influenced by the writings of Sextus Empiricus, the only surviving text of ancient Greek pyrrhonist skepticism, and by the works of some earlier Renaissance authors who had shown interest in philosophical skepticism, and while he was no more a systematic skeptic than he was a systematic follower of any school of philosophy, a strong element of doubt permeates his thought. His longest and philosophically most earnest essay, "Apology for Raymond Sebond," is a historically important discussion of extreme (or pyrrhonist) skepticism. In practice, his interest is not in abstract questions of science or philosophy but in the kind of moral decisions that people make every day of their lives, practical decisions about which of several possible courses of action the individual should choose. In this quest for an experience-based moral philosophy that recognizes the impossibility of absolute certainty and is willing to settle for probability, ancient Stoicism, as found in the writings of Cicero, Seneca, and Plutarch, seems to have been more attractive to Montaigne than any other system, though he had no interest at all in the metaphysical foundations of ancient Stoic philosophy and was merely interested in the making of day-to-day decisions.

Even in his defense of Catholicism, his line of reasoning is not that he can demonstrate the truth of that religion's doctrines but that he can show that the rival Protestant theologians have not convincingly proved that their beliefs are more true than the Catholic ones. Hence he advises holding fast to the traditional system, since doing so seems to offer a better chance of social and political stability. Montaigne may have been a dutiful Catholic, but his writings do not glow with religious warmth. His essay "On Cannibals" is a famous example of the cultural relativism that he drew from the experience of meeting natives from the short-lived French colony in Brazil. In it he suggests that "barbarism" is merely any custom that is alien to our own customs and that a people's religion is determined not by what is true but by where they are born and brought up.

MONTEFELTRO, HOUSE OF. Italian noble family, originally counts of a district in east-central Italy known as the Marches, who came to the city of **Urbino** as imperial and later as papal vicars. Their first important figure, Antonio (1348–1404), incorporated Gubbio and several other towns into his small state and made Urbino his capital. He showed interest in the **humanist** culture that was becoming dominant at **Florence** and took care to have his children educated in Latin literature as well as courtly manners. His son Guidantonio, inheriting a compact and efficient state, enhanced his power and reputation by becoming one of the most highly regarded *condottieri* (mercenary generals) in the service of more powerful rulers. The third in the line of counts of Urbino, Oddantonio, was a debauched scoundrel who abused the wives and daughters of local citizens and was murdered in 1444 after only a year in power.

He was then succeeded by a legitimized half-brother, Federico (1444–1482), who resumed his father's career as a respected and successful condottiere and in 1474 was raised to the rank of duke by Pope **Sixtus IV** as a reward for his military service. Under him and his invalid but capable son Guidobaldo (1472–1508), the ducal court of Urbino became a brilliant center of humanistic culture and polite courtly society, a milieu immortalized as the setting for *The Book of the Courtier* (1528) by Count **Baldassare Castiglione**. Under Guidobaldo, the duchess, Elisabetta **Gonzaga**, a daughter of the ruler of **Mantua**, presided over a highly intellectual and refined court. The ducal couple was childless, and in 1504 Guidobaldo adopted his nephew Francesco Maria della Rovere, who was also the nephew of his overlord Pope **Julius II**, and who succeeded to the throne in 1508, marking the end of the Montefeltro dynasty.

MONTEMAYOR, JORGE DE (1520–1561). Portuguese-born poet, prose author, and singer in the imperial chapel at Madrid. He spent most of his career in the service of **Philip II** of Spain. His poems on religious themes are important contributions to devotional literature. He also wrote a prose dialogue in which fundamental questions of Catholic doctrine are freely discussed. His first volume of verse, both religious and secular, was published at Antwerp in 1554, and an expanded edition came out in 1558. Though Montemayor's kind of open and questioning religious works was not uncommon in the preceding generation, the more rigidly disciplined world of post-**Reformation** Spain found them unacceptable, and in 1559 all of his religious writings were placed on the Spanish Index of Forbidden Books. But that same year he published a prose pastoral romance, *Diana*, which became a literary sensation. It had many reprints and influenced Spanish authors (such as **Cervantes**) who sought to imitate it. It also influenced foreign authors such as **Sir Philip Sidney**, **William Shakespeare**, and the French pastoral novelist Honore d'**Urfé**. The end of Montemayor's life is as obscure as its origins; he seems to have died in Piedmont in 1561; an undocumented legend attributed his death to a duel over a rivalry in love.

MONTEVERDI, CLAUDIO (1567–1643). Italian composer, best known as one of the developers of the opera in the modern sense of the term. Born and trained in Cremona, he spent the first part of his career (1591–1612) in the service of the duke of **Mantua** and the second part (1613–1642) as director of music at St. Mark's in **Venice**, the most prestigious musical appointment in northern Italy. He was trained in the prevailing Renaissance style and in addition to sacred music for use in churches and court ceremonies, he composed some of the finest secular madrigals of Renaissance Italy. But Monteverdi's later madrigals and his operas mark a significant transition in musical style, from traditional Renaissance polyphony, characterized by equality of voices, linear development, and strict observance of counterpoint, to the **baroque** style of the 17th century, which emphasized use of a duet over a supporting bass and permitted dissonances and embellishments not accepted in Renaissance music, and which also gave the orchestral accompaniment a more prominent role than in the past. His first opera, *Orfeo*, produced at the court of Mantua in 1607, is the earliest work still in the modern operatic repertory. His other operas include *Arianna* (1608), of which only a fragment survives, *Il combattimento di Tancredi e Clorinda* (1624), *Il ritorno d'Ulisse in patria* (1640), and *L'incoronzaione di Poppea* (1642). Monteverdi also composed ballets and a great body of church music, especially after his move to Venice.

MONTREUIL, JEAN DE (1354–1418). Chancellor of France in the early 15th century. Though commonly associated with the French **Middle Ages**, he was not only a contemporary but a friend and admirer of the **Florentine humanists Coluccio Salutati, Leonardo Bruni** and **Niccolò Niccoli**, and he admired the works of the early humanists **Petrarch** and **Boccaccio**. He collected a library of **classical** and humanistic books and formed a circle of friends who shared his interests. Thus he is often viewed as a precursor of later French humanism, though his example also shows that even a circle of influential individuals who knew and appreciated the Italian humanists does not necessarily signify the arrival of the Renaissance in countries not politically and socially prepared to embrace a new culture. He was assassinated in 1418 when the **Burgundian** faction at the French court staged a coup d'état and executed royal officials associated with the rival Orléans (or Armagnac) faction.

MORATA, OLIMPIA (ca. 1530–1555). Italian **humanist** and Lutheran refugee. The daughter of Fulvio Pellegrino Morata, physician to the duke of **Ferrara** in the early 16th century, she grew up at court under the influence of the duchess, Renée de France, daughter of King Louis XII, a reform-minded duchess who welcomed to her court a number of early French religious reformers, including **Clément Marot**, Lyon Jamet, and **John Calvin**. Together with the daughter of the duchess, Olimpia studied Latin and **Greek** under a German tutor. She was familiar with **classical** literature and became active as a writer, producing poems, letters, and dialogues that were later edited and published (1558) by the humanist Celio Secundo Curione. At first she did not share the interest in religious reform that motivated the duchess's circle, but the founding of the **Inquisition** in 1542 and the duke's hostility to his wife's religious ideas put Olimpia under pressure to conform to strict Catholic orthodoxy. Her own father, her future editor Curione, her German tutor Sinapius, and a young physician attached to the court, Andreas Grunthler, all were supporters of the German Reformers.

After her father's death, Olimpia was dismissed from the court, probably because her orthodoxy was suspect. In 1550 she married Grunthler, and shortly afterward they moved to his home town of Schweinfurt in Germany. There the couple were openly Lutheran, and Olimpia wrote letters in Latin and Italian to friends back home, recommending **Martin Luther's** books; she also corresponded with Curione, who had settled in **Basel**, and Pier Paolo Vergerio, another Italian religious refugee, who was in Tübingen. When Schweinfurt was conquered during a religious war, she and her husband fled to Heidelberg, but the hardships of their flight undermined her health, and she died a year later.

MORE, THOMAS (ca. 1478–1535). English **humanist**, lawyer, political figure, and Roman Catholic martyr. Born in London, the son of a prominent lawyer, he received an excellent grammar-school education, then spent several years in the household of Cardinal John Morton, archbishop of Canterbury and Lord Chancellor under King **Henry VII**. More attended Oxford University but left without a degree to study law at the Inns of Court in London. He became a friend of the humanist **John Colet**, who had travelled in Italy and had become interested in Italian Renaissance learning. As a young man, More was drawn both to humanistic studies and to a secular career in the law, but he was also attracted by a monastic vocation and lived for a time in a Carthusian monastery in London before choosing to marry and practice law.

In 1499 More met the Dutch humanist **Erasmus**, and the two soon became friends. Erasmus lived for a time in More's home at London and finished the first draft of his famous satire *The Praise of Folly* while staying there. The Latin title of the work, *Encomium Moriae*, is a pun on More's name. More shared Erasmus' conviction that mastery of **Greek** was essential for any serious study of either the **classical** authors or the Bible and the writings of the Christian Church Fathers. The two friends competed in translating the epigrams of the Hellenistic poet Lucian of Samosata, and these translations from Greek into Latin were jointly published. More also wrote original Latin epigrams and poems. He published an English translation (1511) of the life of the Italian philosopher **Pico della Mirandola** written in Latin by his nephew **Gianfrancesco Pico**. He also wrote, in both Latin and English versions (1513), a history of King Richard III, the ruler dethroned by the first **Tudor** king, Henry VII. In it, he depicts Richard as a villain. More's career as a lawyer also flourished, and in 1504 he married and fathered four children.

The advisers to King **Henry VIII** spotted More as a man of great promise, and he began to be drawn into public service, going to the Netherlands in 1515 as a member of an English diplomatic mission. On his return he completed a political and social satire, *Utopia*, an imaginary description of a remote island society that in many ways resembles England and contains both some sharp criticisms of social and political conditions in England and a remarkable description of an ideal society based on the abolition of private property and the mandatory devotion of all citizens to the public interest. Erasmus arranged for the book's publication at **Louvain** in 1516.

In 1517 More became a member of the king's council, abandoning the practice of law for a career as a royal official that culminated in his appointment as Lord Chancellor, the highest judicial office in the land. Although never one of the inner circle who determined royal policy, he was consulted on matters relevant to his legal learning (for example, on the king's divorce from his wife, Catherine of Aragon).

He was one of those who assisted King Henry in writing his *Defense of the Seven Sacraments* (1521) against **Martin Luther**. He was active in the suppression of Lutheran influences in England, justifying his harsh policies in terms of the threat posed by heresy to social stability, and in 1523 he began publishing (at first under a pseudonym) his own tracts against Luther and his English sympathizers, sometimes in Latin but often in English, with the attack being concentrated against William Tyndale, who produced an influential English translation of the New Testament.

More himself came under pressure to endorse Henry VIII's repudiation of papal authority over the English church. In 1532, after the passage of the Act of Supremacy, a Parliamentary statute recognizing the king as head of the English church and repudiating the authority of the **pope**, the king granted him permission to resign the lord chancellorship. Thus he tried to retire quietly from political life, but he continued to publish tracts attacking English Protestants and also responded to anonymous tracts that accused him of inhumane treatment of accused heretics. These attacks on More defended the supremacy of the secular courts over ecclesiastical courts. More's sharp defense of traditional Catholic doctrine and of the independence of the church and its courts from secular authority was risky. In 1533 the royal council ordered him to stop publishing his tracts.

The next year, like all prominent English subjects, More was required to sign an endorsement of an Act of Succession that not only recognized the succession of Henry's offspring by his second wife, Anne Boleyn, but also required explicit endorsement of the king's religious policy. He had no objection to pledging to recognize Anne Boleyn's daughter (the future **Elizabeth I**) as heir to the throne, but he flatly refused to endorse the measures taken against papal authority, which he regarded as the guarantor of Christian unity. He was charged with treason, tried and convicted on 1 July 1535, and a few days later beheaded as a traitor. Whatever may have been his faults as a persecutor of heretics, he willingly gave his life in witness to his ideal of the unity and independence of the church, and was rapidly recognized as a martyr for the Catholic faith. In 1935 the Roman Catholic Church canonized him as a saint.

Although More was ambitious for worldly success, he was also deeply religious, a trait that is evident in many aspects of his life, including a number of spiritual writings. Although a layman and not a professional theologian, he delivered a series of lectures on St. Augustine's *City of God* in one of the London churches. About 1524 he wrote a meditation, *The Four Last Things*, which focused on the vanity and impermanence of all worldly goods. While imprisoned in the Tower of London, awaiting trial and death, he wrote several prayers and meditations, an incomplete meditation on Christ's agony in the garden of Gethsemane, *De tristitia Christi*, and a work that became well known after its posthumous publication in 1553, *A Dialogue of Comfort against Tribulation*. None of these spiritual works was published during his lifetime; some remained in manuscript until the 20th century.

MORISON, RICHARD (ca. 1510–1556). English **humanist**, politician, and religious reformer. Educated at Eton and the new Cardinal College founded by Cardinal **Thomas Wolsey** at Oxford, he also studied at **Padua** and perhaps in Paris before returning to England in 1536 as a protégé of **Thomas Cromwell**, the chief minister of state and the major force pushing the religious policies of King **Henry VIII** toward Protestantism. Morison wrote both religious and political pamphlets upholding royal authority over the church. His tract *A Remedy for Sedition* (1536) emphasized the central role of royal power in creating a stable and powerful nation. After the fall of Cromwell from power in 1540, his public career languished, but with the accession of Edward VI in 1547, he regained favor at court, was knighted in 1550, and sent as ambassador to the court of the Emperor **Charles V**. He lost this position when the Catholic Mary **Tudor** came to the English throne in 1553, and because of the suppression of Protestantism by her government, he settled in Strasbourg, where he died in 1556.

MOSTAERT, JAN (1475–1556). Court painter to Margaret of Austria, who was governor of the Netherlands for her nephew **Charles V**. Mostaert was born and trained at Haarlem. Most of his work consists of portraits, religious paintings, and imaginary landscapes. One of his works represents an incident in the Spanish conquest and settlement in the New World, though the artist himself never left Europe and based his image on written descriptions.

MÜNSTER, SEBASTIAN (1489–1552). German geographer, educated at Tübingen and Heidelberg. He became a Franciscan in 1505 but was converted to Protestantism in 1529 and moved to Switzerland, where he became professor of mathematics at the University of **Basel** in 1536. He was a specialist in **Hebrew** and Chaldean (Aramaic) languages, producing grammars of those languages and an edition of the Hebrew Bible (1534–1535). His *Horologiographia* (1530) was a treatise on sundials. He published an edition of the *Geography* of Ptolemy in 1540. Münster's most influential work was *Cosmographia Universalis / Universal Cosmography* (1544), which is illustrated with woodcuts and maps, not only for Western Europe (where his maps are very detailed) but also for non-European regions (where his maps are often vague because of the lack of reliable information).

MUSSATO, ALBERTINO (1261–1329). Italian scholar and lawyer, conventionally classed as one of the early North Italian "prehumanists," but in some recent scholarship discussed as one of the founders of a genuine Renaissance **humanism** at the very beginning of the 14th century. He was a disciple and friend of the older **Paduan** humanist **Lovato dei Lovati**. Mussato was the illegitimate son of a nobleman whose death when Albertino was 14 left his family in poverty. The youth had to work as a copyist of books in order to support himself and his younger brother and sister. Unable to afford the costly study of law, he was able to become qualified as a notary at Padua. Through native talent and hard work, Mussato soon became a major figure in local politics and an ardent defender of the city's survival as an independent republic in an age when the ambitious lord of Verona, Can Grande della Scala, jeopardized the city's freedom. Mussato was such an effective speaker that he was allowed to plead cases before the law courts despite lack of an academic degree in law. In 1315 the faculty of arts at Padua crowned him poet laureate. The commune knighted him when he was only 35, and he became a member of one of the governing councils in 1296. He worked as administrator of two cities in 1297 and 1309 and represented Padua on diplomatic missions. Mussato served in the army during war against Can Grande in 1314 and spent several months as a prisoner.

But his primary political activity was his eloquent defense of the existing republican constitution in the face of both internal and external pressure to seek security by accepting a *signore* (overlord). In 1325 he was permanently exiled by the Carrara governor of Padua, and he died in exile at Chioggia in 1329, the same year in which Padua formally recognized Can Grande as its lord.

Mussato's most famous literary work was a tragedy, *Ecerinis* (1315), inspired by the Roman dramatist Seneca. This drama, based on the career of the 13th-century adventurer Ezzelino da Romano, was intended to warn his fellow citizens of the dangers of accepting the rule of a tyrant. He also wrote *Historia Augusta*, a chronicle of the Italian expedition of the Holy Roman Emperor Henry VII in 1310–1313. Mussato's earlier poetic writings had followed the **classical** style that Lovato had defined for Latin poetry. In this historical work Mussato extended the new classical style to the writing of Latin prose. His own **guild** of Paduan notaries commissioned him to write an account in Latin verse of an unsuccessful siege of Padua by Can Grande. He also wrote other historical works in Latin prose, a continuation of his *Historia Augusta* and, at the very end of his life, an embittered narrative of the betrayal of Padua into the hands of Can Grande. Beyond the field of history, Mussato wrote pessimistic tracts on fate and political decline, a life of Seneca, and works on moral philosophy conceived in the spirit of Seneca's **Roman** Stoicism. At the very end of his life, his last series of poems, *Soliloquia / Soliloquies*, reflects a religious conversion that made him question the value of the classical studies he had pursued throughout his life. Although later humanists rarely mentioned the humanists of the late 13th century, both **Petrarch** and **Salutati**, the leading figures of later 14th-century humanism, did recognize the two Paduan writers, **Lovato** and Mussato, as their predecessors.

MUTIANUS RUFUS (1470–1527). German **humanist**, born as Konrad Mut at Homburg in Hesse, son of a prosperous merchant. He studied at the famous Latin grammar school of St. Lebwin in Deventer, where the headmaster, **Alexander Hegius**, had introduced a strong element of **classical** humanism into the curriculum. In 1486 he entered the University of Erfurt (B.A. 1488, M.A. 1492) and then spent two years teaching in the faculty of arts while beginning the study of law. During his period at Erfurt he studied under **Conrad Celtis**, one of the first humanists to gain a broad following among German students. In 1494 he left to travel and study in Italy, where he met the Latin poet **Baptista Mantuanus**, popularly hailed as "the Christian Vergil," and one of the leading Venetian humanists, **Filippo Beroaldo**. Mutianus was strongly attracted by the **Neoplatonism** that was becoming influential among Italian intellectuals at this time, but he also studied law at the **University of Bologna** and received a doctorate at **Ferrara** in 1501.

After his return to Germany in 1502, Mutianus worked briefly under his brother, who was chancellor of the county of Hesse. In 1503 he accepted a sinecure as canon of an endowed collegiate church in Gotha near Erfurt, where he spent the rest of his life. This position brought him a secure income and a sheltered existence devoted to study of ancient literature and philosophy, at the expense of a moderate amount of routine liturgical service and a hard-won ability to tolerate the crassly anti-intellectual attitude of his fellow canons. Although located near Erfurt, Mutianus did not participate personally in academic matters, not even when a serious effort to introduce humanistic curricular reforms took place in 1518–1519. But he had acquired a band of young admirers at Erfurt, and many of them looked to him for inspiration and visited him in Gotha. Mutianus thought of himself as a searcher for philosophical truth and was critical of the **scholastic** philosophy and theology of the universities. He also criticized the worldliness and immorality of many of the clergy and ridiculed the church's emphasis on external rituals of the sort that he himself conducted in performing his liturgical duties.

The attack on **Johann Reuchlin** by the theologians of Cologne infuriated Mutianus, and he encouraged his young humanist disciples at Erfurt to support Reuchlin. He probably was privy to the secret composition and publication of the scandalous anticlerical satire, *Letters of Obscure Men*, published anonymously in 1515 by his young admirers **Crotus Rubianus**, **Ulrich von Hutten**, and **Hermann von dem Busche**. Yet while he endorsed the attack on the Cologne theologians in private letters, Mutianus was temperamentally a non-participant. He seems to have been put off by Reuchlin's positive attitude toward the **Jews**, and he played no active role in the defense of Reuchlin, preferring to criticize from the sidelines. The same was true of his criticisms of the church. He complained but took no action. Likewise in the case of **Martin Luther** and the early **Reformation**, he expressed sympathy at first but drew back as the break with Rome became irreversible. Mutianus was one of the most widely respected older humanists of the early 16th century, largely on the basis of the many letters that he exchanged with other German humanists. Aside from the letters, which were not published until the 19th century, he left no written works at all.

– N –

NANNI DI BANCO (ca. 1384–1421). Florentine sculptor of the early 15th century. He was contemporary with the pioneering Renaissance sculptor **Donatello** but showed a strong **classicizing** tendency that is much more closely linked to the Gothic sculpture of the 13th and 14th century than to the new style that was beginning to emerge. His most famous work is the *Quattro Coronati/Four Saints* made about 1410–1414 for one of the niches on the exterior of the church of Or San Michele at **Florence**. Although the figures, especially the heads of two of the four saints, show the results of the artist's study of Roman sculpture, the work, quite unlike the *St. Mark* carved at almost the same time by Donatello, could not be separated from its architectural setting. The bodies of his four figures, however, have a monumental solidity which is unlike medieval classicizing sculpture and suggests the sculpture of the new Renaissance style. Nanni's last commission, not quite completed at his premature death in 1421, is a relief, *The Assumption of the Virgin*, carved for the local cathedral. His treatment of the body and especially of the draperies covering the massive and energetic bodies suggests that he, too, was moving in the stylistic direction that would mark early Renaissance rather than late medieval sculpture.

NAPLES. Principal city of southern Italy, and also the kingdom for which the city served as capital. In the 12th and earlier 13th centuries, it was politically linked with the island of Sicily in a union called the Kingdom of the Two Sicilies. This kingdom was the homeland and political base for the last powerful Holy Roman Emperor, Frederick II (ruled 1198–1250). After Frederick's death in 1250, the **popes** and their French ally, Charles of Anjou, a brother of King Louis IX of France, were able to keep Frederick's heirs from gaining control of

Naples, but a famous uprising of the people of Sicily against Anjou's rule, the Sicilian Vespers (1282), separated Sicily from Naples and eventually brought the island under the rule of the kings of Aragon. Rivalry for control of the mainland kingdom was a major cause of war and political unrest throughout the 14th and 15th centuries and ultimately led to the French invasion of Italy in 1494. This invasion set off the long series of wars that pitted Spain against France and reduced Italy to the level of a battleground for the foreign powers that sought to control the whole peninsula.

The Angevin dynasty controlled Naples from 1268 to 1442, and several of its rulers were important patrons of early Renaissance **humanism**, notably Robert the Wise (1309–1343), who crowned the humanist **Petrarch** as poet laureate in 1341. Ladislas (1386–1414) was a capable military commander and expanded his lands northward into central Italy during a period when the papacy was divided by the **Western Schism**. Under his sister and successor Joanna II (1414–1435), royal power declined, and a decade of war among rival claimants ended in 1442 with the military victory of the king of Aragon, who became Alfonso I of Naples. Alfonso played a major role in the Italian wars at mid-century surrounding the transition of **Milan** from the **Visconti** to the **Sforza** dynasty. Naples was one of the five major Italian powers for the rest of the century. Alfonso left his Neapolitan lands to his illegitimate son Ferrante while Aragon went to his legitimate son John II. Ferrante (1458–1494) was an active and fairly successful player in the game of Italian power politics. His son Alfonso II, however, was unpopular, and the arrival of the French invading army in 1494 brought about the rapid collapse of his rule. Charles VIII of France, asserting his dynastic claim, held power only briefly.

The Aragonese dynasty was restored by Spanish troops sent by King **Ferdinand I** of Spain. The Spanish were briefly driven out by another French invasion led by King Louis XII in 1499, but when King Ferdinand again drove the French out, Naples was partitioned between France and Spain in 1500. The French portion was conquered by Spanish troops in 1502, and in 1504 Ferdinand of Spain dethroned his Neapolitan cousin and made himself king of Naples as well as Spain. Spanish kings retained control of Naples until the end of the War of Spanish Succession in 1713. From 1558 to the end of

Habsburg rule in 1713, Naples, along with Sicily and Milan, was ruled by a royal council in Madrid, with a viceroy based in the city of Naples exercising administrative control.

Under the Angevin rulers (up to 1442), the visual arts remained primarily Gothic in character and were closely linked to French models. The first Aragonese king, Alfonso I, "the Magnanimous," made Naples the seat of all his kingdoms, including Aragon, and his patronage, guided by Renaissance art theorists like **Leon Battista Alberti**, reflected **classical** interests. Alfonso also patronized prominent humanists such as **Antonio Beccadelli** and **Lorenzo Valla**. Valla's famous treatise demonstrating that the basis of the papacy's claim to political power in Italy, the "**Donation of Constantine**," was a forgery, was a striking example of linguistic and historical criticism but functioned as a political tract in favor of Alfonso, who was involved in political disputes with the popes. Alfonso's successor Ferrante also patronized humanist scholars such as **Giovanni Pontano** and **Jacopo Sannazaro**.

NEBRIJA, ELIO ANTONIO DE (1441–1522). Spanish **humanist**, born at Lebrija (or Nebrija) near Seville, son of a Hidalgo family. He adopted the forename Elio (Aelius) as a symbol of his claim to **Roman** ancestry. In 1455 he entered the University of Salamanca, where he received a B.A. degree, and in 1460 he obtained a position in the Spanish College at **Bologna**. Nebrija spent the next decade in Italy, studying theology but also reading current humanistic literature. Upon his return to Spain in 1470, he won the patronage of the archbishop of Seville and in 1475 became lecturer at the University of Salamanca, where he received the chair of grammar and poetry. He married while there, thus foreclosing a career in the church. Throughout his teaching career Nebrija struggled to improve the teaching of Latin and **Greek**. The patronage of a second archbishop of Seville gave him the luxury of spending most of his time on lingistic research while occasionally teaching at the University of Seville. He accepted a professorship at Salamanca about 1505.

Nebrija's philological approach to the study of Scripture and his reliance on the Greek text raised the suspicions of the conservative inquisitor-general, Diego de Deza, who seized his papers and launched an investigation into his orthodoxy. Nebrija wrote an

Apologia/Defense addressed to the primate of Spain, Cardinal **Ximénes de Cisneros**, who intervened in his behalf and secured the return of his papers. In 1509 Nebrija was appointed royal chronicler. Cardinal Ximénes wanted to apply his scholarly talent to the great **Complutensian Polyglot Bible** he was planning to produce at his new University of **Alcalá**, and in 1513 Nebrija moved from Salamanca to Alcalá in order to become one of the editorial team for that project. Before long, however, he challenged the decision that in editing the Latin Bible, textual revisions would be based on authoritative Latin manuscripts but no changes would be introduced on the basis of the Greek and **Hebrew** texts. This conservative textual decision was contrary to Nebrija's discovery of discrepancies between the Latin and Greek texts of the New Testament, but the cardinal refused to change his policy, though he permitted Nebrija to publish three sets of critical notes on the text of the Bible (1514–1516).

Although Nebrija is remembered today mainly because of his biblical scholarship, in his own time he was most famous as a grammarian and **classical** scholar; and his work in those fields was more lasting. His publications include *Institutiones grammaticae* and *Institutiones latinae* (both 1481), the latter being an introductory textbook that was frequently reprinted; a Latin–Spanish dictionary (1492); the scriptural notes mentioned above and one other work on Greek and Hebrew with reference to Scripture (published posthumously, 1563); a vernacular work on Spanish **antiquities** (1499); a lexicon of Latin legal terms (1506); a textbook of rhetoric (ca. 1515); a Latin history of the reign of King **Ferdinand** and Queen **Isabella** (published posthumously, 1545); and critical editions of Pomponius Mela and Persius Flaccus. But his most original and most influential publication was *Gramática ... sobre la lengua castellana* (1492), one of the first scholarly and systematic grammars of any modern European vernacular. Nebrija, who knew the works of the humanist **Lorenzo Valla** well, shared Valla's conviction that language is closely related to political power. Nebrija died at Alcalá and was buried there.

NEOPLATONISM. Philosophical system (or group of systems) derived from the ancient Athenian philosopher Plato (428–348 B.C.); it is called Neoplatonism rather than Platonism because it tends to vary considerably from the actual teachings of Plato and his immediate disciples. It emphasized the importance of spiritual over material reality and valued contemplation and the quest for spiritual perfection more highly than an active life. Neoplatonism was the last major philosophical movement in ancient **Greek** philosophy, developing in the third century of the Christian era, especially at Alexandria in Egypt. Its founder was Ammonius Saccas, who taught at Alexandria in the early third century. He left a great impression on his pupils but wrote no books. His most influential disciple was Plotinus, who moved to **Rome** about 244 and taught there for a quarter-century. Only late in life did he set down his philosophy in written form. After his death his philosophical treatises were collected by his pupil Porphyry into six books called *Enneads*. Porphyry also wrote works of his own, especially an introduction to the *Categories*, a logical work of **Aristotle**, since he insisted that if properly understood, Plato and Aristotle agreed on most issues. Another Alexandrian Neoplatonist was Iamblicus, who merged Platonic and Pythagorean philosophical ideas with Egyptian religion. Also important was Proclus, who developed the idea of divine hierarchies emanating from the one divine being. These Neoplatonic systems were all religious in spirit, emphasizing the spiritual, the divine, and the eternal and belittling the material, the human, and the ephemeral. They presented themselves as systems that could lead the human soul from the material and transitory world to the spiritual and eternal God.

Neoplatonism, which presented itself as an accurate expression of the ideas of Plato himself, was familiar to many of the early Christian intellectuals (both orthodox and heretical ones). St. Augustine of Hippo credited "Platonism" (that is, Neoplatonism) with teaching him the nature of spiritual being and so removing an impediment to his eventual understanding of the Christian concept of God. But Neoplatonism itself was not Christian. In fact, it was a serious rival of Christianity for the spiritual allegiance of educated Greeks and Romans. Its description of humanity's progress from the material to the spiritual and from death to eternal life involved personal perfection through study, ascetic practices, and meditation; it had no place for such central Christian doctrines as the Incarnation, the resurrection of the flesh, the physical existence of a divine being like Jesus or his physical suffering and the shedding of his blood.

Many early Christian heresies arose because of a tendency of Platonizing intellectuals to reinterpret Christianity in Platonic terms—for example, the Docetists, who denied Christ's bodily existence. The Neoplatonists of Alexandria were actively critical of Christianity, which they despised as a materialistic superstition of low-class and uneducated people. Neoplatonic ideas found a harbor within Christianity in the thought of an author known as Dionysius the Areopagite, who actually was a philosophical follower of Proclus but presents himself in his works as the Athenian philosopher converted to Christianity by St. Paul himself, an incident mentioned in the Book of Acts (17:34). His highly spiritualized and hierarchical concept of Christianity presents the religion in largely Neoplatonic terms, and because they were incorrectly believed to be the work of a man taught directly by one of the Apostles, his writings attained almost scriptural authority throughout the medieval period.

The Latin church of the **Middle Ages** knew virtually nothing at first hand about Plato himself or about the genuine Neoplatonic philosophers of the third and fourth centuries. Only one Platonic dialogue, the *Timaeus*, was available in Latin translation. The name of Plato remained current, but only as a memory of an almost-forgotten past. There was Platonic influence on medieval philosophy and theology, but mainly at second hand, through citations in the writings of well-known Roman authors like **Cicero** and St. Augustine, and also from Dionysius the Areopagite. Dionysius' works were received from the Byzantine east in the age of Charlemagne and translated into Latin in the ninth century. At least some of them were known to theologians and ascetics of the 12th and 13th centuries, who accorded apostolic authority to their teachings but were not always quite sure what to make of them. Aristotle was the prevailing ancient philosophical authority; his intellectual method and many of his philosophical doctrines were central to almost all **scholastic** systems.

When early Renaissance humanists like **Petrarch** criticized the rationalism of Aristotle and his scholastic disciples, they sometimes suggested that Plato was a more acceptable thinker, more harmonious with Christianity, but such assertions were based on mere supposition. Petrarch had a few Platonic dialogues in the Greek original, but he could not read them. Only with the re-establishment of Greek studies in northern Italy through the work of **Manuel Chrysoloras** and his Italian pupils in the last decade of the 14th century did it become possible to investigate the thought of the mysterious Plato.

Many of those who learned Greek felt obligated to produce a Latin version of some ancient Greek text. Plato was one of the most alluring subjects of such translations. With the aid of Chrysoloras himself, the Milanese brothers Uberto and **Pier Candido Decembrio** made a pioneering translation of the *Republic*. One of the most active early translators was the **Florentine** chancellor **Leonardo Bruni**. He translated several Platonic dialogues. Other prominent translators of Plato included **Francesco Filelfo**, **Angelo Poliziano**, and the native Greek **George of Trebizond**.

By far the greatest of these Renaissance translators of Plato was the **Marsilio Ficino**, who devoted most of his professional life to translating and interpreting the works of Plato and other ancient philosophers associated with the Platonic tradition. His translation, *Platonis opera omnia / Complete Works of Plato*, first printed in 1484, made the whole body of Plato's works available in a Latin version that remained the basic text used by Latin-reading philosophers until the 18th century. But Ficino in his own philosophy (a commentary on Plato's works in 1496 and the treatises *De Christiana religione / On the Christian Religion* [1476] and *Theologia Platonica* [1482]) understood Plato in the light of the ancient Neoplatonists. In addition to translating Plato he translated the works of the leading Alexandrian Neoplatonists, including Plotinus' *Enneads* (1492), perhaps his greatest translation, dedicated to his patron **Lorenzo de'Medici**. He translated **Hermes Trismegistus'** *Pimander* and other tracts (1471), a collection of vaguely Platonic tracts produced in Roman Alexandria, and he retranslated the works of Dionysius the Areopagite (ca. 1496). The Neoplatonic commentator on Plotinus, Proclus, also attracted the attention of the Ficinian circle at Florence. In fact, the Florentine group associated the Platonic (or Neoplatonic) tradition with other genuine and forged ancient texts that they believed preserved a theosophy, or philosophical wisdom about divine matters, that extended back beyond Plato himself to the Persian sage Zoroaster, the mythical Egyptian sage Hermes, the Jewish **Cabalists**, Orpheus, Pythagoras, the Sybilline prophets, and other even more questionable texts that they found available in Greek.

Ficino firmly believed that these texts, despite their obvious diversity, represented one single tradition of divine wisdom, revealed to humanity at the very beginning of time and passed orally from generation to generation until it was written down in the various texts that he and his colleagues were discovering, translating, and studying. These texts constituted a *prisca theologia* ("ancient theology") that God provided to guide humanity, running parallel to God's revelation to Moses and the Hebrew patriarchs as recorded in the Old Testament. The Neoplatonists were convinced that study of these sages would enrich and revitalize Christianity and that this enriched Christianity would eventually win over by persuasion the followers of all other religions as part of God's plan for the redemption of humanity. The other early leaders of the so-called Florentine **Academy** were **Giovanni Pico della Mirandola** (who was less of a Platonist than the others), **Cristoforo Landino**, Angelo Poliziano, and the patron of them all, Lorenzo de'Medici.

The fundamental philosophical doctrines of Florentine Neoplatonism started from Plato's distinction between the eternal world of ideas and the ephemeral world of matter. Like the Alexandrian Neoplatonists whom they studied, they interpreted Plato in a radically spiritualizing way, regarding the whole universe as permeated by a hierarchy of spiritual beings that emanated from the one God, and viewing the human soul as an inherently immortal spirit that seeks union with God (the true goal of human existence) not only through rational knowledge but also through love, the desire for absolute beauty. The theme of Platonic love was important in Ficino's own philosophical works and passed into the literary world through the *Disputationes Camaldulenses / Disputations at Camaldoli* (ca. 1472) of Landino, the poetry (both Latin and Italian) of Poliziano and Lorenzo de'Medici, and a generation later, such works as *The Book of the Courtier* by **Baldassare Castiglione** and the *Dialogues on Love* of **Leone Ebreo**. In northern Europe, Platonic love was influential in the poems of the French group known as the *Pléiade*, in Edmund Spenser, and in many generations of European poets since the 16th century. These themes are also prominent in the visual arts, beginning with two painters who were themselves members of the Medicean court society, **Sandro Botticelli** and **Michelangelo**, and continuing through the long course of Renaissance and post-Renaissance art.

The concept of an animated universe permeated by spiritual beings also linked Neoplatonism to the study of occultist fields such as magic, **astrology**, and **alchemy**, and to the work of scholars who studied philosophical and scientific questions that would still be regarded as genuine science, such as mathematics, physics, astronomy, and biology. Ficino and Pico themselves pursued both occultist and conventional sciences. Some others affected by Neoplatonism were **Agrippa von Nettesheim, Paracelsus,** such Italian "philosophers of nature" as **Francesco Patrizi** and **Giordano Bruno,** the "Cambridge Platonists" of 17th-century England, and such significant pioneers of modern natural science as **Nicolaus Copernicus** and **Johannes Kepler.** Another earlier Renaissance philosopher who was heavily influenced by Platonism (though not by the Florentine tradition, which had not yet developed) was the German cardinal and philosopher **Nicholas of Cusa.**

NEOSTOICISM. Renaissance adaptation of ancient Roman Stoic philosophy, frequently recommended in the 16th century as a practical philosophy that could help intelligent people cope with the vagaries and violence of the spiritual uncertainty and religious warfare that troubled Europe from the 1540s to the end of the Thirty Years' War in 1648. The ancient philosophers who served as models and sources of inspiration for Neostoics lived in Roman times, though some of them wrote in **Greek.** They included Epictetus, Plutarch, Marcus Aurelius, and Seneca; of these, Plutarch and Seneca were the most frequently read and discussed. Greek Stoicism, which was founded by Zeno at Athens in the fourth century B.C. and emphasized the goal of living in accord with nature, had developed an abstract foundation in the concept of the Logos, or principle of rationality, that lies at the basis of all being, though even Greek Stoicism was primarily concerned with ethical problems. Roman Stoicism had been even more oriented toward concern with the moral problems of life, and this form of Stoic thought was what appealed to Renaissance Stoics. In late **antiquity,** the influential church father St. Ambrose developed a Christianized form of Stoicism as an acceptable guide to moral life, and Stoic texts, especially Seneca's *Letters to Lucilius,* were read and admired in the **Middle Ages.** From the early Renaissance, many **humanists** endorsed Stoicism, with its ideal of duty and self-denial, as a system that was both compatible with Christian asceticism and practical as a guide to living. **Petrarch** addressed one of his imaginary letters to Seneca. His disciple **Coluccio Salutati** also admired Seneca, as did **Leon Battista Alberti**. **Niccolò Perotti** translated the Stoic Epictetus into Latin. At the beginning of the 16th century, thinkers as diverse as **Pietro Pomponazzi**, **Guillaume Budé**, and **Niccolò Machiavelli** incorporated Stoic ideas into their writings, and the greatest **humanist** of that generation, **Erasmus**, edited Seneca's works, while the youthful **John Calvin**, still a humanist and not yet converted to Protestantism, published a commentary on Seneca's book *De clementia*. The age of religious wars, from the 1540s to 1648, represents the peak of Renaissance Neostoicism, as troubled intellectuals found in Stoicism a rational system for maintaining their moral autonomy in a violent age.

The most influential explicitly Stoic moral philosopher of the age was **Justus Lipsius**. His *De constantia / On Constancy* (1584) was his principal work, though he also produced an introduction to Stoic philosophy and an edition of Seneca's works. The French magistrate Guillaume du Vair was the most systematic French Stoic philosopher, but the most influential presentation of Stoic ideas as a means of maintaining the individual's moral autonomy and integrity was the *Essays* of **Michel de Montaigne**, who was not entirely committed to Stoicism as a system (or to any philosophical system) but who upheld many Stoic ideas in essays that had great influence on educated people in France and eventually in other countries.

NICCOLI, NICCOLÒ DE' (1364–1437). Florentine **humanist**. His home at **Florence** became one of the principal gathering-places of enthusiasts for ancient literature, and through his widespread correspondence he directed the search for manuscripts of previously unknown **classical** authors. He had considerable success in this endeavor, being involved in the discovery of the works of the Roman historian Tacitus, who had been little known in the **Middle Ages**, and encouraging his friend **Poggio Bracciolini**, who was probably the greatest manuscript-hunter of the early 15th century. Niccoli was intensely interested in the niceties of good Latin style, but he himself wrote virtually nothing except his many letters. His numerous critics suggested that he wrote so little because his own Latin style was not up to the refined linguistic standards that he criticized others for neglecting. Yet he did build a valuable classical library which was open to his humanist colleagues, and he also was one of the first Renaissance scholars to form a large collection of ancient Roman coins and medals. Although Niccoli had inherited a substantial fortune, he spent so much on books and coins that **Cosimo de'Medici** began subsidizing his collections and eventually acquired many of the treasures left behind at Niccoli's death. Niccoli avoided public office, never married, and devoted himself almost exclusively to the study of **antiquity**.

NICHOLAS V (Tommaso Parentucelli, 1397–1455, elected pope in 1447). Born at Sarzana in northwestern Italy, the son of a physician, and orphaned at an early age, he studied at the **University of Bologna** (ca. 1413–1416), where he became expert in **scholastic** philosophy and especially **Aristotelian** physics. Poverty compelled him to become tutor to the children of two wealthy **Florentine** families, an experience that introduced him to **humanistic** studies and especially to the study of **Greek**. Parentucelli returned to Bologna to complete his master of arts degree (ca. 1420) and then entered the service of Niccolò Albergati, bishop of Bologna, who soon became a cardinal. He accompanied Albergati on diplomatic missions for **Popes Martin V** and **Eugenius IV**. Parentucelli gained valuable ecclesiastical appointments, and in 1444 he became bishop of Bologna. In 1446 the pope made him a cardinal. Shortly after, Eugenius died and Parentucelli was elected pope.

As pope, Nicholas managed to bring about a peaceful end to the schismatic remnant of the **Council of Basel** (1459). He sought peaceful relations with other Italian states. When **Constantinople** fell to the Turks in 1453, he tried to organize a crusade for reconquest of the city, but without success. During his short pontificate he did consolidate papal control of **Rome** itself and conceived an ambitious plan to transform the city into a splendid ecclesiastical capital of Christendom, though only a few of his projects were brought to completion. Nicholas is especially important for the history of the Renaissance because as a pope who had been a humanist, he encouraged humanistic and literary scholarship. He collected a vast library of **classical** manuscripts and intended to sponsor the translation of all of Greek literature into Latin. Nicholas is commonly regarded as the founder of the present Vatican Library. His pontificate marks the first step toward the emergence of Rome as a major center of Renaissance civilization.

NICHOLAS OF CUSA (1401–1464). German philosopher, theologian, mathematician, church reformer, and cardinal. Born Niklas Krebs at Kues in western Germany, he received the nickname Cusanus from the Latin name of his native town. He was educated at Heidelberg, **Padua**, and Cologne. Though his academic doctorate was in canon law and he practiced as a successful lawyer in his youth, he also studied theology and from his experience in Italy acquired an interest in **humanistic** learning. His discovery of a number of lost works of the Roman comedian Plautus gave him a considerable reputation among Italian humanists. He became a priest and accumulated church benefices, and in 1432 he went to the **Council of Basel** as legal advocate of a claimant to the archbishopric of Trier.

Cusanus became a supporter of the council and of the theories of **Conciliarism**, writing *De concordantia catholica / On Catholic Concord* (1433), an influential though moderate defense of conciliar authority as a means of bringing about necessary reforms in the church. He was attracted by the attempt of **Pope Eugenius IV** to negotiate reunion of the Greek Orthodox and Roman Catholic churches and eventually broke with the council, which was increasingly dominated by radical followers of Conciliar theory. He visited **Constantinople** in pursuit of church reunion, travelled widely during the meeting of the **Council of Ferrara-Florence** to win the support of German princes for the pope, and eventually was made a cardinal and appointed to the important bishopric of Brixen. As bishop, he struggled to introduce reforms against the opposition of members of the clergy and the secular princes of the region. His own inflexibility probably contributed to his failure, culminating in 1457 when his enemies forced him to flee from Brixen. Eventually he settled in **Rome**, where he found resistance within the curial bureaucracy to any serious reform just as frustrating as what he had encountered at Brixen.

Throughout this busy period, Cusanus produced some of the most original philosophical writings of the 15th century, drawing inspiration from the growing familiarity of the humanist world with the works of **Plato**, though he died before the movement known as **Florentine Neoplatonism** reached its full development. His most important philosophical work was *De docta ignorantia / On Learned Ignorance* (1440), in which he explored the limits of human ability to gain knowledge of God. Although his innovative concept of learned ignorance elicited attacks from conservative **scholastic** theologians, he continued to produce treatises that raised issues of epistemology long neglected in medieval philosophy. His philosophical work also emphasized the central role of faith in the search for God and made contributions to mathematical theory. His distress over the fall of Constantinople to the Turks in 1453 produced the dialogue *De pace fidei*. It endorsed the unification of all religions (including Christianity, Judaism, and Islam, but on a clearly Christian foundation) as a way to achieve universal peace and concord.

In 1459 Cusanus presented to Pope **Pius II** a sweeping plan for the reform of the whole church, including the papal curia, but despite encouraging words from the pope, nothing of significance came out of his initiative. He also wrote *Cribratio Alkorani / A Critique of the Koran* (1461), which reflected European understanding of Islam in his time. He died while en route to an Adriatic seaport to assist the pope in preparations for a crusade against the Turks. He was buried in Rome, but his heart was buried in his native Kues, where he founded a hospice that still survives for care of the poor.

NOGAROLA, ISOTTA (1418–1488). One of the earliest female **humanists**. The daughters of a noble family of Verona, she and her sister Ginevra were given a humanistic education on orders of their widowed mother. In their youth, both sisters won praise from northern Italian humanists associated with the famous teacher **Guarino Guarini**, himself a native of Verona. The sisters exchanged books and letters with these male humanists. In 1438, however, Ginevra married and abandoned her scholarly activities. Isotta drew back from public expression of interest in secular learning in 1441, partly because she found herself accused of engaging in activities that were not permissible for a respectable **woman**. Even when she received replies to her letters to male scholars, she saw that though some of these letters gave her extravagant praise, others belittled her learning, making it clear that there could be no true scholarly fellowship between their authors and any woman. An anonymous critic accused her (with no evidence) of promiscuity and incest.

Perhaps even more humiliating was the failure of the great educator Guarino, who had trained her own tutor, to reply to her initial letter. When she protested, Guarino did reply but expressed disappointment at

her abject appeal for his approval, warning her that she must stop acting like a woman if she wanted to be esteemed by men for participation in a masculine scholarly world. Her response was to withdraw
entirely from public society. Though not a nun, henceforth she lived
in a single room, where she occupied herself in religious devotions
and studied purely religious texts. This activity was deemed more
suitable for a woman. Lauro Quirini, a learned Venetian nobleman,
outlined for her a rigorous program of private theological study based
on **Aristotle** and the commentators used at the universities. More
emotionaly rewarding was her relationship with Ludovico Foscarini,
who met her when he was governor of Verona. Although Foscarini
admired her, he respected her vow of virginity. Indeed, the one recommendation that she got from nearly all who corresponded with her
and praised her piety and learning was that she must preserve her virginity: that was what was most important for a woman. She and Foscarini exchanged tracts arguing the question whether Adam or Eve
was the more guilty of humanity's original sin. She argued that Eve
was the less guilty, but she did so by emphasizing the inherent inferiority of female nature: Eve could not have been responsible for the
sin, for as a woman she had been created ignorant and imperfect;
Adam had been made perfect, and therefore his was the greater sin.

NOSTRADAMUS (Michel de Notredame, 1503–1566). French
physician and prophet. After the death of his wife and children from
plague, he spent many years as an itinerant plague doctor. Like nearly
all physcians of his time, he was also interested in **astrology** and became known for his prophecies of future events as much as for his
cures of patients. His *Centuries* or *Prophecies* began being published
in 1555. These were collections of verses organized into 10 "centuries," each of 100 quatrains. They are written in an obscure style
modeled on the sayings of ancient oracles and sibyls. There were
many believers in his prophecies, of which the most famous is the
prediction, in a horoscope prepared for Queen Catherine de **Medici**,
that each of her sons would become king, a prediction that nearly did
come true since all but one of them succeeded to the throne in order
of age. Because they claimed to foretell future events all the way to
the year 3797, these verses have continued to be taken seriously by
certain individuals and groups, especially at times of uncertainty and

stress. Nostradamus' prophecies were especially menacing for French Calvinists, and they were his most vigorous critics.

NÚÑEZ DE TOLEDO Y GUZMÁN, HERNÁN (ca. 1475–1553). Spanish **classical** scholar, born at Toledo and often known as Pinciano or Pintianus, a name derived from the Latin name for Toledo. The son of an official at the royal court, he became a member of the military order of Santiago, but instead of spending his life as a crusading warrior, he devoted himself to study of ancient literature. Núñez was educated at Valladolid and about 1490 studied at the Spanish College in **Bologna**, where one of his teachers was the prominent **humanist Filippo Beroaldo** the Elder. After his return to Spain, he became tutor (1498–1510) to the children of the Mendoza family, one of the grandest families of the Castilian nobility. His employer was governor of Granada, and he lived there for a number of years. His humanistic learning, especially in **Greek**, attracted the attention of Spain's leading patron of education, Cardinal **Ximénes de Cisneros**, who recruited him as one of the team of scholars working on the great **Complutensian Polyglot Bible** being prepared at the University of **Alcalá** under the cardinal's patronage. Núñez also taught rhetoric in the **university** but left in 1523 to become the successor of **Elio Antonio de Nebrija** as professor of Greek at the University of Salamanca. His move may have been partly motivated by his support for the Comunero movement, a revolutionary upheaval in the cities of Castile arising from fear that their new **Habsburg** king, the Emperor **Charles V**, was sacrificing Spanish interests for the benefit of his lands in the Netherlands and Germany.

In 1527 Núñez was promoted to the chair of rhetoric at Salamanca, where he spent the rest of his career. His lectures on classical authors such as Lucius Annaeus Seneca, Pomponius Mela, and Pliny the Elder led to his three major publications in the field of **classical** studies, of which his commentary on the *Natural History* of Pliny is perhaps the best known. Although these three authors were Romans, he was an enthusiastic promoter of Greek studies and came to be known by the nickname *el comendador griego / the Greek Commander*, a reminder that he still held the status of an officer in one of the crusading orders. Núñez was also interested in vernacular literature. His commentary (1499) on the long didactic poem *El laberinto de la Fortuna* by **Juan de Mena** was important for Hispanic scholarship. He also published a Castilian translation (1509) of the *History of Bohemia* written by Pope **Pius II** (Aeneas Sylvius Piccolomini), and his *Refranes o proverbios*, a collection of popular sayings and proverbs, was published in 1555, after his death.

NUREMBERG CHRONICLE. A history of the world from the Creation to the end of the 15th centry, compiled by Hartmann Schedel, a physician and collector of books. It was published in both a Latin edition, *Liber chronicarum*, and a German edition, *Das Buch der Chroniken und Geschichten*, both of which appeared in 1493. The books, printed in handsome folio format, have more than 1,800 illustrations printed from 645 woodcuts (many woodcuts were reused several times). These illustrations are more important than the historical text, which is a conventional compilation of events from the Creation to the author's time. Schedel was a member of the Nuremberg **humanist** circle but produced what was essentially a traditional medieval chronicle unaffected by the more tightly organized structure of contemporary Italian humanistic histories by **Leonardo Bruni**, **Niccolò Machiavelli**, and **Francesco Guicciardini**

– O –

OBRECHT, JACOB (ca. 1452–1505). Flemish composer. Born at Bergen-op-Zoom and educated at the **University of Louvain**, he spent most of his career in the Netherlands but visited Italy, mainly the court of the duke of **Ferrara**, in 1487–1488. He returned to Ferrara as head of the duke's choir in 1504 but died of plague the following year. His surviving works include 29 masses, 28 motets, and a number of songs in Latin and Dutch, as well as instrumental music. He was director of choirs in Utrecht, Bergen-op-Zoom, Cambrai, Bruges, and Antwerp as well as several other places in the Netherlands. His compositions often used borrowed themes but treated them in innovative ways. Some of his masses were based on secular songs, others on traditional Gregorian melodies.

OCCULTISM. *See* ASTROLOGY; MAGIC

OCKEGHEM, JOHANNES (ca. 1421–1497). Flemish composer, born in the county of Hainaut. Nothing is known of his musical education, though he may have been a pupil of **Gilles de Binchois**, in which case he would have had an early connection with the dukes of **Burgundy**. He was a singer in the cathedral choir at Antwerp in 1443, but by the mid-1440s he had moved to France, first at the court of the duke of Bourbon and from 1452 in the royal chapel. He remained in royal service through the reigns of kings Charles VII, Louis XI, and Charles VIII. In addition to being a famous composer of masses, motets, and chansons, he taught and influenced the development of important composers of the next generation, men such as **Jacob Obrecht, Heinrich Isaak**, and **Josquin des Prez**. His works include the canon *Alma Redemptoris Mater*. Ockeghem was famous for his skill in counterpoint.

ORLEY, BERNAERT VAN (1490–1541). Flemish painter and designer of tapestries. Born in Brussels and trained by his father, he seems never to have visited Italy but nevertheless became familiar with the Italian Renaissance style of painting, changing from two-dimensional style to a Renaissance style influenced by the paintings of **Andrea Mantegna** and **Raphael**. His designs for tapestries include a *Life of Abraham* and a depiction of *Maximilian's Hunts*, both of which illustrate his move toward more effective treatment of **perspective**.

ORTELIUS, ABRAHAM (1527–1598). Dutch mapmaker and printer. A native of Antwerp, he was trained as an engraver but became a dealer in maps and **antiquities**, travelling widely to collect and sell maps. He became involved in cartography through his acquaintance with the mapmaker **Gerard Mercator**. His *Theatrum orbis terrarum* (1570) was a prototype of the modern world atlas, both in the great number and quality of its engravings and in its attempt to cover the whole world. In 1573 he became geographer to King **Philip II** of Spain. His *Theatrum* went through many reprintings despite the great cost imposed by its elaborate engravings.

OTTOMAN EMPIRE. Islamic state of the Osmanli branch of the Turkish peoples, founded in the late 13th century by Osman I. It continued to be ruled by the sultans descended from him until its dissolution at the end of World War I. The empire was the most powerful political and military force in Renaissance Europe. Its beginnings lay in the Anatolian peninsula, which had been settled by Turks in the late 11th century. Taking advantage of the civil wars among contenders for the throne of the Byzantine Empire, the Ottomans seized control of Gallipoli on the European side of the straits in 1354, and in 1356 the sultan established his capital at Adrianople on the European side. The Turks rapidly pushed northward into the Balkan peninsula, reducing the kingdom of Bulgaria to vassal status between 1369 and 1371, crushing the Serbs at Kossovo in 1389, and then destroying the last vestiges of an independent Bulgarian state in 1393. These victories established an Ottoman rule over the Balkans that lasted until the 19th century.

By the end of the 14th century, the Byzantine Empire was limited to the city of **Constantinople** and a small area around it, and while **popes** and western European rulers talked of a crusade to preserve the ancient Roman capital, they were more interested in exploiting the Byzantine state than in preserving it. In 1396 a crusade organized by the Holy Roman Emperor Sigismund marched southward into the Balkans, but the Ottoman sultan Bayezid destroyed this army in the battle of Nicopolis. Great numbers of Latin knights were captured and, in reprisal for their massacre of all Muslim prisoners, were either put to death or sold as slaves. Bayezid then completed his conquest of most of the Greek mainland and in 1402 demanded the surrender of Constantinople. At this moment, however, Tamerlane, a Turkish prince from central Asia, attacked the Ottomans and demolished their army. The sultan was taken prisoner and died in captivity. Tamerlane soon directed his military efforts elsewhere and died in 1405.

This catastrophe saved Constantinople for more than a generation, but the next sultan, Murad II, reorganized his army and soon was pressing northward into the Balkans and also resuming military pressure on the Byzantine capital. In 1451 a new sultan, Muhammad II (1451–1481) began systematically preparing for the conquest of Constantinople. At the end of May 1453, the Turkish army breached the city's walls and overwhelmed the defenders, ending the last direct remnant of the ancient Roman Empire. Constantinople—now called Istanbul—became and remained the capital of the Ottoman Empire. Then Muhammad rounded out his conquests in the Balkans, driving the Venetians out of the Morea (southern mainland Greece), seizing most of the Greek islands, establishing control over Serbia and Bosnia, and briefly establishing a base at Otranto in southern Italy. His successor Bayezid (1481–1512) faced internal political difficulties. Under Selim I (1512–1520) Ottoman power turned eastward, defeating the Persians and annexing much of northern Mesopotamia, then conquering Syria and Egypt. Under him, the Ottomans also became a sea power. Under Selim's successor Suleiman (1520–1566), the Ottomans reduced the Muslim states of North Africa to vassal status, and the Ottoman navy dominated the western as well as the eastern Mediterranean.

In 1526 Suleiman inflicted a disastrous defeat on King Louis II of Hungary and virtually wiped out the kingdom of Hungary, leaving only the western third in the hands of Louis' brother-in-law, Ferdinand of **Habsburg**, and allowing most of the country to be administered by the leading Hungarian nobleman, John Zápolyai, who became a vassal of the sultan. Suleiman threatened the southern regions of Bohemia and Poland, but his attempt to conquer Vienna and enter southern Germany in 1529 failed after a long siege. The Ottoman state reached its greatest extent in Suleiman's reign. Under the next Sultan, Selim II (1566–1574), the Turks easily conquered the island of Cyprus, but their attempt to end Venetian rule of Crete was thwarted by a fleet of Christian allies in the battle of Lepanto (1571) off the western coast of Greece.

By the end of the 16th century, some of the long-term weaknesses of the empire were becoming evident, particularly the increasing insubordination of its armies and the corruption of its officials. The Ottomans remained powerful even in the later 17th century, besieging Vienna again in 1683, but by the end of that century, they had lost control of most of Hungary to the Habsburgs. By the 18th century, Turkey was on its way to becoming "the sick man of Europe."

– P –

PACIOLI, LUCA (ca. 1445–1517). Italian mathematician and teacher. Born at Borgo San Sepolcro in Tuscany, he became a tutor to a wealthy family in **Venice** and developed his mastery of mathematics under a local teacher. By 1475 he was a teacher at the **University** of Perugia. About this time he became a Franciscan friar and continued to teach mathematics at various places. He was a friend of at least two major artists, **Piero della Francesca** and **Leonardo da Vinci**, both of whom had a strong interest in mathematics. He published several books, including *Summa de arithmetica, geometria, proportione et proportionalità / A Summary of Arithmetic, Geometry, and Proportion* (1494), a Latin edition of Euclid's *Elements* (1509), and a book *De divina proportione / On Divine Proportion* (1509), an expanded version of a work written collaboratively with Leonardo and illustrated by him. The *Summa* was an important book, combining the intellectual mathematics of the academic tradition with the practical mathematics of the abacus, and showing a sophisticated grasp of algebra. It is also significant because it contains the first printed description of the method of double-entry bookkeeping that Italian merchants had developed during the two preceding centuries.

PADUA. City of northeastern Italy, 22 miles (35 kilometers) west of **Venice**. Padua was an important center for communications and travel in the Po river valley. Although the flourishing **Roman** municipality declined in the early **Middle Ages**, the city became one of Italy's leading self-governing **communes** between the 11th and the early 14th century. It was constantly exposed to military and political pressure from ambitious neighboring nobles. It fell under the control of Ezzelino da Romano between 1237 and 1256 but recovered its autonomy after his death. Internal conflicts among the citizens encouraged outsiders to intervene. Although Padua resisted the efforts of the Emperor Henry VII and his ally Can Grande della Scala, lord of Verona, to establish control, the nearby Carrara lords insinuated themselves as commanders of the city's military forces and by the 1320s had become *signori* (lords) of the city. Their rule lasted until 1405, when the republic of Venice established a control that lasted until 1797.

In the late 13th and early 14th centuries, Padua was home to two of the earliest Italian **humanists, Lovato dei Lovati** and **Albertino Mussato.** It was the location of major works of art by **Giotto, Donatello, Andrea Mantegna,** and **Titian.**

Although Padua was a significant commercial power, its main importance was as the seat one of the two greatest Italian universities. In

1222 a large group of students and teachers from the oldest Italian university, **Bologna**, migrated to Padua after a quarrel with the city of Bologna. The university developed gradually during the late 13th and 14th centuries. In 1399 it divided into two separate institutions, a university of civil and canon law and a university of arts and medicine (including not only medical studies but also natural sciences, philosophy, and humanities, and later adding theology). This twofold division persisted until the 19th century. The conquest of the city by the Venetians might have threatened the welfare of an institution controlled by the local government, but the Venetians promised to guard the university's welfare. Under Venetian rule, especially in the 15th and 16th centuries, Padua became the best university in Italy. The Venetian government limited the right of Padua's administration to fill the faculty with native sons and deliberately recruited outstanding professors from other institutions at high salaries. Especially between the hiring of the philosopher **Pietro Pomponazzi** in 1488 and the departure of the mathematician and astronomer **Galileo Galilei** in 1610, Padua led the rest of Europe in several fields, especially in medicine and natural philosophy. In 1540 the medical faculty began the practice of clinical medicine, introducing students to actual medical practice at the bedsides of sick persons. In 1545 Venice authorized a botanical garden (especially useful for pharmacology) which survives, the oldest university botanical garden in Europe.

A clear sign of the university's greatness is the quality of its graduates, including the political philosophers **Paolo Giovio** and **Francesco Guicciardini**; the humanists **Francesco Filelfo**, **Giovanni Pico della Mirandola**, and **Pier Paolo Vergerio**; and the physicians and philosopher-scientists **Ulisse Aldrovandi**, **Girolamo Cardano**, **Gabriele Falloppio**, **Girolamo Fracastoro**, **Francesco Patrizi**, and **Bernardino Telesio**. Foreign scholars also flocked to Padua, including the Germans **Nicholas of Cusa** and **Willibald Pirckheimer**; Hungary's greatest humanist, **Janus Pannonius**; and a brilliant galaxy of English scholars, including **John Colet**, **William Harvey**, **Thomas Linacre**, and **Reginald Pole**.

PALESTRINA, GIOVANNI PIERLUIGI DA (ca. 1525–1594). Italian composer. He was the greatest figure associated with the reform of ecclesiastical music by the Council of Trent (1545–1563), which sought to end the use of "lascivious" or "impure" themes taken from secular songs and to limit the elaborate polyphony typical of late medieval and Renaissance church music. Born in a small town near **Rome**, in the 1530s Palestrina became a choirboy in the basilica of Santa Maria Maggiore at Rome. In 1551 he was put in charge of the choirboys, and in 1555 he became *magister capellae* (master of the chapel) at St. Peter's. Shortly after his appointment, a new **pope**, Paul IV, removed him from the position because he was married. Under a later pope he was reinstated (1571) and spent the rest of his life in that position.

From 1565 Palestrina received a regular salary to compose music for the papal chapel. He wrote much ecclesiastical music, bringing out his first printed collection of masses in 1554. Eventually, he produced 104 settings of the mass and some 250 motets and other musical accompaniments for liturgical acts. In his youth he also wrote many secular madrigals, which were first printed in 1555. Although the 17th century created a myth that his *Missa papae Marcelli / Pope Marcellus' Mass* (ca. 1562) convinced the members of the Council of Trent that polyphonic music could be both reverent and understandable and hence helped to block a total prohibition of polyphonic music in the churches, there is no direct evidence that this is so. He did, however, supervise revision of the chant books used at Rome, making them conform to the regulations enacted at Trent to promote a simpler, more reverent style of singing. For a time he taught music at the new **Jesuit** seminary in Rome. In the following century, his consistent contrapuntal style became the model recommended to those who wanted to learn the art of counterpoint.

PALLADIO, ANDREA (1508–1580). Italian architect. His harmonious and balanced **neoclassical** buildings set a style for palaces, country houses, and churches that spread from his home region in northern Italy throughout Europe. The most famous example of his secular style is the *Villa Rotonda* at Vicenza (1567–1570). He also designed churches, of which the best known is San Giorgio Maggiore in **Venice** (1565). His buildings reflect his desire to apply **Roman** classical forms to modern buildings and to revive the dignity and severity of Roman architecture. Palladio was strongly influenced by the architectural writings of the ancient architect Vitruvius and the

Renaissance architect **Leon Battista Alberti**. In the last decade of his life he served as architectural adviser to the Venetian government. His *Quattro libri dell'architettura / Four Books on Architecture* (1570) was one of the most influential architectural treatises of the Renaissance, and his balanced classical style, as expressed in the Villa Rotonda, powerfully influenced the 17th-century English architect **Inigo Jones**.

PALMIERI, MATTEO (1406–1475). **Florentine humanist**, identified like his older friend **Leonardo Bruni** with exaltation of the active life of the citizen as superior (except for persons embracing a monastic career) to a life of contemplation. Born into a middle-class family, he was educated under the direction of two prominent Florentine humanists, **Ambrogio Traversari** and Carlo Marsuppini. Palmieri held many important public offices, including diplomatic missions to the king of **Naples** and two **popes**. In Latin he wrote a chronicle of world history from Creation to his own times, *Liber de temporibus*; a narrative of the successful Florentine effort to conquer the seaport city of **Pisa** in 1406, *De captivitate Pisarum*; and a biography of Niccolò Acciaiuoli, a prominent Florentine citizen. His long vernacular poem *La città di vita / The City of Life* was an allegory dealing with the fate of the angels who remained neutral during Satan's rebellion against God, and since it depicted the souls of these angels awaiting their turn to be born as human beings and to be purged by the sufferings of human existence so that they could again have an opportunity to choose between good and evil, the church, which firmly opposed the idea of the pre-existence of souls before Creation, later condemned this book.

Palmieri's most important work, however, was *Della vita civile / On Civic Life* (1429). This dialogue deals with questions of child-rearing, the moral life of lay citizens, and the tension between what is "useful" and what is "honest." He quotes heavily from **classical** moralists like Cicero, Plutarch, and Quintilian, but the book also draws on Palmieri's personal experience in public affairs. It emphasizes the importance of a good education as preparation for a life of active participation in family affairs and politics.

PANNONIUS, JANUS (1434–1472). The outstanding figure of Renaissance **humanism** in Hungary and one of the major neo-Latin poets of the Renaissance. His uncle, a prominent bishop, sent him to study at **Ferrara** in the school of the famous schoolmaster **Guarino Guarini**. His brilliance at school impressed his teachers and fellow students, and his poem *Silva Panegyrica* is an important description of the international scope of Guarino's school. From Ferrara he moved to **Padua** to study law and theology. After these studies, in 1458 he visited **Rome** and then returned to Hungary, where he took up the administrative career that his uncle had planned for him. He became an adviser to King **Matthias Corvinus** and was made bishop of Pécs. Pannonius' poems from this period show that he felt isolated in his remote and barbarous homeland and longed for Italy. In 1465 he did return to Italy on an embassy, meeting **Marsilio Ficino** and **Vespasiano da Bisticci**. He became disillusioned with the policies of King Matthias in response to **Ottoman** expansion and together with his uncle joined a conspiracy to overthrow the ruler. The plot was discovered, and Pannonius fled to Italy for safety but got only as far as Zagreb, where he died of pneumonia.

PAPACY. *See* PAPAL STATES; POPES.

PAPAL STATES. The political sovereignty of the **popes** over the city of **Rome** and a more or less extensive surrounding region goes back to Frankish times, when King Pepin and his son the Emperor Charlemagne rescued the popes from domination by the Lombards and local Roman nobles and granted them political control over Rome and its environs. The size and political success of this principality varied through the **Middle Ages**, but as the popes secured an increasingly centralized control over the spiritual affairs of the whole Latin church, they also reached out to establish their temporal rule over central Italy. Their claims to political control extended from south of Rome in a northeasterly direction all the way to the Adriatic Sea and then northward along the Adriatic coast in the direction of the valley of the Po River. The medieval popes often had to struggle against the aristocracy of their capital and of the various regions and also against the citizens of the growing cities within their sphere, who aspired to political independence.

During the absence of the popes at **Avignon** for much of the 14th century, and then during the **Western Schism** of the papacy

(1378–1417), papal control over the city of Rome, and especially over the outlying districts, became weak. Many cities and principalities, though theoretically subject to the popes, had become de facto independent. After the end of the Schism, the popes longed to restore their control over these regions and to pacify the city of Rome itself. This desire to extend the area of papal rule or at least to enforce their rights as overlords meant that the Papal States played an active and often aggressive role in the turbulent politics of Italy during the 15th century. During the long period of relative calm that the policy of **Lorenzo de'Medici** created between 1455 and 1494, the papacy often acted as disturber of the peace, and most of the other Italian states encouraged the princes of virtually independent regions (like the duchy of **Urbino** and the city of **Bologna**) to preserve their independence. Those states were not eager to have a strong, expansionist papal state near their own borders, especially because in the second half of the century, many of the popes were notorious nepotists who tried to set up their own kinfolk as hereditary rulers over portions of the papal territories.

This turbulent political history reached its peak under two men. The corrupt and ambitious Pope **Alexander VI** struggled to put his own son **Cesare Borgia** onto the throne of a principality carved out of the papal territories. The militaristic Pope **Julius II** may have been a warmonger but at least he sought to create a strong political state for the papacy rather than for his own relatives as he extinguished the political independence of **Bologna** and Perugia and ended more than a half-century of Venetian rule over Ravenna. During the 16th century, Julius and his successors tried to manipulate the invading rulers of France and Spain in the interests of papal political authority in central Italy, but it soon became clear that the ultimate victor, Spain, was bringing much of Italy under direct **Habsburg** rule and reducing much of the rest to the status of dependent principalities. The Papal States survived as one of the regional Italian states into the 19th century, when the movement for Italian unification first seized all the outlying territories (1859–1861) and then in 1870 occupied Rome and extinguished the popes' position as rulers of an independent Italian state.

PARACELSUS (1493–1541). Swiss-born physician, known for his rejection of the practices, theories, and authorities of traditional academic medicine. Born at Einsiedeln, the son of a physician, he may never have regularly attended any university or received a medical doctorate, but both his reputation among contemporaries and his many surviving writings show that he had a broad general education, not only in medical subjects but also in mystical religion and **Neoplatonic** philosophy. He incorporated popular remedies and superstitions into his medical practice, and he was broadly sympathetic with **Martin Luther**, not in a theological sense but in reverence for the Bible and willingness to reject traditional authorities. He challenged the value of the ancient authors whose works were the theoretical foundation of academic medicine, such as **Aristotle** and Galen, as well as the medieval medical authority Avicenna, whose principal book he publicly burned during a public festival while serving as municipal physician at **Basel** in the 1520s.

Paracelsus scorned the traditional explanation of illness as an imbalance of the four humors; he rejected the works of Hippocrates and Galen which were the foundation of humoral medicine. Instead, he argued that disease was caused by external agents and must be treated with medicines specific to the ailment. His preferred remedies were based on his study of **alchemy** and included substances derived from toxic plants and minerals. His laboratory techniques and experiments with the modification of substances by distillation and chemical compounding made him a pioneer in the medical applications of chemistry.

Paracelsus had an abrasive, uncultivated manner, and his practice of lecturing in German rather than Latin, together with his contemptuous rejection of conventional medicine, aroused the hostility of academic physicians. Yet he seems to have been strikingly successful at curing patients. While his unconventional ideas and practices led to his having an unstable and itinerant existence, Paracelsus' ideas and practices attracted a loyal body of disciples. They continued to develop and popularize Paracelsan medical ideas through the late 16th and 17th centuries, not only in German-speaking territories but also in England, France, and other European countries. Only a few of his many medical tracts were published in his lifetime, but after his death a great body of Paracelsan medical literature was published, some of it genuine but much of it spurious.

PARÉ, AMBROÏSE (ca. 1509–1590). French surgeon, known as an innovator in surgical treatment of wounds and also as the author of a large number of treatises on surgery, anatomy, and other medical topics. Although trained by apprenticeship rather than by academic study and unable to write in the Latin of accepted medical literature, he demonstrated such broad mastery, combining **classical** knowledge with his own experience, that even many **university**-trained physicians respected his learning. This did not prevent an attack on him by the Paris faculty of medicine in 1575 for the offense of writing on medical subjects in the vernacular.

In the early 1530s, shortly after he had been apprenticed at Paris, Paré became surgeon at the main hospital in the city, but his greatest reputation was as a military surgeon, beginning in 1536 with an appointment to accompany a French army to Italy. He introduced several revolutionary changes into surgical practice, including abandonment of the practice of cauterizing gunshot wounds with boiling oil, for which he substituted the use of salves. He also quit cauterizing amputations with red-hot iron or boiling oil, for which he substituted the use of ligatures to tie off blood vessels, a practice already used in **antiquity**. He introduced new techniques of treating dislocations of limbs. Paré's innovations were so obviously successful in reducing the death rate among wounded soldiers that he gained the protection of leading generals and four kings of France whom he served as principal surgeon (1552–1589).

His published works, though written in French, were successful because they combined a broad base of medical knowledge with specific references to his own experience. His book on treating wounds caused by firearms (1545) was widely used by European armies, and his *Dix livres de la chirurgerie / Ten Books on Surgery* (1564) spread news of his success with the use of ligatures. Paré's collected works were published in French in 1575 and later translated into Latin, Dutch, German, and English.

PARMIGIANINO (1503–1540). Italian painter, usually identified with the emergence of the **mannerist** style of art but also important for his skill at printmaking. Born as Girolamo Francesco Maria Mazzola at Parma, where he was trained by his father and two uncles, he displayed even in his earliest works a skill at draftsmanship and a refined elegance that became hallmarks of his mature work. By the age of 20 he had come under the influence of the older artist **Correggio**. In 1524 he went to **Rome** to study ancient art and the modern works of

Raphael and **Michelangelo**. He also presented to Pope **Clement VII** one of the most striking and unusual of his paintings, *Self-Portrait in a Convex Mirror*, which reproduces with remarkable sophistication the effects of the mirror on the image. The sack of Rome by an imperial army in 1527 disrupted the papal court and caused the young artist to move to **Bologna** and then back to Parma, where he produced his most famous painting, the *Madonna with the Long Neck* (ca. 1535), strikingly mannerist in its bold use of exaggerated, elongated forms and proportions that do not conform to the expectations of a viewer familiar with the works of his High Renaissance predecessors.

PASQUIER, ETIENNE (1529–1615). French antiquarian and jurist. After preparation at the University of Paris, he studied law under the most distinguished jurists of his century. The result of his varied educational background was a strong sense of the relativity of laws, quite contrary to the traditional belief in the primacy and universal validity of **Roman** law. This background and his own strong sense of French identity led him to investigate the historical origins of French laws, customs, and institutions, beginning with the ancient Gauls and continuing through the Frankish, Capetian, and **Valois** reigns down to his own time. This interest in the medieval roots of French laws and institutions was contrary to the narrowly **classical** interests of **humanist** historiography but profoundly harmonious with the strong national sentiment that was growing up in 16th-century France.

Pasquier's researches were compiled into the vast *Recherches de la France / Researches on France*, of which the first volume appeared in 1560, the seventh and last in 1611; two additional books were later edited from drafts left unfinished at his death. He based his historical works not on the narratives of earlier authors but on careful searching for original documents that demonstrated the gradual emergence of the French monarchy as the nucleus of the nation. Pasquier entered the practice of law at Paris in 1549 and had a distinguished legal and judicial career. As legal counsel for the successful effort by the University of Paris to prevent the establishment of **Jesuit** colleges in France in 1564, he portrayed the Jesuits as agents of a papal tyranny that for centuries had encroached on the liberties of the **Gallican** church. During the French Wars of Religion (1562–1598), Pasquier was an outspoken enemy of the extreme Catholics who seized control of Paris in 1588 and fought to block the lawful heir, Henry of

Navarre, from the throne because he was a Protestant. Pasquier was one of the moderate Catholics known as *politiques*, who backed a strong monarchy that could reunify the country and end the civil wars.

PASQUINO. Popular name given to a badly damaged ancient statue discovered at Rome in the late 15th century and relocated to the Piazza Navona, where it still remains. The custom arose among students and **humanists** of decorating this statue with garlands during the annual celebration of St. Mark's Day (25 April). Poets and satirists stuck satirical verses, often criticizing and ridiculing prominent individuals, onto the statue, which (since its true identity as a statue of Menelaus guarding the body of his friend Patroclus was unknown) was nicknamed "Master Pasquino." In 1509 the Roman printer Jacopo Mazzocchi published a collection of these verses, which came to be known as "pasquinades." In the authoritarian and heavily censored atmosphere of Renaissance Rome, these pasquinades provided a rare outlet for political criticism and satire, often sharply worded and indecent. Annual volumes containing the past year's pasquinades continued to be published until the 18th century.

PATRIZI, FRANCESCO (1529–1597). Italian **Neoplatonic** philosopher. Born into a family of minor Croatian nobility, he served for a time under an uncle who was captain of a Venetian warship, then studied at **Venice** and elsewhere before beginning the study of medicine at **Padua** in 1547. There he studied **Greek** and discovered the writings of **Plato** and the Renaissance **Neoplatonist Marsilio Ficino**, which transformed him into an enthusiastic Platonist. After his father's death he abandoned medicine and spent a quarter-century travelling and working in Italy, Cyprus, and Spain. A widely read and learned man, he became a noted polymath and wrote books on many topics, including history, literary theory, and warfare, sometimes in Latin but usually in Italian. In 1571 his *Disquisitiones peripateticae / Inquiries into Peripatetic Philosophy* attacked the philosophy of **Aristotle** and his modern disciples and upheld the superiority of Plato.

In 1577–1578 the University of **Ferrara** appointed Patrizi to the first chair of Platonic philosophy in any European university. In 1592 he moved to the University of **Rome**, again with the title of professor of Platonic philosophy. His major publication, *Nova de universis* *philosophia / A New Philosophy of Universes* (1591), was an encyclopedic presentation of philosophical and scientific knowledge related to the Platonic tradition, including a determined effort to develop a Platonic natural science to replace traditional Aristotelian science. This work also contended that Platonism was fully compatible with Christianity and that Aristotelian philosophy ultimately led to atheism. His book was denounced to the Congregation of the Index on charges of heresy, and after two years of litigation was placed on the Index of Forbidden Books. Neither the papal universty nor any other continued the chair in Platonic philosophy, and traditional **scholasticism** based on Aristotelian principles continued to dominate university faculties for several centuries.

PAZZI CONSPIRACY. Conspiracy intended to end **Medici** political control of **Florence** by assassinating the brothers Lorenzo and Giuliano de'Medici and staging a coup d'état that would bring control of the city into the hands of a number of exiled families, led by the Pazzi, a clan of wealthy bankers. Since the Medici brothers were heavily guarded, the conspirators planned the assassination to take place as they attended mass on Easter Sunday, 26 April 1478. Fortunately for the intended victims, the professional assassin hired to stab the brothers to death refused to commit such a sacrilegious act in a holy place, so that the attack was carried out by two priests who were probably less proficient at murder. Giuliano was killed, but Lorenzo was only wounded. Part of the plot was to have the archbishop of **Pisa**, Francesco Salviati, whom Lorenzo had prevented from taking office because of his ties to anti-Medicean factions, seize control of the city by force. The citizens overwhelmed the armed conspirators and lynched several of their leaders on the spot, including the archbishop himself, whose body was hung by the neck from a window of the Palazzo.

Although local political rivalries motivated the Pazzi family, the main cause of the plot was hostility between Lorenzo and Pope **Sixtus IV** over Florentine foreign policy. The **pope** had intended to make his favorite nephew, Girolamo Riario, lord of the city of Imola, a semi-independent town lying within the **Papal States**. The Florentines had always opposed the creation of principalities for papal kinsmen in territories lying close to their borders, and Lorenzo had refused to support the pope's plan financially, a decision that cost the Medici trading company its position as official papal bank. The Pazzi received the banking position and provided the money for the troops needed to seize control of Imola. A conflict over Sixtus' appointment of Salviati deepened the hostility. Archbishop Salviati, the pope's nephew Riario, and the heads of the Pazzi family were the planners of the conspiracy; whether the pope himself was involved in the plot remains a debated question. Because of the lynching of the archbishop by the pro-Medici mob, the pope excommunicated Lorenzo and laid Tuscany under an interdict. He then declared war on Florence, gaining military help from the king of **Naples**. The defeat of the conspiracy left Florence in a dangerous situation, but eventually Lorenzo succeeded in detaching Naples from the alliance and forcing the pope to make peace.

PEMBROKE, MARY, COUNTESS OF. *See* SIDNEY, MARY.

PEROTTI, NICCOLÒ (1429–1480). Italian **humanist**, born at Fano and educated by both of the most famous schoolmasters of the early Renaissance, **Vittorino da Feltre** at **Mantua** (1443–1445) and **Guarino da Verona** at **Ferrara** (1445–1446). At Ferrara Perotti enjoyed the patronage of the English procurator to the Holy See, William Gray, bishop of Ely, who was studying there. In 1447 Perotti moved to **Rome** and entered the service of the Greek-born Cardinal **Johannes Bessarion**, whom he accompanied to **Bologna** during the years 1450–1455 when Bessarion was papal legate to that city. Perotti was one of the translators employed in the project of **Pope Nicholas V** to make the whole body of ancient **Greek** literature available in Latin translation; his translations included Books I–V of Polybius (1452–1454) and the *Enchiridion* of the Stoic philosopher Epictetus. At a later period he translated the Hippocratic Oath, a homily of St. Basil, and three short works of Plutarch. Pope Calixtus III appointed him papal secretary in 1455, and he was named archbishop of Siponto in 1458, though he continued to serve the papacy as governor of cities in the **Papal States**, including Perugia and Viterbo.

Perotti prepared editions of the Latin authors Pliny the Elder and Martial and produced several independent works, including two treatises on Latin metrics, a book on letter-writing, and his *Epitome*, a collection of translated fables of Phaedrus and Avianus joined to his own poems. His most impressive work was *Cornucopia linguae Latinae*, which had the form of an extensive commentary on Martial but was really a rich and influential storehouse of information on ancient Latin language and literature, first published posthumously (1489) and often reprinted. His other major work was his grammar of the Latin language, *Rudimenta grammatices* (1473), which was widely used on both sides of the Alps and formed the basis for many other humanist textbooks on grammar that were adopted, especially north of the Alps, as part of the humanist campaign for educational reform.

PERSPECTIVE. Technique used by sculptors and painters to create the illusion of three-dimensional reality in an image executed on a two-dimensional surface. Ancient painters had attempted with considerable success to achieve this illusion, but in late **antiquity** the new Byzantine style, for reasons of taste rather than lack of skill, created a pictorial art that deliberately transformed paintings into a pattern applied to an unabashedly flat, two-dimensional surface. In late medieval Western art, interest in the illusion of three-dimensional depth reappeared. The paintings of **Giotto** succeeded in creating an appearance of depth by a composition based on the placement of the figures in relation to each other and to the viewer; his technique did not, however, extend the illusion beyond the foreground of the painting.

Although interest in three-dimensionality is evident in later 14th-century painters, only at the beginning of the 15th century did artists discover and refine rules that guaranteed success in creating the illusion. Among the painters of the Flemish school, especially the brothers Jan and Hubert **van Eyck**, artists learned to suggest depth and three-dimensionality by careful variation of color and shading, a visual trick known as aerial perspective, but they never worked out a set of rules that could be applied by less skilled artists. Almost at the same moment, Italian sculptors and painters were moving toward an alternative technique known as single-point or vanishing-point perspective. In this system, the illusion is created by basing the composition on a set of (invisible) converging lines that come together at a single point in the background, so that each object in the image is scaled appropriately in order to create the illusion that it is not set onto the flat surface of the work but is placed within the apparently three-dimensional world of the work of art. Unlike the Flemish aerial perspective, single-point perspective can be reduced to a set of mathematical rules that any competent artist can master.

Although a biographer of the **Florentine** artist **Filippo Brunelleschi** about 1480 described two panel paintings made by Brunelleschi about 1413 that applied single-point perspective to create three-dimensional space, the earliest surviving work that demonstrates use of the new technique is the relief sculpture *The Feast of Herod*, created about 1425 by **Donatello**. About a decade later, the sculptor **Lorenzo Ghiberti**, in designing the 10 panels of his second set of doors for the Florentine Baptistery, applied the principles of single-point perspective with an ease and assurance that demonstrates full mastery of the new technique. The panel depicting *The Story of Jacob and Esau* is a striking example of this success. In painting, shortly after Donatello's *Feast of Herod*, the painter **Masaccio** produced several works that showed a mature ability to create three-dimensional appearance by applying single-point perspective in a variety of different configurations, represented by his *Holy Trinity* and *The Tribute Money*. Art historians conjecture that Brunelleschi, though he functioned primarily as an architect, was the actual discoverer of the rules on which single-point perspective was based, deriving his new method from careful measurement of examples of ancient architecture and sculpture.

The principles discovered by Brunelleschi and applied successfully by Donatello and Masaccio were codified by **Leon Battista Alberti** in his treatise *Della pittura* (ca. 1435–1436), which reduced the new technique to a set of geometric principles that any artist could learn and apply. Later Italian artists such as **Piero della Francesca** and **Andrea Mantegna** demonstrate increasing sophistication in use of the technique. Mantegna successfully solved the problem of projecting a three-dimensional image onto a vaulted surface. Late in the 15th century, Italian painters also became aware of the type of aerial perspective developed by the Flemish painters and began to combine it with their single-point method. This development is evident in the work of **Leonardo da Vinci**, whose paintings employ a delicate gradation of light and shading known as *sfumato* to enhance the illusion of a three-dimensional image. There is considerable evidence that some artists simplified their task by applying the principle of the *camera obscura* to project images onto the surface of their intended work.

PERUGINO. Nickname for Pietro Vannucci (ca. 1450–1523), an Umbrian painter who began his training with the conservative school of painters active in Perugia but was early subjected to Florentine influence by an apprenticeship to **Andrea del Verrocchio**; he also studied with **Piero della Francesca**. He is especially admired for the high quality of his drawings. By 1472 Perugino had become a member of the Company of Saint Luke, a confraternity of painters at **Florence**, but that same year he moved back to Perugia. Of his early works, *Christ Giving the Keys to St. Peter* (1482), painted in the Sistine Chapel at **Rome** for Pope **Sixtus IV**, is the best known. Perugino also worked at Florence, where he painted *Lamentation over the Dead Christ* (1495) in the Pitti Palace, and one of his most admired works was a series of frescoes in the Collegio del Cambio at Perugia (1496–1500). He seems to have passed out of fashion late in his career; his *Combat Between Love and Chastity* (1505) displeased **Isabella d'Este**, the patron who commissioned it, and the plan to paint a ceiling in the Vatican apartments of Pope **Julius II** fell through because the **pope** had become more interested in Perugino's most famous pupil, **Raphael**.

PERUZZI. *See* BARDI.

PETRARCH (Francesco Petrarca, 1304–1374). Italian poet and **humanist**, commonly ranked as second only to **Dante** among Italian poets and conventionally designated as the first humanist (more accurately, the first humanist to gain a widespread reputation) of the Italian Renaissance. Although Petrarch always regarded himself as a Florentine, he never actually lived in **Florence**. His father, a professional notary, had been banished on politically motivated charges of corruption. The poet was born in the provincial city of Arezzo and lived in Tuscany until about age seven, when his father relocated the family to **Pisa** and then in 1312 to the papal court at **Avignon**, where the father became a curial official. Petrarch grew up in southern France. He received his grammatical education at Carpentras and from an early age developed a passionate love of ancient Latin literature. In 1316 his father sent him to study law, first at the **University** of Montpellier and in 1320 at **Bologna**, the most distinguished law faculty in Italy. He found the law unappealing and remained far more interested in literature. After his father's death in 1326, Petrarch left Bologna and never entered legal practice. He returned to Avignon. There in 1327 he saw the woman who became the idealized Laura of his famous love poems, the Canzoniere, a collection of vernacular lyrics expanded and polished through the rest of his life. Though never ordained as a priest, he became chaplain to Cardinal Giovanni Colonna, a powerful **Roman** aristocrat. In 1333 he travelled in northern Europe, visiting Paris, Ghent, Liège, Aachen, Cologne, and Lyon.

During these travels Petrarch began his lifelong habit of hunting for works of ancient literature previously unknown to him. In Liège, for example, he found the oration *Pro Archaia poeta* by his favorite Latin author, Cicero, an eloquent defense of the social value of literature. A friend he met at Avignon introduced him to the writings of the Christian Church Fathers, especially St. Augustine. In 1335 the **pope** appointed him as canon of the cathedral at Lombez, a sinecure that provided an income but imposed no liturgical duties. He was never ordained to the priesthood. About this time, he wrote a long letter in Latin verse to the pope, urging him to bring the papacy back to its rightful location in Rome. At the end of 1336 he made his own first visit to Rome. He was overwhelmed both by the grandeur of the city and by its decay nearly a millennium after the "fall" of the Roman Empire. He regarded Rome as the rightful ruler of the whole world and developed a strong affection for Italy, expressed in one of his most famous poems, "Italia mia," which laments Italy's disunity and weakness.

Upon his return to France, Petrarch purchased a rural home at Vaucluse and made it a retreat for study and meditation. This period at Vaucluse was productive. He began a number of works that he completed only many years later, including the first version of his collective biography *De viris illustribus / On Famous Men*, his collection of vernacular poems (the *Canzoniere*), his epic *Africa* celebrating the deeds of the Roman hero Scipio, and the first of a long series of allegorical poems that he called *Trionfi / Triumphs*. In 1340 he received two invitations to be crowned poet laureate, one from the University of Paris and the other from the Roman Senate. Inevitably, Rome was the location he preferred, and in April 1341 he was crowned in a ceremony rich in memories of **antiquity**.

Although at that date Petrarch's reputation as a poet was based more on his vernacular lyrics rather than on his uncompleted Latin epic *Africa*, he had become an international celebrity and had developed a strong sense of his own historical mission that recurs throughout his writings. When he got back to Provence, he attempted to learn **Greek**, but he never gained a usable knowledge of the language. In the next few years, as his brother became a monk and he himself became the father of a daughter born out of wedlock, his writings reflected the tension between his worldly desires and his spiritual aspirations. An important product of this period is his *Secretum*, a series of imaginary dialogues with St. Augustine.

While visiting Verona in 1345, Petrarch discovered Cicero's letters to Atticus. The discovery was a triumph, in that he found a major collection of work by his favorite author, but it was also a shock, because these letters made it clear that Cicero was first and foremost an ambitious politician, burning with desire for power, and not primarily the wise and detached philosopher that Petrarch had thought him to be. When he returned to Vaucluse, Petrarch began writing his *De vita solitaria*, in which he lauds the contemplative life but conceives it in terms of an opportunity for study and reflection rather than as a monastic calling. In 1347 the Roman revolution led by the eccentric prophet **Cola di Rienzo**, who aimed to recapture control of the city from the feeble administration of the absentee pope, aroused Petrarch's dream that Roman power could be restored, but Rienzo's inability to distinguish dream from reality ultimately alienated the poet.

The year 1348 brought the crisis of the **Black Death**, and news of the death of his Laura and of several friends during the epidemic moved him to write *Triumphus mortis / The Triumph of Death*. Petrarch also worked on his *Epistolae familiares*, a project inspired by his discovery of Cicero's letters. This was the first of four series of imaginary letters addressed to famous ancient sages. In 1350 he made the jubilee pilgrimage to Rome and for the first time in his life visited Florence, the city he always claimed as his own. His writings had gained admirers there, and he met a number of them in person, notably the other leading Florentine author of his generation, **Giovanni Boccaccio**, who became the chief promoter of his fame in the city. By 1351–1352 he was back in Vaucluse, working on his evolving collective biography of great men, *De viris illustribus*, which by now he had reconceived as covering only ancient Romans, since he had concluded that only Roman history was worth serious study.

Between 1353 and 1361, Petrarch lived in **Milan** as a guest of the ruler. While there, he began writing a treatise on moral philosophy, *De remediis utriusque fortunae / Remedies for Good and Bad Fortune*. In 1361 he moved to **Padua** and later to **Venice**. There he clashed with a number of young aristocrats who passed the word around that Petrarch was a good man but not really learned—by which they really meant that he did not share their enthusiasm for **Aristotelian** rationalism and natural science. They contemptuously dismissed his literary work and his concern with religion. He drafted a clever rebuttal of this criticism, *De sui ipsius et multorum ignorantia / On His Own Ignorance and That of Many Others*. Here he rejected the claims of **scholastic** rationalism (which in Italian universities of the time was non-religious or even anti-religious) to possess absolute truth, arguing instead that the combination of eloquent speech and moral seriousness imparted by humanistic studies was far more useful to human life than the abstruse and anti-Christian philosophy that prevailed in the academic world. In his final years, Petrarch settled in a beautiful mountainous district at Arquà near Padua. His happiness at Arquà and previously at Vaucluse shows that both temperamentally and intellectually he was more suited to the contemplative than to the active life, though in theory he praised both lifestyles. He died at Arquà and was buried there.

Although Petrarch remains famous mainly on account of his vernacular poetry, he always regarded his rediscovery of lost **classical** authors and his Latin treatises on spiritual life, moral excellence, and the need to restore Rome's greatness as far more important. Two ideas dominated his intellectual life: the greatness of Rome and his own special destiny as the person who would restore that greatness.

Behind Petrarch's hunger for fame and the exalted view he had of his own place in human history was an idea that he may be said to have invented, an idea unknown to either the ancient or the medieval world. This was the idea of historical discontinuity. Ancient and medieval historical thought had assumed an endlessly repeated cyclical history, in which there is never any discontinuity or fundamental change. Petrarch's admiration for ancient Rome and his bitter hostility to his own corrupt and disorderly century opened his mind to an unprecedented conclusion: the ancient world of classical Greece and Rome, however admirable, had ceased to exist almost a thousand years ago. Both the political authority and the advanced civilization of Rome had collapsed. Barbarism, expressed in a catastrophic decline of intellectual, linguistic, and literary excellence, had prevailed and had persisted for a thousand years—an age that Petrarch himself in *Africa* labelled a "Dark" Age. The present weakness and disunity of Italy, the unspiritual religion and Avignonese exile of the church, and the low level of contemporary literature and learning were the consequences of this triumph of barbarism. His contempt for the millennium separating ancient Rome from his own time was so deep that he recast his vast biographical project, *De viris illustribus*, to eliminate sections devoted to the lives of Charlemagne and other prominent men of the period that the post-Petrarchan world would come to call the **Middle Ages**.

But though his assessment of his own age was gloomy, Petrarch was not without hope. He believed that Rome could become great and powerful again, and good literature and learning could be restored, through careful study of the literary remains of the dead world of ancient Rome. Italy could be reborn; the corrupt church could be purified; human life could be made worth living if only the moral and political wisdom of the Romans could be rediscovered and made to live in the hearts of modern Italians. The force that differentiates Petrarch from earlier humanists who also revered classical literature such as **Lovati** and **Mussato** was not just his greater literary talent or his deeper knowledge of the ancient world, it was his historical vision of the rebirth—the Renaissance—of the best characteristics of ancient civilization in his own time and through his own efforts. His sense of destiny as the person who would effect a radical turn in human history and usher in a new age of greatness was unique and new. Petrarch's vision of cultural rebirth made him not just a humanist but the first *Renaissance* humanist, a man who believed that he was ushering in a new age in human history.

PETRARCHISM. A style of lyric poetry modelled on the poems of **Petrarch** and his Italian disciples, particularly on the love poetry of his *Canzoniere / Book of Songs*. Influenced by the late medieval Italian poetry of **Dante** and the *dolce stil nuovo* that dominated early Italian lyric, it was consciously embraced by major poets of the 15th century such as **Angelo Poliziano** and **Jacopo Sannazaro**, but the poet and humanist **Pietro Bembo** was the person who established its canonical status in his treatise on vernacular literature, *Prose della volgar lingua* (1525), which designated Petrarch as the perfect model for imitation by poets. Bembo also exemplified the Petrarchan style in his own poetry, published under the title *Rime* (1530). This development occurred at precisely the moment when Italian poetry was beginning to establish a centuries-long dominance over the poetry of other nations. Pioneers such as **Thomas Wyatt** and the Earl of Surrey in England, **Pierre de Ronsard** in France, and **Juan Boscán** in Spain adapted the Petrarchan style to their own lyric poetry. Later Renaissance poets closely associated with the style include **Vittoria Colonna**, **Maurice Scève**, **Philip Sidney**, **Edmund Spenser**, and **William Shakespeare**.

PEURBACH, GEORG (1423–1461). German astronomer and mathematician. He was educated at the University of Vienna (B.A. 1448, M.A. 1453) and then began teaching in the faculty of arts. He probably knew the writings of a noted professor of astronomy at Vienna who died shortly before his arrival, John of Gmunden. Between 1448 and 1453, Peurbach travelled in Germany, France, and Italy. He became court **astrologer** to King Ladislaus V of Hungary and subsequently to the Emperor Frederick III, though his teaching at the university seems to have dealt with **humanistic** rather than mathematical studies. He collaborated with his student **Regiomontanus** in astronomical observations, and in 1454 he completed *Theoricae novae planetarum / New Theory of the Planets*, a traditional Ptolemaic work that was repeatedly reprinted. At the urging of Cardinal **Johannes Bessarion**, Peurbach began work on an *Epitome of the Almagest*, a Latin summary of Ptolemy's Hellenistic astronomical treatise, since he knew no **Greek** and could not provide the fresh Latin translation that Bessarion wanted. His pupil Regiomontanus completed the *Epitome* after his death.

PEUTINGER, KONRAD (1465–1547). German **humanist**. Born into a prominent family at Augsburg, he studied at **Basel** and then at **Padua** and **Bologna**, where he was a pupil of several distinguished legal and humanistic scholars. He visited **Florence**, where he met **Giovanni Pico della Mirandola** and **Angelo Poliziano**, and **Rome**, where he met **Pomponio Leto**. Leto's Roman **Academy** inspired him to found a literary sodality of humanists when he got back to Augsburg in 1488. He became town clerk in 1497 and was named imperial councillor by the Emperor **Maximilian I**, an honor continued under **Charles V**. Peutinger served as a diplomatic representative and representative in the German Imperial Diet for his city and was an official of the Swabian League. Initially he sympathized with **Martin Luther** but like most older humanists drew back after it became clear that Luther's movement was dividing the church.

When Augsburg became Protestant, Peutinger retired from public office and spent the rest of his life on scholarship. He collected and published Roman inscriptions from the Augsburg region (1505) and in 1506 published a volume of reflections on German **antiquity**, a field in which he also edited several important texts, including the *Chronicle of Ursberg*, Jordanes' *History of the Goths*, and Paul the Deacon's *History of the Lombards*. He was also expert in architecture and supervised the construction of the tomb of the Emperor Maximilian at Innsbruck and the renovation of the Augsburg city hall. Peutinger collected ancient coins and accumulated a valuable library of manuscripts, of which the most famous is known by his name, the *Tabula Peutingeriana*, an ancient map of the military road network of the Roman Empire.

PHILIP II (1527–1598). King of Spain from 1556 to 1598, the son and successor of the Emperor **Charles V**. Under him, Spain reached its peak as a military and political power and also entered its Golden Age of literary achievement. He was active in the wars and diplomacy of his time, sincerely conceiving his role as protector of the Catholic faith while at the same time pursuing the dynastic and territorial interests of his own **Habsburg** family. He inherited the Spanish, Italian, and Netherlandish territories of his father but not the German imperial title and the dynasty's hereditary lands in Germany, which passed to his Austrian uncle and cousins. Philip continued his father's wars against the rival kings of France and during the French Wars of Religion (1562–1598) intervened actively but unsuccessfully in the efforts of Catholic extremists to block the succession of the Protestant Henry of Navarre to the French throne. He also faced the **Reformation** in his hereditary Netherlandish provinces, where a combination of local resistance to his ambitious program of political and ecclesiastical centralization with Netherlandish distaste for the harsh measures he used against the growing Protestant movement in the Netherlands led to an uprising and civil war. This conflict divided the Netherlands and led to the de facto independence of the seven northern provinces as the United Netherlands, while the Spanish army eventually was able to regain control of the 10 southern provinces (modern Belgium), which remained under Habsburg rule until the French Revolution.

Closely linked with Philip's military activity in both France and the Netherlands was his abortive attempt to invade and conquer England, the famous Armada expedition of 1588. Philip was also deeply involved in Italian politics (where his interests often clashed with those of the **papacy**) and in the Mediterranean. His navy was a major participant in the great victory of the Christian forces over the **Ottoman Turks** at Lepanto in 1571. His military and political undertakings were frequently impeded by his severe financial problems, which led to three bankruptcies by the Spanish government during his reign. In 1580 he successfully enforced his hereditary claim to the throne of Portugal after the death of the last king of the Aviz dynasty. He ruled Portugal as a separate kingdom but kept its policy closely linked to Spain's.

At least in his intentions, Philip was a good and just king, caring deeply about the welfare (including the eternal salvation) of the many nations entrusted to his rule. He worked hard at the trade of being a king. His greatest flaw as ruler was his inability to delegate authority, so that his painstaking inspection of every document and insistence on making every decision made his government slow and unresponsive to unexpected events. Though deeply Catholic and instrumental in the final effort that brought the Council of Trent to completion in 1563, he did not hesitate to oppose papal policies that he disapproved. He was sensitive to the mystical piety of the greatest religious figure of his reign, St. Teresa of Avila, and sheltered her from those who tried treat her as a heretic. He was an active patron of education, literature, and the arts, continuing a Habsburg tradition of patronizing major artists (**Titian** and **El Greco**, for example) and forming a great royal collection of Renaissance art.

PICO DELLA MIRANDOLA, GIANFRANCESCO (1469–1533).

Italian philosopher and count, nephew of the more famous **Giovanni**

Pico della Mirandola. He is probably best known for his biography of his uncle, published with his edition of his uncle's works (1496) and translated into English by **Thomas More** (1510). He received an excellent **humanistic** education at the court school in **Ferrara** and was influenced by the **Neoplatonic** interests of his uncle, but he was even more strongly attracted by the preaching of **Girolamo Savonarola** at **Florence**, and its effect on him was to turn him against all forms of rationalistic philosophy. As early as 1496, one of his earliest treatises, *De studio divinae et humanae philosophiae / On the Study of Divine and Human Philosophy*, sharply differentiated human philosophy, based on reason, from divine philosophy, based on Scripture, and dismissed the human and rational philosophy as useless or even harmful. The fall of Savonarola and even his execution for heresy did not deflect Gianfrancesco Pico from this radically anti-rationalistic, anti-**Aristotelian** course. Several later treatises followed the same line of argument.

Gianfrancesco's most important philosophical work, probably written sometime after 1510 and published in 1520, was *Examen vanitatis doctrinae gentium*, which is especially important because it marks the first serious attempt to adapt the Pyrrhonist (radically skeptical) philosophical ideas of the Hellenistic philosopher Sextus Empiricus to contemporary intellectual discourse. Gianfrancesco's *Examen* provided a thorough presentation of skeptical principles in philosophy, intended to show that unaided human reason has no ability to discover truth and that only the Bible and the teachings of the church can lead humanity to truth. Gianfrancesco sharply criticized all of the major schools of ancient philosophy, especially Aristotle, the accepted guide for medieval **scholastic** thinkers. He elaborated a devastating critique of the reliability of sensory knowledge, which he regarded as the shaky foundation of Aristotle's thought and of all dogmatic philosophy. Modern scholars do debate, however, whether Gianfrancesco's book, printed in a small edition by an obscure press in his own little principality at Mirandola, had any effect on the later Renaissance authors who developed skeptical points of view, such as **Agrippa von Nettesheim** in Pico's own generation and **Michel de Montaigne**. Neither of these authors mentions the book. Gianfrancesco was also involved in politics. As the son of a count of Mirandola, he inherited the small principality in 1499 but had recurrent conflict with his brothers, was temporarily driven out of power on several occasions, and in 1533 was murdered by one of his nephews.

PICO DELLA MIRANDOLA, GIOVANNI (1463–1494). Italian philosopher and **humanist**. Born the younger son of the count of a small independent principality, he studied canon law at **Bologna** and humanistic subjects and philosophy at **Ferrara** and **Padua**. At Padua, he developed special interest in the thought of **Aristotle** and his major Arabic interpreter, Averroës. He moved to **Florence** in 1484 and became close to the intellectual circle patronized by **Lorenzo de'Medici**, especially to the intellectual star of the Medicean circle, the **Neoplatonic** philosopher **Marsilio Ficino**.

Pico is usually accounted one of the Florentine Platonists, second only to Ficino himself, but his intellectual interests extended far beyond Platonism. In 1485 he spent a year at the **University** of Paris, the principal northern center of **scholastic** philosophy and theology. That same year, he engaged in a literary debate with the Venetian humanist **Ermolao Barbaro**. His open letter *De genere dicendi philosophorum / On the Philosophers' Way of Speaking* disparages humanism as nothing more than stylistic frills and praises philosophy and the traditional philosophical authority, Aristotle. The central principle of his own philosophy was concord, and his treatise *De ente et uno / On Being and the One* aimed to demonstrate that if rightly understood, the two greatest ancient philosophers, Plato and Aristotle, were in fundamental agreement. Pico studied not only **Greek** but also the **Hebrew**, Aramaic, and Arabic languages, for another part of his philosophical program of concord was to master every system of philosophy and theology and to demonstrate that the teachings of all philosophers were harmonious if properly understood.

In pursuit of this idea, Pico compiled a list of 900 philosophical and theological theses which he proposed to defend in public debate against any and all challengers. This list was published in 1486, but even before it came out, conservative critics had charged that many of the articles were heretical and that the whole project erred by implying that the **Jewish** and Islamic religions were on a par with Christianity. **Pope Innocent VIII** prohibited the public disputation, and a papal commission condemned several of the theses, especially those that endorsed the secularist ideas of Averroës or were based on the

Jewish mystical treatises known as **Cabala**. Pico published an *Apologia* defending his opinions but had already agreed to submit to the church's judgment. The pope, after seeing an advance copy of the *Apologia*, condemned all 900 theses (August 1487). Pico decided to go to France to rally support in Paris but was arrested by papal order on the way. Lorenzo de'Medici persuaded the French king to release him, and he then lived in Florence under Lorenzo's protection. Pope Innocent refused to grant him absolution, but the next pope, **Alexander VI**, granted pardon for his errors and his reluctance to submit to the church's decision. Pico spent the rest of his life in Florence, where after the rise of **Girolamo Savonarola** to influence, he became a devoted follower of the great Dominican preacher. At his death, Savonarola was at his side; he was buried in the robe of Savonarola's Dominican order and interred in the Dominican church of San Marco.

Although Giovanni Pico became very close to the friar, unlike his nephew **Gianfrancesco** he did not totally renounce his earlier philosophical convictions. He continued his study of the Semitic languages and in particular pursued his investigation of the Cabala. He was convinced that several ancient religious traditions, not only the Cabala but also the **Hermetic** treatises, the Greek Orphic poems, the thought of the ancient Pythagoreans, and other ancient (or supposedly ancient) religious writings represented distinct but entirely harmonious acts of divine revelation given to the various nations at the dawn of human civilization. All of these ancient traditions were providentially designed to prepare the various nations for the ultimate conversion of all people to Christianity. Pico produced a lengthy commentary on the first 27 verses of the biblical book of Genesis, the *Heptaplus* (1489), in which he applied cabalistic principles to interpret Genesis in a Christian sense. In 1492 he completed and published his treatise harmonizing the philosophies of Plato and Aristotle, *De ente et uno*, which he dedicated to the Florentine poet and humanist **Angelo Poliziano**. His cabalistic studies were also related to his interest in **magic**, since he believed that the occult truths contained in the Cabala could confer power on the enlightened scholar and give him the ability to perform works ordinarily beyond human ability.

While Pico was interested (like his friend Ficino) in magic, he was unusual for his age in his rejection of the pseudoscience of **astrology**. His treatise *Disputationes adversus astrologiam divinatricem*

(1493) attracted much attention as a powerful attack on belief in judicial astrology. Pico argued that belief that the stars controlled human destiny rested on a verbal equivocation, the assumption that the stars were superior ("higher") and the human soul and intellect was inferior and hence subject to astral influence. In terms of physical position (in the Ptolemaic astronomy of the age) the stars were "higher," but what really counted was the fact that according to Neoplatonic principles the spiritual is superior to the material. Thus the human soul or intellect, a spiritual creature, could never be controlled by the material influence of the stars. Indeed, a correct understanding of hierarchy demonstrated that the soul, if properly conditioned, could control the stars, a conclusion that was destructive of belief in judicial astrology but quite compatible with Pico's belief in magic.

The most famous of Pico's writings was a short tract that probably had more influence on modern interpretations than on his own contemporaries. This was the introductory address prefixed to his 900 theses. Though its original title was simply *Oratio*, a later edition lengthened it to *Oratio de hominis dignitate / Oration on the Dignity of Man*. In the scholarship of the 19th and early 20th centuries, this oration was often used as support for the interpretation of Renaissance humanism as a philosophy that glorified human nature and human life in this world. In reality, the main thrust of the oration is to explain and defend Pico's universalist religious conviction that all of the major religions were based on an ancient revelation given to each nation by God. Yet the opening section does present a concept of human nature that was central to Pico's beliefs. As a close but critical reader of Aristotle, he had come to reject the Aristotelian idea of a human nature that is fixed and immutable. In Aristotelian philosophy, the nature of a thing absolutely determines its every action. But in the *Oratio*, Pico proclaimed that the Creator had not given to His human creature any nature at all, but instead had given him something far more precious, absolute freedom. Humankind had been created as a no-nature, a wide-open potentiality, and each human being potentially had the power—and also the responsibility—to shape his own nature by choosing the principles by which he lived. If he chose to pursue spiritual and intellectual goods, he would become spiritual, almost divine; if he chose to pursue worldly and material goods, he would become no more than an animal and would forfeit his blessed status as the child of God. The *Oratio* was a glorification of human nature, but in a deeply spiritual sense, not in terms of either medieval or modern rationalism. It defined the human creature as totally free, subject to no external or internal compulsion, and hence potentially able to become divine.

PIENZA. The small town of Corsignano, home town of **Pope Pius II**, was renamed Pienza and rebuilt in a symmetrical **neoclassical** style by its most famous native, the pope himself. This rebuilding was Pius's most ambitious work of artistic patronage. The plan was carefully laid out by the artist **Bernardo Rosselino**, though it was only partially carried out because of the pope's death in 1464.

PIERO DELLA FRANCESCA (ca. 1420–1492). Italian painter, a native of Borgo San Sepolcro in Umbria and active there and in Arezzo and **Urbino**. His works, which show him to be one of the greatest painters of the mid–15th century, are distinguished by a sense of solemnity and austerity, with solid figures and glowing colors. He was probably trained by a local painter and then worked in **Florence** under **Domenico Veneziano**. His paintings show full mastery of the sophisticated **perspective** and harmonious composition typical of the generation that succeeded **Masaccio**. Piero's remarkable skill in using color, on the other hand, is not typical of Florentine tradition but may be due to his early work with the Venetian-born Veneziano. He also received more academic education than most painters of his time, for surviving documents as well as manuscripts of his treatise on perspective (*De prospectiva pingendi*) show that he wrote **humanistic script** and probably knew some Latin. The treatise on perspective influenced nearly all 16th-century books on the subject. He also wrote vernacular treatises on commercial mathematics (abaco) and on algebra and geometry, and these seem to have been used (in some cases, verbatim) as sources by the mathematical author **Luca Pacioli**, who knew him well and seems to have acquired his manuscripts.

Piero came from a prosperous merchant family and seems to have had an income from the family business, probably the reason why he never organized the usual artist's workshop and also a reason why he did not produce a great number of paintings. His major works include a fresco cycle, *The Legend of the True Cross* (1455–1466) at Arezzo;

an altarpiece, *Madonna with the Duke of Urbino as Donor*, painted for Duke Federigo of Urbino; *The Baptism of Christ; The Nativity of Christ*, often regarded as his last work; and several portraits including the duke and duchess of Urbino (both ca. 1470). His most famous single painting, however, was done for the city hall in his home town at San Sepolcro, *The Resurrection of Christ* (ca. 1460), notable for its severely geometrical design, the **classical** modeling and solidity of its figures, and the effective contrasts of light and shade and also of colors. One of the sleeping soldiers in the painting is thought to be a self-portrait of the artist. He also painted a series of frescoes at **Rome** for Pope **Nicholas V**, but these were replaced in the following century by works of **Raphael**. He was probably the teacher of the Tuscan painter **Luca Signorelli**.

PIERO DI COSIMO (1462–1521). Florentine painter, known mainly for his paintings on themes from classical mythology, such as *The Discovery of Honey*, a work that treats mythology quite differently from the spiritualizing **Neoplatonic** tradition of his contemporary **Sandro Botticelli**. In his treatment, the figures in the pagan myth are not allegories but real creatures of flesh and blood; the work reflects an ancient tradition that regarded the gods as gifted and beneficent humans who were gratefully remembered by posterity and eventually recognized as divine, an explanation of ancient polytheism known as euhemerism that originated in Hellenistic times. According to the art historian **Giorgio Vasari**, Piero was well known in his own time as a maker of ephemeral works for public festivals.

PINTURICCHIO. Popular name for Bernardino di Betto di Biago (ca. 1454–1513), a painter from Perugia who worked in the Umbrian style. Until the influence of **Raphael** brought about a change in popular taste, he was one of the most successful artists of his time. He was trained by **Perugino** and joined his master in **Rome** in 1481 to work on the frescoes of the new Sistine Chapel commissioned by **Pope Sixtus IV**. He also worked for other patrons at Rome, including two other popes, **Innocent VIII** and **Alexander VI**. For the latter, he executed one of his most important commissions, the murals in the Borgia apartments in the Vatican Palace, including the *Disputà di Santa Caterina* (1492–1495).

PIO, ALBERTO, PRINCE OF CARPI (1475–1531). Italian prince, diplomat, and **humanist**. He was the son of the ruler of the small principality of Carpi; his mother Caterina was a sister of **Giovanni Pico della Mirandola**. The death of his father when he was still a small child made it difficult for him to uphold his right to rule the principality, but he finally secured half of the territory in 1490 and the other half in 1512, both times by virtue of a ruling by the Emperor **Maximilian I**. His uncle Giovanni Pico supervised the education of Alberto and his brother, choosing as their tutor the **humanist Aldus Manutius**, whom Alberto Pio later subsidized in his career as the greatest humanist printer of the Renaissance. After Manutius, the **Greek** humanist Marcus Musurus taught Alberto. During a period of the 1490s when his uncle and cousin had gained control of Carpi and forced him into exile, Alberto studied at the University of **Ferrara** under the noted **Aristotelian** philosopher **Pietro Pomponazzi**. At Ferrara he also became a friend of several prominent humanists, including **Pietro Bembo**, and also of the poet **Ludovico Ariosto**, who dedicated poems to him. In 1500 the sale of the other half of Carpi to the duke of Ferrara forced Pio to seek diplomatic support from **Francesco Gonzaga**, marquis of **Mantua**. This relationship eventually led Pio to become a diplomat in the service of his more powerful neighbor, representing Mantua both at the French court and at the papal curia at **Rome**. He briefly lost control of Carpi in 1510 when the French gained the upper hand during their Italian war, but the defeat of the French allowed him to retain control with the aid of the emperor's decision in his favor.

In 1513 Pio became the emperor's ambassador at Rome. He already was a friend of the new Pope **Leo X** and became an active participant in the social and intellectual life of curial society, including membership in the Roman **Academy** and friendship with **Baldassare Castiglione** and the artists **Raphael** and **Bramante**. In 1518 he married a relative of Pope Leo. After his election in 1519, the new Emperor **Charles V** did not renew Pio's appointment as ambassador, but Pio turned to the emperor's enemy King **Francis I** of France and became his ambassador at Rome. In reprisal for this service to France, the emperor confiscated his principality of Carpi, and the disastrous defeat of the French in the battle of Pavia in 1525 ended his rule over the tiny state. Pio was a friend of the second **Medici** pope, **Clement VII,** and after the conquest of Rome by the imperial army in 1527, took refuge with the pope in Castel Sant'Angelo before escaping to France, where he was well received and where he spent the rest of his life.

Pio was religiously conservative. He supported papal inquisitors searching for heretics in his principality, and he denounced **Alfonso d'Este**, duke of Ferrara, to the emperor in 1522 because he had allowed an Augustinian friar to preach "Lutheran" doctrines. He encouraged others to write refutations of **Martin Luther**'s errors and in 1526 published his own treatise against Luther, *Responsio accurata et paraenetica / Accurate Reply and Advice*. Unfortunately for the internal peace of the world of humanists, Pio (like many Italians) was convinced that the Dutch humanist **Erasmus** had prepared the way for Luther's success by his harsh criticism of the church and by his early attempts to shelter Luther from church discipline. He even counted against Erasmus the treatise in which he openly broke with Luther, charging that it was so inept that it had aided the heretic's cause.

This attack on Erasmus was not published until 1529. But Pio's *Responsio* circulated in manuscript among insiders at the papal curia, and Erasmus heard reports of its existence. He tried in vain to establish contact with the refugee Pio and persuade him of his own orthodoxy and good intentions, but by the time he made contact, Pio's book had already been published. Erasmus published a reply (1529) denying that he had caused the **Reformation** or upheld Luther's heretical doctrines, but Pio stubbornly spent the last two years of his life preparing a series of extracts from the works of Erasmus and Luther to prove his contention that Erasmus agreed with the German heretic. This collection of extracts was published by Pio's friends after his death under the title *Twenty-three Books in Erasmus' Publications That Ought to be Revised and Retracted* (1531). Erasmus was furious at what he regarded as Pio's dishonest distortion of his words and published a bitter *Apology* (1532) against Pio despite his own reservations at attacking a man who had died. Pio's books were reprinted in Latin, and the *Responsio* was published in both Spanish and French by conservative Catholics as part of the campaign to label Erasmus an enemy of the Catholic faith.

PIRCKHEIMER, CHARITAS (1467–1532). Abbess of the convent of St. Clare at Nuremberg, which she entered in 1479 and of which she was elected abbess in 1503. She was a member of the wealthy patrician Pirckheimer family, which made education available to its daughters, and her brother **Willibald Pirckheimer**, a noted **humanist** and leading political figure, encouraged her intellectual interests and dedicated editions of **classical** and patristic authors to her. He also introduced her to the artist **Albrecht Dürer** and the humanist **Conrad Celtis**. Celtis dedicated to her his edition of the learned medieval nun Hroswitha of Gandersheim. **Erasmus**, the leading humanist of that generation, praised her educational attainments. Unlike her brother, she opposed **Martin Luther's** ideas from the very first. She used her family and political connections to preserve her convent when the **Reformation** triumphed in Nuremberg, but she could do nothing to reverse the laws that outlawed the celebration of mass and forbade the convent to accept new members. She wrote an account of her struggle (1524–1528) to maintain the convent, *Denkwürdigkeiten / Things Worth Remembering*.

PIRCKHEIMER, WILLIBALD (1470–1530). Member of a prominent patrician family of Nuremberg and one of the leading German **humanists** of the early 16th century. His father pursued a legal career that took the family to Eichstätt, where Willibald was born, and then to Munich, where the father became a councillor to the duke of Bavaria. The boy was privately educated and accompanied his father on diplomatic missions as far afield as Italy. At age 16 he was sent back to Eichstätt for schooling in courtly manners and military affairs. About 1488 he went to Italy, where he studied law at **Padua** and Pavia but spent much of his effort acquiring a broad humanistic education.

In 1495 Pirckheimer returned to Nuremberg, married a local patrician woman, and was promptly elected to the city council. He served as a captain of Nuremberg troops sent to support the Emperor **Maximilian I** in a war against the Swiss (1499), and he wrote a Latin account of that campaign, *De bello Helvetico / On the War Against the Swiss* (1526; first published in 1610). During the war he became a close friend of the Emperor Maximilian I, who appointed him an imperial councillor. He served on the city council from 1495 to 1502 and again from 1505 to 1523. His influence was behind the decision to establish lectureships in **classical** Latin literature at the city's two leading schools (1509). His chief political duty was to represent the city at meetings of the imperial diet and in negotiations and litigation with neighboring aristocrats who encroached on the city's rights.

Pirckheimer's outstanding humanist learning and his education in the law made him effective in this role, and he formed friendships with important political and scholarly figures throughout southern Germany. He was not, however, very popular in his home town, where the dominant mercantile classes found his irascible temper and his outspoken criticisms of the city irritating, and most citizens could not understand why he spent so much effort and money collecting books and trying to found a school of poetry. These same activities made him a heroic figure to humanists throughout Germany, and though they never met in person, he and the leading Northern humanist, **Erasmus**, became friends through frequent correspondence.

In his early years, Pirckheimer's fame among humanists rested mostly on the breadth of his interests (and on his high social status and wealth). His own publications came rather late in his career. He wrote a witty and ironic eulogy of gout, a disease from which he suffered, *Podagrae laus* (1522), and an obituary of the painter **Albrecht Dürer**, who was his close friend and with whom he collaborated in the planning of two books, *Ehrenpforte / The Gate of Honor* (1517) and *Triumphzug / Triumphal Procession* (1526) that were originally planned as propaganda glorifying the Emperor Maximilian. He was known principally as an editor and translator (into both Latin and German) of ancient authors, both patristic (Fulgentius, Gregory of Nazianzen) and classical (Plutarch, Lucian, Theophrastus, Xenophon, Ptolemy), as well as some dialogues falsely attributed to **Plato** and an unpublished translation of the *Hieroglyphica* of Horapollo.

Pirckheimer warmly supported **Martin Luther** in the early years of the **Reformation** and was suspected of being the author of *Eccius dedolatus*, a cutting satire directed against Luther's antagonist Johann Eck. In 1521 Eck evened scores by including Pirckheimer in the list of those to be excommunicated for supporting Luther, though Pirckheimer promptly took steps to free himself from this condemnation. He had hosted Luther in his own home in 1518 and acquired a large collection of Luther's books. He attempted to play the role of mediator between Luther and church authorities and wrote an open letter to **Pope Adrian VI** describing the conditions that had led to the upheaval in Germany. He also published a pamphlet attacking church officials who seemed to be working against a peaceful compromise.

Eventually, as it became clear that the Reformation would produce a split in the church, Pirckheimer moderated his open support for the Reformation but still retained respect for Luther himself. He was deeply offended (as was Luther) by the symbolic or Sacramentarian interpretation of the Eucharist advanced by Protestant leaders in Switzerland and southwestern Germany, such as **Huldrych Zwingli** of Zürich and Johannes Oecolampadius of **Basel**. His treatise against Oecolampadius, *De vera Christi carne et vero eius sanguine / On the True Body and Blood of Christ* (1526), attacked the Sacramentarian opinion, insisting that the consecrated eucharistic elements are really and truly the body and blood of Christ, yet he carefully refrained from endorsing transubstantiation, the medieval theological explanation of that real presence, and he adopted a position that was essentially identical to Luther's. Only gradually, in two later tracts against Oecolampadius, did his growing conservatism bring him to an explicit reaffirmation of orthodox eucharistic doctrine.

Pirckheimer was dismayed by the harsh, controversial tone adopted by all sides to the Reformation debates and also by violent events like the Knights' Rebellion of 1523 and the Peasant War of 1525–1526, as well as by the use of public authority in Protestant cities to suppress traditional religious practices. He blamed extremists on both sides, but gradually his dismay over Protestant radicalism and his determination to protect the sheltered existence of his sisters, including abbess **Charitas Pirckheimer**, in their nunneries led him back to traditional Catholic doctrine and practice. In 1523 he retired from the city council of Nuremberg and spent most of the rest of his life on scholarly work.

PISA, COUNCIL OF. There were two councils of the Western church held at Pisa, neither of which is recognized by the modern Roman Catholic church as genuine. The first of these was summoned by a majority of the cardinals of both rival **popes** during the **Western Schism**. It assembled in 1409 and endorsed the doctrine of **Conciliarism**, according to which a general council of the church is superior to the pope. Since all efforts to negotiate a settlement of the schism had failed, the council declared both claimants deposed and elected a new pope, who took the title Alexander V and was succeeded after his early death by John XXIII. Unfortunately for their plans, the cardinals had not secured advance approval from the major secular rulers, and since the two sitting popes refused to submit, all that the council achieved was to add a third pope to the confusion. The failure of this council did, however, ensure that those who summoned the **Council of Constance** in 1414 took pains to secure widespread political backing and hence were eventually successful in reuniting the church under a single head.

The second **Council of Pisa** (more commonly known as the *Conciliabulum*, or "false council") was even less successful. It was an outgrowth of bitter conflict between Pope **Julius II** and King Louis XII of France and his Italian allies, almost exclusively over issues of territory and political power. Several cardinals, infuriated by Pope Julius' authoritarian ways, co-operated with the French king to call a council with the announced goal of forcing the pope to observe the limits on papal authority upheld by Conciliarism. The actual goal was to dethrone Julius and elect a more pliant leader. The Florentines, who were allied with France, permitted the council to hold its sessions at Pisa, which they controlled. Julius excommunicated and deprived all the rebellious cardinals and laid **Florence** under an interdict. Most of the bishops in attendance were French, and there was virtually no support except from allies of King Louis.

Pope Julius' so-called Holy League to expel the French from Italy had driven French troops from the peninsula by the end of 1512. The council soon transferred its sessions to France. Now even more exclusively French than at its beginning, the council lingered on French soil until 1516, but the new king **Francis I** found that it was more practical to make a direct deal with Pope **Leo X**. He negotiated with the pope the **Concordat of Bologna**, which won papal approval for extensive royal control over the French church; the price paid for this treaty was the dissolution of what remained of the Council.

PISAN, CHRISTINE DE. *See* CHRISTINE DE PIZAN.

PISANELLO, ANTONIO (ca. 1395–1455). Italian artist, known for his paintings (few of which survive), his commemorative medals, and his hundreds of beautiful drawings. Born in Pisa and trained somewhere in northern Italy, he may have painted a historical fresco in the doge's palace at **Venice** between 1415 and 1420, but this does not survive. His earliest surviving painting is an *Annunciation* (ca. 1426) at Verona. By that time, his reputation had been established and he worked for several northern Italian princely courts, especially **Ferrara** and **Mantua**. Pisanello also executed works (now lost) for the duke of **Milan** and **Pope Eugenius IV**. His study of ancient art while at **Rome** led him to develop an innovative type of low-relief portrait medals cast in precious metal; the most famous of these is the portrait of the Byzantine Emperor John VIII Palaeologus during his attendance at the **Council of Ferrara-Florence** in 1438–1439. Pisanello produced portrait-medals for a number of Italian rulers and generals. He also painted portraits, a few of which survive. In the 1960s his only surviving large-scale fresco painting, depicting scenes from a popular Arthurian romance, was rediscovered in the ducal palace at Mantua. His great contemporary reputation rested on the opinion that his portraits were unusually lifelike.

PIUS II, POPE (Aeneas Sylvius Piccolomini, 1405–1464). Prominent Italian **humanist**, diplomat, and cleric, elected **pope** in 1458. He was born near Siena and in 1423 entered the university there. He acquired a broad humanistic education and an excellent Latin style, attributes that won him employment as secretary to a number of high-ranking clergymen. He then became secretary to the **Council of Basel** and embraced its **Conciliarist** ideology. He travelled widely in the interests of the council, forming a knowledge of non-Italian Europe far superior to most Italian humanists of his time. In 1440 he wrote a favorable history of the council, but its increasing isolation and ineffectiveness, together with the threat it now posed of reopening the **Western Schism**, caused him to leave it for a job as secretary to the Holy Roman Emperor Frederick III in 1442. Although Frederick was a famously ineffectual ruler, Piccolomini's imperial office made him a key player in the politics of the Schism, and he negotiated the settlement between the emperor and Pope **Eugenius IV** that ended imperial support for the languishing council. This agreement and his abandonment of Conciliarist doctrine reconciled him with **Rome**, where he became apostolic secretary and was made bishop of Trieste in 1447; he was translated to the see of Siena in 1450 and made a cardinal by Pope Calixtus III in 1456, just in time to be chosen as Calixtus' successor in 1458.

During his years as a Latin secretary, Pius was a prolific author. Many of his letters, both private and official, survive. Until midlife, he led a worldly existence marked by many love affairs, and his most popular literary work was a tragic tale of love, adultery, and suffering, *Historia de duobus amantibus / A Tale of Two Lovers* (1444). He also produced a satire on court life, *De curialium miseriis / On the Misfortunes of Courtiers*; a collection of biographical sketches, *De viris aetate sua claris / On the Famous Men of His Age*; a history of the Emperor Frederick III; and several tracts repudiating the Conciliarist opinions of his youth. After his election as pope, Pius wrote his *Commentarii*, a historical survey of his own career, candidly admitting his earlier unchastity and providing a vivid description of the places and events of his career. As pope, he financed the transformation of his small hometown, Corsignano, into **Pienza**, a model city in Renaissance style. He also issued a papal bull (***Execrabilis***, 1460) outlawing the lodging of appeals from a decision of the pope to a future meeting of a general council. He lamented the fall of **Constantinople** in 1453 and as pope worked diligently but in vain to persuade the Christian rulers to put aside their differences and join in an effort to reconquer the former Byzantine capital. He died while at the port of Ancona completing preparations for the crusade, which never took place.

PLANTIN, CHRISTOPHE (ca. 1520–1589). Printer and publisher at Antwerp from 1555 to his death. He was born in France but about 1548 emigrated to Antwerp, where he worked as a bookbinder and in 1555 received a license to practice the **printing** trade. Although Plantin conformed to the official Catholicism of the **Habsburg** Netherlands, he was a spiritualizing mystic who had little use for the external practices and doctrines of any of the competing religious groups. There is some evidence that his new business received financial support from Hendrik Niclaes, the leader of an underground church known as the Family of Love. In 1562 some of his workers were caught producing illegal Calvinist books and Plantin had to close his press for a year, which he spent at Paris. When he reopened his press in 1563, he took a Calvinist as his partner, but before the end of the 1560s he distanced himself from anti-Catholic and anti-Spanish connections and cultivated the friendship of Cardinal Granvelle, the archbishop of Mechelen and the principal figure in the administration that ruled the Netherlands in name of King **Philip II**.

With royal support, Plantin undertook publication of a scholarly *Biblia polyglotta* (1568–1573), which presented the text of the Bible in five languages. He also won the contract to print royal legislation and the text of the Index of Forbidden Books. Especially profitable was his legal monopoly on the printing of liturgical and religious books for Spain and the Spanish colonies (1571). At his print shop, known as the Golden Compass, Plantin gathered a team of **humanists** who seem to have shared his willingness to conform outwardly to Catholicism while privately following a religion based on universal human brotherhood and personal morality. At this period Plantin's shop had 16 presses and more than 70 employees. When the civil wars of the 1570s and 1580s brought Antwerp under Protestant control for a number of years, he willingly published Protestant and Familist books but remained officially Catholic. When the Spanish army besieged Antwerp in 1582, he founded a branch at Leiden which in 1583 became the official printer to the new University of Leiden. After Antwerp surrendered to the Spaniards in 1585, he returned there and transferred his Antwerp manager, who had been publishing Protestant books while the Calvinists ruled the city, to manage the branch at Leiden. The high quality of his presswork and the excellent scholarship of the humanist scholars with whom he collaborated made Plantin's press an important cultural center and an active printer of humanist and academic books and also of tracts produced by the Catholic **Reformation**.

PLATINA, BARTOLOMEO (Bartolomeo Sacchi, 1421–1481). Roman **humanist** and librarian of the Vatican. Named from the village where he was born, Piadena, he may have received schoolng in Cremona but certainly spent four years as a mercenary soldier in the private army of the *condottiere* **Francesco Sforza**. About 1449 he went to **Ferrara** to study in the school founded by **Vittorino da Feltre**. He became friendly with the duke of **Mantua, Ludovico Gonzaga**, and eventually was hired to tutor the ruler's children. In 1457 he went to **Florence** to study **Greek** under the exiled humanist **John Argyropoulos**. While there, he became close to several prominent Florentines, including the richest and most powerful of them all, Lorenzo de'**Medici**. When his former pupil **Francesco Gonzaga** became a cardinal in 1481, Platina moved to **Rome** and became an active member of the scholarly circle of Cardinal **Johannes Bessarion** and the Roman **Academy** led by **Pomponio Leto**. Platina purchased a curial office as abbreviator that provided him reliable income. A new **pope**, Paul II, who did not like the curial humanists, abolished the college of abbreviators without offering to indemnify officeholders who had purchased their jobs. Platina secured an audience and publicly challenged the pope's action. The pope reacted by having him imprisoned for several months. In 1468 Pope Paul had Platina imprisoned again, together with other members of the Roman **Academy**, on charges of reviving pagan religious practices and plotting against the pope's life. Platina was released after a few months but did not regain papal favor until the accession of the next pope, **Sixtus IV**, in 1471. Sixtus appointed him the first librarian of the Vatican Library in 1475.

Although active as a scholar and an author, Platina did not produce much scholarship of importance. His edition of *De bello Judaico / The Jewish War* by the Hellenistic **Jewish** author Josephus was his most important textual publication. Less significant were his other literary works: a book on personal ethics and health, a guide to foods and cooking, a history of Mantua and the Gonzaga dynasty, a biography of Vittorino da Feltre, a eulogy on his patron Cardinal Bessarion, a treatise on monarchical government for the duke of Ferrara, followed by a treatise on republican government for Lorenzo de'Medici. Far more important was Platina's history of the popes, *Liber de vita Christi et omnium pontificum* (1474), which outwardly lauded the papacy but in its details provided examples of abuses and corruptions that were later cited by Protestant critics. In particular, he used his sketch of the life of Pope Paul II to avenge himself on the pope who had twice imprisoned him and cost him his secure job as abbreviator.

PLATO / PLATONISM in the Renaissance. *See* NEOPLATONISM / NEOPLATONISTS.

PLÉIADE. Collective name for a group of seven 16th-century French poets whose works mark the full development of Renaissance poetic style in France. The principal figure of this group, originally known as "the brigade" but renamed in 1553 after the seven stars of the constellation (and in memory of a group of ancient **Greek** poets), was **Pierre de Ronsard**. He set the fashion for abandoning medieval poetic tradition and following examples from Greek and Latin **classical** literature in order to transform the French language into a suitable medium for serious literature. Ronsard himself listed as other members of the fellowship **Lazare de Baïf, Joachim du Bellay**, Rémi Belleau, Etienne Jodelle, Jacques Peletier, and Pontus de Tyard. The **classical** scholar Jean Dorat is sometimes named as another member. In fact, the roster remains somewhat vague even today, and it changed from time to time as Ronsard dropped some names and added others in order to keep the number at seven. The programmatic book defining the goals of the *Pléiade* was du Bellay's *Défense et illustration de la langue française*, a plea for French poets to imitate the ancients in order to create a great national literature.

PLETHO (common name, Georgios Gemistos, ca. 1355–1452). a Byzantine philosopher and teacher who did much to promote the influence of Plato and the ancient **Neoplatonists** among both Greeks and Latins. He deplored the dominance of **Aristotle** in Western schools, denouncing him as a materialist whose thought was incompatible with Christianity. Nevertheless, modern students of Pletho's thought regard Pletho himself as anti-Christian and neo-pagan, committed to a spiritual and moral religion based on a version of Neoplatonism that revered the ancient Greek gods as symbolic representations of **Platonic** ideas. He began his career as a teacher in **Constantinople**, but in 1409 he moved to Mistra in the Peloponnesus peninsula, which had become the center of a revival of interest in ancient Greek civilization. He spent the rest of his life there except for his trip to Italy in 1437–1440 as one of the Byzantine delegation to the **Council of Ferrara-Florence**. His erudition and especially his harsh criticism of Aristotle and his fervent devotion to Plato made a great impression on the Italian **humanists** whom he met.

The ancient conflict between Aristotelians and Platonists, which had survived in Byzantine civilization, was transplanted into Italian Renaissance thought by Pletho and other Greek delegates, such as **Johannes Bessarion**, a more moderate Platonist, and **George of Trebizond**, a convinced Aristotelian and anti-Platonist. In memoranda written for the ruler of Mistra in 1415 and for the Byzantine emperor in 1418, Pletho called for a radical reorganization of Byzantine society along lines presented in Plato's *Republic* in order to save the imperiled empire from the **Ottoman Turks**. The new society, like Plato's imaginary ancient one, would be divided into three castes—peasants, merchants, and soldiers/rulers. Pletho wanted to abolish the use of mercenary soldiers and to create an army of citizens. He also wanted his reorganized society to enact strict sumptuary laws and to rely on barter rather than money. He regarded the numerous Christian monks as social parasites and urged abolition of all public support for them. While in **Florence** he wrote *A Comparison of Plato and Aristotle* for his Latin friends. His *Laws*, of which only fragments survive, was even more radical, proposing the abolition of the alien cult of Christianity and its replacement by a revived pagan religion, in which the traditional Greek deities functioned as symbols for Platonic ideas. Few if any of his Italian admirers were aware of these opinions.

PODESTÀ. In nearly all independent cities of northern and central Italy, the chief administrative and judicial official. In the 12th and 13th centuries, the emperor appointed the *podestà*; after the 13th century the citizens of the *commune* themselves appointed him. The *podestà* normally convened the governing council and prepared its agenda, but the council had ultimate authority, and he was merely the head of the administrative and judicial system. Quite early, it became usual to prohibit appointment of local men. It seemed safer to bring in a citizen from another Italian city who would not have family and political ties to local factions. Legislation forbade the *podestà* to receive gifts or even to be the dinner guest of a citizen. Terms of office were short, usually six months or a year, and the *podestà* was not normally granted a second consecutive term. **University** training in law was desirable but not essential. Noble rank was ordinarily required. In the larger cities, the duties of the office were limited to judicial matters—control of the local police and the courts.

Although the office of *podestà* was powerful, the shortness of the term and the civilian nature of the office usually prevented the officeholder from acquiring independent political authority. Only one of the dynasties of Italian *signori*, the **Este** rulers of **Ferrara**, used the office of *podestà* as a springboard for seizing power. The other high office normally given to foreigners, the military position of *capitano* *del popolo*, was the usual institutional avenue leading to despotic government. The ruling princes of the 15th century often abolished the office of *podestà* and brought the judicial and police power under their direct control. The title *podestà* was also used for purely judicial officers in smaller, subordinate cities lying within the larger territorial states.

POGGIUS FLORENTINUS. *See* BRACCIOLINI, POGGIO.

POLE, REGINALD (1500–1558). English **humanist**, cardinal, and archbishop of Canterbury, a second cousin of King **Henry VIII**. The king supported Pole's education and early career. Destined from childhood for the clergy, he was educated at a Carthusian monastery and then at Magdalen College, Oxford (B.A. 1515), where his teachers included the humanists **Thomas Linacre** and William Latimer. He received valuable ecclesiastical benefices and in 1521 was sent at the king's expense for further study to the **University of Padua**. There Pole became a close friend of **Pietro Bembo**, Thomas Lupset, and the Belgian humanist **Christophe de Longueil**. In the king's service he secured a declaration by the University of Paris in favor of Henry's plan to divorce Queen Catherine of Aragon, but privately he advised the king to abandon the divorce. After returning to Padua in 1532, Pole became close to the reform-minded Italian "evangelical" movement and underwent a personal conversion to an evangelical Christianity that emphasized the doctrine of justification by faith. He also established connections with the king's enemy **Charles V**, who was the nephew of Queen Catherine and strongly opposed Henry's plans.

In 1536 Pole wrote a treatise defending Catholic unity under papal leadership, *Pro ecclesiasticae unitatis defensione*, which marked his open break with King Henry. Pope Paul III called him to **Rome** and soon made him a cardinal, and from then until he left Italy to help in the restoration of Catholicism in England, he was an influential personage at the curia. Paul III appointed him to the reform commission that produced the *Consilium de emendanda ecclesia*, a candid survey of abuses in the church and proposals for drastic reform. Pole was governor of Viterbo in the **Papal States** in 1541 and one of the papal legates to the Council of Trent, where he was suspected of Lutheran heresy by conservatives. Despite these suspicions, he came within one vote of being elected **pope** in 1550.

With the accession of the Catholic Queen Mary **Tudor** to the English throne in 1553, the pope named Pole legate to England and made him archbishop of Canterbury. He worked closely with the queen in her effort to bring England back to the Catholic faith. He participated in the heresy trials of Archbishop Thomas Cranmer and other Protestant bishops, though he was not favorable to the queen's use of force to hunt and execute heretics among the general population. Pole's dismissal from his position as legate in 1555 by the new Pope Paul IV had less to do with Paul's distaste for the evangelical beliefs of Pole than with the pope's determination to weaken King **Philip II** of Spain, the husband of Queen Mary, because of conflicts between papal and Spanish interests in Italy. Pole died during an epidemic in 1558, on the same day as the queen, leaving England in the hands of her Protestant half-sister **Elizabeth I**.

POLIZIANO, ANGELO (born Angelo Ambrogini, 1454–1494). Italian **humanist** and poet, one of the most learned philologists and textual critics of the 15th century. By 1469 he had moved to **Florence** to attend the university and soon came under the protection of **Lorenzo de'Medici**. He attended lectures by major figures of Florentine Renaissance culture, including **Johannes Argyropoulos, Cristoforo Landino**, and **Marsilio Ficino**, and acquired an outstanding command of **Greek**, a much-admired Latin style, and a strong commitment to **Neoplatonic** philosophy. His translation of a portion of Homer's *Iliad* into Latin (1473), dedicated to Lorenzo, led the latter to invite him to move into the Medici family palace, where he had access to the family's rich manuscript library. Poliziano became private secretary to Lorenzo in 1475 and tutor to his son Piero. His vernacular poem celebrating the victory of Lorenzo's brother Giuliano in a joust in 1475 marks a decisive turn in Italian poetry. He was ordained to the priesthood, and Lorenzo appointed him to two lucrative ecclesiastical benefices. After the bloody **Pazzi Conspiracy** of 1478, which killed Giuliano de' Medici and wounded Lorenzo, Poliziano wrote a Latin account of the event, modelled on Sallust's history of the Catilinian conspiracy. While visiting **Mantua** at Carnival in 1480 he produced another pathbreaking work of Italian poetry, the dramatic poem *Orfeo*, the first Italian vernacular poem written for the stage. During this trip he also became a close friend of the **Venetian** humanist **Ermolao Barbaro**.

In November 1480 Poliziano returned to Florence as professor of rhetoric and poetics. He lectured on both poetry and prose authors, including Quintilian, Statius, Ovid, and the pseudo-**Ciceronian** (but genuinely **classical**) *Rhetorica ad Herennium*. His influential translations from Greek included the Stoic philosopher Epictetus and the historian Herodian. In 1489 he published a work that is still regarded as a landmark in the history of classical philology and textual criticism, *Miscellaneorum centuria prima*, a collection of essays on ancient texts and authors. This work introduced new standards of documentation and citation for identifying the manuscript sources of classical editions. It established Poliziano's central role in the transition from the enthusiastic but unsystematic humanistic editing practiced by early Renaissance humanists to the methods of textual criticism accepted by late Renaissance and modern classical philologists.

Lorenzo de'Medici's premature death in 1492 endangered this quiet and productive scholarly life. Poliziano spent his final years working on a second set of *Miscellanea* (not published in his lifetime) and responding to attacks on his first *Miscellanea* that were partly motivated by hostility to his Medici patrons. He died in late September of 1494, within a few weeks of the deaths of **Pico della Mirandola** and other luminaries of the Medicean intellectual circle. In his last months, like his friend Pico, he fell under the spell of the Dominican preacher **Girolamo Savonarola**.

POLLAIUOLO, ANTONIO DEL (1431–1498). Florentine artist who worked with his brother Piero in **Florence** and **Rome**. Antonio was known mainly as a sculptor; his bronze statuette *Hercules and Antaeus* (ca. 1475) is his principal work in this medium. The two brothers together painted an altarpiece, *The Martyrdom of St. Sebastian* (1475). Antonio also made a highly regarded engraving (his only surviving work in that form), *The Battle of Ten Naked Men* (ca. 1465–1470). His work is striking for its concentration on realistic anatomical structures, evident in the straining muscles of his nude figures, and he is known to have practiced dissection in order to investigate the workings of muscles and tendons.

POMPONAZZI, PIETRO (1462–1525). Italian **scholastic** philosopher, known for his loyalty to the authority of **Aristotle** and especially for his treatise *De immortalitate animae / On the Immortality of the Soul* (1516), which denies that belief in personal immortality can be proved by reason (though he claimed that he accepted the belief as a religious doctrine based on faith). Both before and after publication of this work, which aroused criticism but did not in any way endanger his academic career, he was the outstanding figure among Italian university philosophers of his generation.

A native of **Mantua**, Pomponazzi enrolled at the **University of Padua** in 1484, received a doctorate in arts in 1487, and a doctorate in medicine in 1494. From 1488 he lectured on philosophy at Padua. In 1511 he moved to the **University of Bologna**, where he taught until his death. He was a popular teacher and lectured on a broad range of philosophical subjects, with a special interest in natural philosophy. Pomponazzi's treatise on immortality focused not on the truth about the doctrine but on the question of Aristotle's opinion. Although he conceded that the human intellect is immaterial, he argued that it depends on the body since it is helpless without sensory knowledge. He boldly faced and refuted the objection that questioning immortality would undermine morality, arguing that virtue is its own reward and that actions done out of fear of punishment are base and servile. He published defenses against attacks by his critics in 1518 and 1519.

A slightly less controversial but still hotly debated work was his *De fato / On Fate* (1520), upholding the proposition that all human actions happen out of necessity, not free will, and that what we think is contingency in our actions is merely a product of our lack of self-knowledge. In the same book, however, Pomponazzi also addressed the same question on the basis of faith, relying on the scholastic theologians Thomas Aquinas and Duns Scotus to defend the freedom of the will. A third work of about the same period was *De incantationibus / On Incantations*, in which he made a critical assessment of miracles and tried to establish purely natural causes for apparently miraculous events, including those recorded in the Bible.

POMPONIUS LAETUS. *See* LETO, POMPONIO.

PONTANO, GIOVANNI (1426–1503). Italian **humanist** and diplomat. He was a native of Umbria and was educated at Perugia, but in

1447 he accepted an appointment at the court of King Alfonso of **Naples**. He worked as a tutor at the court and later served as ambassador and as secretary in the royal chancery. Despite his political duties, Pontano was a prolific writer. His efforts in poetry and dialogue form are undistinguished, but his political and moral works show an impressive ability to illustrate his philosophical conclusions with apt instances taken from his own political experience. Between 1468 and 1493 he produced treatises on the ideal prince, on obedience, on bravery, on liberality, and on beneficence. He was a strong defender of monarchy as the best form of government. In addition to his published writings and his official career, Pontano was the principal organizer of an important Renaissance **Academy** at the royal court.

PONTORMO, JACOPO DA (1494–1556/7). Florentine painter, associated with the **mannerist** reaction against the monumental spirit of High Renaissance art, even though his development was strongly influenced by the work of two of the greatest figures of the High Renaissance, **Michelangelo** and the German **Albrecht Dürer**. Unlike his friend and fellow mannerist **Rosso Fiorentino**, his work did not strive for shocking effects or engage in deliberate exaggeration and distortion but instead presented its human subjects as withdrawn and isolated, reflecting the shy, introspective personality of the artist himself. While Pontormo's fresco *The Visitation* (1514–1516) seems to follow the classical, idealized style of the Renaissance, his *Joseph in Egypt* (ca. 1518) already shows traits of mannerism, above all in its sense of anxiety and its unfocused composition. His fresco of *Vertumnus and Pomona* (1520–1521), painted for Pope **Leo X**, is conventional and beautifully executed Renaissance art, but his *Passion* (1523–1526) and especially his altarpiece of the *Lamentation* (1525–1528) again show the disordered composition and the tortured figures that mark the emergence of mannerism. His human figures, well illustrated by his drawing of a young girl (ca. 1526), are moody and withdrawn, far removed in spirit from the masterpieces of the High Renaissance, though not inferior in workmanship.

POPES. Common title for the bishops of **Rome** when viewed in their role as supreme heads of the Roman Catholic Church. The origins of papal sovereignty over the whole church are veiled in the mists of early church history and clouded by controversy between those who support the popes' claims to supremacy and those who regard those claims as a usurpation, such as the Eastern Orthodox churches and (since the **Reformation**) the Protestants. Papal claims to universal supremacy over the entire Christian church were the principal cause, though not the only one, of the final break between the Orthodox Church and the Roman Church in 1054.

Although the papacy experienced periods of weakness and corruption in the early medieval centuries, it never lost sight of its claims to supreme authority. These claims grew during the long period (1076–1250) when popes and the German (or Holy Roman) emperors clashed repeatedly over issues of church patronage and the proper relationship between secular and ecclesiastical rulers. One of the underlying issues in these conflicts was the growing assertiveness of the popes, who by the 13th century were claiming not only spiritual but also political supremacy, including the power to dethrone kings whose policies they judged contrary to the welfare of the church.

Three great popes of the 13th century, Innocent III (pope from 1198 to 1216), Innocent IV (1243–1254), and Boniface VIII (1294–1303), insisted that in case of a conflict of interests, the secular prince must yield because the goal sought by the church, the salvation of souls, is more important than any merely secular goal. Boniface VIII flatly declared that the power of kings came directly through a grant by the pope. The pope possessed ultimate sovereignty in the political as well as the spiritual realm. Pope Boniface found, however, that papal claims to power were far less successful when the pope had to deal with an able king of one of the western European feudal monarchies than with the relatively weak German emperors. King Philip IV of France not only defied papal threats to dethrone him but in 1303 even dared to make an attempt to seize the pope and bring him back to France for trial as a heretic. The pope, a frail and elderly man, died a few weeks after the attack, and the cardinals, instead of penalizing the king, sought to placate him in 1305 by electing a French bishop as pope.

The consequence of this weak response was the so-called **Babylonian Captivity** of the papacy (1305–1377), when all the popes were French. For most of this period, the popes lived at **Avignon** in what is now southeastern France. A great outcry arose not only in

Italy but among many non-French nations that the popes had become pawns of the kings of France. This relocation endangered the prestige of the papacy, but it was nothing compared to the problem created by a disputed papal election in 1378, which ended with the election of two rival popes, producing the **Western Schism** (1378–1417). This caused great spiritual unrest as Europe chose sides between the two (and for a time, among three) claimants; it set loose the ideology of **Conciliarism**, ideas about the nature of authority in the church that challenged the system of papal absolutism created by the 13th-century popes. The Schism was solved only when the secular rulers of Europe, led by the emperor, summoned the **Council of Constance**, which succeeded in removing all three claimants and then in 1417 electing a new pope who was recognized throughout the church.

The prestige of the papacy had been damaged greatly by both the Babylonian Captivity and the Schism. After 1417, the popes were not even able to re-establish securely their traditional political authority in and near Rome. Throughout the 15th century, they strove to expand their secular authority as rulers of Rome and central Italy. Hopes that the return of a universally recognized pope to Rome would mark the beginning of a thorough reform of the church were frustrated. While some popes at mid-century, such as **Nicholas V**, the founder of the Vatican Library, and **Pius II**, who had been a **humanist** scholar himself, fostered the growth of Renaissance culture and made some attempts at church reform, the three popes of the late 15th century, **Sixtus IV**, **Innocent VIII**, and **Alexander VI**, spent most of their energy struggling to expand the **Papal States** and scheming to advance members of their own family as rulers of principalities carved out of papal territories. These three secular-minded popes made the papacy a source of political unrest and military adventurism that disturbed all of Italy. The next important pope, **Julius II**, was an even more ruthless political adventurer, though at least he struggled to strengthen the Papal States rather than scheming to exploit the papal title for the advancement of his family.

The next pope, the well-meaning but self-indulgent and indolent Pope **Leo X**, had to face the early stages of the Reformation crisis in Germany, and it is typical of what the papacy had become that he never even considered the possibility that the real issues in the case of **Martin Luther** involved spiritual questions rather than politics and political ambition. Leo handled the complaints against Luther as a purely administrative matter, insisting that the Reformer must give immediate and unquestioning obedience and had no right, even though he was a qualified theologian, to debate or discuss the important theological issues that he had raised.

As a result of this misjudgment and the pope's concentration on the political problem of electing a new Holy Roman Emperor rather than on the problems of German religious life, the German situation ballooned into a great upheaval that undermined the power of the traditional ecclesiastical authorities in Germany and led to a permanent division of the church. After failing to head off this disaster, the popes who reigned from the mid–1520s to the 1540s resisted the urgings of many of the best clergy and most of the secular rulers to summon a general council to undertake reform and attempt to bring the German heretics back into the Catholic fold. The Council of Trent, which finally did convene in 1545 and met in three stages interrupted by war and political conflict down to its adjournment in 1563, was a triumph for the conservative Catholics who regarded the Protestants as heretics to be condemned and destroyed rather than as misguided brethren to be won back by conciliatory policies. The council reaffirmed all of the traditional doctrines and practices of the medieval church, and it particularly endorsed the universal spiritual power of the popes.

Yet while this council might seem a great victory for the popes, the actual course of ecclesiastical politics in the late 16th and early 17th centuries suggests that increasingly the real decisions on all non-doctrinal issues were being made by the secular princes who had remained Catholic, especially the **Habsburg** Holy Roman Emperors and kings of Spain, and in the 17th century also the kings of France.

Although in many respects the age of the Renaissance and the subsequent Reformation era were not a brilliant period in the history of the papacy, the popes who reigned between mid–15th century and mid–17th century played an active role in the flowering and diffusion of Renaissance culture. From the middle of the 15th century, the papal curia employed leading humanists in influential positions because of their stylistic skills and ability to compose effective administrative documents. The worldly, political popes from Sixtus IV to Leo X employed not only humanist secretaries and advisers but also the finest artists and musicians of the age. Julius II, who aimed to remake Rome into the great metropolis of Christian Europe, dared to demolish the ancient basilica of St. Peter and to replace it with a vast new church built in the best Renaissance style. Though the project was not completed until the mid–17th century, the resulting structure was the present basilica of St. Peter, one of the most splendid churches of the Christian world. Julius and his successor Leo X employed all three of the great masters of Renaissance art (**Leonardo da Vinci**, **Michelangelo**, and **Raphael**) to execute major works at Rome and Florence. The same popes brought to Rome the most brilliant composers and performers from Flanders, the center of Renaissance music, to fill the needs of the papal curia for liturgical music. The papal musical establishment became the greatest center of Renaissance music.

While Florence had been the great center of humanistic and artistic development in the 15th century, by the early 16th century, papal Rome had outpaced it, and Rome remained a major center of humanist learning and especially of artistic creation well into the 17th century. While the popes of the Renaissance did not always fulfill well their duties as spiritual leaders, they made Rome the cultural center of Catholic Europe and a powerful force for the creation and diffusion of some of the greatest achievements of Renaissance civilization.

POPOLO MINUTO / POPOLO GRASSO / GRANDI. Terms used in the early Renaissance to describe the three principal classes in the urban **communes** of northern and central Italy. During the 12th and 13th centuries, as imperial control declined and the cities struggled to assert their own independence, it was natural for the wealthiest inhabitants, those who were rich enough to fight in the cavalry, to assume political leadership. These rich citizens were either the leading merchants or the owners of feudal estates in the vicinity of the city, many of whom built fortified houses in the cities and used their armed retainers to enforce their will. These armed noblemen were variously called *milites*, *nobili*, *magnati*, or *grandi*. Although at first their political dominance was taken for granted, their armed retainers and their fortified urban palaces made them a source of disorder. The far more numerous non-noble citizens—the *popolo*—resented their arrogance and violence.

In a sense, these were conflicts between rich and poor, but the situation was complicated because nearly every city was also divided in complex ways between **Guelfs** and **Ghibellines**. Potentially, the richest non-nobles, called *popolo grasso* (literally, "fat people"), shared many interests with the *grandi*, but usually the *grandi* were unwilling to share power or to accept their own subordination to laws intended to create a peaceful and just civil society. Thus the united *popolo*, rich and poor together, in many cities combined to assert the supremacy of local law over the nobles. In specific terms, this meant suppression of their private armies and demolition of their fortified palaces. This goal was achieved largely by armed conflict, and during the second half of the 13th century, the united *popolo* in most places gained the upper hand and enacted legislation intended to break the power of the *grandi* and in particular to end forever their feeling of being above the law.

In **Florence**, this victory of the *popolo* culminated in the definitive Florentine constitution, the Ordinances of Justice, adopted in 1293 and preserved (though often distorted) until the republic was abolished by Alessandro de'**Medici** in 1532. This constitution restricted voting and office-holding to members of the 21 officially recognized **guilds**—professional and commercial organizations ranging from rich industrial and mercantile groups like the bankers and woolen textile manufacturers to lower-middle-class associations of petty merchants and artisans. No person, no matter how rich, powerful, or nobly descended, had any citizen rights unless he was a member of one of the guilds. All members of any family that had even one single member who had been knighted during the past 20 years were legally declared to be *grandi* or *magnati* and were excluded from political rights. In addition, since the magnates were blamed for frequent acts of violence, the criminal law established by the Ordinances explicitly discriminated *against* the rich and well-born: the penalty for an act of violence committed by a nobleman was far greater than the penalty for the same crime committed by a common citizen.

Among the triumphant Florentine *popolo*, the members of the seven richest guilds—legally defined as the greater guilds (*arti maggiori*)—enjoyed a majority on all governing councils except for a few decades in the 14th century—from 1343 to 1382. Hence for most of the republic's history the wealthy families of the seven greater guilds dominated political life, though the members of the 14 legally defined lesser guilds (*arti minori*) were granted some representation on the *Signoria* and other governing councils in order to give them a sense of participation. This meant that the rich non-nobles—the *popolo grasso*—normally dominated the government if their members were united. During the few decades of democratic reform from 1343 to 1382, the *popolo minuto* (that is, the lower middle class and skilled artisans) gained control of the councils, but by 1382 the leaders of the greater guilds, exploiting the fears caused by pressure for political recognition from the propertyless classes (who had no voice at all in politics), were able to stage a coup d'etat and regain a majority on the governing councils.

Within a few decades of the enactment of the Ordinances of Justice, the restrictions on the *grandi* were relaxed and individual members of magnate families were allowed to enroll in guilds even though they did not conduct any of the businesses associated with their new guild. This concession allowed people from magnate families to have political careers. The reduction of discrimination against rich nobles was facilitated by frequent intermarriages between rich magnates and rich *popolani*. The tension between *popolo grasso* and *popolo minuto* was never entirely resolved, but the granting of a fairly significant minority voice to the *popolo minuto* kept the less wealthy members of the political class quiescent most of the time.

In other cities, similar class conflict between rich and poor was the main force that led to the replacement of republican government by despotic regimes during the 13th and 14th centuries. The acceptance of a dictator was the price paid for law and order. Sometimes the new ruler—the **signore**—seized power on behalf or the *popolo grasso*, but more commonly, the man who eventually acquired dictatorial powers emerged as a champion of the poor against the oppressive actions of the rich. The **capitano del popolo** (commander of the armed forces) was often the person who established his own authoritarian rule.

PORTA, GIAMBATTISTA DELLA (ca. 1535–1615). Neapolitan writer, known for his learning and his authorship of works on science and **magic** as well as for his numerous and successful **neoclassical** dramas. He was deeply learned in scientific and magical lore at a time when the modern distinction between science and magic did not exist. He travelled widely, read omnivorously, and collected artifacts representing natural phenomena. Della Porta's involvement in magic was extensive enough that about 1580 the Neapolitan **Inquisition** questioned him about his beliefs and practices; on its recommendation, in 1610 the **pope** suppressed an association (Academia Secretorum Naturae) that he had helped found for the investigation of nature.

Della Porta insisted that no "black" or diabolical magic was involved in his studies. He also quarreled with several prominent contemporaries, accusing the English scientist **William Gilbert** of stealing and publishing his own discoveries on magnetism and also claiming priority to **Galileo** in the invention of a telescope. He was active in two important scholarly **academies** at **Naples**, the Accademia dei Lincei and the Accademia degli Oziosi. The best known of his writings on science were *De humana physiognomonia / On Human Physiognomy* (1586) and *Magiae naturalis libri XX / Twenty Books of Natural Magic* (1589). The latter was translated into Italian, French, German, and English. His scientific and magical writings contained much information gleaned from his wide reading and his close observation of nature.

Della Porta's parallel career as a playwright developed from his own enjoyment of dramatic presentations at **Naples** during his youth and his interest in the works of the Roman comedian Plautus, which he translated into Italian. His own plays included comedies, tragicomedies, and tragedies, some written in verse and others in prose. They were printed and widely read, beginning with the comedy *L'Olimpia* in 1589 and ending with *La furiosa / The Madwoman* in 1609. These plays strictly observed the neoclassical unities of time, place, and action. Despite his difficulties with the Inquisition, Della Porta was a firm supporter of the Catholic Reformation, a member of a lay society affiliated with the **Jesuits**, and an energetic promoter of use of the arts to promote Christian piety.

PORTUGUESE INQUISITION. The neighboring kingdom of Portugal generally followed Spanish policy on religion. **Pope** Paul III authorized a Portuguese Inquisition in 1536. It was organized on the Spanish model—that is, highly centralized and under royal control. As in Spain, most of the executions occurred in the early decades of its existence, and most of the victims were converted **Jews**. Both the Spanish and the Portuguese inquisitions followed the procedures used by medieval inquisitors. Both national inquisitions also became involved in the censorship of books during their struggle to suppress Protestantism. *See also* INQUISITION; ROMAN INQUISITION; SPANISH INQUISITION.

POSTEL, GUILLAUME (1510–1581). French linguistic scholar, religious reformer, **cabalist**, mystic, prophet of a new age, and (in the opinion of many contemporaries) madman. He was a born scholar, eager to master all languages and to know all knowledge; he eventually published more than 60 books. During his studies at Paris in the 1530s he mastered the three languages emphasized by Renaissance **humanism**, Latin, **Greek**, and **Hebrew**. In 1538 he accompanied a French diplomatic mission to the Turkish sultan at Istanbul, where he had his first serious exposure to the Arabic language and developed a lifelong interest in Christian missions to convert the Muslims. He also bought for the royal library a large collection of books in eastern languages. After his return, Postel lectured (1538–1542) on languages and mathematics at Paris as one of the royal lecturers appointed by King **Francis I**. He also published *Linguarum duodecim characteribus / The Letters of Twelve Languages*, the first comparative study of the grammar and alphabets of a number of eastern languages. He believed that Hebrew, the language in which God spoke with Adam, was the source of all other languages. He thought that knowledge of languages was essential for Christian missions and for the unification of all human societies. He also published the first Arabic grammar in Europe. *De orbis terrae concordia* (1544) was a book justifying Christian doctrines, intended for use by Christian missionaries to the Islamic world.

The concept of the unity of all humans was central to Postel's thought, pursued not only through his plans for missions but also through his efforts to promote moral reform of both the clergy and lay society in Christian Europe. He believed that a divine voice had instructed him to work for reform. His pursuit of the twin goals of religious reform and foreign missions led him to **Rome**, where in 1544 he became one of the early members of the Society of Jesus. Postel's reform ideas were so radical, however, that the **Jesuits** soon expelled him. About this time he discovered the Cabala and became even more convinced of his special mission as the firstborn son of the *restitutio omnium*, a providentially designed new age in human history. In 1546 he went to **Venice**, where he came under the influence of a female mystic who emphasized the need to express one's love of God through service to the poor and sick and who reinforced his mystical interests. His goal of a union of all religions was what had attracted Postel to the Jesuits, and his contact with the mystic whom he called the Venetian Virgin called forth grandiose ideas of a universal church and a universal monarchy, originally conceived as French but later as the Holy Roman Empire. His unrestrained speech and writing brought him before the **Inquisition** at Venice, and he was condemned as a heretic and madman and imprisoned from 1555 to 1559. His vernacular *République des Turcs* (1560) described the **Ottoman Turks** in remarkably positive terms.

In 1560 Postel attended the Council of Trent, where he agitated for a broader, more inclusive Catholicism than was acceptable to the dominant conservatives. He was hostile to Protestantism because it had brought disunity into the life of the church. Yet his dream of unity included winning the support of the Protestants, and he sought contact with a number of scholarly and moderate Protestant leaders, including **Philipp Melanchthon**, and also with radical sectarians like Kaspar von Schwenkfeld. Postel was attracted to the nondogmatic underground religious movement known as the Family of Love. His mystical and prophetic tone attracted many readers distressed by the disunity and corruption of the church.

POZZO, MODESTA (1555–1592). Venetian author, known for her verse romance *Canti del Floridoro* (1581), the libretto for a cantata performed for the doge of **Venice** in 1581, and for two verse narratives written for religious occasions, but chiefly for her dialogue *Il merito delle donne / The Worth of Women* (1600), an imaginary dialogue among seven **women** who denounce the subordination and mistreatment of women by men. Pozzo wrote under the pseudonym Moderata Fonte, and her dialogue was published with a preface by two of her own children. She acquired her education by begging her brother to teach her what he had learned in school, and later, by using her guardian's library. Despite her bitter denunciation of marriage as a form of enslavement for women, she herself was married about 1582 to a Venetian, and though most of her works were written before her marriage, her most important work, *The Worth of Women*, was written while she was married. Pozzo's husband seems to have been sympathetic to her literary aspirations and wrote a preface for one of her religious poems, *The Resurrection of Christ* (1592). She died at age 37 while giving birth to their fourth child.

PRAGMATIC SANCTION OF BOURGES. Legislation issued by King Charles VII in the French Estates General of 1438, defining the **Gallican** (French) Church as an autonomous unit within the total Catholic church and giving only nominal recognition to the **pope** as head of the church. The document imposed major limitations on papal control of the church in France, especially regarding taxation of the clergy and appointments to clerical offices. In practice, it transferred these rights to the king. The papacy never accepted this tradition of "Gallican" autonomy and in 1516 negotiated a concordat (treaty) with King **Francis I** that divided power between the pope and the king, though in practice the king retained control of most major appointments. This concordat effectively nullified the Pragmatic Sanction, and there were bitter but unsuccessful protests by the leaders of the clergy, the **University** of Paris, and the Parlement of Paris. *See also* BOLOGNA, CONCORDAT OF; GALLICANISM.

PRATO, GIOVANNI DA (ca. 1367–ca. 1442). Florentine vernacular author, unusual in a generation when writing in Latin had eclipsed writing in the vernacular. At a time when some **classical** purists disdained the three great Florentine authors of the Trecento, **Dante**, **Petrarch**, and **Boccaccio**, Prato was an outspoken defender of their excellence. He gave public lectures on Dante (1417–1425) and modelled his own works on those of his Florentine predecessors. His most important work is *Il Paradiso degli Alberti*, a romance tracing the author's imaginary pilgrimage to Crete and Cyprus, which ended at a noble castle in Casentino and the villa near **Florence** from which a later editor derived the title for the whole work. The last two segments, in Casentino and the villa del Paradiso, are peopled by contemporary intellectual and political figures, including Petrarch's closest disciple, Luigi Marsili, and **Coluccio Salutati**, the first **humanist** chancellor of Florence. Interest in Dante and Boccaccio is also evident in two other works, *Trattato d'una angelica cosa mostrata per una divotissima visione / Treatise on an Angelic Event Demonstrated by a Most Pious Vision*, and the poem *Philomena*.

PRINTING. The new art of mechanical production of books with movable type emerged in northern Europe, probably at Mainz in western Germany, by the early 1450s. Its immediate and obvious effects were two: it greatly increased the supply of books and reduced their cost (by 80 per cent, according to contemporary evidence), and it facilitated the rapid diffusion of texts and illustrations.

The long-term significance of printing for the history of civilization is even greater. For the **humanistic** and even the artistic and musical side of the Renaissance, the art of printing ensured far more rapid diffusion of new texts and new ideas, and at a cost far less than the cost of hand-copying every single copy. From an early date, the new art was also used for legal forms; for the diffusion of laws, proclamations, and notices by political authorities; and for other public posters and notices. Thus it significantly affected the administrative practice of institutions, both governmental and ecclesiastical. The Renaissance humanists' work of rediscovering, editing, and diffusing newly discovered classical texts was revolutionized, since the standardized nature of the printed text fixed and stabilized a scholar's editorial work on a text in a way impossible when every copy involved error-prone production by hand.

On the other hand, humanistic texts were by no means the dominant product of the early presses. Religious books (such as the Gutenberg Bible and the Mainz Psalter), textbooks for both grammar-schools and universities, books of devotion and meditation, books of popular literature in the vernacular languages—all of these constituted significant portions of the early production. In the long run, no field benefitted more than the natural sciences, since manuscript technology had been even less successful at reproducing comprehensible illustrations than at reproducing accurate texts. The combination of typeset letters with woodcut or copperplate engravings meant that illustrated books, including scientific books that required drawings, could be mass produced accurately for the first time. *See also* ESTIENNE; ELZEVIER PRESS; FROBEN, JOHANN; GUTENBERG, JOHANNES; MANUTIUS, ALDUS.

PULCI, LUIGI (1432–1484). Florentine vernacular poet. His wit and skill as a popular writer won him the patronage of **Cosimo de'Medici**. Urged by Cosimo's daughter-in-law to write a poem on the heroic exploits of the Emperor Charlemagne in support of religion, in 1483 he published his fantastic poem *Morgante maggiore*, drawn from the *Chanson de Roland* and popular verses on the "matter of France," but conceived as a parody of traditional chivalric poetry. It is a mock-epic recounting the adventures of Orlando (the Frankish hero Roland) and his giant friend Morgante. Pulci became a close personal friend of **Lorenzo de'Medici** and seems to have functioned as an irreverent counterweight to the solemn and pretentiously **classical** literature produced by the **Neoplatonists** and **humanists** of the Medici literary circle. He wrote sonnets mocking the ethereal spirituality of the philosopher **Marsilio Ficino** and in particular ridiculing Ficino's defense of the immortality of the soul. Pulci's irreverent tone eventually alienated Lorenzo, and in 1475 he entered the service of a Neapolitan nobleman. In addition to *Morgante*, he wrote an account of a tournament staged by Lorenzo at **Florence** in 1469, a parody of one of Lorenzo's poems, a novella, and a number of other verses. But *Morgante* was the work that made him famous throughout Europe.

– Q –

QUATTROCENTO; QUATTROCENTO STYLE. In Italian, the 15th century, conceived as an historical and cultural epoch. Art historians speak of Quattrocento style as the art produced during the first two-thirds of the 15th century, from **Brunelleschi**, **Donatello**, and **Masaccio** down to the earliest works of **Leonardo da Vinci**, the oldest of the great masters of the High Renaissance style, whose earliest dated work was done in 1473.

QUERELLE DES FEMMES. The "woman question" was a series of literary debates whether **women** are naturally and inevitably inferior to men (as the received wisdom of European writers had held since ancient times) or whether the obvious inferiority of women in intellectual and literary attainments and in nearly all aspects of life was purely a social convention forced on women by the tyranny of men. Some of the first Renaissance authors who expressed sympathy with female complaints of injustice and argued that the low status of women was not inevitable but had been caused by male tyranny were

Mario Equicola in *De mulieribus / On Women* (1500) and the German **occultist Agrippa von Nettesheim**, whose *Declamatio de nobilitate et praecellentia foeminei sexus / Declamation on the Nobility and Superiority of the Female Sex* (1529) was frequently published both in the original Latin and in translations into most of the major vernacular languages. The status of women was also an important theme in one of the major books of manners published in the early 16th century, *The Book of the Courtier* by **Baldassare Castigione**, though its advocacy of women was limited. A more spirited defense of women's rights was **Ludovico Ariosto's** *Orlando furioso*.

The possibility (and actuality) of female succession to the throne made England a center of discussions on this issue. The Spanish **humanist Juan Luis Vives** in his *Instruction of a Christian Woman* (Latin 1523; English translation 1540), written specifically for Queen Catherine of Aragon, advised that the queen's daughter Mary **Tudor** should not inherit the throne because of the inherent weakness of female character. The humanist **Thomas Elyot** in *The Defence of Good Women* (1540) opposed Vives and argued that although normally women should not rule, they have the ability to do so when conditions demand. The actual accession of a woman, Mary Tudor, to the English throne in 1552 made these theoretical debates more real, and since Mary was not only a female monarch but a Catholic one as well, the Scottish reformer John Knox wrote *First Blast of the Trumpet against the Monstrous Regiment of Women* (1558), a work he never repudiated but did find somewhat inconvenient when the death of Queen Mary brought a Protestant woman, **Elizabeth I**, to the throne. Defenses of female monarchy became easier to write when the ruler actually was a woman, and both John Aylmer and **Edmund Spenser** wrote in defense of women's eligibility for the throne, though both authors justified Elizabeth's rule by interpreting it as a special act of divine grace beyond the usual scope of female ability.

Debates about the status of women remained frequent during the 17th century, a period when education of women was often discussed. A woman famous for her own learning, Anna Maria von Schurman (1607–1678), published a treatise in 1638 contending that it is proper for a woman of wealth and leisure to study. **Marie de Gournay** (1565–1645), who avoided marriage in order to devote herself to study and who became a friend of **Michel de Mon-**

taigne and edited his essays, contended that women are intellectually just as able as men but are made inferior because they are excluded from education. The issue of the moral and intellectual equality of women was also discussed by a male author, François Poulain de la Barre, in *De l'égalité des deux sexes / On the Equality of the Sexes* (1673). Despite the theoretical equality of the sexes, the subordination of women in marriage negated much of that equality. A large proportion of the women who became noted for learning either never married or ceased being active scholars after they married.

– R –

RABELAIS, FRANÇOIS (ca. 1494–1535). French author of vernacular prose satires. Born the son of a lawyer at Chinon, he entered the Franciscan order about 1510 and presumably received the typical **scholastic** education provided to members of his order. He and several fellow Franciscans became attracted to **humanistic** studies. Rabelais learned **Greek** and studied **classical** literature, as shown by an admiring letter he wrote to one of the leading French humanists, **Guillaume Budé**, in 1521. In 1523 the Paris theological faculty confiscated secular Greek and Latin books belonging to Rabelais and his fellow Franciscans. His interest in humanism caused him so much difficulty with his order that in 1525 he secured **papal** permission to transfer to a Benedictine monastery, whose abbot became one of his patrons.

In 1527, however, Rabelais left that monastery and spent the rest of his life living as a secular priest. At about the same time he took up the study of medicine, first at Paris but eventually at Montpellier. Henceforth he practiced medicine from time to time but also became an editor of Greek medical texts, especially the works of Hippocrates and Galen. In 1531 he lectured on Hippocrates at Montpellier, and the following year he published an edition of that author's *Aphorisms*. In order to legalize his departure from the Benedictine order, while living at **Rome** in the service of a aristocratic patron, he secured a papal dispensation that freed him from his monastic vows. Then he completed his medical doctorate at Montpellier (1537). Henceforth, he pieced together a living from a combination of medical practice, support by aristocratic patrons, income from two parishes of which he was titular rector, and earnings from his publications.

Those publications included above all his famous satirical novels, humorous prose narratives about the imaginary lives of a family of giants. The first these, *Pantagruel*, appeared in 1532; a second, *Gargantua*, came out in 1534. These books, written in a racy French and full of sexual escapades and gross humor, were condemned by the Paris theologians, but they were so popular that they could not be suppressed despite their obvious sympathy for religious reformers (more for reform-minded humanists like **Erasmus** than for **Martin Luther** and others who broke away from the traditional church). In 1545 Rabelais received from King Henry II (a fierce persecutor of heretics) permission to publish more stories about the adventures of Pantagruel, and his *Tiers livre / Third Book* came out the following year. Much later, he published a *Quart Livre / Fourth Book* (1552) of the adventures of Gargantua and Pantagruel. A fifth book was pieced together from his surviving papers after his death and published in 1562; a more complete version appeared in 1564, but it is likely that considerable parts of this last book were written by another hand.

Rabelais' satires are clearly the work of a man familiar with ancient satirists like Petronius and Lucian, yet they also continue many elements of French popular satire rooted in the **Middle Ages**. Rabelais shelters himself from ecclesiastical censors by his use of irony and shifting points of view. What is perhaps the most famous episode in *Gargantua*, the description of the aristocratic and pseudohumanistic Abbey of Thélème, makes its message so ambiguous that modern critics still debate just what the author meant. Rabelais also published humorous and profitable **astrological** calendars. Although his popular works reflect his interest in humanism and religious reform, the comic spirit predominates, no doubt the reason why his books became and remained popular.

RALEIGH, WALTER (ca. 1554–1618; also spelled Ralegh). English explorer, historian, poet, and courtier. Born of a seafaring family in Devonshire, he studied at Oxford and the Inns of Court. He fought in military campaigns in France and Ireland and became involved in overseas enterprise in 1578 when he commanded a ship in the unsuccessful attempt of his half-brother, Humphrey Gilbert, to plant a colony in North America. Raleigh attracted the favor of Queen **Elizabeth I**, was knighted and given valuable public offices. He commanded expeditions against the Spanish in 1595 and 1616, but his bellicose record and his political links to anti-Spanish political factions offended King James I (1603–1625) and contributed to his being convicted of treason and sentenced to death in 1603. His real offense was involvement in an effort to prevent the accession of James to the English throne. His death sentence was commuted to imprisonment in the Tower of London. He was released in order to carry out an expedition to the coast of Guyana in 1616, but when it failed to produce the anticipated plunder (which the crown would have shared) and led to Spanish diplomatic protests, he was executed in 1618 on the basis of the original conviction of 1603. As a poet, Raleigh produced a number of much-admired lyrics; as a prose writer, he published accounts of expeditions to the Azores and Guyana, but his major prose work was his *History of the World* (1614).

RAMUS, PETRUS (Pierre de la Ramée, 1515–1572). French philosopher, **humanist**, teacher, and Protestant martyr, known in his own time mainly as a critic of traditional **Aristotelian** logic and the whole Aristotelian philosophical tradition. He also criticized the humanistic rhetorical tradition based on the works of **Cicero** and Quintilian and put forward a new dialectic which he viewed not only as a replacement for Aristotle but also as the foundation for a new direction in education and scholarship. In his early career at the **University** of Paris, his *Dialecticae institutiones / Introduction to Dialectic* and *Aristotelicae animadversiones / Observations on Aristotle*, both published in 1543, denied the value and even the authenticity of the philosophical writings attributed to Aristotle and stirred up such bitter conflict that after a formal disputation before a royal commission, the king forbade Ramus to teach at all.

This prohibition was lifted under the next king, Henry II, and in 1551 Henry apointed Ramus to be one of the Royal Readers. His lectures in that position attacked educational tradition, and in 1562 he put forth proposals for drastic reform of the university, such as making physics a required subject in the faculty of arts, adding clinical experience to the requirements for medical degrees, and adding study of the **Hebrew** Old Testament and the **Greek** New Testament to the degree requirements in theology. His proposals recommended the firing of some professors and the addition of new chairs of mathematics, anatomy, botany, and pharmacy. His conversion to Calvinist religion in 1561 explains some of this radicalism. Ramus' work on dialectic was influenced by the humanist **Rudolf Agricola** and by the educational reforms of the Protestant schoolmaster **Johann Sturm** at Strasbourg.

Although Ramus' attack on the Aristotelian tradition reflects concerns about prevailing philosophy that were shared by others, his own elaborate efforts to provide an alternative logic were not successful. His effort in many of his works to organize all learning in accord with his conception of proper method is a significant example of use of the printed book to express relationships in visual form. Ramus was a teacher first of all, and his initial dissatisfaction with traditional university logic was the result of his conclusion that it was unteachable. Some of his more than 50 publications were written (or at least published) in collaboration with Omer Talon (ca. 1510–1562). Ramus had great influence in the late 16th and much of the 17th century, especially in England and other Protestant countries, where his reputation was enhanced by his role as one of the Protestants martyred at Paris during the infamous Massacre of St. Bartholomew's Day in 1572.

RAPHAEL (Raffaele Sanzio, 1483–1520). The youngest of the three major figures of the artistic High Renaissance, known primarily as a painter but also employed as an architect. Born at **Urbino** and initially trained by his father, he subsequently studied at Perugia under **Perugino**. He painted in Perugia, Urbino, and **Florence**, and in Florence he studied the works of **Masaccio, Leonardo da Vinci,** and **Michelangelo.** His paintings at Florence included several of his many Madonnas, such as *Madonna del Granduca* and *Madonna of the Goldfinch,* as well as several portraits. Upon learning that **Pope Julius II** admired his work, Raphael left Florence for **Rome,** where he produced his most famous paintings, including the work commonly regarded as his masterpiece, *The School of Athens* (1510–1511), but also *Galatea* (1513), the *Sistine Madonna* (1513–1514), and a number of portraits, of which the most striking are his revealing portrait of *Pope Leo X with His Nephews* (ca. 1518) and individual portraits of Pope Julius II (1511–1512 and 1515–1516) and many others. His last painting, completed shortly before his premature death, was *The Transfiguration*. Raphael was a popular painter and established a large workshop which trained many of the leading artists of the next generation. After the death of the original architect of the new basilica of St. Peter, in 1514 **Leo X** appointed him chief architect, but his new plan was never put into execution. He designed a number of other secular and church buildings at Rome.

REFORMATION. Although the term is sometimes used to designate efforts of all 16th-century religious groups to reform and revitalize religion, the most common usage is as a label for the religious upheaval that grew out of the challenge of **Martin Luther** late in 1517 to the prevailing doctrines on justification and to the system of penitential discipline based on those doctrines. The refusal of church authorities in Germany and **Rome** to address the issues raised by Luther (who as a professor of theology was authorized to initiate such discussion) and their insistence on immediate and unquestioning submission to authority is now generally regarded as a major cause of the ballooning of what began as a disagreement among professional theologians into a widespread upheaval that by 1521, when Luther publicly refused to submit to papal authority, had produced a split within the medieval Roman Catholic church that dominated the religious history of 16th-century Europe and has continued down to the present. The Reformation was first a German phenomenon, but it rapidly spread to German-speaking Switzerland and the Netherlands and slightly later also to other countries, including all of Scandinavia, England, and France.

Although many aspects of Luther's challenge to authority were influenced by Renaissance **humanism**, the Renaissance and Reformation were distinct movements. Some humanists, mainly the younger ones, became followers (and eventually leaders) of the Reformation, while others (including **Erasmus** and most of the older humanists) remained Roman Catholic despite their continuing complaints about the condition of the church. The earliest followers of Luther referred to themselves as "evangelicals," and after the breakdown of an attempted settlement at the Imperial Diet in 1527 led to a formal protest by the German princes and cities that followed Luther, the term "Protestant" came into use. From the mid–1520s the "Evangelical" or "Protestant" movement split internally into rival groups, since most evangelicals in Switzerland and southwestern Germany concluded that Luther had not separated himself sufficiently from certain Catholic doctrines and practices. These groups were initially called "Sacramentarians" because of their teachings on the sacrament of the Eucharist; they are now often called "Zwinglians" from their first important leader, **Huldrych Zwingli**, or "Reformed," to distinguish them from the "Evangelicals" or "Lutherans."

The Reformation also produced small dissident groups who rejected the claims of all other parties to constitute true Christian churches. Because the usual marker of these groups was their rejection of infant baptism and their practice of rebaptizing adults who joined them, they were called "Anabaptists." After the death of Zwingli in 1531, the largest group of non-Lutheran Protestants eventually came to be called Calvinists, from the name of their outstanding theologian, the ex-humanist **John Calvin**. From the middle of the 16th century, England came to be dominated by a distinct national tradition that rejected papal authority and regarded the king as the earthly head of the Christian community in England; this group is usually called "Anglican."

Roman Catholicism also underwent a series of significant internal reforms that are sometimes labelled the "Catholic Reformation." The older term "Counter-Reformation" is sometimes still used, but it fails to reflect evidence that the reform effort that remained within the old church was already underway before 1517. "Counter-Reformation" also overemphasizes the repressive and disciplinary measures taken against Protestants and thus fails to reflect the strong positive influences that led to a renewed spiritual life that remained explicitly Roman Catholic.

The Reformation, both Protestant and Catholic, had important consequences for education and general intellectual life. The divisions introduced by the Reformation left all of Mediterranean Europe firmly Catholic, while the various Protestant movements became numerous, and often dominant, in much of northern and northwestern Europe. France was deeply divided by the Reformation and between

1562 and 1598 was torn by a series of destructive civil wars caused both by religious disagreements and by political factionalism in an age of weak and incompetent kings. The French Wars of Religion and the Dutch War for Independence (1572–1609) dominated both the political and the religious life of most of western and northern Europe throughout the late Renaissance, and the religious division between Protestant and Catholic was a major force in the outbreak and long duration of the Thirty Years' War (1618–1648), though secular political rivalries among the European powers also played an important part and became increasingly dominant as the war dragged on.

REGIOMONTANUS (Johannes Müller, 1436–1476). German astronomer and mathematician, known primarily because of the astronomical tables (*Ephemerides*, 1474) he compiled and his Latin summary of Ptolemy's *Almagest*, a project begun by his older colleague **Georg Peurbach** and completed by Regiomontanus, who called it an *Epitome* (1463; first printed, 1496). Virtually nothing is known about his life before he entered the **University** of Vienna in 1450. He started teaching there in 1457 and became a close friend of Peurbach, whose work on Ptolemy was stimulated by a visit in 1460 to Vienna by the papal legate, the Greek-born Cardinal **Johannes Bessarion**. Bessarion inspired Regiomontanus to learn **Greek**. Regiomontanus also studied trigonometry and wrote a work, *De triangulis omnimodis / On All Classes of Triangles* (1463–1464; first published in 1533), and another mathematical treatise, *Tabulae directionum / Tables of Directions* (1467–1468). In 1471 he settled in Nuremberg and set up a press for publication of scientific works. His first publication was an edition of Peurbach's *Theoricae novae planetarum / New Theory of the Planets*.

REUCHLIN, JOHANN (1455–1512). German lawyer and **humanist**, famous because of his pioneering role in promoting the study of **Hebrew** in northern Europe, and also because of his controversy with the Dominican theologians of the University of Cologne which gave rise to a savage anticlerical satire, *Letters of Obscure Men*, written in defense of Reuchlin by a group of young humanists.

Reuchlin was born at Pforzheim in Baden and educated in liberal arts at Freiburg, Paris, and **Basel**. He then studied law at Orléans and

Poitiers. He spent most of his career in the law, first as a legal adviser to German princes and then as a judge. His work took him to Italy on several occasions, and he was favorably impressed by the Italian scholars whom he met, including the **Neoplatonic** philosophers **Marsilio Ficino** and **Giovanni Pico della Mirandola** and the Venetian humanist **Ermolao Barbaro**. Reuchlin was one of the first German humanists to become truly competent in **Greek**, and by the 1490s he also had begun to study Hebrew. The **Florentine** Neoplatonists influenced him strongly, and like Pico he extended this interest in Platonic philosophy to include **Jewish Cabala**. He published a Hebrew grammar (1506), a book on Hebrew accents and orthography, and two books on Cabala, *De verbo mirifico / On the Miraculous Word* (1494) and the more knowledgeable *De arte cabalistica / On the Cabalistic Art* (1517). In these books, Reuchlin tried to discover ancient religious truths concealed behind the Hebrew words of Scripture and Cabala. He interpreted Cabala, Neoplatonist philosophy, the works attributed to **Hermes Trismegistus**, and other ancient esoteric writings in a Christian sense, regarding them as providentially designed to prepare the world for conversion to Christianity. Despite these unconventional interests, Reuchlin in most respects was a conservative Catholic and during the early **Reformation** opposed **Luther**. He disinherited his own great-nephew and protégé **Philipp Melanchthon** because of the latter's support of Luther.

Nevertheless, Reuchlin became embroiled in 1511 in a controversy with the Dominican order and the theological faculty at Cologne which created a famous scandal. This controversy began when Reuchlin replied to a request from the Emperor **Maximilian I** by advising rejection of a proposal by a converted Jew, Johann Pfefferkorn, that all Hebrew religious books except the Bible should be destroyed. His opposition to this proposal was based mainly on humanist considerations: the loss of Hebrew learning would be a terrible blow to Christian scholarship. In reply, Pfefferkorn published a slanderous attack, claiming that Reuchlin had taken bribes from rich Jews. Reuchlin's sharp counterattack, *Augenspiegel* (1511), caused the Dominican inquisitor to lodge formal charges that Reuchlin had harmed Christian religion and aided the resistance of Jews to conversion. Litigation over these charges dragged through the ecclesiastical courts for several years. Although temporarily successful in the ecclesiastical courts, Reuchlin finally lost his case when his Cologne opponents appealed the verdict to **Rome**. As an obedient Catholic, he retracted his condemned books and paid the heavy court costs arising from the litigation. But the principal effect of the controversy was the scandalous and anonymous satire *Letters of Obscure Men*, which presented the Cologne theologians as objects of ridicule.

RHETORIC. *See* HUMANISM.

RHÉTORIQUEURS. A group of French vernacular writers, mostly poets and historians, active in glorifying the kings of France and the dukes of **Burgundy** and Brittany during the 15th and early 16th centuries. Covering three generations, they include Georges Chastellain (ca. 1405–1474), Jean Molinet (1435–1507), and **Jean Lemaire des Belges** (1473–1525), all of whom served as historiographers to the dukes of Burgundy, though Lemaire later served the kings of France. All *rhétoriqueurs* had as their primary duty the enhancement of the reputation of the kings and princes at whose courts they served. Much of their writing, including their French plays and a substantial part of their historiographical writing, was in verse. They also wrote in prose, for example *Illustrations de Gaule et singularitez de Troyes / Illustrations of Gaul and Singlarities of Troy* (ca. 1510) by Lemaire, probably the most prominent literary figure in the group. Their admirers regarded them as equals of both **classical** rhetoricians and the early Italian **humanists**, but now they are classed as transitional figures between medieval court poets and court humanists.

RIEMENSCHNEIDER, TILMAN (ca. 1460–1531). German sculptor, best known for his large limewood statues of scenes from the Bible and the lives of the saints. He was born in Thuringia but by 1479 had settled in Würzburg, where he established a large workshop and produced both wood and stone sculpture. His prosperity is reflected in his membership on the city council and a term as burgomaster.

RIENZO, COLA DI (ca. 1313–1354). Roman notary and leader of a popular uprising of the common people of **Rome** against the incompetent administration of the city by the absentee **popes** at **Avignon**. He had become fascinated by the surviving monuments of ancient

Rome and was hostile to the violence of the city's aristocratic clans, whose armed conflicts undermined security of life and property and had led to the murder of his own brother. In January 1343, an apparently spontaneous revolution of the people overthrew the two papal "senators" (representatives) who administered the city. Rienzo was one of the delegation sent by the citizens to justify their action at the papal curia, where his eloquence made an excellent impression. He stayed in Avignon for several months and met the poet and **humanist Petrarch**, who shared Rienzo's dissatisfaction with the absence of the popes from Rome and the chaotic political and social conditions in the ancient capital.

Both the poet and the notary felt nostalgia for Rome's past greatness and dreamed that the city could regain that greatness. While for Petrarch these dreams were confined to the realm of ideas, Rienzo intended to take action. He delivered incendiary speeches decrying the lawlessness of the nobles and reminded his audiences that the Roman people were the original source of all imperial authority and still had a right to revoke the authority of any ruler who failed to govern justly. On the feast of Pentecost 1347 a mob of people approved resolutions imposing the death sentence for murder, raising a citizen militia, placing a citizen army in charge of all fortified places, and conferring on Cola the title "tribune of the people." The uprising was fully successful. Even the aristocratic clans against whom it was directed seemed to accept it.

Unfortunately for himself, Cola's grandiose plans did not stop with the goal of creating law and order in the city. He urged other Italian cities to oust tyrannical rulers and summoned a national parliament at Rome that was intended to restore Italian unity and power—acts that made Rienzo a mythic hero to 19th-century Italian patriots. Although initially Cola's regime was successful in repressing street violence, he proceeded to issue sweeping decrees challenging the political authority of the popes, the Holy Roman Emperor, and the German electoral princes. The pope excommunicated Cola and prepared to drive him from power, but the Roman people themselves, angered by Cola's oppressive behavior, turned against him. Rienzo lost his nerve in the face of a small riot and fled the city in December 1347, after only seven months in power. He took refuge among the heretical Fraticelli in southern Italy.

But Rienzo did not give up his dreams of Roman power though he changed his means. Leaving his hiding place, he secretly travelled to Prague, where he presented himself to the Emperor Charles IV and tried to persuade him to liberate Italy from aristocratic misrule and to restore Roman power. Since Rienzo was already accused of heresy, the archbishop of Prague had him arrested, and in the summer of 1352, the emperor sent him to Avignon to face trial for heresy. At Avignon, however, Rienzo once again made a powerful impression, and a new pope not only released him from prison but in August 1353 sent him back to Rome in the service of the cardinal legate who was dispatched to re-establish papal control. In August 1354 Rienzo managed to regain control of the city. Although the people briefly welcomed his return, his arbitrary and erratic actions stirred up another popular uprising in early October. He tried to escape, disguised as a beggar, but was recognized and killed by the mob.

Rienzo's remarkable career is an example of the chaotic political and social conditions in Rome and central Italy. It is also an example of the ability of memories of ancient Roman greatness to stir the imaginations of contemporaries. Even Petrarch, who shared Rienzo's nostalgia for ancient Rome, was strongly drawn to the Rienzo revolution in its initial phase.

ROJAS, FERNANDO DE (ca. 1475–1541). Spanish dramatist. Born in the province of Toledo to a *converso* family, he studied law and encountered **humanist** influences at the University of Salamanca, graduating about 1499. Shortly before his graduation, he published a play, *Comedia de Calisto y Melibea*, which he claimed to be his own continuation of an anonymous work but probably was entirely his own creation. It was so popular that about 1502 he added five new acts, bringing the total to 21, calling it a *Tragicomedia* instead of a *Comedia*. In its new form, it continued to be popular. Because the action revolves mainly around the character of Celestina, an aging prostitute who acts as go-between in the sexual intrigue that stands at the center of the plot, it has long been known as *La Celestina*. The play presents a bleak picture of a corrupt, greedy, and hypocritical society, directing its barbs against the traditional aristocracy, the newly rich middle class, and the lower classes. After completing the expanded version, Rojas worked as a jurist, serving as mayor of Talavera de la

Reina, where he spent the rest of his life and never produced another literary work. *La Celestina* was rapidly and widely translated into most western European vernaculars and even into **Hebrew** and Latin and is usually ranked as one of the masterpieces of Spanish Renaissance literature.

ROMAN ACADEMY. *See* ACADEMIES.

ROMAN INQUISITION. The last of the major inquisitions to be founded, the Roman Inquisition, was the only one directed primarily against the Protestant **Reformation**. The papal bull founding this inquisition, *Licet ab initio*, was promulgated by Pope Paul III in 1542 and was modelled after the Spanish Inquisition, having a strong central authority (a commission of cardinals that met weekly under the presidency of the **pope** himself) and also having a network of local tribunals. Its tribunals followed the procedural rules common among such bodies, including secret accusations, taking of secret testimony, and in the most serious cases, use of judicial torture. Here, too, the ultimate punishment was the death penalty. Torture and capital punishment could be used only if a bishop or an episcopal vicar was present. In any serious case, the local court could not pronounce final sentence until the supreme congregation at **Rome** had reviewed the documents and had expressed its own judgment, which was binding on the lower court.

Although the procedure was harsh, trials were not merely *pro forma* processing of defendants already doomed. Accusers had to present their charges on oath. The defendant was given legal counsel and a written transcript of the proceedings. Execution was kept in reserve as an ultimate sanction for the most serious cases. Most punishments were interpreted leniently—for example, life imprisonment was usually commuted after three years. The most frequent penalty was the requirement to make public abjuration, an act normally performed outside churches on feast days so that the abjuration of error would be witnessed by large numbers of fellow citizens. Being sentenced to confinement as a rower in the galleys or to death by burning alive were the most severe punishments. The Roman Inquisition was aimed primarily at people who were either supporters of the Protestant heresies or supporters of more moderate teachings (the ideas of reformist

humanists like **Erasmus**, for example) that were thought to favor the Protestants and to undermine the authority of the church. Despite the infamous prosecution of the scientist **Galileo Galilei**, very rarely were individuals tried and punished by any inquisitorial court for abstract philosophical and scientific doctrines. *See also* INQUISITION; POR-TUGUESE INQUISITION; SPANISH INQUISITION.

ROMAN SCRIPT. *See* SCRIPT, HUMANISTIC.

ROMANCE OF THE ROSE. Allegorical dream-poem (*Roman de la Rose*) written in French at two different times in the 13th century by two different poets. Although it is a typically medieval poem written in a medieval century, it had a long-term influence extending to the time of **Chaucer**, who translated portions into English, and even into the 16th century, when the French poet **Clément Marot** edited it for publication. It was probably the most widely read poem of the **Middle Ages**.

   The first portion, which seems to be the product of a member of the aristocracy and expresses the romantic tradition of chivalric literature, was the work of Guillaume de Lorris, who wrote it about 1237. It describes the hero, a lover who pursues his inaccessible lady (the Rose) against the opposition of abstract characters such as Envy and Jealousy, and it breaks off as the lady (the Rose) is held captive in a fortified castle. The second part, much longer and written about 1280, was the work of Jean de **Meung** (also called Jean Clopinel), who was born about 1250, seems to have received a classical education, and probably lived until the early 14th century. The tone of this second part is radically different from that of the first. Jean de Meung loaded his continuation with prolix and irrelevant detail apparently intended to show his familiarity with ancient literature. This portion abandoned the idealistic tone of Lorris' work for a cynical expression of distrust in the church, the aristocracy, and in particular the honor of **women**.

ROME. The city of Rome during the Renaissance stood for two related but distinct entities. First and foremost it was the Eternal City, the idealized capital of the ancient Roman Empire, which in turn was viewed as the culminating element in the ancient **classical** civilization that was the ideal of the whole Renaissance. This idealization of

Rome was not entirely lacking from the culture of the **Middle Ages**, but in some medieval thinkers it was qualified by aversion to the pagan religious identity and the worldly spirit of the pre-Christian city. Beginning with **Petrarch** in the 14th century, the concept of a rebirth of high culture after a millennium of barbarism implied restoring the literary and artistic standards of ancient Rome at its height. For many Renaissance intellectuals, especially the so-called "civic **humanists**" of **Florence** and later of **Venice**, it also meant recapturing the self-sacrificing patriotism which, at least according to the views promoted by the ancient Roman historians, had been the primary cause of the ancient city's rise to greatness.

But Rome was also the ecclesiastical capital of medieval Latin Christendom, already the principal Christian center of the western empire before the political dissolution of the Roman state in the fifth century. Above all, it was the seat of the papacy, which was accepted throughout western Europe as the principal religious authority. During the early Renaissance, the actual residence of the **popes** was not at Rome but at **Avignon** on the southeastern border of France (1309–1377). Even then, however, the basis of papal authority was "Roman," and the overwhelmingly French papal curia of that period still referred to itself as the "Roman" curia, a practice that Petrarch treated with ironic bitterness. During the **Western Schism** (1378–1417), when there were two or even three rival popes, one of these lines established itself in control of Rome while the other returned to Avignon. After the election of a universally accepted pope, **Martin V**, in 1417, papal control of Rome remained tenuous at best. His successor, Pope **Eugenius IV**, was driven from Rome by an uprising among the nobility and spent nine years (1434–1443) in exile, most of them in Florence. Only under the next pope, **Nicholas V** (1447–1455), did the papacy re-establish itself securely in Rome.

Nicholas V is important in the history of papal Rome because he had the ambition of redeveloping Rome as the central city of the whole Christian world, both politically and culturally. His ambitious plans to rebuild the city into a grand and flourishing metropolis remained little more than dreams until the early 16th century, when Popes **Julius II** and **Leo X** made papal Rome Italy's principal center for the patronage of Renaissance art and humanistic scholarship. This ambition was compromised and deflected in more conservative directions by the outbreak of the **Reformation** and the disastrous Sack of Rome in 1527 by the army of the Emperor **Charles V**, but it was not ended. Already under Pope Paul III (1534–1549), later popes resumed the effort to develop the city into a suitable capital for Catholic Christendom, using the arts as an integral part of their goal of reasserting the power and magnificence of Rome. Examples of this continuing effort include the completion of the basilica of St. Peter under Paul V (pope, 1605–1621), the addition of Gianlorenzo Bernini's *baldachino* to the high altar of St. Peter's under Urban VIII (pope, 1623–1644), and the addition of the great colonnade that frames the approach to the basilica (designed in 1656–1657 under Pope Alexander VII).

In the history of Renaissance Rome, the most spectacular single incident is the infamous Sack of Rome, the conquest and unrestrained looting of the papal capital on and after 6 May 1527 by the army of the most powerful Catholic ruler in Europe, the Emperor Charles V. Although wars between popes and Catholic rulers had been common since the 11th century, the violence of this incident shocked contemporaries, many of whom (including many orthodox Catholics) regarded it as a judgment of God on the corruption and worldliness of the church. It has often been taken as the terminal date of "the Renaissance," a judgment that is debatable even with regard to Italy and certainly is invalid for the rest of Europe. But the incident did break up the galaxy of artistic and literary stars who for the preceding two or three decades had made Rome the center of Renaissance culture. Several leading Roman humanists were killed in the violence and others left the city and returned only much later or never. Major artists, including **Jacopo Sansovino** and **Parmigianino**, left to seek their fortunes elsewhere. There was eventually a partial recovery, but Rome never again became the predominant center of Renaissance culture, and the mood of gloom and insecurity caused by the plunder never entirely disappeared, perhaps because the incident proved that like the other Italian states, the papacy could not maintain its political autonomy in the face of the struggle between France and Spain for control of Italy.

RONSARD, PIERRE DE (1524–1585). French poet, the leading figure of the group of poets that called itself *la Pléiade*. Born into a noble family and trained as an aristocratic page in the service of two children of King **Francis I**, Ronsard was educated in Latin and **Greek** by tutors. In the early 1540s he began writing poetry in both Latin and French, and after the death of the duke of Orléans in 1545, he lived in the home of the **humanist Lazare de Baïf**, where he continued his study of Greek and Latin under the scholar and poet Jean Dorat. He also studied under Dorat at the University of Paris (1547–1549). In the late 1540s and the 1550s the group of young poets, all educated in humanism and all attracted by Italian poetry, came together in an effort to create a French poetic style inspired by the **classics** and the Italian poets and distinct from medieval French poetry.

Ronsard published his first collection of poems in the new style, *Les quatres livres des odes / Four Books of Odes*, in 1550. Although the ode, a genre with classical origins, remained one of his favorite forms, he also adopted the Italian sonnet. His collection *Les amours* (1552) was modeled on the *Canzoniere* of **Petrarch**. Ronsard's love poems were so laden with mythological references that another member of the poetic group published a commentary to explain them. He published a second collection of *Amours* in 1555. Two later collections of lyrics, mostly sonnets, appeared in Ronsard's collected works in 1578, *Sonnets et madrigals pour Astrée* and *Sonnets pour Hélène*. The poet also aspired to write a national epic in the new style and in 1572 published the first four books of *La Franciade*, a work he never completed. He also functioned as a court poet. In this role he wrote poems defending the policies of Catherine de **Medici** toward the French Huguenots. His last poems (*Les derniers vers*) were composed on his deathbed in 1585.

RORE, CIPRIANO DE (1516–1565). Flemish composer, who like many of his nation spent much of his career in Italy as a composer of secular madrigals and sacred music. After study under **Adriaan Willaert** at **Venice**, where he was a singer at St. Mark's, he entered the service of Duke Ercole II of **Ferrara** about 1550. In 1561 he entered the service of Ottavio **Farnese**, duke of Parma. Rore spent 1563 as the successor to his teacher Willaert at Venice but returned to Parma in 1564. He is best known for his numerous madrigals, many of which are settings for poems by **Petrarch**. What made his madrigals most impressive was his sensitivity to the poetic rhetoric of the texts he was using.

ROSSELLINO, BERNARDO (1409–1464). Tuscan sculptor and architect, active mainly in **Florence**, Siena, and other Tuscan cities but also able to attract commissions from **popes Nicholas V** and **Pius II**. His most famous work as a sculptor is the tomb he executed for the Florentine chancellor **Leonardo Bruni** in 1444. He achieved even greater fame as an architect. He worked for both Nicholas V and Pius II at **Rome**, but his most famous commission was the remodeling of the entire city of **Pienza** for Pope Pius, who wanted to transform his native town into a model city rebuilt in a **classical** style.

ROSSO FIORENTINO (Giovanni Battista di Jacopo Rosso, 1494–1540). Florentine painter, later active in France. From the early 1520s he was one of the young artists whose work marks the transition from the balanced, harmonious style known as High Renaissance to the "mannered" style that emerged at **Florence** about 1520 and is known as **mannerism**. Trained in the Renaissance style by Andrea del Sarto (1486–1530) at Florence, by 1521 he had produced his *Descent from the Cross*, a treatment of a sacred theme that violates all conventions of the genre and defiantly rejects the stylistic tradition in which the painter himself had been trained. The exaggerated emotions of the figures, the use of color, the strange expression and posture of the dead Christ and other human figures are extreme examples of the deliberate exaggeration, the studied disharmonies, and the emotionalism and violence that define the mannerist style. In 1524 Rosso went to **Rome** but left after the disastrous Sack of Rome in 1527. After a brief stay in **Venice**, he accepted an invitation from the king of France, **Francis I**, to work in France, where his principal work was in the king's chateau at Fontainebleau. Other paintings that show his radical new style are *Moses Defending the Daughters of Jethro* (1523) and *Dead Christ* (1526).

RUBENS, PETER PAUL (1577–1640). Flemish painter. He worked in the **baroque** style and became the most internationally famous artist of northern Europe, admired for the lush colors, energetic spirit, and sensual, fleshly human figures typical of his works. His father, a prominent Protestant, fled Antwerp to escape Spanish persecution. After his death the family returned to Antwerp, and Peter Paul grew up a pious Catholic and loyal subject of the Spanish king. Trained by several leading Antwerp painters, he also received a good **humanistic** education and always reflected the tradition of Renaissance **classicism** in his works, a tendency strengthened by eight years in Italy that began in 1600 at **Venice** and **Mantua**, took him to **Rome** in 1601, and gave him a chance to study the works of the major Renaissance painters. In Italy he became successful both as a painter and as a courtier, receiving valuable commissions for paintings in churches at Rome and also serving as a member of a Mantuan embassy to **Naples**.

In 1608 Rubens hurried back to Flanders because of his mother's fatal illness, intending to return promptly to Italy, but he received a commission to paint an *Adoration of the Magi* in 1609. The Spanish regents of the Netherlands then appointed him court painter, granted him valuable exemptions from taxes and other privileges, and helped him secure commissions that established him as the leading artist of the Spanish Netherlands, including two triptychs executed for churches in Antwerp, *The Raising of the Cross* (1609–1611) and *The Descent from the Cross* (1611). Rubens set up a large and productive workshop and produced much-admired paintings with both religious and secular themes, culminating in a vast commission to provide 39 ceiling paintings for the new **Jesuit** church at Antwerp, a task completed (with the aid of many assistants) in the single year 1620. In 1621 he began serving as a secret diplomatic representative of the Archduchess **Isabella**, using his fame as an artist and collector of **antiquities** as a cover for political negotiations in the Dutch Republic, England, France, and Spain.

At Paris in 1622 the queen-mother of France, Marie des Médicis, commissioned a series of works for the Luxembourg Palace commemorating her career as queen and regent of France, including allegorical scenes like *Henry IV Receiving the Portrait of Marie des Médicis* and *Marie des Médicis, Queen of France, Landing in Marseilles*. The lavish colors and classicizing tendencies of Rubens' mature baroque style are also evident in the sensuous *Garden of Love* (ca. 1630–1632). In the late 1630s he designed and co-ordinated the workshop production of a series of mythological sketches for a hunting lodge built near Madrid by Philip IV of Spain. Not long before his death he produced a striking self-portrait depicting himself as an aging but poised and elegantly dressed knight. His influence is visible in the work of successors not only in the Netherlands but also in Italy, Spain, and France.

RUCELLAI. Family of wealthy **Florentine** patricians prominent in the cloth trade, politics, and cultural life during the 15th and early 16th centuries. Giovanni di Paolo (1403–1481) built the noted family palace and the new façade of the church of Santa Maria Novella, both designed by **Leon Battista Alberti**. Giovanni's family ties to the exiled Strozzi family left him out of favor with the dominant **Medici** family. His son, Bernardo di Giovanni (1448–1514), however, married into the Medici family and became a political adviser to Lorenzo de'Medici. He was a philosophical disciple of **Marsilio Ficino** and the author of several works written in Latin, including a history of the French invasion of Italy in 1494 and an antiquarian study of the city of **Rome**.

After Lorenzo's death in 1492, Bernardo turned against Lorenzo's son and successor Piero de'Medici, who was expelled by a popular uprising in 1494. The new republican regime, however, was far too subject to influence from the lower classes to suit Bernardo. He withdrew from politics in 1502 and voluntarily left the city in 1506. He laid out the elegant family gardens in the city, the Orti Oricellari, which became famous both for their many exotic plants and for the intellectual discussions among Florentine politicians and scholars that began in his time and continued under the patronage of his son Cosimo Rucellai (1495–1519). The discussions in the garden often dealt with political questions and have attracted the attention of modern scholars, especially because one of the participants was **Niccolò Machiavelli**.

RUDOLF II (1552–1615). **Habsburg** king of Hungary and Bohemia; Holy Roman emperor from 1576. He is remembered mainly for his cultural patronage after he transferred the seat of imperial rule from Vienna to Prague in 1583. The court painters whom he supported were late representatives of the artistic style known as **mannerism**, and he patronized other mannerist artists who did not settle at his court, of whom the most prominent was **Giovanni da Bologna**. Rudolf also collected the works of earlier artists, especially **Albrecht Dürer** and **Pieter Brueghel the Elder**. He was a collector not only of paintings but also of weapons, clocks, scientific instruments, rare animals and plants, and other curiosities. His intellectual interests included Renaissance **occultism**, and his patronage attracted such notorious figures as **John Dee** and **Giordano Bruno**. As a political leader, although he opposed Protestantism in general, he sought vainly to bring about a lowering of religious tension in Germany, in opposition to the aggressively anti-Protestant policies of his Habsburg cousins in Spain and the German lands. In his final years, which were marked by mental instability and by a long and unsuccessful war with the **Ottoman Turks**, the rest of the Habsburg family forced him to yield the crown of Hungary to his ambitious younger brother, Matthias, who had been his political and personal rival and who eventually succeeded him as emperor and king of Bohemia. Rudolf never married and so left no heir eligible to claim his thrones.

– S –

SÀ DE MIRANDA, FRANCISCO DE (1480/90 to 1558). Portuguese poet and dramatist. The son of a canon of Coimbra, he grew up in the royal court at Lisbon and received a doctorate in law. Some of his early poems were published in 1516. He spent six years (1520–1526) in Italy and probably wrote two comedies, *Os estrangeiros / The Foreigners* and *Os Vilhalpandos / The Vilhalpando Family*, while abroad, though they were not produced until after his return home. He married and sometime before 1530 settled as a country gentleman in northern Portugal, where he wrote most of his later works. He introduced italianate literary forms such as sonnets, eclogues, and elegies into Portuguese literature, yet he also continued to write in traditional Portuguese verse forms.

SACHS, HANS (1494–1576). Nuremberg shoemaker, poet, and playwright, who devoted much of his literary output to making propaganda for the Lutheran **Reformation**. Born the son of a tailor, he attended Latin school for eight years and at age 15 was apprenticed to a shoemaker. He travelled through much of Germany during his five years (1511–1516) as a journeyman, then returned home, married, and became a master of his trade in 1520. Aside from occasional attendance at trade fairs at Frankfurt-am-Main, he spent the rest of his life in Nuremberg.

From the early 1520s, Sachs became an outspoken supporter of **Martin Luther**, and his most famous poem, the lengthy allegory *Die Wittenbergisch Nachtigall / The Wittenberg Nightingale* (1523), attacks the corruption of the church and provides versified explanations of Luther's doctrines. It was reprinted many times and made its author famous. His four prose dialogues on Reformation themes, such as *Disputation Between a Canon and a Shoemaker* (1524), were part of the campaign to convert Nuremberg itself to the Lutheran cause.

For many years, Sachs was the leader of the **guild** of Meistersinger in the city, a group of artisans who presented public solo performances of their own musical compositions. His 4,000 songs, many of which are still unpublished, drew on biblical, **classical**, and medieval themes. Better known as literary works today, however, are his 80 carnival plays (*Fastnachtspiele*), short plays which present incidents and characters from daily life. His other dramas, some 130 tragedies and comedies, attract little attention from German readers today. In the late 18th century, the German author Goethe revived interest in Sachs and other Meistersinger from Nuremberg and other south German cities, and a century later, the composer Richard Wagner presented a highly romanticized picture of Sachs and his peers in the opera *Die Meistersinger*.

SACK OF ROME. *See* ROME.

SACROSANCTA. *See* CONSTANCE, COUNCIL OF.

SALUTATI, COLUCCIO (1331–1406). Italian **humanist**, notary, and chancellor of the republic of **Florence**; in the latter role, he became one of the most influential figures in the diplomacy of his time. Born near Florence, he received his education in **Bologna**, where his exiled father served the local ruler. He studied the notarial art (1348–1350) and worked as a private notary and then as secretary of several city governments until 1374, when he received an administrative job in Florence that led the following year to his appointment to the powerful position of chancellor. He held this position for the rest of his life. His success as the administrator of Florentine foreign policy in a dangerous period and as an effective propagandist for the republic's opposition to the political intrigues of the **papacy** and the aggressive military expansion of **Giangaleazzo Visconti**, duke of **Milan**, made him famous throughout Italy.

More than a decade before moving to Florence, Salutati's interest in ancient literature and history brought him into contact with the Florentine admirers of the humanist **Petrarch**. He developed a widely admired style of **classicized** Latin, though he used it only in his private correspondence and literary publications, retaining the traditional notarial Latin of the late **Middle Ages** for his official papers. His letters of propaganda in favor of Florentine foreign policy contained many references to events in ancient and medieval history that cast Florentine republicanism in a favorable light and Milanese despotism in an unfavorable light.

As the holder of an influential public office, Salutati gathered a group of younger humanists around his person (including leading figures of the next generation such as **Leonardo Bruni, Poggio Bracciolini, Pier Paolo Vergerio**, and **Antonio Loschi**), encouraged their studies, promoted their careers, and maintained contact after they left Florence to pursue careers elsewhere. His diplomatic correspondence and access to courier service enabled him to create a network of educated men in many parts of Italy who shared his interest in ancient language and literature. Although Salutati never had leisure to gain an effective mastery of **Greek**, he realized that ancient Latin literature could not be understood thoroughly unless humanists also knew Greek language and literature, and in 1397 he was instrumental in bringing the Byzantine scholar **Manuel Chrysoloras** to Florence as a teacher of Greek, a move that was the real beginning of Greek studies in Renaissance Italy.

Like Petrarch but unlike his young humanist disciples, Salutati was deeply concerned about religious questions such as the relation between predestination and free will. His major book *De laboribus Herculis / The Labors of Hercules* (written in two parts, 1382 and 1381–1391) interpreted the myths about the ancient demigod as symbols of Christian truths. Later in life, Salutati's Christian outlook led him to express reservations about excessive devotion to pagan literature, producing some tension between him and secular-minded disciples such as Leonardo Bruni. He also revered the great Florentine vernacular authors of the 14th century, especially **Dante** and **Petrarch**, with a respect that was not fully shared by his more narrowly classicist followers.

Although Salutati vigorously defended the excellence of Florence's republican constitution and insisted that Florence itself had been founded under the **Roman** republic and not by Julius Caesar, the first emperor, he was also more respectful than followers like Bruni toward the medieval Holy Roman Empire and the leading role of the papacy in Italian political life. His political leadership, his own classical studies and Latin prose style, and his many efforts to arouse sympathy for humanistic studies throughout Italy enhanced the role of Florence itself in the emergent humanistic culture, and he was the individual most responsible for the city's rise to be the intellectual center of Italian Renaissance humanism.

SANNAZARO, JACOPO (1458–1530). Neapolitan **humanist** and poet. During his youth at **Naples**, he was a member of a circle of local humanists led by **Giovanni Pontano**. During the 1480s and 1490s he developed a reputation as a poet in both Italian and Latin. When his patron, King Frederick of Aragon, was dethroned and exiled to France, he shared the exile until the king's death in 1504 and then returned home to his rural villa, where he spent the rest of his life, busy writing but removed from court life and politics. In Latin he wrote Virgilian-style *Piscatorial Eclogues* and a Christian epic on the birth of Christ, *De partu Virginis* (1526). His most important poetry, however, was his vernacular pastoral poetry, especially the lengthy *Arcadia* (1502 and 1504). This work, with its many allusions to **classical** poets and modern ones like **Dante** and **Petrarch**, describes an imaginary society of cultivated shepherd-poets and provides an allegorical account of his own romantic quest for the woman he loved. Arcadian pastoral poetry had great influence on later Renaissance literature, not only in Italy but also in England, in the work of Sir **Philip Sidney**; in Spain, in the romances of **Jorge de Montemayor** and **Miguel de Cervantes Saavedra**; and in France, in the pastoral poetry of **Honore d'Urfé**.

SANSOVINO, JACOPO (1486–1570). **Florentine** architect and sculptor, born Jacopo Tatti. He was a pupil of Andrea Sansovino, whose surname he took when he followed his master to **Rome** in 1505. His early career was in Rome, but after the Sack of Rome by the imperial army in 1527 he settled in **Venice**, where he did his most important work. His most famous architectural work was the Biblioteca Marciana in Venice, which was begun in 1536 and completed a decade after Sansovino's death; it was praised by **Andrea Palladio** and subsequent critics because of its historically correct usage of the **classical** architectural orders.

SANTILLANA, IÑIGO LÓPEZ DE, MARQUIS OF (1398–1458). Castilian aristocrat, poet, and book-collector, often regarded as the crucial figure in introducing Renaissance learning into Spain, though he himself had only a limited command of Latin. His own poetry was written in Castilian, though it did employ **classical** rhetorical devices and cite classical authors, most of whom the author probably read in Italian or Castilian translations. He was also a noted collector of manuscripts, especially translations of the classics.

SARPI, PAOLO (1551–1623). Venetian monk and author, known primarily for his historical works, including a sharply critical *History of the Council of Trent* (1619), and for his theological and political services to the republic of **Venice**. Although he rose to high office within the Servite order and resided at the court of Pope Sixtus V at Rome (1585–1588), he became increasingly critical of the papacy as an institution, an opinion reflected in his history of the council, which portrays the **popes** of the 16th century as ruthless manipulators of the council, determined to undermine the authority of councils and to establish their own undisputed primacy within the church. A similar cynical interpretation of papal policy is evident in his other historical works, such as his *Treatise on Benefices* (not published until 1675), which contrasts the voluntary poverty and devotion of the early church with the wealth and power of the contemporary institution, and his *History of the Interdict* (1625), a strongly pro-Venetian account of the conflict between the papacy and Venice in 1606–1607.

During the latter crisis, Sarpi became a theological adviser to the republic despite a papal sentence of excommunication. His defense of the right of secular governments to control the clergy and their properties influenced 17th-century theorists of absolute monarchy. As adviser to the Venetian government, Sarpi established political and ideological connections with foreign Protestant officials and private individuals in Germany, France, the Netherlands, and England who shared the city's hostility to the political ambitions of **Habsburg** Spain and the papacy. His writings on philosophical and religious theory, never published in his time but now partially collected under the title of *Pensieri / Thoughts*, suggest that late in life he held a materialist and determinist view of the world and doubted an afterlife and divine providence, though he recognized the social utility of religion as a device to control the uneducated.

SAVILE, HENRY (1549–1622). English historian and textual scholar. Educated at Oxford, he became warden of Merton College in 1585 and provost of Eton in 1596. His principal scholarly works were a collection of early English chronicles, *Rerum Anglicarum scriptores* (1581) and the first complete edition of the **Greek** text of the works of St. John Chrysostom (1610–1612). He was also one of the scholars involved in preparation of the Authorized (King James) version of the Bible. In 1619 he endowed the Savilean professorships of astronomy and geometry at Oxford.

SAVONAROLA, GIROLAMO (1452–1498). Dominican friar, a native of **Ferrara** but best known as the spellbinding preacher who after the expulsion of the **Medici** from **Florence** in 1494 dominated the city's political life in order to impose political, religious, and moral reform. He entered the Dominican order at **Bologna** in 1475 after an education that included **humanistic** studies and the study of medicine. He studied theology until 1482, when he began his preaching career at the Florentine convent of San Marco, at first with little success. Recalled to Bologna in 1487 to direct the education of the order's novices, he matured into a compelling preacher. From about 1485, his sermons began warning of impending doom because of God's wrath over the worldliness of the church and the sins of the people.

In 1490 Lorenzo de'Medici requested the order to send Savonarola back to Florence. His preaching became more and more sensational and ominous, and his enthusiastic hearers included many of the leading Medicean intellectuals, including **Marsilio Ficino, Giovanni Pico della Mirandola, Angelo Poliziano**, and the artists **Sandro Botticelli** and **Michelangelo**. Although he remained close to the Medici and attended Lorenzo on his deathbed in 1492, his sermons denounced tyranny and social injustice, and increasingly they claimed direct divine inspiration. Elected prior of the friary of San Marco, Savonarola imposed strict observance of the Dominican rule. Recruits flocked into the monastery. His dire prophecies became more specific, warning of an avenging leader who would conquer Italy.

The French invasion of Italy in 1494 seemed to be the fulfillment of his prophecies, and after the expulsion of Piero de'Medici and the Medicean political faction, Savonarola's sermons demanded reforms far more radical than those proposed by the patricians who had succeeded the Medici in power. Florence was destined to be the New Jerusalem that would lead the world through the age of Antichrist and into an age of Christian perfection and peace. He appealed directly to the people for support against reluctant politicians, staging mass demonstrations at which "vanities," including lewd books and pictures, immodest clothing and cosmetics of women, playing cards, and dice were publicly burned.

The foreign policy that Savonarola supported was contrary to the interests of Pope **Alexander VI**, who in 1497 excommunicated him and all who supported him or heard him preach. The **pope** also imposed economic penalties that harmed the city's trade, thus encouraging Savonarola's Florentine opponents, who had never ceased denouncing him as a false prophet and a threat to social order. His decision to execute several patricians who had conspired to restore the Medici to power harmed his popularity, since the accused were executed without any right of appeal. Savonarola's fall from power, brought about by collaboration between the pope and the local opposition, was rapid. An attempt by one of the Dominicans in April 1498 to demonstrate Savonarola's divine inspiration by undergoing ordeal by fire was a fiasco that undermined popular support. The city's armed guard arrested Savonarola and two other friars. Under torture, the friars confessed that Savonarola's prophecies were false. When Savonarola then attempted to recant his own confession, he and his two fellow friars were convicted of heresy and on 23 May 1498 hanged and burned.

The execution left power in the hands of patrician families who pursued a far more cautious program of anti-Medicean political reform. After a brief period of persecution, Savonarola's populist supporters, the *Piagnoni*, hailed him as a martyred saint. Despite his execution as a heretic, his sermons and other writings were repeatedly published in Italian and translated into other languages. The reputation of Savonarola as an inspired prophet remained strong among the poor of Florence and many other Italian communities for several decades, and during the last desperate uprising of the Florentines against Medici rule in 1527–1530, *Piagnone* preachers participated actively, proclaiming Christ king of the city and once again demanding the moral purification of society.

SCALA, BARTOLOMEO (1430–1497) and ALESSANDRA (ca. 1475–1506). Italian **humanists**, father and daughter. Bartolomeo served as chancellor of the Florentine republic from 1465 until his death. Born the son of a poor miller in the small Tuscan town of Colle, he moved to **Florence** to study at the local **university**. In 1454 he moved to **Milan** to study under **Francesco Filelfo**. He returned to Florence about a year later. Although qualified to practice law, by 1457 he had become private secretary in the service of Pierfrancesco de'Medici, an appointment that for the first time brought him into the circle of the politically powerful **Medici** family. This connection led to his appointment as chancellor in 1465. Scala's authority was greatest during the hegemony of Lorenzo de'Medici over Florence (1469–1492), for he was a useful agent of Lorenzo's active foreign policy. He had much less influence on Lorenzo's son Piero de'Medici. After the fall of the Medici from power in 1494, he was dismissed for three days by the anti-Medicean regime and then restored to office, though his salary was cut and his role in government reduced. Despite his administrative duties, Scala wrote several books, of which the most important was his *History of Florence*. Other works included *De consolatione / Consolation*, written in response to the death of Giovanni de'Medici (1463); *Apologi centum / A Hundred Apologues* (1481), and *De legibus et iudiciis / On Laws and Legal Judgments* (1483), which he dedicated to Lorenzo.

His daughter Alessandra Scala received a humanistic education from her father but also studied with Johannes Lascaris and **Angelo**

Poliziano. The latter admired her ability despite his personal dislike for her father. Her eloquent performance in a presentation of Sophocles' *Electra* in **Greek** drew praise from contemporaries, and she corresponded with the Venetian female humanist **Cassandra Fedele**. Alessandra married the Greek scholar and soldier Michele Marullo but after his death in military service in 1500 spent the rest of her brief life in a convent.

SCALIGER, JOSEPHUS JUSTUS (1540–1609). French literary and linguistic scholar. The son of an expatriate Italian **humanist, Julius Caesar Scaliger**, he seems to have believed his father's false claim of descent from the della **Scala** dynasty that had ruled **Verona**. He studied at Paris under some of the most famous French scholars of his time, **Adrien Turnèbe** and Denys Lambin, both of whom became royal readers in **Greek**, and the legal scholar Jacques Cujas. In 1562 he became a Calvinist, and in 1593 he accepted an appointment to the faculty of the **University** of Leiden, where he spent the rest of his life. Scaliger's early work as a textual scholar focused on Latin poets such as Catullus, Tibullus, and Propertius, and especially the astronomical poet Manilius. His edition of the surviving fragments of the lexicographer Festus (1575) introduced him to the study of archaic Latin.

Perhaps because his Protestant faith made him less inclined to spare the works of Christian saints from critical inspection, he proved beyond a doubt (though it was doubted by conservatives) that the treatises of the Christian author known as Dionysius the Areopagite could not possibly be the work of a first-century Athenian philosopher converted to Christianity by St. Paul himself, as the medieval church believed, but was an author of the sixth century. Thus he transformed pseudo-Dionysius from a major witness to the beliefs and practices of the apostolic age into a minor and late patristic author whose authority on issues of theology and hierarchical organization deserved little weight. Scaliger also did important work on historical chronology that involved reconciling the various dating systems of ancient societies so that the chronological relationships between those societies could be established accurately.

SCALIGER, JULIUS CAESAR (1484–1558). Italian **humanist**, father of **Josephus Justus Scaliger**. Born Giulio Bordone, the son of a painter of miniatures who settled in **Venice**, he claimed to be descended from the della **Scala** family that had formerly ruled **Verona**. For a time he was a Franciscan friar, then worked for the Venetian printer **Aldus Manutius**, served for a time as a soldier, and studied medicine at **Padua**. By about 1525 he was practicing medicine. In 1524 Scaliger moved to southwestern France and entered the service of Antonio della Rovere, bishop of Agen. There he married and became successful both as a physician and as a **classical** scholar. He wrote several books on scientific and philosophical subjects. He engaged in polemics against the leading northern humanist, **Erasmus**, criticizing the Dutch humanist's attack on **Ciceronian** Latin even though Scaliger himself did not write in a strictly Ciceronian style. He also published attacks on **Girolamo Cardano** and **François Rabelais**. His criticisms of Cardano and his works on botany and zoology reveal him to be a philosophical follower of **Aristotle**, and he wrote an influential *Poetics* (1561) that expounds a strongly Aristotelian theory of literature.

SCÈVE, MAURICE (ca. 1501–ca. 1564). French poet, a member of the group known as *La Pléiade*, especially important for bringing **Neoplatonic** influence into French poetry. He was born into a prosperous family of Lyon and received an excellent **humanistic** education. His mistaken belief that he had discovered the tomb of **Petrarch's** Laura appears in his **emblem** book *Délie* (1544), a series of love poems in the italianate sonnet form. Other important works were *La saulsaye / The Willow-Grove* (1547), a pastoral poem, and *Microcosme* (1562), a philosophical poem.

SCHISM, WESTERN (1378–1417). Also known as "the Great Schism." Division within the Roman Catholic Church caused by disagreement over which of two (and for a time, three) claimants to the position of **pope** had been lawfully elected. It originated in the aftermath of the election of Pope **Urban VI** (1378–1389) as successor to Pope Gregory XI, who the preceding year (1377) had finally succeeded in re-establishing **Rome** as the seat of the papal administration and had brought the predominantly French college of cardinals back from **Avignon** to Rome, thus ending the so-called **Babylonian Captivity** of the papacy. The election of Urban VI was tumultuous, with large crowds of Roman citizens gathered outside the electoral conclave, threatening the lives of the cardinals if they did not elect an Italian rather than another French pope. Although all but one of the cardinals acquiesced in the election of Urban (who was an Italian, the former archbishop of Bari), many of them claimed that the fear of mob violence had forced them to make the election and that therefore the whole process was illegal.

When the new pope proved disrespectful of the traditional privileges of the cardinals and showed signs of erratic behavior, the French cardinals left Rome, reassembled beyond the pope's reach, formally declared the earlier election invalid, and then elected one of their own group, **Clement VII** (1378–1394), as pope. Since Pope Urban held firm control of Rome, Clement VII and the majority of the cardinals returned to Avignon. Thus there were two rival claimants, one at Rome and one at Avignon. Since each claimant excommunicated his rival and all of his rival's supporters and then filled up his college of cardinals with new appointees, the division was institutionalized. When either claimant died, his cardinals elected a successor. Thus the division was not limited to the lifetime of the first two claimants: there were not only two popes but also two colleges of cardinals and two papal administrative systems. The rival popes sought support of rulers and prelates in all parts of Catholic Europe, so that the various nations divided into pro-Roman and pro-Avignonese groups. Since each side excommunicated the other, half of Europe seemed doomed to eternal damnation for supporting a false pope, and no one was quite sure which half it was.

This spiritual crisis produced many attempts to resolve the schism, either by negotiation between the two rival popes or by mediation of secular rulers, but all efforts based on compromise or mediation proved unsuccessful. Eventually, appealing to the practice of the early church, many university theologians and canon lawyers adopted the theory of **Conciliarism**, insisting that a church council, not the pope, was the ultimate authority in the church. The first attempt to put this theory into practice, made by groups of cardinals from both Rome and Avignon, was the **Council of Pisa** that assembled in 1409, declared both claimants deposed in the interests of unity, and then elected a new pope. This action added a third claimant rather than solving the problem.

Eventually, the Holy Roman Emperor Sigismund gained the backing of most European rulers and summoned a new council, the **Council of Constance**, which convened in southern Germany in 1414, dominated by Conciliarist theorists who optimistically hoped that the new council not only would bring an end to the Schism but also would enact far-ranging reform legislation. Meaningful reform proved difficult to enact, but in 1417, after deposing one of the three popes, persuading a second to abdicate, and forcing the third to flee to Castile, the council elected a new pope, **Martin V**, who was universally recognized. The Schism was at an end. The experience left papal authority weakened and for a generation continued to inspire demands for reform and insistence that the Conciliarist decrees enacted at Constance, *Haec Sancta* and ***Frequens***, were a permanent part of the church's laws and required that councils must be summoned at frequent intervals.

SCHOLASTICISM. Term used as a generic label for the various forms of philosophy and theology developed in western European **universities** from the late 11th or early 12th century. All of these "scholastic" systems of thought were broadly **Aristotelian**. They accepted Aristotelian logic and Aristotelian terminology as standard practice in debating intellectual questions. Aside from their broad agreement on the status of Aristotle as a methodological guide, however, these schools did not share a common set of doctrines on broad philosophical and theological issues. From almost the beginning, there were many "scholasticisms." The term really meant little more than "the philosophy taught in the schools"—that is, in the universities. The founders of scholasticism, such as the theologian Peter Lombard (ca. 1100–1160) and the philosopher Pierre Abélard (1079–1142), accepted Aristotelian logic as their guide to rational discourse, but they knew only a limited number of Aristotelian works at first hand.

In the early years of the 13th century, however, as almost the whole corpus of the Aristotelian writings known today was translated into Latin (mostly from Arabic rather than directly from **Greek**), Aristotle became an overwhelming presence not just in logic but also in virtually every philosophical subject, including natural science and even Christian theology. On many disputed questions, philosophers and theologians soon found that they did not agree on just what his writings meant. The 13th century, when Aristotle's works were newly discovered, was the golden age of scholastic philosophy and theology, distinguished by the careers of such figures as Albertus Magnus (1206–1280) and Thomas Aquinas (1224/5–1274). The great task was to assimilate the new Aristotelian learning and to define its relationship to philosophical and theological doctrines such as God's creation of the world out of nothing and the immortality of the human soul. On both these and other doctrines, Christian thinkers had to contend with a radically secular way of interpreting Aristotle associated with the Arabic commentator and philosopher Ibn Rushd (in Latin, Averroës, 1126–1198), whose understanding of Aristotle denied the philosophical validity of belief in both the creation of the world and the immortality of the individual soul.

Even in its greatest century, scholasticism was divided into contending schools, sometimes defined by the authority of a leading figure (for example, Thomism, based on the thought of Thomas Aquinas) and sometimes defined by the tradition of a particular university or by the prevailing opinion within a religious order (Aquinas among the Dominicans and Bonaventura [1221–1274] among the Franciscans). These divisions continued to multiply in the following generations, so that scholastic philosophy came to be divided into a great number of contending schools or traditions, a point used against it by its critics among the **humanists** of the Renaissance but admitted by leading scholastic thinkers as well. From the greatest figure of late 13th-century scholasticism, John Duns Scotus (ca. 1270–1308), stemmed an influential tradition known as Scotism, which criticized Aquinas as excessively rationalistic and became dominant at many universities. It was still influential in the 16th century. Another powerful school of thought was known as Nominalism, which had its roots in philosophical and theological controversies of the earlier **Middle Ages** but in its late medieval formulations looked upon the English Franciscan William of Ockham (ca. 1285–1347) as its founding authority.

Though potentially radical in its implications for theology, Nominalism produced few challenges to Catholic orthodoxy. It was, however, critical of the older forms of scholasticism associated with Albertus Magnus, Aquinas, and Duns Scotus. Followers of these older schools of thought came to be known as the *via antiqua*, while several academic traditions that arose out of the criticism of the "realist" views of the older schools on the question of universal ideas came to be known as the *via moderna*, "the modern way." Especially in Germany and at Paris, there were sharp divisions between the *Antiqui* and the *Moderni*. Some German universities (Erfurt, for example) were fully committed to the *via moderna* during the 14th and 15th centuries, while others (such as Cologne and **Louvain**) became just as firmly committed to the *via antiqua*. At a few German universities, the faculty of arts was formally divided into two sections, one following the *via antiqua* and the other, the *via moderna*. In practice, the division often narrowed down to the choice of different sequences of textbooks for the study of arts subjects, especially dialectic.

Although some modern historians have argued that the *via antiqua* was more open to humanistic influences and others have viewed the *via moderna* as more receptive, there is no convincing evidence that the problems faced by humanists who wanted to reform the faculties of arts were significantly different because of the "way" that prevailed locally. In 15th-century Paris, the king for a time intervened to forbid use of "modern" textbooks and to give a monopoly to followers of the *via antiqua*, but this effort proved unworkable, and the *via moderna* not only survived but was probably the more influential tradition in the study of logic at Paris by the end of the 15th century. Although the humanists wanted to reform the arts faculties of universities in order to give more attention to their own favorite subjects, thus decreasing the time students were required to devote to dialectic and natural philosophy, most of them had no intention of abolishing all scholastic studies. They wanted better-written and less abstruse textbooks to be used and eventually succeeded in getting rid of old textbooks and substituting books more congenial to their ideas of good education. Yet they neither destroyed nor wanted to destroy scholasticism in general. Even the Protestant **Reformation** did not lastingly break the hold of scholasticism on the academic world. **Martin Luther** set out to drive scholasticism and all forms of Aristotelian philosophy out of his own university at Wittenberg, but the alternative set of textbooks and subjects put forward to replace Aristotle was not very successful. By the 1530s, under the leadership of Luther's close associate **Philipp Melanchthon**, both Aristotle and some parts of traditional scholasticism were gradually and quietly reintroduced in the Wittenberg faculty of liberal arts, though not in theology.

Scholasticism, somewhat reformed under the influence of humanism, remained dominant in all European universities until the late 17th century, when the rise of the new quantitative approach to natural science and the intellectual collapse of Aristotelian metaphysics and natural philosophy began the gradual demolition of scholasticism as the dominant intellectual tradition of European higher education. Even then, in conservative Roman Catholic countries like Spain, Portugal, and Italy, the revival of the Thomist tradition and its close alliance with post-Tridentine Catholic theology preserved a scholastic intellectual tradition that remained powerful into the 20th century. In general, scholasticism has come to be regarded as a significant philosophical tradition of the past which might still have valuable insights, more in some fields such as moral philosophy and metaphysics and less—much less—in others, such as natural science.

SCHONGAUER, MARTIN (born between 1435 and 1450; died 1491). Alsatian painter and engraver, trained by his father, a goldsmith of Colmar. He is one of the most important German painters of the late Gothic period. As an apprentice he may have traveled in Spain and the Netherlands, and the obvious influence of **Rogier van der Weyden** suggests that he spent time in Flanders. He spent most of his career in Colmar but moved in 1489 to Breisach, where he executed a series of frescoes, *The Last Judgment* (ca. 1489–1491). Other surviving paintings include his Orlier Altarpiece (ca. 1465–1470), *The Virgin of the Rose Garden* (ca. 1473), and *The Adoration of the Shepherds* (ca. 1480) as well as several smaller paintings, including two representing the Holy Family. He also left a number of pen and ink drawings. From the perspective of modern art historians, however, his most important work is his body of 116 copperplate engravings. These prints made him famous and influenced not only German artists like Hans Burgkmair and **Albrecht Dürer** but also **Michelangelo** and **Raphael**. The most famous of them was *The Temptation of St. Anthony.* Schongauer seems to have been the first German artist to sign his engravings, and he signed all 116 of them.

SCRIPT, HUMANISTIC. Letter-forms developed by **humanists** of the late 14th and early 15th centuries who disliked the elaborate and often nearly illegible handwriting that dominated not only informal writing but also official documents and the copying of books in the high and late medieval period. (These medieval letter-forms are now commonly called "gothic" or "blackletter.") The Florentine chancellor **Coluccio Salutati** experimented with simplified letter-forms that he found in some of his oldest manuscripts of ancient authors, but the person who transformed these beginnings into a dictinctively new type of writing was Salutati's young disciple **Poggio Bracciolini**. While still living in **Florence** before 1404, Poggio seems to have used a striking new script. This style was based on the handwriting found in the best and oldest manuscripts of **classical** authors available in Florence. Poggio and Salutati assumed that this clear, legible handwriting was the script used by the ancient Romans, hence they labelled it *antiqua littera* ("ancient letter") or "Roman letters," being totally unaware that the manuscripts they admired were written in what palaeographers now call Carolingian minuscule, a script developed by Frankish scribes of the ninth century. The new humanistic handwriting was probably also influenced by letter-forms found in ancient Roman inscriptions.

For many Italian humanists, it came to be the preferred script for copying books, especially classical Latin books, though traditional medieval forms of handwriting continued to dominate the writing of legal documents, business records, and vernacular books. While the earliest printers after 1450, being Germans, used "gothic" letters, eventually the new "roman" letters were widely used in Italy for the **printing** of classical literary texts. Gothic or blackletter typefaces remained in use for many purposes, and north of the Alps they remained dominant even longer, though the spread of Italian humanism led to the use of the "roman" typefaces (still called by that name in modern typography) by some printers and for some purposes, such as the printing of Latin.

Humanistic script also followed a second, closely related line of development. Since the "roman" letters were not cursive, they could not be written so rapidly as cursive scripts. A second Florentine associate of Salutati, the humanist **Niccolò Niccoli**, developed an alternative handwriting that was also modelled on the supposedly "ancient" (but actually Carolingian) manuscripts but was cursive, suited to more rapid, informal copying, with ligatures joining letters and a slanted, sloping apearance. This was the script that later came to be known as "**italic**." Its use for the printing of books is associated especially with the great Venetian printer **Aldus Manutius** at the end of the 15th century. Thus the Florentine humanists of the early 15th century originated the two major humanistic scripts on which most modern typefaces are based, roman and italic.

SFORZA. Dynasty that ruled the duchy of **Milan** between 1450 and its expulsion by a French army in 1499, and again for intermittent periods in the first third of the 16th century. Its founder, Francesco (1401–1466), was the son of a successful *condottiere*; Francesco succeeded his father and became one of the most successful professional generals of his century. The last duke of the old **Visconti** dynasty died without legitimate heirs in 1447, leaving only an illegitimate daughter, Bianca Maria. She had been married to her father's most successful general, Francesco Sforza. Bianca Maria claimed the ducal throne, but the citizens of Milan reacted to the death of the last male Visconti by declaring the ducal office abolished and their old republican constitution restored. Facing many military challenges by predatory neighboring states, the leaders of the new republic hired Francesco Sforza to defend them, and by 1450 Sforza, having beaten off invasions by foreign powers, seized control of Milan and established himself and his wife as duke and duchess. Unlike the last of the Visconti, he was an effective political as well as military leader, and his diplomatic skill led to a revolution in the traditional power alignment of the Italian states that enabled Milan and **Florence** to impose on the other Italian powers a general peace treaty, the Treaty of Lodi (1454), that stabilized the internal relations of the Italian peninsula for 40 years, ending a period of frequent wars among the Italian powers.

Francesco's political and military talent was not inherited by his son Galeazzo Maria Sforza, who abused his authority to seize the property and the women of prominent Milanese citizens and was murdered in 1468. Galeazzo Maria's young son, Giangaleazzo, held the title of duke from 1476 to 1494, but real power was in the hands of his uncle, Ludovico Sforza, nicknamed "il Moro." Ludovico reduced his nephew to a mere figurehead until the nephew's death in 1494. This de facto usurpation of power enraged the young duke's in-laws, the royal family of **Naples**, and also the **Medici** leader at Florence, Piero de'Medici, who had married a Neapolitan princess. Ludovico feared that he might be attacked by a coalition of hostile Italian powers led by Naples and Florence. He sought to escape this danger by encouraging the king of France, Charles VIII, to enforce a dynastic claim of his own to the throne of Naples. Although Ludovico probably desired nothing more than a diversionary threat of intervention, the actual result was the famous French invasion of Italy in 1494, which precipitated a series of wars that soon drew Spain into the fighting as a rival to the French for control of Italy. This struggle ended in 1559 with a settlement that left most of the peninsula directly or indirectly in the hands of the king of Spain.

For Ludovico, the French invasion and the resulting action of Spain and several Italian allies in expelling the French from Naples initially relieved the political and military insecurity he had feared. After his nephew's death in 1494 (poisoned by the uncle, according to popular rumor), he assumed the ducal title. But the death of Charles VIII in 1498 brought to the French throne King Louis XII, who as a direct descendant of a princess of the Visconti dynasty had a hereditary claim not only to Naples but also to Milan itself. Louis XII staged a second French invasion of Italy in 1498, this time beginning with the conquest of Milan and the dethronement of Ludovico Sforza. Louis claimed the throne of Milan for himself and held Ludovico as a prisoner in France for the rest of his life. In the chaotic years that followed, Ludovico's son Massimiliano and then his younger son Francesco II enjoyed brief periods of rule at Milan whenever the Spaniards held the upper hand over the French, but when Francesco II died in 1535, the Emperor **Charles V** (who was also king of Spain) claimed the duchy for himself, ending Sforza rule forever and establishing Spanish control of the duchy that lasted until 1706.

Under the immediate successors of the first Francesco Sforza, Galeazzo Maria and Ludovico il Moro, the Sforza court at Milan became an important center of the courtly variety of High Renaissance culture. The Sforza rulers made their court a major center of Renaissance music and art. The original architect of the new basilica of St. Peter at **Rome, Bramante,** began his career in the service of the Milanese dukes, designing the cathedral in the Lombard university town of Pavia and the churches of Sant'Ambrogio and Santa Maria della Grazie in Milan. In the period of Ludovico's domination, **Leonardo**

da Vinci painted his *Last Supper* in Santa Maria delle Grazie and also served the duchy as military engineer and architect.

SHAKESPEARE, WILLIAM (1564–1616). England's greatest dramatist. The son of a successful merchant and alderman of Stratford-on-Avon, he was educated in the excellent local school and learned enough Latin to become familiar with many **classical** authors, but he never attended a **university**. In 1582 at age 18 he contracted an imprudent and probably rather unhappy marriage necessitated by the bride's pregnancy. This early marriage, coinciding with a reversal of his father's fortunes, seems to have thrown William on his own resources. The years following it are virtually undocumented, but sometime before 1590 William (unaccompanied by his family, who remained in Stratford) had settled in London, active as a poet and also on the flourishing London stage. The first hard evidence for his literary career is an attack by another playwright, Robert Greene, charging that Shakespeare's success was due to plagiarism. Both in his earliest plays and those he wrote at the end of his career, Shakespeare worked with collaborators; some of these are known, others are a matter of speculation.

Thirty-seven surviving plays are attributed to Shakespeare, including comedies, tragedies, history plays, and romances. In addition, during a long closure of the London theaters by plague, he wrote two lengthy narrative poems, *Venus and Adonis* (1593) and *The Rape of Lucrece* (1594), both dedicated to the Earl of Southampton. He also produced a significant body of *Sonnets* (ca. 1593–1603; published in 1609). The peak of Shakespeare's achievement rests in the great tragedies *Hamlet* (ca. 1599–1601), *Othello* (ca. 1603–1604), *King Lear* (ca. 1605–1606), and *Macbeth* (ca. 1606–1607), but his comedies, such as *Twelfth Night* and *A Midsummer Night's Dream*, most of which appeared in the mid-1590s, are also major achievements. In his English history plays dealing with the political turmoil of Lancastrian England, he not only created the remarkable comic figure of Falstaff but also traced the political and personal maturation of the future King Henry V. These history plays constitute a new genre in the development of drama, unlike any classical model. Yet he also wrote several plays with classical themes, of which *Julius Caesar* is probably the most widely admired. Even one of his comedies, *The*

Comedy of Errors, an early work (ca. 1590), conforms closely to **neoclassical** standards; the influence of the Roman comedian Platus is obvious. Shakespeare's later plays are often classed as tragicomedies or romances and are rather somber in tone, especially the last of his major plays, *The Tempest* (ca. 1611). This play seems to be a work of farewell, and Shakespeare retired to Stratford after it, though he returned to the stage in 1613, writing *Henry VIII* and, with the collaboration of John Fletcher, *Two Noble Kinsmen*. After these productions, he abandoned the theater entirely, probably because of ill health.

Shakespeare prospered in the theater, becoming one of the owners of the successful theatrical company for which he wrote, acquiring a respectable home in Stratford for his family, and as early as 1598 attracting praise from other writers for his plays and sonnets. Several of his plays were published in his lifetime, some of them in quite defective form and evidently all without the dramatist's permission. In 1623 two of his former colleagues brought out a folio edition of his collected works, including most of those now known. In the centuries since his death, many critics have challenged Shakespeare's authorship of the plays and poems, which have been attributed by various critics and at various times to various individuals, including Edward de Vere, the earl of Oxford, **Francis Bacon**, and **Christopher Marlowe**—the last being a particularly impressive "true author" since he died before most of Shakespeare's major plays were written. Essentially, all these efforts, even when presented by skillfull and learned advocates, are rooted in an aristocratic snobbery that refuses to believe that a man of such humble origins could have become so great an author. By any reasonable standard of judgment, the question is easily resolved: Shakespeare wrote Shakespeare.

SIDNEY, MARY (1561–1621). English writer and literary patron, sister of **Philip Sidney**. She made the suggestion that led to her brother's writing the *Arcadia*, which he dedicated to her. Her marriage to Henry Herbert, earl of Pembroke, made her countess of Pembroke. After her brother's premature death, Mary used her patronage to encourage works in praise of him, of which the most important was **Edmund Spenser**'s *Astrophel*. She took charge of Philip's literary estate, preparing editions of his *Arcadia* in 1593 and 1598. In 1592 she published her own translations of works by French authors Philippe de Mornay and Robert Garnier; and in 1602 she allowed publication of her dialogue in praise of *Astrea* in a book by Francis Davison. Most of Mary Sidney's writings, however, circulated only in manuscript, including an English translation of at least a portion of **Petrarch**'s *Trionfi* and two of her own poems. She also continued her brother's work of translating the Psalms from the French Huguenot Psalter of **Clément Marot** and Théodore de Bèze.

SIDNEY, PHILIP (1554–1586). English poet and soldier, the eldest child of an aristocratic family, brother of Robert Sidney, earl of Leicester, and of the writer **Mary Sidney**. He was educated at Christ Church, Oxford, where he received an excellent **humanistic** education. After this study, he travelled on the Continent, and while in Paris he witnessed the infamous St. Bartholomew's Day massacre of French Protestants in 1572. Sidney also visited Italy, Germany, Bohemia, Poland, and the Netherlands. Queen **Elizabeth I** regarded him as such a valuable member of her court that she limited the length of his foreign sojourn. In 1578 he wrote a masque, *The Lady of May*, in which the queen herself played the leading role. His public letter (1579) to the queen urging her not to marry the duke of Alençon, one of her foreign suitors, angered her, and he may have been banished from court for a time. But in 1583 Sidney was knighted. He married a daughter of Sir Francis Walsingham, one of the most powerful political figures in England. In order to prevent him from joining an expedition to the New World planned by Sir Francis Drake, the queen appointed him governor of the city of Flushing in the Netherlands, which the English occupied militarily. Two years later he was killed in battle with Spanish troops. He was hailed as a hero and received an elaborate funeral in London.

Three of Sidney's writings had great influence. *The Defence of Poetry* (1585) defends the value of the poetic imagination and is strongly influenced by **Platonism**. This work presents the author's own survey of earlier English literature and urges English poets to create in their own language a literature equal to that of the ancient Greeks and Romans. His second major work is the pastoral romance *The Countess of Pembroke's Arcadia*, written about 1580 for his sister Mary and published posthumously in 1590. It was influenced by earlier Arcadian works by **Jacopo Sannazaro** and **Jorge de Montemayor**. Also posthumous was his collection of sonnets, *Astrophel and Stella* (written 1580–1584 but unpublished until a pirated edition appeared in 1591). Sidney also began the English translation of the Psalms completed by his sister. The biography written by his friend and fellow poet Fulke Greville presents him as a heroic figure and even as a sort of Protestant martyr, since his death in battle occurred as part of England's resistance to the greatest Catholic power of the century, the Spain of **Philip II**.

SIGNORE. The Italian term was used for a dictator, usually a professional military man, who seized control of an independent Italian city, establishing authoritarian rule though in some cases preserving (while also controlling) the institutions of the previous republican system. Although most of the larger cities of northern and central Italy had gained their independence during the 12th and 13th centuries under republican constitutions, many of them accepted a *signore* during the 13th and 14th centuries, sometimes seeking a defender against aggressive neighbors but more often seeking internal peace and stability after periods of violent conflict between rival political factions. In most cases, the *signore* tried to stabilize his position by acquiring a traditional feudal title such as duke, marquis, or count, and also by transforming what often began as a personal authority into a dynastic lordship inheritable by his descendants. Examples of such regimes were the **Visconti** (and later the **Sforza**) in **Milan**, the **Este** in **Ferrara**, and the **Gonzaga** in **Mantua**. Only rarely did a *signore* rise to power exclusively through military power. Most commonly, they used a combination of political manipulation and force, presenting themselves as protectors of the general interest against selfish factions among the wealthy citizens who traditionally dominated all Italian city-republics.

Some *signori* organized regimes that lasted for several centuries, while other such lordships collapsed during the lifetime of the founder and many more within a generation or two. By the 15th century, only two of the larger Italian republics, **Venice** and **Florence**, preserved their medieval republican constitutions relatively intact. Most Italian **communes** became *signories*. This development meant that despite the strongly republican spirit associated with early **Pad-**

uan humanism and later with Florentine intellectual life during the early 15th century (a tendency often called "civic humanism"), the new humanistic learning, vernacular literature, and art of the Italian Renaissance proved readily adaptable to a monarchical political system. The Italian term for the rule of such a *signore* is *signoria*. The latter term was also used for the most powerful executive council of the republic of Florence, the *Signoria*.

SIGNORELLI, LUCA (ca. 1450–1523). Italian painter, born in the Tuscan town of Cortona and probably trained by **Piero della Francesca**. His artistic style, however, also suggests the influence of Florentine painters such as **Antonio del Pollaiuolo** and **Andrea Verrocchio**. His early works include frescoes in the Santa Casa at Loreto and some of the original paintings in the Sistine Chapel at **Rome**. Two frescoes, only one of which, *The Testament of Moses*, survives, were probably his contribution to a joint project there that involved several leading artists. In the years preceding the death of **Lorenzo de'Medici** in 1492, he won commissions in **Florence**; *The Court of Pan* comes from this period. The peak of Signorelli's career came in 1499 when he was commissioned to complete a cycle of frescoes on the end of the world for the Chapel of St. Brizio at Orvieto, begun a half-century earlier by **Fra Angelico**. This cycle of six paintings occupied him from 1499 to 1503. Although Signorelli received additional commissions such as decorating the apartments of Pope **Julius II** in the Vatican and making paintings for the Petrucci palace in Siena, during the last two decades of his life he was eclipsed by the young painter **Raphael**. Signorelli was especially skilled as a draftsman, and his chalk sketches represent a high point in that branch of Renaissance pictorial art.

SIGONIO, CARLO (ca. 1522–1584). Italian **humanist** and historian. A native of Modena, he taught humanistic subjects there and at **Venice** before moving to the **University of Padua** in 1560 and then to the **University of Bologna** (1563–1584). He made his literary reputation by his lectures and publications on Aristotle's *Rhetoric* and *Poetics*. His greatest importance, however, was as a historian of ancient **Rome**. Beginning during the 1550s with a series of editions and commentaries on Roman inscriptions and Livy's history, during the following decade he published historical studies showing how the aristocratic families of the republican period had gradually been forced to share power with the plebeians. Sigonio then turned to the history of the later Roman empire and the **Middle Ages**, subjects that were far more contentious because they dealt with the early history of the Christian church. His *De regno Italiae / On the Kingdom of Italy* (1574 and 1580) and *De occidentali imperio / On the Eastern Empire* (1574) were the earliest general survey of the history of Italy from Roman times to the 12th century. He moved next to the history of the ancient Hebrews and the history of the church.

Sigonio's works dealing with the historical development of the church and the papacy proved highly sensitive, for he used local city archives and other newly available sources that led to new conclusions and did not harmonize with traditional historical accounts. For example, in explaining the rise of papal political authority in Italy, he omitted any mention of the document known as the **Donation of Constantine**, no doubt because he knew that **Lorenzo Valla** had shown it to be a forgery. Since the papacy still used this document to justify its political claims, ecclesiastical censors in Rome sharply criticized his work. Sigonio came under pressure to include specific reference to the Donation and to revise other sections of his history of Italy that traced papal power in Italy to grants given by Charlemagne and his successor Louis the Pious. He had based his account on surviving medieval documents, but his conclusions were unacceptable in Rome because they confirmed Protestant charges that the **popes** had usurped the secular political authority they claimed over all of Christendom. The censors accused him not just of historical error but also of false doctrine, since the church taught that all political authority had been transferred by Christ to his successor, St. Peter, and by Peter to each of his successors as bishop of Rome, down to the present in unbroken line.

In the end, Sigonio's later historical works were not placed on the Index of Forbidden Books. But he was faulted for not hewing to the post-**Reformation** party line and embracing the whole traditional history, even the parts that were mythical. Though his books were not forbidden and he was not directly penalized, it was not permissible to reprint them in any part of Italy until the 18th century, though they were eagerly reprinted and even translated under Protestant auspices in Germany. Siginio was one of the last great critical humanists of the Italian Renaissance, for his troubles made it clear that even for a scholar who went out of his way to compliment the papacy on every possible occasion, free exercise of critical judgment was not allowed. The censors demanded total conformity to the official historical account.

SIXTUS IV (Francesco della Rovere, 1414–1484; pope from 1471). Born near Savona to a merchant family of modest means, Della Rovere rose to prominence through the Franciscan order. Unlike most **popes** of the Renaissance period, who tended to be canon lawyers if they had any university education at all, Della Rovere studied theology in his order and at the **University of Padua**, where he received a doctorate. He then became a professor of theology at Pavia and several other universities. He became minister general of the Franciscan order in 1464 and was made a cardinal in 1467. He was an outsider in the papal election of 1471 but eventually emerged as the candidate whom backers of his rivals were willing to accept.

Although his career as a friar gave Sixtus a reputation for piety and high principle, his personal piety did not keep him from adopting policies that make his pontificate a significant turning point toward the extreme nepotism and political ambition typical of the Renaissance papacy. He had promised in the electoral conclave not to appoint new cardinals without consulting the other cardinals, but he promptly appointed two of his nephews, Pietro Riario and Giulio della Rovere (who later became Pope **Julius II**). Eventually he named six of his relatives to the Sacred College. In addition, Sixtus based his policy as ruler of the **Papal States** largely on the goal of promoting his family's interests. His attempt to create a principality for his nephew Girolamo Riario led to bitter conflict with the republic of **Florence**, and the efforts of **Lorenzo de'Medici** to block the emergence of a powerful Riario state on the borders of Florence produced the scandalous **Pazzi Conspiracy** of 1478, a conspiracy between Riario and a group of disgruntled Florentine exiles to murder Lorenzo and his brother. Whether the pope himself was privy to the plot is undocumented, but persons very close to him were the prime movers. The outcome was a protracted and dangerous war between Florence and a coalition led by the pope.

In order to finance his aggressive foreign policy and wars, Pope Sixtus also increased the old abuse of selling curial administrative offices. Although his private morality seems to have remained beyond reproach, the same cannot be said for many of the relatives whom he advanced to high office, so that his reign as pope marks a period of blatant luxury and moral corruption that gave the Roman Curia a bad reputation throughout Europe.

The luxury of the papal court did have a positive side. Sixtus reorganized and expanded the Vatican Library, constructed a new papal chapel in the Vatican (named the Sistine Chapel after him) and employed some of the century's finest painters (**Sandro Botticelli**, **Bernardino Pinturicchio**, **Domenico Ghirlandaio**, **Pietro Perugino**, and **Luca Signorelli**) to decorate it, and rebuilt a number of churches at Rome. Thus he made the papacy a major patron of Renaissance art.

SLUTER, CLAUS (ca. 1380–1406). The most important non-Italian sculptor of the International Gothic style. A native of the Netherlands, which was ruled by the dukes of **Burgundy**, he spent most of his career working for Duke Philip the Bold in the old Burgundian capital at Dijon. His most famous works were done for the Carthusian church at Champmol near Dijon. Most of his other work was on a less monumental scale, including portions of churches such as tombs and pulpits; most notable of these, also at the Carthusian monastery, is the *Moses Well*, a remarkable artifact depicting Old Testament prophets such as Moses and Isaiah. Sluter's figures are individualized persons, precise not only in the texture of costume and skin but also in the presentation of a unique personality, as if they were portraits. Although his work is more reminiscent of 13th-century French cathedral sculpture than of 14th-century Italian Gothic **classicism**, its skill in depicting personality is quite different from earlier Gothic sculpture.

SMITH, THOMAS (1513–1578). English **humanist** and statesman. After study at Cambridge University, he continued his education abroad at Paris and **Padua**. He taught **Greek** at Cambridge from 1535 to 1540 and was involved in the attempt of several Cambridge humanists, led by **John Cheke**, to introduce the pronunciation of Greek proposed by **Erasmus**, rather than the traditional one based on medieval Byzantine practice. This effort was opposed by the conservative chancellor of Cambridge, Bishop Stephen Gardiner, who regarded it as disrespectful of tradition. Smith was a noted collector of books and under Queen **Elizabeth I** served abroad as an ambassador. He is best known as the author of *De republica Anglorum / On the English Polity* (written in 1563 but not published until 1583), a concise and well informed account of the actual workings of English law and government in his time. In this work he distinguishes England, despite its having a king, from contemporary states because it is a commonwealth in which power is shared among crown, nobility, burgesses, and yeomen. Indeed, he classes England not as a monarchy but as a "democracy."

SODERINI, PIERO (1452–1522). Florentine political leader, elected to a life term as *gonfaloniere della giustizia* (head of the *Signoria*, the central policy-making body of the republic) in 1502. Previously, the *gonfaloniere*, like the other eight members of the *Signoria*, had been selected by lot to serve a two-month term. The heads of the anti-Medicean political factions who gained control of the government after the expulsion of the **Medici** in 1494 and the execution of **Savonarola** in 1498 concluded that in such dangerous times, the city must have a stronger executive authority, someone like the doge in Italy's other great republic, **Venice**. While they did not want a dictator, they realized that having the whole membership of the *Signoria* turn over every two months had created a dangerous lack of continuity. The reformers' solution was to grant the leader of the *Signoria* a life term. Soderini seemed the ideal person to hold this position. He belonged to a wealthy aristocratic family, yet his reputation for moderation and his good personal character made him acceptable to the less aristocratic members of the population.

As *gonfaloniere* Soderini did prove to be a capable administrator who stabilized the government's shaky financial situation. Since **Florence** lacked strong military resources, his foreign policy relied on the city's traditional alliance with France and on careful neutrality in the wars stirred up in Italy by Pope **Julius II**, who was allied at various times with the Spanish and the Venetians. The greatest triumph of his foreign policy was the reconquest of the port city of **Pisa**, which had thrown off Florentine rule in 1494 when the **Medici** regime collapsed. Soderini benefitted from the services of the most brilliant civil servant that Florence ever had, **Niccolò Machiavelli**. Unfortunately for Soderini, his cautious neutrality and reliance on French political and military support became a liability after an alliance between the **pope**, the Venetians, and the king of Spain in 1512 forced King Louis XII to withdraw his troops from Italy. The victorious allies then decided to punish Florence for its pro-French neutrality by sending an army to re-establish the Medici family's control of the city. Soderini was forced to resign and go into exile. The lifetime office that he had held was abolished.

SPANISH INQUISITION. The evil reputation of the Inquisition rests less on the record of the medieval inquisitors than on a very different institution, the Spanish Inquisition. After 711, when most of Spain and Portugal were under the rule of Muslim princes, the peninsula became a religiously pluralistic and fairly tolerant society. As the reconquest of Spain and Portugal by the surviving Christian kingdoms of the north proceeded, strong pressures for conversion to Christianity developed and from the 14th century often involved mob violence against non-Christians, mostly **Jews**. In the face of these periodic acts of terrorism, many Spanish Jews gave in and were baptized. But both the clergy and their gentile neighbors suspected that these *conversos* continued to observe Jewish religious practices in secret.

In 1478 the monarchs, **Ferdinand** and **Isabella**, asked the **pope** to authorize a special tribunal in Castile to inquire into the religious beliefs and practices of *conversos*. This tribunal was organized in Castile in 1480 and in 1483 was extended to Aragon. Although authorized by papal authority, the Spanish Inquisition was essentially a royal institution. Unlike its medieval predecessor, it had a strong central authority, headed by a clergyman (normally a Dominican or Franciscan friar) and a governing council of clergymen, the Suprema, all appointed by the rulers. Eventually, 16 local tribunals were formed, scattered throughout the country.

In the early period of its existence, 90 percent of those prosecuted were converted Jews. The accused were encouraged to denounce themselves and (provided they had no prior offense) were often let off with warnings. During the first half-century, some 2,000 *conversos* were condemned to death. Very few people who were not of Jewish ancestry were executed. After 1530 the number of executions declined. Since the Inquisition had no jurisdiction over unconverted Jews and Muslims and the inquisitors contended that the presence of any Jews in Spain tempted *conversos* to relapse into Judaism, in 1492 a royal edict required all remaining Jews to become Christians. This decree ended the existence of a recognizable Jewish community in the country and led to the exile of thousands of people. Similar pressure to convert was brought against the large Muslim minority, beginning in 1502 for Castile and in 1525 for Aragon. In both regions, the majority submitted though those Muslims who refused were allowed to emigrate.

At first, these forcibly converted Muslims, or *moriscos*, were sheltered by landlords who needed their agricultural skills. Pressure to abandon the use of Arabic language and Islamic customs became so intense that in 1568 the Moors of Granada rebelled. It took two years of military campaigning to restore control of the countryside. Finally, in 1609, the government decided that neither preaching nor supervision by the Inquisition could control this population. Some 350,000 people, all of them at least nominally Christian, were deported, most of them settling in Muslim North Africa. Jewish *conversos* also continued to suffer from suspicion and increasingly from active discrimination, expressed in policies of *limpieza de sangre* ("purity of blood") which excluded people of known Jewish descent from the most attractive positions in the church, the universities, and the civil service.

From about the middle of the 16th century, the Inquisition also acted to protect the country from the spread of Protestant doctrines. Though Spain had very few Protestants, there were some trials and executions. By the 1540s, not only real Protestants but also reformist Catholics who looked to the Dutch **humanist Erasmus** for inspiration were exposed to prosecution. Other targets of the Inquisition included the numerous followers of popular mysticism, the *alumbrados*. The Spanish Inquisition was also extended to Spanish dependencies in Sardinia and Sicily and, beginning in 1571, to the Spanish colonies in America. *See also* INQUISITION; PORTUGUESE INQUISITION; ROMAN INQUISITION.

SPENSER, EDMUND (ca. 1552–1599). English poet. He is best known for his allegorical romance *The Faerie Queene* (1590, 1596).

Born in London, he was educated at the Merchant Taylors' School, an institution that emphasized the value of **humanistic** education to prepare boys for public service. He entered Pembroke Hall, Cambridge, as a sizar (a student supported by work as a servant) and received his B.A. degree in 1573 and M.A. in 1576. In 1578 he became personal secretary to the bishop of Rochester, then entered the household of the Earl of Leicester in London, where he became a friend of **Sir Philip Sidney**. Spenser married in 1579 and not long afterward became private secretary to Lord Grey of Wilton, the new lord deputy of Ireland. Stationed first in Dublin and then in Cork, he acquired a number of administrative positions that permitted him to hire a deputy to do most of the work while keeping most of the income for himself. He also engaged in land speculation. Though Lord Grey soon left Ireland, Spenser lived there for the rest of his life.

Publication of the first part of *The Faerie Queene* in 1590 brought literary fame and also an annual stipend from the queen. An uprising of Irish peasants in 1598 destroyed his country estate. Although he regarded Ireland as his home, his sympathies lay with English colonists like himself, not with the native Irish.

In Ireland Spenser won the patronage of Sir **Walter Raleigh**, who introduced him at the royal court when he visited London in 1590 to present the first three books of *The Faerie Queene* to Queen Elizabeth. In addition to *The Faerie Queene*, Spenser published a satire directed against Lord Burghley, *Mother Hubberds Tale*, which was suppressed by the government. In 1579 he made his contribution to a major Renaissance literary genre, the pastoral poem, with *The Shepheards Calendar. The Faerie Queene*, which was originally planned for 12 books but never completed, was a poetic romance. It aimed to glorify England and its queen, who appears in the poem as Gloriana. In 1591 Spenser published *Complaint*, a collection of his poems. His *Colin Clout's Come Home Againe* (1595), dedicated to Raleigh, is an allegorized account of his visit to the royal court in 1590. His prose dialogue *A Veue of the Present State of Ireland* (1596, first published in 1633) advocated harsh enforcement of English hegemony in the troubled Irish colony. Spenser was not very convincing in writing allegory or constructing a coherent narrative for his long poems, but his mastery of poetic forms and his remarkable facility in exploiting the resources of the English language made him famous in his own time and have maintained his rank as one of the major English poets. He died in 1599 while visiting London and was buried in Westminster Abbey.

SPONDE, JEAN DE (1557–1595). French poet, son of a **Calvinist** who served as secretary to the queen of Navarre. He studied at the University of **Basel**, graduating in 1580. In 1588 he published a series of prose meditations on the Psalms. His poems are written in an elaborate style that is often called **mannerist** or **baroque**. His collection of poems, *Essay de quelques poèmes chrétiens* (1588), centered on religious themes, especially the sharp contrast between man's insignificance and God's omnipotence. In this collection, *Stances de la Cène* shows a Calvinist position on the Eucharist, while the *Sonnets de la mort* have no particularly Calvinist viewpoint and emphasize instead the vanity of all worldly things. Sponde also wrote a substantial body of love poems, *Les amours*, published posthumously in 1597. French Protestant authors agonized about the propriety of producing anything but works devoted to the Bible, and Sponde's insistence on pursuing his own poetic direction may have been one cause of his conversion to Catholicism shortly before his death.

STAMPA, GASPARA (ca. 1523–1554). Venetian poet and musician, noted both for her poems and for her singing and playing the lute. Born at **Padua** to a Venetian mother and an impoverished Milanese nobleman and jewel merchant, she and her sister and brother received from their father an education in **Greek**, Latin, modern languages, and music. After the father's death in 1531, the family moved back to **Venice** in order to promote the musical careers of both daughters. Gaspara wrote many sonnets and other lyrics dealing with love from a specifically female perspective, criticizing the way in which **women** were denied any independence in negotiating their own social and romantic relationships. Her *Rime*, published posthumously by her sister in 1554, give much attention to the psychology of a woman in love. These poems reflect the poet's own attachment to a nobleman unwilling to marry a woman whose social position was lower than his own. Stampa was a disciple of the poetic theories of the Venetian **humanist Pietro Bembo** and, following Bembo's ideas, took **Petrarch** as her poetic model.

STEVINUS, SIMON (1548–1620). Flemish physicist, engineer, and mathematician. His most notable achievement was the introduction of decimal notation into European mathematics. Little is known of his early life. A native of Bruges, he worked there and in Antwerp as a city financial clerk. Sometime between 1571 and 1577, he travelled in Poland, Prussia, and Norway. In 1581 Stevinus settled at Leiden and two years later matriculated in the **university**. Later he entered the service of the Dutch government as an engineer and in 1604 became quartermaster-general of the army. He also tutored Maurice of Nassau, prince of Orange, in mathematics and wrote several textbooks for his pupil. As a military engineer, he designed systems for flooding territory to guard against Spanish attacks. The government often consulted Stevinus on matters of defense and navigation, and he administered the personal domains of the prince of Orange. He also organized a school of engineers at Leiden.

By his time, Renaissance textual scholarship had recovered the major scientific works of **antiquity**, and his own writings reflect the assimilation of this ancient knowledge while also demonstrating ability to push beyond what the ancient scientists had done. Stevinus wrote nearly all of his works in the Dutch vernacular, and his treatises covered a vast range of scientific topics, both theoretical and applied. His books are clearly written and carefully organized, and they reflect the combination of theoretical science and practical application that was typical of the new Dutch republic. His first book, *Tafelen van Interest* (1585), reflected his commercial experience and made public the tables of interest that previously had been kept confidential by banking firms and insurance underwriters. His short booklet *De Thiende / The Decimal* (1585) introduced the use of decimal fractions and explained their usefulness. That same year, he wrote a general treatise on arithmetic and algebra. Stevinus also wrote a mathematical work on the treatment of **perspective** in art, a treatise on the mathematical basis of tuning musical instruments, and a series of other books making practical applications of mathematical knowledge. His *De Beghinselen der Weegconst / Principles of the Study of Solids* (1586) is his major work on mechanics, dealing principally with statics.

Stevinus was the first Renaissance author to develop and continue the work of Archimedes, discussing the theory of the lever, rules for determining the center of gravity of an object, and, most important, the law of the inclined plane. His next work in that field, *De Beghinselen des Waterwichts / Principles of Hydrostatics*, is the first systematic treatise on hydrostatics since Archimedes. He also wrote a treatise on the design of windmills for operating drainage pumps, and he designed systems of sluices and locks to be used in the management of water. Stevinus' principal book on astronomy, *De Hemelloop / The Course of the Heavens* (1608), was an endorsement of the Copernican system antedating the full acceptance of **Copernicus** by **Galileo**. His works on astronomy were related to Dutch interest in navigation, and he produced several specialized treatises, including one on the determination of longitude by use of the deviation of a magnetic needle from the astronomical meridian. Several of his publications were related to his experience as a military engineer, including a treatise on fortification and a detailed discussion on laying out a military encampment.

Stevinus even wrote on political and social issues. His *Het burgherlick Leven / Civic Life* was a guidebook for communities facing civil disorder. He defended religion as socially necessary to develop moral character in children, and in the face of the religious wars and persecutions of his generation, he argued that an individual who dissents from the prevailing religion is obliged either to conform or to emigrate. Toward the end of his life, Stevinus collected and published many of his mathematical works in *Wisconstighe Ghedachtenissen* (two volumes, 1605–1608), a work that appeared almost simultaneously in Latin and French translations.

STURM, JOHANN (1507–1589). German **humanist** and educator. Born at Schleidan in the Rhineland, he studied at **Louvain**, learning **Greek** from Rutger Regius, with whom he collaborated in publishing editions of Greek texts for teaching. In 1529 he went to Paris for further study. There he became involved in efforts to ally King **Francis I** with the German Protestants. In 1536 Sturm moved to Strasbourg to teach in the new Protestant town school, and when it was reorganized in 1538, he became the school's rector. The city govenment intended to use the school to educate Christian citizens, but Sturm emphasized broader aims, such as the need for study of natural philosophy and ancient literature, and especially for mastery of Latin. His educational theories and practices were described in his *De literarum ludis recte aperiendis / On Correctly Establishing Literary Studies* (1538) and in a collection of letters explaining his educational theories to his own teachers, *Classicae epistolae sive scholae Argentinenses / Letters for the Classes of the Strasbourg School* (1565 and 1573). The underlying principle of his school was to proceed in a sequential order so that students moved from simpler to more complex problems. The school's great success spread his method and his writings throughout Germany.

Sturm also edited and published editions of Latin and Greek texts for use in teaching. Cicero was the most important author studied; nine of Sturm's 14 editions were **Ciceronian** works. Sturm edited several Greek rhetoricians, **Aristotle**'s *Nicomachean Ethics*, and a collection of **Plato**'s dialogues for student use. He published commentaries on Cicero's orations, three treatises on the education of nobles and princes, and a collection of his correspondence with the English educator **Roger Ascham**. His educational treatises and editions of **classical** authors were reprinted frequently. Sturm laid great emphasis on rhetoric, for he believed that rhetorical skill permitted orderly solution of social problems and promoted the general welfare of society. Despite the success of his school, he was dismissed as rector in 1581 because he opposed the introduction of Lutheran doctrines to replace the Reformed doctrines of Martin Bucer that had prevailed in the early Strasbourg **Reformation**.

SYPHILIS. Venereal disease which became a major health problem in every part of Europe from the 1490s. The name comes from a poem published in 1530 by the physician **Girolamo Fracastoro** describing the illness and cure of a shepherd affected by the disease. Modern scholars disagree whether this was an entirely new disease or merely an epidemic occurrence of a disease long established in Europe. Most contemporary opinion regarded it as new and usually attributed its appearance to the infection of sailors from the ships of **Christopher Columbus** by women of the West Indies. This "Columbian" theory of its origin has been challenged, but most modern students of the question have concluded that while the evidence is not conclusive, the disease was new to Europe and was probably imported from the West Indies.

Anthropological research has found no evidence of syphilitic lesions in human remains from European burials before 1492 and does find such evidence in American Indian remains. There is no clear evidence of syphilitic symptoms in the medical literature of Europe, the Muslim world, India, or China before 1493, and references to the disease become increasingly frequent after the 1490s. The first such references come from Spain in the 1490s; a Spanish physician wrote a treatise on the disease between 1510 and 1520, reporting that he treated victims of the disease at Barcelona in 1493. A Spanish **humanist** published a Latin poem at Salamanca in 1498 in which he described a disease he named *las buvas*, characterized by a sore on the genitals. The preceding year, the physician to Pope **Alexander VI** published a tract on what he called "the French disease," describing 17 cases he had attended. The army of King Charles VIII of France suffered an outbreak of the disease in December 1494 while besieging **Naples**, and Naples had frequent political and commercial contact with Spain.

Thus the conventional accounts of the time attribute the introduction of the disease to sailors from Columbus' ships. The disease then spread rapidly, especially among soldiers and sailors, first in Spain and then in the kingdom of Naples, where French troops contracted it and carried it back to their homeland, thus beginning its rapid spread throughout Europe. The role of the French army explains why it was early named "the French disease" or "the French pox," though in France it was "the Neapolitan disease." All 16th-century accounts agree that the infection, affecting populations that had no natural immunity, was malignant, fast-moving, and quickly fatal. Because of its sexual transmission, it was often viewed as a judgment of God on human sinfulness. Modern anti-Columbians contend that before the 1490s the disease was simply misdiagnosed as leprosy or some other skin ailment or as one of the other venereal diseases known to be common in the **Middle Ages**. Complicating the discussion is the fact that the bacterium that causes the disease, *treponema pallidum*, is bacteriologically indistinguishable from the agents that cause yaws, pinta, and a number of less deadly skin diseases. Syphilis spread with epidemic rapidity, caused great alarm among European populations, and led to desperate but almost always futile efforts to find medicines that would cure it.

– T –

TABORITES. *See* HUSSITES.

TALLIS, THOMAS (ca. 1505–1585). English composer and organist, noted for his mastery of counterpoint. He was organist at a Benedictine abbey at Dover in 1532 and then at Waltham Abbey until the dissolution of all remaining monasteries by King **Henry VIII** in 1540. Tallis then became a gentleman of the Chapel Royal, a position he held until his death. During the reign of Edward VI (1547–1553), he composed music for the new Anglican liturgy, but some of his best compositions were made during the Catholic restoration under Queen Mary I (1553–1558), including the mass *Puer natus est nobis* and several much-admired motets. Tallis passed easily and apparently with no qualms of conscience into the service of **Elizabeth I** (1558–1603), under whom he composed music for both Latin and English liturgical texts, though most of his work was still for Latin liturgies. He composed several settings for Archbishop Matthew Parker's English Psalter. From 1570, his colleague in the Chapel Royal was the man who became the leading English musician of the next generation, **William Byrd**. In 1575 Tallis and Byrd published the collection *Cantiones sacrae*, to which each of them contributed 17 motets. That same year, the crown granted them a 21-year monopoly for **printing** music and music paper, but this privilege did not turn out to be so lucrative as they hoped, and after two years they petitioned successfully for an annual pension. Tallis also composed secular vocal and keyboard works, but his importance lies in the field of sacred music.

TARTAGLIA, NICCOLÒ (Niccolò Fontana, 1499–1557). Italian physicist and mathematician. He grew up at Brescia, where at age 12 he suffered the facial wounds that made him a stammerer (the meaning of *Tartaglia*) during French pillaging of the city. His father's early death left him in great poverty, but his love of mathematics and determination to learn enabled him to get an education. He worked as a teacher of *abaco* (commercial arithmetic) at Verona from about 1516 until 1534, when he moved to **Venice** to teach mathematics. Tartaglia was a close student of the Latin translations of ancient **Greek** mathematical authors and edited several of them. His *Opera Archimedis / Works of Archimedes* (1543), which reprints the medieval translations made by a pupil of Thomas Aquinas, William of Moerbeke, included *On Floating Bodies*, which was a major influence on the criticism of **Aristotelian** physics. From this tract, Tartaglia himself derived the hydrostatic principles underlying his treatise on the raising of sunken vessels, *Travagliata inventione / A Hard-won Discovery* (1551) as well as his posthumously published table of specific gravities. His Italian translation of Euclid's *Elements* (1543) was the first translation of this fundamental geometrical text into any European vernacular. Other works include *Nova scientia / New Science* (1537), a treatise on mechanics which advances an influential theorem defining the proper elevation (45 degrees) for attaining the maximum range for a cannon and which also shows some significant departures from Aristotelian physics; *Quesiti e inventioni diverse / Various Questions and Inventions* (1546); and his last work, *General trattato di numeri e misure / General Treatise on Numbers and Measures* (1556), a survey of pure and applied mathematics. Tartaglia's greatest single mathematical discovery, the solution for cubic equations, was made at **Verona**. This discovery led to a quarrel with **Girolamo Cardano**, who published it in 1545 (without Tartaglia's permission, but giving him credit) after Tartaglia had divulged it to him in secret.

TASSO, TORQUATO (1544–1595). Italian poet. He was born at Sorrento in the kingdom of **Naples**, the son of a court poet who later followed his patron, the prince of Salerno, into exile. The son accompanied his father as he sought new patrons at various princely courts. Young Tasso received a thorough **classical** education, culminating in study of law at **Padua** and **Bologna**. His real interests, however, were in poetry and philosophy, and he abandoned the potentially lucrative study of law in order to write poetry and study philosophy. His chivalric romance *Rinaldo* (1562) laid the foundations of his reputation as a poet. In this early period Tasso began work on a poetic narrative of the First Crusade and also on his *Discorsi dell'arte poetica / Discourses on the Art of Poetry*. The latter was finally completed and published in 1587. He left Bologna without a degree in order to become court poet to the Cardinal Luigi d'**Este**, brother of the duke of **Ferrara**, thus entering the risky career of a courtier that his father had hoped he would avoid by studying law.

In 1575 Tasso completed his poem on the crusade, then titled *Gerusalemme liberata / Jerusalem Liberated*, but instead of risking publication, he sent the text to several literary critics whom he asked to judge both its literary qualities and its religious and political orthodoxy. Since some of the critics expressed objections, he spent great effort responding to their criticisms. Apparently the stress of this process led to a nervous breakdown marked by several instances of violent behavior that cost him favor at court, led to seven years of imprisonment as a madman, and made him fear that he would never recover the manuscript of his treasured poem. Eventually he did regain possession of his manuscript and in 1581 published it along with an "allegory" or lengthy preface that emphasized its orthodoxy and wholesome nature.

Tasso wrote and published many short lyric poems, participated in pamphlet debates over the relative merits of his own epic poem and **Ludovico Ariosto's** *Orlando furioso*, and wrote several dialogues and a treatise on the dialogue as a form of literature, *Discorso dell'arte del dialogo*. After his release from confinement in 1586, he completed a play, *Torrismondo* (1587), published a lengthy religious poem, *Le sette giornate del mondo creato / The Seven Days of the Creation of the World* (1594), and a work on the theory of the heroic poem, *Discorsi del poema eroico* (1594). He also worked on revision of his epic account of the First Crusade, trying to make it conform to church doctrine and to the practice of ancient epic poets. In 1593 the new version appeared under a new title, *Gerusalemme conquistata / Jerusalem Conquered*. Literary critics have tended to favor the earlier version over the revision. Early in his career, Tasso also made an important contribution to the Renaissance fashion for pastoral themes, writing and staging the pastoral drama *Aminta* for the Este court. He also wrote many letters, of which about 1,500 survive. Despite his periods of insanity, he was early recognized and honored as a great poet. After his release from confinement, aristocratic patrons sheltered him. Tasso died while living at **Rome**.

TAVERNER, JOHN (ca. 1490–1545). The most important musician of England in the first half of the 16th century. He began as a boy chorister at Tattershall near Lincoln and from 1525 to 1530 was organist and choir director at the new Cardinal College, Oxford. He wrote eight masses and numerous Latin motets. His mass *Gloria tibi Trinitas* was reportedly performed at the great diplomatic conference at Calais known as the Field of the Cloth of Gold in 1520. It is important in the history of English music later in the century because the *cantus firmus* of the Benedictus at the words "in nomine Domini" became the basis for instrumental variations by his successors that as a group are called *In nomine*. Taverner was attracted by Protestant beliefs and briefly imprisoned in 1528 but later participated under the direction of the king's chief minister, **Thomas Cromwell**, in the dissolution of the English monasteries.

TELESIO, BERNARDINO (1509–1588). Italian philosopher of nature. Born at Cosenza and educated there by an uncle who taught him both Latin and **Greek**, he studied philosophy at **Padua** and received his medical doctorate in 1535. **Aristotle** and Galen dominated teaching at Padua, but Telesio rejected the Paduan tradition of interpreting Aristotle according to the ideas of the Muslim philosopher Averroës. His reading of both Aristotle and Galen in the original Greek made him critical of medieval **scholasticism** in general. Telesio undertook a new synthesis of these ancient authors and in 1565 published at **Rome** his major work, *De rerum natura iuxta propria principia / On the Nature of Things According to Their Own Principles*. At Cosenza he founded an Accademia Cosentina to encourage study of natural philosophy. Other writings on natural philosophy were published posthumously as *Varii de naturalibus rebus libelli / Brief Treatises on Natural Subjects* (1590). Although critical of some aspects of Aristotelian natural science, especially the *Physics*, Telesio followed the ancient philosopher on some questions. He regarded sensory knowledge as primary and reason as merely a tool to be used when discussing subjects that permitted no direct observation. He was not, however, a genuine empiricist and made no use of experiment or measurement.

THOMAS À KEMPIS (1380–1471). Monk of the religious community of St. Agnietenberg near Zwolle in the Netherlands, part of the Windesheim Congregation of Augustinian canons regular. Born at Kempen near Cologne in western Germany, he came under the influence of **Geert Groote**, the founder of the late-medieval spiritual movement known as *Devotio Moderna*. Although too young to have known Groote in person, he admired his ideas and wrote his biography. Thomas' fame comes from his probable authorship of an influential book of religious meditations, *The Imitation of Christ*, written in Latin but soon translated into Dutch, French, High German, and other western European languages. This book is hostile to the speculative theology of **scholasticism** and emphasizes personal religious experience by the individual over the external and ritualistic aspects of religion. Yet in it Thomas still gives the sacraments of the church, especially the Eucharist, a significant role in spiritual life. His book constantly quotes from the Bible and is notable because it does not refer to any other source.

TINCTORIS, JOHANNES (ca. 1435–1511). Flemish music theorist and composer. A native of Nivelles near Brussels, in his youth he studied both law and theology, earning a double doctorate in civil and canon law. He became a priest and a canon at Poperinghe and may have been a singer at Cambrai under **Guillaume Dufay**. In 1463 he was choirmaster at Orléans, but like many talented Flemish musicians, he moved to Italy and after about 1472 spent at least 15 years in the service of Ferrante of Aragon, king of **Naples**. Between 1484 and 1500 Tinctoris was attached to the papal chapel in **Rome**. The outstanding manual of counterpoint in the 15th century, *Liber de arte contrapuncti / Book on the Art of Counterpoint* (1475), was one of his 12 treatises on musical theory. In it he sharply criticized the dissonances in the music of the preceding half-century and laid down strict rules for introduction of dissonances. Another influential work was his dictionary of musical terms, *Terminorum musicae diffinitorium* (1495). Though he was important mainly for his writings on musical theory, four masses, two motets, and several chansons by him survive.

TINTORETTO (Jacopo Robusti, 1518–1594). Venetian painter, usually associated with the **mannerist** tradition and known for his portraits and religious paintings. He was the only major figure of the Venetian school of painting actually born in **Venice**. The identity of his teacher is unknown, but by 1539 he was an independent master. He closely studied the works of **Michelangelo** and also those of his Venetian contemporary **Titian**. Tintoretto's first important work was the *Miracle of St. Mark Rescuing a Slave* (1548), painted for a Venetian confraternity, the Scuola di San Marco. He produced several other paintings of St. Mark for this confraternity. In 1564 he executed *The Apotheosis of St. Roch* in the chapel of that saint's confraternity, and the following year he created his most important painting, the *Crucifixion*. He produced several other paintings for the confraternity of St. Roch and became a member himself. The best known of these is his *Christ Before Pilate* (1566–1567).

Tintoretto's last major work, *The Last Supper* (1592–1594), when compared with the painting on the same subject by **Leonardo da Vinci**, provides a striking example of the difference between a High Renaissance and a mannerist treatment of the same theme. He also painted many portraits, including one of himself.

TITIAN (Tiziano Vecellio, ca. 1487–1576). The leading Venetian painter of the 16th century. He was born in northern Italy to an aristocratic family and was trained at **Venice**, first under a mosaicist, Sebastiano Zuccato, but chiefly under the prominent painter **Gentile Bellini**. He may also have worked under Giovanni Bellini and **Giorgione** before becoming an independent master. His early *Bacchanal* (1518) pursues an openly pagan theme and reflects the influence of ancient art as well as familiarity with engravings representing the great works of the High Renaissance at **Rome**. The animated quality of his painting is also evident in his religious works such as *Madonna with Members of the Pesaro Family* (1526). His most notable religious works were the *Assumption of the Virgin, The Entombment*, and *Christ Crowned with Thorns*.

After the premature death of **Raphael**, Titian became the most sought-after portraitist of the century. A striking individual portrait, *Man with the Glove* (1520), demonstrates the qualities that led to his dominance. His first portrait of the Emperor **Charles V** (1533) established his international reputation. The most striking reflection of human character in his portraits is *Paul III and His Grandsons* (1546), which demonstrates his ability to capture the dominating personality of its central figure, the **pope**. Titian executed several additional portraits and other works for Charles V, who granted him a patent of nobility, and he later served the emperor's son, **Philip II** of Spain, beginning with a portrait (1550–1551) but also including works based on **classical** mythology.

As the greatest representative of the Venetian Renaissance tradition, Titian made striking use of color and lighting. He also made designs for several woodcuts that were printed and diffused widely throughout Europe and so spread his reputation far beyond Italy and Spain.

TOMICKI, PIOTR (1464–1535). Polish bishop and royal chancellor, an important patron of Polish **humanism** and an admirer of the great

Dutch humanist **Erasmus**. Born into a noble family and educated at the court of his uncle, Tomicki accompanied the uncle on an embassy to the Emperor Frederick III in 1486 and remained in Germany until 1488 to study at Leipzig with a private tutor. In 1489 he entered the **University** of Cracow (B.A. 1490, M.A. 1493) and then, after a visit to the imperial court at Vienna, studied law at **Bologna**, where he took a doctorate in canon law in 1500. Next he visited **Rome**, where he observed the procedures of the papal chancery. Later in 1500 Tomicki returned home and became chancellor to the bishop of Cracow, for whom he undertook many political and diplomatic missions. He also served the next bishop of Cracow (1503), but in 1506, when Sigismund I, a brother of his first Polish patron, became king, he became a secretary in the royal chancery. He travelled widely on diplomatic missions and through royal patronage accumulated valuable ecclesiastical benefices.

In 1514 Tomicki became bishop of Przemysl and vice-chancellor of the realm. In 1520 he was translated to the see of Poznán and in 1525 to Cracow. As bishop of Cracow, the principal residence of the monarch, and as vice-chancellor, he had great influence on both domestic and international policy. He supported a pro-**Habsburg** foreign policy and a religious policy of firm resistance to Lutheran influences. He secured royal edicts forbidding the importation of books from Germany (1523) and study by Polish students in German universities (1520 and 1534).

Tomicki's study in Italy had given him a taste for Italian customs, including use of a strictly **classical** Latin style in documents of the royal chancery. He founded a humanistic palace school in his own household to educate the sons of Polish nobles as preparation for university study. He subsidized study abroad for gifted students and hired foreign humanists to teach in his own school. As chancellor of the University of Cracow, he favored "**trilingual**" study (classical Latin, **Greek**, and **Hebrew**) of the Erasmian sort and tried to persuade Erasmus to settle at the Polish court. Tomicki even tried to win the German humanist **Philipp Melanchthon** for the Cracow faculty, hoping to detach him from the doctrinal influence of the arch-heretic **Martin Luther**. His patronage supported his own nephew **Andrzej Krzycki**, a celebrated neo-Latin poet, the Hebraist Jan van Campen, the Hellenist Jerzy Liban, and the physician Jan Antonin, a special friend of Erasmus.

TOSCANELLI, PAOLO (1397–1482). Florentine astronomer, mathematician, and cartographer, best known in his own time as an outstanding mathematician but most famed in modern times because his
geographical ideas and his map depicting non-European parts of the
world may have encouraged **Christopher Columbus** in the formula-
tion of his plan to reach eastern Asia by sailing west. Toscanelli studied mathematics at the University of Florence and medicine at
Padua. At Padua he became a friend of the German scholar **Nicholas
of Cusa**. Toscanelli practiced medicine in **Florence** from 1424, and
since **astrological** knowledge was an important part of 15th-century
medicine, he was expert in that field and in the closely related field
of astronomy. He observed and mapped comets and was one of the
first to conclude that comets are celestial rather than meteorological
(that is, superlunary rather than sublunary) objects. His family's involvement in the spice trade may have attracted Toscanelli to speculate about routes to the oriental source of spices. His miscalculation
of the circumference of the earth, based on rejection of the accurate
figures of the ancient astronomer Eratosthenes and his acceptance of
other Hellenistic astronomers (including the standard authority,
Ptolemy) who greatly underestimated the circumference, may have
encouraged Columbus to seek his new route to Japan and China. If
the letters are not later forgeries (a hotly debated issue among Columbus scholars), Columbus corresponded with Toscanelli, receiving a
letter and a map that encouraged the plan that he carried out (unsuccessfully, as far as reaching East Asia was concerned) in 1492.

TRAVERSARI, AMBROGIO (1386–1439). Florentine monk and **humanist** who made the study of ancient Christian authors (the Church
Fathers) his scholarly specialty, though he also studied and wrote
about pagan authors and translated from **Greek** into Latin the *Lives
of the Philosophers* by Diogenes Laertius, an important source for
Renaissance understanding of ancient philosophy. Born in Portico, a
village of the Romagna, he came to **Florence** in 1400 and entered the
Camaldolese monastery there. He claimed to have learned Greek
through private study, though he probably had some help from a native Greek who resided in the same monastery. His mastery of Greek
and of ancient Latin literature attracted the attention of the wealthy
Florentine humanist **Niccolò Niccoli**, who opened to him his private

library of manuscript books. Traversari's monastery became the meeting-place of the influential humanist circle (including the physician **Paolo Toscanelli** and a great patron of Florentine humanism, **Cosimo de'Medici**) that flourished during the 1420s.

Traversari was a close student of the works of Latin Church Fathers such as St. Jerome, Lactantius, and Tertullian, but his mastery of Greek led him to the study and translation of Greek Church Fathers, including Athanasius, Basil, [pseudo-]Dionysius the Areopagite, Ephraem, Gregory of Nazianzen, and John Chrysostom. These translations opened the little-known world of ancient Greek Christian literature to Latin-reading Western scholars. Like many humanists, Traversari valued this patristic literature far more highly than the prevailing **scholastic** theology of the **universities**. In 1431 he became general of his order, an administrative position that forced him to travel widely to inspect and reform Camaldolesian communities throughout Italy. He wrote a narrative of these journeys, the *Hodoeporicon*, and carried on an extensive correspondence, much of which is preserved. Traversari was one of the papal legates at the **Council of Basel** in 1435 and was a member of the Western delegation at the **Council of Ferrara-Florence**, where his command of Greek and his expertise in Greek patristic literature gave him a prominent role in the negotiations to reunite the Greek and Latin churches.

TRILINGUAL COLLEGE. A **humanistic** educational institution that taught all three of the ancient languages in which **classical** literature, the Bible, and patristic writings were written, **Hebrew**, **Greek**, and (classical) Latin. The founding of institutes for the teaching of these three languages and for study of the ancient texts written in them was one of the major demands of the "biblical humanists" of the late 15th and early 16th centuries. The first school organized along these lines was the College of San Ildefonso in the new **University of Alcalá**, founded by Archbishop **Francisco Ximénes de Cisneros** (formally established in 1499; instruction began in 1509). In 1517 a similar institution, the *Collegium Trilingue*, was founded at the **University of Louvain**. The appointment of a group of scholarly specialists as Royal Readers to lecture on similar subjects by King **Francis I** in 1530 marks a parallel development in France, though these lectures did not have a real institutional foundation until much later in the

16th century; eventually, they developed into the **Collège Royal**. Although not conventionally labelled a trilingual college, the **University** of Wittenberg under the leadership of **Martin Luther** in 1519 underwent reforms that by classicizing the teaching of Latin and adding permanent chairs of both Greek and Hebrew transformed it also into a trilingual institution.

TRITHEMIUS, JOHANNES (1462–1516). German Benedictine abbot, theologian, and **humanist**, famous for his learning and efforts at monastic reform but also for his interest in **magic, astrology**, and other occult sciences. He was born at Trittenheim and studied at Heidelberg, where he associated with the leading German humanists of the time, **Conrad Celtis** and **Johann Reuchlin**. He became abbot of the Benedictine monastery of St. Martin at Sponheim in 1485 and made it a center of learning, collecting a large library. His monks, however, resisted his efforts to reform their lives and make their community a center of learning. Conflict became so bitter that in 1506 he moved to the monastery of St. Jacob at Würzburg, where he served as abbot until his death. The **Habsburg** emperor **Maximilian I** was his patron, and he dedicated several works to the ruler.

Trithemius wrote a treatise on the importance of monastic scriptoria, *De laude scriptorum / In Praise of Scribes* (1492) and a number of influential chronicles and biographical collections, including *De viris illustribus ordinis sancti Benedicti / On Famous Men of the Order of St. Benedict* (1492; first published 1575); *Annales Hirsaugienses / Annals of [the Monastery of] Hirsau* (1509–1514; first printed in 1690; first partial edition, 1602); *Catalogus illustrium virorum Germaniae / A Catalog of Famous Germans* (1491–1495; first edition before 1501); *Chronicon Sponheimense / Chronicle of the Abbey of Sponheim* (1495–1509; first printed in Trithemius' *Opera historica*, 1601); *Chronicon successionis ducum Bavariae et comitum Palatinorum / Chronicle of the Succession of the Dukes of Bavaria and the Counts Palatine* (1500–1506, printed 1544); *De scriptoribus ecclesiasticis / On Ecclesiastical Authors* (1494). Trithemius also wrote works on monastic life and administration, on theology, on the lives of saints, on the spiritual life, as well as a collection of sermons (published in 1516), and many letters, of which about 250 survive. In his historical works, he tried to trace links between modern Germans and the ancient Trojans and Druids, sometimes inventing documentary sources on his own when he could not find the evidence he needed. He endorsed **trilingual** study of Latin, **Greek**, and **Hebrew**.

Like many contemporaries who investigated recondite ancient sources, Trithemius believed that the universe is permeated by spiritual and astrological forces, and though he warned against dealing with demons, he was convinced that Christian theology was compatible with magic (that is, types of magic that refrained from invoking demons). Three of his published works dealt with such material, *De septem secundeis / Concerning the Seven Secondary Intelligences* (1508), which taught that human history runs in cycles defined by the cyclical ascendancy of certain astrological influences; *Steganographia* (not published till 1606, but previously circulated in manuscript), a study of secret writing or cryptography that invoked angelic spirits; and a less radical cryptographical tract, *Polygraphia*, where he omitted reference to angelic and demonic forces but applied materials from ancient **Hermetic**, Pythagorean, and **cabalistic** literature in his system of secret handwriting.

Trithemius' involvement in these occultist studies became a public issue because the French humanist Charles de Bouelles, after being allowed to read the manuscript of *Steganographia* during a visit to Trithemius in 1504, denounced him as a practitioner of forbidden magical arts. A denunciatory letter of Bouelles, which was widely circulated in manuscript and print, seemed to confirm other unsettling reports about Trithemius' interest in magic. Trithemius tried to defend himself in a treatise that is lost but is probably summarized in the introduction to his *Polygraphia*, published in 1514. A younger German enthusiast for study of the occult arts, **Agrippa von Nettesheim**, also visited Trithemius in 1510 and presented him with a copy of his own magical work, *De occulta philosophia*.

TUDOR DYNASTY. Ruling family of England from the accession of King **Henry VII** in 1485 to the death of Queen **Elizabeth I** in 1603. Henry Tudor in 1485 claimed the throne by right of descent from the Lancastrian branch of the English ruling family, but in reality he became king because of his victory over the last Yorkist king, Richard III, in the battle of Bosworth, which marks the end of the **Wars of the Roses**. Henry's hereditary claim was weak, both because the Lancastrian claim itself was inferior to the claim of the Yorkists and because his own line of descent from the last undisputed English king, Edward III (1327–1377), was shadowed by a possibly illegal marriage. He took steps to strengthen this claim by marrying Elizabeth of York, the eldest surviving child of King Edward IV. Thus while Henry's own claim to the throne might be disputed, he ensured that his children, descended from Edward III through the Yorkist ancestry of their mother and also through his own more disputable Lancastrian descent, would have an unimpeachable hereditary title. Henry VII kept the throne not because of his hereditary claim or even his military victory but because of his political ability. A shrewd, cautious, and determined man, he took steps to weaken the great aristocratic clans who had run riot during the Wars of the Roses and to strengthen his own personal and institutional power as king. He also managed royal finances so carefully that he soon had a sound financial basis for his government.

By the time of his death in 1509, Henry VII left his son **Henry VIII** the sound political and fiscal foundations that made the second Tudor a far more impressive figure at home and abroad than his father had been. Henry VIII's ambitious foreign policy and wars eroded the monarchy's fiscal basis but did not destroy it, thanks in part to the confiscation of monastic properties that he carried out in the 1530s. Henry VIII's reign is noted mainly for a religious policy that marks the beginning of the Protestant **Reformation** in England. His personal life is notorious for his complicated marital history, which produced direct conflict with the papacy and led to his first moves toward religious change, beginning with his abolition of the authority of the **popes** over the church in England. Henry's theological traditionalism acted as a restraint on those of his advisers who wanted to move the English church closer to Continental Protestant doctrines and practices.

At Henry VIII's death in 1547, his son Edward VI was still a minor. The king's uncles, first the duke of Somerset and then Somerset's rival, the duke of Northumberland, set the country on an openly Protestant religious path. Edward VI, however, died in 1553 at age 15 and was succeeded by his half-sister Mary I (1553–1558), the elder of Henry VIII's two daughters. Despite the growth of a strong Protestant movement among the educated classes under Edward, the nation was still largely Catholic (or at least not firmly Protestant) in 1553.

Mary quickly gained control of the country and executed the ring-leaders of a plot to keep her from the throne. Her most urgent goal was to restore the Roman Catholic religion in England, and in the short run, she was successful. Many of the leading Protestants fled into exile. Mary carried through Parliament the legislation restoring England's allegiance to the papacy and reversing the religious poli-cies of her brother and her father, though she was not strong enough to undo the vast tranfers of landed property from the suppressed monasteries into the hands of powerful aristocratic families.

Mary tried to strengthen her position by marrying King **Philip II** of Spain, who became king consort but was not given any continuing political authority if his wife died without children. Mary's effort to enforce Catholic orthodoxy involved a level of religious persecution that gave her an evil reputation among later English Protestants though it was not particularly bloody by the standards of the 16th century. Her greatest mistake in these persecutions occurred when she passed from the early executions of Henry VIII's archbishop of Canterbury, Thomas Cranmer, and several other Protestant bishops to her later policy of hunting out and executing heretics among the com-mon people.

When Mary died in November 1558 without children, the throne passed to her younger sister Elizabeth I, who was not a fanatical Protestant but whose personal religious preferences and political af-filiations favored a slightly more moderate restoration of the openly Protestant policy of Edward VI's reign. Elizabeth was by far the greatest of the Tudor monarchs, having much of the tough political realism of her grandfather Henry VII and showing great skill in choosing loyal and effective statesmen to administer the realm. Un-der her, England, which had been politically weak and militarily hu-miliated during the short reigns of Edward and Mary, played a major role in international politics and in 1588 defeated the naval expedi-tion, the Armada, sent by Philip II of Spain to conquer England. Eliz-abeth's greatest failure was her refusal to marry. At her death in 1603, the Tudor dynasty came to an end and the crown passed into the ea-ger hands of King James VI of Scotland, descended from a daughter of the first Tudor king, Henry VII.

Under the Tudors, English culture was strongly affected by Re-naissance influences coming directly from Italy and indirectly through France and the Netherlands. Henry VII, a tight-fisted ruler with little munificence in his soul, made a few moves toward royal patronage of the new trend; his son Henry VIII was more supportive of the new culture but was too preoccupied by foreign wars and other political interests to become an active patron of Renaissance art and literature. Edward VI and Mary I both reigned for too short a time to have much impact on English culture, except for the spread of Protestant religious beliefs among the educated classes in Edward's time. Elizabeth's cultural role was more important. Though she herself was not particularly generous to the arts and **humanistic** learning, she had received an excellent humanistic education and gathered about her a circle of courtiers who became patrons of the new culture, especially in the fields of poetry and drama. Thus the English Renaissance reached its peak much later than the Italian, flowering mainly during the reign of Elizabeth and her first Stuart successor, James I (1603–1625).

TULLIA D'ARAGONA (1508–1565). Roman poet and courtesan, one of a number of sophisticated Italian prostitutes who wrote poems dealing with love from a **woman**'s point of view. In 1547 she published a collection of poems and a dialogue, *The Infinity of Love*.

TURKS. *See* OTTOMAN EMPIRE.

TURNÈBE, ADRIEN (1512–1565). French **humanist** and **classical** scholar. A native of Normandy, he studied in Paris, receiving his M.A. degree in 1532. He became professor of **Greek** at the **University** of Toulouse and in 1547 succeeded Jacques Toussain, one of the two original royal lecturers in Greek at Paris. In 1561 he moved to the lectureship in Greek and Latin philosophy. Turnèbe was director of the royal press from 1552 to 1556 and published new editions of the Greek dramatists Aeschylus and Sophocles. He also edited an anthology of early Greek gnomic poets, including Theognis. In Latin scholarship, Turnèbe produced editions and commentaries on Ausonius, Horace, Juvenal, Lucretius, Martial, Persius, and Varro. His scholarship on **Cicero** was especially important because he investigated the Greek sources of Cicero's philosophical works. Also of great importance for the development of classical scholarship was his *Adversaria*, a collection of emendations and scholia on classical authors (three parts, 1564, 1565, and 1580). Turnèbe exerted great influence on the leading French classical scholar of the next generation, **Josephus Justus Scaliger**.

– U –

UCCELLO, PAOLO (1397–1475). Florentine painter. Originally trained as a goldsmith and apprenticed to **Lorenzo Ghiberti** about 1407–1412, when Ghiberti was working on his first set of doors for the cathedral's baptistery, Uccello executed his early works in the International Gothic style. Even after he changed his style to incorporate the new Renaissance manner, his works continued to display a love of detail and a use of color and graceful drawing that reflect Gothic influence. In the Renaissance aesthetic associated with **Filippo Brunelleschi, Donatello**, and **Masaccio** in **Florence**, Uccello focused on the problem of linear **perspective** as most essential to a successful painting. His best-known work is a series of three panel paintings depicting a recent Florentine military victory, *The Battle of San Romano* (ca. 1455). Earlier examples are a monochrome fresco for the Florentine cathedral representing the English *condottiere* Sir John Hawkwood on horseback (1436) and *The Deluge*, another monochrome fresco executed in the church of Santa Maria Novella about 1445. Uccello's use of perspective was never entirely successful. His figures have a somewhat unrealistic appearance despite the success of the three-dimensional illusion. Other works by Uccello include *St. George and the Dragon* and *The Hunt* (both ca. 1460). Most of his work was done in Florence, but before his conversion to Renaissance style, he spent the years 1425–1431 in **Venice**, where he created mosaics for the basilica of St. Mark.

UDALL, NICHOLAS (1505–1556). English schoolmaster, translator, and playwright. He was educated at Winchester School and Corpus Christi College, Oxford, and early developed a sympathy for the doctrines of **Martin Luther**, though during the Catholic restoration under Queen Mary I, he conformed to the established religion and continued to enjoy favor at court. From 1534 to 1541 Udall was headmaster of Eton College but was discharged for misconduct in a complicated case that involved theft of silver plate belonging to the college but also seems to have included sexual abuse of one or more students. His loss of this position proved irreversible, though his reputation seems not to have been permanently harmed. Udall had a lifelong interest in Roman comedy, publishing in 1533 a bilingual (Latin-English) collection of phrases from the plays of Terence, *Floures for Latine spekynge selected and gathered out of Terence*, intended to help schoolboys learn to converse in Latin. In the time of Queen Mary, he presented dialogues and interludes before the queen, probably acted by boys from Westminster School, of which he was headmaster from 1554 until his death.

The most important product of Udall's interest in the Roman dramatists Terence and Plautus is an original play in English, *Ralph Roister Doister*, which seems to have been performed in 1553 or 1554 by Westminster boys. In it he adopts the tightly structured plot of the Roman comedians rather than the loose, episodic structure of medieval English drama. His characters are borrowed from his Roman sources but transformed into Englishmen and joined with other characters derived from English tradition. This is commonly regarded as the first English comedy and constitutes an important step toward the rich comic literature of the Elizabethan period.

In the 1540s Udall was involved in the translation of works of the **humanist Erasmus**, publishing an English version of selections from Erasmus' *Apophthegmata* (1542) for use by students, while his translation of Erasmus' Paraphrase of the gospel of St. Luke about 1545 was part of a program of translations of Erasmus' spiritual writings encouraged by Henry VIII's last queen, Catherine Parr, and other Protestant sympathizers at court. These Paraphrases were not published until 1549, when the government of Edward VI was moving toward an openly Protestant religious policy. He also translated a work on the Eucharist by the Protestant theologian Peter Martyr Vermigli.

UNIVERSITIES. The university as known in the European world was a creation of the 12th and 13th centuries. **Bologna**, which was Italy's oldest university, emerged out of the teaching of law in that city during the late 11th century and gradually developed institutional forms and practices during the 12th century. Paris, the archetype of a very different sort of university, grew out of the earlier cathedral school of the city's bishop and gradually developed institutions and customs during the 12th century as the **guild** (in Latin, *universitas*) of masters was organized and took control of teaching and the qualification of students for degrees, though the ecclesiastical authority still retained a monopoly on the formal conferring of degrees, normally done by the bishop's chancellor on recommendation of the faculty. Paris received a royal charter in 1200, and in 1231 the **papacy** issued its own charter defining and limiting the authority of the chancellor and also recognizing the existence of the guild of teachers.

The University of Bologna was legally a corporation of students who banded together to secure an education and to defend their rights against oppressive actions (such as excessive rents) by local citizens. But the city government appointed the professors, and the professors in each field of study formed a college which defined the conditions of eligibility to teach (essentially, the requirements for degrees). At Bologna and the other Italian universities, the organization of students was dominant, no doubt because the Italian universities arose as institutions for the teaching of professional subjects, law and medicine, and students arrived as young men with most of their pre-professional education already completed. This Italian organizational pattern also prevailed in Spain and southern France.

The Northern universities, however, followed the organizational pattern developed at Paris during the 12th and 13th centuries. They were controlled by the guild of teachers. Students were kept in a distinctly subordinate role, no doubt because students entered at a much younger age, usually 13 or 14 years. While they were expected to have already attained competence in Latin, they had to pass through the academic program of the faculty of liberal arts, receiving bachelor of arts and master of arts degrees from the university, before they were eligible to enter one of the professional faculties. Most Northern universities were organized into four faculties, a faculty of liberal arts, which more and more concentrated instruction on those subjects (such as logic) that were judged useful for success in the three higher faculties; a faculty of theology; a faculty of law (commonly subdivided into canon law and civil law); and a faculty of medicine. But not every university taught in all faculties. In all Northern universities, the faculty of liberal arts, which enrolled boys at an early age and conferred B.A. and M.A. degrees, was by far the largest because graduation with its degrees was required for entry into the three higher (that is, professional) faculties.

Italian universities differed in structure as well as in governance. At Bologna and **Padua**, the faculty of arts was combined with (and subordinated to) the faculty of medicine, and the faculty of law was for centuries organized as an entirely separate university. In the Italian universities, there was no separate faculty of theology. All or nearly all teaching of theology occurred within the study-houses of the various monastic orders, and a college of theologians (including some graduate theologians who never taught at all) examined candidates and granted theological doctorates in the name of the university.

Once established on one or the other of these two lines (the Bologna model or the Paris model), the program of studies in each faculty rather quickly became fixed, and introduction of changes met resistance. There were differences from one university to another, but the program in each of the four faculties was sufficiently standard that students and professors could move from one university to another fairly easily, a process facilitated by the practice of conducting all instruction in Latin. Universities multiplied in number. By 1400 there were already 29 in Europe. New foundations continued through the 14th and 15th centuries. In 15th-century Germany, many of the new foundations were made by rulers of the semi-independent principalities. During the 16th century, Germany also developed several new universities intended to meet the needs of rival religious groups and to ensure that local boys could receive their education close to home without danger of doctrinal contamination. By 1601 there were 63 European universities. Only England, a relatively small country, resisted the temptation to found new universities: Oxford and Cambridge remained the country's only universities until the 19th century, though England also developed a unique set of institutions, the Inns of Court, to prepare men for the practice of English common law. Although Paris had several thousand students, most medieval universities were small. Especially in the North, many young men entered the university, remained for a few years (sometimes, but not always, engaging seriously in study), and then departed without taking any degree at all.

The tight organization and highly articulated traditional programs of these universities made them resistant to the desire of Renaissance **humanists** to change the program of studies, especially in the faculty of liberal arts, in order to give greater emphasis to the study of ancient languages (**Greek, Hebrew**, and **classical** Latin). This situation could breed conflict as academic reformers struggled to introduce new humanistic courses and to reduce the time spent on the study of old medieval textbooks and the subjects most useful for traditional **scholastic** subjects. In Italy, such conflict seems to have been rare, largely because the liberal-arts subjects were incorporated into the professional faculties of law and medicine and because the students, older by several years when they first enrolled, had already completed most of their study of the liberal-arts subjects in lower schools or with the aid of tutors.

In some Northern European universities, however, the effort to introduce humanistic educational reforms led to internal conflict, with the senior faculty, who controlled the university, stubbornly trying to preserve the same studies and textbooks that had been used in their own education and exploiting their power within the institution to silence, punish, or even expel reformers who pushed too hard for change. In Germany, the friction between defenders of medieval tradition and humanistic educational reformers became extremely heated in several places and sometimes produced open conflict. The use of printed pamphlets and manifestoes became common, and both conservatives and reformers appealed to external authorities—the city council, the regional prince, or even the pope or the emperor—to help them overcome their rivals.

The movement for university reform in Germany began to win the upper hand in some places (such as Erfurt, Wittenberg, and Vienna) in the first two decades of the 16th century, but the academic reformers made their most rapid gains in places where the **Reformation** triumphed, since the territorial princes who made the decision whether or not to adopt the Reformation were generally the patrons and ultimate rulers of the territorial university and favored humanistic educational reforms as a way of preparing the next generation of Protestant leaders. In a number of places where Catholicism retained control, such as Ingolstadt, where the dukes of Bavaria upheld the old religion and used the universities as a source of intellectual defense against Protestant heresy, the political authority also intervened in favor of humanistic educational reforms. Other universities, such as Cologne, strongly resisted both humanistic educational changes and

Protestant heresy, though most of these anti-humanist schools suffered both in enrollment and in revenues.

Even in places where humanist educational reformers gained substantial success, the reformers neither attained nor desired a total abolition of all parts of the medieval scholastic tradition. The humanist program of study did not embrace all branches of academic learning, but chiefly defined changes needed in the *studia humanitatis* (humanism). In most fields of natural philosophy and dialectic, traditional textbooks and philosophical practices survived. In particular, the authority of **Aristotle** as the guide to the methods and problems of university study, though criticized on some points of detail, remained dominant because there was no alternative set of treatises that could match the orderly, systematic, and generally clear writings of Aristotle. Though an increasing number of students of natural philosophy (especially in Italy, where the universities had developed a flourishing tradition of scientific study) became dissatisfied with Aristotelian science, Aristotelian ideas of scientific logic, and Aristotelian assumptions about the nature of reality (metaphysics), there was no viable substitute, and scholastic science, though modified almost everywhere to some degree by humanistic influence, survived intact until the middle of the 17th century, when the non-Aristotelian natural science developed by **Galileo** and other dissatisfied scientific investigators finally began to overturn the centuries-long domination of Aristotle as the guide to the methods and basic principles of scientific learning.

URBAN VI (pope, 1378–1389). Bartolomeo Prignano, archbishop of Bari, was elected **pope** by a badly divided college of cardinals subject (to an extent that remains debatable) to the pressure of a mob of Roman citizens who feared that if the large French majority among the cardinals chose another French pope, the papacy would move back to **Avignon**, where it had resided from 1309 to 1377. Although a clear majority of the cardinals voted for Prignano and attended his enthronement, his behavior in the months following his election, especially his treatment of the cardinals, was so arrogant and arbitrary, perhaps even demented, that the French majority turned against him. The French cardinals left **Rome** and reassembled outside Urban's reach, charging that his election had been invalid because of pressure by the mob. They then elected one of their own number, who took the name **Clement VII**. The French pope did return to Avignon, while Urban remained in control of Rome. This disputed election marks the beginning of the **Western Schism**, during which two and even three rival popes competed for the support of the Christian community.

URBINO. Small Italian city in the Marches, a region of east-central Italy. Founded under the Roman republic, in the 12th century Urbino came under the control of the **Montefeltro** dynasty, who originally ruled as imperial vicars and later as vicars for the papacy. The **popes** claimed overlordship of the city but during the early 14th century exerted so little control that the city became a virtually independent state. The head of the dynasty, Count Antonio, had been deposed by the papal legate in 1369 but in 1375 returned as *signore* (lord) of the city under an agreement to share power with the citizens. In general, the council directed routine internal affairs but the prince controlled foreign policy, extended his rule over neighboring regions, and developed an effective mercenary army. By the 1380s the papacy had recognized this arrangement and legalized Antonio's rule by again recognizing him as papal vicar.

Under Count Guidantonio (ruled 1404–1443), the ruler became one of the most important Italian *condottieri*, hiring himself and his army out to other Italian cities that needed effective military forces. After the aberrant reign of Oddantonio, who was assassinated during his second year in retribution for oppressive actions, his illegitimate half-brother Federico (1444–1482) succeeded to the throne and resumed his father's successful career as a *condottiere*. In 1474 Pope **Sixtus IV** rewarded Federico's military service by granting him the title duke of Urbino. Under Federico and his son Guidobaldo (1482–1508), Urbino reached its peak as a small but formidable Italian power and a center of Renaissance culture. The Montefeltro line became extinct with Guidobaldo's death, and rule over the city passed into the hands of Francesco Maria della Rovere, nephew of Pope **Julius II**, who persuaded Guidobaldo to adopt the nephew as his heir.

During the 16th century, caught up in the great-power rivalries and ruled by the della Rovere family, which transferred the seat of government to Pesaro, Urbino declined in importance. Previously, the

Montefeltro court was a significant center of patronage for artists and writers, and at its peak, a lively intellectual life developed around the person of the duchess, Elisabetta **Gonzaga**, since Duke Guidobaldo himself was a lifelong invalid. The intellectual life of this circle is reflected in the influential *Book of the Courtier* by one of its members, Count **Baldassare Castiglione**. The greatest figure in the artistic history of the city is the painter **Raphael**, who was born there and initially trained there by his father, a painter at the Montefeltro court.

URFÉ, HONORE D' (1568–1625). French author of the late Renaissance, remembered primarily for his pastoral romance, *L'Astrée*, of which the first part was published in 1607 and the fourth in 1627, after the author's death. D'Urfé's secretary saw this fourth part through the press and later published a fifth part supposedly based on his notes. The shepherds and shepherdesses who populate the romance are aristocrats who have fled the complications of life at court and inhabit an idealized landscape modeled on the author's native Forez region in east-central France. The action involves the dilemmas caused by the romantic attachments of the characters. Although the author adopts the conventions of Platonic love, the narratives follow the ins and outs of the characters' romances. The work shows the influence of ancient **Greek** romantic tales but also of Italian pastoral authors such as **Jacopo Sannazarro** and **Torquato Tasso**.

D'Urfé was born into an aristocratic family and brought up amidst a rich environment of literary and artistic activity. He received his formal education at the **Jesuit** Collège de Tournon. He was deeply involved in the extremist Catholic League during the civil wars of the 1580s. His other works include *Epistres morales* (1598–1608), a set of philosophical meditations in letter form; a body of pastoral poems; and an unpublished epic poem.

UTRAQUISTS. *See* HUSSITES

– V –

VADIANUS, JOACHIM (Joachim von Watt, 1484–1551). Swiss **humanist**, physician, and religious reformer. Born at St. Gallen into a prominent family of merchants and civic officials, he was educated at the local grammar school and then at the **University** of Vienna, where he associated with the humanist **Conrad Celtis** and received B.A. (1504) and M.A. (1508) degrees. During an episode of plague at Vienna he interrupted his studies (1506–1507) and for a time taught school at Villach in Carinthia. He also visited **Venice** and **Padua** while away from Vienna. After returning to Vienna, he taught at the university, lecturing on **classical** authors, especially those who wrote on geography. He produced a commentary on Book 7 of Pliny's *Natural History* (1515) and another on Pomponius Mela (1518). His edition of Mela reflected a preference for authors who based their geographical writings on direct experience rather than on the reports of others. Vadianus personally visited Polish salt-mines and climbed Swiss mountains to extend his understanding of topics that today would be classed as geological. His mastery of humanistic Latin and his publications marked him out as a leading scholar.

The Emperor **Maximilian I** crowned Vadianus poet laureate in 1514, and he became professor of rhetoric and poetry and rector of the university in 1516, on his way to a doctorate in medicine (1517). He conducted an active correspondence with other humanists. Although the path to a successful university career was open, he chose to return to his native St. Gallen, where he settled in 1520 after an extensive journey through eastern Germany and Poland. In 1519 he married a daughter of the patrician Grebel family of Zürich. His return to St. Gallen involved his appointment as town physcian, and he succeeded his father as a member of the small council, the principal agency of local government.

Aside from practicing medicine, Vadianus' other goal was to spread humanistic culture in his native region. He established close ties with the humanist community at **Basel** and in the summer of 1522 during a visit there met **Erasmus**. At Basel he assisted in the editorial work on a new edition of the *Helvetiae descriptio / Description of Switzerland* by another prominent Swiss humanist, **Henricus Glareanus**. He also published an enlarged version of his edition of Pomponius Mela. By the early 1520s he had also become deeply interested in the movement for religious reform. He read many of the works of **Martin Luther** and had long known the major Swiss Protestant leader, **Huldrych Zwingli**. Vadianus organized a biblical study group and lectured to its members on the early Christian creeds and the book of Acts. His interest was not so much in dogmatic disputes as in questions of practical religion.

Vadianus led the establishment of a Reformed church at St. Gallen on the pattern created at Zürich, and his election as mayor (*Bürgermeister*) of St. Gallen in 1526 made him a leader of both the religious **Reformation** and the political life of his city. When the local Benedictine abbey was secularized in 1529, he acted to preserve its valuable collection of manuscript books, and in general he pursued a moderate, though clearly Protestant, religious policy. Vadianus spent most of his later years engaged in historical work. The manuscripts of the abbey constituted the major source for a history of the abbey, a history of the city, a history of the Lake Constance region, a history of monasticism, and histories of the Roman emperors and Frankish kings. He also conducted an extensive correspondence, of which some 4,000 items survive.

VALDÉS, ALFONSO DE (ca. 1500–1532). Spanish **humanist**, the leading figure among Spanish admirers of **Erasmus**. His family were Spanish *conversos*, and one of his uncles, a priest, was burned at the stake by the **Inquisition** in 1491 on charges of secretly continuing **Jewish** religious practices. Alfonso's education is not well documented, but he was probably tutored by an Italian humanist attached to the royal court in Valladolid, Pietro Martire d'Anghiera. He may have studied at the new **University of Alcalá**. Valdés was a member of the Emperor **Charles V's** secretarial staff at Brussels and Aachen in 1520 and then at Worms in 1521, where he witnessed the hearing of **Martin Luther** before the Imperial Diet. He returned to Spain in 1522 and entered the service of the imperial chancellor, Mercurino Gattinara. In 1525 he edited official reports of the battle of Pavia in which Spanish troops captured King **Francis I** of France. By early in 1526 he was secretary for Latin correspondence in the imperial chancery. During the rapid spread of Erasmus' popularity in Spain in the middle 1520s, Valdés was one of the Dutch humanist's warmest supporters, helping to organize the defense of Erasmus' orthodoxy by the court humanists against the unsuccessful attempt of the Spanish religious orders to secure a condemnation of Erasmus' writings.

Valdés' *Diálogo de las cosas ocurridas en Roma* (subtitled *Lactantio*), an exculpatory and pro-Spanish account of the notorious

Sack of **Rome** by the imperial army in 1527, caused the papal nuncio at the imperial court, **Baldassare Castiglione**, to attack Valdés (and Spanish policy) as disrespectful of the Supreme Pontiff. Valdés' other major work was his *Diálogo de Mercurio y Carón / Dialogue Between Mercury and Charon*, completed in 1528. It combines the Erasmian concept of the "philosophy of Christ" with sharp criticism of the clergy. This dialogue also reflects a kind of inward spirituality that is reminiscent of the contemporary popular Spanish mystics known as *alumbrados* (the enlightened ones).

Valdés accompanied the imperial court to Italy in 1529, attended the coronation of Charles V by the **pope** at **Bologna**, and accompanied the emperor on his trip to Germany in 1530. After the death of the chancellor Gattinara in 1530, Valdés took over his role as the leading mediator at the imperial court between Catholics and Protestants. He attended the imperial diet at Augsburg in 1530, negotiated directly with **Philipp Melanchthon** and other Protestant leaders, and joined Melanchthon in the vain effort to seek a peaceful reunification of the church. At the emperor's request, Valdés prepared a Spanish translation of the Lutheran Augsburg Confession. Despite the failure at Augsburg, he remained active in court service, attending the coronation of Charles' brother Ferdinand as king of the Romans, accompanying the court on its travels in the Netherlands and Germany, and attending the imperial diet at Regensburg in 1532. In October of that year, he contracted plague while in Vienna and died.

VALDÉS, JUAN DE (ca. 1509–1541). Spanish **humanist** and religious writer, younger brother of **Alfonso de Valdés**. He shared his brother's reformist religious interests but was much closer to the heretical *alumbrado* movement that was becoming widespread in Spain. Like Alfonso, he probably was tutored by the Italian humanist Pietro Martire d'Anghiera. Unlike his brother, he was directly involved with the mystical *alumbrados* ("the enlightened ones"). In 1523–1524 he attended religious meetings at Toledo that would later be defined as centers of heresy. About 1526 Juan entered the **University of Alcalá**, where he remained until 1531, establishing close connections with the influential circle of **Erasmian** humanists and reformers there. It remains uncertain whether he ever completed an academic degree at Alcalá.

Valdés' first published book, *Diálogo de doctrina cristiana* (1529), led to his being summoned before the **Inquisition**, though he initially escaped any penalty. His opinions, however, were dangerous in the Spain of this time, and when he learned that a second set of charges was being prepared, he fled to Italy, arriving at the papal curia in **Rome** in August 1531. His position at Rome, unlike that in Spain, was not precarious since he was well-connected through his brother and his humanist contacts. He acted as an imperial agent while in Rome. Popes **Clement VII** and Paul III granted him the revenues of two churches in Spain, though he never was ordained as a priest.

Valdés settled permanently at **Naples** in 1535. There he became close to a former papal protonotary, Pietro Carnesecchi, who many decades later would be executed for heretical doctrines that probably derived from Valdés. Valdés' connections in Spain and Naples brought him into the highest levels of Neapolitan intellectual society, and he became leader of a religious conventicle known as "the Kingdom of God." Some of this group became Protestants and eventually fled north of the Alps, while others became leading figures of the early Catholic **Reformation**. Valdés' own beliefs upheld justification by faith and rejected good works as a way to salvation, but there is no evidence that his theology was derived from German Protestant theologians.

The conventicle included intellectuals and aristocrats of the highest rank, including the young widow Giulia **Gonzaga**, Bernardino Ochino (general of the new Capuchin order, who was already secretly Protestant and fled to Geneva in 1542), Pietro Martire Vermigli (who joined Ochino in his flight to Geneva), and the Roman noblewoman and poet **Vittoria Colonna**. Other members of the Neapolitan conventicle, including the humanist cardinals **Reginald Pole** and Gasparo Contarini, remained Catholic but inclined to an "evangelical" emphasis on justification by faith. One of the most influential spiritual books of the 16th century, the anonymous *Il beneficio di Cristo / The Benefits of Christ* (1543), was the work of someone in touch with the Valdesian group at Naples. It is usually attributed to an "evangelical" Benedictine monk, Benedetto da Mantova, and the text was prepared for publication by the humanist Marcantonio Flaminio, one of the members of Valdes' conventicle at Naples.

Valdés' *Diálogo de doctrina cristiana* is a catechism, perhaps the first of the century, published several months before **Martin**

Luther's *Shorter Catechism*. In it he used Erasmian terminology but went beyond Erasmus' ideas and promoted the illuminist ideas of the Spanish *alumbrados*. Valdés wrote another statement of his spiritual views, his *Alphabeto cristiano*, which may have been published in 1536 (though no surviving copy antedates 1545). Other, shorter works on religion, published only posthumously, included a catechism for children, first published in 1544 or 1545; *Le cento e dieci divine considerazioni / A Hundred Ten Divine Considerations* (published by his Italian follower Celio Secondo Curione in 1550); and a collection of five short theological treatises (published in 1545). He also produced commentaries on Psalms 1–41, not published until the 19th century; on Paul's epistle to the Romans and on 1 Corinthians (published at Geneva by a Spanish refugee in 1557); a Spanish translation of the gospel of Matthew (not published until 1880); and several short tracts. In addition, Valdés left a significant collection of unpublished letters. He probably wrote commentaries on additional books of the New Testament, but these have not survived. He also wrote *Diálogo de la lengua / Dialogue on Language* (ca. 1535), a pioneering linguistic study of the Spanish language.

Valdés died at Naples in August 1541; his will, of which only a summary survives, affirms his belief in the doctrines by which he has lived but does not make it clear what those doctrines are. It is probably significant, however, that his will makes no mention of papal authority, does not invoke any saints, and does not contain the pious phrases used in traditional Catholic wills.

VALLA, LORENZO (1407–1457). Italian **humanist**, active mainly in **Rome** and **Naples**, often regarded as the ablest humanist scholar of the 15th century. He is remembered especially for his innovative approach to linguistic and textual criticism. He was critical of his fellow humanists, most of whom he regarded as incompetent, and engaged in many of the bitter personal feuds for which Italian humanism is notorious. Valla was born in Rome, where his father was an official in the papal curia. His early education was under the direction of private tutors, but prominent curial humanists coached him, including **Leonardo Bruni**, the future **Florentine** chancellor, and Giovanni Aurispa, a prominent Hellenist. Later, Valla studied under **Vittorino da Feltre** at **Mantua**.

From the very beginning of his career, Valla seemed to have a knack for offending people and stirring up controversy. In an age when other humanists idolized **Cicero**, he wrote a book (1428) comparing Cicero's Latin style unfavorably with that of the recently rediscovered works of the Roman rhetorician Quintilian. This brash act won for him the enduring hostility of the influential humanist **Poggio Bracciolini**. His treatise on moral philosophy, *De voluptate / On Pleasure* (1430) shocked readers by arguing that pleasure is the highest goal of human life, a claim that made most readers regard him as a pagan and an Epicurean. When he taught at the **University** of Pavia in 1431–1433, his open contempt for the leading medieval commentators on Roman law infuriated the powerful law faculty and was the probable reason why he was not reappointed. He taught briefly at **Milan** and Genoa and spent time in Florence, where he met some of Italy's leading humanists. He seems to have got along well with the Florentines, but he found no enduring place there. In fact (with good justification in some cases) he regarded most earlier and contemporary humanists as incompetent, and he was not at all shy about letting his opinions become known. He became involved in several of the vicious personal feuds which are one of the least attractive characteristics of Italian humanism. Before he was 30, he had gained a reputation for arrogance and quarrelsomeness. He obviously thought himself brighter and more learned than any of his peers, and while he probably was right, making this opinion known through constant negative shots at others was not a way to promote his own ambition for recognition and reward.

Valla's fortunes took a turn for the better when he entered the service of Alfonso of Aragon, king of **Naples**, in 1435. The years he spent at Naples (1435–1448) were the most productive period of his life. About 1437–1440 he completed the work that had the greatest influence on his own contemporaries, *De elegantiis linguae latinae / The Elegances of the Latin Language*. This book was a practical guide to **classical** Latin style, vocabulary, usage, and grammar, immensely useful to all who wanted to develop a genuinely classical style of Latin. Its method was inductive, drawing on instances of actual usage in ancient texts and basing its conclusions on ancient practice. *Elegances* was a huge literary success. When **printing** was introduced into Italy, the book was printed early (1471) and often. By the time of the death of the Dutch humanist **Erasmus** in 1536, 59 editions of this lengthy text had been published, not counting more than 50 editions of the widely used epitome or abridgment that Erasmus produced in 1529.

In the long run, *Elegances* was even more important than contemporaries realized because it was the most systematic statement of a linguistic principle that became the foundation of later Renaissance textual scholarship and all modern philology. Valla seems to have been the first person to realize clearly that language is a social product, undergoing constant change from generation to generation. This principle meant that the efforts of earlier humanists to write a vaguely "classical" Latin were inherently misguided, because they regarded the language written by authors separated by several centuries as one single language, and thus they wrote an eclectic jumble of words and usages that no ancient author had ever used. Instead, Valla insisted, the good stylist must focus attention on a single author, or at least on the authors of a single generation, and must confine vocabulary and grammatical practices to those used by the model generation. This idea of linguistic evolution, which is the foundation of all subsequent philological scholarship, explained why Valla found the Latin of his humanistic predecessors deficient.

Valla's awareness of the constant changes that occur in any language over time made it possible for him to attain a new level of proficiency in the critical evaluation of manuscripts and the philological reconstruction of ancient texts. It also set a standard by which corrupt texts and forgeries could be detected. Valla applied this philological approach to his editions of Latin authors and to translations of Greek authors such as Aesop's *Fables*, Xenophon's *Cyropedia*, and part of Homer's *Iliad*. The most famous application of Valla's philological criticism, however, was *De falso credita et ementita Constantini donatione declamatio / A Declamation on the False and Forged Donation of Constantine* (ca. 1440), a short treatise that was really intended to be a political tract defending his employer, the king of Naples, against the attempts of the pope to claim political overlordship over the kingdom of Naples. The papacy for centuries had cited the Donation of Constantine, which purported to record the gift of political overlordship over Rome and the whole Latin half of the Roman empire to Pope Sylvester I by the Emperor Constantine, as one of the major foundations for papal claims to political (rather than just spiritual) authority over the western half of the Roman empire. Valla's tract subjected this document to critical examination. He easily demonstrated on grounds of law, political propriety, lack of contemporary corroborating evidence, and (most important) linguistic analysis that the Donation of Constantine is a crude forgery that has no value at all as the legal foundation of a territorial and political claim by the pope. The papacy simply ignored his tract, continuing to cite the Donation until the early 19th century as if it were valid historical evidence. Since both King Alfonso and Valla himself soon settled their political quarrel with the pope, the text was not widely circulated. It was first printed in 1519 as part of a general attack on papal authority by the humanist **Ulrich von Hutten**. The book thus became Protestant propaganda reflecting negatively on the spiritual as well as the political claims of the papacy, a use that Valla himself never intended.

One other product of Valla's insights into philology was a set of textual notes on the New Testament, in which he applied his thorough mastery of **Greek** to clarify obscure passages in the traditional Latin Vulgate text and to suggest corrections of what he regarded as obvious errors in the Latin translation. This work attracted little attention among his contemporaries and remained unpublished. In 1504, however, the Dutch humanist Erasmus discovered a manuscript copy in a monastic library, and he published it the next year. His study of Valla's *Adnotationes in Novum Testamentum / Notes on the New Testament* was one of the influences that impelled Erasmus toward the preparation of his famous edition of the Greek New Testament.

Valla was far more interested in philosophical and theological questions than most humanists of the early 15th century. His *Dialecticae disputationes / Dialectical Disputations* (1439) was an assault on the categories of **Aristotle** and his followers and hence a fundamental attack on the underlying assumptions of medieval **scholastic** philosophy. The effect of his criticism was to shift emphasis from metaphysical issues to linguistic (especially rhetorical) ones. Also in 1439 Valla addressed a more specific philosophical issue in his *Dialogus de libero arbitrio / Dialogue on Free Will*. Contrary to the predominant opinion among scholastic theologians, he maintained that while humans can determine the outcome of secular affairs through reason, their actions cannot determine their eternal salvation, since this depends exclusively on faith and divine grace. In the 16th century, **Martin Luther** remarked favorably on Valla's opinions on free will and grace.

Valla was a prolific author. In 1440 he published a tract, *De professione religiosorum / On the Profession of the Religious*, which challenged the idea that members of monastic communities had a better claim on salvation than laypersons. Also while still at Naples, he composed a *History of King Ferdinand of Aragon* (1446), his royal patron, and in a rebuttal to an attack on it by a rival Neapolitan humanist, Bartolomeo Facio, he produced an *Antidotum* to Facio which is mostly invective but contains a remarkable reconstruction of the text of Book Four of Livy's *History of Rome*.

Valla had long desired appointment as a curial official. His reputation for disputatiousness may have kept him from securing his desired position early in his career. The hostility of the influential humanist papal secretary Poggio may also have barred his way. His views on moral philosophy, assiduously misinterpreted as anti-Christian by his rivals, his unwelcome criticism of the monastic life, and his critical assessment of the Donation of Constantine, to say nothing of some theological and philosophical issues that brought him to the attention of the Neapolitan **Inquisition**, made Pope **Eugenius IV** suspicious. The accession of the humanist Pope **Nicholas V** (1447–1555) opened the way for Valla's advancement. In 1448 the new pope invited him to Rome, initially as a lecturer at the pontifical university, then as a curial official. He was named a canon of St. John Lateran and in 1455 became an apostolic secretary, thus completing his rise to the upper ranks of the papal bureaucracy.

After moving to Rome in 1448, Valla composed two "antidotes" to his most persistent and dangerous critic among contemporary humanists, Poggio, and two satirical dialogues. More significant was his inaugural lecture for his course at the papal university, which emphasized the historic importance of the church as an agency in preserving Latin language and literature during the chaotic centuries after the dissolution of the western Roman Empire. One of his last works, pronounced before members of the Dominican order at Rome, was *Encomium Sancti Thomae Aquinatis / An Encomium of St. Thomas Aquinas* (1457). In it, Valla praised the Dominican saint and theologian as a holy man but belittled his philosophical and theological work because it was based on the pagan philosopher Aristotle rather than on the Bible and the early Church Fathers. The most he would grant was that Aquinas was a man of great ability and had done remarkably well, considering the barbarous age into which he had the misfortune to be born.

VALOIS DYNASTY. French royal dynasty between 1328 and 1589. The last strong king of the medieval Capetian dynasty, Philip IV (1285–1314), left three sons (Louis X, Philip V, and Charles IV) who ruled in succession between 1314 and 1328. At the death of Louis X in 1316, leaving daughters but no son, the French aristocracy accepted his younger brother rather than one of his daughters in order to avoid having a female ruler. Their legal experts justified this decision by citing an old feudal law, the "Salic Law," that forbade female succession among the Salian Franks. When Charles IV also died without a male heir in 1328, the French nobles acknowledged his cousin, Count Philip of Valois, insisting that the "Salic Law" excluded not only a female heir but also any male heir descended from the female line and hence that King Edward III of England, whose mother was a daughter of Philip IV, was not entitled to the throne. Edward III lodged a legal protest but later acknowledged the Valois claimant, Philip VI, as king of France. Yet Edward never fully accepted his own exclusion, and when he declared war on France in 1337 (mainly over quite different issues), he also reasserted his claim to the French crown. The war that opened in 1337 was the beginning of the **Hundred Years' War**.

After the expulsion of the English armies from France in 1453, the Valois kings consolidated their power and rebuilt the authority of the monarchy, which now had effective control over most of the territories that were legally part of France. When the duke of **Burgundy**, Charles the Rash, was killed in battle by the Swiss in 1477, leaving only a daughter as his heir, the Valois king, Louis XI, immediately occupied the duchy of Burgundy and thus effectively completed the territorial unification of France in the form it had throughout the rest of the Renaissance period. The Valois dynasty survived two further breaks in direct father-to-son succession in 1498 and again in 1515 when rulers died without leaving a son. In each case, a male cousin of the deceased king came to the throne. The second of these, **Francis I** (1515–1547), is the ruler most clearly identified with the emergence of Renaissance culture in France. His son Henry II left four sons, three of whom succeeded to the throne in turn, Francis II, Charles IX, and Henry III, and none of whom produced a male heir. These last three Valois kings ruled during the chaotic civil wars known as the French Wars of Religion (1562–1598). After the assassination of Henry III in 1589 by a Dominican friar, his Protestant cousin Henry of Navarre successfully asserted his claim to the throne, ruling as King **Henry IV** (1589–1610), the first king of the Bourbon dynasty.

VAN DER GOES, HUGO (ca. 1440–1482). Flemish painter, active at Bruges until 1478, when he entered a monastery. Although he painted for a brief period after he became a lay brother, he suffered from profound depression and abandoned his art. His best-known work is the *Portinari Altarpiece* (ca. 1476), executed for a wealthy Florentine businessman active in Bruges and placed in his family chapel in **Florence**, where it was much admired. Other works include *The Fall of Man* (ca. 1470), a *Lamentation* (ca. 1470), the *Monforte Altarpiece*, treating the Adoration of the Magi (ca. 1472), and two late works which are sometimes interpreted as showing evidence of the artist's emotional instability, a Nativity (ca. 1480) and *The Dormition of the Virgin* (ca. 1480), depicting the death of Mary.

VAN DER WEYDEN, ROGIER (ca. 1399–1464). Flemish painter, in his own time considered second only to **Jan van Eyck** among Northern European artists. Influenced by both van Eyck and **Robert Campin**, he produced a large body of brilliantly colored and exquisitely detailed paintings in a number of genres. His earliest major work, *Deposition from the Cross* (ca. 1435), is notable for its striking depiction of emotion. In 1450 Rogier made the jubilee pilgrimage to **Rome** and left behind two paintings that show Italian influence, *Virgin and Child with Four Saints* (also called the *Medici Madonna*) and *Farewell at the Tomb*. In general, however, his work after 1450 shows little significant Italian influence. He painted many portraits, among which the most striking are *Portrait of Francesco d'Este*, *Portrait of a Lady*, and *Philippe de Croy*, the latter paired with the most striking of his treatments of the theme *Virgin and Child*.

VAN EYCK, HUBERT AND JAN. Flemish artists, brothers. Another brother, Lambert, and a sister, Margaret, were also painters, but almost nothing is known about their work. Relatively little is known about Hubert, the elder of the two famous brothers. He seems to have headed a workshop at Ghent and to have died in 1426. Only one painting is securely attributed to him, *Three Marys at the Tomb*, and it survives only in a copy painted about 1440. Several early van Eyck paintings are variously attributed to Hubert or Jan, such as *The Crucifixion* and *The Last Judgment*, both dated 1420–1425. Some art historians have even speculated that Hubert was a fictitious artist, though this is not the prevailing view.

Jan van Eyck, on the other hand, is a well documented figure with many surviving paintings, some of them signed and dated. He was born about 1490, worked in the 1420s in Holland and at Lille, but was also active as a member of the court of Duke Philip the Good at Bruges. He not only served as the duke's court painter but also became a member of diplomatic delegations in 1426 and 1427 and executed an extensive mission in Spain and Portugal in 1428–1429. The most famous van Eyck work is the *Ghent Altarpiece*, also known as the *Altarpiece of the Lamb*, a collection of panels that quickly became an object of admiration for visitors to the Netherlands. This vast work seems to have been begun by Hubert but was left unfinished when he died in 1426. At some later date, probably not until the early 1430s, Jan took over the project. Since it was finished by 1432 and Jan would have had no time to work on it before January 1430, it seems likely that much of the work had been completed (or brought close to completion) by Hubert before his death, but there is no way to determine which panels are mostly the work of Hubert and which the work of Jan. The most striking parts of the altarpiece are the central panel in the lower range of the open altarpiece, *The Adoration of the Lamb*, a symbolic eucharistic scene inspired by the Book of Revelation, and the two nude figures of Adam and Eve placed at the far left and right of the upper range of panels.

Jan settled in Bruges in 1430, married, and purchased an elegant house. After completing the great altarpiece, he continued painting, recognized as the greatest figure of the Flemish school of painting. Many of his works survive. Among the best known of them are Madonnas, of which *Madonna and Child with Saints Michael and*

Catherine (1437) and *Madonna with Chancellor Nicolas Rolin* (1435) are noteworthy. Jan painted many portraits, of which the early *Portrait of Tymotheos* (1432), probably a portrait of the court musician **Gilles Binchois**, and *Man in a Red Turban* (ca. 1433), perhaps a self-portrait of the artist, are the most striking. In a class by itself is his *Arnolfini Wedding Portrait* (1434), which is more than a wedding picture of an Italian merchant and his bride, but is intended to be a legal record of the marriage and contains a number of striking symbolic elements including a representation of the artist himself reflected in a mirror, present because he is a witness to the wedding vows. The work of Jan van Eyck (especially, but not exclusively, the great altarpiece) was widely admired, not only in the Netherlands but in many parts of Europe. Some of the earliest enthusiastic descriptions of his work were written by Italian travellers.

VARCHI, BENEDETTO (1503–1565). Florentine **humanist**. He studied law at the Universty of **Pisa** and **Aristotelian** philosophy at **Padua**, but because of his inherited wealth was free to devote much time to mastering **Greek** and Provençal. His support of the uprising against **Medici** rule of **Florence** in 1527 forced him into exile, but in 1543 Duke Cosimo de'Medici permitted him to return to the city, where he became a member of the ducal court, joined the Florentine **Academy**, and lectured on **Dante** and **Petrarch**. In 1547 Cosimo asked Varchi to write a history of Florence, and his *Storia Fiorentina*, based on careful use of documents and frank in its criticism of some of the Medici, is now regarded as his principal work, but it was not published until 1721. His contemporaries admired him for his vast memory, his rich linguistic knowledge, and his poems in both Latin and Tuscan. He wrote a comedy, *La suocera / The Mother-in-Law*, orations, works of literary criticism, and a grammar of the Provençal language. Varchi's treatise *Ercolano* was a contribution to contemporary debates on language and supports the humanists' contention that usage is more important than authority and reason in determining good practice in any language. He defended the use of the contemporary Florentine form of Tuscan against critics who attacked usages not found in the great 14th-century writers. On the other hand, as a great admirer of the "Three Crowns" (Dante, Petrarch, and **Boccaccio**), he also argued that a good stylist must be familiar with the language as used by the best writers of the past.

VASARI, GIORGIO (1511–1574). Italian artist and architect, best known as the author of a highly influential history of art. The son of an artisan of Arezzo, he received a good vernacular education and had sufficient command of Latin to read works in that language, but not to write in it. He moved to **Florence** in 1524 as a member of the household of Alessandro and Ippolito de'**Medici** and maintained connections with important literary figures of his time. His artistic training began in Arezzo, where he worked with a French glass painter, but later he associated with more important artists, including Andrea del Sarto and **Rosso Fiorentino**. Vasari had strong support from the Medici family and from important figures at the papal curia. As a painter, he was highly productive, heading a large workshop and accepting commissions great and small. His *Deeds of Pope Paul III*, painted for the **pope's** grandson **Alessandro Farnese** in 1546, and his paintings in the Palazzo Vecchio at Florence (1555–1572) were his most notable achievements as a painter. He was also an architect. The Loggia of the Uffizi Palace in Florence (1560) was inspired by **Michelangelo's** Laurentian Library. He designed the De Monte chapel in the Church of San Pietro in Montorio at **Rome**, and rebuilt the Gothic church of the Pieve in Arezzo.

As a painter and architect, Vasari was successful and competent, but not especially memorable. His greatest achievement was literary, his book *Le vite de'più eccelenti architetti, pittori, et scultori italiani / The Lives of the Most Excellent Italian Architects, Painters, and Sculptors* (1550; enlarged edition, 1568). In this book he expresses admiration for **classical** art as a standard of excellence and notes its decline in the fourth century. The art of the subsequent period (medieval art) was inferior, in part because it produced images that were flat rather than natural-looking. He attributed the beginning of a revival of good art to the late 13th century because of the paintings of **Cimabue** and especially **Giotto**. He defined a second era of "rebirth" that began with the paintings of **Masaccio** and the sculptures of **Donatello**. The third and most perfect period was defined by the works of the three great High Renaissance artists, **Leonardo da Vinci**, Michelangelo, and **Raphael**.

In general, success in realistic representation of nature was the standard by which Vasari judged the quality of each age and each artist. His three-part division of Renaissance art, and his definition of medieval art as inferior and Renaissance art as a new age of artistic glory, influenced all subsequent art critics and historians, and while his denigration of medieval art was largely abandoned during the 19th century, his categories for classifying Renaissance art still are influential. His book also provided useful biographical information on individual artists, especially useful for those of the High Renaissance period since many of their pupils and other contemporaries were still alive when he wrote.

VEGA, GARCILASO DE LA. *See* GARCILASO DE LA VEGA.

VEGA CARPIO, LOPE FÉLIX DE. *See* LOPE DE VEGA.

VENEZIANO, DOMENICO (ca. 1410–1460). Italian painter, probably a native of **Venice**, who settled in **Florence** in 1439 and under the influence of the works of **Masaccio** adopted the new Florentine Renaissance style of painting, though his use of color is reminiscent of the Venetian tradition. Very little is known about any part of his career, especially its beginning, and his productivity seems to have been rather limited. Yet he influenced later Florentine painting with his typically Venetian emphasis on color and light, and the ablest painter of the next generation, **Piero della Francesca**, is recorded as one of his assistants in the execution of a major commission, a fresco cycle of scenes from the life of the Virgin in the church of St. Egidio at Florence, which does not survive. The Renaissance art historian **Giorgio Vasari** attributed to him the introduction of oil paints into Tuscan art. This claim is no longer tenable, but he may have been among the earliest Tuscans to use oil effectively.

Veneziano's best-known surviving work is the so-called St. Lucy altarpiece, a colorful and striking series of paintings for the church of Sta. Lucia de'Magnoli at Florence, which subsequently was divided. The central panel, *Madonna and Child with Saints* (ca. 1445), is now in the Uffizi Museum in Florence, but the predella panels are scattered. Other works of reasonably certain attribution are the early *Adoration of the Magi* (1439–1441), the *Carnesecchi Madonna* (ca. 1440), and three renditions of the Virgin and Child. One of his last works is *Saints John the Baptist and Francis* (1445–1461).

VENICE. City of northeastern Italy, center of a substantial territorial state during the Renaissance period, an active participant in Italian political and military affairs, and one of only two major Italian city-states to retain its republican political forms into the later Renaissance. Venice was founded during the sixth and seventh centuries when refugees fleeing the invasion of Italy by the Germanic Lombards took refuge on a small cluster of islands just off the Adriatic coast. By the year 1000 these small communities had coalesced into a municipality ruled by an elected duke (*doge* in the Venetian dialect) and several councils representing the merchant community. The city became rich from foreign trade, especially in luxury commodities (spices and cotton and silk cloth, among others) obtained through trade with the Muslim world and the Byzantine Empire. Early Venice had close contacts with **Constantinople** and regarded itself as in many respects a Byzantine rather than a western European community.

The city profited from the crusades by providing shipping and naval support to the crusaders, in return for which it acquired a share in the loot and (more important) commercial privileges in the Byzantine Empire and in the crusading states of the Levantine coast. During the 14th century, Venice contended with the rival commercial city of Genoa in a series of wars, mostly fought at sea. The War of the Chioggia (1379–1380) ended in a definitive victory for Venice, which from that time was the dominant commercial power in the eastern Mediterranean and acquired a number of island colonies (especially Crete). Although Venice had profited from its long relationship with the Byzantines, the fall of Constantinople to the **Ottoman Turks** in 1453 was not a total loss. Venice retained control of many of its island colonies and developed an active commerce with the new Turkish rulers. In the 16th century, as the Turks became an increasing naval threat, Venice contributed significantly to the Christian fleet that defeated the Turks at Lepanto in 1571. Venice remained a significant maritime power into the 17th century but gradually lost status as Mediterranean commerce declined in importance.

During its early history, Venice was exclusively a sea power and neither had nor desired territory in mainland Italy. Toward the end of their struggle with Genoa, however, the Venetians joined alliances against **Giangaleazzo Visconti**, the ambitious duke of **Milan**, whose expansion into northeastern Italy threatened to disrupt the city's food supply and trade links through the eastern Alpine passes to northern Europe. Venice took advantage of the temporary collapse of the Milanese state after the death of Duke Giangaleazzo (1402) to acquire a large mainland territory and by 1422 had brought Verona, Vicenza, **Padua**, and Belluno under Venetian rule. These territorial acquisitions changed the relationship of Venice to the rest of Italy. Before 1402, Venice studiously avoided involvement in Italian political conflicts. But with a mainland empire to defend, the republic could no longer function solely as a sea power tending to its business in the eastern Mediterranean.

The revival of Milanese territorial expansion after 1425 forced Venice to fight on land in order to maintain its food supplies and access to its markets in northern Europe. Although the Venetians were unable to prevent the accession of **Francesco Sforza** to the Milanese throne and only reluctantly approved the peace treaty of 1454 that recognized his title, the settlement left Venice secure in its mainland territories, a situation that prevailed until the French invasion of Italy in 1494. In the ensuing chaos of wars, alliances, and betrayals that left the rival kings of France and Spain in contention for control of Italy, Venice was often gravely threatened, especially during the War of the League of Cambrai (1509–1517), which was essentially a plot by the **pope**, the emperor, Spain, France, and several Italian powers to attack and loot the Venetian mainland state. When political conditions stabilized between 1530 and 1559, Venice was the only Italian state to avoid control by the ultimately victorious foreign power, Spain. Although the city's relative power gradually grew less, it survived as an independent republic until conquered by Napoleon Bonaparte in 1797.

The success of Venice in preserving its independence and maintaining control of most of its mainland territories was due partly to its isolated geographical location offshore. But the main reason for its survival was that its republican political system provided a remarkably stable and competent government that played the game of international politics with great skill. The other major Italian republic, **Florence**, had an unstable and frequently violent political history and ended up as a duchy ruled by the **Medici** family. The very different republican constitution of Venice provided considerably less political freedom but gave the city an orderly administration that endured. The city began with a government consisting of the *doge*, who was popularly elected for life, and a number of councils dominated by the wealthy merchants. In 1297 the leading families of the mercantile aristocracy, originally numbering some 200 families, declared the permanent closure of the Great Council, the largest of the city's conciliar bodies. This assembly of some 240 members had already usurped the right to elect the *doge*. The closure of the Great Council meant that henceforth all executive and judicial offices and all powers of legislation were in the hands of a legally defined noble class. Non-noble citizens (that is, members of families not represented on the Great Council) could never hold any civic office with real political power, though they could receive administrative appointments and serve as salaried employees. A handful of additional families were added to the nobility in the 14th century, but after 1380, the membership was permanently sealed.

Since the Great Council was too large to formulate policy, a Senate of 60 members did most of the real work of government, making the Grand Council mostly a pool of men eligible for high office. The Senate appointed ambassadors, conducted and determined foreign policy, chose the important magistrates, and appointed governors for the island colonies and the subject cities on the mainland. A particularly notorious part of the constitution was the **Council of Ten**, created in 1310 after a faction of aristocrats had plotted a revolution. This council, appointed by the Senate, maintained internal security. Although careful rotation of its membership kept any individual member from being powerful, as a group this council had great power. It could arrest, interrogate secretly, torture, or do anything else it judged necessary to ferret out plots. It was always alert to make sure that the *doge* was not plotting with outside forces to introduce foreign troops and seize power for himself, and in 1355 it arrested and executed a sitting *doge* who had conspired to do just that. This was an incredibly complex political system, but it functioned with remarkable efficiency. Despite occasional personal misdeeds and peculations, the Venetian nobility maintained a high standard of dedication to public service.

Venice had a large ecclesiastical establishment and was deeply observant of the external forms of religion, an observance reflected in the prominent role of the clergy in the many processions and ceremonies that embellished public life. The city treasured the supposed relics of St. Mark, acquired from Egypt at great cost in the ninth century. It had many elegant and costly churches (137 in 1493) and a large population of priests, monks, and nuns. Wealthy men and women left large sums to churches, monasteries, and hospitals, and Venetians of every rank participated in the *scuole* or fraternal organizations that financed poor relief, care of orphans, assistance to the sick, and other social services. Yet even while it was enthusiastically pious and strictly orthodox, the city was in many ways very secular and rationalistic in its management of religion. Members of the clergy were totally excluded from eligibility for all political offices and from the deliberations of the Senate and Great Council. The city appointed all bishops in its territories. Although Venice remained solidly Catholic during the **Reformation**, both individual heretics and heretical books and ideas were common. The local government exercised its own censorship of the press but refused to allow the papacy or any other external agency to exercise any control that might endanger the profitability of the local press, which had made Venice the greatest publishing center of Renaissance Europe. The city had its own inquisition, appointed and controlled by its own secular government.

After the **Roman Inquisition** was created, the city insisted on having its own observers present whenever papal inquisitors held a trial of a Venetian citizen. While it expected its own citizens to be loyal Catholics, it did not trouble the many foreign Protestants (especially Germans) who came there to do business or to study at its great **university** in Padua. Neither did it tolerate any open proselytizing by foreign heretics among its own citizens. Although direct confrontation with the papacy on ecclesiastical matters (as distinct from purely territorial and political issues) was difficult for any Catholic state of the Renaissance, Venice lived through a period of papal interdict during the War of the League of Cognac after 1509 and a far more difficult period of interdict in 1606, when the city government required the clergy to administer the sacraments of the church in defiance of the papal interdict.

Even in the Renaissance period itself, Venice was widely hailed as the most beautiful city in the world because of its location on many small islands and the use of bridges and boats rather than streets and wheeled vehicles for most local traffic. The principal church, the basilica of St. Mark, was a medieval structure (11th century) showing strong Byzantine influence. The Doge's Palace, the central location of government, was built in the 14th century and has many Gothic elements. Venetian art remained very traditional, but a distinctive Venetian Renaissance style of painting emerged in the work of the **Bellini** family. The Venetian style became influential beyond the Veneto region through the work of Giovanni Bellini's short-lived pupil **Giorgione** and Gentile Bellini's extremely long-lived pupil **Titian**, who is generally acknowleged as the city's greatest painter and worked not only in Venice but also for leading Italian and foreign rulers. His successors were the realist painter **Veronese** and the **mannerist Tintoretto**, both of whom were highly regarded.

Venice was also traditional in educational and literary culture and adopted the new Renaissance **humanism** rather slowly. Florentine humanism dominated the 15th century, though Venice, with its long tradition of contact with the eastern Mediterranean, was a principal point of contact for the entry of **Greek** language and literature into the West. The transplanted Byzantine bishop and scholar **Johannes Bessarion** willed his rich library of Greek **classical** and patristic texts to the city of Venice, not to Florence or papal **Rome**. By the end of the 15th century, the Venetian humanist **Ermolao Barbaro** was one of the most highly regarded humanist scholars in Italy, attaining a reputation rivalled only by his Florentine contemporary **Angelo Poliziano**. From late in the 15th century, the city had several of the rare female literary figures of the Italian Renaissance, **Cassandra Fedele** being active from the 1480s, the courtesan-poets **Gaspara Stampa** and **Veronica Franco** in the earlier 16th century, and **Lucrezia Marinella** toward the end of that century. The city had a rich society of **academies** and informal salons where both Latin and vernacular literatures were discussed. It had many private schools and tutors and maintained at public expense two excellent schools, the Latin grammar-school at San Marco and a more advanced school on the Rialto for lectures in philosophy. The intellectual life of the city was also influenced by the **scholastic** culture of the nearby University of Padua, which came under Venetian control in the early 15th century.

Venice was the center of a rich musical culture in the 15th and 16th centuries, and the basilica of St. Mark was second only to the papal curia at Rome as a center of church music. The choir directors and organists of St. Mark's included some of the greatest figures in early music, even though many of them in the earlier period came from the region of northern France and Flanders dominated musically by the court of the dukes of **Burgundy**. Figures like **Adrien Willaert, Cipriano de Rore, Gioseffo Zarlino, Andrea** and **Giovanni Gabrieli**, and **Claudio Monteverdi** were associated with St. Mark's for important parts of their careers, and Venice shared with several princely courts a central role in the development of Italian opera in the opening decades of the 17th century.

VERGARA, JUAN DE (1492–1557). Spanish **humanist** and priest, the most influential Spanish follower of the Dutch humanist **Erasmus**, whom he met in the Netherlands in 1520. Born at Toledo and educated at the **University of Alcalá**, he attracted the attention of the university's patron, Cardinal **Ximénes de Cisneros**, and about 1514 was made a fellow of the College of San Ildefonso, the principal center of humanistic studies in Alcalá. Also in 1514 he received the M.A. degree, and during this period he participated in the editorial work on the **Complutensian Polyglot Bible**, a project sponsored by Cardinal Ximénes. Vergara was a skilled Hellenist and in addition to work on the biblical project produced new Latin translations of **Aristotle**. About 1516 he became secretary to the cardinal. In 1517 he completed a doctorate in theology at Alcalá. He travelled with the imperial court to the Netherlands and Germany in 1520–1521 and entered the service of Guillaume de Croy, the successor to Ximénes as archbishop of Toledo.

When Cardinal de Croy died in 1521, Vergara became chaplain to the Emperor **Charles V**. In 1523 he was offered the chair of rhetoric at Alcalá but declined it, and in 1524 he became secretary to the next archbishop of Toledo, Alonso de Fonseca. This position near to the center of ecclesiastical power in Spain made it possible for him to promote the growth of "Erasmianism" in Spain and also to influence the outcome of the Valladolid Conference of 1527, summoned to hear charges of heresy and impiety brought against the books of Erasmus by the mendicant friars. The conference adjourned without either condemning or endorsing Erasmus, an outcome that at the time appeared to be a great victory for the Erasmians.

In 1533, however, Vergara was arrested on suspicion of having tried to bribe witnesses against his half-brother, who had been arrested by the **Inquisition** on charges of sharing the heresies of the mystical *alumbrados* ("the enlightened ones"). Vergara's connection with Erasmus became a basis for additional charges of promoting heresy, and even the efforts of his patron Archbishop Fonseca and his friend the **inquisitor**-general Alonso de Manrique could not secure his release. Vergara was imprisoned for two years, then tried and convicted of holding heretical opinions, and forced to make public recantation. He was heavily fined and imprisoned for a year in a monastery to do penance. He was released in 1537, but his conviction and imprisonment had undermined both his health and his reputation, and he lived the rest of his life in retirement at Toledo. His fall from such a high position marks the radical turn of the Spanish church away from the reformist humanism of Erasmus and the rapid destruction of the Erasmian movement in Spain.

VERGERIO, PIER PAOLO (1370–1444). Italian **humanist** and educator. A native of Capodistria in Venetian territory, he studied at **Bologna** (1388–1390) and while there also taught dialectic, an experience that turned him against the contentious wrangling of logicians and toward interest in the moral philosophy and rhetorical eloquence of the **classical** authors Seneca and **Cicero**. Vergerio also wrote a Latin comedy inspired by the Roman playwright Terence. He then moved to **Padua** to study medicine and law (1390–1397).

Having become interested in the works of the pioneering humanist **Petrarch**, Vergerio went to **Florence** and with the collaboration of the city's chancellor and leading humanist, **Coluccio Salutati**, completed an edition of Petrarch's unfinished Vergilian epic poem, *Africa*. His efforts to win patrons either in **Venice** or at the court of Padua were unsuccessful. In 1398 he moved to Florence and became one of the cluster of talented young humanists who studied **Greek** under the Byzantine scholar **Manuel Chrysoloras**. Late in 1399 Vergerio returned to Padua to renew his efforts to gain a place at the ruler's court, and about the same time he completed a doctorate in civil law. He later added a second doctorate in canon law. While campaigning to be appointed tutor to the Paduan ruler's son, Vergerio composed his most important book, *De ingenuis moribus et liberalibus studiis / On Honorable Character and Liberal Studies* (1403), which recommended study of humanistic subjects (history, moral philosophy, and eloquence or rhetoric) as the best way to prepare a young man for a life marked by ethical behavior and political responsibility. This book had great influence on both the theory and the practice of education in 15th-century Italy.

After the Venetians annexed Padua in 1404, Vergerio moved to **Rome**, where he attracted attention by his orations on St. Jerome, whom he praised as the prime example of an appropriate balance between classical learning and Christian commitment. He gained employment at the court of Pope Gregory XII and also the patronage of his old friend Cardinal Francesco Zabarella, whom he accompanied to the **Council of Constance** in 1414. Later, he accompanied the Holy Roman Emperor Sigismund on a long journey to the royal courts of Spain and Portugal in pursuit of an end to the **Western Schism**. He spent the rest of his life at Buda and Prague in the service of the emperor and in 1421 represented Sigismund at a colloquy seeking to end the religious division between **Hussites** and Catholics in Bohemia. After Sigismund's death in 1437, he lived in retirement at Buda, where he died.

VERGIL, POLYDOR (also Polidoro Virgilio, ca. 1470–1555). Italian **humanist** and historian. A native of **Urbino** and a priest, he entered papal service and accompanied Cardinal Adriano Castellesi to England when the cardinal became collector of Peter's Pence in that country. By 1502 he had become the cardinal's deputy, and in 1508 he became archdeacon of Wells. Vergil spent almost all the rest of his life in England, returning to Urbino only in 1553. His early writings included a collection of proverbs, *Proverbiorum libellus* (1498), which was a precursor of the more famous *Adagia* of **Erasmus**. The following year, he published *De inventoribus rerum / On the Inventors of Things*, a collection of essays on the persons he believed to have been the originators of human actions and inventions, ranging from religion and matrimony to more identifiable innovations like the art of **printing**. For Europe as a whole, this was his most famous publication.

Vergil's scholarly reputation made him a welcome figure at the court of King **Henry VII** and his successor **Henry VIII**, and with royal encouragement he wrote a history of England, *Anglica historia*, which originally extended to the death of Henry VII in 1509 and was first published in 1534. As an Italian who had come as a papal functionary but who also held a valuable English benefice, Vergil quietly conformed to the religious changes associated with the early English **Reformation**, though he avoided any historical publication covering the reign of Henry VIII until he had returned to Italy in his old age; then he published an extension carrying the story down to 1538. Because Vergil had resided at the English court so long and had such close connections with prominent persons there, his history is an important source for the early **Tudor** period. His denial of the legendary history of King Arthur offended many later English writers even though in 1525 he published an edition of the history of Gildas, one of the few literary sources for the history of Britain in the centuries following the end of Roman rule. The later chroniclers Raphael Holinshed and Edward Hall used his *Anglica historia* as a major source.

VERONESE, PAOLO (Paolo Caliari, 1528–1588). Venetian painter, born at Verona into a family of stonecutters and trained there under Antonio Badile. He was influenced by the work of the **mannerist** painters **Giulio Romano**, who had worked in Verona, and **Parmigianino**. Veronese began his career in his home town but received commissions from patrons at **Venice** and in 1555 settled there. His specialty was decorative ceiling paintings, of which the earliest, produced in 1553 for the rooms of the **Council of Ten** in the doge's palace, made his reputation, combining remarkable political allegory with a technical mastery of foreshortening and illusionism that made the figures seem lifelike when viewed from below. He continued with *The Coronation of the Virgin* (1555) as part of the sacristy ceiling in the church of San Sebastiano, following in 1556 with three pictures of the story of Esther on the nave ceiling of the same church. In 1557 Veronese was one of seven artists commissioned to produce competitively a number of roundels in the ceiling of the newly completed Library of St. Mark, and his representation of *Music* was awarded the prize by the distinguished judges, the painter **Titian** and the designer of the building, **Jacopo Sansovino**.

Even more famous was the series of ceiling decorations depicting feasts that he painted for the refectories of monasteries. The earliest of these was *The Wedding at Cana* (1562–1563) for the Benedictine monastery of San Giorgio Maggiore, but the most notorious was his *Last Supper* for the Dominicans of Santi Giovanni e Paolo. After its completion, the artist was summoned before the Venetian **Inquisition** to explain why he had included representations of Germans (Lutherans, perhaps), **Jews**, dwarfs, and drunkards among the vast throng depicted in what at best was a very unconventional picture of the Last Supper. Since the inquisitors were not impressed by his plea for poetic license, he agreed to add an inscription identifying the work with an entirely different theme, which he now called *Feast in the House of Levi*. His later works included *Allegory of the Battle of Lepanto* (1574) and *Apotheosis of Venice* (1577), both executed for the ducal palace.

VERROCCHIO, ANDREA (Andrea Cione, ca. 1435–1488). Florentine artist, primarily known as a sculptor. Born the son of a kiln worker and initially trained as a goldsmith, as early as 1463 he received a major commission for a monumental bronze sculpture, *The Incredulity of St. Thomas*. Another early work was a tomb for two members of the **Medici** family in San Lorenzo at **Florence**, *Piero I and Giovanni de'Medici* (1472). For a fountain at a Medici family villa he produced *Putto with a Dolphin* and a *David* that directly challenged the much-admired earlier treatment of the same figure by **Donatello**. Both of these works are thought to date from the 1460s or 1470s. His most widely known work, also in a sense a challenge to Donatello, is his *Equestrian Monument of Bartolomeo Colleoni* (ca. 1483–1488), a monumental bronze statue erected at **Venice** in honor of one of the city's most successful mercenary generals. Verrocchio headed a large workshop which trained many younger artists, of whom the most famous was **Leonardo da Vinci**. In his own time he was also a famous and successful painter, though the attribution of his works is often disputed. Even his most important painting, *The Baptism of Christ* (ca. 1475–1485), is known to have been retouched (if not repainted) by Leonardo. Many of the Italian artists of the next generation show traces of his influence.

VESALIUS, ANDREAS (1514–1564). Physician and anatomist. Born in Brussels, he was the son of an apothecary who served the Emperor **Charles V**. After study at the **University of Louvain**, he began the study of medicine at Paris, where he found the traditional anatomy lectures useless. He then returned to Louvain, took a baccalaureate in medicine (1537), and moved on to the University of **Padua**, the premier medical faculty in Europe, where he received a medical doctorate later that same year. He was immediately appointed professor of surgery, with the duty of conducting anatomical dissections. His early *Tabulae anatomicae sex / Six Anatomical Tables* (1538), produced jointly with a pupil of the painter **Titian**, was based on the ancient Greek anatomist Galen, whose work relied on animal dissections. But Vesalius' experience in dissections convinced him that Galen's book, the standard textbook on anatomy, was full of errors, and he began criticizing Galen in his lectures.

Beginning in 1540 he worked on a new manual of anatomy, *De humani corporis fabrica / On the Structure of the Human Body* (1543), for which he employed a skilled German painter and woodcut engraver, Jan Steven van Calcar (known in Italy as Giovanni Flammingo), whose illustrations reflect Vesalius' new anatomical discoveries even more accurately than the book's Latin text. Vesalius also produced a shorter text for use by students, his *Epitome*. This book was quickly translated into German. A considerably revised Latin edition appeared in 1555. That same year, Vesalius joined the Spanish court, where he found the scientific climate less favorable than Padua had been. In 1564 before leaving on a pilgrimage to the Holy Land, he accepted reappointment to the faculty at Padua, but he died on the return trip later that same year. His *De fabrica* is generally regarded as the first significant step toward abandonment of the authority of Galen and the introduction of new material based on direct experimentation.

VESPASIANO DI BISTICCI. *See* BISTICCI, VESPASIANO DI.

VIÈTE, FRANÇOIS (1540–1603). French mathematician, important for the development of trigonometric tables and algebraic notation. The son of a lawyer and notary at Fontenay-le-Comte in Poitou, he was educated in law at Poitiers, receiving a baccalaureate in 1560 but abandoning that profession in 1564 to become tutor to the daughter of an important noble family. He moved to Paris in 1570, and in 1573 King Charles IX appointed him counsellor in the Parlement of Rennes, where he remained for six years. In 1580 Viète became a privy councillor and *maître des requêtes* in the Parlement of Paris. Having been banished from court through the influence of political enemies, he spent the years 1584–1585 in the provinces. After the accession of King Henry IV in 1589, he returned to court, deciphering coded messages captured during the war with Spain. In 1602, however, he was dismissed from royal service.

Viète's first mathematical tract, *Principes de cosmographie*, began as one of his lectures as a tutor. Other works include *Canon mathematicus seu Ad triangula* (1579), *In artem analyticam isagoge* (1591), and *De aequationum recognitione et emendatione* (1615), edited and posthumously published by a Scottish friend. Viète's mathematical innovations include being the first mathematician to use letters of the alphabet to represent known and unknown quantities, invention of the term "coefficient," and use of the cosine law for plane triangles. He also published the law of tangents. In 1592–1595 he engaged in a public dispute with the noted scholar **Josephus Justus Scaliger**, who erroneously claimed to have solved the problem of squaring the circle.

VILLANI, GIOVANNI, MATTEO, and FILIPPO. Florentine mercantile family, known principally for their description of **Florence** on the eve of the period when it became a major center of Renaissance **humanism**. Giovanni (ca. 1275–1348) travelled to **Rome** for the papal jubilee in 1300 and after seeing the ruinous ancient capital declared that Rome, the old metropolis, was sinking while his city, Florence, was rising. Confident of the great destiny lying before Florence, he undertook to write its history, beginning, in good medieval fashion, with the Tower of Babel and providing a largely uncritical account until he got to his own times, which he described with shrewd insight into the civic life he knew from personal experience. Giovanni served three terms as one of the priors and held several significant administrative jobs. He also endured a period of exile. As an experienced businessman who had travelled in France and Flanders in 1302–1308 and had worked as manager of the **Peruzzi** bank's branch at Bruges, he had an interest in numbers that led him to include not only his famous estimate of the number of students in Florence but also much other statistical information on population, food consumption, cloth production, public works, and churches. Modern research has in general found these estimates remarkably accurate. Giovanni died in the **Black Death** of 1348. His brother Matteo continued the history of

Florence down to 1363, when he also died of plague, and Matteo's son Filippo added one book covering one additional year.

Giovanni's description of the large number of boys and girls attending school in the city (between 8,000 and 10,000 in vernacular schools and 550 to 600 boys learning Latin grammar) is often cited, both as an indication of widespread literacy and as evidence of the more restricted availability of Latin education. Filippo Villani, who was one of the city's early humanists and served as chancellor of the commune of Perugia and as lecturer on **Dante** in the Florentine *Studio* (1401–1404), is also known for his work *Famous Citizens of the City of Florence*, a collection of biographical sketches of local citizens, written in Latin.

VILLON, FRANÇOIS (1431–ca. 1463). French poet, usually classed as a late medieval rather than a Renaissance author since his works lack the **classicizing** style associated with the French Renaissance. Yet his poetry was admired by leading figures of the Renaissance, including **François Rabelais**, who cites him in *Pantagruel* and makes him appear as a character in the *Quart livre*, and **Clément Marot**, who published the first collected edition of his works in 1533. Villon was born in Paris to a poor family and brought up by one of his relatives, a chaplain, whose surname he adopted. Thanks to this patron, he was able to study at the **University** of Paris (B.A., 1449; M.A., 1452). Villon seems to have led a disorderly and violent life, belonging to a gang of ruffians and in 1455 getting involved in a brawl that ended with his killing a priest, a crime for which he received a pardon from the king. Late the following year Villon participated in the theft of a large sum from the Collège de Navarre, and when the theft was discovered, he left Paris and remained in the provinces until 1461. In 1461 he was imprisoned for an unknown crime but was one of the prisoners pardoned in honor of the formal entry of King Louis XI into the city of **Meung**. In 1462 he was involved in another fatal conflict and was imprisoned though not identified as the murderer. He appealed his sentence to the Parlement, which commuted it to an exile of 10 years in 1463. A few days later, Villon disappeared from Paris, and there is no further record of him.

Villon's poems are full of topical references and personal satires which even his Renaissance editor, Marot, could not fully understand. They refer to events in his life, and they also parody legal language and traditional ideas of courtly love, often in a scatological manner. His collected *Lais* circulated from 1456, and his *Testament* from 1462. Some of Villon's poems are written in the argot of the Parisian criminal class.

VIRTÙ. Italian term, derived from the Latin *virtus* and frequently used in Renaissance discussions of human character. The term, like its Latin source, does not mean "virtue" in the conventional modern sense, though it does imply "goodness" in contrast to "vice." Above all, it denotes the qualities that made a man (the source-word of *virtus* is *vir*, the **classical** Latin word for a high-status man) admirable, such as intelligence, competence, and energy. **Niccolò Machiavelli** in particular employs it to describe the qualities needed in a successful ruler, but it was a common word, used by many authors and always having a complimentary connotation. When used with reference to things, it implies power or efficacy, such as the *virtù* of a medicine or a weapon.

VISCONTI. Italian ruling family who established themselves in the late 13th century as *signori* ("lords") of **Milan**, which they made the center of a powerful principality that by 1400 aspired to control all of central and northern Italy and perhaps even aimed at securing a royal title. The family's control of Milan grew out of the violent factional struggles between **Ghibellines** and **Guelfs** in the 13th century for control of the city's government. Authoritarian rule was first created by the rival Guelf family of Della Torre, but in 1277 they were overthrown by a Ghibelline conspiracy led by the local archbishop, Ottone Visconti. Since Ottone, ruling as a bishop, could not pass his lordship on to his descendants, he arranged for his nephew Matteo Visconti to be elected *capitano del popolo*, leader of the city's armed forces, first for a 10-year term and then for life. Though the Visconti were temporarily displaced by their Della Torre rivals in the early 14th century, the interruption was brief, and the family ruled Milan and a growing set of subject cities and rural districts until it became extinct in 1447 and was shortly afterward replaced by the **Sforza** dynasty. In the middle of the 14th century, the principality was ruled jointly by three Visconti brothers, with Milan and the old Lombard capital at Pavia being the two principal centers of power.

The greatest figure of the dynasty was Giangaleazzo Visconti (1351–1402), who succeeded his father in 1378 and in 1385 deposed his last surviving uncle, the brutal and violent Bernabò. Having united the whole principality in his own hands, Giangaleazzo consolidated his power, capitalized on the wealth and commercial importance of Milan, and established an effective and largely beneficent internal administration. But he also was ambitious to expand his territories and through shrewd manipulation of inter-city rivalries and the use of military force made himself a growing threat to the independence not only of other small states in Lombardy but also of the wealthy and powerful republics of **Venice** and **Florence**. Significantly, as he annexed conquered regions, he did not incorporate them into the territory subject to the city of Milan but ruled them in his own person, thus reducing his dependence on the political voice of the Milanese people. He brought this political development to its peak in 1395 when he purchased the title duke of Milan from the Holy Roman Emperor Wenceslas, thus acquiring a hereditary title under which he could solidify personal control of the whole state.

Giangaleazzo's military expansion eventually united the Venetians and Florentines against him. His enemies (especially Florentine **humanists**) depicted him as an unprincipled tyrant while representing themselves as defenders of republican institutions and Italian liberty. Giangaleazzo's military power and diplomatic skill posed a serious threat to both of the great republics, and the Florentines in particular seriously feared that they would be conquered and incorporated into his territories, a fear increased by his success in taking over **Pisa**, Siena, Perugia, and **Bologna** (1398–1402).

His unexpected death of plague in 1402 seemed the salvation of Florentine independence. It was, however, a disaster for Milan and the large state that he had built, which rapidly collapsed and never entirely recovered under his successors. At the time of Giangaleazzo's death, both of his sons were minors. The states that had come to fear Visconti power, particularly the Venetians, quickly seized territory that Giangaleazzo had added to his principality; in the case of the Venetians, their move to seize the easternmost provinces of the duchy marks the beginning of their direct involvement in mainland politics. Several of the subjugated cities threw off Milanese rule. The elder of Giangaleazzo's sons, Giovanni Maria (1402–1412), was mentally deranged and proved to be so dangerous that he was assassinated. The younger son, Filippo Maria (1412–1447), was a far better ruler and managed to stabilize the duchy and restore control over the western part of his father's territories, though the Venetians kept control of the lands they had seized in the east. Filippo Maria came to be a danger to both the Venetians and the Florentines. His territories and power never equalled his father's, but he was a successful duke except for his failure to produce a legitimate heir.

At his death in 1447, Filippo Maria left only his illegitimate daughter Bianca Maria, whom he had married to his ablest mercenary general, Francesco Sforza. The Milanese succession crisis produced another round of wars as the citizens of Milan tried to re-establish their republican form of government while at the same time defending their independence and their territories from ambitious neighbors, especially the Venetians. Eventually they had to turn to Francesco Sforza to beat off the foreign invaders, but after doing so, he seized control of the city and declared himself and his wife duke and duchess of Milan. The success of this seizure of power inaugurated a long period when the duchy of Milan was ruled by this new Sforza dynasty.

VITRY, PHILIPPE DE (1291–1361). French composer and poet, also bishop of Meaux. His contemporary **Petrarch** knew and admired his French poetry, but he is best known as one of the leading figures of the new musical style known to contemporaries as *ars nova*. He wrote four treatises on the *ars nova* style. His surviving compositions include a number of motets.

VITTORINO DA FELTRE (Vittorino Ramboldoni, 1378–1446). Italian **humanist**, scholar, and educator, the son of a notary of Feltre. About 1390 he entered the **University** of **Padua**, where he studied dialectic, rhetoric, and philosophy and also canon law, but his deepest interest was in the *studia humanitatis*—that is, in humanism. His teacher at Padua, Giovanni Conversino da Ravenna, had been a pupil of **Petrarch**. Next Vittorino studied rhetoric with Gasparino Barzizza, an early leader in the effort to introduce humanistic reforms into the curriculum of schools and universities. In 1410 Vittorino completed his doctorate in arts. Since he was poor, he had to earn a living by teaching introductory Latin language and mathematics. In 1415 he moved to **Venice**, where he studied **Greek** under **Guarino da Verona** and **George of Trebizond**, once again supporting himself by teaching Latin to schoolboys. Vittorino returned to Padua in 1419 and became a successful teacher there. Like other masters, he took students as boarders in his own home, and he reduced his fees for those who (like himself in earlier years) were poor. In 1422 the university appointed him Barzizza's successor in the chair of rhetoric, an appointment that committed him to a secular career; previously, he had considered entering a monastery. As a university professor, however, he found that the prevailing teaching style conflicted with his own preferred methods and also that his students could not be given the careful moral supervision that he had provided for his private pupils. In 1423 he resigned his professorship and settled in Venice to found his own Latin grammar school.

That same year, however, Vittorino received an invitation from **Gianfrancesco Gonzaga**, marquis of **Mantua**, to organize a school at the Mantuan court for the children of the ruler and prominent courtiers. The opportunity to educate and shape the character of a future ruler was attractive to him, and after making sure that he would be allowed to conduct the school according to his own preference, he moved to Mantua. This school at Mantua, which he called La Casa Giocosa / The Pleasant House, was one of the earliest and most influential Italian schools specfically organized to teach the humanities. The students included members of the ruling family, sons of local nobles, and promising students from poor families to whom he could offer free education and connections with the rich and powerful that would promote the students' future careers. These scholarship students made up about half of the enrollment; there were about 70 students in all, including a few girls.

Vittorino insisted that it must be a boarding school, even for the children of the ruler, since he wanted to impart strict moral and religious training and to insulate his adolescent students from the moral corruption and cynicism of court life. The program of study focused on the humanistic subjects of grammar, rhetoric, history, poetry, and moral philosophy and involved study of both Latin and Greek. It also included mathematics, music, philosophy, and religion. Since he was educating boys who would be future rulers and high officials—and hence also soldiers—Vittorino included physical training and military exercises. Religious instruction and regular participation in religious services and sacraments were an important part of the school's atmosphere.

The ultimate goal of the educational program was to prepare pupils to be useful members (and leaders) of society. The school soon developed a reputation extending far beyond Mantua, so that prominent families throughout Italy strove to get their sons admitted to study with Vittorino. A number of men who became leaders of the next generation of humanists studied there, including **Niccolò Perotti** and **Lorenzo Valla**. This school, together with the contemporary court school conducted at **Ferrara** by Guarino da Verona, established a model for the humanistic grammar school that became the ideal of Renaissance education throughout Italy and later throughout Europe.

VIVES, JUAN LUIS (1492–1540). Spanish **humanist**, born into a family of *conversos*. He was educated in his native city of Valencia and then at the **University** of Paris (1509–1512), where he disliked the traditional **scholastic** curriculum and eventually left without taking a degree. He settled in Bruges, which became his principal home for the rest of his life. In 1517 he became tutor to Guillaume de Croy, the aristocratic cardinal and archbishop-elect of Toledo, and accompanied his 19-year-old pupil to the **University of Louvain**. Vives was permitted to lecture at Louvain despite his lack of a formal university degree. He had attracted the favorable attention of the French humanist **Jacques Lefèvre d'Etaples** at Paris and of the Dutch humanist **Erasmus**, who settled in Louvain in 1517, about the same time that Vives arrived there. Both Erasmus and his friend **Thomas More** admired Vives' command of Latin. His treatise criticizing scholastic education, *In pseudodialecticos*, also attracted Erasmus and More to him. In 1522 he received an offer of the chair of rhetoric at the **University of Alcalá** in his native Spain, in succession to the great Spanish humanist **Elio Antonio de Nebrija**. Almost simultaneously, however, he learned that the **Spanish Inquisition** had arrested his father on charges of relapsing into **Jewish** religious practices. The father was executed in 1524, and though the humanist's mother had died in 1509, she, too, was accused of apostasizing into Judaism, was tried in 1528, and her body was exhumed and burned. Prudently, Vives declined the offer from Alcalá and never again returned to his native country.

In 1523 he visited England and accepted an offer from Cardinal **Thomas Wolsey** to teach **Greek** at Oxford. In 1524 he returned to Bruges and married the daughter of a Spanish *converso* family settled there. His wife remained in Bruges when he returned to England, where he had formed friendships with influential persons such as Thomas More, Bishop John Fisher, and the royal physician **Thomas Linacre**. In 1527–1528 he served as tutor to Princess Mary **Tudor**, daughter of **Henry VIII** and his Spanish queen, Catherine of Aragon. His support for Queen Catherine during Henry's effort to secure a divorce cost him the king's favor, and for a time in 1528 he was held under house arrest but was eventually permitted to return to Bruges. Late in 1528 he briefly returned to England as adviser to Queen Catherine, but since she refused to follow his advice on how to conduct her opposition to the divorce, he returned to the Netherlands, living mostly at Bruges.

At the urging of Erasmus, Vives edited St. Augustine's *City of God*, accompanied by his own commentary (1522). He dedicated this work to Henry VIII but it did not interest the king. His *De institutione feminae Christianae / On the Education of a Christian Woman* (1524) was dedicated to Queen Catherine, who was more receptive, and he also gained the queen's interest with his *De ratione studii puerilis / On the Method of Educating Children* (1536), a guide to education written for Princess Mary. Later he wrote a work *De officio mariti / On a Husband's Duties* (1529), dedicated to the Spanish duke of Gandia. Vives wrote several textbooks that were widely used in schools, including *Introductio ad sapientiam / Introduction to Learning* and a collection of dialogues designed to assist in the study of Latin (1538). Vives also made a major contribution to contemporary social theory with his *De subventione pauperum / On Poor-Relief* (1525), which addressed the much-debated issue of the relief of poverty, and he published two political tracts on resistance to the Turks and on issues of war and peace among Christians.

VOSSIUS, GERARDUS JOANNES (1577–1649). Dutch **humanist**, a major representative of the late flowering of Renaissance culture in the independent Netherlands. In his lifetime he was recognized as a great scholar, and his publications summed up much of what Renaissance humanistic scholarship had achieved. His widespread correspondence extended his influence throughout Europe. Born at Heidelberg, where his father, a prominent Dutch Calvinist, had taken refuge during the war for independence, Vossius received his education at the Latin school in Dordrecht and in 1595 entered the **University** of Leiden, where he received the M.A. degree. He became rector of the Latin school at Dordrecht (1600–1615) and then regent of a college for ministers at Leiden. Although he preserved neutrality in the conflict between the Arminians and the strict Calvinists, he was dismissed after the latter faction gained political control of the republic. In 1622 he became professor of eloquence and history at Leiden and in 1632 became the first rector and professor of history and politics in the Athenaeum Illustre at Amsterdam.

Several of Vossius' publications dealt with church history, including *Historia Pelagianismi / History of Pelagianism* (1618) and *Dissertationes tres de tribus symbolis / Three Disquisitions on the Three Creeds* (1642). In secular history he wrote *Ars historica / The Art of History* (1625), *De historicis Graecis / The Greek Historians* (1623), and *De historicis Latinis / The Latin Historians* (1627). His works as a rhetorician and grammarian included *Institutiones oratoriae / Introduction to Oratory* (1606), *Poeticarum institutionum libri tres / Three Books of Lessons on Poetics* (1647), *Aristarchus, sive de arte grammatica libri septem* (1635, a work on Latin grammar), *De vitiis sermonis / On Errors in Language* (1645), and *Etymologicon linguae Latinae / Etymological Dictionary of the Latin Language* (1662). He also published a work on **classical** mythology, *Theologia gentilis* (1641), a work on the structure of the arts and sciences, *De artium et scientiarum natura ac constitutione* (posthumous, 1695), and a number of highly successful textbooks.

– W –

WARS OF THE ROSES. Series of sporadic civil wars among contending factions of the English royal family and their aristocratic supporters (1455–1485). The underlying causes of the wars were the unresolved questions of the extent of the king's personal authority, the transformation of the higher nobility into military adventurers and subcontractors during the **Hundred Years' War**, and the inability of the crown's traditional sources of revenue to meet the financial needs of government. More immediately responsible, however, was the periodic insanity of King Henry VI, which made it impossible to establish firm royal control over the agencies of government and produced bitter rivalries among factions of the high nobility who had become financially dependent on their ability to control royal patronage and revenues. The ruling Lancastrian dynasty had usurped the throne by force in 1399, and the king's illness motivated Richard, duke of York, to rebel aganst his own exclusion from the council of regency set up to run the government during the king's incapacity. A further cause of civil war was recriminations over the defeat of the English in the final campaign of the Hundred Years' War.

The internal struggle led to the death of Duke Richard of York in battle, the dethronement of Henry VI by Richard's son Edward, duke of York, in 1461, a brief restoration of Henry VI by the Lancastrian faction in 1470, and a resurgence of Yorkist power with the aid of the duke of **Burgundy** in 1471. Once restored to power, the Yorkist king, Edward IV, managed to impose a measure of internal order, but his early death, leaving two minor sons in charge of his brother, Richard, duke of Gloucester, ended in the usurpation of the throne by Gloucester (who ruled as Richard III from 1483 to 1485), and he in turn was defeated and killed in battle by a distant relative of the Lancastrian kings, Henry **Tudor**, who took the throne as **Henry VII**. The new Tudor dynasty ruled England until the death of its last direct member, **Elizabeth I**, in 1603.

The term "Wars of the Roses" is something of a misnomer. According to tradition, the white rose had been the symbol of the house of York and the red rose, of the house of Lancaster, but the term was applied only later, no doubt as part of the successful propaganda of Henry VII, who married the daughter of the Yorkist king Edward IV, to present his victory as a permanent solution of the dynastic problems that had led to civil war. Traditional historiography associates the beginning of the English Renaissance with the new Tudor dynasty and records the Wars of the Roses as the last act in English medieval history, but this is largely a product of Tudor propaganda: the wars occurred during a period when Renaissance art and **humanistic** culture were reaching their peak in

Italy and when influences from Italy were already beginning to attract educated persons in both England and France.

WEBSTER, JOHN (ca. 1578–ca. 1625). English dramatist, best known as the author of two violent and melodramatic revenge tragedies, and the probable author of several others. He was the son of a prosperous London coachmaker and merchant tailor, was apprenticed to his father's trade, and was admitted to the Merchant Taylors' Company in 1603. But at least a year earlier, he seems to have been already involved in the theatrical world, perhaps as an actor and probably as a collaborator with other dramatists. Two of the three plays generally ascribed to him are now regarded as works of highest quality, *The White Devil* (1612) and *The Duchess of Malfi* (1614). A third play, the tragicomedy *The Devil's Law Case* (ca. 1617–1619), is also highly regarded. The attribution of another tragedy, *Appius and Virginia* (ca. 1608), is debated; it may have been written in collaboration with John Heywood. Several comedies have also been ascribed either to Webster or to him and other collaborators, including *Northward Ho* and *Westward Ho* (ca. 1605–1606, both probably collaborations with Thomas Dekker), *Any Thing for a Quiet Life* (ca. 1621, perhaps with **Thomas Middleton**), and *A Cure for a Cuckold* (ca. 1624, ascribed to him and William Rowley).

WECHEL. Family of printers active in Paris, Frankfurt-am-Main, and Hanau, 1526–1627. Christian Wechel, born near Antwerp, became a Paris bookseller about 1518 and acquired a **printing** shop in 1526. In 1550 his will transferred the Paris firm to a nephew, Andreas Wechel, and other properties in Cologne to another nephew, Simeon Wechel. Andreas fled from Paris after the St. Bartholomew's Day massacre of Huguenots in 1572 and re-established his business successfully at Frankfurt. When he died in 1581, two sons-in-law, Claude de Marne and Jean Aubry, also Protestant refugees, took charge of his press. At the same time, Johann Wechel, whose relation to the others is not clear, moved from Cologne and began printing in Frankfurt. Because Frankfurt was becoming strongly Lutheran and hostile to **Calvinism**, Jean Aubry moved his firm to Hanau, where Calvinism was predominant. In 1613 Clemens Schleich, Marne's son-in-law, reunited the two German branches, but the business did not prosper during the

Thirty Years' War, and by 1627 it had become a merely local operation. For most of its existence, the Wechel family was linked to Calvinistic Protestantism and also to Renaissance **humanism**. Chrétien printed Book Three of **François Rabelais'** *Pantagruel* and many editions of **Erasmus'** works. Andreas at Paris was the main printer used by the French Calvinist philosopher **Peter Ramus**. But once it settled in Germany, the firm was distinguished mainly by publication of neo-Latin literature, **classical** philology, and works by Ramus and his followers. In the 1590s the family also produced many editions of a **Neoplatonic** or **Hermetic** sort, including books by **Giordano Bruno**, **John Dee**, and **Giambattista della Porta**.

WEYDEN, ROGIER VAN DER. *See* VAN DER WEYDEN, ROGIER.

WILLAERT, ADRIAAN (ca. 1490–1562). Flemish composer. He was trained by Jean Mouton in Paris but spent most of his career in Italy. By 1515 he was in the service of Cardinal Hippolito d'**Este** at **Rome** and travelled to **Ferrara** in the cardinal's household. After the cardinal's death in 1520, he entered the service of Duke Alfonso I d'Este at Ferrara, and in 1527 he became *maestro di cappella* at St. Mark's in **Venice**, one of the principal musical appointments in Italy. Willaert made visits home to Flanders in 1542 and 1556–1557 but spent the rest of his career at St. Mark's. He trained many leading musicians of the next generation, including **Cipriano de Rore**, **Andrea Gabrieli**, and **Gioseffe Zarlino**. Most of his work was in the form of motets for church use, though he also was an early composer of madrigals, a secular genre in which he followed the tradition of the Venetian humanist **Pietro Bembo**, who in turn was responsible for the revival of **Petrarchan** influence in Italian poetry. More than most Franco-Flemish composers of his time, Willaert was strongly influenced by **humanism** and by native Italian musical practices. He paid great attention to the stress of Latin pronunciation, took care never to permit a rest to interrupt a word or thought, and insisted that **printers** of music place each syllable of a word directly under the matching musical note. His major publication was a collection of motets and madrigals, *Musica nova* (1559).

WILSON, THOMAS (ca. 1525–1581). English **humanist** and royal official. Born in rural Lincolnshire, he studied as a King's Scholar at

Eton College (1537–1542), where he was a pupil of **Nicholas Udall**, and then moved to King's College, Cambridge (B.A. 1547, M.A. 1549). At Cambridge he was associated with the group of humanists known as "Athenians" for their support of the **Erasmian** method of pronouncing **Greek**, an issue that gave rise to sharp controversy with the traditionalist chancellor of the **university**, Bishop Stephen Gardiner. While teaching at Cambridge after completion of his degrees, Wilson was tutor to two sons of the Duchess of Suffolk, who was a patron of the regius professor of divinity, the noted German Protestant theologian Martin Bucer. With the death of King Edward VI and the accession of Queen Mary I, who was determined to restore Catholicism in England, Wilson decided to leave the country, not only for fear of persecution but also because several of his patrons had been executed for attempting to prevent Mary's succession to the throne. He went to **Padua**, where he joined his fellow exile **John Cheke** in perfecting his Greek and also began the study of civil law; he took a doctorate in law at **Ferrara** in 1560. While working as a legal advocate in **Rome**, he was arrested by the **Roman Inquisition** on charges that his books on logic and rhetoric contained heretical doctrine. He survived only because in 1559 a Roman mob stormed the inquisitorial prison and set all prisoners free.

Since the Protestant **Elizabeth I** was now ruling England, Wilson returned home in 1560. Having found the career of humanist scholar insecure and financially unrewarding, he now pursued a career at court. He began with a number of administrative and judicial appointments and because of his legal training and his residence abroad was also sent on embassies to Portugal and the Netherlands. Beginning in 1563, he was elected to every Parliament that sat during the rest of his life. About 1577 he shared with Sir Francis Walsingham appointment as principal secretary of the Privy Council. Despite his explicit renunciation of a scholarly career after his return from Italy, he continued to write and study the **classics**. During his time at Cambridge, his closest associates had become convinced of the need for learned books in the English language, and most of Wilson's published books contributed to that cause. His *Rule of Reason* (1552) is an early example of a logic textbook written in English. His best known and most influential work, *The Art of Rhetoric* (1553), shows little originality but presents a useful introduction to rhetoric based on ancient authors such as **Aristotle**, **Cicero**, and Quintilian. His later publications include a *Discourse upon Usury* (1572), which condemned charging of interest as a form of extortion and repeated sentiments he had expressed as a member of Parliament. Wilson also continued his interest in Greek literature and published the first English translation of Demosthenes' *Olynthiacs* and *Philippics* (1570).

WIMPHELING, JAKOB (1450–1528). German **humanist** and clergyman, known as an influential but generally conservative figure among the reform-minded humanists of the early 16th century. Born at Sélestat in Alsace and educated in the excellent local Latin school and then at Freiburg-im-Breisgau (B.A. 1466), Erfurt, and Heidelberg (M.A. 1479, licentiate in theology 1496), he was ordained as a priest and served churches near Heidelberg during his theological studies. He also taught in the faculty of arts. In 1484 he became cathedral preacher at Speyer but returned to the Heidelberg faculty in 1498. Although Wimpheling's candidacy for appointment as a cathedral canon at Strasbourg in 1501 was unsuccessful, he remained in that city from 1501 to 1515, supporting himself by income from other church offices, tutoring children, and editing and authorship of more than 40 books for local printers. In 1515 he moved back to Sélestat and spent the rest of his life there.

Initially, Wimpheling was sympathetic to **Martin Luther**'s criticism of indulgences and corruption among the German clergy and at the papal curia. But as he realized that Luther's theology was contrary to traditional doctrine and that the unity of the church was in danger, he broke with Luther and worked to prevent Lutheran preachers from functioning in Sélestat. His last years were spent in isolation, since Catholic leaders had not forgiven him for his denunciations of ecclesiastical corruption while those humanists who had become Lutheran regarded his opposition to the **Reformation** as a betrayal.

During his literary career, in which he published more than a hundred books, Wimpheling produced Latin poems, a Latin school drama modelled on Terence, *Stylpho* (1484), and a number of pedagogical works that endorsed study of **classical** authors but also warned repeatedly against the moral corruption that lurked in pagan poets. These books included *Elegantiarum medulla / Kernel of Elegances* (1493), *Isidoneus germanicus / A Guide for Germans* (1497), and especially the influential *Adolescentia / Youth* (1500). Teachers, he recommended, should use classical texts in order to develop good Latin style in their pupils but should be very careful in selecting which authors to teach, avoiding sensual authors and concentrating on those who inculcated sound moral principles.

Wimpheling's conservatism became clear in a controversy between him and a more radical humanist, Jakob Locher, of the **University** of Ingolstadt, who attacked **scholastic** education in ways that Wimpheling, despite his own earlier criticisms of the scholastics, could not endorse; his *Defensio theologiae scholasticae et neotericorum / Defense of Scholastic Theology and the Moderns* (1510) upheld scholastic theology. He also wrote a manual for the education of princes (*Agatharchia*, 1498) and a number of works that show that even a quite conservative humanist could engage in bitter denunciation of clerical immorality, especially among the monks and friars, and could denounce the corrupt patronage system that neglected dedicated and well-educated priests (like himself) and conferred the best appointments on well-connected but unqualified persons. Wimpheling also edited the writings of others, especially while working for the flourishing **printing** industry in Strasbourg. He edited works of **Sebastian Brant, Giovanni Pico della Mirandola**, and **Erasmus**, but also medieval theologians such as Jean Gerson, Heinrich von Langenstein, Bernard of Clairvaux, and Ludolph of Saxony. Despite his conservatism and his diminished influence during the Reformation crisis of his last years, Wimpheling was one of the most influential reformist humanists of the early 16th century and insisted that education must combine cautious study of classical literature with inculcation of Christian piety.

WITCHCRAFT. In the law of every European nation in the later **Middle Ages** and the Renaissance, witchcraft was a crime punishable by severe penalties, including death, and at certain specific times and places, a "witch craze" developed in which a significant number of individuals were accused, convicted, and executed. The idea of witchcraft involved two elements. First, the witch was a *maleficus*, an evildoer, who employed supernatural powers in order to inflict actual harm on one or more victims, causing death, bodily injury, illness, impotence, or some other observable misfortune that was attributed to the action of the witch. Study of judicial records suggests that in cases where charges of witchcraft were instituted by members of a local community, this was almost the only kind of accusation made, especially in countries like England, where witchcraft cases were tried in secular courts and torture was never applied in witchcraft prosecutions.

But since the 13th century, **scholastic** theologians had associated the kind of witchcraft that caused (or was believed to cause) specific harm with the second element in witchraft prosections, belief that the witch disavowed Christ and the Christian God and engaged in worship of the devil. This worship was believed to involve not only some formal act of repudiating God but also some inverted parody of Christian worship, directed not to God but to the devil. In most developed form of witchcraft lore (as in the Faust legend of the 16th century), the new witch would sign a formal written contract, often written in blood, with the devil and would defile consecrated communion hosts stolen from a church or consume human flesh (often described as the flesh of innocent babies) or venerate excrement with the same observances used by orthodox believers during veneration of the sacrament. In return for worshipping the spirit of evil, the witch would receive the supernatural powers by which he or she caused harm to individuals. Witches would also acquire other supernatural powers, and they would gather periodically to worship their diabolical master, dancing naked, engaging in sexual intercourse with demons, and (according to some theorists) flying through the air to remote mountaintops where these orgies—the witches' sabbath— took place.

The first concept of witchcraft—limited to malevolent infliction of specific harm on specific individuals—was no novelty in the Renaissance period; indeed, belief that some individuals possessed supernatural powers and used them to inflict harm goes back to the earliest human societies. But the association of this primitive conception of witchcraft with the accusation of formal devil-worship and blasphemous rejection of God and defilement of Christian symbols was essentially a product of the late Middle Ages, based on the theories of highly educated theologians. In the 13th century, scholastic theologians debated whether the blasphemous and obscene actions performed at the witches' sabbath were physically real or existed only in the deluded minds of witches. Even so judicious a thinker as Thomas

Aquinas (usually acknowledged as the greatest of the scholastic thinkers) concluded that the actions of the witches' sabbath were physically real. This development of an intellectual doctrine of witchcraft seems to have resulted from an association of the harmful acts of witches with belief that any form of heresy involved a renunciation of God and hence involved worship of the devil, the inverse of God. The campaign of Dominican, Franciscan, and other mendicant inquisitors to destroy adherents of medieval heretical groups like the Albigensians and the Waldensians often led to accusations that such heretics engaged in immoral acts (especially sexual ones) and met secretly to worship the devil.

The emergence of this learned pseudoscience of witchcraft among clerical intellectuals culminated in the writing of a number of treatises defining witchcraft, indicating methods for identifying witches, and justifying punitive action. The most famous of these tracts, the *Malleus maleficarum / The Witches' Hammer*, was published by two German Dominican inquisitors, Heinrich Krämer and Jakob Sprenger, in 1487. Three years earlier, these beliefs had been given official status by Pope **Innocent VIII** in the papal bull *Summis desiderantibus*. The papal bull and the tract by Krämer and Sprenger together mark the emergence of a highly developed theological and legal justification for the pursuit and punishment of witches. The clerical witchcraft treatises laid more emphasis on the apostasy and devil-worship of the witch than on specific harmful acts, and the baneful effects of the theologians' beliefs are illustrated by the trial records: wherever ecclesiastical courts, dominated by these theories, tried cases of heresy (in most Continental countries and in Scotland), witches were persecuted more relentlessly and more clearly for worshipping the devil than for harming individuals, whereas in England and other countries where witches were tried in secular courts and laymen not indoctrinated by study of the witchcraft manuals conducted the trials, prosecution of witches (though by no means uncommon) was less severe and involved accusations of specific harmful acts against individual victims.

The inquisitorial procedure adopted in ecclesiastical courts in some ways made trials more rational because formal judicial action replaced the "swimming" (dunking) of witches or other primitive ordeals. But the inquisitorial procedure also allowed secret testimony by unidentified accusers. Theoretically, since testimony of two eye-witnesses to the defendant's criminal actions was required for conviction, proof of charges might seem difficult. But since an alternative basis for conviction was confession by the accused, and since inquisitorial procedure permitted the application of torture to elicit confessions, an accused witch might have very little chance of acquittal. In some jurisdictions, as at **Rome** and in the Parlement of Paris, torture was used sparingly, but in other regions, judges were less cautious. In England, where secular courts conducted the trials, torture was never used and conviction depended on testimony that could convince juries composed of laymen.

Trials involving both kinds of accusations—harmful actions and formal worship of the devil—seem to have occurred first in western Switzerland, Savoy, and Dauphiné during the early 15th century. Significantly, perhaps, these were regions where medieval heretical groups still survived, so that the association between fear of heresy and the hunt for witches is clear. Witchcraft trials of the inquisitorial sort occurred in various continental countries during the 15th century—least commonly in Italy and Spain—but then seem to have declined gradually until the middle of the 16th century, when by far the greatest wave of mass prosecution of witches took place, concentrated mainly in regions destabilized by religious conflict and foreign or civil war, such as western Germany (especially the ecclesiastical principalities of the south and west), eastern France, parts of Switzerland, and Scotland.

The total number of individuals accused, convicted, and executed as witches can be only roughly estimated, but recent estimates suggest that altogether during the 15th, 16th, and 17th centuries, about 100,000 people were brought to trial, with about half of these being found guilty and executed. In regions where hysteria took control, the effects were severe. According to contemporary reports, in the year 1586 in the diocese of Trier in western Germany, there were two villages in which only two women were left alive at the end of a wave of prosecutions. At Quedlinburg in Saxony in 1589, a town of about 12,000 people, 133 convicted witches were burned on a single day. In England, where the prohibition of torture restrained but did not prevent convictions and executions, trials of witches flourished during the disorderly period of the Civil Wars. Between 1645 and 1648 nearly 300 witches were tried and most of them sentenced to death, compared to only 125 trials and only 47 executions during the long reign of **Elizabeth I**. After the end of the Civil Wars restored social stability, prosecution of witches became increasingly rare in England. The infamous witch-craze of colonial Massachusetts in 1692 is closely linked to a period of great tension caused by Indian raids on frontier settlements.

One of the most striking features of the witchcraft delusions is the high percentage of **women** accused. In the early 15th century, when witchcraft was closely linked with heresy, a large proportion of the accused were men. But over the whole period when prosecution of witches was common, about 80 percent of the accused were female. In part this was because women were most closely involved in types of activity that might seem exposed to the intervention of evil spirits. They were the most likely to be locally known (and sometimes admired rather than feared) as healers, dispensers of herbal and other remedies. In addition, almost all those most closely involved in the most awesome and mysterious (at least to men) of human experiences, childbirth, were female, and midwives who attended women at childbirth and other women who cared for very young infants and might be suspected of causing their deaths or ailments were often subject to charges of witchcraft.

Modern social historians have noted that in many places, most of the accused were elderly, perhaps somewhat demented women who lived alone, might well have sharp tongues and antisocial habits, and in particular might feel vengeful when poverty drove them to beg for aid from neighbors who turned them down. If some misfortune happened to a denying neighbor shortly after the refusal, the latent guilt felt by the neighbor might produce suspicions that the beggar had taken revenge through witchcraft. The prevailing misogyny of educated clerical inquisitors suggested that women by their very nature were morally weak and sexually insatiable, so that they might be easily seduced by a devil offering the sexual orgies of the witches' sabbath as well as an ability to exercise power over potential victims.

There were always some who opposed the pursuit and execution of accused witches. Before the emergence of theological support for belief in the physical reality of the witches' sabbath, the prevailing view was that while witchcraft was both illegal and sinful, the face-to-face pacts with the devil and the sabbath were not physically real but mere delusions induced by the power of Satan. This view had been part of church law since the 10th century but had been outweighed by scholastic witchcraft doctrine in the 13th century. In the 16th century, the German physician Johann Weyer and the Englishman Reginald Scot argued that the contract with the devil was a delusion and that witches should be regarded as mentally ill rather than criminal. The excesses of the witch craze eventually undermined the credibility of the accusations. In particular, the use of torture, which was applied not just to secure confessions but also to force accused witches to name all the people they knew as fellow witches, created a moral swamp in which each confession produced a list of new defendants who were tortured until they provided the names of still more alleged witches. This procedure explains why when a wave of prosecutions began, it tended to grow exponentially until the list of accused became so large and so incredible that the whole process was discredited. Johann Weyer inveighed heatedly against the use of torture to force victims of the courts to produce false accusations.

By the late 17th century, while common folk in the countryside might still believe in (and fear) witches who inflicted specific kinds of harm, the educated classes became increasingly incredulous. In England, the last recorded execution of a woman for witchcraft occurred in 1684. In 1712 an English jury convicted an accused woman of being a witch but the judge, who had ridiculed the prosecution throughout the trial, secured a royal pardon so that the accused could be released. In 1736 the English and Scottish laws against witchcraft were repealed, and thereafter, witches could be charged with no legally recognized offense other than fraud. In Germany in 1679, the archbishop of Salzburg sentenced 97 witches to death. Germany executed its last witch in 1775; Switzerland, in 1782; Poland was apparently the last European nation to execute witches, burning two victims in 1793.

WITZ, CONRAD (ca. 1400–ca. 1446). German painter whose work reflects the spread of the influence of Flemish painters into other regions of northern Europe. His father was a painter who worked at the court of Philip the Bold, duke of **Burgundy**, and as a youth he accompanied his father to Burgundy and the Netherlands. He settled in

Basel in 1434 and did most of his work there. Witz's best-known painting, *The Miraculous Draught of Fishes* (1444), seems to reflect the influence of the Master of Flémalle, now usually identified as **Robert Campin**. Though Campin's influence is reflected in the draperies of the human figures, the landscape background suggests the influence of the brothers **Van Eyck**. A few fragments of a fresco *Dance of Death* painted in the Dominican cloister at Basel survive. Other known works include two wings of the *Heilspiegel Altarpiece* (ca. 1435–1438); an *Annunciation* panel for an altarpiece for a Dominican convent at Basel; the St. Peter Altarpiece (central section is lost but the wings survive, including the *Miraculous Draught* and *Liberation of St. Peter from Prison*); *Meeting at the Golden Gate*; and *SS. Catherine and Mary Magadalen in a Church*. Less certainly attributed are *Holy Family and Saints in a Church*, a fragment of a *Virgin and Child*, *Decision on the Redemption of Man*, and a panel with a *Nativity* on the outside and a votive scene on the inside, parts of a dismantled altarpiece. Despite the high quality of his work and his contemporary reputation, Witz had little influence on later German art, since the success of **Rogier van der Weyden** brought about a change of taste that made Witz's paintings seem old-fashioned.

WOLGEMUT, MICHAEL (1434–1519). German painter and engraver, who became the leading artist in Nuremberg and established a large workshop there. He is best known because **Albrecht Dürer** was his apprentice for three years. As a painter, he produced altarpieces in Zwickau and Schwabach, and he probably completed the *Hofer Altarpiece* (ca. 1485), for which his master Hans Playdenwurff held the commission but had probably left unfinished at his death in 1472. Aside from being Dürer's teacher, Wolgemut is best known for the many engravings he produced for the Nuremberg **printing** industry. His woodcuts illustrated the *Schatzkammer der wahren Reichthümer des Heils / Treasury of the True Riches of Salvation* and *Der Schrein Od'Schatzbehalter / The Cupboard or Treasure Chest* (both 1491) and, most important, the famous *Weltchronik / Chronicle of the World* by Hartmann Schedel, also known as the *Nuremberg Chronicle*.

WOLSEY, THOMAS (ca. 1472–1530). English clergyman and statesman. Born the son of an innkeeper and butcher at Ipswich, Wolsey was educated at Magdalen College, Oxford, where he became master of the affiliated grammar school. In 1501, however, he left Oxford and entered the service of a series of powerful men. He was talented and ingratiating and soon became chaplain to King **Henry VII**, then almoner to young King **Henry VIII**, who recognized his energy and competence and appointed him to increasingly important administrative offices. The king made him bishop of Lincoln in 1514 and elevated him to the archbishopric of York in 1515.

Later that year, Wolsey became chancellor, the highest office in the kingdom. He accumulated enormous political influence and personal wealth; foreign ambassadors and native petitioners quickly identified him as the person whose favor was crucial to their success. As chancellor he worked to expand the jurisdiction of the Court of Chancery and the Court of Star Chamber. Responding to the king's ambition to play a major role in European politics and war, Wolsey increased the revenues of the crown through forced loans, browbeaten out of reluctant lenders. In Parliament, he pushed hard for new taxes and even tried (but failed) to levy taxes without parliamentary authorization. Although some of these activities were socially beneficial, Wolsey's ruthless drive to increase royal power and his own splendor was resented, all the more because of his humble origins. As long as he was useful to the king, he seemed secure. When Henry decided to end his marriage to Queen Catherine of Aragon and sought papal approval for a divorce, however, he expected Wolsey to produce results. His failure to secure approval of the divorce cost Wolsey his favor at court. He was dismissed as chancellor in October 1529. A year later, after he had retired to his archdiocese at York, he was summoned to court on charges of treason. He died on the journey south.

Wolsey was in many ways a corrupt and worldly cleric, entering the clergy and taking high office solely for the power and wealth he could get, not out of any spiritual concern. He kept a mistress and fathered a son and a daughter. He used his control of church patronage to secure sinecures for his son. He was a notorious pluralist, holding one or another bishopric in addition to York, as well as the abbacy (and revenues) of the rich abbey of St. Albans.

Yet however worldly his motives may have been, Wolsey did take measures to prevent the spread of Lutheran heresy; he encouraged reform of both secular and monastic clergy (though not of his own life);

and he showed special concern for the education of future priests. He founded a **humanistic** school in his home town and undertook the foundation of a splendid new college at Oxford, Cardinal College (1525), which he intended to make into a showplace of the new humanist learning. Wolsey's fall from power in 1529 left arrangements for the new college still in progress, and there was danger that its endowment would be seized by the crown, but it survived and later was reorganized as Christ Church, one of Oxford's most splendid colleges. Wolsey extended patronage to a number of humanist scholars, employed some of the ablest artists, and built several palaces, of which Hampton Court, later seized by the king, was the most famous. Yet most contemporaries judged that his patronage of arts and letters arose more from his desire for display and elegance than from any true devotion to learning and the arts.

WOMEN. Although obviously half of the population of Renaissance Europe was female, the role of women in the high culture, especially the Latin-based **academic** culture and **humanist** movement of the period, was very limited, a generalization which is also true of political life, large-scale business enterprise, the fine arts (both music and visual arts), and even vernacular literature. Continuing the misogynistic culture of medieval Europe, Renaissance society excluded women from any leading role in public life. One prominent student of the place of women during the period has stated flatly that for women, the Renaissance was not a renaissance at all, but a period of declining status, and while this conclusion has been challenged, there is considerable evidence that in at least some respects, the restrictions on women's participation in society increased during the centuries (14th through 16th or early 17th) usually covered by the term "Renaissance."

Women's proper role in society, as defined by most opinion in that age, was largely limited to the domestic sphere, and even in family life, both legally and actually, women were always supposed to be under the control of some male authority: first by the father, then by the husband, and if the woman were widowed, in many regions finally by either male children or the male relatives of her deceased spouse. The course of a woman's life was clearly defined: first as daughter and virgin, then as wife and mother, and finally as widow. Only a wealthy widow had any real chance of being more or less independent and in charge of her own life. Even in that case, her independence in many regions was greatly restricted by the property rights of her sons and her husband's kinsmen.

Until the **Reformation**, women theoretically had the option of continuing to live in a virginal state by entering the monastic life. Since, however, most female monasteries expected postulants to present a dowry upon entry, in practice only women from relatively prosperous families had the option of becoming nuns. In the 13th and 14th centuries, especially in urban areas, informal communities of single women sprang up outside the monastic orders, but since such groups did not have official approval and were not subject to supervision and control by male clergy, they often faced suppression by authorities who feared that unsupervised communities of females either would fall into heresy or would become prostitutes. After the Catholic Reformation became strong from about 1550, church authorities were even less tolerant of unofficial communities of unmarried females living together.

Religion did remain one field in which some activity by women was socially acceptable, but almost always in a role clearly subordinated to control by the exclusively male clergy. There were a few exceptions, such as the influential 14th-century **Catherine of Siena**, who became an outspoken agitator for reform of the church and was later canonized, but such figures were notable mainly for their rarity. In the first half of the 16th century, some devout Italian intellectuals were stirred by a quest for spiritual authenticity based on the Bible, a movement known as *evangelismo*. The poet **Vittoria Colonna** became a central figure among such a group of "evangelicals" at **Naples** (some of whom became Protestants while others became early leaders of the Catholic Reformation). But Colonna was not only a member of an ancient and influential Roman aristocratic family but also a wealthy woman who was widowed early in life, had no children, and never remarried, thus managing to establish an independent existence that was extremely rare for women in any part of Renaissance Europe.

Despite their limited status in society, women did have some rights in theory and even in practice. The dowry that a woman brought into her marriage remained legally her property, and if the marriage were dissolved by annulment or the death of her husband, she had in theory a right to control that part of the total resources of her marital household. On the other hand, during the course of a marriage, actual administration of the dowry was in the hands of the husband, and if he dissipated it through ill fortune or bad management, the woman had no recourse. Women of the higher classes (royal, aristocratic, and bourgeois) were more closely controlled than peasant women or women of the poorer urban classes, because their marriages involved important political and economic relationships and valuable properties. While European brides were never purchased as was done in some cultures, the daughters of prominent families were married off by their parents (essentially, by their fathers), who used the marriages of daughters (and sons, too) in order to make political or business connections. Lower-class women, on the other hand, often had considerably more independence in choosing whom and when to marry, though the fundamental cause of this independence was that they were poor and hence their marriage did not involve the pursuit of extraneous material goals.

In most parts of Europe, women of royal and noble families and also women of the wealthy business classes (especially in Italy, the most economically developed region) married young, in their early or mid-teens, and were given to husbands considerably older than the bride: upper-class Florentine males usually did not marry until their late 20s or early 30s. Among the lower classes, however, women often deferred marriage until somewhat later and married men only slightly older than themselves. In part this was because poor girls often had to work as household servants or in other common occupations in order to save money for dowries that were modest but still regarded as essential for successful establishment of a new household. Since no effective contraceptive methods were available, young wives could look forward to bearing many children. Wealthy families often regarded large families as desirable since the children's marriages could be used to promote the general interest of the father's family. Social historians have noted that in northwestern Europe from the mid–14th century (that is, after the **Black Death**), women of the peasant and artisan classes tended to defer marriage until their mid-20s, a practice that not only allowed them to earn money for their dowries but also had the practical effect (whether intended or not) of producing fewer offspring and hence fewer claimants to a share of the family's agricultural lands or urban workshop when one generation gave way to the next.

The role of women in the scholarly, artistic, and literary life that formed the center of Renaissance civilization was limited not only by the subordination of women to their family role but also by the unavailability of education for women. At every level of society, women had far lower rates of literacy than men, and this was especially true in rural districts and among the poor. In the cities, women of the higher and middle classes had some opportunity to receive an elementary education in which they learned to read, write, and do simple arithmetic. But in the view of contemporary society, even this modest level of education was of marginal utility for women. What they had to learn was how to cook, sew, manage a household, rear children, and participate in religious devotions.

As for any more advanced learning, only a handful of privileged women from the upper classes had a chance to learn Latin, the essential tool for participation in the humanistic studies of the Renaissance. A few princesses were able to study in the palace schools created for the education of their brothers; of these, the humanist academies at the courts of **Ferrara** and **Mantua** were the best known, but only the daughters of the ruling prince and their closest companions were privileged to share the instruction. A somewhat larger number of women from noble and wealthy mercantile families had the opportunity to learn Latin and a few carefully selected (and morally proper) works of ancient Roman literature from tutors hired by their fathers, usually for the education of sons but occasionally for daughters alone. No **university** would have permitted a woman to attend its classes, though the issue was unlikely to arise since virtually no woman had the command of Latin expected of entering university students. The first recorded conferral of an academic degree on a woman did not occur until 1678, when Elena Lucrezia Cornaro Piscopia, a member of a Venetian noble family, was awarded a doctorate in philosophy. Society in general opposed the very idea of a learned woman, since it had no use for such a creature. In any case, prevailing theory held that women's minds were inherently unsuited to intense intellectual effort. A learned woman, like a woman who claimed political authority, was viewed as something unnatural—a sort of monster.

Two developments during the Renaissance centuries slightly mitigated the exclusion of women from learning. First, the invention of

printing in the second half of the 15th century gradually worked to spread literacy (at least in the vernacular languages) more widely through all levels of society. Urban women of the middle and patrician classes often were able to read and now had access to reading matter to a degree never before known in human history. Especially from the second half of the 16th century, as an increasing body of **classical** texts and other serious literature became available in translation, both men and women who had been excluded from higher education had access to books that presented information and ideas previously available only to the learned elites. Second, while printing from the very first had made certain types of religious literature (mainly prayers, meditations, and lives of the saints) available to women, the Protestant Reformation emphasized the right and responsibility of all Christians to read the Bible.

From the time of its first leader, **Martin Luther**, Protestantism promoted the founding of schools open to all levels of society, to girls as well as boys, though the higher schools remained just as firmly closed to females as ever. These gains for women were limited. Women might read the Bible in Protestant regions, but except for the very early period of the Reformation (the 1520s), they were not allowed to discuss it in public or to preach it, and their reading was always supposed to occur under the guidance of their fathers or husbands.

Even the few women who became truly learned found that if they married, they had lost their personal control over leisure for study since they were subject to the authority of their husbands. In addition, once married, they would be pregnant and engaged in child-rearing most of the time. For most learned women, continued study implied refusal to marry, and since in virtually all cases an independent life as a single person was unthinkable, there was seldom a niche in society where a woman could develop her intellectual interests while remaining single. In countries that remained Catholic, there was theoretically always the monastic option, but the reading and activities of nuns were supervised closely (especially after the Reformation) by the clergy and by monastic superiors.

To the horror of conservative moralists, the vagaries of dynastic succession produced a few princesses who were not only well educated but actually became rulers, such as Queen **Isabella** of Spain, Isabella's granddaughter Mary **Tudor**, who ruled England briefly

(1553–1558), and Mary's half-sister **Elizabeth I**, one of the greatest political figures of the 16th century. Though all of these women were educated and intellectually active, their deep involvement in politics kept any of them from pursuing an active literary and intellectual life beyond their early years.

When the question turns to identifying serious female intellectuals, modern scholarship has been able to find very few women who were able to share actively in the scholarly and intellectual life of Renaissance humanism and vernacular literature. All of the Italian women who excelled as humanist scholars or successful authors were privileged daughters of highly educated fathers. Examples are **Laura Cereta**, **Cassandra Fedele**, **Lucrezia Marinella**, **Olimpia Morata**, **Isotta Nogarola**, **Modesta Pozzo** and **Alessandra Scala**. Even these able and highly privileged women were denounced by conservative clergy and scholars, who in some cases publicly accused them of using their studies as a cover for sexual relationships with men. When they tried to establish personal or epistolary contact with humanist scholars whose works they admired, they either received no response at all or were sternly admonished to guard their chastity—a quality which all their male counterparts (and the women themselves) regarded as far more essential in a woman than any level of erudition.

Earlier in time than these was **Christine de Pizan**, the daughter of an Italian physician at the court of King **Charles V** of France, who as a young widow was able to earn her living as an author of French vernacular works. She wrote an eloquent defense of the intellectual capability of women if only they were allowed access to education. Italian women generally led the way among female authors of vernacular literature. Most married women found that their obligations as wives and mothers effectively terminated their literary careers. Few unmarried women found it possible to live a single life devoted to study even if they could endure the isolation and hostility that such a career generated. Hence some of the most successful female writers of the Italian Renaissance were courtesans—that is, high-class prostitutes—such as **Veronica Franco**, **Gaspara Stampa**, and **Tullia d'Aragona**.

France in the 16th century produced female vernacular authors of more respectable social status, such as **Louise Labé**, a talented poet from a modest artisan family; **Margaret of Navarre**, queen of Navarre and sister of King **Francis I** of France, who was active both as a patron and as an author of spiritual treatises and prose fiction; **Madeleine and Catherine des Roches**, a mother-daughter pair of poets belonging to the class of ennobled judicial officials; and **Marie de Gournay**, a close friend and literary executor of **Michel de Montaigne**. England did not produce female authors of real distinction until the second half of the 17th century, but the poet **Aemilia Lanyer** gained some success with her volume of poems in the first decade of the 17th century. Spain in the 16th century produced one major female author of spiritual works, the mystic and monastic reformer Teresa of Ávila, who was suspected of being a heretic or a fraud but was fortunate to have the wholehearted support of King **Philip II** and was canonized as a saint in 1622. Her career, however, belongs to the Catholic Reformation movement and not the Renaissance. Though she was an inspiring writer on religious topics, she had a very modest educational background—no Latin and not much reading except for devotional literature.

The most comfortable role for energetic and educated women of the upper classes was as patrons and admirers of male scholars and poets. Margaret of Navarre played this role in 16th-century France in addition to her own literary career. A number of female members of Italian princely families were patrons of writers and artists and created highly intellectual court societies. The Venetian noblewoman **Caterina Cornaro**, after beng pressured by the government of **Venice** into exchanging her rule as queen of Cyprus for nominal lordship of the town of Asoli in Venetian territory, became patron of an influential literary circle, including the ablest Italian poet of the early 16th century, **Pietro Bembo**. The duchess of Mantua, Isabella d'**Este**, daughter of the ruling prince of Ferrara, who as a girl was tutored in Latin and **Greek** by the headmaster of the famous court school at Ferrara, was the central figure of a brilliant circle of poets, humanists, and authors who made Mantua an important center of Renaissance civilization. At the court of **Urbino**, the duchess Elisabetta **Gonzaga** created a distinguished society that is reflected in the most famous literary work describing the Italian court culture of the late 15th century, *The Book of the Courtier* by **Count Balsassare Castiglione**. In early Tudor England, **Lady Margaret Beaufort**, the mother of King **Henry VII**, though not personally learned, was a generous patron of university education, strongly influenced by her spiritual adviser, Bishop John Fisher. Thus a handful of intelligent women privileged by high social status and great wealth were able to do much to shape Renaissance culture. Margaret of Navarre was the only one of these to become a literary creator in her own right, and even she lacked the Latin-based education that would have opened to her the ancient and modern literary works not available in translation.

In the visual arts, no female artist of great reputation emerged until the second half of the 16th century, and in each case, the artist enjoyed unusual privileges that opened to her a career ordinarily available only to men. **Sofonisba Anguissola**, the first female painter to win a widespread reputation and to produce a significant body of work, was unusual in that she was not the daughter of an artist. She was the daughter of a Piedmontese nobleman who had her tutored by a skilled painter of Cremona. More typical of the few female painters was **Lavinia Fontana**, daughter of an artist from **Bologna**. The greatest female painter of the late-Renaissance (or **baroque**) period was **Artemisia Gentileschi**, daughter of a successful pupil of **Caravaggio**. She was trained at **Rome**, and an incident in her training illustrates why entry into an artistic career was regarded as perilous for a woman. At age 16 she was raped by an artist to whom her father had entrusted her for training in **perspective**, and although (unusually for the time) her father brought legal charges against the rapist and secured a conviction, the guilty man was let off with a light penalty.

In Italy, but not in Northern countries like England, women were permitted to appear as performers on the stage, but since actresses were conventionally regarded as little better than prostitutes and were generally controlled by male producers and directors, few of them achieved personal fame and respectability. One rare exception is the Italian actress **Isabella Andreini**, whose contemporary reputation emphasized her high moral character as well as her abilities as a performer.

Many of these outstanding women expressed in their own literary and artistic works a keen awareness of the limitations that society placed on women. While they defied those limitations and demonstrated that women could become scholars, authors, and artists if given the chance, they often tended to justify their own activity by claiming that they had exceeded (rather than fulfilled) the capabilities of female nature. *See also QUERELLE DES FEMMES*; WITCHCRAFT.

WYATT, SIR THOMAS. *See* HOWARD, HENRY, EARL OF SURREY.

WYCLIF, JOHN (ca. 1330–1384). English theologian, professor of theology at Oxford. His teachings were condemned as heretical, but Wyclif himself had such powerful support from the royal family that he could not be punished, though he was forced to retire from Oxford. Wyclif himself, his political role in representing the English monarchy in a conflict with the **papacy**, and the doctrines regarding ecclesiastical authority and the sacraments for which the archbishop of Canterbury declared him heretical in 1382 are very much a part of medieval rather than Renaissance history, but his followers, the **Lollards**, were numerous until driven underground by royal persecution in the early 15th century. The movement survived as an underground heresy of simple laymen into the early years of the English **Reformation**, though the degree to which it influenced the course of the Reformation in England is debatable. Wyclif's theology also had some influence on the Czech theologian **John Huss** and the **Hussite** religious movement that became the majority religion of the kingdom of Bohemia during the 15th century. Since Wyclif's Lollard followers stubbornly clung to his teaching that all Christians should have free access to the Bible in their own language, one effect of his career is that in pre-Reformation England, unlike most continental countries, possession of the Scriptures in English translation was regarded as *prima facie* evidence of heretical belief. Thus the opinion of **Erasmus** and other Christian **humanists** of the early 16th century that the Bible ought to be accessible to the people seemed far more dangerous in England than in many continental countries, where vernacular copies of parts of the Bible were relatively common and were eagerly sought by simple folk.

– X –

XIMÉNES DE CISNEROS, FRANCISCO (1436–1517). Castilian friar, archbishop, cardinal, church reformer, and statesman; in modern Spanish, the patronymic is often spelled Jiménez. Born into an impoverished family of the lower nobility, he was early intended for the church. Educated under the direction of an uncle and sent to grammar school at the town of Alcalá de Henares, he proceeded to the **University** of Salamanca, where he graduated as a bachelor of laws in 1460. He then pursued a career in the secular clergy, successfully cultivating patrons and accumulating valuable benefices. About 1484, however, Ximénes underwent a spiritual conversion and renounced his pursuit of high office and wealth by entering the Observant (that is, reformed and strict) branch of the Franciscan order. Although he lived an isolated life as a friar, he maintained some contact with the royal court and his former ecclesiastical patrons and thus attracted the attention of **Queen Isabella** of Spain, who in 1492 summoned him to be her confessor.

Even at court Ximénes led a highly ascetic life, but his position as the queen's spiritual adviser made him an influential figure and eventually led him to high offices of the sort he had rejected when he became a friar. His initial use of his new influence was in reform of his own order, the Franciscans. In 1495 the queen enhanced his ecclesiastical authority by having him appointed archbishop of Toledo, the primatial see of Spain and reputedly the richest bishopric in Christendom. In 1496 Ximénes became visitor of the entire Franciscan order, and the preceding year, a papal bull had authorized him to visit (that is, inspect) and reform all regular clergy in his diocese, a power extended in 1499 to cover all parts of Spain. He strove to compel undisciplined mendicant communities to return to strict observance of their original rules, though his ruthless energy in pushing such changes aroused bitter opposition. His religious zeal for conversion of non-Christians and his great influence over the pious queen suggest that he probably was a major force in the ruler's infamous decision in 1492 to expel all **Jews** from Spain unless they converted to Christianity. After the conquest of the Muslim kingdom of Granada in 1492, he also began bringing such great pressure on the Muslim population that he precipitated rebellions.

The death of Queen Isabella in 1504 and then of her son and heir Philip in 1506 left the unified Spanish monarchy in jeopardy since King **Ferdinand** of Aragon had no legal claim to personal rule in the Castilian half of the country. The archbishop brokered a dynastic agreement under which Ferdinand became regent of Castile until his and Isabella's grandson Charles, prince of the Netherlands (the future

Emperor **Charles V**, born in 1500), attained his majority. Grateful to Ximénes for pushing through this arrangement against the opposition of many Castilian nobles, Ferdinand had Ximénes made a cardinal and appointed him inquisitor general (head of the **Spanish Inquisition**) in 1507. When Ferdinand himself died early in 1516, the nobles again made a bid for power until Prince Charles, now king of both Castile and Aragon, should reach his majority, but Ximénes maintained control, created a powerful military force to preserve order, and prepared the way for Charles to take power as soon as he reached Spain. The cardinal himself died in November 1517 while on his way to meet the young king upon his landing in Spain.

Ximénes was not only a vigorous church reformer and a shrewd and loyal servant of the Spanish monarchs but also a patron of Renaissance learning. He wanted the secular clergy of Spain to undergo the same kind of sweeping disciplinary reform that he had struggled to impose on the monastic orders. But he was convinced that the Spanish church could not be effectively reformed unless it had a new leadership based not on aristocratic kinship and court intrigue but on personal competence, learning, and spiritual devotion. In 1499 he began the creation of the new **University of Alcalá**, which he conceived as a center for the training of future leaders for the church (and also for the secular administration). He created within the university a well-endowed institute, the College of San Ildefonso, where students not only would receive book-learning but also would live under close moral supervision in an atmosphere intended to produce pious as well as learned graduates.

– Z –

ZARLINO, GIOSEFFO (1517–1590). Italian composer and music theorist. One of several talented students of **Adriaan Willaert**, the Flemish choirmaster of St. Mark's at **Venice**, he was a native of Chioggia and from childhood aimed at a career in the church. He was educated by Franciscan friars and joined that order in 1536. Also in 1536 he was a singer at the cathedral of Chioggia. He studied theology and took minor clerical orders. In 1541 he moved to Venice to study with Willaert, and in 1565 he succeeded his fellow pupil **Cipri-**

ano de Rore in the influential position at St. Mark's once held by their teacher.

Zarlino published two influential books on music theory. The first was *Istitutioni harmoniche / Principles of Harmony* (1558), which was translated into French, German, and Dutch and which included discussion of counterpoint and the various modes defined by **classical** writers on music and also rules to guide composers in underlaying words to polyphonic music. His second book was *Dimostrationi harmoniche*, a collection of dialogues that supposedly reflect conversations of friends meeting in 1562 at the home of the ailing Willaert. His theoretical writings were sharply attacked by his own former pupil **Vincenzo Galilei**, and his *Sopplimenti musicali / Musical Supplements* (1588) was in part intended to reply to Galilei's criticisms. In 1589 he published a four-volume collection of his writings.

Zarlino's position at St. Mark's required him to compose many musical works, but few of them survive. He produced both motets and madrigals, and he composed a mass for the consecration of the Venetian Church of Santa Maria della Salute as well as the music for a pageant celebrating the naval victory of the Christian powers over the Turks at Lepanto in 1571. In his writings Zarlino disagreed with extreme **classicists** who dismissed all modern music as defective because it did not conform to ancient theory, but he did believe that music had declined at the end of the ancient world along with all other forms of learning and that a great Renaissance of music had recently taken place, in which his master Willaert was "a new Pythagoras." In 1583 he was offered the bishopric of Chioggia but declined the honor, preferring to remain in his influential musical office at St. Mark's.

ZASIUS, UDALRICUS (1461–1535). German **humanist** and jurist. A native of Constance, he attended the cathedral school there and in 1481 entered the **University** of Tübingen, where he received a B.A. degree. He then became a court clerk in the service of the bishop of Constance and rose to be head of the episcopal chancery. Concurrently, he also worked for the municipal government. He later served as town clerk at Buchhorn, Baden im Aargau, and eventually Freiburg-im-Breisgau, where he moved in 1494 and where he spent the rest of his career.

Only after becoming clerk at Freiburg did Zasius begin formal study of law at the local university. In 1496 he left the position of clerk and became head of the city's Latin school, employment that enabled him to pursue his studies. In 1499 he resigned his teaching position in order to study full time, and in 1501 he became doctor of both laws. Although Zasius held a recognized legal doctorate, he acquired most of his very substantial legal learning through private study. He began teaching the course on Justinian's *Institutes* in 1500 as a substitute for a professor and in 1501 repeated the course while also teaching poetry and rhetoric. He returned to the position of town clerk in 1502 and also served as legal counsel to the university. In 1506, after a lengthy campaign of pressure by both town and students, the faculty appointed Zasius professor of law despite resistance by some of his new colleagues. The salary was low, and he always supplemented it by working as a legal adviser and by offering room and board to students. In 1508 the Emperor **Maximilian I** gave him the honorary title of imperial councillor. His lectures in praise of law were eventually published as part of his *Lucubrationes* in 1518.

One of Zasius' duties after reappointment as town clerk was to prepare a book of legal precedents valid in the local municipal court, together with a legal code defining the customs, statutes, and privileges of the town and linking these to the relevant sections of **Roman** law. The city's law code adopted in 1520 is mostly his work. It was one of the most important legal codifications of his time, since it melded together the traditional local law and the principles of Roman law. This code remained in force until the 19th century and influenced the legal codes of other German municipalities.

At first, Zasius' reputation as a jurist spread by word of mouth, a process speeded by the striking success of the men he trained in winning important positions in the administrations of German princes, prelates, and towns. His work in law was closely linked to his development as a humanist, and he created a broad network of influence by correspondence with other humanists, including **Sebastian Brant**, Geiler von Kaysersberg, **Jakob Wimpheling**, and the younger Thomas Wolf. He also had contact with **Conrad Celtis, Gianfrancesco Pico della Mirandola, Willibald Pirckheimer** and **Mutianus Rufus**. His favorite student, **Bonifacius Amerbach**, who later became professor of law at **Basel**, brought him into touch with **Eras-**

mus. In the earliest years of the **Reformation**, Zasius expressed sympathy for the teachings of **Martin Luther**, but as he realized that Luther's movement was dividing the church and also learned that Luther had contemptuously burned a copy of the canon law, he turned against the Saxon reformer, earlier and more bitterly than most German humanists did. When Erasmus moved to Freiburg after the city of Basel had become officially Protestant in 1529, Zasius welcomed him and helped arrange for his place of residence.

Although Zasius did not begin publishing early in his career, he produced a number of influential legal works, including an early (1508) tract urging the forcible baptism of **Jewish** children; his collected essays on law, the *Lucubrationes* (1518); a treatise against the theologian Johann Eck (1519), dealing with Eck's defense of the legality of charging interest on loans; and *In usus feudorum epitome* (1535), a study of feudal law. His works were collected and published as his *Opera omnia* (1550) in seven volumes that included his lecture courses and his formal legal judgments. Although Zasius had much of the bumptious combativeness typical of an autodidact, he became influential in the development of German humanism, in his professional field of jurisprudence, and in the very early stages of Catholic opposition to the Reformation.

ZWINGLI, HULDRYCH (1484–1531). Swiss religious reformer, the first major figure of the Reformed (later often called Calvinist) branch of Protestantism. Although he primarily figures in history as a leader of the **Reformation** in Zürich and as the first systematic defender of the Sacramentarian doctrine of the Eucharist, Zwingli began his career as a young priest who was attracted to **humanism**. He studied **classical** languages at Bern (1496–1498) and then pursued traditional **scholastic** subjects at the **University** of **Basel** (B.A. 1504, M.A. 1506). When he moved from Basel to become pastor at Glarus, he continued his study of **Greek** language and the Church Fathers, and these interests led him to the study of the Bible and into the circle of young Swiss admirers of the biblical humanist **Erasmus**.

Zwingli matured as a preacher at Glarus and the great pilgrimage center at Einsiedeln, and when he moved to Zürich as the city's principal preacher in 1519, he cast aside the liturgical calendar of Scripture readings and began preaching chapter by chapter through the

Gospel of St. Matthew. His early preaching was inspired by Erasmus' biblical scholarship and conception of religion as the "philosophy of Christ," but his sermons increasingly reflected Lutheran influence, more than Zwingli ever acknowledged or even realized, though he honored Luther as a great religious leader. At Zürich, Zwingli moved from a reform-minded humanism to an evangelical or Protestant perspective. He led the city in its sharp break away from traditional Catholic doctrine and religious practice and then worked to spread his ideas through the rest of Switzerland, an effort that generated conflict with those Swiss cantons that remained firmly Catholic, giving rise to a civil war that in 1531 led to his death in battle.

Bibliography

INTRODUCTION

This bibliography is intended to serve readers of English-language publications, though a handful of especially important works that have
never been translated from other languages are included. The selection
of titles reflects the dictionary's emphasis on the Renaissance as a cultural force, but it provides a broad range of reference works that can
guide interested readers to material on political, social, and economic
history that are only lightly treated here. In particular, the section on
textbooks includes useful general accounts that also contain bibliographical sections directing the reader to more specialized publications.
The final section of this bibliography suggests books on the social, political, and economic background that cast light on other aspects of the
general history of the chronological period covered (basically the 14th,
15th, and 16th centuries) with some overlap into the early 17th century.

One saving grace of the emphasis on English-language publications
is that English-speaking (and writing) scholars have made major contributions to the study of the Renaissance, especially the study of Italy,
the birthplace of the new culture. This has many causes, but one of them
is that because of the policies of the Nazi regime in Germany between
1933 and 1945, a number of talented scholars who normally would have
had their careers at German universities spent their most productive
years at universities and institutes in the United States, Canada, and
Great Britain. These scholars (Hans Baron, Felix Gilbert, Paul Oskar
Kristeller, and Erwin Panofsky are perhaps the most eminent examples,
but there were many others) thus trained English-speaking students to
investigate the history of Europe, especially Italy, in this fertile period
of European history.

Readers interested in pursuing Renaissance topics further will find
that four North American periodical publications and at least one in the
United Kingdom focus on the study of these centuries: *Renaissance
Quarterly* (a publication of the Renaissance Society of America), the
Sixteenth Century Journal (a publication created by the Sixteenth Century Studies Conference), *Archiv für Reformationsgeschichte / Archive
for Reformation History* (a bilingual joint publication of the German
Verein für Reformationsgeschichte and the Society for Reformation Research), and *Renaissance and Reformation* (a publication of the Canadian Society for Renaissance Studies and the Centre for Reformation

and Renaissance Studies at Victoria University, University of Toronto) in Canada. In the United Kingdom, the journal *Renaissance Studies* is a publication of the Society for Renaissance Studies.

I. WORKS OF REFERENCE

1. Encyclopedias and Biographical Collections

Bracken, James K., ed. *Reference Works in British and American Literature*, 2nd ed. Englewood, Colo.: Libraries Unlimited, 1998.

British Writers, vol. 1 (*William Langland to the English Bible*) and vol. 2 (*Thomas Middleton to George Farquhar*). Ian Scott-Kilvert, general editor. New York: Charles Scribner's Sons, 1979.

Contemporaries of Erasmus: A Biographical Register of the Renaissance and Reformation, ed. by Peter G. Bietenholz and Thomas B. Deutscher, 3 vols. Toronto: University of Toronto Press, 1985–1987.

Cosenza, Mario Emilio. *Biographical and Bibliographical Dictionary of the Italian Humanists and of the World of Classical Scholarship in Italy, 1300–1800*, 2nd ed., 6 vols. Boston: G.K. Hall, 1962–1967. (The first four volumes are a rather disorderly collection of photocopied raw notes; vol. 5, *Synopsis*, will be the part most helpful to general readers.)

The Dictionary of Art, ed. by Jane Turner, 34 vols. London: Macmillan, 1996.

Dictionary of Literary Biography. [A series of biographical articles on authors of many periods and regions.] Detroit, Mich.: Gale Research, various dates. Published volumes dealing with Renaissance literature are:

British Prose Writers of the Early Seventeenth Century, ed. by Clayton D. Lein, series vol. 151 (1995).

British Rhetoricians and Logicians, 1500–1800, vol. 1, ed. by Edward A. Malone, series vol. 236 (2001)

Elizabethan Dramatists, ed. by Fredson Bowers, series no. 58 (1987).

German Baroque Writers, 1580–1660, ed. by James Hardin, series no. 164 (1996).

German Writers of the Renaissance and Reformation, 1280–1580, ed. by James Hardin and Max Reinhardt, series vol. 179 (1997).

Jacobean and Caroline Dramatists, ed. by Fredson Bowers, series vol. 58 (1987).

Seventeenth-Century British Nondramatic Poets, ed. by M. Thomas Hester, series no. 121 (1992).

Sixteenth-Century British Nondramatic Literature, ed. by David A. Richardson, 4 vols., series nos. 132 (1993), 136 (1994), 167 (1996), and 172 (1996).

Dictionary of Scientific Biography, ed. by Charles Coulston Gillispie, 16 vols. + 2 Supps. New York: Charles Scribner's Sons, 1970–1990.

Encyclopedia of the Renaissance, ed. by Paul F. Grendler et al., 6 vols. New York: Scribner, 1999.

Encyclopedia of World Art, 15 vols. + 2 Supps. New York: McGraw-Hill, 1958–1987.

The New Grove Dictionary of Music and Musicians, 2nd ed., ed. by Stanley Sadie, 29 vols. London: Macmillan, 2001.

The Oxford Dictionary of the Renaissance, ed. by Gordon Campbell et al. Oxford: Oxford University Press, 2003.

The Oxford Encyclopedia of the Reformation, ed. by Hans J. Hillerbrand et al., 4 vols. Oxford: Oxford University Press, 1996.

2. Bibliographies and Guides

Archiv für Reformationsgeschichte / Archive for Reformation History, Part 2: *Literaturbericht / Literature Review*. Gütersloh: Gütersloher Verlagshaus Gerd Mohn, 1972–. (Annual.)

Bibliographie Internationale de l'Humanisme et de la Renaissance. Geneva: Librairie Droz, 1965–. (Lists publication in all Western languages; publication lags behind the calendar: the volume for 1996 publications appeared in 2000.)

Brady, Thomas A., Jr., Heiko A. Oberman, and James D. Tracy, eds. *Handbook of European History, 1400–1600*, 2 vols. Leiden: E. J. Brill, 1994–1995.

The Cambridge Companion to English Literature, 1500–1600, ed. by Arthur F. Kinney. Cambridge: Cambridge University Press, 2000.

Fletcher, Stella. *The Longman Companion to Renaissance Europe, 1390–1530*. London: Longman, 1999.

Giraud, Yves, et al. *La Renaissance*, 3 vols. Paris: Arthaud, 1972–1974.

Hadfield, Andrew. *The English Renaissance, 1500–2001*. Oxford: Blackwell, 2001.

Hager, Alan, ed. *Major Tudor Authors: A Bio-bibliographical Critical Sourcebook*. Westport, Conn.: Greenwood Press, 1997.

Harner, James L. *English Renaissance Prose Fiction, 1500–1660: An Annotated Bibliography of Criticism, 1984–1990*. New York: G. K. Hall, 1992.

Hattaway, Michael, ed. *A Companion to English Renaissance Literature and Culture*. Oxford: Blackwell, 2000.

ITER: Gateway to the Middle Ages and Renaissance. An on-line bibliography of publications, sponsored by the University of Toronto Libraries in cooperation with the Renaissance Society of America and the Arizona Center for Medieval and Renaissance Studies. Full access is available to members of the Renaissance Society of America and to patrons of subscribing libraries. Website: www.itergateway.org.

Kohl, Benjamin G. *Renaissance Humanism, 1300–1550: A Bibliography of Materials in English*. New York: Garland, 1985.

The Longman Handbook of Early Modern Europe, 1453–1763, ed. by Chris Cook and Philip Broadhead. Harlow, England: Longman, 2001.

Moseley, William W., et al., eds. *Spanish Literature, 1500–1700: A Bibliography of Golden Age Studies in Spanish and English, 1925–1980*. Westport, Conn.: Greenwood Press, 1984.

The New Cambridge Bibliography of English Literature, vol. 1 (600–1660), ed. by George Watson. Cambridge: Cambridge University Press, 1974.

The Oxford Companion to Art, ed. by Harold Osborne. Oxford: Clarendon Press, 1970.

The Oxford Guide to English Literature in English Translation, ed. by Peter France. London: Oxford University Press, 2000.

Ribner, Irving, and Clifford Chalmers Huffman, eds. *Tudor and Stuart Drama*. Arlington Heights, Ill.: AHM Publishing, 1978.

II. SOURCES AND CONTEMPORARY WORKS

1. Individual Authors, Collected Works

Erasmus, Desiderius. *Collected Works of Erasmus*. Toronto: University of Toronto Press, 1974–. (A collaborative project to produce English translations of all works of Erasmus; still in progress. Where they have been completed, these are generally the best English translations available.)

———. *Colloquies*, 2 vols., trans., ed., and annotated by Craig R. Thompson. Vols. 39 and 40 of *Collected Works of Erasmus*. Toronto: University of Toronto Press, 1997.

———. *The Correspondence of Erasmus*. [A subset of the *Collected Works* series, 12 volumes completed to date.] Toronto: University of Toronto Press, 1974–.

———. *The Erasmus Reader*, ed. by Erika Rummel. Toronto: University of Toronto Press, 1990. Selections from several of the author's most important works, English texts from the *Collected Works of Erasmus*.

———. *Praise of Folly and Letter to Maarten van Dorp, 1515*, trans. Betty Radice. Harmondsworth, England: Penguin, 1971. (The best recent English translation, also incorporated into the Toronto *Collected Works of Erasmus*.)

More, Thomas. *The Complete Works of St. Thomas More*, ed. by Louis L. Martz et al. 15 vols. New Haven: Yale University Press, 1963–1997. (Latin and English texts of the Latin works appear on facing pages.)

Robin, Diana, ed. *Filelfo in Milan: Writings, 1451–1477*. Princeton, N.J.: Princeton University Press, 1991.

Shakespeare, William. *The Annotated Shakespeare*, ed. by A. L. Rowse, 3 vols. New York: C. N. Potter, 1978.

———. *The Complete Works of William Shakespeare*, ed. by David Bevington, 4th ed. New York: Longman, 1997.

2. Individual Authors, Single Works

Alberti, Leon Battista. *The Family in Renaissance Florence*, trans. Renée Neu Watkins. Columbia: University of South Carolina Press, 1969.

———. *On Painting and On Sculpture: The Latin Texts of De pictura and De statua*, ed. with translation [into English] by Cecil Grayson. London: Phaidon, 1972.

Boccaccio, Giovanni. *The Decameron*, trans. Mark Musa and Peter Bondanella. New York: Norton, 1982.

Camões, Luís de. *The Lusiads*, trans. William C. Atkinson. Harmondsworth, England: Penguin, 1952.

Castiglione, Baldassare. *The Book of the Courtier*, trans. Charles S. Singleton. Anchor Books, A186. Garden City, N.Y.: Doubleday, 1959.

Cellini, Benvenuto. *The Autobiography of Benvenuto Cellini*, rev. ed., trans. George Bull. London: Penguin, 1998.

Cereta, Laura. *Collected Letters of a Renaissance Feminist*, ed. and trans. by Diana Robin. Chicago: University of Chicago Press, 1997.

Cervantes Saavedra, Miguel de. *The Ingenious Hidalgo Don Quixote de la Mancha*, trans. John Rutherford. London: Penguin Books, 2001.

Erasmus, Desiderius. *Colloquies*, trans. Craig R. Thompson, 2 vols. Vols. 39–40 of *Complete Works of Erasmus*. Toronto: University of Toronto Press, 1997.

Guicciardini, Francesco. *The History of Florence*, trans. Mario Domandi. Philadelphia: University of Pennsylvania Press, 1972.

———. *The History of Italy*, trans. Sidney Alexander. New York: Macmillan, 1968.

Machiavelli, Niccolò. *Discourses on Livy*, trans. Harvey C. Mansfield and Nathan Tarcov. Chicago: University of Chicago Press, 1996.

———. *The Florentine Histories*, trans. Laura F. Banfield and Harvey C. Mansfield, Jr. Princeton, N.J.: Princeton University Press, 1988.

———. *The Prince*, trans. Harvey C. Mansfield, 2nd ed. Chicago: University of Chicago Press, 1998. (The most recent of many translations.)

Margaret of Navarre / Marguerite de Navarre. *The Heptameron*, trans. P. A. Chilton. Harmondsworth, England: Penguin, 1984.

Montaigne, Michel de. *Complete Essays*, trans. Donald M. Frame. Stanford, Cal.: Stanford University Press, 1958.

———. *The Complete Essays*, trans. M. A. Screech. New York: Penguin Books, 1991.

More, Thomas. *Utopia*. Ed. [and trans.] by Edward Surtz, SJ. New Haven, Conn.: Yale University Press, 1964. (The best of many translations.)

On the Eve of the Reformation: Letters of Obscure Men, trans. Francis Griffin Stokes. New York: Harper & Row, 1964. (Anonymous, but usually attributed to Crotus Rubeanus and Ulrich von Hutten.)

Petrarch [Francesco Petrarca]. *Petrarch's Secret; or, The Soul's Conflict with Passion: Three Dialogues Between Himself and S. Augustine*, trans. William H. Draper. Westport, Conn.: Hyperion Press, 1978; repr. of ed. London: Chatto and Windus, 1911. (Latin title: *Secretum.*)

———. *The Sonnets of Petrarch*, trans. Anna Maria Armi. New York: Grosset & Dunlap, 1968. (Italian and English on facing pages.)

Pius II, Pope. *Memoirs of a Renaissance Pope: The Commentaries of Pius II: An Abridgment*, trans. Florence A. Gragg, ed. by Leona C. Gabel. New York: Capricorn Books, 1962.

Rojas, Fernando de. *La Celestina: The Spanish Bawd, Being the Tragi-Comedy of Calisto and Melibea*, trans. J. M. Cohen. Baltimore, Md.: Penguin, 1964.

Ronsard, Pierre de. *Selected Poems*, trans. and ed. by Malcolm Quainton and Elizabeth Vinestock. London: Penguin, 2002.

Sidney, Philip. *An Apology for Poetry*, ed. by Geoffrey Shepherd. New York: Thomas Nelson, 1973.

Spenser, Edmund. *The Faerie Queene*, ed. by Thomas P. Roche and C. Patrick O'Donnell, Jr. Harmondsworth, England: Penguin, 1978.

Thomas à Kempis [probable author]. *The Imitation of Christ*, trans. Leo Sherley-Price. Harmondsworth, England: Penguin, 1952.

Valla, Lorenzo. *On Pleasure / De voluptate*, trans. A. Kent Hieatt and Maristella Lorch. New York: Abaris Books, 1977. (Latin and English texts.)

———. *The Profession of the Religious and Selections from The Falsely-Believed and Forged Donation of Constantine*, trans. Olga Zorzi Pugliese, 2nd ed. Toronto: Victoria University, 1994.

———. *The Treatise of Lorenzo Valla on the Donation of Constantine: Text and Translation into English*, ed. and trans. by Christopher B. Coleman. New Haven, Conn.: Yale University Press, 1922. Reissued, New York: Russell & Russell, 1971.

3. Anthologies and Collections

Brucker, Gene, ed. *The Society of Renaissance Florence: A Documentary Study*. Harper Torchbooks, TB 1607. New York: Harper & Row, 1971.

——, ed. *Two Memoirs of Renaissance Florence: The Diaries of Buonaccorso Pitti & Gregorio Dati*, trans. Julia Martines. Prospect Heights, Ill.: Waveland Press, 1991.

Cassirer, Ernst, et al., eds. *The Renaissance Philosophy of Man*. Chicago: University of Chicago Press, 1948. (Highly influential collection of English translations of works by Francesco Petrarca, Lorenzo Valla, Marsilio Ficino, Giovanni Pico della Mirandola, Pietro Pomponazzi, and Juan Luis Vives.)

Emerton, Ephraim, ed. *Humanism and Tyranny: Studies in the Italian Trecento*. Cambridge, Mass.: Harvard University Press, 1925.

Fallico, Arthur B., and Herman Shapiro, eds. *Renaissance Philosophy*, vol. 1: *The Italian Philosophers*; vol. 2: *Renaissance Philosophy: The Transalpine Thinkers*. New York: Modern Library, 1967–1969.

Garin, Eugenio, ed. *La disputà delle arti nel Quattrocento*. Florence: Vallecchi, 1947.

——, ed. *L'educazione umanistica in Italia: Testi scelti e illustrati*. Bari: Laterza, 1959.

——, ed. *Il pensiero pedagogico dello umanesimo*. Florence: Giuntine, Sansoni, 1958.

——, ed. *Prosatori latini del Quattrocento*. Milan: R. Ricciardi, 1952.

Gordan, Phyllis Walter Goodhart, ed. and trans. *Two Renaissance Book Hunters: The Letters of Poggius Bracciolini to Nicolaus de Niccolis*. Records of Civilization, Sources and Studies, no. 91. New York: Columbia University Press, 1974.

Gundersheimer, Werner L., ed. *The Italian Renaissance*. Englewood Cliffs, N.J.: Prentice-Hall, 1965.

Halsall, Paul, ed. *Internet Medieval Sourcebook*. Fordham University Center for Medieval Studies. Includes material on the Renaissance. Website: 150.108.2.20/halsall/sbook.html

King, Margaret L., and Albert Rabil, Jr., eds. *Her Immaculate Hand: Selected Works by and about the Women Humanists of Quattrocento Italy*. Medieval & Renaissance Texts & Studies, no. 20. Binghamton, N.Y.: Center for Medieval and Early Renaissance Studies, 1983.

Kohl, Benjamin G., and Ronald G. Witt, eds. *The Earthly Republic: Italian Humanists on Government and Society*. Philadelphia: University of Pennsylvania Press, 1978.

Kors, Alan C., and Edward Peters, eds. *Witchcraft in Europe, 1100–1700: A Documentary History*. Philadelphia: University of Pennsylvania Press, 1972.

Rebhorn, Wayne A., ed. and trans. *Renaissance Debates on Rhetoric*. Ithaca, N.Y.: Cornell University Press, 2000.

Ross, James Bruce, and Mary Martin McLaughlin, eds. *The Portable Medieval Reader*. New York: Viking Press, 1949. (Despite the title, many of the selections are from authors of the 14th and 15th centuries.)

———, eds. *The Portable Renaissance Reader*. New York: Viking Press, 1953.

Watkins, Renée Neu, ed. *Humanism and Liberty: Writings on Freedom From Fifteenth-Century Florence*. Columbia: University of South Carolina Press, 1978.

III. TEXTBOOKS AND GENERAL WORKS

1. Textbooks

Bartlett, Kenneth R., ed. *The Civilization of the Italian Renaissance*. Lexington, Mass.: D. C. Heath, 1992.

Black, Robert, ed. *Renaissance Thought: A Reader*. London: Routledge, 2001.

Cochrane, Eric, and Julius Kirshner, eds. *The Renaissance*. Readings in Western Civilization, vol. 5. Chicago: University of Chicago Press, 1986.

Dannenfeldt, Karl H., ed. *The Renaissance: Basic Interpretations*, 2nd ed. Lexington, Mass.: D. C. Heath, 1974.

Dunn, Richard S. *The Age of Religious Wars, 1559–1715*, 2nd ed. New York: W.W. Norton, 1979.

Elton, Geoffrey R. *Reformation Europe, 1517–1559*, 2nd ed. Oxford: Blackwell, 1999.

Ergang, Robert. *The Renaissance*. Princeton, N.J.: D. Van Nostrand, 1967.

Estep, William R. *Renaissance and Reformation*. Grand Rapids, Mich.: Eerdmans, 1986.

Ferguson, Wallace K. *Europe in Transition, 1300–1520*. Boston: Houghton Mifflin, 1962.

Grendler, Paul F., ed. *An Italian Renaissance Reader*, 2nd ed. Toronto: Canadian Scholars' Press, 1992.

Grimm, Harold J. *The Reformation Era, 1500–1650*, 2nd ed. New York: Macmillan, 1973.

Jensen, Delamar. *Reformation Europe: Age of Reform and Revolution*, 2nd ed. Boston: Houghton-Mifflin, 1992.

———. *Renaissance Europe: Age of Recovery and Reconciliation*, 2nd ed. Boston: Houghton-Mifflin, 1992.

Johnson, Paul. *The Renaissance: A Short History*. New York: Modern Library, 2000.

Kohl, Benjamin G., and Alison Andrews Smith, eds. *Major Problems in the History of the Italian Renaissance*. Lexington, Mass.: D. C. Heath, 1995.

Nauert, Charles G., Jr. *The Age of Renaissance and Reformation*. Lanham, Md.: University Press of America, 1982.

Rice, Eugene F., Jr., and Anthony Grafton. *The Foundations of Early Modern Europe, 1460–1559*, 2nd ed. New York: W. W. Norton, 1994.

Spitz, Lewis W. *The Renaissance and Reformation*, reprint ed., 2 vols. St. Louis, Mo.: Concordia Publishing House, 1980.

Tomlinson, Gary, ed. *Source Readings*, vol. 3: *Renaissance*, rev. ed. New York: W. W. Norton, 1997.

Weinstein, Donald, ed. *The Renaissance and the Reformation, 1300–1600*. Sources in Western Civilization, 6. New York: Free Press, 1965.

2. General Interpretations

Bouwsma, William J. *The Culture of Renaissance Humanism*. Washington, D.C.: American Historical Association, 1973.

——. "The Two Faces of Humanism: Stoicism and Augustinianism in Renaissance Thought," in *Itinerarium Italicum: The Profile of the Italian Renaissance in the Mirror of Its European Transformations*, ed. by Heiko A. Oberman, with Thomas A. Brady, Jr., pp. 3–60. Leiden: Brill, 1975. Reprinted in Bouwsma, *A Usable Past: Essays in European Cultural History*, pp. 19–73. Berkeley: University of California Press, 1990.

——. *The Waning of the Renaissance, 1550–1640*. New Haven, Conn.: Yale University Press, 2000.

Burckhardt, Jacob. *The Civilization of the Renaissance in Italy: An Essay*, [trans. S. G. C. Middlemore], 3rd ed. New York: Phaidon, 1950. (There are many editions by other publishers, all using the same translation.)

Burke, Peter. *The European Renaissance: Centres and Peripheries*. Oxford: Blackwell, 1998.

——. *The Renaissance*. Atlantic Highlands, N.J.: Humanities Press International, 1987.

——. *The Renaissance Sense of the Past*. New York: St. Martin's Press, 1969.

Cassirer, Ernst. *The Individual and the Cosmos in Renaissance Philosophy*, trans. Mario Domandi. Oxford: Basil Blackwell, 1963.

Dresden, Sem. *Humanism in the Renaissance*, trans. Margaret L. King. London: Weidenfeld & Nicolson, 1968.

Eisenstein, Elizabeth L. *The Printing Press as an Agent of Change: Communications and Cultural Transformations in Early-Modern Europe*, 2 vols. Cambridge: Cambridge University Press, 1979.

Ferguson, Wallace K. *The Renaissance in Historical Thought: Five Centuries of Interpretation*. Boston: Houghton Mifflin, 1948.

Hay, Denys. *The Italian Renaissance in Its Historical Background*, 2nd ed. Cambridge: Cambridge University Press, 1977.

Kelley, Donald R. *Renaissance Humanism*. Boston: Twayne Publishers, 1991.

Mommsen, Theodor E. "Petrarch's Conception of the 'Dark Ages,'" *Speculum* 17 (1942): 226–42. Reprinted in Mommsen, *Medieval and Renaissance Studies*, ed. by Eugene F. Rice, Jr. Ithaca, N.Y.: Cornell University Press, 1959.

Nauert, Charles G. *Humanism and the Culture of Renaissance Europe*. Cambridge: Cambridge University Press, 1995.

Porter, Roy, and Mikulás Teich, eds. *The Renaissance in National Context*. Cambridge: Cambridge University Press, 1992.

Roth, Cecil. *The Jews in the Renaissance*. New York: Harper & Row, 1965. Originally published by the Jewish Publication Society of America, 1959.

Steinberg, S. H. *Five Hundred Years of Printing*, 2nd ed. Harmondsworth, England: Penguin, 1961.

IV. RELIGION AND THE CHURCH

Birely, Robert. *The Refashioning of Catholicism, 1450–1700: A Reassessment of the Counter Reformation*. Washington, D.C.: Catholic University of America Press, 1999.

Hay, Denys. *The Church in Italy in the Fifteenth Century*. Cambridge: Cambridge University Press, 1977.

Kamen, Henry. *The Spanish Inquisition: An Historical Revision*. London: Weidenfeld & Nicolson, 1997.

Monter, William E. *Frontiers of Heresy: The Spanish Inquisition from the Basque Lands to Sicily*. Cambridge: Cambridge University Press, 1990.

Oakley, Francis. *The Western Church in the Later Middle Ages*. Ithaca, N.Y.: Cornell University Press, 1979.

O'Malley, John W. *Praise and Blame in Renaissance Rome: Rhetoric, Doctrine, and Reform in the Sacred Orators of the Papal Court, c. 1450–1521*. Durham, N.C.: Duke University Press, 1979.

———. *Trent and All That: Renaming Catholicism*. Cambridge, Mass.: Harvard University Press, 2000.

Ozment, Steven. *The Age of Reform, 1250–1550: An Intellectual and Religious History of Late Medieval and Reformation Europe*. New Haven, Conn.: Yale University Press, 1980.

V. HUMANISM AND INTELLECTUAL HISTORY

1. General Studies

Bentley, Jerry H. *Humanists and Holy Writ: New Testament Scholarship in the Renaissance*. Princeton, N.J.: Princeton University Press, 1983.

Boas, Marie. *The Scientific Renaissance, 1450–1630*. New York: Harper & Row, 1962.

The Cambridge History of Later Medieval Philosophy, ed. by Norman Kretzmann et al. Cambridge: Cambridge University Press, 1982.

The Cambridge History of Medieval Political Thought, c. 350–c.1450, ed. by J. H. Burns. Cambridge: Cambridge University Press, 1988.

The Cambridge History of Political Thought, 1450–1700, ed. by J. H. Burns. Cambridge: Cambridge University Press, 1991.

The Cambridge History of Renaissance Philosophy, ed. by Charles B. Schmitt et al. Cambridge: Cambridge University Press, 1988.

Copenhaver, Brian P., and Charles B. Schmitt. *Renaissance Philosophy*. A History of Western Philosophy, 3. Oxford: Oxford University Press, 1992.

Goldberg, Jonathan, ed. *Queering the Renaissance*. Durham, N.C.: Duke University Press, 1994.

Goodman, Anthony, and Angus MacKay, eds. *The Impact of Humanism on Western Europe*. London: Longman, 1990.

Grafton, Anthony. *Commerce with the Classics: Ancient Books & Renaissance Readers*. Ann Arbor: University of Michigan Press, 1997.

——. *Defenders of the Text: The Traditions of Scholarship in an Age of Science, 1450–1800*. Cambridge, Mass.: Harvard University Press, 1991.

Hale, John. *The Civilization of Europe in the Renaissance*. New York: Atheneum, 1994.

Huizinga, J[ohan]. *The Waning of the Middle Ages: A Study of the Forms of Life, Thought and Art in France and the Netherlands in the Fourteenth and Fifteenth Centuries*, trans. F. Hopman. London: Edward Arnold, 1924.

——. *The Autumn of the Middle Ages*, trans. Rodney J. Payton and Ulrich Mamnitzsch. Chicago: University of Chicago Press, 1996. A retranslation of the precedng item; the relative merits of the two versions are debated.

Huppert, George. *The Idea of Perfect History: Historical Erudition and Historical Philosophy in Renaissance France*. Urbana: University of Illinois Press, 1970.

King, Margaret L. *Women of the Renaissance*. Chicago: University of Chicago Press, 1991.

Klaits, Joseph. *Servants of Satan: The Age of the Witch Hunts*. Bloomington: Indiana University Press, 1985.

Kristeller, Paul Oskar. *Renaissance Concepts of Man and Other Essays*. New York: Harper & Row, 1972.

——. *Renaissance Thought: The Classic, Scholastic, and Humanist Strains*. New York: Harper & Row, 1961.

——. *Renaissance Thought II: Papers on Humanism and the Arts*. New York: Harper & Row, 1965.

Mandrou, Robert. *From Humanism to Science, 1480–1700*, trans. Brian Pearce. Harmondsworth, England: Penguin, 1978.

Margolin, Jean-Claude, and Sylvain Matton, eds. *Alchimie et philosophie à la Renaissance*. De Pétrarque à Descartes, vol. 57. Paris: Librairie Philosophique J. Vrin, 1993.

Popkin, Richard H. *The History of Scepticism from Erasmus to Spinoza*. Berkeley: University of California Press, 1979.

Porter, Roy, and Mikulas Teich, eds. *The Renaissance in National Context*. Cambridge: Cambridge University Press, 1992.

Quillen, Carol Everhart. *Rereading the Renaissance: Petrarch, Augustine, and the Language of Humanism*. Ann Arbor: University of Michigan Press, 1998.

Rabil, Albert, Jr., ed. *Renaissance Humanism: Foundations, Forms, and Legacy*, 3 vols. Philadelphia: University of Pennsylvania Press, 1988.

Rice, Eugene F., Jr. *The Renaissance Idea of Wisdom*. Cambridge, Mass.: Harvard University Press, 1958.

Rummel, Erika. *The Humanist-Scholastic Debate in the Renaissance and Reformation*. Cambridge, Mass.: Harvard University Press, 1995.

Schmitt, Charles B. *Aristotle and the Renaissance*. Martin Classical Lectures, vol. 27. Cambridge, Mass.: Harvard University Press for Oberlin College, 1983.

Shumaker, Wayne. *The Occult Sciences in the Renaissance: A Study in Intellectual Patterns*. Berkeley: University of California Press, 1972.

Siraisi, Nancy G. *Medieval & Early Renaissance Medicine: An Introduction to Knowledge and Practice*. Chicago: University of Chicago Press, 1990.

Skinner, Quentin. *The Foundations of Modern Political Thought*, 2 vols. Cambridge: Cambridge University Press, 1978.

Struever, Nancy S. *Theory as Practice: Ethical Inquiry in the Renaissance*. Chicago: University of Chicago Press, 1992.

Trinkaus, Charles. *"In Our Image and Likeness": Humanity and Divinity in Italian Humanist Thought*, 2 vols. Chicago: The University of Chicago Press, 1970.

Walker, D. P. *The Ancient Theology: Studies in Christian Platonism from the Fifteenth to the Eighteenth Century*. Ithaca, N.Y.: Cornell University Press, 1972.

———. *Spiritual and Demonic Magic from Ficino to Campanella*. Studies of the Warburg Institute, vol. 22. London: Warburg Institute, University of London, 1958.

Weiss, Roberto. *The Renaissance Discovery of Classical Antiquity*. Oxford: Basil Blackwell, 1969.

Wilcox, Donald J. *In Search of God and Self: Renaissance and Reformation Thought*. Boston: Houghton Mifflin, 1975.

Wilson, N[igel]. G[uy]. *From Byzantium to Italy: Greek Studies in the Italian Renaissance*. Baltimore, Md.: Johns Hopkins University Press, 1992.

Witt, Ronald G. *In the Footsteps of the Ancients: The Origins of Humanism from Lovato to Bruni*. Leiden: Brill, 2000.

Yates, Frances A. *Giordano Bruno and the Hermetic Tradition*. Chicago: University of Chicago Press, 1964.

2. Education

Black, Robert. *Humanism and Education in Medieval and Renaissance Italy: Tradition and Innovation in Latin Schools from the Twelfth to the Fifteenth Century*. Cambridge: Cambridge University Press, 2001.

Charlton, Kenneth. *Education in Renaissance England*. London: Routledge and Kegan Paul, 1965.

Chartier, Roger, Marie-Madeleine Compère, and Dominique Julia. *L'Education en France du XVIe au XVIIIe siècle*. Paris: Société d'Edition d'Enseignment Supérieur, 1976.

Curtis, Mark H. *Oxford and Cambridge in Transition, 1558–1642*. Oxford: Clarendon Press, 1959.

Farge, James K. *Orthodoxy and Reform in Early Reformation France: The Faculty of Theology of Paris, 1500–1543*. Studies in Medieval and Reformation Thought, vol. 32. Leiden: E. J. Brill, 1985.

Garin, Eugenio. *L'educazione in Europa (1400–1600): Problemi e Programme*. Bari: Laterza, 1957.

Grafton, Anthony, and Lisa Jardine. *From Humanism to the Humanities: Education and the Liberal Arts in Fifteenth- and Sixteenth-Century Europe*. Cambridge, Mass.: Harvard University Press, 1986.

Grendler, Paul F. *Schooling in Renaissance Italy: Literacy and Learning, 1300–1600*. Baltimore, Md.: Johns Hopkins University Press, 1991.

———. *The Universities of the Italian Renaissance*. Baltimore: Johns Hopkins University Press, 2002.

Hartfelder, Karl. *Philipp Melanchthon als Praeceptor Germaniae*. Nieuwkoop, Netherlands: Mouton, 1964.

Huppert, George. *Public Schools in Renaissance France*. Urbana: University of Illinois Press, 1984.

Kagan, Richard L. *Students and Society in Early Modern Spain*. Baltimore, Md.: Johns Hopkins University Press, 1974.

Kearney, Hugh F. *Scholars and Gentlemen: Universities and Society in Pre-Industrial Britain, 1500–1700*. Ithaca, N.Y.: Cornell University Press, 1970.

Leader, Damian Riehl. *A History of the University of Cambridge*, vol. 1: *The University to 1546*. Cambridge: Cambridge University Press, 1988.

Lebrun, François, Lear Quénart, and Marc Venard, eds. *Histoire générale de l'enseignement et de l'éducation en France*, vol. 2: *De Gutenberg aux Lumières*. Paris: Nouvelle Librairie de France, 1981.

McConica, James, ed. *The Collegiate University*, vol. 3 of *The History of the University of Oxford*, ed. by T. H. Aston. Oxford: Clarendon Press, 1986.

Moran, Jo Ann Hoeppner. *The Growth of English Schooling, 1340–1548*. Princeton, N.J.: Princeton University Press, 1985.

Simon, Joan. *Education and Society in Tudor England*. Cambridge: Cambridge University Press, 1966.

Woodward, William Harrison. *Studies in Education During the Age of the Renaissance, 1400–1600*. Classics in Education, no. 32. New York: Teachers College Press, 1967; repr. of ed. 1906.

——. *Vittorino da Feltre and Other Humanist Educators*. Classics in Education, no. 18. New York: Teachers College Press, 1963; repr. of ed. 1897. (Appended are educational treatises by Pier Paolo Vergerio, Leonardo Bruni, Aeneas Sylvius Piccolomini [subsequently Pope Pius II], and Battista Guarino.)

3. Italy

Baron, Hans. *The Crisis of the Early Italian Renaissance: Civic Humanism and Republican Liberty in an Age of Classicism and Tyranny*, rev. ed. Princeton, N.J.: Princeton University Press, 1966.

Bentley, Jerry H. *Politics and Culture in Renaissance Naples*. Princeton, N.J.: Princeton University Press, 1987.

Bernardo, Aldo S. *Petrarch, Scipio, and the "Africa": The Birth of Humanism's Dream*. Baltimore, Md.: Johns Hopkins University Press, 1962.

Bouwsma, William J. *Venice and the Defense of Republican Liberty: Renaissance Values in the Age of the Counter Reformation*. Berkeley: University of California Press, 1968.

Brucker, Gene A. *Renaissance Florence*. New York: John Wiley & Sons, 1969.

Cochrane, Eric. *Florence in the Forgotten Centuries, 1527–1800: A History of Florence and the Florentines in the Age of the Grand Dukes*. Chicago: University of Chicago Press, 1973.

D'Amico, John F. *Renaissance Humanism in Papal Rome: Humanists and Churchmen on the Eve of the Reformation*. Baltimore, Md.: Johns Hopkins University Press, 1983.

Field, Arthur. *The Origins of the Platonic Academy of Florence*. Princeton, N.J.: Princeton University Press, 1988.

Fubini, Riccardo. *Humanism and Secularization: From Petrarch to Valla*, trans. Martha King. Durham, N.C.: Duke University Press, 2003.

Garin, Eugenio. *Italian Humanism: Philosophy and Civic Life in the Renaissance*, trans. Peter Munz. New York: Harper & Row, 1965.

Gilbert, Felix. *Machiavelli and Guicciardini: Politics and History in Sixteenth-Century Florence*. Princeton, N.J.: Princeton University Press, 1962.

Godman, Peter. *From Poliziano to Machiavelli: Florentine Humanism in the High Renaissance*. Princeton, N.J.: Princeton University Press, 1998.

Hankins, James. *Plato in the Italian Renaissance*, 2 vols. Leiden: E. J. Brill, 1991.

——, ed. *Renaissance Civic Humanism: Reappraisals and Reflections*. Cambridge: Cambridge University Press, 2000.

Holmes, George. *The Florentine Enlightenment, 1400–50*. New York: Pegasus, 1969.

King, Margaret L. *Venetian Humanism in an Age of Patrician Dominance*. Princeton, N.J: Princeton University Press, 1986.

Rowland, Ingrid D. *The Culture of the High Renaissance: Ancients and Moderns in Sixteenth-Century Rome*. Cambridge: Cambridge University Press, 1998.

Seigel, Jerrold E. *Rhetoric and Philosophy in Renaissance Humanism: The Union of Eloquence and Wisdom, Petrarch to Valla*. Princeton, N.J.: Princeton University Press, 1968.

Struever, Nancy S. *The Language of History in the Renaissance: Rhetoric and Historical Consciousness in Florentine Humanism*. Princeton, N.J.: Princeton University Press, 1970.

Trinkaus, Charles. *The Poet as Philosopher: Petrarch and the Formation of Renaissance Consciousness*. New Haven, Conn.: Yale University Press, 1979.

Weinstein, Donald. *Savonarola and Florence: Prophecy and Patriotism in the Renaissance*. Princeton, N.J.: Princeton University Press, 1970.

Weiss, Roberto. *The Dawn of Humanism in Italy*. London: [University College, London], 1947.

4. Britain

Bush, Douglas. *The Renaissance and English Humanism*. Toronto: University of Toronto Press, 1939.

Erickson, Carolly. *The First Elizabeth*. New York: Summit Books, 1983.

Gleason, John B. *John Colet*. Berkeley: University of California Press, 1989.

Hudson, Winthrop S. *The Cambridge Connection and the Elizabethan Settlement of 1559*. Durham, N.C.: Duke University Press, 1980.

Maccaffrey, Wallace T. *Elizabeth I*. London: Edward Arnold, 1993.

MacQueen, John, ed. *Humanism in Renaissance Scotland*. Edinburgh: University of Edinburgh Press, 1990.

Mayer, Thomas F. *Thomas Starkey and the Commonweal: Humanist Politics and Religion in the Reign of Henry VIII.* Cambridge: Cambridge University Press, 1989.

McConica, James Kelsey. *English Humanists and Reformation Politics Under Henry VIII and Edward VI.* Oxford: Clarendon Press, 1965.

Neale, John. *Queen Elizabeth.* New York: Harcourt Brace, 1934. (Reprinted as *Queen Elizabeth I.* New York: Doubleday, 1957.)

Scarisbrick, J. J. *Henry VIII.* Berkeley: University of California Press, 1968.

Tillyard, E. M. W. *The Elizabethan World Picture.* London: Chatto & Windus, 1943.

Warnicke, Retha M. *Women of the English Renaissance and Reformation.* Westport, Conn.: Greenwood, 1983.

Weiss, Roberto. *Humanism in England During the Fifteenth Century,* 2nd ed. Oxford: Basil Blackwell, 1957.

Woolfson, Jonathan, ed. *Reassessing Tudor Humanism.* New York: Palgrave Macmillan, 2002.

Yates, Frances A. *The Occult Philosophy in the Elizabethan Age.* London: Routledge & Kegan Paul, 1979.

5. France

Bowen, Barbara C. *The Age of Bluff: Paradox & Ambiguity in Rabelais & Montaigne.* Urbana: University of Illinois Press, 1972.

Desan, Philippe, ed. *Humanism in Crisis: The Decline of the French Renaissance.* Ann Arbor: University of Michigan Press, 1991.

Febvre, Lucien. *The Problem of Unbelief in the Sixteenth Century: The Religion of Rabelais,* trans. Beatrice Gottlieb. Cambridge, Mass.: Harvard University Press, 1982.

Kelley, Donald R. *Foundations of Modern Historical Scholarship: Language, Law, and History in the French Renaissance.* New York: Columbia University Press, 1970.

Renaudet, Augustin. *Préréforme et humanisme à Paris pendant les premières guerres d'Italie (1494–1517),* 2nd ed. Paris: Librairie d'Argences, 1953.

Simone, Franco. *The French Renaissance: Medieval Tradition and Italian Influence in the Shaping of the Renaissance in France,* trans. H. Gaston Hall. London: Macmillan, 1969.

Stone, Donald. *France in the Sixteenth Century: A Medieval Society Transformed.* Englewood Cliffs, N.J.: Prentice-Hall, 1969.

6. Germany, Switzerland, and the Netherlands

Bernstein, Eckhard. *German Humanism*. Boston: Twayne Publishers, 1983.

Evans, Robert John Weston. *Rudolf II and His World: A Study in Intellectual History, 1576–1612*. Oxford: Clarendon Press, 1973.

Hoffmeister, Gerhart, ed. *The Renaissance and Reformation in Germany: An Introduction*. New York: Frederick Ungar, 1977.

Moeller, Bernd. "The German Humanists and the Beginnings of the Reformation," in *Imperial Cities and the Reformation: Three Essays*, trans. H. C. Erik Midelfort and Mark U. Edwards, Jr. Philadelphia: Fortress Press, 1972.

Overfield, James H. *Humanism and Scholasticism in Late Medieval Germany*. Princeton, N.J.: Princeton University Press, 1984.

Smith, Pamela H. *The Business of Alchemy: Science and Culture in the Holy Roman Empire*. Princeton, N.J.: Princeton University Press, 1994.

Spitz, Lewis W. *The Religious Renaissance of the German Humanists*. Cambridge, Mass.: Harvard University Press, 1963.

Strauss, Gerald, ed. *Pre-Reformation Germany*. New York: Harper & Row, 1972.

7. Eastern Europe

Davies, Norman. *God's Playground: A History of Poland*, 2 vols. New York: Columbia University Press, 1982.

Fiszman, Samuel, ed. *The Polish Renaissance in Its European Context*. Bloomington: Indiana University Press, 1988.

Maczak, Antoni, Henryk Samsonowicz, and Peter Burke, eds. *East-Central Europe in Transition, from the Fourteenth to the Seventeenth Century*. Cambridge: Cambridge University Press, 1985.

Segel, Harold B. *Renaissance Culture in Poland: The Rise of Humanism, 1470–1573*. Ithaca, N.Y.: Cornell University Press, 1989.

8. Spain

Bataillon, Marcel. *Erasme et l'Espagne*, rev. ed., ed. Daniel Devoto and Charles Amiel, 3 vols. Geneva: Droz, 1991. (This study of the Spanish Erasmian movement has never been translated into English, but there is a Spanish translation: *Erasmo y España*, trans. Antonio Alatorre. Mexico: Fondo de Cultura Economica, 1950.)

Castro, Américo. *The Spaniards: An Introduction to Their History*, trans. Willard F. King and Selma Margaritten. Berkeley: University of California Press, 1971.

López Estrada, Francisco, ed. *Siglos de Oro: Renacimento*. Barcelona: Crítica, 1980.

VI. ART AND MUSIC

1. Art: General Works

Antal, Friedrich. *Florentine Painting and Its Social Background*. London: Kegan Paul, 1948.

Baxandall, Michael. *Painting and Experience in Fifteenth-Century Italy*. Oxford: Clarendon Press, 1972.

Beck, James H. *Italian Renaissance Painting*. New York: Harper & Row, 1981.

Benesch, Otto. *The Art of the Renaissance in Northern Europe*, rev. ed. London: Phaidon, 1965.

Berenson, Bernard. *Italian Painters of the Renaissance*, rev. ed. London: Phaidon, 1967.

Bialostocki, Jan. *The Art of the Renaissance in Eastern Europe: Hungary, Bohemia, Poland*. Ithaca, N.Y.: Cornell University Press, 1976.

Blunt, Anthony. *Art and Architecture in France, 1500–1700*, 5th ed., rev. by Richard Beresford. New Haven, Conn.: Yale University Press, 1999.

——. *Artistic Theory in Italy, 1450–1600*. Oxford: Clarendon Press, 1962.

Brown, Jonathan. *Painting in Spain, 1500–1700*. New Haven, Conn.: Yale University Press, 1998.

Christensen, Carl C. *Art and the Reformation in Germany*. Athens: Ohio University Press, 1979.

Cuttler, Charles D. *Northern Painting from Pucelle to Bruegel: Fourteenth, Fifteenth, and Sixteenth Centuries*. New York: Holt, Rinehart & Winston, 1968.

Edgerton, Samuel Y., Jr. *The Renaissance Discovery of Linear Perspective*. New York: Basic Books, 1975.

Emison, Patricia A. *Low and High Style in Italian Renaissance Art*. Garland Studies in the Renaissance, vol. 8. New York: Garland, 1997.

Freedberg, S.J. *Painting in Italy, 1500 to 1600*, 3rd ed. Pelican History of Art. New Haven, Conn.: Yale University Press, 1993.

——. *Painting of the High Renaissance in Rome and Florence*, rev. ed., 2 vols. New York: Hacker Art Books, 1985.

Friedländer, Max J. *Early Netherlandish Painting*, trans. Heinz Norden, 14 vols. New York: Praeger, 1967–1973.

Friedländer, W. F. *Mannerism and Anti-Mannerism in Italian Painting*. New York: Columbia University Press, 1957.

Gilbert, Creighton. *History of Renaissance Art: Painting, Sculpture, Architecture Throughout Europe*. New York: H. N. Abrams, 1973.

Goffen, Rona. *Renaissance Rivals: Michelangelo, Leonardo, Raphael, Titian*. New Haven, Conn.: Yale University Press, 2002.

Harbison, Craig. *The Mirror of the Artist: Northern Renaissance Art in Its Historical Context*. New York: H. N. Abrams and Prentice-Hall, 1995.

Hartt, Frederick, and David G. Wilkins. *History of Italian Renaissance Art: Painting, Sculpture, Architecture*, 5th ed. New York: Harry N. Abrams, 2003.

Jardine, Lisa, and Jerry Brotton. *Global Interests: Renaissance Art Between East and West*. Ithaca, N.Y.: Cornell University Press, 2000.

Landau, David, and Peter Parshall. *The Renaissance Print, 1470–1550*. New Haven, Conn.: Yale University Press, 1994.

Lee, Rensselaer W. *Ut pictura poesis: The Humanistic Theory of Painting*. New York: W. W. Norton, 1967.

Meiss, Millard. *Painting in Florence and Siena after the Black Death: The Arts, Religion and Society in the Mid-Fourteenth Century*. Princeton, N.J.: Princeton University Press, 1951; reprinted as Harper Torchbook TB 1148, New York: Harper & Row, 1964.

Muller, Theodor. *Sculpture in the Netherlands, Germany, France and Spain, 1400–1500*, trans. Elaine and William Robson Scott. Pelican History of Art. Baltimore, Md.: Penguin, 1966.

Murray, Linda. *The High Renaissance and Mannerism: Italy, the North, and Spain, 1500–1600*. New York: Oxford University Press, 1977.

Murray, Peter, and Linda Murry. *The Art of the Renaissance* [to about 1500]. New York: Frederick A. Praeger, 1963.

Osten, Gert von der, and Horst Vey. *Painting and Sculpture in Germany and the Netherlands, 1500–1600*, trans. Marry Hottinger. Pelican History of Art. Baltimore, Md.: Penguin, 1969.

Panofsky, Erwin. *Early Netherlandish Painting*, 2 vols. Cambridge, Mass.: Harvard University Press, 1953.

——. *Renaissance and Renascences in Western Art*, 2nd ed. Stockholm: Almqvist & Wiksell, 1965.

——. *Studies in Iconology: Humanistic Theories in the Art of the Renaissance*. New York: Harper & Row, 1972.

Paoletti, John T., and Gary M. Radke. *Art in Renaissance Italy*, 2nd ed. New York: H. N. Abrams, 2002.

Partridge, Loren H. *The Art of Renaissance Rome, 1400–1600*. New York: H. N. Abrams, 1996.

Pope-Hennessy, John. *An Introduction to Italian Sculpture*, 3 vols. London: Phaidon, 1955–1963.

Rosand, David. *Painting in Cinquecento Venice: Titian, Veronese, Tintoretto*, rev. ed. Cambridge: Cambridge University Press, 1997.

Seymour, Charles, Jr. *Sculpture in Italy, 1400–1500*. Pelican History of Art. Baltimore: Penguin, 1966.

Seznec, Jean. *The Survival of the Pagan Gods*, trans. Barbara F. Sessions. New York: Pantheon, 1953.

Shearman, John. *Mannerism*. Harmondsworth, U.K.: Penguin Books, 1967.

Snyder, James. *Northern Renaissance Art: Painting, Sculpture, the Graphic Arts from 1350 to 1575*. Englewood Cliffs, N.J.: Prentice-Hall, 1985.

Tomlinson, Janis. *From El Greco to Goya: Painting in Spain, 1561–1828*. New York: H. N. Abrams, 1997.

Wittkower, Rudolf. *Architectural Principles in the Age of Humanism*, 3rd ed. New York: W. W. Norton, 1971.

Wohl, Hellmut. *The Aesthetics of Italian Renaissance Art: A Reconsideration of Style*. Cambridge: Cambridge University Press, 1999.

Wölfflin, Heinrich. *Classic Art: An Introduction to the Italian Renaissance*, trans. Peter and Linda Murray, 3rd ed. New York: Phaidon, 1968.

2. Art: Studies of Individual Artists

Baxandall, Michael. *Giotto and the Orators: Humanist Observers of Painting in Italy and the Discovery of Pictorial Composition*. Oxford: Clarendon Press, 1971.

Beck, James. *Raphael*. New York: H. N. Abrams, 1976.

Bouchier, Bruce. *Andrea Palladio: The Architect in His Time*, rev. ed. New York: Abbeville Press, 1993.

Clark, Kenneth M. *Leonardo da Vinci*, rev. ed. Baltimore, Md.: Penguin, 1967.

Cole, Bruce. *Giotto and Florentine Painting, 1280–1375*. New York: Harper & Row, 1976.

——. *Masaccio and the Art of Early Renaissance Florence*. Bloomington: Indiana University Press, 1980.

Davies, Martin. *Rogier van der Weyden*. London: Phaidon, 1972.

De Tolnay, Charles. *Michelangelo*, 2nd ed., 5 vols. Princeton, N.J.: Princeton University Press, 1969–1971.

Friedländer, W. F. *Caravaggio Studies*. Princeton, N.J.: Princeton University Press, 1955.

Gibson, W. S. *Bruegel*. New York: Oxford University Press, 1977.

Goffen, Rona. *Giovanni Bellini*. New Haven, Conn.: Yale University Press, 1989.

Gudiol, J. *Domenikos Theotokopoulos, El Greco, 1541–1614*, trans. Kenneth Lyons. New York: Viking, 1973. Reprinted, New York: Greenwich House, 1983.

Hartt, Frederick. *Michelangelo*, 3 vols. New York: H. N. Abrams, 1965–1976.

Hope, Charles. *Titian*. New York: Harper & Row, 1980.

Lightbown, Ronald. *Piero della Francesca*. New York: Abbeville Press, 1992.

Pacht, Otto. *Van Eyck and the Founders of Early Netherlandish Painting*, ed. by Maria Schmidt-Dengler, trans. David Britt. London: Harvey Miller, 1994.

Panofsky, Erwin. *The Life and Art of Albrecht Dürer*, 4th ed. Princeton, N.J.: Princeton University Press, 1955.

Perlingieri, Ilya Sandra. *Sofonisba Anguissola: The First Great Woman Artist of the Renaissance*. New York: Rizzoli, 1992.

Pope-Hennessy, John. *Donatello: Sculptor*. New York: Abbeville Press, 1993.

Saalman, Howard, *Filipo Brunelleschi: The Buildings*. University Park: Pennsylvania State University Press, 1993.

Strieder, Peter. *Albrecht Dürer: Paintings, Prints, Drawings*, trans. Nancy M. Gordon and Walter L. Strauss, rev. ed. New York: Abaris Books, 1989.

Whiting, Roger. *Leonardo: A Portrait of the Renaissance Man*. London: Barrie and Jenkins, 1992.

3. Music

Atlas, Allan W. *Renaissance Music: Music in Western Europe, 1400–1600*. New York: W. W. Norton, 1998.

Brown, Howard Mayer, and Louise K. Stein. *Music in the Renaissance*, 2nd ed. Englewood Cliffs, N.J.: Prentice-Hall, 1999.

Cuyler, Louise Elvira. *The Emperor Maximilian I and Music*. London: Oxford University Press, 1973.

Kisby, Fiona, ed. *Music and Musicians in Renaissance Cities and Towns*. Cambridge: Cambridge University Press, 2001.

Perkins, Leeman L. *Music in the Age of the Renaissance*. New York: W. W. Norton, 1999.

Reese, Gustave. *Music in the Renaissance*, rev. ed. New York: W. W. Norton, 1959.

Sternfeld, Frederick W., ed. *Music from the Middle Ages to the Renaissance*. London: Weidenfeld & Nicolson, 1973.

Walker, D. P. *Studies in Musical Science in the Late Renaissance*. Studies of the Warburg Institute, vol. 37. London: Warburg Institute, University of London, 1978.

VII. VERNACULAR LITERATURE

1. General Works

Bush, Douglas. *English Literature in the Earlier Seventeenth Century, 1600–1660*, 2nd ed. Oxford History of English Literature, vol. 5. London: Oxford University Press, 1962.

Green, Otis. *Spain and the Western Tradition: The Castilian Mind in Literature from El Cid to Calderón*, 4 vols. Madison: University of Wisconsin Press, 1963–1966.

Greenblatt, Stephen. *Renaissance Self-Fashioning: From More to Shakespeare*. Chicago: University of Chicago Press, 1980.

Hunter, G. K. *English Drama, 1586–1642: The Age of Shakespeare*. Oxford: Clarendon Press, 1997.

King, John N. *English Reformation Literature: The Tudor Origins of the Protestant Tradition*. Princeton, N.J.: Princeton University Press, 1982.

Lewis, C. S. *English Literature in the Sixteenth Century, Excluding Drama*. Oxford History of English Literature, vol. 3. Oxford: Clarendon Press, 1954.

Sypher, Wylie. *Four Stages of Renaissance Style*. Garden City, N.Y.: Doubleday, 1955.

Tilley, Arthur Augustus. *The Dawn of the French Renaissance*. New York: Russell & Russell, 1968; reprint of ed. 1918.

——. *The Literature of the French Renaissance*, 2 vols. New York: Hafner, 1959.

Weinberg, Bernard. *A History of Literary Criticism in the Italian Renaissance*, 2 vols. Chicago: University of Chicago Press, 1961.

Wilson, F. P. *The English Drama, 1485–1585*. Oxford History of English Literature, vol. 4, part 1. London: Oxford University Press, 1969.

2. Biographies and Studies of Individual Writers

Ackroyd, Peter. *The Life of Thomas More*. London: Chatto & Windus, 1998.

Augustijn, Cornelis. *Erasmus: His Life, Works, and Influence*, trans. J. C. Grayson. Toronto: University of Toronto Press, 1991.

Bakhtin, Mikhail M. *Rabelais and His World*, trans. Helene Iswolsky. Cambridge, Mass.: MIT Press, 1968.

Bergeron, David Moore, and Geraldo U. de Sousa. *Shakespeare: A Study and Research Guide*, 3rd ed. Lawrence: University Press of Kansas, 1995.

Bergin, Thomas G. *Petrarch*. Twayne's World Authors Series, no. 81. New York: Twayne Publishers, 1970.

Boyle, Marjorie O'Rourke. *Petrarch's Genius: Pentimento and Prophecy*. Berkeley: University of California Press, 1991.

Chambers, Edmund K. *William Shakespeare: A Study of Facts and Problems*, 2 vols. Oxford: Clarendon Press, 1930; reissued, 1966.

Chambers, R. W. *Thomas More*. London: Jonathan Cape, 1935.

Close, Anthony J. *Miguel de Cervantes: Don Quixote*. Cambridge: Cambridge University Press, 1990.

De Grazia, Sebastian. *Machiavelli in Hell*. Princeton, N.J.: Princeton University Press, 1989.

Fox, Alistair. *Thomas More: History and Providence*. New Haven, Conn.: Yale University Press, 1982.

Frame, Donald M. *Montaigne: A Biography*. New York: Harcourt, Brace & World, 1965.

Guy, John. *Thomas More*. New York: Oxford University Press, 2000.

Hamilton, A. C. *Sir Philip Sidney: A Study of His Life and Works*. Cambridge: Cambridge University Press, 1977.

Hayes, Francis C. *Lope de Vega*. Twayne's World Authors Series, no. 28. New York: Twayne, 1967.

Hexter, J. H. *More's Utopia: The Biography of an Idea*. Princeton, N.J.: Princeton University Press, 1952.

Hoffmann, George. *Montaigne's Career*. Oxford: Clarendon Press,

Huizinga, J[ohan]. *Erasmus of Rotterdam*, trans. F. Hopman. London: Phaidon, 1952.

Kristeller, Paul Oskar. *The Philosophy of Marsilio Ficino*, trans. Virginia Conant. New York: Columbia University Press, 1943.

Marius, Richard. *Thomas More: A Biography*. New York: Knopf, 1984.

McNeil, David O. *Guillaume Budé and Humanism in the Reign of Francis I*. Geneva: Droz, 1975.

Ridolfi, Roberto. *The Life of Girolamo Savonarola*, trans. Cecil Grayson. New York: Knopf, 1970.

——. *The Life of Niccolò Machiavelli*, trans. Cecil Grayson. Chicago: University of Chicago Press, 1963.

Screech, M. A. *Montaigne & Melancholy: The Wisdom of the Essays*. London: Duckworth, 1983.

——. *Rabelais*. Ithaca, N.Y.: Cornell University Press, 1979.

Silver, Isidore. *Ronsard and the Hellenic Renaissance in France*, 2 vols. St. Louis, Mo.: Washington University, 1961.

Tetel, Marcel. *Montaigne: A Biography*. Twayne's World Authors Series, no. 317. New York: Twayne, 1974.

Tracy, James D. *Erasmus of the Low Countries*. Berkeley: University of California Press 1996.

Wells, Stanley. *Shakespeare: A Life in Drama*. New York: W. W. Norton, 1995.

Wilkins, Ernest Hatch. *Life of Petrarch*. Chicago: University of Chicago Press, 1961.

Witt, Ronald G. *Hercules at the Crossroads: The Life, Works, and Thought of Coluccio Salutati*. Durham, N.C.: Duke University Press, 1983.

VIII. POLITICAL AND SOCIAL BACKGROUNDS

Black, J. B. *The Reign of Elizabeth, 1558–1603*, 2nd ed. The Oxford History of England. Oxford: Clarendon Press, 1959.

Braudel, Fernand. *Capitalism and Material Life, 1400–1800*, trans. Miriam Kochan. London: Weidenfeld & Nicolson, 1973.

——. *The Mediterranean and the Mediterranean World in the Age of Philip II*, trans. Sian Reynolds, 2 vols. New York: Harper & Row, 1972.

Cheyney, Edward P. *The Dawn of a New Era, 1250–1453*. New York: Harper & Brothers, 1936.

Cipolla, Carlo M. *Before the Industrial Revolution: European Society and Economy, 1000–1700*, trans. Marcella and Alide Kooy, 2nd ed. New York: W. W. Norton, 1980.

Cohen, Elizabeth S., and Thomas V. Cohen. *Daily Life in Renaissance Italy*. Westport, Conn.: Greenwood, 2001.

Collinson, Patrick, ed. *The Sixteenth Century, 1485–1603*. Oxford: Oxford University Press, 2002.

Elliott, John Huxtable. *Imperial Spain, 1469–1716*. New York: St. Martin's Press, 1963.

Finlay, Robert. *Politics in Renaissance Venice*. New Brunswick, N.J.: Rutgers University Press, 1980.

Fox, Alistair, and John Guy, ed. *Reassessing the Henrician Age: Humanism, Politics, and Reform, 1500–1550*. New York: Basil Blackwell, 1988.

Gilmore, Myron P. *The World of Humanism, 1453–1517*. New York: Harper & Brothers, 1952.

Green, V. H. H. *Renaissance and Reformation: A Survey of European History Between 1450 and 1660*, 2nd ed. London: Edward Arnold, 1964.

Guy, John. *Tudor England*. New York: Oxford University Press, 1988.

Hay, Denys. *Europe in the Fourteenth and Fifteenth Centuries*. New York: Holt, Rinehart and Winston, 1966.

Huppert, George. *After the Black Death: A Social History of Early Modern Europe*. Bloomington: Indiana University Press, 1986.

Knecht, R. J. *Renaissance Warrior and Patron: The Reign of Francis I*. Cambridge: Cambridge University Press, 1994. (A revision of his *Francis I* [same publisher, 1982].)

——. *The Rise and Fall of Renaissance France, 1483–1610*, 2nd ed. Oxford: Blackwell, 2001.

Koenigsberger, H. G., George L. Mosse, and G. Q. Bowler. *Europe in the Sixteenth Century*, 2nd ed. London: Longman, 1989.

Lane, Frederic C. *Venice: A Maritime Republic*. Baltimore, Md.: Johns Hopkins University Press, 1973.

Larner, John. *Culture and Society in Italy, 1290–1420*. New York: Charles Scribner's Sons, 1971.

Logan, Oliver. *Culture and Society in Venice, 1470–1790: The Renaissance and Its Heritage*. London: B. T. Batsford, 1972.

Lynch, John. *The Hispanic World in Crisis and Change, 1598–1700*, rev. ed. Oxford: Blackwell, 1992.

———. *Spain, 1516–1598: From National State to World Empire*, rev. ed. Oxford: Blackwell, 1992.

Mackie, J. D. *The Earlier Tudors, 1485–1558*. The Oxford History of England. Oxford: Clarendon Press, 1952.

Martines, Lauro. *Power and Imagination: City-States in Renaissance Italy*. New York: Alfred A. Knopf, 1979.

Miskimin, Harry A. *The Economy of Early Renaissance Europe, 1300–1460*. Cambridge: Cambridge University Press, 1975.

———. *The Economy of Later Renaissance Europe, 1460–1600*. Cambridge: Cambridge University Press, 1977.

Molnar, Miklos. *A Concise History of Hungary*, trans. Anna Magyar. Cambridge: Cambridge University Press, 2001.

O'Connell, Marvin R. *The Counter Reformation, 1559–1610*. New York: Harper & Row, 1974.

Parker, Geoffrey. *Philip II*, 3rd ed. Chicago: Open Court, 1995.

Spitz, Lewis W. *The Protestant Reformation, 1517–1559*. New York: Harper & Row, 1985.

Sugar, Peter F., general ed. *A History of Hungary*. Bloomington: Indiana University Press, 1990.

Wiesner, Merry E. *Women and Gender in Early Modern Europe*, 2nd ed. Cambridge: Cambridge University Press, 2000.

About the Author

Charles G. Nauert is professor emeritus of history at the University of Missouri—Columbia. He received his doctorate in history from the University of Illinois at Urbana-Champaign and taught at Bowdoin College, Williams College, and the University of Missouri. At Missouri his teaching specialty was the Renaissance-Reformation period of European history. There he served as chairperson of the Department of History, held the special Middlebush Chair in History for a term, and in 1991 received the Thomas Jefferson Award presented by the four-campus university system. He has been active in the American Historical Association, the Society for Reformation Research, the Renaissance Society of America, and the Sixteenth Century Studies Conference. He was president of the Sixteenth Century Studies Conference in 1978, and in 2002 the Conference named him the first recipient of its Bodo Nischan Award "for scholarship, civility, and service." His publications include many articles and book reviews, three books on Renaissance topics, a book-length article on Renaissance commentaries on Pliny the Elder, and the introductions and textual annotations to volumes 11 and 12 of *The Correspondence of Erasmus*. He served as the first general editor (1979–1996) of the book series "Sixteenth Century Essays and Studies." In 1998 colleagues and former students honored him with a Festschrift, *In Laudem Caroli: Renaissance and Reformation Studies for Charles G. Nauert*.